# The Scope of Social Architecture

# The Scope of Social Architecture

Edited by C. Richard Hatch

VNR VAN NOSTRAND REINHOLD COMPANY
NEW YORK   CINCINNATI   TORONTO   LONDON   MELBOURNE

Copyright © 1984 by Van Nostrand Reinhold Company Inc.

Library of Congress Catalog Card Number: 81-11437
ISBN: 0-442-26153-5

Manufactured in the United States of America

Published by Van Nostrand Reinhold Company Inc.
135 West 50th Street
New York, New York 10020

Van Nostrand Reinhold Company Limited
Molly Millars Lane
Wokingham, Berkshire RG11 2PY, England

Van Nostrand Reinhold
480 Latrobe Street
Melbourne, Victoria 3000, Australia

Macmillan of Canada
Division of Gage Publishing Limited
164 Commander Boulevard
Agincourt, Ontario M1S 3C7, Canada
15 14 13 12 11 10 9 8 7 6 5 4 3 2 1

**Library of Congress Cataloging in Publication Data**

Main entry under title:

The scope of social architecture.

   Includes index.
   1. Architecture and society—Addresses, essays,
lectures.   I.  Hatch, C. Richard.
NA2543.S6A65      720′.1′03      81-11437
ISBN 0-442-26153-5               AACR2

COLUMNS, Volume 1
**A Publication of the New Jersey Institute of Technology**

Edited and with an Introduction by C. Richard Hatch

# Preface

Giancarlo De Carlo, architect in Milan,
founding member of Team 10, editor of the
review *Spazio e Società*

## Beyond Postmodernism

We could say it all began when Walter Gropius disconsolately remarked on the disagreeable fact that an occasional good modern building in no way improves the overall physical environment, which is subject instead to inexorable and continuous deterioration. At that time, Gropius had already moved to the United States and was about to construct the occasional mediocre modern building himself, after making the Harvard architecture department one of the two strongholds for the Europeanization of American architecture. The other stronghold was Chicago, where Mies van der Rohe was head of the architecture department at IIT and was about to construct a considerable series of variations on his model of the "neutral skyscraper."

The liberating/repressive effects of these two strongholds in that period account for much of the contradictory behavior of contemporary American architecture, on the one hand trying hard to go back to the roots of classical culture, known only through neoclassical manipulations, and on the other hand wanting to establish an independent identity.

We can take the disconsolate exclamation of Gropius as the first sign of the schizophrenia that was to afflict the Modern Movement in the following 40 years. At that time the Movement had already lost the conviction that progress, mechanization, and the "esprit nouveau" would automatically generate the "great Cartesian grid," within which architecture, and then the world, would finally reach universal reason. Two ways out of the resultant state of insecurity were found: ecumenism and attempted alliance with power.

In fact, these two paths ran together as one. Ecumenism amounted to accepting any architectural manifestation of the present and past as modern (as long as it was celebrated), and to affirming a continuity which was to prove that nothing had changed. Ecumenism effectively reestablished an institutional legitimacy, the prerequisite to a reinstatement in the power-relationships existing between institutions. So it was that a long, hard voyage against the stream ended at a point which was the opposite of that originally aimed for. At the outset, in fact, the goal had been to free architecture from the demands of power and the opportunistic distortions of the long period of academicism, and to give it an immediacy of representation and expression once more, so that everyone everywhere could understand and use it.

Ecumenism and interest in the expectations of power brought back into the Modern Movement uncertainty and yearning for academicism. These symptoms have gradually worsened and have resulted in the present great confusion.

Uncertainty began to manifest itself in an eager desire to involve architecture in ever-larger programs. If the physical environment could not be improved by the insertion of occasional good modern buildings, well, then the attack had to be directed at the physical environment as a whole.

It so happens, however, that every part that is attacked, no matter how large, turns out to be only a fraction of a still greater whole that eludes control. So, inevitably, the dimensional and temporal range of proposals had to be continually expanded. At the same time, the longing for control implies the acquisition of instruments and methods that are unusual for architecture. These instruments were taken from specializations involved in quantitative processing. They were therefore ineffective, and even misleading, when applied to the qualitative problems that lie at the heart of every architectural question. But the most serious aspect of the affair was that large-scale and long-range evolutions broke the working level into two: on one hand, the abstractions of statistical calculation, technological hazard, and formalistic sophistication; on the other hand, the pseudo-realistic attempt at rationalizing everything, thus complying with all the expectations of capitalist speculators and state bureaucracy. Similarly, the conceptual level also broke into two parts: on one hand, rejection of the everyday, the personal, and different; on the other, exaltation of the universal, standardization, and unification.

This dualism (in a movement that aimed at making architecture universal) robbed human beings of the chance of using architectural language to express themselves, to communicate, and to organize and shape their space to the measure of their individual and social existences.

The organization and formation of physical space has been divided into categories based on the dimensions of the sphere considered. Within each category, theory was separated from method, method from instruments, analysis from project, project from realization, understanding from action, experience from use, exercise from memory, and so forth.

Even the idea of architecture has been split up into "exceptional architecture" and "ordinary architecture." The first is for special circumstances and is left to the judgment of the critics, finally able to blow the dust off their old critical tools that had already proved exhausted for the figurative arts. The second is intended for the mass demand for houses and services and so is entrusted to the judgment of experts in economic planning and technical organization operating within the domain of political decisions.

Incidentally, we might point out that all sorts of ways have been pursued to legitimize the "duality" of architecture: musings on occasional brief notes in Wittgenstein, exhumations of some marginal work by Heidegger, presented as the Word. It is more important, however, to point out that under this "duality" alibi, architecture has quickly reached its maximum possible confusion. The connection "ordinary architecture-political decision" has helped distort the hard-won principle according to which architecture should demonstrate awareness and political responsibility (should be answerable to society for its choices and the effects of its operation). This connection has opened the way to a series of twisting syllogisms such as "architecture is the work of politicians," "making architecture is making politics," "architecture is political action," etc., etc. And so it was that between the mid-1960s and the early 1970s we saw the invasion of a crowd of frantic cats with a mind to human sciences, administration, social engineering, or political procedure and convinced that architec-

ture could be the wonderful boots that in seven league jumps would carry them to the height of the revolution.

The association "exceptional architecture—artist piece," on the other hand, has contributed to the accelerated development of the many Beaux Arts mannerisms, which, for the sake of ecumenism, had been drawn into the Modern Movement. And so it is that in the mid-1970s we had a second invasion—symmetrical, specular, and complementary to that which preceded it. The newcomers were emotionally opposing—but in fact integrating—merely verbal architecture, and proposed merely visual architecture, ready finished and significant at the moment it is drawn.

This time it was a mixed bunch of eclectics unconsciously or deliberately unaware of the problems of the present and therefore unable to articulate new languages. Their feverish interest was addressed to every kind of revivalism: neo-monumentalist, neo-rationalist, neo-realist, neo-Beaux-Arts, neo-dada, neo-hyperrealist, neo-Siedlungen, neo-EUR, neo-Stalin Allee, neo-villa at Garches, neo-beach hut with vague De Chirico overtones.

The two groups eye each other from opposite banks; they even nod to each other—after all, both of them owe their fortune above all to the other. This fortune may seem quite relevant since the first group is establishing itself in all the ganglia of the bureaucratic machine—from public administration, to production, to political parties—while the second group, with Mafia-like skill, is tending to widen its control over reviews, exhibitions, competitions, and in general

over the mass media, whose fatuity it seems to know well.

If we now wonder who could possibly like these two groups, we find that both are very welcome to a third group (ever-present in architecture, and also in the Modern Movement) of neutral professionals, organized in planning groups at the service of capitalist investment and state bureaucracy's prestige, selling standard typologies and oppressive technologies, collaborating in the neo-colonization of the Third World and the perversion or the whole world with an architectural output for pure consumption, destitute of any substance or quality. The fatuous incompetence of the others is the best legitimization for their own ruthless efficiency: that's why they are very glad of the present turn of events.

But the two groups also please and reassure bureaucrats, as they can expect a pile of inconclusive reports on one hand and heaps of unbuildable competition projects on the other. Reports on nothing and projects about nothing guarantee immobilism and reinforce conservatism. They also please the critics who at last can concentrate only on "artist pieces," which are open to the most traditional type of art criticism and save one from the hard work of having to sort out the complex interconnections that an architectural event keeps weaving.

The lucubrations of verbal architecture please those historians, sociologists, economists, psychologists, psychiatrists, and so forth, who try to drown the faintness of their specific instruments in any kind of interdisciplinary cacophony. The lucubrations of visual architecture please fashionable museums and gallery owners, exhausted by too many retrospectives and inclined to test the market (now deaf to the torments of contemporary painters and sculptors) with the "naiveté" of the pastels and models of the architects. But both kinds of lucubrations please, most of all, those who exercise power because they hope to have gotten rid at last of the annoying goad of modern architecture: a busybody, perhaps, but also stimulating, ready to criticize, full of proposals, and debunking (in its best moments, at least).

Probably it was the realization of this vacuum that some time ago led certain critics to declare that architecture was dead. But this statement did not sound convincing, it being quite plain after all that architecture has to go on existing as long as there are human beings on the earth and there is a need for organized and formed physical space. However, the vacuum was there; so the debate shifted to the identification of the corpse, and recently someone confirmed that there was indeed a dead body, but that it belonged to the Modern Movement. The place and date of decease were subsequently established. At the same time, there was a desperate search for an alternative presence, which was finally found and christened Postmodernism. (We aren't sure yet if this naming was given by those who identified the corpse or is perhaps the invention of two architects in a bar in New York one spring morning. Eclectics, with their well-known marked regard for history, are very punctilious in their debates on primogenitures).

When all is said and done, however, all this is of little importance. Most of the components converging in the present confusion would not even be worthy of consideration, if they were not symptomatic of a more widespread involution, going beyond their own intrinsic irrelevance. These components are variously annoying according to their cultural background. In fact, we can't give the same weight to the various "visualists": the upholders of Nazi neoclassicism and of Fascist metaphysical deserts, the dandyism of the English, the Talmudic sarcasm of certain New York groups, the semantic urgency of the Madrid architects, or the missionary pedantry of the discoverers of Las Vegas (who have arrived at a Chippendale decor loaded with such bigoted irony that it really does need to be taken seriously).

The various currents share certain more-or-less common characteristics: unawareness of the system of relations and of the process that an architectural event generates in space and time, concentration on the object and even on the solipsism of the gesture, lack of concern or even disdain for the character of place, disregard for use—therefore also for users—and indifference to the conflicts of society in which architecture is inevitably involved.

The most alarming characteristic they share is their acceptance of a notion of architecture entirely regulated by the ruling bureaucracy, intended for the quality-lacking human standard of the petit-bourgeois universe, where the architect simply loads simulacra on the space-product in order to make it more attractive to the market.

Nevertheless, there are certain architectural proposals that reveal restlessness, doubt, critical ferment, and often also talent, so that it is quite possible that in a further development they will become more structured, changing from knots of confusion into cues for active disorder. Indeed, contemporary architecture *needs* active disorder—not confusion, not passive order—to accelerate its pace, to go forward with greater dialectic energy, to face the problems posed by the various social contexts and by its own being, to reexamine critically its stock of ideas and achievements, to revise its techniques, and to recover all the dimensions of architecture and once more base them on the principle that the process of organizing three-dimensional space is indivisible, although possible configurations are as many as the contexts which generate and experience them. Despite the present confusion (and the little energy devoted to tackling it) this operation is now under way. The scarcity of records about it is because most recorders are tuned to the academic channels, while the movement is following new routes and is spreading in complex, noninstitutional zones.

For this reason, the present volume of COLUMNS: ARCHITECTURE & SOCIETY is particularly welcome. Its emphasis on process, on the involvement of users, and on the democratic control of the environment—argued with concrete examples from both Europe and America—confronts the Postmodernists on their home ground and points to new and fruitful directions for architecture. *Affetuosi saluti!*

# Acknowledgments

My involvement with the issues discussed here dates back to the early 1960s when I organized the Architects' Renewal Committee in Harlem (ARCH), the first of the Community Design Centers. This book is part of a continuing effort to define and encourage the social practice of architecture.

I wish to recognize first the contributions of ordinary people all over the world who, through their involvement with buildings and their collective struggle to humanize the city, have taught us about social architecture. I want also to thank all those architects who work with them, and especially those who have provided materials for this book.

*The Scope of Social Architecture* required extensive time and travel, which was made possible in the first instance by the Brunner Scholarship Fund of the New York Chapter of the American Institute of Architects. The Research Foundation of the New Jersey Institute of Technology and its Director, Dr. Arnold Allentuch, were also extremely helpful and generous. I owe both a great deal.

The translations of the material from Cuba, Italy, France, and Spain are mine. I take responsibility for any errors; I wish I could take credit for the good ideas. Barbara Conner typed the manuscripts—frequently again and again until we agreed we had them right. My wife Maureen has been an invaluable critic. Mario Quilles did a splendid job on book design and production. My thanks to them, too.

C. Richard Hatch
Professor
School of Architecture
New Jersey Institute of Technology

# Table of Contents

# Part 3: The Neighborhood and the City

# The Scope of Social Architecture

# Introduction

C. Richard Hatch
School of Architecture
New Jersey Institute of Technology

## Toward a Theory of Social Architecture

Nearly 25 years ago, Aldo Van Eyck issued an urgent warning: the contemporary city was being transformed into "mile upon mile of organized nowhere;" place and occasion were being removed from the modern world. In response, he called on architects to "get closer to the shifting center of human reality and build its counterform—for each man and all men, since they no longer do it themselves." Van Eyck's message raised difficult questions. Why do not—or cannot—men in our time determine their reality and its counterform? Can the architect alone replace the missing efforts of all men? And if, as architects, we have profound disagreements with the human reality shaped by contemporary society, how are we to build?

The answer lies in the power of architecture not merely to reflect reality, but also to change it. It is true that in a class society architecture is given the task of making manifest the power of property. It is asked to objectify the hierarchical structure of human relationships. It is called upon to build a convincing claim for the legitimacy of the social order. How then can architecture contribute to liberation? How can we provide an effective, alternative counterform for a society that does not yet exist? This book is an effort to respond to these questions, to define social architecture, and to provide a guide for practice. The commentaries and case studies contained here constitute an international debate on the goals, methods, and scope of social architecture. Collectively they form a moral argument for an architecture of social change and an implicit denunciation of

the alternative directions which are so much in evidence.

Most architectural journals today are crowded with unbuildable projects. Galleries exhibit paper architecture. We are told, in an essay on Aldo Rossi by Peter Eisenman, that

Rossi's drawings are not merely drawings "of" architecture, nor are they to be taken as metaphors "of" architecture, they are architecture.

Modern architecture once sought social standing by attaching itself to engineering rationalism. Today professional legitimacy and design validation are sought in connections with envied, achieving fields like structural linguistics and conceptual art. Architecture, seeking a prestige that remains just beyond its grasp, attempts once again to associate itself with the wealthy and powerful and with forms that suggest their earlier periods of dominance. Alex Tzonis and Liane Lefaivre have characterized the present moment as essentially narcissistic:

The preoccupation with formalism, hedonism, graphism and elitism has allowed architects to shift with easy conscience from practical measures to the realm of mental constructs. This is an attempt . . . to deny the separation between reality and desire, and to turn inward for approval to the closed world of peers and the office drawing board, where everything becomes possible. This collective narcissism has helped blur the distinction between wielding profes-

sional tools and acting effectively on the manmade environment.

This is no time to escape into beauty, to ally architecture to what Herbert Marcuse once called "the holiday function of art." Ten years ago we were told that this generation would have to build as much as all earlier generations in America combined. Daily statistics reminded us of the housing deficit, the spreading deterioration of cities, the environmental cost of suburban sprawl. But little was done; the need remains. However, our social and environmental problems are not limited to unmet material needs. Everywhere we see evidence of alienation, the fraying of the social fabric, the breakdown of community. Commercial architecture contributes to these trends. Academic architecture—postmodernism—is in retreat from these painful realities. Social architecture, limited so far in its adherents and its armamentarium, remains to probe, to test, to propose solutions that at once satisfy immediate needs and open up new visions of life and work.

Not long ago, Giancarlo De Carlo set out the steps that describe the trajectory of most building projects:

1. Function established
2. Location chosen         } Owner
3. Financing arranged

4. Spatial organization defined
5. Form and structure drawn         } Architect
6. Construction overseen

3

| 7. | Use | *Users* |
|---|---|---|
| 8. | Management, repair | |
| 9. | Recycling | Owner |
| 10. | Demolition and replacement | |

A world that comes into being, defines human activities, structures time and space, nearly excludes users, and then changes or disappears in response to the invisible hand of the market is a comparatively recent phenomenon. It is the result of the transformation of everyday life and the redefinition of the city which have accompanied the rise of capitalism. Steadily, the scope of involvement in housing, in work, and in city life has been narrowed. The final consequence is not only the loss of autonomy, of competence, of the city itself, but the loss even of the need for these things. The alienated user accepts these limitations as inevitable. Social architecture does not.

The 26 projects from 12 countries presented here share a view of architecture as an instrument for transforming both the environment and the people who live in it. The scale ranges from individual dwellings to neighborhoods to the city as a whole. All these levels of involvement are considered important: step-by-step, members of contemporary society must rediscover their need and their ability to shape the world in which they live.

Contributors to this volume—with one exception all are architects—were asked to describe the political context of their projects, to lay out their social objectives and relate them to the completed designs, and to evaluate the results, providing directions for future work. The book is divided into three sections, corresponding to the scope of the projects presented.

## Part 1: The Dwelling

The smallest scale is that of personal living space, the dwelling itself. This section includes model self-help schemes, as well as sophisticated, adaptable housing, such as Herman Hertzberger's Diagoon Houses and SAR-inspired projects, now quite common in Europe. John Carp, the present director of SAR in Holland has contributed a history of the organization's work since its inception under John Habraken in 1964.

Issues at this scale include the politics of self-help, the value of various techniques for design participation, and the effects of participation on resident satisfaction. Perhaps the knottiest problem that arises in this section is the appropriateness of a focus on the manipulation of private dwelling space. Here, as in all three sections of the book, certain salient issues have been singled out for discussion by informed commentators. Commentaries follow the project reports; when they deal with more than one project, they typically appear following the first to be discussed.

## Part 2: The Building Ensemble

This intermediate scale encompasses groups of buildings and small settlements. Projects range in size from Christopher Alexander's use of the pattern language to create a cluster of homes in Mexicali to Ralph Erskine's community on Byker Hill in Newcastle and Lucien Kroll's *zone sociale* at the new medical school in Brussels. Here the scope of involvement extends to the form of the building itself, its common spaces, and its site. At this level new issues are introduced: the need for a common language to facilitate communication, the difficulty of maintaining the professional commitment required by participatory design, the desirability of pluralism or populism in architectural expression, and the relationship between architecture and the creation of community.

## Part 3: The City

At the largest scale, the neighborhood and the city, citizen control constitutes a crucial test for democracy. Effective participation at the urban scale is in its rudimentary stages, although the quite different reports from Chadwick Floyd (of Moore Grover Harper) on the use of TV in urban design, from Boston's Southwest Corridor Project, and from two Community Design Centers show us that progress is continuous. Bologna, a socialist city, and Cuba, a socialist nation, offer us examples which go well beyond what we have achieved. They offer valuable lessons and a reminder of what remains to be done.

Issues raised at this level are complex and profound. They include the search for innovative methods for involving citizens in shaping the world they live in. New formal means to increase the transparency and legibility of the city are required. The miles upon miles of organized nowhere must be transformed into places worthy of our affection and commitment.

Together these projects illustrate the diversity and vitality of social architecture today. They offer somewhat different answers to fundamental cultural questions. They reflect different views of the correct relationship between architect and user, architecture and the public. There are, however, certain common themes that bind them:

1. The conviction that participation is crucial to the redirection of architecture and the city it creates.

2. An understanding that architecture is a form of public discourse and, as such, has the responsibility to reveal the social forces that condition it.

3. A belief in the contingent nature of present society and a view of history that clarifies the tasks confronting social architecture.

4. A response to Van Eyck's question about how to build: we should build so as to encourage critical reflection and the development of many-sided human beings, rich in needs.

## The Loss of the Traditional City

Architects are accustomed to dealing with needs quantified in terms of families to be housed, work stations or hospital beds to be provided. There is a more fundamental level of needs that, has at its source, drives to community, to competence, and to self-actualization. Perhaps the best way to examine these needs—and the task before social architecture—is to trace the changes that have taken place in everyday life since the beginning of the modern era and the loss of the traditional city.

For more than 100 years, writers on architecture have returned to the pre-industrial town for models of a saner, more organic society. Allowing for the tendency toward mythicization, and with full knowledge that for many life was nasty, brutish, and short, there is still much to learn from looking backward. The most important lessons lie in the radical circumscription of human roles and powers that are the result of the growth of the capitalist economic order.

The traditional city was no utopian democracy. Its spatial order was the order of the palace, cathedral, and market, representing the nobility, the clergy, and the merchant class. These institutions of political, spiritual, and economic power determined the form of the city. But down the lesser streets, in the smaller squares, there was considerable autonomy and a rich social life. The spatial subdivision of the traditional city corresponded to the gross division of labor and hence to the structure of the guilds, which dominated the sphere of production. Each guild was a parish, and within the parishes each household was a complete economic unit. Every dwelling was workshop, warehouse, training school, and home for family and apprentices. A garden at the rear dooryard guaranteed sustenance in good times and bad.

The workday started with the sun. In decent weather, shop doors were thrown open; work spilled out into the streets. The pace was steady, but not rushed. There was time for conversation with neighbors and passing strangers. In such towns, a simple walk to market was an education in political economy and technics.

As the guild regulated employment, wages, quality, and prices, competitiveness and suspicion did not yet discolor all social relations. Visual clues to status were not great. The houses of the journeymen and the masters shared a street, a common wall, and a common style. On religious holidays and civic occasions, all classes mingled freely. If they did not share power equally, they had a common understanding of the social order and a mutuality of interest in regard to the city itself. The encircling wall which distinguished an urban way of life and thought from the attitudes of the rurals beyond was the symbol of their bond. But this fusion of urban form and urban life was under pressure almost from the beginning. As Lewis Mumford has written in *The City in History:*

The economic history of the medieval town is largely a story of the transfer of power from a group of protected producers, earning a modest living,

achieving a state of relative equality, to a small group of wholesale merchants, engaged in large scale transactions for the sake of immense gains.

The story of the United States is, of course, a replication of this history under the special conditions of America. The self-governing towns of early New England remind us of what society might be without the distorting influences of class and wealth. These towns had the same quality of social and economic transparency as their earlier European counterparts, but considerably greater liberty, and they produced a very special sort of citizen. Alexis de Tocqueville's classic description tells us about the meaning of the town for the inhabitant:

. . . its wealth is the aim of his ambition and future exertions. He takes part in every occurrence in the place; he practices the art of government in the small sphere within his reach . . . he acquires a taste for order, comprehends the balance of powers, and collects clear practical notions on the nature of his duties and the extent of his rights.

The history of Newark provides us with an example of the fundamental social transformation which was just underway when Tocqueville was first published. Founded in 1666 by New England Puritans, by the time of the Civil War Newark was the nation's largest industrial center. But in 1820, the city's population barely exceeded 8000.* Craft production was the rule, and shops were small, averaging eight men. Following the traditional pattern, they were usually attached to the owner's house. Women and children played important roles in the workshop as well as the home. The family was the basic unit of production as well as of reproduction and consumption.

Each worker owned his own tools. Access to the tools and the knowledge of how to use them could be obtained only through apprenticeship and was protected both by custom and regulation by craft associations. Apprentices and journeymen were treated well, coming as they did from within the same

community and living under the same roof with the master craftsman and his family. Each could reasonably expect to become a self-employed master himself one day.

These small groups of craftsmen made entire products in their independent shops. Social status was linked to the quality of production. As specialized workers, they were already tied into an exchange economy. And as products made in this way were stamped with the personalities of their makers, economic interdependence was felt as personal interdependence. Exchange was the glue that made these artisan households a community.

Between 1790 and 1860, first in England and then in the U.S., wholesale merchants transformed themselves into industrialists and launched a revolution that quickly put an end to this way of life. After 800 years, the traditional city was replaced by a new type of habitat, a new *mentalité,* a new mode of production, and a new set of social relationships. Liberal historians view the results of the industrial revolution, on balance, as the slow but steady expansion of opportunity and choice. The alternative and more telling interpretation of the events focuses on the substitution of one set of freedoms for another, the sharp erosion of control over crucial areas of life, and the steady shrinkage of needs until only one, the need to consume, remains.

The central instrument in this profound restructuring of life was the factory. Two significant features explain the power of this invention: the use of machinery faster and more skillful than human hands and the spatial organization of hands (and it is to hands that workers were reduced) into specialized buildings under surveillance and control. The rationalization of work and the productivity of the ever-improving machines created impossible competition for the artisan class. Little by little they were forced to close their shops and enter the factories. The traditional nexus between life and work was broken. The family lost its role and its independence; its livelihood now depended on the chance sale of its members' labor time. Merchant capitalists had long since conceived the products of nature as commodities to be bought cheap and sold dear. Now industrial capitalists reduced human beings to a commodity—work—to be bought at the lowest market price.

---

* I am indebted here to Susan E. Hirsch's excellent *Roots of the American Working Class,* 1978.

5

To complete the revolution, space, the third and final factor of production, had to join the ranks of commodities. Land, which had always had a special significance in western political culture, became an "investment." Speculation in social space became a principal route to wealth. Artisans, who had once enjoyed independence and security, building and modifying their workshop homes as needed, now lived precariously at the whim of the markets in land and labor. Uncertainty became the only fixed rule of life.

## Loss of Control

In Newark, by 1860, almost all crafts, with the exceptions of blacksmithing and carpentry, were either fully industrialized or well on their way to being so. Less than 9 percent of male heads of households were self-employed, owning their own shops. The remainder, possessing neither tools nor skills that were not generally available, were losing control over the conditions of work. Hours were up. Wages were down. There was no longer any likelihood that workers would one day rise to ownership.

Once forced to give up control over tools and materials (the means of production), workers everywhere found that personal control of other crucial areas of life was also stripped away. No longer did they exercise discretion over the place of work, the pace of work, or the product of work. No creativity was desired—or permitted. The ever-finer division of labor, far from refining the skills of specialized workers, ensured that each need know less and less about production. This process of deskilling spread from the factory to the office and may only now be reaching its apogee with the universal dissemination of computers. It has two consequences of overwhelming importance. Adam Smith recognized the first at the very beginning of industrialization. In *The Wealth of Nations,* he wrote, with less exaggeration than one would like:

In the progress of the division of labour, the employment of the far greater part of those who live by labour, that is, of the great body of the people, comes to be confined to a few very simple operations, frequently to one or two. But the understandings of the greater part of men are necessarily formed by their ordinary employ-

ments. The man whose whole life is spent in performing a few simple operations, of which the effects too are, perhaps, always the same, or very nearly the same, has no occasion to exert his understanding, or to exercise his invention in finding out expedients for removing difficulties which never occur. He naturally loses, therefore, the habit of such exertion. . . . The torpor of his mind renders him, not only incapable of relishing or bearing a part in any rational conversation, but of conceiving any generous, noble, or tender sentiment, and consequently of forming any just judgment concerning many even of the ordinary duties of private life. Of the great and extensive interests of his country he is altogether incapable of judging . . .

The second consequence, no less significant, relates to the effects of deskilling on the relations between workers. As is widely recognized, each step in the rationalization of work increases the interchangeability of workers in their jobs. This homogenization of labor which reduces distinctions between workers intensifies the competition between them. In a society where unemployment is maintained at a high level, this competition colors all human contacts and exacerbates ethnic and racial conflict. It is not going too far to say that the famous shift from *gemeinschaft* to *geselschaft* is the result of the capitalist institution of a competitive market in labor.

Outside the workplace, everyday life changed as well. The city was now conceived as a machine to make money. Its primary function came to be the aggregation of labor for production and markets for consumption. To this end, first railroads, then highways, created regional supercities. The market in land allocated each location to the most profitable use. The new industrial division of labor became a spatial ordering principle. In the contemporary city it is mapped geographically, first as the segregation of functions—institutionalized as zoning—and then as the separation of classes. The wealthiest take up key positions at the center of culture and power or at the fringe in locales of established prestige. The remainder of the population distributes itself according to income and race unevenly over the territory of the metropolis. The planned paucity of public spaces and common

rituals ensures little face to face contact and the separate development of each group.

The medieval town opened its heart and its doors: work, courtship, worship, exchange, even the terrible justice of the gallows went on in public view. Firmly established rules regarding architectural styles and the modes of dress associated with the various trades helped the eye to understand the structure of life and work. Earlier, I described a walk through a traditional city as an education in technology and a lesson about the common interdependence of citizens in the urban economy. It is no longer so easy to learn the truth about the life of our cities. The spatial structure of the city of capitalism isolates people and activities and sharply limits the legibility of the manmade environment.

The new opacity of urban form was first noted by Frederick Engels in his description of Manchester in 1845:

The town itself is peculiarly built, so that a person may live in it for years, and go in and out daily without coming into contact with a working-people's quarter or even with workers . . . outside [the city of Manchester] lives the upper and middle bourgeoisie . . . in free, wholesome country air, in fine comfortable homes . . . and the finest part of the arrangement is this, that the members of the money aristocracy can take the shortest road through the middle of all the laboring districts to their places of business, without ever seeing that they are in the midst of the grimy misery that lurks to the right and left. For the thoroughfares leading from the Exchange in all directions out of the city are lined, on both sides, with an almost unbroken series of shops, and are so kept in the hands of the middle and lower bourgeoisie which, out of self interest, cares for a decent and cleanly external appearance and *can* care for it. True, these shops . . . are more elegant in the commercial and residential quarters than when they hide grimy working-men's dwellings; but they suffice to conceal from the eyes of the wealthy men and women of strong stomachs and weak nerves the misery and grime which form the complement of their wealth.

Economic historians like David Gordon point out that this now familiar environmental pattern has the additional benefit of making the rich invisible to the poor and shielding the new concentrations of wealth from scrutiny.

The natural outcome of the sum of the changes in everyday life that we have been cataloging is an epidemic of alienation.* The principal causes can be summarized this way:

1. Society has been fragmented into "interests" that are the unavoidable effect of a competitive market in labor. Community is almost unknown; society is reduced to an aggregation of fearful and mutually suspicious individuals.
2. The development of the economic order imposes an ever narrower division of labor. This is an effective obstacle to shared knowledge and understanding. This problem is exacerbated by the opacity of the city—a product of the segregation and separations that delimit experience.
3. Further, docile specialization at work has measurable negative effects on participation in family and community life.** The number of roles we are comfortable playing shrinks, and with it the memory of what were formerly important human needs.
4. There has been an inversion of ends and means in regard to work. Work is no longer performed for itself, or as a way of satisfying one's own needs or those of one's family. What

work now creates is not ours, not what we want or need. It is done for others; what is produced is theirs. Life begins only when the workday ends.

We are confronted with an extraordinary paradox. The economic system that created the greatest cornucopia of social wealth the world has ever seen also produces impoverished individuals. Human capacities and desires shrink to those that the market can satisfy at a profit. Needs formerly considered the most important are lost, among them the needs for many-sided competence and for creativity. Together, these losses imply a greater loss, the loss of the need for architecture and for the city, that is, for rich social existence.

This change, which followed the destruction of the traditional city, was recognized early by John Ruskin. In a prophetic address to the Royal Institute of British Architects in 1865, he said:

All lovely architecture was designed for cities in cloudless air; for cities in which piazzas and gardens opened in bright populousness and peace, cities built that men might live happily in them, and take delight daily in each other's presence and powers. *But* our cities . . . which are mere crowded masses of store, and warehouse, and counter, and are therefore to the rest of the world what the larder and cellar are to a private house; cities in which the object of men is not life, but labour; and in which all chief magnitude of edifice is to enclose machinery; cities in which the streets are not avenues for the passing procession of a happy people, but the drains for the discharge of a tormented mob, in which the only object in reaching any spot is to be transferred to another; in which existence becomes mere transition, and every creature is only one atom in a drift of human dust, and current of interchanging particles, circulating here by tunnels underground, and there by tubes in the air, for a city, or cities, such as this no architecture is possible—nay, no desire of it is possible to their inhabitants.

Rekindling the desire for architecture and for the city is the task that social architecture sets for itself. Through the production of architecture, it tests new roles, restores old needs, and produces

new ones. The making of architecture is grasped as an opportunity to help users reflect on their roles, on themselves, and on their very power of reflection. At its best, social architecture aims to create and develop critical consciousness. As Paolo Freire has written (in "Education as the Practice of Freedom"):

. . . hope coincides with an increasingly critical perception of reality. Society now reveals itself as something unfinished, not as something inexorably given; it has become a challenge rather than a hopeless limitation.

Social architecture defines three principal strategies for carrying out its difficult task. These strategies reflect the complex character of architecture as process, form, and content. Each is called upon to make a specific contribution to critical awareness and rich human needs. In the realm of process, we will consider new meanings for *participation*. Form will be called upon to provide *rational transparency*. Content will be discussed as *the structure of experience*. Together they posit a radical alteration in the relationship between people and the built world.

## Participation

The widespread acceptance of the principle of user participation in housing and urban development is the major achievement of social architecture in the recent past. As a result, architecture has shaken off the shibboleth of universal norms and begun to reflect the diversity of individuals and aspirations in a plural society. It is true that the goals of participation have been limited in many cases to individual satisfaction, and that design participation has not yet extended, as it must, to the workplace. However, when contrasted with the anomic production of commercial architecture and the elitist cultural models of the postmodern academics, design participation has proved its value.

Think, for example, of Atwells Avenue in Providence or UHAB's sweat equity rehabilitation in Harlem, both described in the book. For the first time, the people of that Providence Italian neighborhood found the means to express their institutions, their sense of occasion and place. In Harlem, black Muslims, against all odds, built homes

---

* Alienation is a notoriously slippery concept, but also a necessary category. I use it here not in the personal psychological sense of estrangement or anomie, but to describe a society—a congeries of institutions, ways of livelihood and means of life—in which human beings seem to be in the grip of events, unable to comprehend or control the forces they have themselves set in motion. As this state of affairs, from within society, may well seem to be "normal," it is useful to consider Bertell Ollman's analogy of alienation to health and illness (see *Alienation*, 1976): "We only know what it is to have a disease because we know what it is not to." Only with difficulty, of course, can we know what it is not to live in alienation. To form an idea of what society—and life—could be like without it, we must add together our memories of our peak experiences: the intense pleasure of creative work, heightened awareness when falling in love, the exhilaration of collective effort, perhaps in sports, the youthful desire to take on new challenges. . . . There is no reason why life should not approach this as a steady state. The European Situationist slogan sums up the desire: "Vivre sans temps mort."

** For a thorough discussion of the relationship between participation and the sense of political efficacy, see Carole Pateman, *Participation and Democratic Theory*, 1970.

and a mosque for themselves. In both cases, ordinary people, with the support of architects, were able to give form to their lives and cultures.

Other projects reported here emphasize different outcomes of participation. John Sharratt who works in Boston is concerned with preventing the displacement of working class communities through gentrification and institutional expansion. Architects writing from Cuba focus on the difficult problem of housing a growing population. To increase production, Cuban architects have refined a small number of building systems specifically to accommodate large-scale participation of unskilled workers in construction. Cuban architects are aware of the shortcomings of some aspects of their new communities, but they accept the fact that the provision of housing and the solidarity that grows out of collective building are more important now than formal experimentation.

Many architects express disappointment with the quality of participatory architecture. To them, it is banal when it conforms to familiar models and chaotic when it expresses the choices of participants. Those who criticize on aesthetic grounds ignore either the necessity of social change or its difficulty. They seem to wish to go beyond without going through the present cultural moment. But the projects we are dealing with here, for the most part, still have one foot imbedded in the old system of relations and the needs and tastes that come from it. The other has found a foothold in the future, and it is this leap that qualifies these projects as social architecture. Each project begins with people as they are—and moves them toward a better understanding of themselves and their alternatives. At the same time, their designers are groping toward forms which can speak intelligibly about new relationships and needs. The process is slow; no single participatory effort can take more than a few steps forward. Yet each project gives its participants a taste for the power of architecture. One important function of participation is the creation of demand, the rekindling of desire. . . .

Since the rise of participatory practice there have been architects who, dismissing the limitations inherent in the popular lack of experience of good design, have gone so far as to describe professional leadership as a restriction of the inalienable right to environmen-

tal self-determination. The vocal opposition attacks any collaboration between designer and user as an abdication of the architect's *raison d'être.* Overlooked in the debate between formalists and populists is the central argument for participation. The story of Orcasitas makes the point clear.

In Orcasitas at the edge of Madrid, participation transformed a marginal squatter settlement into a cohesive political organization, capable of demanding and obtaining roads, utilities, schools, and, eventually, new housing. The sophistication of the local leadership and the talent of the volunteer architects held the promise of significant innovations in design. But when the time came to build, the people of Orcasitas insisted on conventional apartment towers based on upper-middle-class models. At that moment, the former squatters had achieved what surely had formerly appeared to them as impossible. They had stood up to a dictatorial government and won. Land they had nearly lost was theirs forever. Their new homes were spacious and safe. If their image of architecture was little changed, they themselves were not. It is on this transformation that participation must focus.*

The true significance of participation lies in its effects on the participants, not on architecture. When alienation has reached extreme levels, the need to overcome it must be produced. Participation in the making of architecture represents an almost unique opportunity to evoke this need. Participation is the arena in which people can relearn environmental competence, experience the pleasures of collective work, and develop the ability to question the nature of the manmade world. I believe there is a fundamental drive to competence, a basic need for human beings to become the subjects of history and not its objects. It has been difficult indeed to express this drive since the loss of the traditional city, but there is evidence that it has not been utterly suppressed.

Jean Piaget, for instance, in *The Origins of Intelligence in Children,* presents findings that children focus on those aspects of the world around them that they can affect in valued ways. Piaget concludes that "we demand a

knowledge of effects and to be ourselves producers of effects." Psychologist Robert White, stimulated by Piaget's propositions, reviewed the related literature in a well-known article, "Motivation Reconsidered: The Concept of Competence," In his summary, he writes that there is a need to deal with the environment and to do so continuously and effectively:

Dealing with the environment means carrying on a continuing transaction which gradually changes one's relation to the environment. Because there is no consummatory climax, satisfaction has to be seen as lying in a considerable series of transactions, in a trend of behavior rather than a goal that is achieved. It is difficult to make the word satisfaction have this connotation, and we shall do well to replace it [in order to explain what human beings seek] by "feeling of efficacy. . . ."

Sociologist Talcott Parsons found important reinforcement for this drive to competence in American institutions. In a paper entitled "Definitions of Health and Illness in the Light of American Values and Social Structure," Parsons wrote that:

. . . even so complex and highly differentiated a society as our own can be said to have a relatively well-integrated system of institutionalized common values at the societal level. Ours I shall characterize as a pattern emphasizing "activism" . . . "worldliness," and "instrumentalism."

He argues that the most highly valued roles and tasks—and hence individuals—are those that demonstrate mastery over the social or physical environment, that successfully pursue practical ends, and that illustrate a belief in achievement and general progress. Parsons then defines somatic and mental illness *as the inability to incorporate or respond to these common values.* He makes the point that the development of industrialization, urbanism, and mass communications has made the problem of capacity to meet these demands more urgent. In an especially arresting phase, Parsons writes, "The alienation involved in the motivation to illness may then be interpreted to involve alienation from a set of expectations which put particular stress on independent achievement."

---

* Evidence of their transformation comes not only from their political success, but also from the fact that in the second phase of construction they are already talking about more adventuresome designs (see page 279).

And he notes that, "Recovery is defined as a job to be done in cooperation with those who are technically qualified to help...."

Clearly, architects are among those who are qualified to help in recovery from the distress that accompanies inability to shape a responsive environment. Participation is the means, and the richer the experience—the more aspects of the total process opened for involvement,* the higher the degree of participant control, the more comprehensive the education that accompanies participation—the greater the impact on alienation will be, the further the recovery toward health.

Earlier in this essay, I cited Giancarlo De Carlo's list of steps which describe the production of the environment. This list was originally included in order to illustrate the increasing marginalization of the user in the manmade world. Now it must be seen as a checklist of decisions to be brought back, one by one, under user control.** Christopher Alexander and his associates have given us an example of what can be expected from an extension of participation. In their description of the families with whom they planned and built a small community in Mexico, they write:

They have shaped the world as they have shaped themselves. And they

_____

* Participation is also a way of overcoming the debilitating division of labor in society. Cuban architecture since the Revolution pays particular attention to this potential (see my Commentary on page 361ff). Of more immediate import to architects working in the United States and Europe is Lucien Kroll's medical school project, which introduces the possibility of nonalienated work. Kroll insisted that the *construction workers* be given certain design responsibilities. The men building concrete walls and columns were encouraged to line the forms with beautiful materials picked up in the fields on their way to work. Masons were called on to revive old skills and to elaborate freely on themes laid down by the architect. Their exhilaration is evidenced by the inventions they left behind, their pride by reports of workmen bringing wives and children to the site on their days off to exhibit their creativity. In *The Stones of Venice,* Ruskin called to our attention the consequences of the modern divorce of manual and intellectual work. Considering the effect on building workers of the architect's desire for perfection and control, he warned us that we are "put to a stern choice. You must either make a tool of the creature, or a man of him. You cannot make both."

** Of course, as the scale of decisions extends from the dwelling to the city, the definition of user moves from individual to group to polity. In this regard, see the SAR chart of participatory levels on page 26.

now live in the world they have created for themselves ... watching the water trickle through the common land, looking after the neighbors' children, waiting to help friends.... They have become powerful, and are powerful, in a way that almost takes the breath away.

The paramount purpose of participation is not good buildings, but good citizens in a good society.

## Rational Transparency

It is a fundamental precept that sound decisions require shared and accurate knowledge of the world. At the same time, it is acknowledged that the manmade world is increasingly less a source of reliable information. The mute quality of the urban environment is frequently attributed to the reductive code of the International Style. However, there are more fundamental factors at work. I have referred to the isolating effects of the division of labor. Role differentiation tends to subdivide society into groups with basically different relationships to the urban scene. The segregation of functions and the spatial separation of social classes have also been pointed to as causes of deepening environmental opacity.

Given this opacity, the complexity of modern life, and the narrowness of each individual's view from within it, architecture becomes crucial as a source of information. Abstract entities like the state, the system of justice, and the labor market control the pattern of our lives. They are important elements in a vast social structure of which we are a part. Yet this underlying reality is as intangible as it is pervasive. We cannot know it directly. In an important sense, it is mediated for us by architecture. In this context, architecture is the concrete manifestation of the institutions that make up society. Much of what we know of these institutions and their meanings we know from the large array of building types and styles we encounter. Architecture is also the reification of social roles and a set of three-dimensional statements about power relationships. To break the code of architecture at the scale of the city is to grasp the structure of society. Conversely, to comprehend our real situation, we require an architecture which bares its content—an architecture of rational transparency.

The task of social architecture as form, then, is to make legible the institutions, relationships, and values that are at the heart of social life. These must be expressed in a manner that makes them available to reason, reveals their contingent nature, and brings what is accepted without thought into the realm of critical consciousness. This legibility will require the careful employment and extension of familiar architectural languages. It will not do, if honest communication is the aim, to introject new systems of meaning, whether derived from an admired past or the architect's fertile brain. And for a time at least, architecture must cease to aspire to the condition of art.

It is the nature of art to impose order and meaning on an extrinsic subject. In classical theory, art uses visible materials to reveal a metaphysical reality which is not directly apprehensible, e.g., religious doctrine or philosophical truth. The romantics redefined this goal to include authentic experience: art as the expression of the artist's character and feelings. The avant garde now speaks of past art as the subject for art today. Architecture surely contains all these possibilities, but none is appropriate to the present moment. Architecture today must reveal its content precisely and without rhetoric. What we need now is architecture *degree zero*—a radical functionalism that refuses to hide—not in the name of formal order and not for beauty's sake—what it knows about life.

Functionalism has been caught for years in a confusion about just which of a building's many functions should control expression. This is not the place for a full discussion of the issue, but it should be made clear that the functional design I am proposing is not that of a Louis Sullivan or a Mies van der Rohe. Sullivan, in "The Tall Office Building Artistically Considered," for example, describes the stacked floors of office workers as essentially identical and without interest. To give form to the office tower he is forced to fall back on the tripartite organizational scheme of the traditional Italian palazzo. An historical *parti* is invoked where a careful examination of the individual groups at work could have been the basis of architectural form. Mies' decision to concentrate on structure as function is another reversal of ends and means. Beyond building type *per se*, we learn precious little about the specific activities

9

and people behind his elegant walls. Knowledge of the world is a human need, and architecture can only satisfy that need if functional design comes to mean communication of everyday life.

The SAR projects, with their clear separation of Support and Infill—related realms under communal and individual control, respectively—offer one approach to rational transparency. Klostermuren in Sweden, with its consciously adopted family of forms, represents a straightforward, complementary approach. The preservation program for Bologna is a more complex example. The architect in charge, Pier Luigi Cervellati, calls the city's historic core "the collective memory of the population." With its medieval form, it still speaks of the pre-industrial unity of life and work. To reawaken the collective memory, Bologna combines programs of urban information, neighborhood governance, and preservation approaches that knit together the traditional fabric and adapt landmark structures for collective needs. By increasing the legibility of the original code and contrasting it with new uses at prominent points, Bologna approaches transparency and offers itself for reappropriation by its citizens.

## The Structure of Experience

Rational transparency calls on buildings to reveal their true nature and meaning. However, any new legibility will have limited impact if at the same time the pattern of uses within the city and its districts is not changed. It is the spatial distribution of people and their activities that shapes our experience of everyday life—and our consciousness in turn. If we can accept the principle that human beings need first to comprehend the world before they can change it, then the ordering of urban activities—the spatial structure of experience—becomes of central concern.

Kroll's is the most important effort reported here to condense activities and connect diverse populations, but Ralph Erskine's Byker plan also responds to this need. In addition to the expected shops and services, the Byker plan contains small and mid-size workshops to encourage production within the quarter. Cuba, as an expression of egalitarianism, is steadily reducing the importance of its city cores and replanning its urban districts as substantially self-contained entities, each with equal opportunities for education, work and

culture.

The task of overcoming the opacity of the city, however, is one that, for social architecture, lies largely in the future. In our own country, architects have led the city away from a traditional integration of activities into functional zoning. The case for exclusive land use areas was based on the need to quarantine noxious uses, preserve property values, and rationalize transportation. When effects on workers (assumed to be largely male) were considered, they were restricted to those that might affect them as tools in a system of production, not as whole men with rich needs. No one asked about the effects on women and children. But the need for architecture as the structure of experience is summed up succinctly in Louis Kahn's memory of Philadelphia, "where as a small boy walking through it," he could find "what he wanted to do his whole life."

The making of cities where people can discover themselves out of our present situation requires a total overhaul of contemporary ideas of zoning and urban design. The deprivation experienced in the sanitized cores of our cities, with their faceless office towers and anonymous streetscapes, has often been described. An equal number of critics has remarked on the sterility of purely residential districts. Robbed of these human uses and the people associated with them, the industrial parks and loft districts of suburb and city, where millions spend their waking hours, are cruelly monotonous.

Previously, land uses were brought together or separated on planning maps to promote economic efficiency. Now they must be juxtaposed spatially to present the full panoply of urban life. Movement through the new city should be designed to reveal the rich and complex collective effort of which we are a part and on which we depend. There are few industries today so noisy or dangerous that they must be excluded from participation in the city of experience. Computer networks and telecommunications reduce the office sector's need to dominate central locations. New York's (or London's) dispersion of theatres and art galleries indicates that the concentration of culture is not a law of nature. Measures will be needed to limit the agglomeration and density of uses and to control land prices. Planning and economic development policies must be redirected to encourage a self-

sustaining mix of production, residential, and service activities over the entire territory of the city. The urban designer's concern will be with parcellization and grain: there is, surely, a correct spatial range for activities that responds at the same time to economic requirements and the goals of transparency and experience. The city as education is the next central task for social architecture.

## Architecture and Morality

I have proposed three principles to define social architecture. Together, participation, rational transparency, and the city as education are the contribution architecture can make to overcoming the alienation that marks us and the society in which we live. Social architecture as presented in this book is consciously an architecture "in-between"; it avoids idealistic utopias but continually addresses the need to challenge received ideas and propose alternatives. Social architecture insists that the process of conceiving and producing the manmade world involves moral choices. The power of architecture can continue in the service of the *status quo,* or it can be harnessed to a program of social change. As social architecture in its practice and theory not only proposes the world transformed, but also suggests the means of its transformation, stern choice is again put to us as architects. At the beginning of the rapid transformation of the traditional city, Henri de Saint-Simon wrote:

> The Golden Age of the human race is not behind us at all, it is ahead, it lies in the perfection of the social order; our forefathers have never seen it; our children will reach there some day. It is up to us to trace the path for them.

These are difficult times. They demand architects grounded in history, technically prepared to build and allied to those who need them most. This is the continuing path of social architecture, and if we trace it assiduously, it will lead us to that world where aesthetic is not the quality of isolated objects, but of life itself.

# 1: The Dwelling

# Diagoon Houses
# Delft, Holland

Dutch architect Herman Hertzberger is well known in this country for his Centraal Beheer office building in Apeldoorn and the recently built music center for Utrecht. Earlier, he built a small series of "carcase houses" in Delft that are described in the following article. In these dwellings, as in his larger buildings, Hertzberger eschews the SAR distinction of Support and Infill and the technological bias of industrialized systems, and recognizes the difficulties inherent in involving users directly in design.

Against this process he sets his concept of "appropriation." He asserts a central role for the architect in creating form—but not the static and alienating form of the postmodernists. Instead, he argues, what matters is the interaction of form and user, until they "mutually take possession of each other." The modifications, accommodations, additions, and personalizations that have taken place in the 10 years since the Diagoon Houses were constructed constitute solid support for his position. In the Commentary that follows, five families in the Diagoon houses tell what it is like to live in space designed to be "appropriated" through active intervention.

1. Project for a community of carcase houses showing how residents might elaborate the basic unit.

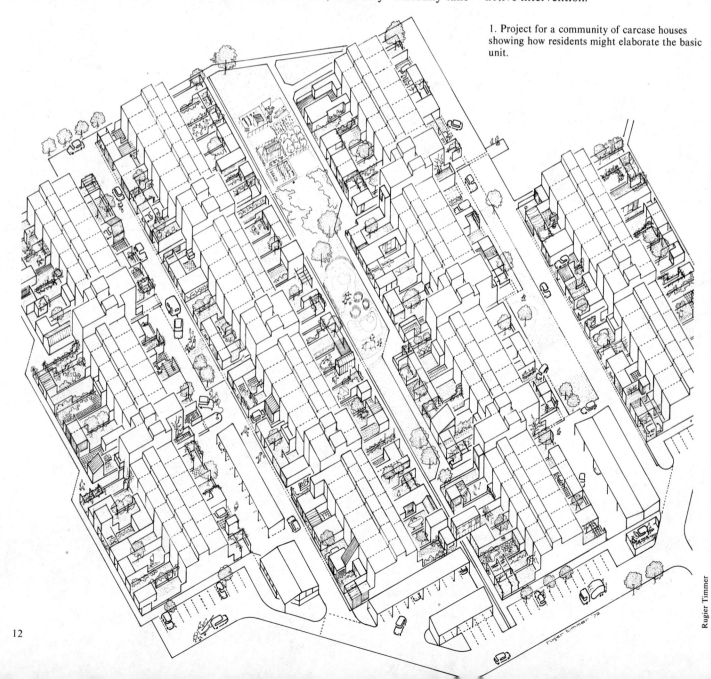

Rugier Timmer

# The Interaction of Form and Users

**Herman Hertzberger, architect**
**Amsterdam**

This is a sketch, with an optimistic tint, of what we can do at present—with some practical suggestions offered to those to whom architecture seems to have lost its point.

It is not the outward form wrapped around the object that matters to us, but form in the sense of inbuilt capacity and potential as a vehicle of significance. Form can be filled with significance, but can also be deprived of it again, depending on the use that's made of it, through the values we attach or add to it, or even deprive it of. All this is dependent on the way in which users and forms react to and play on each other. The fact that we put "form" in a central position with respect to such notions as "space" or "architecture" means in itself no more than a shifting of emphasis. What we are talking about here is in fact a notion of form different from that which presumes a formal and unchanging relationship between object and viewer. The case we want to put forth is that it is the capacity to absorb, carry, and convey significance that defines what form can bring about in the users, and conversely, what the users can bring about in the form. What matters is the interaction of form and users, what they convey to each other and bring about in each other, and how they mutually take possession of each other.

When one considers the conditions under which people live—or subsist— all over the world, it seems absurdly pretentious even to pose the question whether, as an architect, one can make even the very slightest contribution. Everywhere it has been the people themselves who, without even a minimum of outside help, have gone on making do with the given conditions. With seemingly inexhaustible vitality, and usually with the help of what others regarded as waste material, they have often produced surprising and touching results. We could set out by assuming, as many do, that all of what architects do is unnecessary, since people, left to themselves, could provide for their own needs

better than we can provide for them, if only we give them the room. But would this not be to abuse the invention and apparently limitless adaptability with which people, however confined their circumstances, make do with the impossible, making the unusable useful and the uninhabitable habitable?

Wherever the architect effectively determines the environment of people on a large scale and gives it form in word and deed, he in fact contributes, as is continually being demonstrated, to the perpetuation and extension of a world where everything is too cold and too large: a grim underworld of gravestone skyscrapers, passages, lifts, tunnels, and pipes through which people circulate and are transported and manipulated, a world of empty squares and

2. The Diagoon Houses in Delft today.

smooth, rejecting, untouchable walls between the asphalt that is spewed out as a choking crust over steadily enlarging areas of our towns.

This whole misformed world is in fact no more than a gigantic storage system where nobody really feels at home and everybody is an outsider. This is a no-man's-land, from which none of us can disengage himself but in which no one is really involved—a world of alienation.

The architect, as we know, has never been very human: throughout history he always served the happy few and never the great number. Since building costs money, he was always on the side of money: the wrong side. Or did he just stand for the wrong things? He has occupied himself with pyramids, temples, cathedrals, palaces, and office buildings, and more often allowed himself to be exploited as a tool for repressing the

people than helped them to liberate themselves. Partly as a result of his forced marriage with aesthetics, he has existed more to honor and celebrate the established order of the few than to stimulate better conditions for the many, more a servant of the repressors than of the repressed.

Ordinary people used to build their own houses until they could no longer do so because they had been chased from their own territory; when they were bereft of everything—work, land, and house—the architect still did not do his job, but went on to put the flourish on the organization, refining the alienation process instead of combating it. In order to make any real contribution, architects have to use everything they influence or create to support the people in the struggle against alienation from their surroundings, from each other, and from themselves. They must combat the continually self-extending inhospitableness of the no-man's-land by providing the people with an appropriate environment which has scope for everyone: an arena in which each can play as many parts as he has within him, so that everyone can become more truly himself.

Everything we make has to offer a helping hand to the people to let them become more intimate with their surroundings, with each other, and with themselves; it has to do with making shoes that fit instead of pinch. And if there's any truth in the postulate that the solid matter making up our built environment is the mold in which human behavior is cast since, unable to disengage ourselves from it, we have no alternative but to adjust, then the architect and town planner must set themselves to altering the mold, exploiting every possibility of making the world less abstract, less hard and alien, a warmer place, friendly, more hospitable, more appropriable—a world, in short, that is relevant to its inhabitants.

Designing ought to mean a better disciplining of the material, with an eye to getting more in return for your money. Everything that is given a deliberate form should function better, should do its work, be appropriate for the job expected of it by different people in different situations at different moments, and this in endless retake. Making something new each time would be not only useless, but impossible. What is possible is to present the same things in

such a way that something new can be read into them. What matters with forms, just as with words and sentences, is how they are read, what images they evoke in the "reader." Seen through a different eye and in different situations, a form will evoke other images and acquire new significance. And it is this experimental phenomenon that provides the key to a new notion of form which we can use to make things adjustable to more situations.

## Diagoon: Experimental Carcase Houses

The idea determining the "carcase houses," eight prototypes of which have been built in Delft, is that they are on principle incomplete. The plan is to a certain extent indefinite, so that the occupants themselves will be able to decide how to divide the space and live in it and where they will sleep and eat. If the composition of the family changes, the house can be adjusted and, to some degree, enlarged. What has been designed should be seen as an unfinished framework. The carcase is a half-product which everyone can complete according to his own needs.

Many people are of the opinion that, because of their relatively high building costs, these houses don't make much sense as an experiment, and indeed we have not been able to prevent their being occupied by a group that is much too select in terms of income and motivation. And apart from that, it is a very limited number of houses, so that whatever conclusions we make cannot be taken as generally valid. But they are meant to show what should be possible today as a response to the sort of housing demands we suspect many people have. It is an attempt to get away from a number of persistent stereotypes that still dominate housing.

Architects must not just show what is possible. They must also, and especially, show what should be possible for everyone. What matters is that there is a lot to learn from how the occupants react in individual situations to the superabundance of instigators they are offered. We must not forget that things have been put into practice here, however insufficiently, which we are sometimes tempted to brush off too easily. It is too readily forgotten that changes take place very slowly and that it is essential that each step be built on the ex-

perience of the preceding one. This is valid not only for architects, but also for other specialists, and especially for the authorities with their regulations that are changed only when new hard facts come to light in practice. The starting point for the design of houses is still the conception formed by authorities, investors, sociologists, and architects about what people want. This conception cannot be more than a stereotype to which perhaps everyone seems by and large to conform, but to which no one person completely conforms. It is the collective interpretation by a few of the individual wishes of many. What do we really know about everybody's individual wishes, and what should we do to find out? The study of human behavior, no matter how painstakingly undertaken, can never bore through the thick skin of conditioning which dominates that behavior and prevents the emergence of a real personal exercise of the will. Because we shall never come to know what each person really wants for himself, no one will ever be in a position to devise for others the houses which

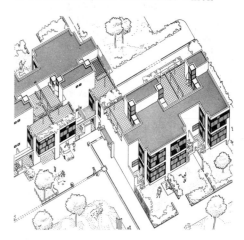

3. Axonometric view of the Diagoon project.

each individual would find appropriate to himself.

When people were still individually building their own houses, they were not free either, since every society is for the individual simply a basic given pattern to which he is subsidiary. Everyone is doomed to be whatever he wants to be seen as by others. That is the price that the individual pays to society in order to remain an insider, and so he is simultaneously possessor of and possessed by a collective pattern of behavior. Even if people built their own houses they could not escape from this, but instead of having to accept the fact

4. Theme and variations: alternate uses of the house's many levels.

5. Diagoon plans and section.

that there is only one place to put the dining table, everyone would at least be able to interpret the collective pattern in his own personal way.

Each Diagoon house fundamentally consists of two fixed cores, with a number of floors differing in height by half a story forming the living units. These can take on any function: living area, sleeping area, study, and play, sitting, or dining area. In each unit, a part can be divided off to make a room and the rest is an indoor balcony looking onto the living hall which runs the full height of the house. These balconies, which could be furnished individually by the members of the family, together form the living area for the family as community. There is no longer a strict division between living area and sleeping area (with its forced "going up-stairs"). Each member of the family has his own part of the house and the big communal living room.

One might assume that in fact we only have to make unemphatic empty cartridges, as neutral as possible, so as to allow the occupants optimal freedom to fulfill their specific wants. However paradoxical it may seem, it is very questionable whether such a degree of freedom might not have a paralyzing effect, since, although in theory very many possibilities then present themselves, you will still not be able to make

6., 7., 8. Interior views showing residents' transformations within the adaptable spatial order.

the choice that is most appropriate for you. It is like the sort of menu that offers such an endless array of dishes that instead of making you hungry it dulls your appetite.

Not only is it a necessary condition for every act of choosing that the propositions can be grasped (and must thus be limited), but the chooser must also be able to imagine the possibilities one by one as ideas within, and as part of,

his frame of reference and thus be able to "connotate" them with images from his own experience. Freedom in terms of possibilities can only be exploited when the chooser gets a chance to use them to evoke associations in himself, and thus to form his own judgment by putting them next to images that were already present in him, either consciously or in his unconscious. When the image called up by the new stimulus is compared with the images already collected in previous experience, it is recognized and put to the test as a useful addition to the world he believes in—his familiar personal environment—to become another brick added in the build-up of his personality.

If this is so—that the mechanism of choice can be activated only if there is recognition of, or identification with, the images already stored in experience—then with everything we make and propose, we are concerned with doing our utmost to evoke such associations in the users. The more associations something evokes, the more people (and the more of their personal situations) will be able to resonate with it; precisely those associations will be evoked in the user that

Willem Diephraam

are relevant for him at that moment. Each form should, therefore, instead of being neutral, contain the greatest possible variety of propositions that, without limiting the various users to one specific direction, can constantly initiate associations in them.

If we take, for instance, a dark space or niche, then for most people it will suggest something of a safe corner, but for each individual it has a different emphasis, relevant to his personality. Thus it can have connotations of a secluded corner to sit in, quiet study corner, bed niche, darkroom, or storage place for food or other belongings. If it is to have the capacity to summon up all these kinds of associations and be able to contain them, every house should somewhere have such a dark niche. In a similar way, small rooms, tower rooms, attics, cellars, and windows under the eaves induce other trains of association. The richer the variety a house offers in this respect, the greater is its capacity to suit the richly varied reference worlds of its occupants.

The bareness and uninhabitability of most new buildings becomes obvious in this regard and is in sad contrast with what an old house has to offer. One need only think of the inexhaustible possibilities in old houses for converting and furnishing them in as many ways as there are people. Even when, like new buildings, their designs were based on a stereotyped scheme, they have much more to offer because of their greater richness in qualities that give impulse to new associations, making them always appropriate for others and allowing themselves to be appropriated.

Houses should, not only inside but also on the outside, permit occupiers to convert them to their own needs. Internally, it is especially the needs of family members that matter; outside it is relations with others that are involved. Here the starting point is that it must be possible, without being obligatory, for everyone to identify and define his own territory. It must be made possible to extend the interior at the cost of your own exterior space.

Diagoon facades were designed as a framework that can be filled in freely by the occupants with either glass or solid panels. The framework is a constant and represents, one might say, the order within which everybody's individual freedom and all freedoms together can be acted out and be contained. The

Willem Diephraam

9. The roof greenhouse was added by the owners.

10,11. The architect provides the cues; families interpret them according to their needs and those of their neighbors.

12. Finding new uses for common elements.

13. Diagoon Houses in the process of being appropriated by their inhabitants.

framework is devised to accept all infills conceivable within the set regulations, in the sense that the sum of the various infills together will always amount to a coherent work.

With every intervention on the outside you will have something to do with your neighbor, and to avoid your taking advantage of your freedom at the cost of his, a mutual decision will always be necessary. This state of affairs can give rise to conflict situations. People no longer sit safely within the walls of their own little castle, protected from one another by the authorities, but are dependent upon one another, and this is what society really means.

How much you have to do with your neighbor depends very much on the sort of boundary there is between gardens. A fence is based on the idea of isolating two areas as much as possible. Leaving them completely open, however, means that you cannot avoid being seen by each other, that you cannot get out of each other's way, and that you cannot hold a conversation without knowing that your neighbors, whether they want to or not, are listening in. But who would have the nerve, in a situation where this openness is an obvious part

of the design, like a proviso in the social contract, to go and make a partition whenever it suits him? By suggesting not more than the beginnings of a wall at the boundary between premises as an invitation to which everyone can give his answer, we legalize, as it were, the measures that everyone individually would like to take but, left on his own, would hesitate to begin. Neighbors will then perhaps be induced to consult each other and agree about what kind of separation should be made and even make a communal activity of building it. There is a chance that they will decide on making something in which the emphasis is less on separation than on joint use. In Delft, a low line of perforated blocks separating backyards makes the foundation for a brick wall, or fence posts can be propped in the perforations. If one does not want visual separation, then there need be no more than a low wall or some greenery.

These houses all have a roof terrace as well as a garden, and this is perhaps a bit of an exaggeration in view of the extra costs involved. But, nonetheless, roof terraces have specific possibilities and can in many ways provide a substitute where it is difficult or impossible to

14,15,16. Over the years, Diagoon residents have made good use of the possibilities afforded by the design of the houses.

make a garden. They have the advantage that they are almost always sunny since they are not shaded by surrounding buildings. Between neighboring roof terraces, a construction of bars has been provided as definition and boundary of the two areas. Bars invite one to hang up or fix things, especially lightweight things of a less permanent character, such as sailcloth or reed matting. You can also let plants climb up them, or tie your wash line on them. Perhaps the reason that bars offer such a strong incitement in every situation is that things can be fixed on them without any great complications, so that it's an obvious thing to do.

The ground at the front of the houses has been kept public. Although this land, strictly speaking, belongs to the houses, front gardens have not been anticipated. The boundary between the houses has not been indicated, and the area has not been handled in a way that suggests any private claim. It has been paved with concrete tiles which, since they are used on all Dutch pavements, suggest the idea of a public street. The occupants are beginning to remove some of the paving and to plant greenery. The paving stones have been retained to form a path to the front door, or wherever people want to bring their cars near the house. Every resident takes over that part of the area for which he has something in mind, and he makes use of as much as he needs and not more than he can cope with. The rest is left open and remains public and accessible by everyone. If we had started with the idea of division into private yards, no doubt everyone would have done his best to make something of it for himself, but a strict, built-in division between private area and public street would have been established. Now an in-between area has been created in the intermingling zone of the strictly private areas (the houses) and the public domain (the street). In this in-between area of public and private, the individual and collective claims mingle and conflicts are solved and reconciled. It is preeminently here that everyone plays the roles which show what he wants to be, how he wants to be seen by others. And here is revealed what the individual and society have to offer each other.

Just as on the garden side of each house, a screened-off corner has been provided as extension of the house on the street side—a porch where you are

protected waiting at the door, where departures can be delayed, and where you can sit outside in front of your house. This front terrace can, if you like, be built upon to make a storage space for bicycles.

However far the designer goes, it is the occupants who go on to put the finishing touches to a building once they have taken it over, constantly changing and renewing it, and constantly taking more complete possession of it. They interpret the building in their own way, and the more diverse the ways in which the building allows for completion, the more people there will be who can feel at home in it. What architects should be making is the wall on which everyone can write down, in his own way, whatever he wants to communicate to others. The information which remains under discussion will be legible for a long time; that which is no longer relevant will be submerged by other accounts, the distinctive marks of other and different inhabitants. This is tangibility in its most literal sense, and it is the opposite of the unassailability of a world of order and neatness, the alienated world from which we want to wrest ourselves.

Whatever goal architecture may have set for itself, it can be meaningful today only if it is making a contribution to the improvement of living conditions and circumstances. Form must improve conditions or, rather, must lend a helping hand to people, inciting them to make their own improvements.

Apart from being helpful when it is a smoothly running apparatus, form, in the guise of instrument, can also help improve living conditions by clarifying the responsibility and relationships of those involved with it and bringing to light the scope each person has for freedom of action, as well as showing where, by whom, and in what ways he is oppressed. What we can do is to open up the scope of form so that revaluation becomes easier, thus enabling established ideas and values to be phased out and replaced, in order to make way for better relationships.

To adapt to changes is difficult—for the repressed as well as for the repressors—since established certainties must be traded in for an appeal to the imagination. Changes cannot be imposed. Only when they are generated by the people themselves can they awaken awareness and be assimilated as such.

# Commentary on Diagoon Houses

## FIVE FAMILIES SPEAK OUT*

Taken from *This is Not a House for Lazy People* with the permission of the Stichting Experimentele Woningbouw. Translated by Oscar Trugler.

### FAMILY 1

*Since I've lived here, I've become much more easygoing. I've begun to live with more freedom.*

**He:** One has the feeling of a large living space, and not of sitting between four walls. It isn't just the space, but also the playfulness of it—those varied corners play a role. The home is never dull, but rather full of movement and changing form.

From the very first day we lived here, we began calling everyone by their first name, something we didn't do in our old apartment. It's different with the neighbors further down who don't live in the Hertzberger houses. They don't have many kind things to say about us. Their children also have little contact with ours.

**She:** This is a wonderful home to do things in just because there is no specific place to do them. I had the immediate feeling that one could throw down some hay anywhere and just lie down.

There are so many possibilities. For instance, one can eliminate a wall and create a dining room or bar. This could not be done as readily in any other house.

Because of this home we stay busy and feel more modern. I've become much more easygoing since I moved here. I feel much freer.

### FAMILY 2

*At work I'm still a perfectionist, but I'm less so at home.*

**He:** What is nice about this house is that if you leave the doors open, you can talk to everyone in the house no matter where you are. Often you don't listen consciously, but you hear more, you live more with each other. I like the contact we have with one another—much more than my parents had with me.

### FAMILY 3

*In this house one feels no restrictions. Just the opposite: one is stimulated to change and complete it.*

**He:** There is not one extra wall or door. One is constantly within calling distance of the others. That is the beauty of this home, all spaces blend into one another, giving the

feeling that everyone is together. The house gives everyone more to experience.

**She:** Alive with the sun. . . . In the morning I sit downstairs, in the afternoon when I'm busy, upstairs in the sun, or on the balcony outside. One can use the entire house, which is a great advantage. One is in motion all day long:

Everyone can go his own way in this home and find his own corner.

### FAMILY 4

*Up until now, I haven't seen a house which is more attractive.*

**He:** I like the house because of its form. It deviates from the normal pattern—right-angled rooms with doors on four sides. Because of the multilevel concept, one is not in enclosed spaces, but rather one can see throughout. One has the sense of a large space, although it's only 190 m² in area. This is a discovery of Hertzberger's that I find remarkable: because of the design, one only needs half stairs, as opposed to the usual high staircase we do not like. In a normal house, there is one living room, but in this home we have a maximum of living situation possibilities. One can sit in front, in the rear, upstairs, downstairs, and on the roof terrace. Sometimes together, sometimes apart. However we always remain in contact with each other. When we have company, my wife can still follow the conversation from the kitchen. If I want, I can withdraw with my work to the tower room.

**She:** It's a great house. There are spots here where you can hang a hammock to lie down. There are corners when you can just fit a table with some comfortable chairs. When I'm in the kitchen, I'm still near everything.

---

*The resident interviews presented here were completed in September, 1978 by the staff of the *Stichting Experimentele Woningbouw* (Experimental Housing Research Foundation) in Hoevelaken and are condensed and reprinted by permission.

There is a pleasant atmosphere among all the residents. We are friendly, but when one wants to be alone it's possible. The families here are not constricted or restrained. They have chosen something quite different from other homes. From this fact alone I felt sure these would be friendly people, which they indeed are.

## FAMILY 5

*I'm happy that many people tell me, "I'd never want such a house." Because then I don't feel so guilty.*

**He:** It's a wonderful design concept of Hertzberger's. I immediately recognized this ... the whole organization, light, entry, and proportions. I still just sit sometimes and take it all in. I get a pleasant feeling looking at the forms, especially in the light. Something really special and nice emanates from this house.

I'm happy many people tell me, "I'd never want such a house." I don't feel so guilty then, being one of the few to have a house like this.

What is also unique is that the house never feels lonely and empty with only two people and it isn't full with 50. Everyone spreads out over the whole house.

I did have a wall installed. In that respect we're old-fashioned. I believe a bedroom needs a door and a wall. To all sleep in one giant space doesn't appeal to me.

**She:** I'm much more conscious of space in this house. We live in the whole house, especially on Sunday, when we wander from one corner to the next. One searches for the right spot for each special moment of the day.

## Summary

Residents are positive about the overall design and critical of the details.

- In general, there is approval of the openness of the Diagoon, where contact with others is continually possible.
- The house is experienced as captivating, playful, and challenging. It can be changed and the design suggests the exploitation of the many possibilities.
- Everyone is pleased with the materials, even though the walls give off much dust.
- Every part of the home is lived in. However, the concept that every floor can be lived on is more theory than practice. Usually the living room is located near the kitchen and the bedroom near the bathroom. No family lives upstairs and sleeps downstairs.
- Some find it a house that must be worked on and completed, others find that it doesn't need to look conventionally perfect.
- When one inhabitant completes an alteration (e.g., making the carport into a hobby room), it stimulates neighbors to undertake similar projects.
- Within the home, individuals don't bother one another. A stereo upstairs and a TV downstairs don't conflict. However, the noise insulation between adjacent houses leaves much to be desired.
- Even though the homes are spacious, there is a feeling that a family cannot have more than two children here. Although there is positive spatial contact with children, it is believed children will want more privacy and their own rooms when they get older.
- The inhabitants have trouble with the weekly incursions of architects and students who want a quick look around. But this has given the homes extra status.
- The houses clearly stand out from the surrounding neighborhood; this has led to clannishness.
- None of the present inhabitants want to move. If they should be forced to move, they would all want homes similar to these.

# SAR: Supports for Participation

*Dwelling is indissolubly connected with building, with forming the protective environment.*

*N.J. Habraken,* Supports: an Alternative to Mass Housing

With *Supports* (1961) and *three r's for housing* (1970), John Habraken launched the counterattack against mass housing, the *chemin du grue*, the bureaucrats' dream of a standardized dwelling unit for a standard family. Pointing out that dwelling is an act, not a product, Habraken argued that the architect's task is to create a system through which individuals and families can house themselves. In 1965, he organized the Stichting Architecten Research (SAR) at the Technical University of Eindhoven to develop the architectural and institutional means for returning control over urban housing to its users. In the early years, SAR's emphasis was on the design of prefabricated Infill components and the new forms of high-density residential structures that would accept them in the endless variations needed to satisfy a heterogeneous population. These structures, which Habraken dubbed Supports, had been prefigured in the early 1930s by Le Corbusier in the famous "viaduct building," included in his Obus Plan for Algiers. With its ability to accept the most diverse architectures—Louis XVI, Moorish, International Style—while structuring the space of the city with its own powerful form, this proposal fascinated a generation of architects. Although the *form* of the building reappeared in a number of places, notably the Pedregulho housing project in Rio de Janeiro (A. E. Reidy, 1952), the concept of individual dwelling design within such a common framework remained almost unexplored until SAR showed the way.

The influence of SAR on architects in Holland and throughout Europe has been significant. A good number of housing projects that adopt the SAR distinction between Support and Infill and that have permitted residents to design their own dwelling plans have now been completed. In a recent conversation in Cam-

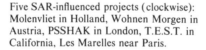
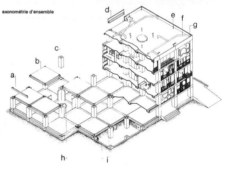

Five SAR-influenced projects (clockwise): Molenvliet in Holland, Wohnen Morgen in Austria, PSSHAK in London, T.E.S.T. in California, Les Marelles near Paris.

bridge, where he is on the faculty of the Department of Architecture at MIT, John Habraken selected the Molenvliet housing complex at Papendrecht as the best single example of SAR principles. A description of this project by its architect, Frans van der Werf, is included in this section along with SAR-inspired designs from Britain, Austria, France, and the United States.

John Carp is the new Director of SAR. In the following article, he describes the historical circumstances in which SAR's critique of mass housing arose, the development of a series of techniques for implementing user-control of the dwelling environment, and some of the problems raised by the architectural profession and the bureaucracy that always seems to surround subsidized housing. Carp concludes by explaining how SAR's focus on user-control has steadily widened until today SAR concentrates on increasing participation at the level of the neighborhood, the city, and even the planning of the region.

22

# Twenty Years of SAR

John Carp, architect, Director of the
Stichting Architecten Research (SAR),
Eindhoven

## DWELLING AS AN ACT

The basic SAR principle is this: the user constitutes the kernel of the entire environmental decision-making and production process. John Habraken, the first Director of SAR and now at the Department of Architecture at MIT, argued that almost all the problems of mass housing can be traced to the fact that the user does not play his proper role, and more frequently than not, plays no role at all. The absence of the user creates an abstract design situation in which architects cannot hope to arrive at the correct decisions. Habraken's critique of mass housing is, of course, very much related to the Dutch context. Holland is a singular case because nearly 85 percent of all housing is subsidized and hence subject to the regulations and mechanisms of bureaucratic control. Holland is unusual also in that 60 percent of all housing is rented rather than owned, which extends the condition of mass housing—the absence of user control—beyond the design stage and into the phase of inhabitation.

In his well-known book, *Supports, An Alternative to Mass Housing*, Habraken explained the crucial distinction between housing and dwelling:

A dwelling is only a dwelling *not* when it has a certain form, *not* when it fulfills certain conditions which have been laid down after long study, *not* when certain dimensions and provisions have been made to comply with municipal by-laws, but only and exclusively when people come to live in it. The igloo is as much the dwelling of the Eskimo as the bamboo hut of the Javanese. *The notion "dwelling" is entirely subjective and is certainly not related to any particular form.*

The human act, in this case the act of dwelling, determines what a dwelling is. But this single truth is totally meaningless in mass housing, for to employ this method the tangible form of the dwelling must be known . . . before the occupier is in any way concerned.

And he proposed an answer:

The conclusion must be that the return of consultation and involvement on the part of the users, in the most literal sense, must be accepted.

On the strength of this book, Habraken was invited by other architects to start SAR in 1965, and its history since then is the story of the elaboration of this basic aim. The first activity of SAR was to look into the architectural consequences of this principle and translate them into concrete recommendations. Habraken had already provided the framework in his book. In housing, he proposed to distinguish two spheres of control: the realm of the community and the realm of the individual user. To make these realms tangible, he coined two terms: *Support* embodies all the communal decisions about housing, the "detach-

able units" (*Infill*) embody the individual decisions. Note that these terms do not describe a technical or functional distinction. They describe a situation in which control of the housing process is divided between community and individual. The precise line of division is still very much a matter of definition, negotiation, and even struggle.

First of all, the notion of such a division had to be propagated. Images had to be produced of what buildings would look like when their initiation, design, and production involves users. Examples were drawn up of what a Support would look like, how a Support could be subdivided into different dwelling types and sizes to suit future occupants, and finally, how these occupants could create individual solutions for their floor plans. A design method was devised to handle the technical problems that arose because of this new division of control. Rules for modular coordination were developed to ensure that detachable units of different sorts would fit into Supports. An evaluation method was drawn up to simplify judgments about the capacity of Support proposals to accommodate varied dwelling sizes and types and maximize the flexibility of their floor plans. This method consists of a step-by-step analysis of the spatial properties of a proposed design. The method was called *SAR 65* after its year of introduction. The current edition includes numerous examples of Supports, detailed information on modular coordination and dimensioning, and a full explanation of the evaluation method. It is available in an English version as *Variations* (The MIT Press, 1976).

In the early 1970s, builders, materials suppliers, developers, planners, and consulting engineers were invited to join the architects in SAR. This was a logical step because in the early years of its existence SAR had developed working relationships with these groups, and the first sponsors had reached the conclusion that what SAR was after was not an exclusively architectural affair, but needed the expertise and cooperation of all the other parties involved in housing. This conclusion becomes inevitable when comparing the current goals of SAR with the original ones. The original aims had a much more limited scope, laying much emphasis on stimulating industrial production of dwelling components in order to increase the utility of the built environment. It is interesting to realize that SAR dropped its emphasis on industrial production at the time it opened up its membership to industry. By showing concern with production,, SAR had managed to eliminate some of the antagonism between architects and builders. This is a very important aspect of SAR, because bridging this gap forms the basis of its effectiveness: SAR's stand is interdisciplinary and must remain so.

The statutes were revised in 1973, and SAR now has as its stated objectives:

1. To investigate what measures can be taken to improve the

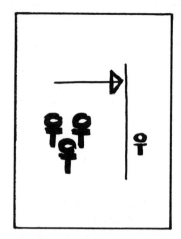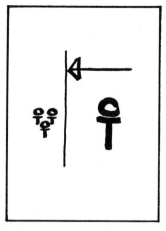
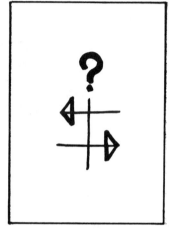

In *three r's for housing* (1970), John Habraken defined housing as the meeting point of the public and private realms. But mass housing programs had pushed the boundary between the realms to far. The individual was getting lost. SAR set itself the task of redefining the roles of all the parties involved in housing production.

utility of the built environment and specifically the dwelling environment

2. To develop design methods that can stimulate these measures

3. To promote these measures and design methods, the Foundation aims especially at

4. Investigating those measures in the decision and production process that will lead to control over the environment by its users

It should be clear that a vehement debate has accompanied the progress of SAR—and it has not at all been considered negative. On the contrary, this debate plays an essential role. Not only the methods, but many of the underlying ideas have been modifed as a result, largely because the debate did not remain on an academic level. If that had been the case, architects would have settled the matter with a shrug of the shoulders. No, the debate has been carried on at a practical level as well, due to the very special way SAR is organized. The sponsors (practicing architects, building industries, developers, etc.) put into practice the ideas and methods we develop. Their activities have a laboratory function, giving practical feedback on the academic research of the SAR office. Let us examine the responses to SAR's propositions from architects and others in the housing field.

## ON THE IDEA

In general, the principal idea of user control was favorably received. Almost no one opposed it in principle. But its elaboration into the two spheres of control, community and individual, raised doubts, especially because SAR did not specify where the division between those two realms of control should lie (this should be a matter of negotiation). The usual comment was that, in this case, there would not then be much hope for the user. There has been considerable discussion within SAR about whether or not to demarcate this line. The stand of the SAR office has been to refuse to do this because it would be contrary to our ideal of a dynamic process. We feel that the line of division should be a political decision and that SAR should concentrate on the technical measures which will facilitate the necessary political debate. Recently, SAR has developed a concept of the democratic processes needed to arrive at such decisions at all levels of environmental control.

Another widespread concern focused on the notion introduced in *Supports* that the design of "detachable units" would further industrial production of housing components. Rather than offering a benefit to the user in terms of economy and choice, critics feared industry would manipulate users, reducing them to mere consumers as was already occurring in other spheres of life. Initially SAR responded to this criticism by pointing out that the manipulation of the user could never become worse than it was already. In fact, mass housing reduces the dwelling to a consumer article and the dweller to a consumer. Choice between consumer products would at any rate be choice! Later, as we will see, SAR took another approach to this point of debate, one which relates to our ideas on democratic processes.

## ON THE METHOD

The SAR design method aroused considerable debate as well. This was not so much of a political as of a professional nature. The debate focused on topics like design freedom and design content. The modular proposals of *SAR 65* rocked architects considerably. However, the debate did not so much concern the principles of the approach as the modular tools that accompanied it.

SAR introduced a 1M–2M tartan grid* as a reference system for the positioning of all elements of Support and Infill. This grid contains modular increments of 3M, which many designers consider too coarse for their purposes. However, to SAR this increment was necessary to enable one position to differ in a meaningful way from the next. Apart from its positive effects on type reduction, this is also needed in order to distinguish meaningful increments in the utility value of spaces. This need to differentiate spaces functionally refers very much to the evaluation procedures that constitute the other part of the method. Throughout we emphasized that modular coordination is no more than a tool, that it does not prevent designers from introducing angles or even curves, and that designers can deviate from the increment and bands of the tartan grid when they wish

---

*The modular proposals of *SAR 65* are a refinement of the agreements drawn up by ISO, the International Organization for Standardization. The internationally approved basic module of M ( = 10 cm) and the preferred module of 3M ( = 30 cm) have been combined to form the 1M-2M tartan grid. The 3M module is incorporated in this grid because the 1M bands as well as the 2M bands lie at 3M increments.

This grid was originally proposed by SAR to separate Support and detachable units. This would be achieved by the rule that these two categories of material meet in the 1M band.

The sponsors of SAR take a leading role in the development of standards, as may be witnessed in many projects such as the Papendrecht scheme. These modular proposals have had quite an impact abroad as well. A good example is the Mémé building at the UCL Medical School in Brussels, by Lucien Kroll. Many people are surprised to learn that this spectacular building has been designed on the 1M-2M grid. This is the best proof that this grid does not stand in the way of architectural expression.

to do so. The grid, however, shows where and to what extent the deviation occurs so the appropriate measures can be taken to solve problems that arise.

A final draft for a Dutch modular standard in housing has recently been brought out by a government-appointed committee. The draft still meets a lot of professional resistance, but this will surely dwindle when the Ministry of Housing makes the "bonus" available. This bonus consists of a procedural advantage in the plan evaluation process by the Ministry. Projects that follow the modular standard may be submitted as rough sketches on a 3M grid, giving the spatial properties only. The benefit is plan approval at a very early stage and much freedom for further elaboration.

Let us now consider the debate on the SAR evaluation method.* Once again the criticism of SAR had many aspects, some concerning the method as such, others the tools that form the method. Much of the opposition had as its background certain professional conceptions of architectural freedom. The main argument was that the SAR approach was rationalizing the design process when much of the process is properly irrational. This argument was countered first of all on a dialectical level by saying that declaring part of the design process irrational is a mystification. It only serves to keep part of the process outside of discussion. Architects should open up their profession, especially when dealing with the user directly.

Later on, this uncompromising stand was mitigated. The SAR office realized that the argument was not as simple as that. What really had confused the discussion was that the method had been introduced, or had come across, as a *design* method. However, it is only an *evaluation* method. Its ouput is never more than the input. Secondly, the method deals only with one *aspect* of design, the aspect we later decided to call the *physical planning aspect*. This aspect concerns the utility value of spaces. This value is expressed in the capacity of a space to

accommodate spaces and elements of a lower order. This capacity, and nothing else, can be analyzed by means of the method. Psychological, sociological, economic, and structural aspects of housing schemes cannot be evaluated with this method, and of course these aspects are of equal importance. Site planning also remained outside of the scope of the method.

The evaluation method deals only with different orders of structure and space in the abstract. As a result of this reflection, another consideration concerning the design process was introduced by SAR, i.e., the distinction between *model* and *plan*. The modeling phase precedes the plan phase. The modeling phase consists of putting order in the major design elements according to their level of environmental intervention (Infill, Support, housing site) and arriving at syntheses of these elements on each level in the form of generalized spatial representations; these are called *models*. For example, during the planning phase, sites are tackled with these models, resulting in *plans*. In the design process, the models are adjusted to the site characteristics and vice versa. This approach creates a two-way flow of information—from the smaller scales upwards during the phase of designing the models and from the larger scales downwards during the planning phase. This two-way process is also an essential requirement for user participation. The modeling phase is very useful in encouraging users to express their requirements, as well as in simplifying the sorting-out of conflicts in these requirements.

## FROM DWELLING TO CITY

SAR received yet another kind of feedback that led to an altogether new field of research—ideas concerning "urban tissue" and the large-scale planning method that we brought out subsequently. This started a comment on the impact of the idea of Supports. It was said that giving the user control of the internal layout, equipment, and finishing of his dwelling would be only a marginal expansion of his control and would contribute only marginally to man's environment. And that was where the problems were considered to lie: not so much in the interior of the dwelling as in the organization of the dwelling environment. New housing estates were rejected by the users as being too large in scale, monofunctional, and monotonous—in short, uninhabitable. The postwar gain in quality at the level of the dwelling had been accompanied by an incredible loss of environmental quality. Our task, then, was to consider whether the SAR could draw up a methodical approach to tackle the design of the dwelling environment while simultaneously supplying a basis for user control at this level. The method, *SAR 73* (once again named for the year of publication), distinguishes yet another decision level: The levels of Infill and Support are now followed by the *tissue level*.

Like the dwelling plan giving the form for the rooms and the Support plan giving the form for the group of dwellings, the tissue plan gives form to the housing site and the city district. It is SAR at the level of urban design. A notable distinction of the SAR tissue level is that it is both physical (roads, pipes, etc.) and spatial—it deals with thematic urban spaces such as streets, squares, and parks. In fact, the tissue method concentrates first of all on these public urban spaces, following the observation that it is mostly the properties of these spaces that determine the character of the environment.

The method continues by introducing some formal distinctions and tools needed for describing the character of tissues. The environment consists of spatial elements and built elements

---

*The evaluation method is a step-by-step analysis starting with the most general description of a Support, i.e., its zoning principle. This zoning principle is established on the basis of criteria like dwelling depth, access type and so forth. A *zone* is a piece of dwelling territory that has a specific functional meaning, e.g., lying along the facade, or lying in the interior of the dwelling; zones are separated by areas called *margins*. The second step in the analysis is to establish the dimensions of the chosen zones and margins. The zone sets the minimum standard for certain functions that one wants to accommodate. The margin adds extra area. Zone plus margin represents an ample standard for these functions. The third step consists of an analysis of a section of zone plus margin, such as may be delimited by bearing walls. This analysis, the sector analysis, establishes the capacity to contain certain functions in the direction perpendicular to the zone width. With these two analyses, the functional capacity of a sector is known and therefore can be used as a design element in the Support design or it can be modified to improve its ability to accommodate different Infill.

After sectors have been arranged according to the zoning principle, dwelling territories of various types and sizes can be studied by considering clusters of sectors. This introduces a next step in the sequence of analysis, i.e., the analysis of basic variants. A *basic variant* is a dwelling program that can be contained by a sector group. The number of basic variants that can be accommodated is a measure of the capacity of the sector group. In addition to the capacity of a sector group to contain Infill plans, the capacity of a Support to contain sector groups (=dwelling territories) should also be studied. The more different sector groups that can be accommodated, the higher the capacity of the Support.

These analyses will produce the general layout of the Support. In order to establish the detailed distribution of Support material, the final step in the analysis consists of the analysis of subvariants. A subvariant is an elaborated floor plan based on a basic variant. One basic variant may have various subvariants, sharing a functional program but differing in elaboration. With these steps of analysis, the evaluation method of *SAR 65* has been described. It will be clear that this evaluation deals with one design aspect only, i.e., "capacity." Other aspects such as the technical or architectural quality form no part of the analysis. But the method does allow the architect to evaluate technical or architectural starting points for their functional quality.

that have a certain relationship. These elements can be further distinguished into common elements that follow a theme and special elements that do not, that in fact break the rules of the theme. *SAR 73* uses many historic Dutch examples to illustrate its ideas on the tissue, i.e., the continuity of the built elements (the building blocks) and the elements of space (the streets and garden courts), together forming the thematic elements and the nonthematic elements—those that distinguish themselves because they occur only occasionally (the churches and the squares). Historic examples are useful because they illustrate

the limited number of themes that result from interrelating these basic elements.

In the past, there was a general acceptance of what an urban environment should look like. This created a clear context and freedom for elaboration at lower decision levels, i.e., the building and the dwelling. The clear structure of the built environment also reduced the necessity of strict land-use regulations. In old towns, the form of the tissue and the Supports is self-evident. This regulates to a large extent the various functions that will and will not be accommodated. In old towns, function follows form just as much as form follows function. Furthermore, these towns demonstrate that there is no need for a strict separation of functions such as CIAM proposed. Historic towns show how spatial themes can regulate urban planning processes. It is evident that we will need different themes to suit the requirements of today. In drawing up such themes, morphological considerations should at least be equally important as functional considerations.

Like *SAR 65,* the tissue method introduces the principle of zones and margins, but at a new scale. Another similarity with *SAR 65* is that the method is an aid for drawing up models and not a "quick fix" for the design of plans. In fact, the necessity to distinguish between model and plan became apparent first during the research on *SAR 73*. However, the introduction of this distinction did not put criticism to an end. The method, and really the focus on the tissue level as such, was intended to ensure that architects and city planners would no longer mind only their own business.

This notion was not very welcome at first. It is only very recently that many urban designers have come to the conclusion that the built environment should follow distinct patterns and rules. The freedom that currently exists to elaborate site plans into any conceivable shape is no longer considered a benefit. The resulting chaotic townscape is all too evident. But architects are still reluctant to accept the reinstitution of definite urban design prescriptions, even in the form of zones and margins. In our opinion, this is quite unjustified. We are convinced that the use of tissue models will both give comprehensible form to the public realm and stimulate architectural expression rather than hamper it. The proof of this is shown by our historic towns like Amsterdam. The straightforwardness of the tissue plan, for example the constraints created by the pattern of canals, formed and still forms an excellent framework for architectural elaboration. One can even argue that a clear and straightforward tissue plan is essential for a dynamic environment that responds in a flexible way to new requirements. Along the Amsterdam canals, one can witness many building activities—modifications as well as completely new structures. It is difficult to imagine how a new town district would accommodate such activities. The loose and chaotic contemporary urban fabric gives no clear indication of what to do or where to do it.

## THE LEVELS RECONSIDERED

As has been said, the tissue level closes the gap between architecture and planning, or rather between the other SAR levels of dwelling plan and Support plan and city planning. Our contact with the planning discipline brought us to the realization that the levels SAR had "discovered" were congruent with the levels that were already embodied in law. In Holland, the Physical Planning Act describes three planning levels—the regional plan, the urban structure plan, and the land use plan—as the plans that organize the functions and physical structure of the province, the municipality, and the city district, respectively. Another

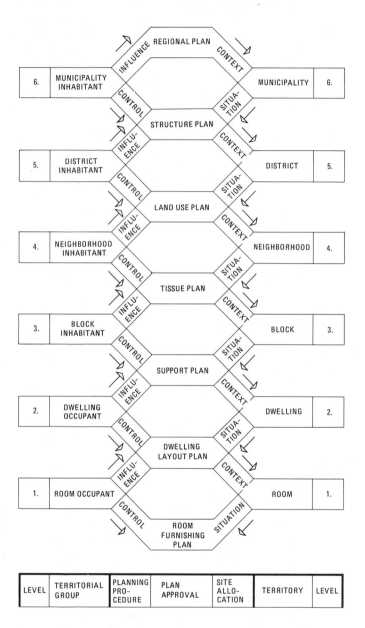

SAR's Levels of Control. The chart shows the desired relationships of influence or control— from the spatial level of the private room all the way up to the neighborhood, the city, and the region.

very important characteristic is that such plans are approved by democratic bodies (the elected houses of representatives at the provincial and local level). Apart from representation through these elected bodies, the required planning process allows the citizen to exercise a measure of direct influence. For this purpose, plans have to be laid on the table for criticism for fixed periods of time. In short, in the public sphere, a system of planning levels already exists linking up planning decisions at the territorial levels established by our democratic system.

This observation produced the shock effect that usually accompanies the discovery of the obvious. What SAR really had been trying to do instinctively was to translate procedures that already exist in the public sphere into the private sphere. After all, the public law sphere had all along adopted user-control as the main planning principle. Public authority can overrule private property interests and enforce land uses and infrastructure measures by means of its plans.* The conclusion was that "the user" can and must manifest himself at the different territorial levels that can be distinguished, that these territorial levels exist in the public sphere as well as in the private sphere, that these territorial levels communicate with each other concerning planning decisions by means of planning levels, and that the plans at each level constitute contracts between the higher and lower territorial levels involved. So, as what we call an urban structure plan constitutes a contract between a municipality and its districts, a Support plan is the contract between the users of the building and individual inhabitants of its dwellings. Planning control, comprising initiative as well as management, can be restored to the user by a universal approach that unites democratic procedures and the planning process.

To date, SAR principles of user control have been explored at three levels—control of individual Infill plans, control of dwelling unit distribution, and control of the Support—in widely differing schemes such as "Wohnen Morgen," PSSHAK (Adelaide Road), and Molenvliet, which are described in this volume. The results, measured in terms of user satisfaction, in these and other SAR-influenced projects have been gratifying. However, the emphasis we now put on the tissue level, and in fact on user control of the entire chain of decision making up to and including the level of regional planning, makes it clear that we at SAR still have much to do to win general acceptance of the democratic processes of planning and design in which we believe. SAR's focus today is on elaborating the mechanisms that will extend the principles of user control from Infill and Support to the larger environment.

---

*The notion of public control of land use is well established in Dutch culture. First of all, the Dutch territory has been densely populated for a considerable time; this implies that rules had to be set to prevent territorial conflict and to make maximum use of every inch of the country. Furthermore, in large parts of the country the soil conditions were such that urban settlement patterns were the obvious answer. Most towns in the western part of the country are built on a thick layer of peat, making the construction of houses and infrastructure very costly. Public land-use control was logical under these circumstances.

The second reason for the specific Dutch condition is the vulnerability of its territory, necessitating a strong social organization. Holland was constantly in danger of being flooded by the sea or overrun by its big neighbors. The territory had to be defended constantly. The Dutch Waterboards are the oldest public institutions of Holland, dating from before the establishment of the municipalities. People could be summoned up at short notice to reinforce dikes, dig canals, and so forth. Even the Dutch military defenses have been based on water management. Large parts of the country could, and still can, be flooded purposely, creating the so-called Dutch Water Line. In this way the Spanish occupation forces were literally flushed out as they laid siege to Leiden in the late sixteenth century.

# SAR/Molenvliet
# Papendrecht, Holland

Frans van der Werf was barely out of architecture school when he won a national competition in 1969 to build 2400 dwellings in the small city of Papendrecht in Holland. Sharing John Habraken's belief that dwelling is an act, van der Werf proposed a Support/Infill scheme in which each tenant would be responsible for the design of his own apartment. The Support, he said, would express the collective beauty, and the Infill the individual beauty of the people and their place.

One section of the Molenvliet project was completed and occupied in 1978. Van der Werf worked personally with each prospective tenant family on the interior planning. This process was studied closely by Dutch sociologist Ans Gotink, who was also responsible for a later evaluation of the residents' attitudes. A summary of Gotink's quite positive report on the impact of participation on dwelling satisfaction follows van der Werf's description of the technical and social aspects of the project.

1. SAR at home in Holland: 108 adaptable dwellings shown in the architect's original rendering.

# A Vital Balance

**Frans van der Werf, architect**
**Werkgroep KOKON, Rotterdam**

The project in Papendrecht is an experiment in the social production of housing. In Holland, the basic housing needs of most people are provided by non-profit housing societies that are subsidized by the government. These organizations have tended to produce either high density row houses or apartment blocks of a few basic types. This approach to mass housing has provided quantity, but not quality. More and more people are living in standardized dwellings designed *for* them, without their having any say in the matter. The apartment plans reflect national standards for specific categories of people: single workers, families of different sizes, the elderly, and students. This system of production takes no account of the differences between individuals or the special needs of many families.

But I know that no two people or families are alike. Each needs a special, personal environment in order to develop and grow. And this in turn demands participation—interaction between the human being and the environment. I believe that this participation is a human need. I also believe that direct involvement in the satisfaction of an individual's own needs opens the way to more comprehensive social contact.

I agree with John Habraken and SAR that dwelling is an act, and an act that takes place in two domains: that of the individual and that of the community. Only when we have agreed what decisions belong to the sphere of the community (the tissue plan and the Support) on the one hand, and to the individual (the Infill) on the other, can we be clear about the nature of participation and the degree of influence or control we are proposing. This view requires a new organization of the building process and a new, adaptable architecture.

Because dwelling is not an artifact, but an interaction between people and their environment, the physical environment the architect provides must be capable of simple alteration to meet the needs of new inhabitants. The Support-

Infill distinction permits this constant adaptation without affecting the realm of the community. The changing nature of family life presents a powerful argument for a residential architecture that permits spatial adjustments and internal reorganization to meet the ways we may live in the future. In addition, Holland, with its former colonies and its foreign workers, has become a multicultural nation. Only the participatory production of housing will allow each group to have satisfactory dwellings.

## Urban Structure

The Support and Infill concepts have not emerged solely from the need for participation. I believe that there is an underlying, universal principle that is served by this distinction: the clarity of urban structure. The structure of residential districts can be provided by the common form of the Support buildings. The personalized Infill makes the separate Supports different from one another. This approach offers cohesion, and merges individual buildings into an entity in which the elements of the Support are recognized throughout the whole complex. We are talking, then, about the idea of a main theme in which variations are encouraged. The theme—the Support structures—makes variation possible and legible.

The design of a Support is the design of housing *when the desire of the larger community for a particular urban structure is known but the specific needs of the future users are not.* They will come along later to make their Infill dwellings in accordance with the possibilities inherent in the Support. The Support design (space, materials, utilities) places limits on what can be realized within it, and the Support generates dwellings by stimulating participation.

To rationalize this generating process, SAR has developed a method involving *zones, margins,* and *sectors.* In the plans for our housing at Papendrecht, as in all SAR Support structures, $\alpha$ zones are the areas in which there is adequate daylight (as defined by local codes). $\beta$ zones are those interior areas without sufficient natural

2. The SAR planning grid divides the space between lines of structure (called Sectors) into zones and margins. Designated by greek letters, zones and margins give the maximum and minimum dimensions for rooms and indicate locations for specific uses—at the exterior, near the stair, along the wet walls, etc.

29

light and ventilation. Margins are the transitional areas between these zones and between the $\alpha$ zone and the exterior (a place for terraces and balconies, perhaps). A sector is the area between bearing walls that can be freely divided. When zones, margins, and sectors are given precise dimensions they constitute a *model* for a Support—and each model can be evaluated for its Infill variation potential. But a model for a Support is not yet the design of a building. It is a *parti:* a system of organization of foundations, bearing walls, floors, ducts, and roofs. The translation of this *parti* into specific materials, with specific dimensions, on a specific site becomes the Support design. Within the theme of the design, nonthematic elements may appear as deformations called for by the context, or they may be added: a special stair or a particular way of turning a corner. In terms of our musical analogy of themes and variations, these moments are the *cadenzas.* So a Support need not be rigid and confining. In fact, it leads us to a significant new way of making cohesive urban form.

## The Urban Tissue

Just as the Support is characterized by thematic elements—dwelling space, structure, and services—so the urban tissue is made up of thematic open spaces (squares, streets, courts, passages) and the buildings which form them. An urban tissue designed according to SAR principles can be used in numerous ways and can evolve over time. This approach to urban design enables us to create space and material without fixing for all time the human activities that will animate it. This does not mean that we ignore the function of the streets or the life of public places. Quite the contrary. Working this way, we start with the idea that the shape of the public spaces generates their functions. In other words, thematic spaces in an urban tissue, given specific location and dimension, will stimulate desirable activities.

The urban tissue, then, is the formal structure of a residential environment in which a chosen theme in urban design is laid down and then enriched through the addition of particular, nonthematic elements such as a major shopping street or a school; variation appears again at this level without loss of coherence.

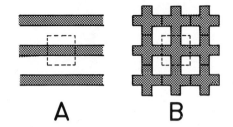

A    B

3

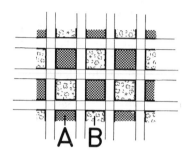

A B

4

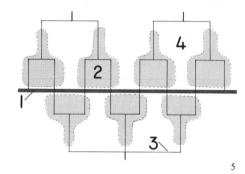

5

3. Stages in the development of the site plan: building depth and width of related open space established. These dimensions were then applied to a bi-directional building pattern.

4. The open spaces within the two-directional grid are differentiated into entry courts and garden courts.

5. Schematic site plan shows central street (1), building zones (2), internal roads (3), and green areas (4).

6. SAR concept of zones and margins at the tissue level: A areas are built up in all cases, B margins can become either part of A or of C, open spaces.

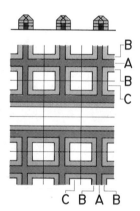

6

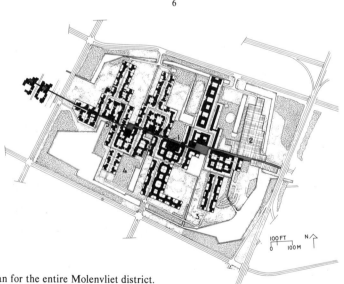

7. Site plan for the entire Molenvliet district. Only a small portion was built in the end.

## Molenvliet at Papendrecht

Our Molenvliet project is a small portion of the original proposal for 2800 dwellings on an adjacent site. But we were concerned from the outset with establishing an urban tissue and a Support structure that would work at this larger scale. The elements of the urban tissue are:

- Traffic streets
- Entry courtyards
- Garden courtyards (including children's play areas)
- Connecting alleys

The building theme is high density (higher than usual in Holland, and part of the experiment), low rise, gallery-access apartments. The following relationships have been established and structure the project as a whole: entry and garden courtyards alternate in checkerboard fashion; alleys connect the courtyards to one another and to the streets. Had the larger project been carried out, this tissue plan would have permitted many architects to contribute to the new community, making free and varied use of the margins, without losing the harmony implicit in this theme, its variations, and the cadenzas provided by the sports hall, schools, and shops.

Let us now turn to the completed project. Molenvliet should be seen as a test fragment where the tissue plan has become a specific site plan and home to some 350 people.

## Levels of Decision

In accordance with SAR practice, we distinguish four levels or scales of design, each with its own specific decision-making process and list of concerned participants—from government ministers at the highest level to housing society officials, neighbors, and inhabitants as one moves down the list:

Level 1: Overall plan of the district which locates the building sites, the major circulation system, and the green areas
Level 2: The tissue plan in the form of open spaces and building zones as described above
Level 3: The plan of the Supports themselves which will accommodate
Level 4: The Infill—partitions, mechanical equipment, and facade ele-

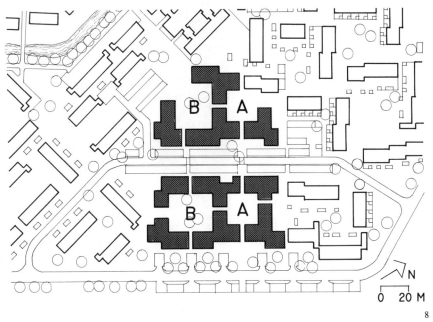

8. The completed portion of the scheme consists of four courtyards: entry courts are marked A, garden courts B.

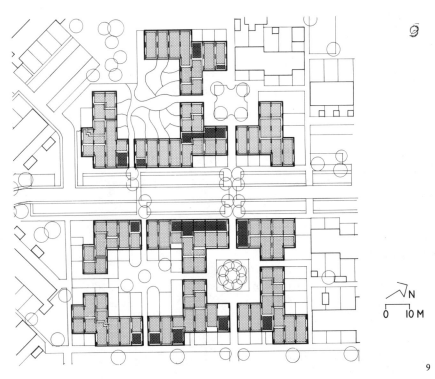

9. Drawing shows the subdivision of the Support into dwelling units. This is one of many possible ways to use the interior space. Dark areas are circulation and storage.

ments of the dwellings, shops, offices, etc., as required by the program. Let us focus on Levels 3 and 4.

In Molenvliet, the concept of the Support has the following characteristics:

- Duplex apartments, stacked to give a four-story building height, the maximum permitted by the local building laws
- Small gardens for ground floor units, large terraces for those above
- Gallery access for the upper level units, reached by stairways in the courtyards
- Pitched roofs, which mean home in Holland (and probably almost everywhere else)

Structurally the Support is made of the following elements, all laid out using the 10/20 cm SAR planning grid:

- 20-cm concrete floor slabs with regular openings for staircases and mechanical chases
- Concrete piers, 20 × 140 cm, arranged in bays of 480 cm (15′9″)
- 45° timber roof elements parallel with the piers and two bays wide (these provide useful attic space)
- Precast concrete lintels and a fixed wood member at doorhead height which acts as framework for facade Infill elements
- *In situ* concrete stairs and access galleries

Everything else is under the control of the inhabitants and thus, by definition, is not part of the Support.

The Infill assembly kit for each dwelling unit was prefabricated and delivered to the site as a complete package. Each kit contained:

- Gas heater
- Kitchen group, including fixtures and cabinets
- Bathroom group(s), including fixtures and cabinets
- Wiring components
- Facade elements (windows, doors, frames)
- Interior partitions as required
- Closet and storage units

To maximize the subsidy available to the project sponsor from the government, I made up a set of plans for the Support showing the economically opti-

10

10. The Support and the tissue model—beyond this point the users are in charge.

11. Ground floor plan

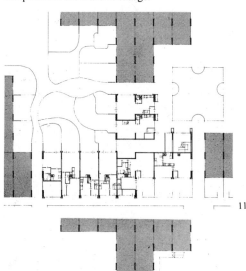

11

12. Second floor plan.

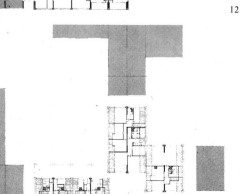

12

13. Third floor plan.

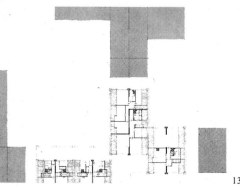

13

32

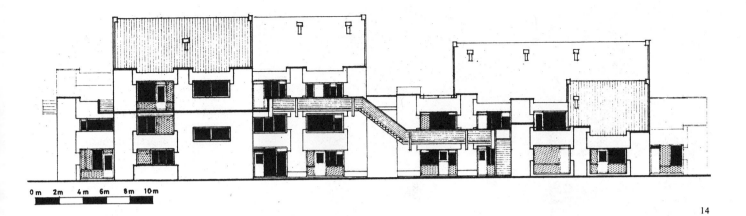

0 m  2m  4 m  6m  8m  10 m

14

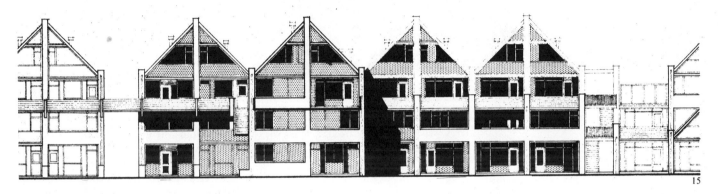

15

16

17

14,15. Elevations. The architect, to obtain financing approval, did a set of drawings with conventional interior layouts and unit mix. Both were changed appreciably when the users got involved.

16. The Support beginning to receive its Infill.

17. The roofs are on—and the Infill kits stand on their pallettes ready to be used.

18

18. The architect working at design participation.

19. A sketch made by the architect during one of these conversations with a future resident, later turned into a proper measured drawing to be approved by the users before construction.

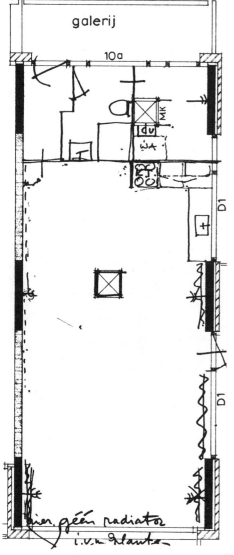

19

mal organization of dwelling units which it could accommodate. Costs were computed and code approval was given on the basis of these plans.

## Participation in Design

The final plan of the Supports at Molenvliet is entirely different from the drawings I prepared for budget calculations. This is because the Infill—Level 4—was designed by the inhabitants, and reflects the varied sizes of families, cultural differences, stages in the life cycle, and the special needs of the handicapped who have come to live there.

As each Support began to take shape, prospective tenants were selected by the housing society on the basis of need and length of time on the waiting list. At first there was a series of general information meetings at which the concept of the experimental project was explained and aspects of management, rent, and services were laid out. Each household was given information on the Molenvliet scheme and shown the size and location of the apartment which was intended for them. Some of the tenants were not happy with the situation we had chosen for them, but were able to switch with others right on the spot. It quickly became clear that there was a greater than predicted need for small units. The SAR concept permitted this problem to be solved without any building redesign: 16 large apartments were split into 32 smaller ones, each with its own front door and outside space.

When every household had been allocated a dwelling space according to its wishes, blank floor plans were distributed and appointments for planning sessions were set up. Each family then met privately with the architect, a representative of the housing society, and the sociologist who followed the experiment from beginning to end (see Commentary by Ans Gotink). Two sessions of 45 minutes each were scheduled for each tenant. At first, we talked candidly about lifestyles, habits, and customs of eating, sleeping, and bringing up children. Sitting around a table we started talking:

*Should spaces be open or closed? How important is an entry room for you? Do your children sleep in one room? Where do they play? What kind of activities do you do as a*

20a

20b

20c

20a,b,c. Different ethnic backgrounds, life styles, hobbies, and tastes determine the choices users have made.

21. When a man confined to a wheelchair moved in, the building system made it easy to alter the facade to improve his view and access.

21

*group? Do you have hobbies? Where do you want to locate the bathroom, the washer/dryer? What happens when grandmother comes for a couple of days?*

I tried to open their minds to new ideas, to get them to express their feelings about the act of dwelling. Everyone had his own story, his own individuality. Occasionally people hesitated and gave no answers, waiting for me to speak as a specialist. In such cases I insisted that we were talking about their lives and their home, not mine. We took the empty Support plan and started together to define the front, to locate the internal staircase. Gradually we elaborated a rough floor plan, using every inch of space to come to a solution. The future occupants went home with this sketch plan to think it over. When they left, new clients came in with their blank Support plans, new faces, different lives and stories.

Here are some examples which demonstrate the adaptability of the scheme. A married couple of about 60 years of age was allocated a two-story unit. As they laid it out, the upper level became *one space* for sleeping, cooking, and eating: only the bathroom was enclosed. The entry floor was reserved for receiving visitors. In another family, the father worked nights and slept during the day. Their layout isolated the master bedroom so that the family could function easily during the daytime.

A nurse got an extra room, 1.50 m wide, separated from her living room— even though Dutch codes don't permit such things! And there was a family that started by giving central place to a very large aquarium before dividing up the remainder of their dwelling space. Finally, an Indonesian family demanded and got a single bedroom large enough for the entire group.

In the second session, comments on the first sketch plans were dealt with. Some tenants brought scale cutouts of furniture. Others had completely worked-out plans. The SAR 10/20 grid made it relatively simple for ordinary people to make detailed plans. We worked together to refine the schemes and located equipment, electrical outlets, windows, and doors. A selection of exterior paint colors was made from a palette I proposed.

Too little time had frequently been scheduled and the talks went on into the evenings. Most people were pre-

22. An entry court in the occupied housing.

23. A view from a terrace shows different facade decisions within the continuous Support.

pared to wait for their future neighbors to finish in order to make the fullest use of their opportunity to plan their own apartment layouts. For many of the future inhabitants it was a great experience to visit the site a few months later to find, in the empty shell of the Support, a neat package of partitions, frames, and fixtures sitting on a large pallet and covered by a tarpaulin— ready to put in place in accordance with their own drawings! At this stage in the construction the Support-Infill division was clearly visible as both a division of control and a division of production.

**Tenant Alterations**

Tenants at Molenvliet have altered

their dwellings both to personalize them further and to correct mistakes made in the original planning. We knew at the outset that mistakes were bound to be made. Not all the aspects of each layout were discussed by the future inhabitants and the architect. Living patterns are not something that can be made totally clear in two sessions of 45 minutes. Sometimes after moving in, a room was found to be smaller than it had seemed on the plans. Or the amount of daylight was disappointing. In some cases the location of kitchen equipment turned out not to be efficient. On the other hand, there were some pleasant surprises when space and light turned out to be quite special and better than anticipated.

36

24

24. The garden courts are for children.

For whatever reason, then, some tenants wanted alterations in their apartments after they had moved in. With the approval of the housing society, partitions were removed or repositioned. In other cases, new partitions either still in stock or ordered directly from the suppliers were put in place. A number of facade elements were changed to give either more or less light. For example, one family with a severely handicapped father asked to have the window sills in the living areas lowered to provide a view from wheelchair height. The Support-Infill division enabled us to make these changes quickly and inexpensively. Interior walls, except for the few which are part of the Support, are non-bearing and can be easily removed by loosening a screw fitting. All piping is accessible, and the electric wiring is surface-mounted in base and ceiling moldings and can be extended as required. Only modifications to the cen-

tral heating system and the bathroom tile required skilled labor because we had to build these in the traditional manner.

What happens when a new tenant moves in? As a result of the participation process and the flexibility of the building system, each apartment is different. Some interiors are so specific and personal that there is a chance that a new tenant would refuse it. Surely the answer has by now become clear: The spatial organization of the Support, the SAR planning grid, and the modular construction make it relatively easy for new tenants to see the possibilities inherent in the space they are given and to make their own dwellings.

We like to say that dwelling is an act in which tenants appropriate space and give it value. We believe that this has happened at Molenvliet. If you visit the homes now, you will notice everywhere how much painting and carpentry the tenants have added, how much of themselves they have added to these units which have become their homes.

## Lessons from Molenvliet

Housing is an act in the public realm at the same time that it is an act in the realm of the individual. For this reason, the architectural concept must distinguish between those decisions (design elements) which belong to the collective sphere and those (the Infill components) which belong to the individual. In Papendrecht, the Support expresses the collective beauty, the Infill an individual beauty. Together, they reflect the vital balance which is essential to community. And at Molenvliet that is what we sought to build: a contemporary version of the traditional village, with people living together, keeping up their houses and gardens, and constantly adapting and remodeling them by using all kinds of materials and colors.

# Commentary on Molenvliet

Ans Gotink, Sociological Institute, State University of Utrecht

## PARTICIPATION AND SATISFACTION

There is a difference between participation of inhabitants in housing rehabilitation schemes and in newly built dwellings. The first type of participation deals with a group of known inhabitants who are dissatisfied with their dwellings—dwellings that are no longer fit to live in. In cases like this, residents often demand direct involvement in finding a solution to their problems. The second type of participation is quite different. Discontent on this level is not clearly manifested as in redevelopment areas. People who are going to live in newly built areas don't organize themselves. As a rule, they don't know each other. But the inhabitants of our new housing areas are not as happy with their new dwellings as the urban planners and architects of the 1960s and 1970s believed they would be. So the experts began to explore ways to overcome the public dissatisfaction with much new housing. They proposed new plans with more variations and choice of styles. A few wanted to try participation—working with future inhabitants, to find out how they wanted to live. In Holland, there are only a few examples of participatory housing design—and even fewer that have been the subject of sociological inquiry.

Since its inception, the Institute has been studying the Molenvliet project in Papendrecht. This building project has been doubly subsidized by the central government—once because it's for lower income families and once because of its experimental nature. Both the architectual design and the participation of the future inhabitants in the decision-making process are experimental. The local housing association received these subsidies on the condition that there be a sociological investigation. Although it was not the purpose of this research to inquire specifically into the effects of participation on the future inhabitants themselves (the accent was on an evaluation of the participation process itself and its impact on the housing), still a number of interesting effects became clear.

Before these results are presented, a brief description of the project and the process of participation is necessary. Our findings will be described in regard to the experiences of the inhabitants in the participation process and especially to the effects of participation on the residents' satisfaction and the community life of the inhabitants. These outcomes will be compared with those of other recent projects.

## DESCRIPTION OF THE PROJECT AND PARTICIPATION

Molenvliet contains 122 dwellings at a density of 37 dwellings per acre. Almost every dwelling is different. There are small apartments for young people who live on their own, "normal" apartments for young families, duplexes for big families, special dwellings for the elderly and invalids, and so forth. The houses are built around four courts in this plan, two of them with private gardens. Those that don't have gardens have terraces, and their front doors are on a gallery overlooking a courtyard.

The people who live here rent their dwellings from a nonprofit housing association. For all the people involved, Molenvliet represents the first time that they have participated in the housing design process. Participation in this case involved establishing the floor plans of their apartments, selecting the colors of the exterior window and door frames, and deciding upon the amount of glazing in the facades. Unfortunately, there was no resident participation in the site selection or planning.

About 60 percent of the tenants we found in 1978, one year after the project was completed, participated in the design of their homes. The others, selected too late to be involved, got a finished dwelling—the usual situation when you ask a housing society for accommodation. Those who did participate designed their own dwellings with the aid of the architect. Most had a minimum of two half-hour sessions with van der Werf over a two-week period. Of course, there were many restrictions in making the floor plans—for instance, the shape and overall size of the dwelling, the location of the stairs, the entry, and the main vertical duct (for electricity, water, and gas). Then, of course, there were the rules of the government housing ministry, the fire brigade, the housing society, and the architect himself.

Soon after the meetings between the architect and the tenants in which the designs of the dwellings were finished, we asked all the parties involved to evaluate this type of participation and the way it was carried out. It should be made clear that none of these tenants had ever participated in housing design before. For most of them, agreeing to get involved in this project was the only way to get a dwelling. They had little choice and mostly they just wanted a dwelling at an acceptable rent. However, in spite of this and the restrictions mentioned above, it seemed to these people to be a tremendous experience to get involved in making their own living space. They gave a very positive account of this type of participation.

However, the amount of information they had before going to talk with the architect was deemed insufficient. The same can be said about the time available to make decisions. Instead of two weeks, people felt they needed at least a month to think about their schemes. Twenty percent of the tenants had some difficulty in making their own floor plans, especially the young families. The older people seemed to be more conscious of their needs, perhaps because they had more experience with different ways of living—or perhaps they are less demanding than are younger people.

The architect was able to fulfill all the wishes of the majority of tenants in making his floor plans (65 percent). But afterwards, various organizations had to approve the floor plans before they could be built. As a result, in one-third of the cases the residents' plans could not be used without alterations. Unfortunately, there was no discussion of changes with the tenants, which led to the withdrawal of a number of people. However, two years after the design participation, when the families had lived in their dwellings for a year, they were still very positive about the process and its results (92 percent would want to repeat the process and 65 percent want more participation should they move to another housing project).

## RESIDENTS' SATISFACTION

After a year in residence, three-fourths of the tenants were satisfied or very satisfied with their floor plans. Only a few were dissatisfied. However, this does not mean that everything is fine, because one-third of the tenants wanted a different layout. At this point we found an important difference between people who did participate and those who didn't. There was a greater likelihood that someone who didn't participate wanted a new floor plan than someone who did participate ($\gamma = .64$). (See Table 1.) We saw the same result when we looked at the degree of overall satisfaction with the housing ($\gamma = .66$).

What did they really want to change? Some mentioned interchanging the living and bedrooms. Others wanted a larger living room, kitchen, hall, or bathroom; still others wanted an open staircase instead of a closed one, or another location for the staircase, toilet, or entry. The usual reasons given were more space, light, and convenience. Half of the group that was not satisfied found a solution by altering their floor plans, for instance by moving partitions or changing doors and windows (one large bedroom can be made from two little ones). Others were not able to find a solution in their dwelling or in this project (there are a few tenants who found a more satisfactory dwelling in the same project) and wanted to move. Again, there was a correlation with the degree of participation: there was a much greater chance that those who didn't participate wanted to leave ($\gamma = .60$).

Of course, the final judgment these tenants made about their dwellings and about this project was based on many more elements than those they could control here (through the participation process). There were a lot of experimental elements in which the tenants had no voice. We also asked their opinion about these elements. Although in general the residents were positive, they were negative about the high density and the street that divides this project into two parts.

The overall judgment of the tenants at Molenvliet is not as interesting as their evaluation of specific design elements. The average rating is a 7 on a 10-point scale, and there is only a small difference between the two groups, participants and nonparticipants. One can only see the difference in satisfaction between these two groups when one looks directly at those elements that have been the objects of the design participation. We think that if participating tenants had more control over more elements and had a wider range of choice, there would have been a greater difference in their expressed satisfaction.

## COMMUNITY LIFE

The development and maintenance of contacts between the residents of a neighborhood is important to community life. Here the architect set out to create a project with many possibilities for residents to come into contact with each other by planning courtyards, building at high density, and grouping people who are heterogeneous as to age and state of the family.

We distinguished between two kinds of contacts. First, there are close contacts like visiting at home, and second, there are casual contacts such as talking with each other on the gallery or in the courtyards. When we interviewed the tenants, we asked them to show us on a map of the project the families' apartments they frequently visited and tell us how many times they spoke with other residents. The contacts they had before they came to live in this project were left out of consideration because we wanted to measure the effect of the experimental design on the amount and kind of contacts in the Molenvliet project the Meerzicht project (Zoetermeer), the Kasbah (Hengelo), and Geestenberg (Eindhoven)—all experimental architectural designs but without the participation of residents in the decision-making process.

However, most of the people at Molenvliet were satisfied with the quality and quantity of contacts they had (91 percent). Nearly one-half of the inhabitants thought it was easier to meet others in this project than in a "normal" new project. We agree with Michelson* when he says that the need for contact is very high just after the moving into a new dwelling and neighborhood, that is, in the first year of residence. But we noted only a few collective activities. There was an action to get play equipment for the children to use in the courtyards, a volleyball club was started, and there is a tenants' committee. Because there was no resident participation in planning the collective environment (courtyards, street, etc.)—the local government opposed the idea—this could not affect the frequency of contacts, as was hoped by the architect. We can only speculate about the influence of individual participation in dwelling design on the number of contacts between the residents, but we feel that this type of participation had no effect on the frequency of the contacts and visits between the residents.

## CONCLUSION

The most interesting result of the Molenvliet project in Papendrecht is the effect participation had on the satisfaction of the residents of this project.

We believe the results of the sociological inquiry prove that resident participation is worthwhile even for renter families. The tenants really enjoyed being able to participate in design, and those who did show a higher degree of satisfaction with *whatever* they were able to decide on themselves (see Table 1). Participation, we found, also leads to a lower incidence of moving. We conclude that this type of participation (with direct contact between the architect and future tenants) should be generalized and expanded to experiment with more influence for those directly involved on overall project planning.

*Michelson, W., "Determinism by the urban environment," from *Man and his Urban Environment: a Sociological Approach*, Addison-Wesley, Reading, Mass., 1970.

### Table 1. The Influence of Participation on Resident Satisfaction, Presented by Gammas ($\gamma$).

| | Percentage of People Who Did Participate | Percentage Who Did Not Participate | Total Percentage | Gamma ($\gamma$) |
|---|---|---|---|---|
| Would prefer another dwelling in the project | 7 | 23 | 13 | .59 |
| Intended to move | 15 | 42 | 25 | .60 |
| Dissatisfied with the floor plan | 14 | 43 | 24 | .66 |
| Dissatisfied with the project (1 to 6 on a 10-point scale) | 24 | 30 | 26 | .13 |
| Dissatisfied with the project density | 41 | 44 | 42 | .06 |
| Dissatisfied with the participation process | 0 | 10 | 4 | — |

**(The number of current residents who did participate is 71; the number who did not participate is 40.)**

# SAR/Wohnen Morgen
# Hollabrunn, Austria

The competition was called *Wohnen Morgen,* "The Dwelling of Tomorrow." The Vienna office of architects Ottokar Uhl and Joseph Weber found in this an opportunity to introduce SAR principles into Austria "to make housing more democratic." The project, which consists of three large, low rise blocks, is located in Hollabrunn not far from the Czechoslovakian border.

The architects developed a set of useful techniques to assist future users in designing their individual dwellings. They found that the participants' interest in the building design was so great that it grew to encompass much more than apartment layout. Prospective dwellers became actively involved in issues of orientation, fenestration and views, selection of mechanical systems, the design of collective facilities, and the quality of construction—and "even threatened to find other dwellings if their wishes were ignored."

1. "The Dwelling of Tomorrow:" a general view of the completed project.

# Democracy in Housing

**Ottokar Uhl, architect**
**Vienna**

The objective of participation by future dwellers in the planning of their homes is to make housing more democratic. Users must have the right to participate in design with architects and planners, and to abandon the role of mere consumers. By this process, the dwelling loses much of its character as a commodity, and the user participates in determining its economic value. To permit participation in the design of dwellings, certain structural and administrative conditions must be met. Those who were up to now responsible for housing, i.e., construction companies, builders, and architects, must provide the following prerequisites.

## Construction Conditions

Allowance for Delayed Decisions—The user must be given enough time to make decisions slowly and to revise them if discussion within the family generates a better solution. The consideration of late decisions must be made feasible by suitable planning methods. Alterations in use which might become necessary in the course of time must be possible in each individual dwelling by reorganizing the layout (adaptability). Fluctuations in family size must also allow the alteration of the size of the dwelling (flexibility).

## Administrative and Legal Conditions Required

A New Type of Sale or Rental Contract—this would give the size and location of the dwelling, but not its floor plan, thus securing a new right of use.

Individual Calculation—participation of the prospective dweller in the planning process will require increasingly individualized cost calculations.

Information and Consultation—guidance as to construction possibilities, equipment, and alternate layouts must be offered by professionals.

Direction—the user has the right to take part in planning and to give orders to the designers.

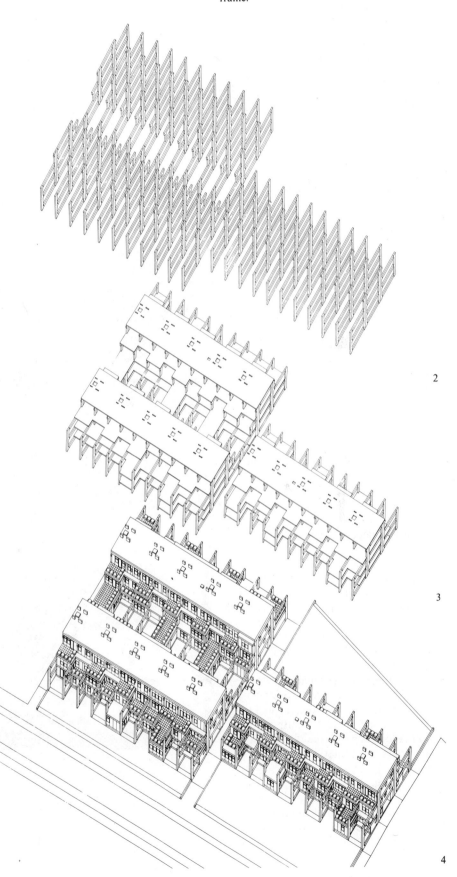

2

3

4

Joint Administration—the participation process does not end with the completion of the project. Users must also have the right to control management in housing cooperatives.

## Financial Presuppositions

Housing costs must be determined by the regulations of social (publicly subsidized) housing programs and must not exceed these limits. It is only in this way that planning participation can claim to be an innovation.

## The Process of Participation

For a design competition with the title "The Dwelling of Tomorrow," the office of Uhl and Weber produced a project which provided just the basic structure, thus allowing for a large variety of dwelling types. It was our fundamental idea that the Infill of the structure should be made according to the wishes of the future users. The project was awarded the first prize, and planning started in July, 1972. The builder was a nonprofit housing cooperative which welcomed the participation of the future dwellers in the planning process. The Austrian *Bundesministerium für Bauten und Technik* subsidized this project through its housing research fund.

In order to provide a methodological framework for the participation process, we decided to use the SAR methodology developed in Eindhoven under the direction of John Habraken. The reasons for this decision were the following:

● The basic idea of separating the Support (the primary structure) from the Infill (the secondary elements) has positive implications for the development of independent but compatible production of public/private decision making in housing
● The tartan grid (modular coordination system) developed by SAR is based on the commonly accepted European 30-cm standard, but, in addition, allows for the free placement of materials in alternating 10/20-cm bands
● The concept of zones, margins, and sectors permits analysis and evaluation of dwelling layout alternatives by means of a clear and comprehensive notation system.

Thus, the methodology has both the capacity for open planning and the means for technical implementation without being tied to any particular construction system or any particular material.

Since the users joined the architects only in a late stage of development, they had no influence on the city planning level of decision making. It is, however, desirable to have the dwellers participate right from the beginning—even in the search for a site. In the case of the Hollabrunn project, the users were able to make the following decisions:

1. Subdividing the primary structure into individual dwellings (types).

5

6

The outer shape of the building was determined by the users.
2. Size of dwellings. As the users could determine the location of facades within certain limits, the size of dwellings could be tailored to individual needs without interfering with the neighboring apartments.
3. Subdivision of the dwelling into rooms. The construction system (primary structure) permitted almost any room layout. With the supply system (chases and ducts) we had designed, even service elements could be situated practically anywhere on a floor.
4. Organization of the facade. By means of a number of different facade elements that could be com-

bined in any order, users could match the facades of dwellings to needs and floor plans.

5. Finishing of the dwellings. The users had the option to do certain jobs themselves (like painting, tiling, floor covering, etc.) and to be credited with the money saved.

January, 1974 marked the beginning of the participation phase, which coincided with the beginning of construction. Regular meetings were held in Hollabrunn which were attended by prospective dwellers, the architects, and representatives of the housing coopera-

Gert Schlegel

7

5,6,7,8. The architects and representatives of the cooperative housing society met frequently with future residents during the design phase.

8

tive. Detailed information concerning dwelling size, layout possibilities, costs, and construction schedules, as well as blank floor plans, was distributed to all participants to be taken home for discussion with family and friends. (Only the structure and the location of the vertical service elements were shown on these blanks. Examples of actual floor plans were given to participants *only if they expressly asked for them*.) In addition, a 1:200 scale model of the project was put on display and kept "up to date" to show construction and occupancy progress. This allowed the participants to see themselves in the context of everyone else's decisions and to visualize the impact of their own decisions. Interestingly, even during preliminary discussions, most users had already formed strong and divergent feelings about such matters as sun, light, location, view, and so forth. Most important was a good, unobstructed view—to have other dwellings, or even trees, in front of windows was considered undesirable.

By October, consultations were under way concerning final floor plans, decisions on facade treatments, and communal service facilities. Some of the participants not only designed their own layouts, but criticized the plans provided by the architects as examples and offered suggestions for future improvements. The majority managed to solve all their problems during the general consultation sessions or in individual sessions with the architects. It is truly remarkable that none of the participants gave up their right to determine the layout of their own dwellings (except for a few who planned to rent their dwellings to someone else).

9

10

9, 10,11. Prospective occupants worked with models to lay out their dwellings and design facades.

11

44

## Influence of Participation on the Design of the Project

Before the participation process started, the original concept of planning envisaged long buildings with a consistent east-west orientation and with "open" structural walls. Although we knew that the north and south sides could have had windows as well, we preferred closed end walls to achieve a clear planning concept and to give all dwellings the same status. So windows were provided in the east and west facades only. This decision was supported by clear physical requirements—that each dwelling should be surrounded by heavy construction elements with good insulating properties.

The basic design also provided a uniform supply system. The internal staircases were surrounded by U-shaped chases to which service could be con-

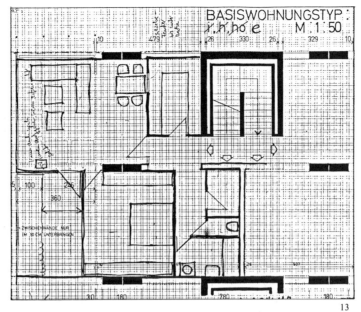

13

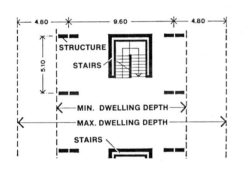

12

12. Basic building plan provided by the architects.

nected directly. This would have produced only interior bathrooms and kitchens. Both concepts had to be abandoned as soon as the future users started participating in the planning.

Twenty-nine out of 34 users wanted to have daylight in their kitchens. In the dwellings at the north and south ends of the buildings, most kitchens got windows in the end elevations. In some cases, even living rooms were shifted into the "dark zone" and bathrooms ended up in areas we had intended to be sleeping rooms, and vice versa.

These are just a few examples, but the users had a great number of wishes related to nearly every sphere of planning and included matters like quality of construction, heating systems, construction costs and schedules, and the design of areas of joint use. The prospective dwellers expressed their feelings very vigorously and even threatened to find other dwellings if

their wishes were ignored. Within the given technical and financial possibilities, we managed to satisfy most of them.

When construction got into the final phase of interior work, the interest of the future users in their new homes became so strong that they actually hindered the progress of work on the site by their constant visits. The problem was solved by introducing a weekly "consulting hour for users" which

13. One family's apartment sketch.

14. Overall model showing unit types, construction phasing, and occupancy progress.

14

45

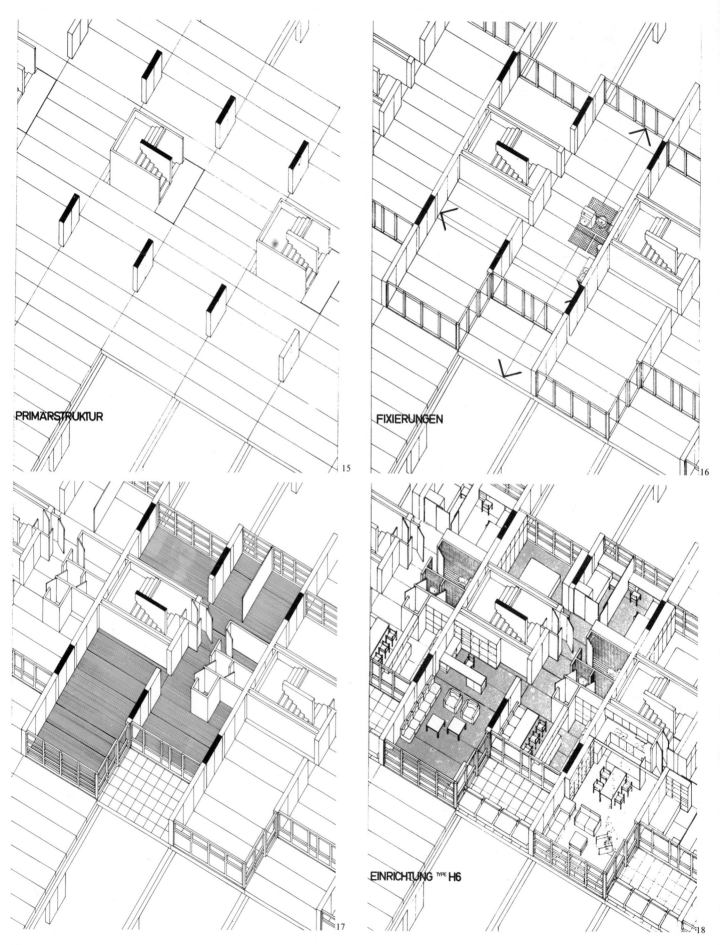

PRIMÄRSTRUKTUR

15

FIXIERUNGEN

16

17

EINRICHTUNG TYPE H6

18

46

yielded agreeable side effects: the time-consuming path of decision making from the user via consultant via housing cooperative via architect to the craftsman was reduced to a far less bureaucratic affair by establishing personal contact between user and construction worker.

## The Technical Conception of the Project

The completed project consists of three buildings, each 51 m long. This is the first of a total of three stages of construction. Most dwellings are oriented east to west. Their size varies from 38 to 150 m². Each building has three floors. The dwellings on the ground floors have gardens. All those on the upper floors have terraces and/or loggias.

The Support is a concrete skeleton made from prefabricated columns and beams. The floor/ceiling slabs were cast on site and connected by using prefabricated stairs. The facade consists of modular prefabricated sandwich elements of room height, 60 or 120 cm in width, which can be arranged in any combination. The walls between dwellings and against staircases are of plaster blocks. Within the dwellings partitions are plasterboard on metal frames.

About 70 percent of the units can expand *outward* without interfering with other dwellings (e.g., type e can grow from 72 to 92.5 m² on the same level). In this way the dwelling can be adjusted to family size or to increasing standards as the user's income increases. This also allows for the correction of mistakes which might have been made in the initial planning. Due to this also, the volume and form of the buildings are to an important extent determined by the users.

## The Results

The buildings have been in use since November, 1976, and the following preliminary conclusions can be drawn.

Even in social housing, users can and want to participate in planning.

Participation demands greater organizational efforts and leads to higher costs. In Hollabrunn, these were about five percent of the total construction costs; they were covered partly by government housing research funds, and partly absorbed by the architects' office. A survey turned up the following interesting fact: users would be ready to accept a five percent smaller dwelling in return for the right to take part in planning.

The planning of homes can be quickly learned. Each dwelling planned by its user differs from the others in floor plan as well as in elevation. Participation in creating and managing one's home increases the use value of a dwelling, and helps users to understand dwelling as a basic right—and not as alms granted by social welfare.

Participation must be made possible by:

1. A suitable method of building planning
2. A suitable construction technology
3. The architect's comprehension of his new role

It is especially this comprehension which is enlarged and solidified by the common effort to comply with the demands of each individual dweller: through personal contact we *can* build individualized homes. In view of the growing centralization of planning and industrialized construction, participation represents the necessary decentralizing counterweight. The democratic rights of users must be broadened.

Further participation projects have been realized in Austria by other architects and builders, and more projects are in the planning stage or under way. Participation in social housing is still not generally accepted in Austria, but the architects who believe in participation are determined to proceed on their way whenever the possibility arises.

19

15. The fixed structural and circulation elements of the Support.

16. The primary structure is subdivided according to family size and needs.

17. Infill elements create the dwelling as the residents have designed it with the architects.

18. A Type H6 Unit—one of many possible ways to organize space within the Support.

19. Wohnen Morgen with Hollabrunn in the background.

# SAR/Adelaide Road Estate
# Borough of Camden, London

PSSHAK—Primary Support Structures and Housing Assembly Kits—was originally a thesis project done at the Architectural Association School of Architecture in London by Nabeel Hamdi and Nick Wilkinson, now a staff member at SAR in Eindhoven.

Hamdi took the almost pure idea of the permanent Support and the detachable, prefabricated Infill kit of parts into the Greater London Council (GLC) soon after completing his studies, and stuck with the idea until the first true, SAR-based PSSHAK was built and occupied

in the London Borough of Camden in 1979.

Although the GLC bureaucracy was deeply troubled by the sometimes-idiosyncratic design ideas of the future tenants in the Adelaide Road PSSHAK, Hamdi was able to give them substantial freedom and to incorporate some very nonregulation dwellings in this 45-unit project. Not only were tenant wishes accommodated, but as a result of the planning meetings and site visits during construction, residents report that before occupancy "already there was the em-

bryo of a village feeling. . . ."

Interestingly, even though he succeeded in creating a full-fledged PSSHAK, Hamdi is himself critical of certain aspects of the design process and of the entire kit-of-parts concept. He now believes that the benefits of PSSHAK homes can be achieved better with less emphasis on industrialized components and more emphasis on co-operative control and management. He is currently refining his approach to housing as a member of the MIT Department of Architecture.

1

# PSSHAK: Primary Support Structures and Housing Assembly Kits

**Nabeel Hamdi, architect**
**London**

In March, 1977, the London Housing Aid Center published its report: "Housing in London—The Continuing Crisis." That report brought to light many frightening indications of the housing crisis which are as important today as they were then. The report summarized the problems as follows:

1. Opportunities for house purchases have been severely restricted by the decline in new building, cuts in local authority lending, and restrictive Building Society loan policies.
2. The private rental market is inexorably in decline, and rents of most of the few new units are beyond the reach of all but the wealthy.
3. Opportunities for moving to New Towns are being threatened by Government policies.
4. Local Authority building programs are going to slump due to rising costs.
5. Rehabilitation and improvement of decaying properties in both the public and private sectors has collapsed.

The Housing Aid Center then drew the inescapable conclusion, "that unless present policies are revised, London is heading for a housing disaster in the 1980s."*

Despite the current crude surplus of housing units to households, few would doubt that statement—expressed in the increasing number of people on local authority waiting lists, the number of households currently in temporary accommodation, and the number of older projects now classified as structurally deficient or lacking in basic amenities. Local public authorities, previously focused on the task of satisfying the numerical demand for housing units, are now burdened with the legacy, not of shoddy building, but of a housing stock which is the wrong size, difficult to rent, and becoming obsolete at an ever-

*Christine Hammond, *Housing in London: The Continuing Crisis,* March, 1977, SHAC (The London Housing Aid Centre).

1. A view from Adelaide Road. A conventional exterior masks the first use of SAR flexibility in British Council Housing.

increasing rate. The Ministry of Housing in 1978 was ready to admit that difficult-to-rent housing was not merely a question of housing surplus, but a reflection of the fact that "hard-up applicants, who know they have a high priority for re-housing, are now a good deal more choosy."

The widely celebrated British housing process was undoubtedly successful at producing houses. But it was at the same time widening the gap between those who could afford to own their properties—to have control—on the one hand, and those who for lack of choice (approximately 35 percent of Britain's housing is in public ownership) rent from local authorities. Politically and socially, this state of affairs is clearly no longer tenable. For one thing, the dependence of public authorities on scale for economy makes it almost impossible for them to deal with the abundance

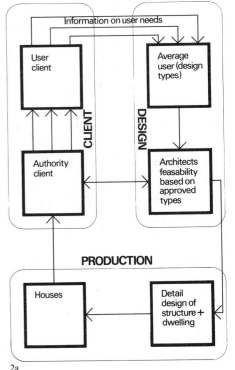

2,2a. The standard approach to public housing emphasizes the "typical" family. PSSHAK explicitly recognizes the idiosyncracies of users and the changing nature of the modern family.

The Greater London Council

2a

now of smaller sites in inner urban areas—it is uneconomical. For another, and as a corollary, its methods of design, production, and management rely on abstractions of needs, standards, and costs. Bureaucratically distilled into convenient "package deal" solutions, they create an unmistakable council house stigma. Some of the "products" may well be architecturally significant, attracting many visitors and bestowed with awards of one kind or another, but in fact, we are discovering them to be socially divisive, resented by tenants, and inflexible in the face of changing standards.

It is against this background that the PSSHAK effort should be assessed.

## Project Objectives

John Habraken set out his ideas for an alternative approach to mass housing in 1961 in his book *Supports*. This, together with the subsequent work of

SAR, proposes a fundamental restructuring of the decision-making hierarchies in housing—a new framework for housing production derived from basic principles. The most fundamental of these tell us that:

- Dwelling must be an act, not a product
- The user must be the key to housing design
- The appropriation of resources for housing production, maintenance, and management should support *user action* rather than centralized, bureaucratic initiatives

In the following pages, I shall attempt an evaluation of SAR concepts based on the project I have recently completed for the Greater London Council (GLC) at Adelaide Road in London. In general terms, the intention was to develop and test SAR ideas within the framework of a very large housing agency, and as a response to

the problems it was facing with its tenants and the public. Specifically, the objectives can be summarized as follows:

1. The development of a Support, designed to meet current standards for space, planning, and finishes, in a way which enables the user to interpret these freely according to his needs and quirks.
2. The development of a standard structure which could accommodate a wide variety of dwelling types (from 1 to 8 persons) in which the mix need not be decided until a late stage in the contract, and one which could be adapted simply to meet changing demand.
3. The design of dwellings which can be simply adapted and upgraded, piecemeal, to meet changing space and equipment standards.
4. An arrangement of physical form which capitalizes on the benefits of standardization for building, but

3. The Support at Adelaide Road consists of load-bearing cross walls and reinforced concrete floor slabs pierced for possible stairs and ducts. The location of the main stair maximizes unit flexibility. The shell includes primary electrical and mechanical systems.

4. Alternative dwelling mixes which can be accomodated in the 3-story blocks. Letters refer to unit types and numerals to number of occupants. The mix can change over time.

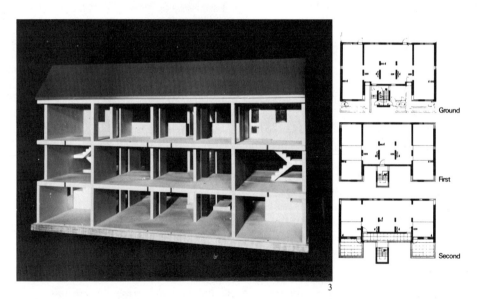

3

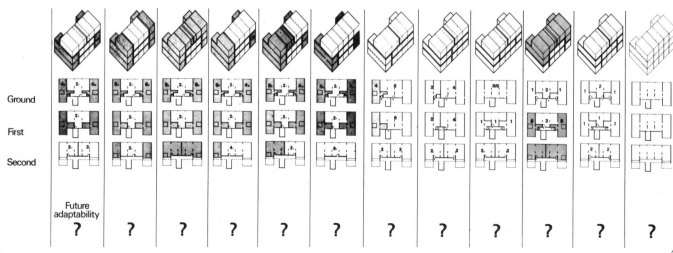

Ground

First

Second

Future adaptability

? ? ? ? ? ? ? ? ? ? ? ?

4

which is not, as a result, uniform functionally.

## PSSHAK—In Theory

The foundation of the PSSHAK approach rests on the separation of the building structure from the internal space-dividing elements of the dwelling units. This enables dwelling sizes and dwelling mix to be varied independently of the structure, and allows the number and sizes of rooms in any apartment to be modified with the use of an adjustable system of internal fitments. This facilitates initial user involvement in design, and modernization to suit waiting list requirements and changing family needs becomes a more practical proposition than usual.

The divergence from traditional housing methods that PSSHAK entails has considerable repercussions on housing management procedures. Housing authorities using PSSHAK will be able to make late-stage modifications to their building programs, and need not necessarily finalize the dwelling mix until the development reaches a fairly advanced phase. Since the inbuilt flexibility of the PSSHAK housing structure allows the incorporation of a greater range of housing alternatives than is normally the case, the ability of housing authorities to accommodate atypical households is assured. The range of accommodation can extend to include special groups, such as extra-large families and the handicapped. But where PSSHAK differs most from present housing methods is in its central recognition of the role of the user in the housing process, and the success or failure of the experiment depends greatly on the degree of active participation which is elicited.

## The Client Bodies

As a housing authority, the GLC is predictably unremarkable in its operations, although until recently, very convincing in its achievements. Its decision-making hierarchy is shaped, like most large bureaucracies, in pyramidal fashion. At the top is the housing committee, composed largely of politicians locally elected. Its primary task is policy making and budget approvals; it also has final veto power over all housing schemes.

Next is the Housing Department, composed of a number of sections, all under the Director of Housing. It is he who has the task of protecting the interest of the housing committee, housing management, and the user. The Director of Housing is the contact man for the architect on the job, he is "the client." He formulates project programs, and through his various consultants (mostly realtors and housing engineers), sets the number of different dwelling types, decides on the inclusion of facilities—such as for play and the elderly—and oversees standards. He approves new dwelling plans where they vary, for whatever reason, from the prescribed "plan type" or "preferred plan." His requirements are incorporated in a document, the "Housing Information File," on the basis of which specific projects are developed. This convenient package, therefore, represents the designer's tool, set up to streamline design and production, and to guarantee the project safe passage through the various regulatory bodies and approval procedures.

Beyond the GLC (which also includes building codes control, the fire authorities and building inspectors who must all approve plans), the architect encounters both the local planning authority and central government. It is within the local borough's jurisdiction to determine appropriate densities, layouts, building scale, and architectural styles. In order to qualify for central government subsidy, plans have to comply with minimum/maximum space standards, based on the recommendations of the 1961 Parker Morris committee, and with the government's famous "cost yardstick."*

By linking the space standards to subsidy and costing procedures, the process which enabled careful design to suit particular circumstances was replaced by a product—"the Parker Morris house"—which could be indiscriminately applied irrespective of the context.

Finally, there is that anonymous mass, referred to as "tenants," whom this entire process, we are told, is in-

---

*How is the yardstick devised? Nobody knows for certain! The ambiguities of the yardstick were best illustrated when, during the early 1970s, many bids were coming in well over the limits due to increased material and labor costs. The Ministry was able to authorize many contracts, however, through a system of "market allowances," which in many cases were 30 percent and even 50 percent over yardstick, and which left quantity surveyors in disarray attempting to disentangle costing procedures.

tended to serve. To qualify for a council house, each family must rank high on a points system designed to assess family qualifications and the extent of need for housing or rehousing. Applicants are filed on a computerized list, which also handles transfers and exchanges of accommodation. When a housing unit becomes available for rent, the computer identifies those either at the top of the list, or most "appropriate" for the type of accommodation being offered. Generally, three offers are made, each approximately two weeks before the household would have to move in. If none is accepted, the family is dropped to the bottom of the list.

Architects, needless to say, never meet their user clients, and must rely on the interpretations set out by the Director of Housing. PSSHAK at Adelaide Road was an effort to change this process in a fundamental way—from within the GLC.

## Site and Project Description

The 1.395-acre (0.565-hectare) Adelaide Road site is zoned for residential development at a density of 100 ppa (247 ppha). The site was vacant, and bounded to the north by the four- and five-story houses of the Eton Villas conservation area. To the south is Adelaide Road, and beyond is the Primrose Hill railway complex, set in a cutting. An existing GLC housing estate lies to the east. To the west is Eton Road.

It was considered important that the scheme relate sympathetically to the scale of building in the surrounding area, particularly to the Eton Villas conservation area. The design of the site also aimed at safeguarding the privacy, daylight, and prospect from the rear of the existing buildings in nearby Provost Road, and has managed to preserve a good number of the existing hardwood trees. Another major priority was for as many dwellings as possible to be provided with either private gardens or balconies, and with individual front doors to all dwellings at ground level.

### Accommodation Requirements

The scheme can accommodate a maximum of 64 dwellings (one- and two-person apartments) and a minimum of 32 dwellings (eight-person houses and two-person apartments) in 8, three-story blocks. The accommodation is presently broken down into the following unit

5. PSSHAK's eight 3-story blocks are organized along interior walkways. Dwellings have individual front doors and either gardens or balconies.

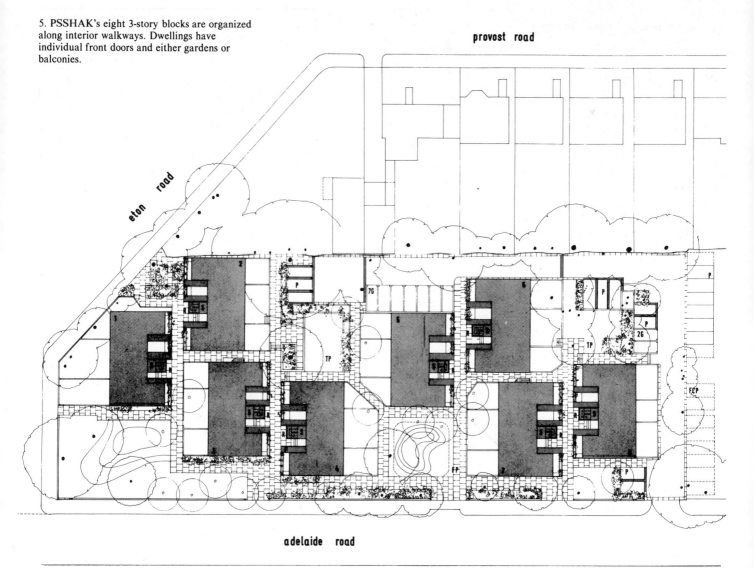

provost road

eton road

adelaide road

N

| 1 person flats (elderly) | 2 |
|---|---|
| 2 person flats (elderly) | 15 |
| 2 person flats | 13 |
| 3–4 person maisonettes (duplexes) | 9 |
| 3–4 person flats | 1 |
| 5–6 person houses | 4 |
| 7–8 person houses | 1 |
| Total number of dwellings | 45 |

The program also called for a common room for all residents. District heating, by central gas-fired boilers, heats individual radiators in all dwellings. To begin with, 26 parking spaces have been provided, but there will ultimately be a total of 35.

## PSSHAK In Practice

### The Support

The first stage of the PSSHAK process involves the construction of a basic structural shell, with load-bearing crosswalls and reinforced concrete floors pierced in the appropriate places to provide for long-term flexibility. The shell includes primary mechanical and electrical service connections.

External walls at Adelaide Road are of brick/block cavity construction, with good quality facing brick. The pitched roofs have black roof slates, and windows are of a softwood, horizontal pivot type. The screening and orientation of the blocks aimed to shield them from the noise of Adelaide Road, but as an extra precaution, fixed plate glass was specified for the Adelaide Road elevations.

## Assembly Kits

The second stage of the PSSHAK construction process is concerned with the installation of a kit of parts (Assembly Kit) within the completed structure. This kit is completely independent of the structure and consists of factory-produced components which form the internal layout and finishings once the dwellings are rented and detailed requirements can be determined.

The use of the kit should also mean that the dwellings will be capable of modernization in the future, and will accommodate future changes in housing standards. It will be possible to change the layout of flats on any particular floor without interfering with those above or below, thus avoiding the need for residents to move while alterations are being carried out.

The Assembly Kit, supplied by the Bruynzeel Company of Holland, consists of vertical service ducts, partitions, doors, cupboards, kitchen units, bathrooms, and stairs. All partitions in the Bruynzeel system are of a softwood frame covered with 16-mm-thick parti-

6a,b,c,d. Views of PSSHAK.

All photos The Greater London Council

6a

6c

6d

6b

cle board panels, ready for decoration. Within bathrooms, the frame is faced with 16-mm waterproofed particle board with a melamine plastic finish. Door frames are of high impact PVC or hardwood. Cupboards are made of standard partition elements, with PVC door frames and 18-mm-thick doors. Electrical wiring and fittings were included in the kit, ready to set in place.

Kitchen units were set against a 16-mm, melamine-faced particle board which lines the main structural walls and which carries service and cupboard units. All exposed pipework in bathrooms and kitchens is chrome-plated copper piping. Bruynzeel also provided free-standing cupboard units, with or without shelves, as wardrobes or linen closets.

## Site Organization

An important objective of the PSSHAK method is to rationalize traditional building processes and speed construction on site. The Assembly Kit is an entirely dry process and, together with the careful erection sequence which has been devised, it should result in a substantial saving of time on site. Industrialization of the finishing package allows a greater degree of control over

production and could lead to an improvement in quality. Delivery of the package in the form of complete house sets was intended to reduce labor content. Other cost reductions will be in painting and decorating.

Due to the construction method used for this development, it was anticipated that the contract period would be 15 months. In fact it was more like 40, although many dwellings were handed over prior to this. A wide range of problems, both technical and procedural, caused delays.

7. Elements of the Assembly Kit. All the Infill was supplied by the Dutch firm of Bruynzeel.

7c

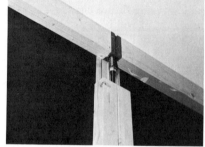

7b

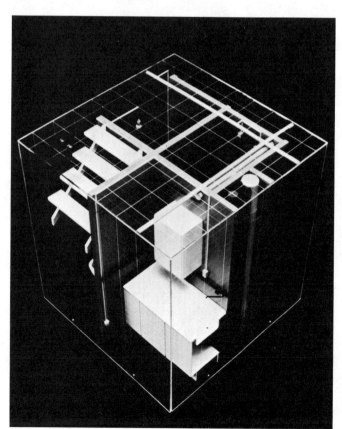

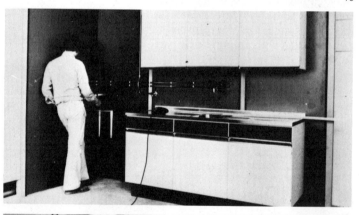

7a

## Cost

The difference in cost between building with PSSHAK and building with traditional methods is minimal. Nevertheless, we anticipated savings in design and construction time due to simplification of precontract and construction procedures. In assessing the overall economics of the system, it is also necessary to take into account savings which might be made in future modernization. These savings should be substantial, compared with the current high cost of improvements.

## The Participatory Exercises

The first meeting with prospective tenants was held in September, 1976, in the offices of the GLC. Families were invited in groups of 12 to hear about the project and the procedures which were to be adopted in working out dwelling plans. The meeting involved a description, with slides, of the planning forms and checklists in the design manual which was distributed. Discussion covered aspects of rent, pets, completion dates, car parking, the kind of heating system proposed, private gardens, availability of playgrounds, recreation rooms, and the management cooperative* that was to be formed.

Many tenants were clearly suspicious at these first meetings, others bewildered, some elated. As one tenant later wrote to me: "The ideas presented were fully understood by me and my family, although there were some present who appeared lost. I got quite enthusiastic in explaining to some my interpretations of it, as I saw it." Many expressed the view, that whatever else, the meetings presented a good opportunity to establish some sense of community prior to moving in—a rare opportunity with Council developments. In the words of

*There are essentially three types of cooperatives in Britain, all of which have as their main intention the involvement of participants in decision making. The first is a *management cooperative* in which associations of residents have collective responsibility for some or all of the management functions, but do not own the property. The second is a *nonequity cooperative,* similar to subsidized coops in the US, in which residents collectively own the property, but have equity limited to the nominal purchase price. The third kind is *coownership.* Here, residents collectively own and manage the property and share in the equity through an entitlement to market value on leaving. While Adelaide Road has become a management cooperative, the residents' ultimate goal is coownership.

one tenant: "I was immensely pleased to see the people who were to live around me, especially after my present disappointing and alarming experience of neighbors."

A number of similar group meetings were held, after which tenants had about two weeks to study the design manual and call back with queries aimed at clarifying the meaning of the manual and checking on the practicality of some of their ideas. Tenants' abilities to interpret the information, to establish priorities, and to draw schematic plans varied considerably. One tenant wrote: "The handbooks we found easy and helpful, and to my surprise, I found great enjoyment in drawing the plans.

8. A furnished interior with Bruynzeel shelving and partitions.

9. Prospective tenants were called together by the GLC to hear about the possibility of participation.

My husband and I had long discussions on what we would most like, from the area allowed us, and after he supplied a block of graph paper, I outlined about a dozen sketches, and set to work experimenting."

Another woman later wrote:

I found the handbooks amusing, easy to understand and very helpful, and it inspired me to visualize my new flat and all the possibilities for it. The slides and information at the meeting helped me consolidate the ideas—I went home and set to work immediately on designing my new flat, and retired to bed finally at 2:30 A.M.! I found the questionnaire easy to answer, and it was to prove useful at the later stage of drawing up plans with the architect. I found making the plans very exciting and made photostat copies and got all my friends to help. My class of children at school also wanted to be involved and drew up plans from the mundane to space age living!

Not all found the information so clear: "The handbook," wrote another tenant, "although I cannot suggest any way to make it easier, was not easy to follow, but on reading it over a few times, and discussing it with my family, we found we could formulate the kind of place we wanted within the limited space at our disposal."

After a two-week period, families returned their completed checklists, and in many more cases than anticipated, drawings of desired dwelling plans. What was lacking—and this reflected the nature of my design manual and procedures—was expression in more comprehensive terms of symbolic and other personal values related to the space and its arrangement, as opposed to purely functional needs.

Tenants' plans were carefully checked against practical criteria: bathroom/service ducts, door swings, scale, and so forth. Where plans were not included, care was taken to avoid a translation of a tenant's checklist requirements into a set solution, but rather to understand the implication of what was desired within the constraints set by the Support in order to have a more meaningful discussion at the site meetings.

Site workshops were conducted over a period of a month, with approximately three hours allocated to each

10. Every future occupant received a copy of the architect's guide to apartment planning.

11. A page from the Tenant's Manual: basic instructions on reading plans.

12. Planning aids from the Tenant's Manual.

family. The workshops were a team effort, between architect, kit manufacturer, and the Housing Department of the GLC, to establish in detail each family's needs. Families visited the unfinished space they were to occupy, and were able to visualize more completely the plan, to come to grips with the scale of the dwelling as a whole. Many families had brought with them photos and cutouts of furniture which they intended to move in. These were turned into quick models to ensure the "fit" would be right. The Assembly Kit was described and its options fully explained. Tenants' plans were set up in model form, and the ensuing discussions covered layout, location of doors, furniture,

arrangement of kitchen units, position of socket outlets, light switches and lights, as well as other detail items.

The results were diverse and predictably rich in the variety of plans produced: elderly persons opting for accommodation on the third floor, when normally they would be located on the first or second, the introduction of interconnecting doors between dwellings to safeguard an elderly neighbor, the option for two bedrooms in a two-person apartment, where a single double room is standard, the combination of two small yards into one for communal use, the decision to gain access to one bedroom through another to save space, living rooms, often divided into two

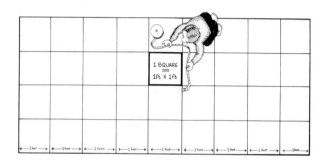

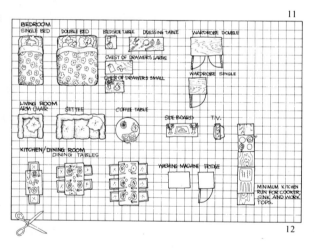

areas—formal and family, the variety of interpretations for dining/kitchen, dining/living, and so on.

Throughout this process, and in the presence of representatives of the Director of Housing, housing management, and the supplier of the kit, plans were checked against project budgets, allocated on the basis of the yardstick and a "standard plan" which I had drawn up for the housing committee to attract the maximum subsidy. While costs represented a key constraint, many trade-offs were possible. An elderly couple was able to benefit from a separate bathroom which was not wanted by another family. Doors, cupboards, and partitions, which proved in excess to many (the standard plan was intentionally over-provided with material at the budgeting stage), were utilized by others who were creating hobby rooms, separate dining areas, or additional bedrooms.

For a period of about a month following the site workshops, tenants were able to call back with adjustments and changes of mind, after which final plans were drawn up by the Bruynzeel people, on the basis of which kits were calculated and ordered.

Tenants' first responses to nearly completed apartments were varied. While most felt that what they saw met their expectations, others expressed concern. The overall size of many dwellings seemed smaller than anticipated. As one tenant put it:

> . . . having seen the near finished project, I should have commented and questioned more rigorously . . . it is not easy for a layman to visualize the finished article at the drawing board stage, as it were . . . I think the manner of response of the persons involved closely reflects the situation from whence he is seeking to escape.

Many tenants were happy to accept anything, simply to move from their existing, unsatisfactory council housing.

The possibilities of the Assembly Kit, together with the opportunities for planning, it seems now, were overstated despite efforts to the contrary, with the result that expectations were sometimes too high. It was interesting to read some tenants' initial responses: "The handbook conjured up visions of a domestic paradise," wrote one tenant; and another reflected that, "It inspired me to visualize my new *ideal* flat."

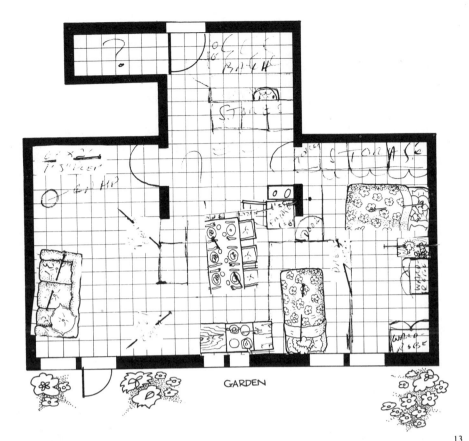

GARDEN

13

14

## An Assessment of Ideologies

Habraken defined the physical Support as representing those elements of the built environment which the *public* controls and about which the user has no direct say. Conversely, "detachable units" (Assembly Kits) represent the decision-making field of individual users. This ideological concept requires an understanding that there are "limits" to the activities of each participant (the public and the individual users)

13. Scissors and pins lead to a preliminary layout.

14. Tenants meet with architect Hamdi to discuss their ideas.

which should be *negotiated* on the basis of mutual needs, abilities, and resources. The decision-making hierarchy of the GLC, which I have already briefly described, together with current housing legislation, is an immense stumbling block to this process. At this stage, both the Support and the Infill are owned by the GLC. Although the present layouts have been determined largely by the residents, any future changes must be approved at County Hall. In other words, tenant action needs official approbation.

The proper balance, therefore, between public and private decision making has not existed at Adelaide Road. What Habraken called the "theoretical division" of Supports and detachable units, became, in the hands of the public authority, a technique for dealing with bureaucratic problems, not tenant needs. For example, various political maneuverings prevented the cooperative from being set up at any early enough stage to involve tenants in discussions of site layout, car parking facilities, public amenities, landscaping, and public versus private open space. The Support became everything to do with the "outside" and detachable units—some aspects of which tenants could influence—"inside." This convenient and simplistic interpretation of the idea fitted well with the predominantly British notion that you can do what you like, so long as you do it *in* your home (keeping in mind that, in this case, it was not in fact *your* home at all, but the public's). This, of course, represents the basic paradox and the stumbling block of most public housing initiatives. The range of user choice deemed reasonable by the authority found physical expression in a "kit of parts," manufactured in "package deal" fashion for the user. This notion itself now seems ideologically doubtful. The consumerist approach, the antithesis of participation, is perpetuated—the *status quo* is ruthlessly safeguarded.

Andrew Rabeneck, a well known British housing critic, described his thoughts thus:

It seems to us that the assembly kits or detachable units are a red herring. They are important only as part of the 'supports' concept as a whole, as a means of providing occupants with a tool for exercising individual choice within the community-provided sup-

port structure. However, the search for a perfect kit of parts within an adaptable shell seems paradoxical . . . we think this is because the objects themselves have little to do with the 'act of dwelling' in the sense a cooker has to do with the act of cooking— they are simply not important, beyond simple functional requirement.*

Rabeneck is quite right in pointing out the contradiction between the flexibility of a Support and the utilization of a single,"perfect" set of Infill components to subdivide and service it. A single kit of parts is important to those who would encourage industrialization and to housing agencies bent on streamlining production, but it is not central to the Supports concept. I no longer believe that the sort of Assembly Kit used at Adelaide Road is necessary as far as participation is concerned—perhaps not even desirable. As a next step, we should explore the practicality of providing unfinished shells to be finished as tenants see fit, using a combination of "off-the-shelf" and craft techniques.

## Detachable Units—An Evaluation

Whatever the ideological arguments, managing the delivery and erection of the detachable units turned out to be fraught with difficulties. It is true that much of this was associated with the decision on cost grounds to select a Dutch manufacturer, and the subsequent, inevitable problems of meeting British codes and construction procedures.

Installation was subcontracted to a firm that had wide experience in plasterboard partition systems and who bid on the contract on the basis of the man-hour requirements estimated by the supplier. Any additional time involvement was to be calculated on a flat rate basis, avoiding, thus, the inclusion of a hefty contingency sum in the contract to cover the project's experimental nature.

Initial delivery of components, once they had been calculated on the basis of tenants' plans, was made to the subcontractor's warehouse where components were shelved under their various categories—posts, facing panels, screws, and so forth. While direct delivery to site would have simplified operations,

*Andrew Rabeneck, David Sheppard, and Peter Town, "Housing Flexibility," special issue of *AD,* November, 1973.

lack of space necessitated a two-stage delivery program. It was originally hoped that deliveries might be made directly to each of the blocks, but this required blocks to be complete buildings according to an agreed timetable—an operation deemed risky in view of the likely delays (which did occur) due to inclement weather and sporadic supply of materials and labor. Furthermore, it would have required the Dutch supplier to presort components and deliver in dwelling packages, which proved uneconomical in terms of loading each container truck to full capacity. More seriously, the notion that an apartment block could be entirely free of other trades when the time came to install the kits proved unrealistic in terms of conventional construction scheduling. Erection of the kits was substantially hampered by the continued presence of other trades completing the installation of radiators, gas supplies, and cabinet work.

Upon delivery from the warehouse to the site, many kits were incomplete. This was due to many factors—the subcontractor's omitting parts, the manufacturer's inability to interpret the complex dwelling schedules, damage during delivery to warehouse and site, and the fact that house plans had been subject to last-minute changes by tenants. All this resulted in delays, claims for reimbursement, and the fact that when the work reached "kitting out" the last block, there were substantial shortages of components.

The mechanical services, prefabricated to include all pipework, also proved complex in terms of site operations. The supplier had tested each section (running from floor to ceiling), and was able to guarantee good workmanship. The subcontractor fixing the units, however, had similarly to guarantee joining—one unit to the other—for the full height of each block. The heating contractor, who made connections to his hot and cold water tanks in the roof space, had similar responsibilities for that part of the work, while the gas company—insisting on control of final installation—was in and out to fix the supply at the base of the duct and final distribution to meters and stoves. What is telling about this is that the intentions originally argued—the kit would "simplify site operations" and minimize conventional delays resulting from the usual "trades waiting on trades"—were not borne out.

There were also problems related to workmanship in building the shell. The kit required tolerances within the shell to be accurate. This includes the position of windows, radiators, inspection chambers, floor to ceiling heights, and width of openings. Many adjustments were required as the kit was being installed—both to the kit and to the shell—to make up dimensional differences, to secure a good fit of kit to Support. And there were problems with the components themselves: plastic cornices which fractured on installation, hardwood heads to timber posts breaking when the pressure required to hold partitions in position was applied.

A number of other technical problems arose. I am less concerned about these, since, whereas the management issues restricting participation are inherent to the system and require fundamental changes, site management and technical problems were largely teething troubles, easily worked out if the resultant benefits were considered worthwhile.

## PSSHAK in Use

The Adelaide Road estate is now fully occupied with seemingly happy tenants and the cooperative is in full swing. It received its registration certificate from the Registrar of Friendly Societies on June 28, 1979. Frequent meetings are held to educate members in the principles of cooperatives and in the management and accounting of their resources. Many adjustments have already been effected to the site based on common concerns—signage to the development, gates to control entry into the estate, a more accurate parking allocation system.

Within the limitations set by legislation, prevailing bureaucracy, and current attitudes, the project has been a success. We have a reusable housing shell, one which can be continuously adapted as circumstances dictate. Families have been involved earlier than usual, with greater decision-making powers. We see this reflected in the care and enthusiasm they exhibit. A crucial question which remains is: what kind of an administrative framework would facilitate a fuller participatory role for users? What is the proper role of the architect? How do we replace the existing, entrenched bureaucracy?

"If architects have a professional fu-

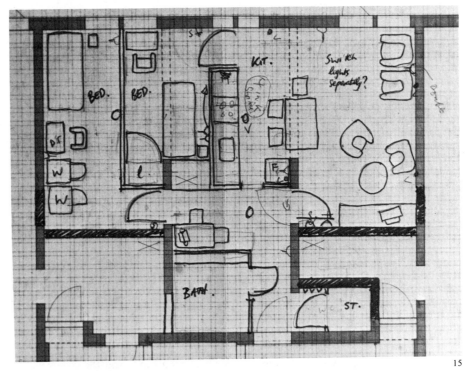

15

15. A refined version of the plan following the meeting with the architect.

16,17. Under Council housing rules, a two-person flat has only one bedroom. PSSHAK enabled this mother and daughter to plan their home with two bedrooms within the alloted space.

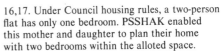

16

17

Richard Davies/The Architectural Press

ture at all, it is . . . as 'skilled understanders,' enabling people to work out their problems:" Colin Ward to the architecture students at Sheffield University in March, 1976. This statement, in my view, provides an essential insight into the meaning of participation for designers. It does not attempt to define at random and in the abstract what each party should do—what participation is. That is left to be *negotiated,* depending on context. We cannot be sure of our precise roles out of context. And that context is the place, the people, the resources available, and the cultural and regulatory rules which apply. It is a common fault that, having dismantled one set of design formulae, we should substitute others which, although freer and more participatory in nature, are nevertheless restrictive when it comes to action, because they anticipate that action.

Too many designers, in place of participation, have accepted a kind of environmental determinism—the belief that if one defines the activities likely to take place, assesses furniture and equipment requirements of the space in question, then one can design around these needs. It is in these terms that housing managers within local government profess to have accumulated enough experience about users to pass judgment on their needs without much question. Their designs, they argue, are even based on attitude surveys. This suggests why public housing officials in Britain have never investigated the potentials of participation: they have believed that it always existed.

Peter Hall sums up the current dilemma aptly:

How then can we involve participants in decision-making in such a way that politicians, and designers do not feel that their responsibility and prerogatives are being diminished? How do we prevent the thousands of contradictory perceptions and notions of the public from being digested by the politicians to produce a compromise answer to them?*

One of the ways, of course, in which this has been done is to mandate participatory programs, to absorb them within the existing framework, and to declare them as part of official policy.

This too frequently becomes simply and naively the process of displaying completed or half-completed, unintelligible plans in town halls, for comment and consultation—the professional seeking the public's stamp of approval. In most cases, all the major decisions have already been taken, while it remains firmly the prerogative of the authorities to decide which "bits and pieces" are left to be manipulated by the user.

There is a better way. Public authorities *do* have a significant role to play as "skilled enablers," that is, predominately in structuring appropriate economic and political frameworks for user initiative, in making available resources of money and skills, and in providing education and information to citizens and professionals on the techniques and methods of participatory housing production.

The Supports idea represents a return to basic principles in structuring our housing programs. And the issues will not be fully explored if one's starting point is the *product* itself. That may be very disappointing for architects, but a concentration on *process*—and especially a larger role for the user—is essential if we hope to escape from our perpetual housing dilemma.

---

*Peter Hall, "The Planners and the Public," *New Society,* March 22, 1973.

# Commentary on SAR

John F. C. Turner, architect, Director
of AHAS: Housing & Local Development, London

## THREE BASIC CRITERIA FOR EVALUATION

This essay attempts to clarify what I now see to be the essential criteria for evaluating any work, including housing projects such as SAR's Molenvliet, Papendrecht, and PSSHAK's Adelaide Road. My comments are intended as propositions to be tested, using my own perception of these projects and their kind as an illustration of the framework which should be used for deciding on a particular course of action in any field. The discussion also continues my long-term work on "appropriate technology" for housing. I hope to move toward firmer conclusions through correspondence with readers concerned with the issues raised in the field of housing and local development.

My premise is that without personal responsibility for the production and use of vital goods and services, energy will be wasted and life will be shortened.

There are three parts to this argument, each of which refers to a different sphere of relations and aspect of the reality we perceive. The first, personal responsibility, implies local control and refers to relationships between people in the first place. The second, the production and use of vital goods and services, refers to what people and their organizations and institutions actually do, and so to the relationships between (interrelated) people and the environments they make and maintain. The third part, about energy and life, deals with the overall relationship between civilization and the universe of nature, that is, between society, together with its culture and built environment, and the biosphere. I assume that we all recognize this trinity of relationships in everyday experience: the more-or-less distinct and separately variable relationships we have with other persons, with what we or they do or have done, and with nature. No consideration is complete and nothing is seen as a whole unless all three dimensions are viewed in space and in time.

From the point of view I am trying to establish and in the view I am trying to clarify, there are three key issues in any field of action, corresponding to the three spheres of relations. The first is the issue of *authority*, which determines and is a consequence of the ways and means by which people relate to one another in any society. The second is the issue of *economy*, the values placed on what is done through the transformation of resources into goods and services by people, their organizations, and institutions. The third issue, which subsumes the other two, is that of *life* itself. Many people apparently assume that knowledge and powers of decision and control both are and should be with those who have more formal education and whose higher status and position enables them to see more. My co-workers and I believe that understanding and knowledge of needs and resources is rooted in firsthand experience so that there is no correlation between social status and real authority. Political, moral, and intellectual power, in other words, are different and, more often than not, in conflict. In the familiar view, economy is evidently a matter of productivity in the industrial sense and of financial costs in the bankers' sense. This conception conflicts with the view that economy is a matter of the use of all available resources and of the usefulness of the goods and

services produced, irrespective of the ratios between hours worked and production and of costs and prices. If we were to pursue the discussion into the third sphere, we would frequently also reach an impasse over our interpretations of the final goals. Common political language is full of direct and indirect references to material progress in the urban-industrial sense, a language denying the reality of entropy and the second law of thermodynamics.* We do recognize and respect this law so that the ultimate criterion concerns the use of energy: the more energy used, the less life there can be ultimately.

I am *not* accusing friends like John Habraken, Frans van der Werf, and Nabeel Hamdi of the perhaps caricatured opinions I have just described. But I do think that much of the work that they have done in the past conflicts with much of what they say and write—and with which I agree. Indeed, I have a great deal in common with the Supports concept as pioneered by Habraken at a time when I was only starting to articulate my own and closely parallel ideas. As I and others have been saying for some years, it is evident, from the point of view I share with SAR, that a technological application that is not complemented by institutional innovations is counterproductive. In effect, I believe that the experiments with industrialized and merely technical interpretations of the Supports principle actually decreases the scope for personal responsibility in housing and that it demands excessive energy and, therefore, it cannot be life-enhancing.

In the first place, the purely formal and technological separation of Support and Infill strengthens the separation of local and central powers. The added use of industrially-supplied components, coordinated to match the centrally determined modular design of the Support structures, increases the division of labor and the separation of production and use. The possibility of manipulating dwelling components in order to rearrange internal space is a trivial advantage for which essential freedoms are sacrificed. People who want to make their own housing decisions demand freedom to live where they need to for their own social, economic, or environmental reasons. If central planners and authorities decide on the installation of the Support systems or infrastructures, then they either tie users down to the specific sites they prepare or society must carry the costs of un- or underused infrastructures in order to provide an adequate range of choice. If people are not free to choose where they live—from an adequate range of alternatives—then they cannot easily choose their neighbors. And one suspects that the systems imposed will standardize forms of tenure and financing, even if there is some flexibility with regard to the volume and arrangement of domestic living space. To the apparently considerable extent that users are locked into specific forms of construction that are highly industrialized, they are reduced to the status of passive users or "consumers" of subsystems that they can only

---

*The references to the law of entropy (or the second law of thermodynamics) are fully explained in *Entropy, A New World View*, by Jeremy Rifkin, Viking Press, New York, 1980.

assemble. As these tend to be complex, and as the materials and components they are made from are difficult to use or modify or combine with other materials using hand tools, user-control is further reduced. The increased separation of production from use extends the reified domain of consumerism, the ultimate form of alienation.

All of these tendencies increase both material and social costs. Even allowing for all the distortions of reality when only financial measures are used, it still seems that the very high monetary costs of these SAR-influenced experiments reflect significant demands on relatively scarce and costly resources. Many highly industrialized materials and components are commercially cheaper, but when they are tied into coordinated systems, their design and production, storage and delivery, and, even their assembly and subsequent maintenance tend to be more complicated and expensive. Technical mistakes, which are practically inevitable at the design stage, are often very difficult and expensive to put right. All these complications, together with the administrative tasks of component allocation and matching variable plans with individual households (or, at least, different sets of components and the supervision of their assembly) demand exceptionally high proportions of professional and administrative work; this, of course, is not directly productive and yet is highly paid. All these material costs are complemented by social ones as anticipated above. The inhibition and frustration of capabilities and demands that people have create or increase personal anxiety that can often be released only by anger. We see this expressed by increased and often exaggerated demands on the suppliers and authorities to which the users are subject. Systems that limit the scope of personal responsibility and control either inhibit personal growth, maturation, or fulfillment, or they redirect frustrated energies into demands on others.

Both the inhibition of personal responsibility and its often perverse redirection into extraneous and often destructive activities further increase dependence on mechanical and administrative substitutes. The organizations required by industrialized production and centralized planning and supply increase the distance between producers and users. The greater the physical or managerial distance, the less understanding and knowledge the planners and organizers can have of both needs and resources at both ends of the whole process: at the workbench or in the field and where the products are used or consumed. Producers are increasingly separated from users; the division of labor and of production and consumption in space, time, age, and sex, as well as class, simultaneously reduces understanding and increases the power of management. But this ultimate practice of the principle of divide and rule is self-defeating. Cut off from the roots of knowledge and, therefore, genuine authority, management is incompetent and often corrupted by unaccountable power. Workers and users—producers and consumers—lose respect for pseudo-authority and lapse into apathy or violence as their frustration rises. Unable to make proper or full use of locally-available material resources—often the most plentiful, but often highly variable—and finding mechanical and electronic systems more profitable or administratively convenient, a viciously counterproductive circle is accelerated.

This argument has led to the conclusion that any ways and means that increase dependency on large organizations and capital-intensive technics are bound to waste resources and are bound to use high proportions of those that are least renewable and plentiful and the most polluting. In the final analysis it is a matter of energy and, therefore, of life. Those that understand the very simple second law of thermodynamics (which states that all matter and energy can only be changed in one direction, that is, from usable to unusable, or from available to unavailable, or from ordered to disordered) know that the biosphere itself, like everyone's own life, has a limited span. The only realistic goal in life is to live fully, and this demands a wise use of energy. Any activity which demands more than the necessary amount of energy for the necessary support of life is intrinsically destructive. This, then, is the vital criterion: does the activity take more life away from other people, in other places or in the future, than the life it gives?

In spite of the good intentions, I am afraid that projects like Papendrecht and Adelaide Road do inhibit more life than they can generate. Of course, this accusation should be contested. Only through further investigation and discussion can we find the measures and indicators of the now evidently vital criteria and learn to design socially and biologically responsible housing.

# Response to Turner

Nabeel Hamdi

Turner's three basic criteria for evaluation are indisputably important. The ambiguities emerge in connection with means rather than ends, given prevailing circumstances in the UK, and with the way in which these basic criteria are interpreted as a basis for action. Let me start with Turner's reference to the separation of Support and Infill as reinforcing the hierarchy of central and local powers. This is a position that can now be clearly recognized as counterproductive. It is unfortunate, but I suppose inevitable, that the projects built so far should have emphasized this hierarchical separation—after all, they were built within the established frameworks of public housing, frameworks that at least produced a large quantity of houses.

My personal position with the Supports idea has become clearer as projects have been completed and occupied and as my discussions with colleagues continue. It begins with the reassertion of "community" (rather than the individual "user") as the effective power in decision making. The clearest institutional support for this idea is the cooperative, and the many forms (both formal and informal) that this can take. In relating Supports to this notion, a number of issues became clear. For example, the Support and Infill as a physical manifestation of who does what must be determined through negotiation and not static theory. It is a reflection of the shared values of a community and not the standards prescribed by a public agency. Given this position, the role of public agencies emerges as one which provides appropriate institutional frameworks to reinforce particularity, rather than to absorb it into the universal body of public housing. Housing is an arena in which policies of least intervention should operate simultaneously with those of maximum support.

Needless to say, a gap exists between what is said and what is in fact done in projects such as Adelaide Road. I find this neither discomforting nor remarkable, given prevailing circumstances. Of course, no real change will come without the kind of institutional changes that Turner and many others have described. As a designer, my position is explicit and therefore vulnerable. In working within the existing framework, the intent is to enable ideas to infiltrate and challenge—with the hope of changing—current attitudes and procedures, generating the need for alternative frameworks for design and management. It is a mode of working that recognizes design as being both political and social, as a *responsive* rather than *pioneering* act, conducted in a contextual rather than theoretical setting. It is also a mode of working which, in my view, gives substance to the otherwise ambiguous ritual of design.

The project at Adelaide Road, despite its acknowledged shortcomings, represents the very thin end of a rather large wedge. In pragmatic terms, it provides a structure that is reusable, albeit under the control of a public agency. It does therefore reflect current standards, but in a way which, for house and house layout, are modifiable. The process did require architect, housing managers, and users to negotiate dwelling plans and equipment, an unprecedented level of user intervention in public housing, limited as it may seem. The physical parts themselves are made in ways that permit incremental change to respond to changing needs, despite a relatively capital-intensive mode of production. A cooperative is being attempted in recognition of the importance of community, although at a late stage when design and production could not be influenced by the coop. Given the massive waste of energy and money in conventional renovation of the existing housing stock the levels of underoccupancy in the Greater London area, the numbers of people on waiting lists and classified as homeless, and the numbers of dwellings deemed difficult to rent, I draw the conclusion that the idea, even as built at Adelaide Road, must "add to life," modest as this contribution may be.

In general, therefore, I agree with Turner's comments, but not his rejection of the Supports idea. Whether our tools are the appropriate ones to achieve the goals which have been set out, and about which there is considerable agreement, is in my view an area for continued research and discussion.

# SAR/Les Marelles
# Boussy-St. Antoine, France

The most technically sophisticated of the Support/Infill projects reported in this volume, Les Marelles was designed and executed by architect Georges Maurios and his social scientist partners in the Paris firm *environnement et comportement* (environment and behavior). They set out to test two hypotheses in this condominium housing project in a rather bleak Paris suburb: future inhabitants are competent space planners, and when people participate in dwelling design they develop special feelings about them-

selves and their homes. They found that they were right—but not quite in the ways they had predicted when embarking on Les Marelles.

The designers were struck by the depth of the residents' involvement, the housing issues on which they focused, and the anxiety that was provoked by the unfamiliar process of making one's own environment.

As Les Marelles was built as a shell to be sold by the square meter, Maurios' team came up with an instructive set of

design aids, equipment selection catalogs, and cost-estimating guides for prospective purchaser-participants. These provide a model to follow in extending this concept to other countries and categories of users.

In her Commentary, Katherine Coit, an American planner teaching in Paris, describes the experiment at Les Marelles as a reaction against official housing policy and the counterproductive, traditional role of the architect in housing development.

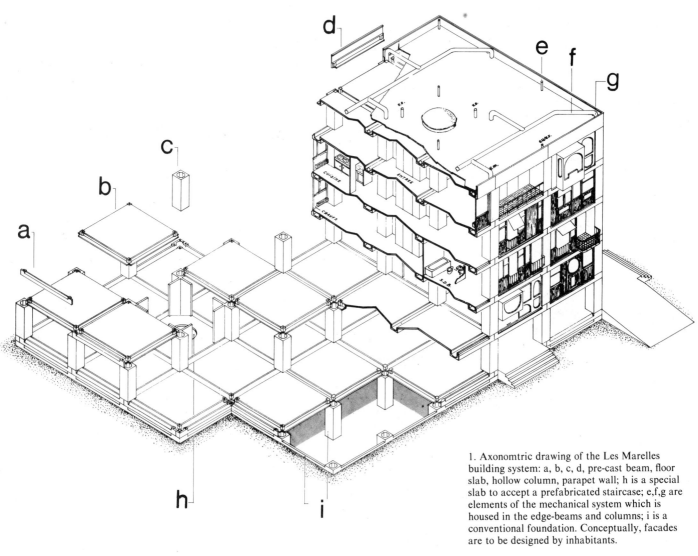

1. Axonomtric drawing of the Les Marelles building system: a, b, c, d, pre-cast beam, floor slab, hollow column, parapet wall; h is a special slab to accept a prefabricated staircase; e,f,g are elements of the mechanical system which is housed in the edge-beams and columns; i is a conventional foundation. Conceptually, facades are to be designed by inhabitants.

# The Limits of Flexibility

**Georges Maurios, architect**
*environnement et comportement,* Paris

In the mid-1970s, more than 500,000 dwellings were being produced each year in France. Almost all of them were delivered to their present occupants completely finished and entirely conceived and planned by architects and the other narrow specialists ordinarily concerned with the production of dwellings. This phenomenon can be interpreted in two different ways: the specialists are so much like future inhabitants that they can properly think and decide for them, or the inhabitant is incapable of making proper decisions by himself.

It is in relation to this situation that one should examine our experiment in housing design and construction at Les Marelles. All too often ordinary people say when looking at a new building: One can see that the architect doesn't live here. This is another indication of the lack of concordance between the desires of inhabitants and the choices made by housing specialists. With this in mind, we established as our primary postulate the following: all people have the right to plan their own dwellings. It was our objective to give to each future occupant both the power and the means to conceive of personalized plans—if not for the building as a whole at least for their own space within it. We were quite sure that in this way, housing satisfaction would be greatly increased.

## Experimental Hypotheses

With the support of the Ministry of the Environment and the Quality of Life, Les Marelles was conceived as an experimental project. At the outset, we formulated two hypotheses to guide our work: future inhabitants are *quite capable* of making concrete plans for their dwellings, and specialists such as architects and engineers should provide, instead of leadership, support and technical assistance in this process. Second, when people participate in the conception of their dwellings, they develop special feelings about themselves and about their homes.

In order to verify or to test these two hypotheses, it was necessary to create an institutional framework in which the inhabitants were able, in fact, to make plans and then to occupy and use the space they planned. To satisfy these requirements, we came up with a method of planning, construction, and financing which put these powers in the hands of future inhabitants. This experiment focused on the interior planning of individual dwellings. For that reason, we separated the project into two distinct phases:

1. Phase A involved site planning and the determination of overall building plans. This was under the control of the architects. Future inhabitants were then given the possibility of choosing the location of their dwelling within the buildings already under construction and also the amount of floor area which they wished to occupy.
2. Phase B had to do with the planning and subdivision of the interior dwelling space, and this was left entirely to the inhabitants—with the assistance of our office.

## The Building Project

Les Marelles is situated in Boussy—Saint Antoine in the planning area of Val d'Yerres, 300 m from the suburban railroad station (30 minutes by train to the Gare de Lyon), 200 m from a large shopping center, close to the forest of Sénart, and in the neighborhood of a school complex and other recent apartment projects. The program called for the development of medium rise apartment houses to be offered on a condominium basis, and benefiting from special interest rates offered by a state–supported housing bank, Crédit Foncier. The floor space to be constructed was approximately 7100 m², which represented somewhere between 70 and 104 dwellings, depending upon their final size. This total area was divided between three buildings, which are three and four stories high. The scheme provides 33 terraces for upper level apartments. The ground level apartments all have private gardens.

Children's play areas and general landscaping were well under way when the experiment in dwelling planning began. As no dwelling partitions had been put in place by the architects, potential occupants found large, open loft spaces when they visited the project for the first time. To them was given the possibility of determining how much floor area they needed, what orientation they would choose, where they wished to be within the building complex, and then, finally, the possibility of laying out a dwelling according to their own desires.

## Constraints and Opportunities

Before turning to the planning freedom accorded to future occupants, let us examine some of the limitations at work in this project. Les Marelles was conceived within the ordinary framework of building codes, financial regulations, condominium laws, and technical limits. Hence there were several types of constraints at work:

1. Financial Restrictions—The project was made possible by the special loan conditions offered by Crédit Foncier. This involved two consequences: (a) The overall cost of the project, including certain aspects of the participation experiment, had to be within the price or the cost guidelines of the bank. (b) In order to take advantage of these special loan conditions, each purchaser had to fall into a very precise income bracket. This, of course, made it impossible for either the relatively poor or the relatively rich to participate in this experiment. Because all of the families who moved in had incomes which were more or less the same, the differences in apartment sizes are very small.

2. Building Codes—Every dwelling completed under this experiment had to conform to the standard building codes, to the electrical code, and also to the special construction requirements of Crédit Foncier. Further, the zoning regulations required us to provide 1.4 parking places or garage spaces for each dwelling. In turn, the developer had to require each future occupant to purchase a garage which added almost 10 percent to the dwelling price.

3. Legal Constraints—The condominium law which governed this project called for *clefs en main* (keys in hand). This means that a dwelling is not truly sold until it is delivered complete. A purchaser may drop out of the program at any moment and for any reason, even after two-thirds of the construction of a personally planned apartment had been completed.

4. Technical Constraints—The planning of the common areas of the buildings and of the structural system was, of course, done by the architects. The flexibility of the interior space is tied to the nature of the structure—light conditions, bay sizes, locations of chases, and so forth.

On the other hand, our project provided the following areas of choice to the purchaser:

1. Within the limits set by the bays and the column bands (about 15 m² and 3 m², respectively), inhabitants could determine the floor area for their individual dwellings.

2. They had the right to select colors for exterior panels from a range provided by the architect.

3. They could choose the location of the bays to be purchased and determine the precise plan for subdividing the space within their apartment.

4. They could select from an extensive catalog the quality and quantity of finished materials and cabinetwork for their own units.

## The Support Structure

The structural system calls for only three precast concrete elements, factory fabricated, easily transportable, and of more or less equal weight. These members form a hollow structural skeleton that provides a three-dimensional network of chases for plumbing and ventilation. The columns contain the primary chases. At each floor level, pipes and ducts spread out horizontally through the channel beams in a secondary network of services. Of each four columns, two contain plumbing. The other two are reserved for mechanical ventilation. This conjuncture of structure with both vertical and horizontal services removes any constraints on the locations of bathrooms and kitchens, and permits total flexibility in the design of individual dwellings.

## The Design Experiment

The theoretical maximum number of dwellings which could be contained within the structures at Les Marelles was 104. Our experiment lasted one full year (from April, 1974 to April, 1975). In that time, 16 families accepted the challenge to design their own dwellings. Nine were able to see the project through to the end and now live at Les Marelles. Of the seven who dropped out, five were forced to do so for economic reasons and two others because of family changes.

There are a number of reasons why so few families participated in the planning of apartments at Les Marelles. The location, which we had not proposed, is quite far from the city and in an environment composed largely of single family homes. In addition, given that we are talking about the purchase of the dwelling with payments over 15

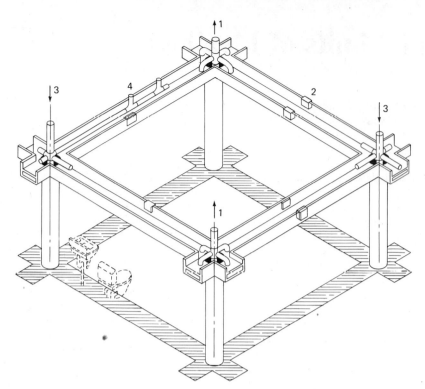

2. U-shaped beams and hollow columns carry HVAC ducts, plumbing lines, and electrical power. Dotted lavatory and wc indicated that bathrooms (or kitchens) may be located at any corner of the grid. Availability of fresh air and exhaust ducts around the perimeter makes subdivision simple.

years, the economic climate in France combined with the unfamiliarity of this kind of project, its innovative aspects, the complexity of the experiment, and the mode of financing with its income floors and ceilings, discouraged certain potential purchasers.

Our experiment was conducted in two phases. First, there was a systematic observation of the behavior of the purchaser families during the design and planning of their dwellings. In this work they used models and other materials provided by the architects. Second, in a post-occupancy evaluation carried out through visits and discussions, we attempted to compare the space in use with the ideas of use expressed by each inhabitant's original plan.

Throughout the study which we carried out at Les Marelles, the following conclusions seemed clearly to emerge. The object of our experiment was to permit people to plan their own dwellings. We soon learned that the choices that we were offering were far from being the most important, and far from being as important as we thought at the outset. One might put it this way: if we hadn't *fixed* the musical score in advance, in effect we were only permitting the occupants to compose within a single octave.

There were too many restrictions on their liberty, on their freedom of design. Their choices were hemmed in by the construction system and by the economic system in which the experiment took place. The costs per square meter certainly limited the freedom of planning. And, even more importantly, it turned out that the values and history of each family and each individual sharply limited experimentation with the flexibility we had provided. At the same time, we have learned how important each small detail is in dwellings, how much meaning it has for those who planned it.

3

4

3. The Support under construction.

4. Support interior ready to receive plumbing and electrical lines.

5. Les Marelles as delivered to new residents—ready to be made into a home using a catalog kit-of-parts.

5

Each dwelling plan, in fact, has a very specific significance. Every family group has a certain number of roles and rituals that help it to continue. We found that danger lurked in the process of elaborating plans for a new dwelling. The danger is the possible collapse of a way of life, of a self image, of a family image and *modus vivendi*. All these are challenged and could be destroyed by a change of context—the new dwelling and, more specifically, involvement in its planning.

The difficult decisions were not those that had to do with the locations of partitions or windows, but those that had to do with the relationships between people in the household. If the present occupants' plans are what they are, one must not search for the cause in lack of imagination. These same families demonstrated their great capacity for decision and for symbolic representation in the realm of furnishing and decoration within their apartments. The explanation seems more truly to lie in the fact that families maintain themselves through a structure of relationships between the members, and between the family and the outside world, and the space plan is a representation of this structure of relationships.

The first step in designing the dwell-

ing plan seemed to consist largely of determining the nature of this family structure, and then making sure that the plan within our structures at Les Marelles would not shake it. An unusual plan, a new arrangement of activities, a new spatial framework for family members, all these seemed to threaten the group. Ironically perhaps, most families' interest in our experiment at Les Marelles did not consist so much in the possibility of changing their way of life, but in the possibility of continuing a way of life established in an earlier dwelling. Ordinarily, a family that moves must adapt its structure to the new dwelling plan with all the awkwardness that this can entail. Due to the flexibility we had provided, these threats to family stability could be avoided. Each purchaser could create a familiar environment, taking into full consideration his or her interior constraints—economic, psychological, and familial.

### Reviewing the Hypotheses

Let us return to our experimental hypotheses: inhabitants are capable of planning their own dwellings. Architects should act solely as technical advisers. And the fact of participation in

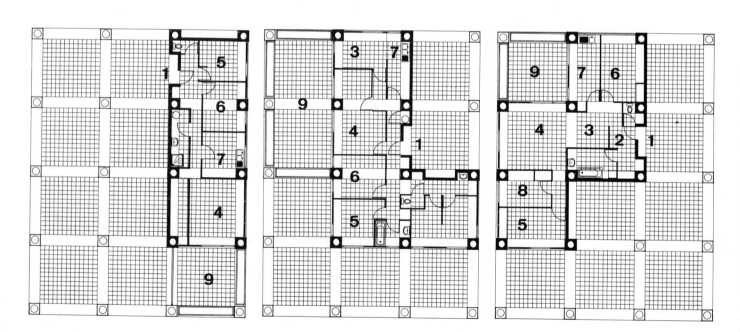

6. Six examples of apartments. 1: Entry. 2: Foyer. 3: Dining Room. 4: Living Room. 5: Master Bedroom. 6: Bedroom. 7: Kitchen. 8: Study. 9: Terrace. 10: Professional Office or Studio.

personal dwelling design brings with it particular behaviors and attitudes which can be measured. It is not on a statistical plane that we can verify these hypotheses, but by looking at the ensemble of determinants which led people to choose Les Marelles and make their own plans.

We have discovered a great deal about the multiple meanings of the dwelling for each inhabitant. A dwelling is something which has a role at once very important, and yet secondary. The importance of dwelling was clear to us from the depth of emotion shown by participants and by their willingness to come to grips with the constraints, to return many times to the office and the site, to give up a great deal of free time in making the plans, and then to wait between 6 and 12 months before being able to occupy their completed dwelling. In addition, through numerous passionate discussions on this and that point, it became clear to us that those who participated considered their dwellings as extensions of themselves. A very important matter because it required that individual relationships be given form, and that each member's territory within the dwelling be delineated. A very important issue in relation to the world outside, demonstrated by the de-

sires to purchase a home and to make a dwelling within which one will remain.

On the other hand, the dwelling seemed of secondary importance in the sense that it is a reflection of something more basic. It is the expression of power relationships within the family. And decisions about the dwelling are conditioned by terribly important outside considerations, such as price and location. In fact, all of these things seemed more important in the choice of housing than the right to plan.

However, participation in planning did permit a partial satisfaction of certain of the aspirations that people brought with them. In the realm of the imagination—for a moment freed—we saw people dream of grand living rooms and spacious bedrooms, of swimming pools in place of bathtubs. But we also noticed throughout the process how quickly the participants returned to the realm of possibility, how ready they were to conform to present social norms. No one attempted to make a plan that was totally new and which represented a new form of life. No one contested the fundamental rules of the game. Participants were only able to make dwellings within the reality which was theirs in 1974 and 1975.

We learned a great deal from watch-

ing the participating families make their plans. Each dwelling has its own history. Nothing in any plan was a matter of chance. Everything drawn had importance. No space was purely functional. Each says something specific about its designers. In fact, the importance of a project like Les Marelles lies in the fact that it permits people to create dwellings which they feel have deep meaning in their lives. In this case, they were able to give meaning to space before inhabiting it.

After the inhabitants had been in their apartments for a month, we went back to check on their satisfaction with what they had designed. We found that the dwellings seemed to them to provide the right image for their idea of family life. We also found that the new inhabitants hadn't considered the process of design at Les Marelles as a chance to experiment, but much more as a chance to get what they felt they needed within the economic and psychological constraints which operated on them. They were pleased that here they had not had to adapt to the whim of an unknown architect. The number of rooms, the grouping of activities, the circulation system, the openings onto terraces, all these are theirs—the successes as well as the failures. They had to make their

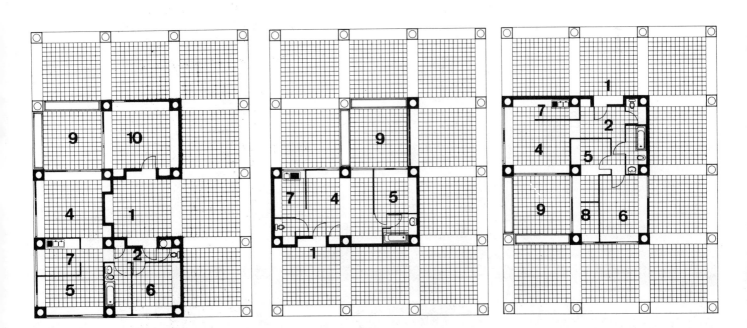

own plans, but they do not have to live in a dwelling designed for someone else. Whatever constraints there are are the residents' own and they can live with them.

## Lessons from Les Marelles

What lessons do we learn from the experiment at Les Marelles? The experiment concerned not the form, but the process of making a dwelling. Here it was the user and not the architect who made the decisions. A number of different problems flow from this fact.

### In the Sphere of Production

All of the usual arrangements are disturbed. The usual procedure for conceiving, contracting, and producing dwellings no longer functions. The ordinary division of responsibilities is upset. The scheduling of trades is altered. Everything is more complicated. Obstacles appear on all sides. First we must redefine the roles of all of the actors in housing production.

7b

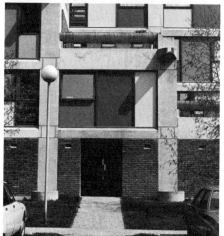

7a

7a,b,c. Support and Infill: views of Les Marelles.

7c

## In the Sphere of Use

We have initiated a major change of role. We have changed the passive consumer of dwelling space into an active participant in the creation of the dwelling. It seems to have positive effects.

## In the Sphere of Design

As decision making moves into the realm of the user, everything must be sires to purchase a home and to make a dwelling within which one will remain. and costs of each choice—architectural and economic—must be spelled out. There must be recognition that each user decision has serious consequences —for family structure, for the family's pocketbook, and for the satisfaction that the dwelling will provide in daily use.

Some families found the situation filled with anxiety. They backed away, citing difficulties in obtaining credit, or saying the color selection didn't satisfy them, or they didn't know how to make a plan. But for those who followed the process through to the end, satisfaction is tremendous: one does not easily change one's mind or engage in self criticism when the involvement has been so total. Things that don't seem to work are minimized or excused or made

| Nb. | MAILLE | CHENEAU | CHENEAU DE FACADE OU MITOYEN | CHENEAU D'ACCES |
|---|---|---|---|---|
| 1 | 15,21 m2 | 2,92 m2 | 2,34 m2 | 0,90 m2 |
| 2 | 30,42 m2 | 5,85 m2 | 4,68 m2 | 1,81 m2 |
| 3 | 45,63 m2 | 8,77 m2 | 7,02 m2 | 2,71 m2 |
| 4 | 60,84 m2 | 11,70 m2 | 9,36 m2 | 3,62 m2 |
| 5 | 76,05 m2 | 14,62 m2 | 11,70 m2 | |
| 6 | 91,26 m2 | 17,55 m2 | 14,04 m2 | |
| 7 | 106,47 m2 | 20,47 m2 | 16,38 m2 | |
| 8 | 121,68 m2 | 23,40 m2 | 18,72 m2 | |
| 9 | 136,89 m2 | 26,32 m2 | 21,06 m2 | |
| 10 | 152,10 m2 | 29,25 m2 | 23,40 m2 | |

## SURFACE QUE VOUS CHOISISSEZ

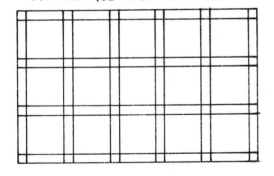

## EXEMPLE

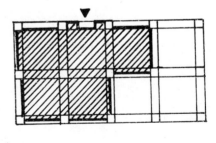

| | Nombre | Surface |
|---|---|---|
| | 5 | 76,05 m2 |
| | 5 | 14,62 m2 |
| | 5 | 11,70 m2 |
| | 1 | 0,90 m2 |
| Surface utilisable | | 103,27 m2 |

8. Space-planning guide from the users' handbook prepared by the architect.

| DESIGNATION | QUANTITES EXECUTEES Q. | PRIX UNITAIRES VALEUR MAI 74 P.U. | PRODUIT VALEUR MAI 74 Q. x P.U. |
|---|---|---|---|
| **A- INTERIEURES** | | | |
| 01.  Porte isoplane, dimensions : 0,80 x 2,02,  40 mm d'épaisseur, avec imposte 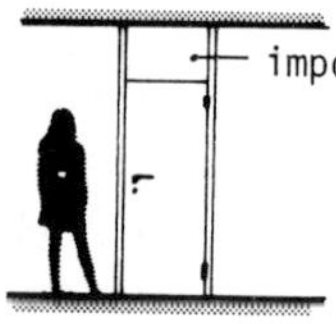 | U. | 341,40 | |
| Plus value pour bec de cane à condamnation (fermeture pour W.C., salle de bains,...) | U. | 10,50 | |
| 02.  Plinthe en bois (sur poteaux et cloisons séparatives entre logements) | ml. | 5,90 | |
| 03.  Portes de placard KAZED   2.50 x  60 | U. | 566,90 | |
| 2.20 x  60 | U. | 547,10 | |
| 2.50 x  90 | U. | 665,80 | |
| 2.20 x  90 | U. | 631,60 | |
| 2.50 x 120 | U. | 820,60 | |
| 2.20 x 120 | U. | 788,20 | |
| 2.50 x 150 | U. | 928,60 | |
| 2.20 x 150 | U. | 806,20 | |

9a

| DESIGNATION | QUANTITES EXECUTEES Q. | PRIX UNITAIRES VALEUR MAI 74 P.U. | PRODUIT VALEUR MAI 74 Q. x P.U. |
|---|---|---|---|
| **B - EXTERIEURES** | | | |
| 01.  Dépose et repose des 2 premiers éléments de façades | | inclus dans le prix d'achat des mailles | |
| 02.  Dépose et repose d'un élément de façade (après les 2 premiers)   - jusqu'à 90 de large | U. | 108,80 | |
| - 120 et 150 de large | U. | 144,40 | |
| 03.  Panneaux de façades avec vitrage supertriver : | | | |
| sur rez de chaussée exclusivement ) type 1   220 x  90 | U. | 896,40 | |
| ) type 3   220 x 150 | U. | 1.148,70 | |
| type 2   220 x  90 | U. | 1.443,00 | |
| type 4   220 x 150 | U. | 1.786,10 | |
| type 5   220 x  90 | U. | 1.155,80 | |
| type 6   220 x 150 | U. | 1.660,50 | |
| sur terrasse exclusivement ) type 12  190 x  90 | U. | 792,90 | |
| ) type 13  190 x 150 | U. | 1.296,90 | |

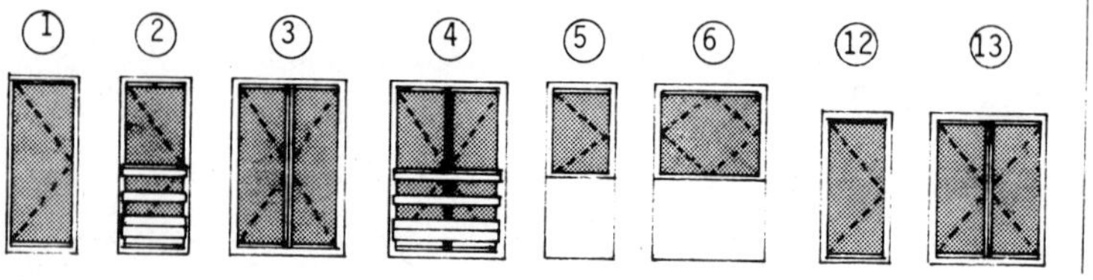

① ② ③ ④ ⑤ ⑥ ⑫ ⑬

TOTAL

9b

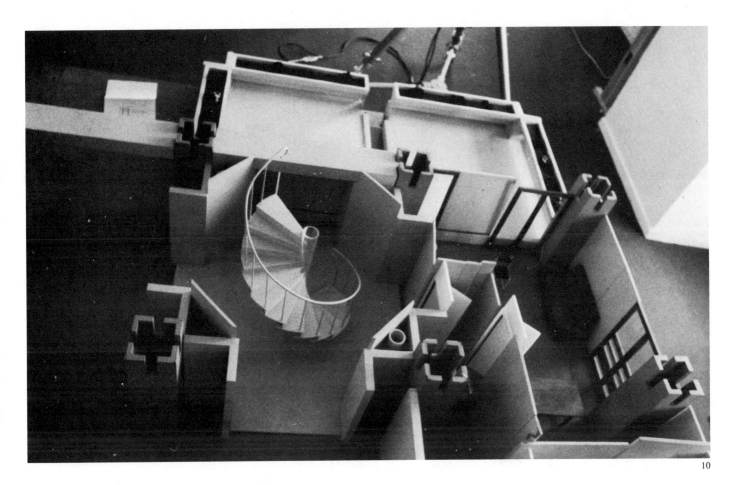

10

the responsibility of others. The pleasure taken in the completed dwelling is enormous. The apartment becomes "my home." The sociologist working with our group reported the appearance of a special consciousness among those who had participated. They felt themselves part of a special group—those who had made their own dwellings and who were responsible for them. They were anxious to retain control of the habitat, and they were afraid that their power would soon disappear and they themselves would sink back into anonymity.

From an architectural point of view, while not particularly innovative, as we said, the majority of the plans would not have been designed by an architect, nor would they have been accepted by a developer for fear that they would not sell. The most idiosyncratic plans are those for the biggest apartments in which the largest number of persons was expected to live.

A final point for political consideration: At Les Marelles, it was the inhabitants themselves who introduced the constraints in the development of dwelling plans. It was neither a distant bureaucracy nor a faceless architect who set the limit and the style. It was

9a,b. Pages from the users' handbook showing some of the interior doors and windows available on order and their prices.

10. The model used by buyers to plan their apartments.

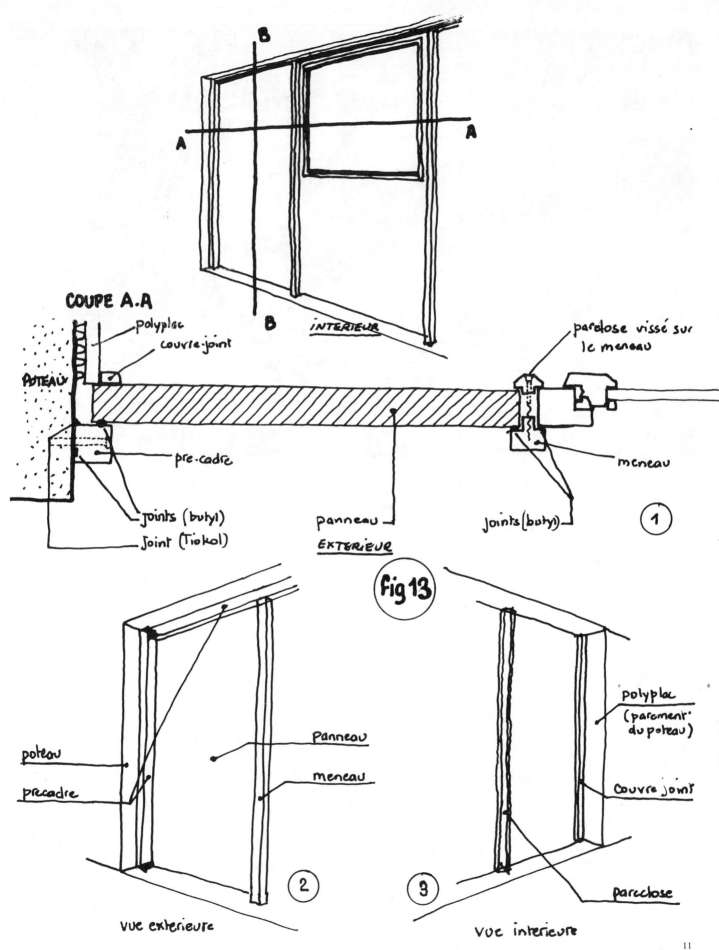

**COUPE A.A**

polyplac

couvre-joint

POTEAU

pre-cadre

joints (butyl)

Joint (Tiokol)

B

B

INTÉRIEUR

parclose vissé sur le meneau

meneau

Joints (butyl)

panneau
EXTÉRIEUR

① 1

**Fig 13**

poteau

precadre

Panneau

meneau

② 2

vue extérieure

polyplac
(parement du poteau)

Couvre joint

parclose

③ 3

vue intérieure

74

11

the purchasers themselves who fit their image of dwelling to the realities of price and location. This self-imposed reduction in expectation is easier to accept. There are no scapegoats. Nothing has been obviously imposed. Every household was responsible for its own dwelling and all of its important features. And the residents are satisfied with what they have made.

This experiment has been carried out with financial assistance from CORDA (Ministry of Cultural Affairs) and of the organization Plan Construction (Ministry of the Environment).

12. Whether the enormous flexibility of the Les Marelles building system will be utilized by the residents remains to be seen.

11. The architect also wrote and illustrated a manual for modification and repair to encourage continuing transformation and refinement of the living space. The page shown describes the installation of facade panels.

# Commentary on Les Marelles and MHGA

Katharine Coit, University of Paris (UP7)

## HOUSING AND THE *COURANT AUTOGESTIONAIRE*

To understand the significance of French experiments in participation and self-managed collective housing (see MGHA, Part 2), they must be seen as a reaction both to the predominant trends of French official housing policy and to the traditional working class movement's attitude to housing and urban questions.

From across the Atlantic, France would seem to be continually fermenting revolutionaries, social criticism, and radical action of all sorts from 1789 to May, 1968. Socialist and communist ideologies are firmly implanted among a large part of the population, and the parties that represent them obtained a majority in the last elections. Strangely enough, progressive and "politicized" as are the working classes and their unions and parties concerning the struggle over production, the same cannot be said about protest concerning housing and neighborhoods. There have been urban issues in the past—the Paris uprising of 1870 was sparked because the government rescinded rent control policy and the *Communards* took over the city. And the restructuring of Paris by Haussmann brought about the deportation of the working classes to the periphery amid a certain amount of protest. But it is important to note that since the Commune, urban action has rarely if ever joined forces with working class action in the factories. Furthermore, urban struggles lag way behind workplace struggles (with a few fortunate exceptions) in the mass support developed, in the militancy of the leaders, and in the concessions obtained.

Lack of momentum in this field cannot be said to be due to a lack of cause for complaint. Since the Second World War, the larger cities, and especially Paris, have suffered from a severe housing shortage. Whole families have been crowded into one or two rooms in run-down buildings. Until recently, bathrooms and private toilets were a luxury for the middle and upper classes. Until 10 years ago, the shantytowns that had sprung up around all the industrial centers were witness to the unavailability of any housing at all for the poor. At the same time, rents have soared and real estate speculation is rampant.

The official response to the crisis has been to build public housing in quantity—as much as possible, as soon as possible, as cheap as possible, with little regard to transportation or to the essential services, schools, and shops. To the postwar condition of overcrowded, unsanitary, and dilapidated housing, another dimension has been added to the housing problem. The new *grands ensembles*, often gerry-built, high rise, dormitory suburbs were put in isolated spots with little if any possibility of jobs or entertainment nearby, creating employment problems for the women and the young not able to commute long distances. On the other hand, rents and living expenses are high, too high to be borne by one wage earner per family. These new

housing developments show a general breakdown of neighborliness and community. Mental illness, suicide, and delinquency rates are high.

The disregard of the inhabitants' needs, the repeated standard plans, and the poor quality of the construction have caused a certain amount of hostility to the new public housing estates. Tenant movements are spreading slowly, and there has been resistance to the further destruction of older working class areas.* Probably because of the rapid deterioration of the buildings and the social problems they create, rather than because of these isolated actions by the tenants, the government has recently renounced housing towers and the location of large numbers of units in one area.

In France, in spite of a highly centralized society, and a working class movement whose attention is turned elsewhere, there have been attempts to resist the dominant tendency. Efforts both to provide opportunities for local participation in housing and urban planning, and to combat the isolating and alienating effects of the housing policy, have been made. The two cases presented here are examples of these attempts. They resemble each other in that they are efforts to give people decision-making powers concerning their homes. They differ very much in the way they go about it and in their overall intent.

In the case of Les Marelles, the future inhabitants are given the possibility of drawing up plans for their homes. The role of the architect is reduced to that of technical help. On the one hand, the experiment showed how much the participants became emotionally involved in this task. Maurios says, "their housing can be considered an extension of themselves." On the other hand, so many restrictions were involved that the inhabitants had no real power of decision over anything but the interior design. The location, the environment, the form (i.e., an apartment rather than a single family dwelling), the cost, the financing, the neighbors, and the pattern of daily life were all determined for them.

---

*The lack of concerted action on urban questions cannot be attributed to a lack of analysis. Much research in urban sociology, city planning, urban economics, and geography has been inspired recently by the critical approach of such writers as Henri Lefebvre, Michel Foucault, Henry Coing, and Chombart de Lauwe. The tendency has been to analyze how capitalist relations of production affect daily life and the form of housing, how the State maintains control in subtle ways through urban policy, and how capitalism reproduces urban space whose primary aim is to boost productivity and profitability. See, for examples, the reviews *Espaces et Société* and *Recherches*. A colloquium of the Centre de Recherche Urbaine (CRU) summarized some of these points of view; see *Amenagements Urbain et Mouvements Sociaux*, CRU, Paris, 1978.

This government-supported experiment does not attempt to deal with the major issues of the French housing crisis. On the contrary, occupying people with only one aspect of their housing camouflages other critical problems such as the deportation of workers to the far suburbs, the high cost of housing, and the paucity of services. The case is exemplary, however, in the way that it upsets the traditional institutions and transforms the role of the architect: "competencies are questioned." Furthermore, there were truly original designs: "most of the plans could not have been designed by an architect." Because of the extent and the complexity of the housing problem, however, it remains only a partial response.

The MHGA—the Movement for Collective Self-Managed Housing—encourages the future inhabitants to draw up the project themselves, but also brings families together in a semi-communal fashion to collectively manage the housing after it is built. There is a much greater involvement in decisions regarding location, cost, and life style—the initiative coming from those involved. The obvious drawback to this form of housing production is that it is limited to those with incomes high enough to be able to buy urban space.

Young as it is, the Movement is expanding rapidly, a sign that it answers certain needs and fulfills certain aspirations. The name alone indicates its intentions. "Self-managed" implies adherence to a political current or ideology. The Movement includes militants or ex-militants of left wing parties and groups that have been trying to develop this tendency (called in France the *courant autogestionaire*). Their aim is to put into practice their ideas and to create living examples of self-managed communities. They are part of a struggle that opposes hierarchy, bureaucracy, centralization, authoritarianism, over-specialization, and technocracy in government, political parties, unions, and all associations.

The collective aspect of the Movement can be seen not only as a desire to regroup with friends to share equipment and space, but also as a means of mobilizing dissipated energies and reuniting scattered efforts. They explicitly refuse social segregation and make sincere efforts to develop close ties in their neighborhoods by offering the use of their communal space. Recently, the MHGA has created a Société Coopérative Ouvrière de Production (SCOP) to sponsor the development of self-managed housing for low and moderate income families. Its first project will be 40 units in small groups of from 5 to 10 families for the city of Chambery (Isère). The participants are drawn from the lists of those waiting for public housing. The MHGA will provide all the necessary design and technical assistance. The creation of the SCOP is indicative of the goal the Movement has set for itself of spreading the action to lower income tenant groups. MHGA refuses to be merely an attractive housing solution for those groups who can afford to refuse the isolating and alienating effects of the normal housing conditions in France.

It remains to be seen whether the Movement will gather enough momentum to become a major factor in France, or whether it will continue to be a marginal alternative to dominant housing trends. At present, the Movement gives us an example of the role of architecture in the struggle for social transformation and the creation of humanistic communities where solidarity, equality of power, and creativity are essential values.

# SAR/T.E.S.T.
# El Centro, California

Although no SAR housing has yet been built in the United States, many of the initial arguments for the concept have particular force at this time. Housing that involves the user in design and construction and that can be enlarged or upgraded over time as resources permit is surely a logical direction in the face of government cutbacks, record interest rates, and exorbitant land and materials costs. Helmut Schulitz, a German-trained architect in Los Angeles, has taken two important steps toward popularizing SAR principles in the US First, he has developed a coordinated "open" building system that utilizes construction components already in series production and second, he has demonstrated its effectiveness in the design of his own home in Beverly Hills (for more information on this house, see *Progressive Architecture*, October, 1977). Now he has applied this system to the problem of low rise, high density housing in a typical small American city. This project, which Schulitz calls a "framework concept," deals with the crucial issues of cost, construction, zoning, and democratic decision making. It is a valuable contribution in the present housing crisis.

1. The architect's home in Los Angeles demonstrates the T.E.S.T. principles.

# A Framework for Housing Redevelopment

**Helmut Schulitz, architect**
**University of California at Los Angeles**

The attempt of the high density housing project in El Centro is to find a framework regulation that will give new incentive to inner-city housing development by creating better conditions for living, and a proper response to a population of largely Mexican origin, as well as to the hot, dry, desert climate. It is a response to observations of American inner-city housing in general and addresses the issues of (1) zoning, (2) decision making, and (3) construction methods.

A main feature of the framework is a different approach toward use of open space. The framework permits development on a lot-by-lot basis or as large-scale projects. It encourages the participation of those who will eventually occupy the space, and limits central decision making to the communal infrastructure and urban design functions.

The framework is strongly related to the construction method, which makes use of SAR concepts and employs "open systems" prefabrication.

The housing project is part of a larger redevelopment project for downtown El Centro (a city of 25,000 in the desert region of Southern California, 10 miles from the Mexican border). It is at the same time a response to common technical problems with American inner-city housing in general and is therefore, I think, of much wider application than just the special El Centro situation.

## Zoning

It seems that for the largest part of the American population the dream will continue to be the single family house. But inner-city lots are now too expen-

sive for single family housing. R-3 density zoning, which is common in American cities,* is from the outset a compromise—a continuation of single family house mentality. Accepting single family house land subdivision, it tries to protect privacy through side yard setbacks. While single family houses are typically oriented towards front and backyards, R-3 buildings overcrowded the smaller, California cities and were forced to orient towards the setback-side yards. Privacy was lost, and outdoor spaces were unusable. Since the typical R-3 buildings turned out to be no substitute for single family housing, inner-city housing develop-

---

*R-3 is the typical designation given to districts intended for row houses and low rise multiple dwellings. In El Centro, minimum lot width is given as 50 feet, and a minimum of 800 sf of lot area is required for each dwelling unit.

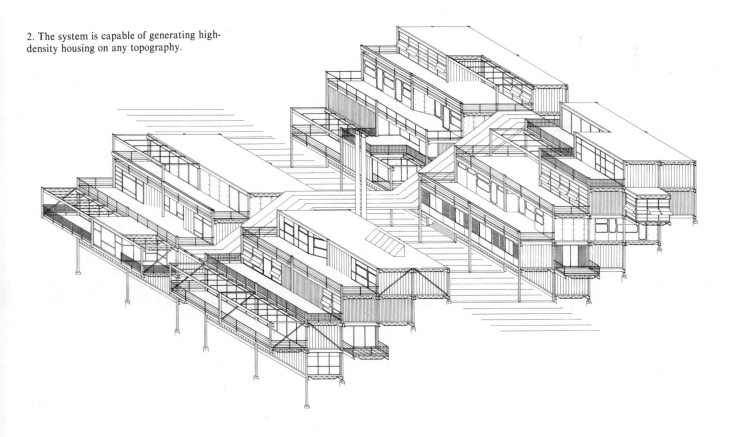

2. The system is capable of generating high-density housing on any topography.

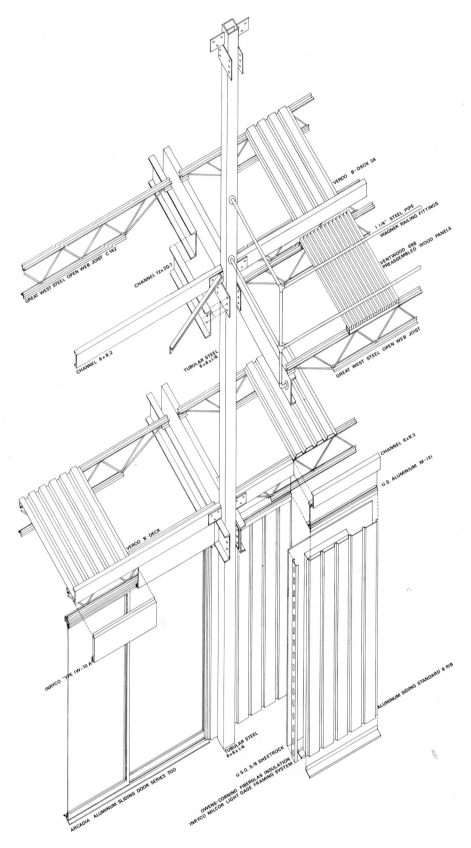

VERCO B - DECK 24

1 1/4" STEEL PIPE

WAGNER RAILING FITTINGS

VENTWOOD 688
PREASSEMBLED WOOD PANELS

GREAT WEST STEEL OPEN WEB JOIST C-142

CHANNEL 12 x 20.7

CHANNEL 6 x 8.2

TUBULAR STEEL
6 x 6 x 1/4

GREAT WEST STEEL OPEN WEB JOIST

CHANNEL 6 x 8.2

U.S. ALUMINIUM M-121

VERCO B - DECK

ALUMINUM SIDING STANDARD 8 RIB

INRYCO TYPE IW-10 A

TUBULAR STEEL
6 x 6 x 1/4

U.S.G. 5/8 SHEETROCK

OWENS-CORNING FIBERGLAS INSULATION
INRYCO MILCOR LIGHT GAGE FRAMING SYSTEM

ARCADIA ALUMINUM SLIDING DOOR SERIES 700

3. Exploded view of skin and structure shows one set of catalog building materials which fits the flexible, modular system.

ments for higher densities became a losing proposition: those who could afford it moved to the suburbs or into mobile home parks.

The large number of underutilized and vacant lots in the downtown area of El Centro point to the dilemma. The downtown R-3 housing area shows four typically different conditions:

- Vacant lots
- Single family houses on R-3 lots
- Up to four small houses on individual lots; many of these houses are, in addition, structurally substandard and constantly threatened with being torn down
- Multifamily buildings with little outdoor space except for sideyards

The aim of this housing project in El Centro is to find a new framework which would give new impetus to inner-city development by avoiding the current zoning drawbacks, while achieving the same densities allowed under the current law.

The rules are set up in such a way that they allow for:

- A different use of open space, based on zero setbacks and zero sideyards. Instead of sideyards and setbacks, outdoor spaces could be privately used for courtyards or terraces.
- Building forms that are climatically more suitable to the El Centro desert condition than the typical R-3 developments already built in the area. The orientation of windows is no longer limited to east-west exposure. Buildings are constructed around courtyards which create pockets of cooler air and allow for easy shading devices. Similar building forms have been developed and tested in hot desert climates for thousands of years, although choice of materials and exterior appearance here is quite different.
- Building forms that are at a scale similar to the single family units that exist in the area today and thus preserve the character of the area. This also allows the residents to identify their house as a distinct unit.

**Decision Making**

The difficulties with piecemeal, lot-by-lot redevelopments have in many cities resulted in a strategy to rebuild through planned unit development with central

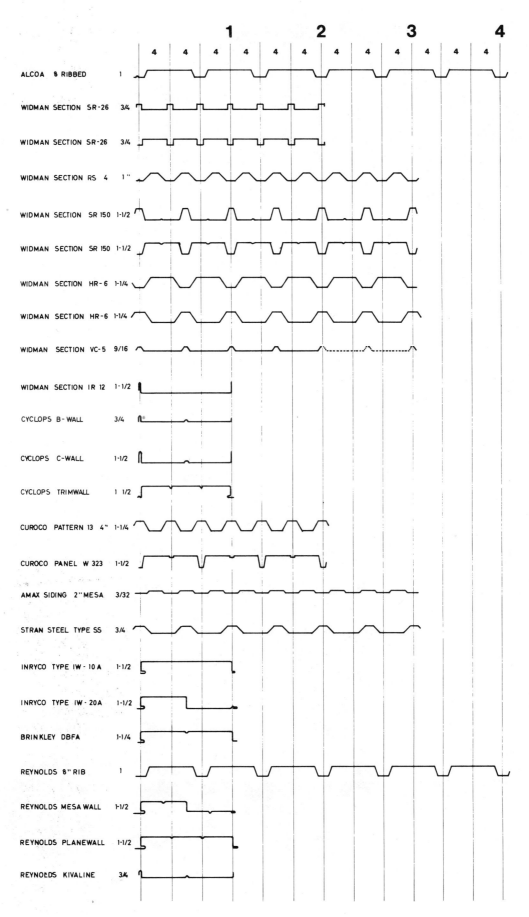

4. A page from the T.E.S.T. catalog lists
compatible metal skins available on the market.

decision making. This has often required bulldozing of entire city blocks and rebuilding at a massive scale. The special zoning district proposed for El Centro is set up so that development can take place both on individual lots and/or at a large scale. It attempts to decentralize decision making and to leave as much of the decision power as possible with the individual homeowners.

This approach has the advantage that little of the existing housing stock in good condition would have to be destroyed, and no large-scale land acquisition would be required. This also means that years of negotiations and preparatory work which have become so typical of inner-city redevelopment projects could be avoided, and rebuilding could start immediately on a piecemeal basis.

With regard to the individual dwelling unit, the framework encourages the participation of those who will eventually occupy the space. This framework is strongly related to the construction method. The future resident is able to choose among seven different types of units, each with several subvariations in terms of size and room number. A total of 30 variations or alternative plans are currently documented. Theoretically, the system makes an unlimited number of variations possible.

The project uses the T.E.S.T. building method which offers a number of interchangeable subsystems. This enables the residents to influence not only the plan but the final appearance of their dwelling by selecting components and materials of their own choice. Although all buildings reflect a rational

5. El Centro. Project site indicated by dotted line.

6. Typical in-depth lot development with wasteful sideyards.

7. Vernacular cluster housing is the inspiration for the El Centro urban design regulations.

and systematic construction process, each dwelling unit could be different in form and materials from the ones next door.

The townhouses could be built and rented, sold as completely finished buildings, or they could be erected as a basic shell only, at very modest cost, to be finished later by the residents through self-help with their own unskilled labor. The building system also facilitates change over time as family requirements or tastes change.

## Building Construction Method

The housing system is an open system building method which makes maximum use of prefinished industrial components from manufacturers' catalogs. The El Centro project uses primarily wood elements. It has the following features:

- It makes it possible to use highly developed, prefabricated building components without investment in production facilities, and instead relies on the production capabilities of existing industry
- It cuts down on onsite labor
- It enables residents to choose from a large number of different building elements to create personal living spaces according to their own imaginations

The T.E.S.T. building method consists of a catalog of compatible components and a set of rules governing their coordination. These rules are based on modular coordination principles, and are an extension of the research work of the SAR group in Holland, adapted to American conditions.

The rules of the new zoning are:

1. The district must comprise a minimum of one block.
2. The total amount of open space must equal the open space required in the traditional R-2 (two-family house) and R-3 zone. (The idea of the zero setback zone is to use open space more efficiently: more useable courtyards and backyards rather than useless sideyards and setbacks.)
3. If pedestrian access paths to the dwelling units are placed perpendicular to the street, these paths should be a minimum of 10 feet per 50-foot lot. Such paths should not have dead-ends, but connect street to

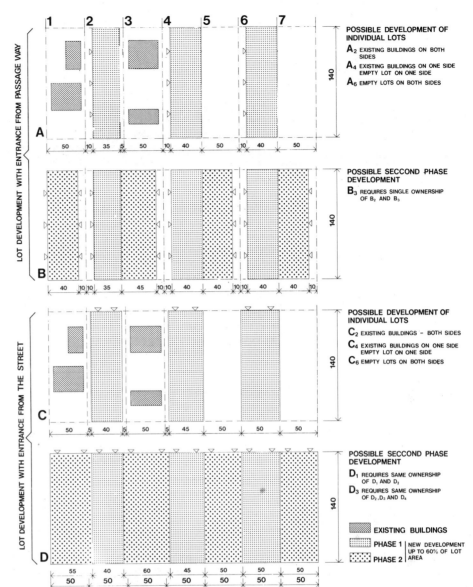

8. Proposed zero setback regulations for residential redevelopment.

alley. Access paths would be placed adjacent to each other wherever possible, resulting in a 20-foot access strip. If access paths for two lots are adjacent to each other, a 4-foot strip of the path may be added to private courtyards or may be privately landscaped; no building, however, should extend into this strip.

4. No windows necessary to light a room should be placed on the zero sideyard side. If windows are placed there, they should be located not less than 6 feet above the floor of the rooms. (No "right-of-view" can be derived from a window placed on the zero sideyard line.)
5. Building roofs should be designed to drain onto the lot upon which the building is located.
6. During the time of transition from the traditional R-2/R-3 zones to a zero sideyard and setback zone, the rights of existing buildings should be protected by a sideyard of 5 feet. This sideyard can be reduced if the total distance to the adjacent, existing building exceeds 12 feet.

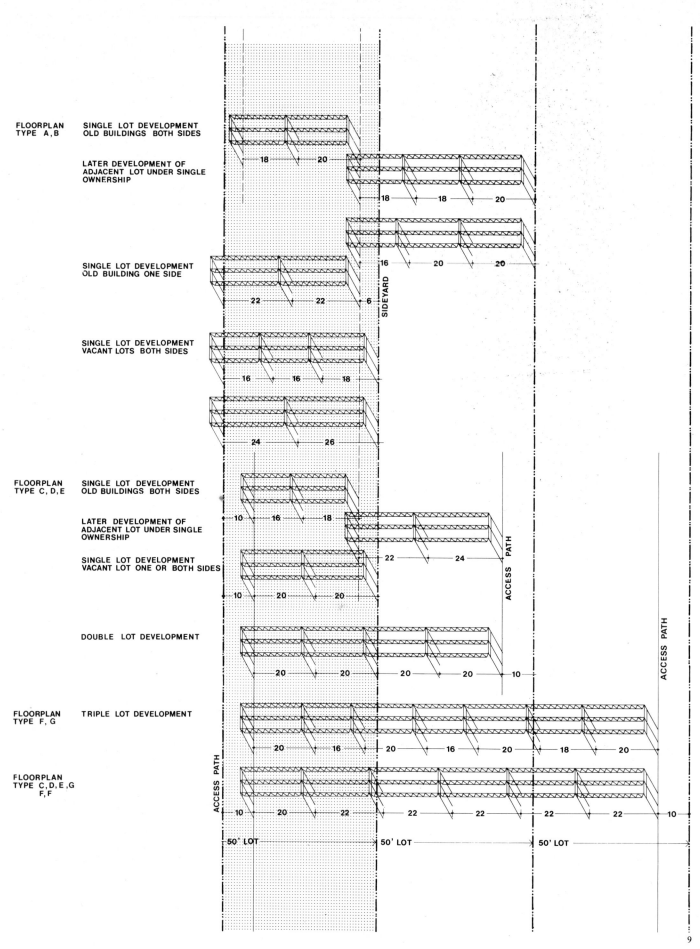

FLOORPLAN
TYPE A,B     SINGLE LOT DEVELOPMENT
OLD BUILDINGS BOTH SIDES

LATER DEVELOPMENT OF
ADJACENT LOT UNDER SINGLE
OWNERSHIP

SINGLE LOT DEVELOPMENT
OLD BUILDING ONE SIDE

SINGLE LOT DEVELOPMENT
VACANT LOTS BOTH SIDES

FLOORPLAN
TYPE C,D,E     SINGLE LOT DEVELOPMENT
OLD BUILDINGS BOTH SIDES

LATER DEVELOPMENT OF
ADJACENT LOT UNDER SINGLE
OWNERSHIP

SINGLE LOT DEVELOPMENT
VACANT LOT ONE OR BOTH SIDES

DOUBLE LOT DEVELOPMENT

FLOORPLAN
TYPE F,G     TRIPLE LOT DEVELOPMENT

FLOORPLAN
TYPE C,D,E,G
F,F

SIDEYARD

ACCESS PATH

ACCESS PATH

ACCESS PATH

50' LOT     50' LOT     50' LOT

9

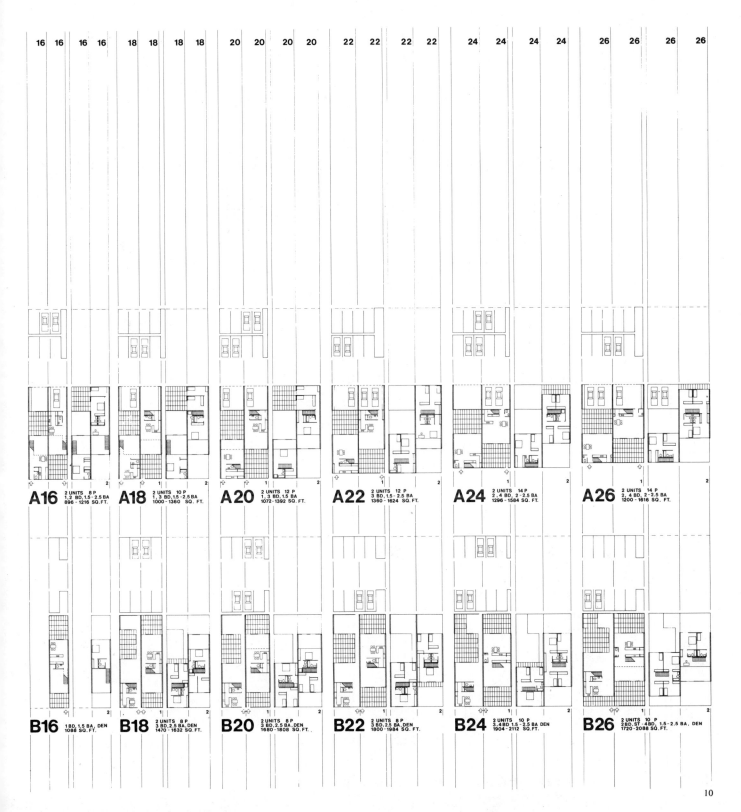

16  16    16  16        18  18    18  18        20  20    20  20        22  22    22  22        24    24    24    24        26    26    26    26

**A16** 2 UNITS  8 P
1,2 BD, 1.5 - 2.5 BA
896 - 1216 SQ. FT.

**A18** 2 UNITS  10 P
1, 3 BD, 1.5 BA
1000 - 1360  SQ. FT.

**A20** 2 UNITS  12 P
1, 3 BD, 1.5 BA
1072 - 1392 SQ. FT.

**A22** 2 UNITS  12 P
3 BD, 1.5 - 2.5 BA
1360 - 1624  SQ. FT.

**A24** 2 UNITS  14 P
2, 4 BD, 2 - 2.5 BA
1296 - 1584 SQ.  FT.

**A26** 2 UNITS  14 P
2, 4 BD, 2 - 2.5 BA
1200 - 1616  SQ.  FT.

**B16** 1 BD, 1.5 BA, DEN
1088 SQ. FT.

**B18** 2 UNITS  8 P
3 BD, 2.5 BA, DEN
1470 - 1632 SQ. FT.

**B20** 2 UNITS  8 P
3 BD, 2.5 BA, DEN
1680 - 1808 SQ. FT.

**B22** 2 UNITS  8 P
3 BD, 2.5 BA, DEN
1800 - 1984 SQ. FT.

**B24** 2 UNITS  10 P
3, 4 BD, 1.5 - 2.5 BA, DEN
1904 - 2112 SQ. FT.

**B26** 2 UNITS  10 P
2 BD, ST - 4 BD, 1.5 - 2.5 BA, DEN
1720 - 2088 SQ. FT.

10

9. Diagram showing development patterns for
small and large lots utilizing the full array of
unit types possible with the T.E.S.T. system.

10. The flexible grid and large kit of alternative
parts generates tremendous variety at high
density and reasonable cost. Plans for units A16
(16 feet wide) to G80 (80 feet wide) are shown
on this and the following two pages.

16 16 16 16   18 18 18 18   20 20 20 20   22 22 22 22   24 24 24 24   26 26 26 26

**C20** 4 UNITS 8 P
3 BD, 2.5 BA
1129 - 1312

**C22** 4 UNITS 8 P
2 BD, ST - 3 BD, 2.5 BA
1104 1448 SQ. FT.

**C24** 4 UNITS 8 P
2 BD, ST - 3 BD, 2.5 BA
1296 - 1584 SQ. FT.

**C26** 4 UNITS 8 P
2 BD, ST - 3 BD, 2.5 BA
1408 - 1688 SQ. FT.

**D32** 4 UNITS 5 - 6 P
1 BD, 1.5 BA
768 - 832 SQ. FT.

**D36** 4 UNITS 6 - 8 P
2 BD, 1.5 BA
1104 SQ. FT.

**D40** 4 UNITS 8 P
2 BD, 2 BA
1236 SQ. FT.

**D44** 4 UNITS 8 P
2 BD, 2 BA
1184 - 1360 SQ. FT.

**E32** 3 UNITS 5 P
1 - 3 BD, 1.5 - 2.5 BA
1024 - 1472 SQ. FT.

**E36** 3 UNITS 6 P
2 - 3 BD, 1.5 BA
1176 - 1472 SQ. FT.

**E40** 3 UNITS 8 P
2 - 3 BD, 2.5 BA, DEN
1472 - 1712 SQ. FT.

**E44** 3 UNITS 8 P
2 - 3 BD, 2.5 BA, DEN
1624 - 1888 SQ. FT.

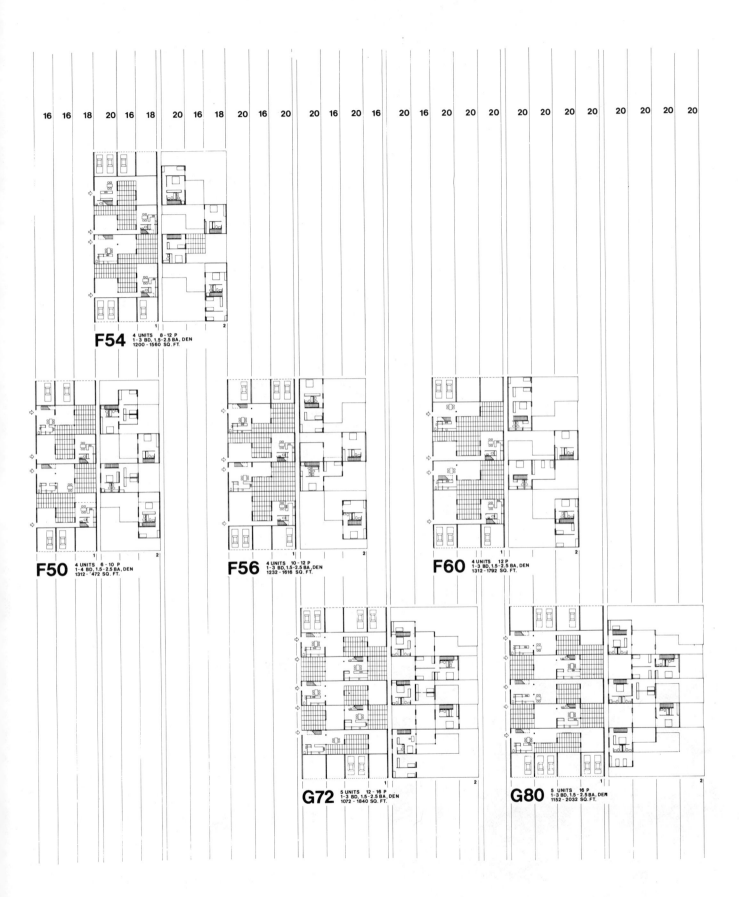

16  16  18  20  16  18  20  16  18  20  16  20  20  16  20  16  20  16  20  20  20  20  20  20  20  20  20  20  20  20

**F54**  4 UNITS   8 - 12 P
1 - 3 BD, 1.5 - 2.5 BA, DEN
1200 - 1560 SQ. FT.

**F50**  4 UNITS   6 - 10 P
1 - 4 BD, 1.5 - 2.5 BA, DEN
1312 - 472 SQ. FT.

**F56**  4 UNITS   10 - 12 P
1 - 3 BD, 1.5 - 2.5 BA, DEN
1232 - 1616 SQ. FT.

**F60**  4 UNITS   12 P
1 - 3 BD, 1.5 - 2.5 BA, DEN
1312 - 1792 SQ. FT.

**G72**  5 UNITS   12 - 16 P
1 - 3 BD, 1.5 - 2.5 BA, DEN
1072 - 1840 SQ. FT.

**G80**  5 UNITS   16 P
1 - 3 BD, 1.5 - 2.5 BA, DEN
1152 - 2032 SQ. FT.

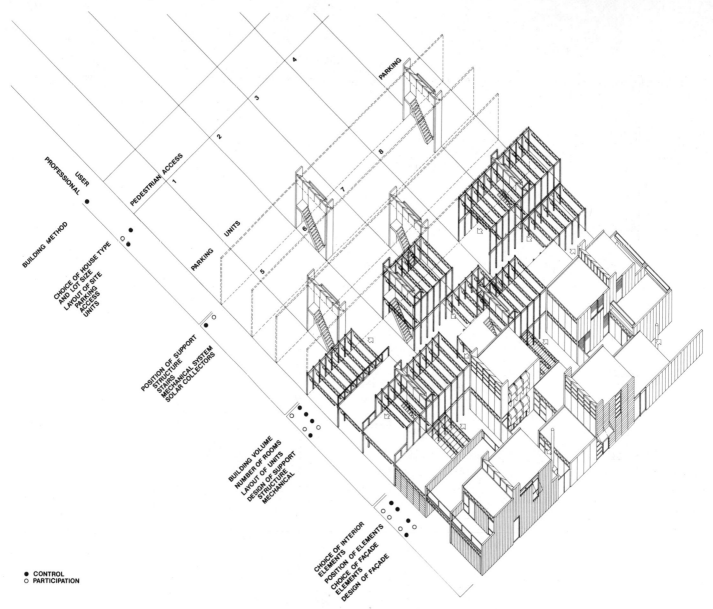

USER
PROFESSIONAL

BUILDING METHOD

CHOICE OF HOUSE TYPE
AND LOT SIZE
LAYOUT OF SITE
PARKING
ACCESS
UNITS

PEDESTRIAN ACCESS

PARKING

UNITS

PARKING

POSITION OF SUPPORT
STRUCTURE
STAIRS
MECHANICAL SYSTEM
SOLAR COLLECTORS

BUILDING VOLUME
NUMBER OF ROOMS
LAYOUT OF UNITS
DESIGN OF SUPPORT
STRUCTURE
MECHANICAL

CHOICE OF INTERIOR
ELEMENTS
POSITION OF ELEMENTS
CHOICE OF FAÇADE
ELEMENTS
DESIGN OF FAÇADE

● CONTROL
○ PARTICIPATION

11

11. Site development diagram indicates how
design participation and control are shared
between architect and user.

12. Land use pattern for El Centro.

13. El Centro project model: SAR adapted to US
conditions.

12

# Commentary on SAR

Joseph Wasserman AIA, New York

## AN AMERICAN VIEW OF SUPPORTS

Architects concerned with multifamily housing design have long been troubled by the fact that they had to crank out standard apartment layouts for nameless typical families, knowing full well that the standard design is often a compromise and offers a poor fit to the needs of many, if not most, of the occupants. Add to this the rigid minimum room sizes (read maximum) promulgated by HUD and other governmental housing agencies, and the result is an almost fully standardized and homogenized product. Because of this, architects have long fantasized about ways to build apartments in which the occupant simply rents or purchases a volume of space, in which he is almost totally free to create whatever personalized layout he may wish. In the fanciest dreams, this even includes rearranging plumbing and exterior walls and making outdoor terraces and garden rooms at will—all within a cube of space that has sometimes been described as two or even three stories high. Clearly this is a great idea—and one has to wonder why it has so rarely migrated from the drawing board to reality.

John Habraken and SAR have worked for nearly 20 years evolving building systems, building standards, and building designs to achieve flexible schemes in which occupants are personally involved in their "housing process," particularly the layout of their individual apartments (or assigned spaces). Naturally, implementation of this system goes far beyond mere tools. The allocation and administration of housing must also be adapted to permit the user to shape his environment.

With nearly 20 years invested in this idea, an institute in Eindhoven to perform the necessary studies, and the generation of considerable interest among housing designers in Europe, one should now be able to look at the finished product and judge the results. The movement is ongoing, but at a slow pace. It has not won the instant conversion of the housing industry, or the various national housing authorities, or even of housing consumers in large numbers. The best projects—Molenvliet in Holland and the GLC's Adelaide Road—are quality, small, walk-up housing developments, several cuts above the typical project. User satisfaction is apparently high, but it is not clear that this is primarily due to the use of a flexible housing system. For even without the flexibility in unit layouts permitted here, the care and attention lavished on the overall project design is exceptional, the sites and neighborhoods are better than average, the budgets were higher than average, the skill and attention of the architects and municipal authorities was certainly greater than usual and, more to the point, the early and intense involvement of the future tenant group was effective in creating a "community" even before one was physically extant. All of these assets may be by-products of the Habraken system, but they could and probably should occur whether or not a flexible housing system is employed. The results of the system as shown in pictures and plans are modest indeed. Rearrangements are possible, but

most of the apartments are organized, out of necessity, along conventional lines. Variations involve such things as the position of dining relative to living and kitchen areas, and the size and location of bedrooms, particularly the ability to subdivide larger sleeping space into smaller bedrooms. It is rarely possible to create a radically different space configuration within the *highly* constrained overall space limitations of the English, Dutch, or Swedish national housing standards. The same would be true here with our HUD minimum property standards.

There has been little written about the problems associated with administering a system of flexible unit design. However, there must be many. Consider the fact that future occupants must be identified and assigned to space in the project far in advance of occupancy, an event that is something hardly possible to envision in the American system, especially in the dominant nonsubsidized field where tenant selection is rarely made far in advance of occupancy. It is true that most public housing authorities maintain long lists of persons who desire housing and are qualified. But individual family needs evolve over time. In our socially and physically fluid society, it may be unrealistic to expect that potential occupants will remain committed to a particular project literally (as in the Adelaide Road example) years in advance of occupancy.

As family needs change, are the individual families free to rearrange their space—move walls, wiring, plumbing? Do they do it themselves? Do they have to have the "landlord" perform the changes? Who pays for the changes? In what condition do they leave the apartment when the tenancy terminates? Is the owner prepared to go through a similar process of reshuffling the interior layout when a subsequent tenant moves in? These questions do not, as yet, have answers. Until they do, my guess is that few if any public authorities in the United States would ever consider offering such a program, worthwhile as all might agree it to be. I see little hope that SAR methodology will soon be applied in the US to subsidized housing or market rate rental housing. But, clearly the *idea* has an enormous appeal, and should not be discarded just because it is more, perhaps much more, trouble to implement.

I strongly believe that initially the idea will find, and in a sense perhaps has already found, currency in the private housing market. As multifamily housing goes more and more away from rental to coop and condominium ownership, the buyers (owners) will certainly want to personalize their apartments. Many will gladly pay a premium for this freedom of organization and potential for future change. The typical American single-family dwelling built with modular stud partitions and dry wall partition facings has always lent itself to swift and economical rearrangement. Even the shell is modifiable at reasonable cost. Porches, bigger living rooms, and extra bedrooms are often added to basic houses. Attics and basements have traditionally been used for expansion space. Surely, similar systems will evolve for the urban multifamily dwelling that is replacing the single-family house in response to demographic and economic changes.

In reality, the system *has* been adopted and with considerable enthusiasm. My home base is New York City. In the last five years, the major housing market has been in the conversion of older loft-type buildings to residential use. Special tax considerations have been a strong part of the incentive for recycling these older buildings. But clearly the public has fallen in love with the possibilities that these larger, higher, more flexible spaces offer the occupant to shape and personalize his environment. Our analysis of buyers indicates that there are three distinct buyers and markets:

1. A truly built-out interior for those who cannot envision "fixing" up their own space. Normally the builder offers a standard layout; he loathes building out "to suit" as the contract negotiations and problems of on-site coordination can be utterly horrendous.
2. A dwelling unit in which everything is built out except the space-dividing partitions, i.e., finished floor and wall and ceiling coverings, bath, kitchen, and basic storage.
3. A raw, open space module, in which only piping and electricity is provided in otherwise "rough" space. The tenant is obliged to finish his space however he chooses.

Our experience indicates that in *every* price category and even in varying quality neighborhoods there are buyers who want each of these options, and in the best of all possible worlds, each would be offered.

This discussion may seem to have strayed some considerable distance from the original consideration of the SAR system and the ideas of John Habraken. But, it is worthwhile in the light of the developing American market to look more closely at what SAR *says*, rather than what has been done to date in the European context. SAR sees the architect as the one person in the process who should bridge the gap between human needs and technical possibilities, and who should take the initiative in opening possibilities for the future involvement of the occupant (to which may be added: reasonable and do-able). SAR then puts forth a design methodology that I find unnecessarily complex. It boils down to a heightened awareness on the part of the designer of the various options available to the occupant, and a need to consciously test these options in the design phase and then compromise as few as possible in the working out of structure, fenestration, heating, plumbing, and partitioning. Our firm's work on "lofts" was an excellent exercise for us, as we were obliged to lay out the apartments in several ways to test the adaptability of the space configurations. Once we felt we had flexible, but variously usable space, the contract documents were completed, omitting partitions. We located electrical outlets, heating convectors, and AC units in such a fashion that they would be adaptable to several interior layouts. Of course, had these been new structures we would have used more systematic methods.

As I see it, the real value of the SAR system, American style, is to heighten the designer's and user's imagination, leading to more thoughtful planning of interior layouts that will offer a greater variety of spaces, especially regarding kitchen/dining/living arrangements and to bedroom size and allocation. Of course, this can be facilitated with a systematic and demountable partitioning system, but it has yet to be demonstrated that an aesthetically acceptable system is cost effective. We can still tear out drywall and replace it more cheaply than anything else. It would, however, be extremely useful to have available prefabricated and demountable storage units.

I believe that we are not far away from the moment when developers will seriously consider marketing "cubes of space," and we will see Le Corbusier's hanging gardens actually realized. In New York, new cooperative apartments are now in construction which are the contemporary equivalent of the customized country estate. The potential for flexible design schemes that these luxury apartments invite should percolate down and affect the planning and development of much high-density housing. Step-by-step it may even be possible to radically alter the outlook, procedures, and methods by which our housing agencies serve up their standardized product.

We have, as a country, emerged from a rather sobering period in which architects, especially those of us who specialized in housing design, have learned, sometimes most painfully, that a better apartment or even a better-designed apartment project did very little to cure the pathology of a sick neighborhood and a deprived society. These better projects have deteriorated just as fast as the standard housing authority product. We learned that housing is simply one element, albeit an important one, in the total picture of a man's life and his feelings of worthiness. It is essential for the occupant to have a real stake in his dwelling. Middle-class Americans have traditionally gotten there by having a vested interest to defend, protect, and advance. Nothing serves this purpose better than a man's house. To the extent that we create housing that the occupants own, care about, and can design and modify to suit, we will be ahead in the business of making a better, saner, safer society.

SAR's method may have limited direct appeal to the American housing industry, but the message can be interpreted to produce a vastly superior product—as one important element of a stronger community environment.

# Response to Wasserman

It is at the same time heartening as well as frustrating that Wasserman interprets the SAR message almost exactly as we wish it to be understood. I agree entirely with his conclusions: how the SAR ideas should be adapted to the American context and how, in fact, market developments are already converging in the direction of these ideas. My frustration is because I realize that apparently we have once again not been very clear about the basic issues and potentials of the SAR idea at the outset. As has happened with so many others, Wasserman's perception of the SAR message was at first very much obscured by the SAR method.

Let me be clear. The method is secondary to the notion of user control. In fact, any approach that can achieve this aim is good. SAR appreciates fully the important contributions made by so many others who have recognized this main issue, but approach the solution in their own way. There is just one marginal note to add: it would be beneficial to the architectural profession if some general agreement could be reached on an approach. Everyone doing the same thing in a different way does not make much sense. This is why SAR makes an effort to formalize its approach into a method.

Wasserman pays considerable attention to the differences between the housing context of the US and European countries like Holland. The US distinguishes itself by policies which rely upon the private sphere to resolve housing needs. In Europe the public sector has a far greater stake in housing, with Holland as an extreme example. Wasserman concludes that the growing dominance of ownership in private housing, even multifamily, will be more conducive to the SAR idea than the tenant situation that prevails in the public solution. To a certain extent he is right, especially in respect to the condominium type of housing which is so much more developed in the US than with us. It appears that the distinction Habraken introduced between shared and individual responsibilities within a housing project can be applied most directly to this type. The next question is whether the communal part of the project may not be rented instead of co-owned. In fact, this is a solution we advocate for our government-financed housing associations, i.e., to consider a mixture of renting and ownership. The user will rent the serviced space and will own the internal subdivisions, equipment, and finishings. This will allow the public to continue regulating the housing market, offering user control "where it matters."

Such a solution has its own characteristics, presenting advantages as well as new problems. I mention this solution in order to introduce yet another level in the legal, financial, managerial, etc., terms of the main notion that shared responsibilities and individual responsibilities should be distinguished. I do this to emphasize that the possible elaborations are many. It is essential that such elaborations be tested in practice. In this respect, I am very pleased to find that Wasserman not only engages in such experiments, but also that he puts forward strong arguments for others to do the same. I agree entirely with his conviction that giving the occupants a real stake in housing will make a better, saner, and safer society. Although it may sound like a minor consideration, I would like to add that it will be good for the architects' profession as well. We need the proper social context not just for conscience's sake, but also to sort out our professional toolkit. I have no doubt that the discussion on methods will continue as well—and I welcome it.

John Carp
SAR
Postbus 429
5600 AK Eindhoven

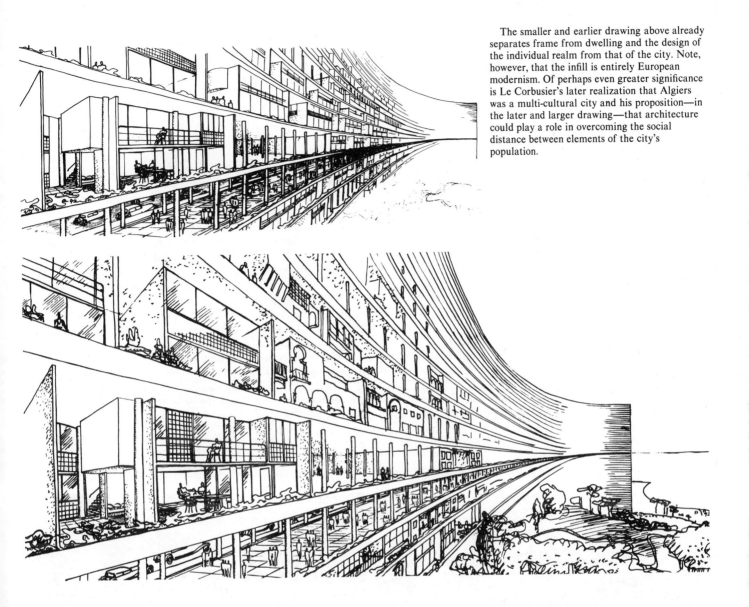

The smaller and earlier drawing above already
separates frame from dwelling and the design of
the individual realm from that of the city. Note,
however, that the infill is entirely European
modernism. Of perhaps even greater significance
is Le Corbusier's later realization that Algiers
was a multi-cultural city and his proposition—in
the later and larger drawing—that architecture
could play a role in overcoming the social
distance between elements of the city's
population.

# Black Road GIA
# Macclesfield, UK

Architect Rod Hackney moved into the Black Road district of Macclesfield not knowing that his house and others around it were scheduled to be cleared to make way for a large-scale redevelopment project. When the working class homeowners and tenants formed an Action Group to oppose demolition, they turned to their resident architect for assistance. Under the slogan, KEEP IT UP, BLACK ROAD!, they convinced the local Council to change the project designation to General Improvement Area (GIA), thus making rehabilitation loans and grants available. Working together, the people of Black Road and their architect planned, supervised, and worked on the rehabilitation of all the houses and the creation of common seating and play spaces—and in the process transformed a deteriorating neighborhood into a real community.

Since the completion of Black Road, Hackney has organized similar improvement schemes in other sections of Macclesfield, and in Birmingham, Cleator Moor, Millom, and Carlisle. He has fought successfully to gain recognition of the importance of neighborhood-based redevelopment efforts from the Department of the Environment and the backing of the once-suspicious and rather elitist RIBA. Colin Ward recently called him "my architectural hero, who commands the greatest respect for his humility in imposing no kind of architectural censorship on his clients." He has, of course, critics as well as admirers and has been accused of fighting fiercely to preserve the *status quo* and of conscientiously teaching the poor "to administer their own poverty." There are also those (see Commentary by Tom Kay) who question whether Hackney's approach is quite as general a solution as he assumes it is. The arguments on both sides are difficult to resolve, depending as they do on estimates of the true capacity of an economic and political system to house its people and on the value one places on autonomy and local initiative. In the bleak political and economic climate that threatens to prevail in the United States for some years to come, regardless of what one prefers, there may be crucial lessons in Rod Hackney's experience in Black Road.

1. The architect (second from left) with Black Road neighborhood leaders.

# Community Architecture and Self-Help

**Rod Hackney RIBA**
**Community Architect in Macclesfield**

The policies of mass clearance and comprehensive redevelopment which reached a peak in Britain in the 1960s have been halted. On reflection, many large schemes have proved disastrous beyond all measure. Apart from the astronomical cost—about £100,000 a unit over the 60-year loan period—the new tower and medium rise blocks failed to improve upon the rows of terrace houses that were bulldozed to make way for them. The general result is a multitude of unpopular and expensive modern units, doubtfully constructed and planned and, worst of all, now posing a whole new range of social and management problems.

Recent building in this country on open spaces originally cleared for the continuation of the high and medium rise housing policy has taken the form of the more acceptable two and three story terraces, which may alleviate some social problems connected with high rise buildings. Nevertheless, they are still expensive substitutes for the dwellings they replace.

Now that most of us acknowledge that the British financial position is a delicate one, it is understandable that housing funds, like all other aspects of the public economy, have had to be cut back. Expensive clearance and redevelopment have failed, and small-scale infill and rehabilitation have become financial and social necessities.

The Housing Act of 1974 emphasized the need for public participation in future programs, but how many housing agencies, particularly local authorities, can honestly say that their endeavors to encourage public participation will go beyond a few well-publicized meetings? Indeed, are there not many officials who still regard the general public as a spanner in the machinery of the local authority administration?

One might also ask: Is the public at large willing or even able to participate in the manner outlined in the recent housing legislation? Unfortunately, if some working relationship is not ef-

fected between the professionals and the public, then, on the next swing of the housing pendulum, say in the late 1980s, the government would have every reason to state that the participation programs have failed miserably, together with the program of rehabilitation. With the industrial momentum increasing, lubricated by North Sea oil, the only sensible course would then be a return to a more controlled product, again replacing the old housing with new building on a large scale.

Despite the limited financial budget available, there is a good chance that many inroads into solving the housing problem can still be made during this next decade by emphasizing the practical benefit of public participation. The Housing Act which may well have been an interim political measure to tide us over our financial troubles, could therefore, with public participation, prove to be a whole new way of tackling the housing situation. It will involve the owner-occupier, tenant, and landlord to an extent never really envisaged by most of the people involved in the housing sector. It will require confidence on the part of residents and foresight on the part of officials.

With shorter hours being worked and less overtime required, the climate seems opportune for residents to get involved with self-help on an ever-increasing scale. Indeed, without it, local authorities will only be able to scratch the surface of the housing problem. Unless you have public participation, the finances available can only be spent in one of two ways: either spread thinly over many houses, which in effect would give those attended to nothing more than a glorified "paint-and-make-good" job, or given to a few privileged areas to produce reasonable schemes of improvement, but leaving the bulk of substandard housing unattended, thus producing blight at an unprecedented rate.

Take a look at the building operations involved in improvement and repair. A large percentage of them do not

require skill. These jobs could easily be done by the house occupier providing he is willing and able. It is a matter of cooperation and coordination between the public, the skilled worker, and the professional manager. It does not mean that builders will lose out on the work available. The skilled trades would still be needed, although they may be acting in the capacity of subcontractors, rather than general contractors. Neither does it mean that professionals will be ousted, although their role will become one of community relations and personnel management, rather than the straightforward application of design skills they were trained in.

Standards need not decline with self-help; on the contrary, as the example which follows illustrates, they may very well improve. Costs will be greatly reduced, and a worthwhile exercise will have been carried out with those most intimately involved in rehabilitation—that is, the residents—having played a major role in their housing improvements and repairs. Think of the extra social benefits which accrue, of the pride of the participants, and of the reduction in vandalism.

To help to understand this line of reasoning, let us consider the example of the Black Road General Improvement Area in Macclesfield, Cheshire. The Macclesfield experiment is the first completed self-help rehabilitation project in Britain, and it in many ways foreshadowed the legislation outlined in the Housing Act of 1974. The account is written in chronological order to help explain the progress of the scheme from start to finish.

Macclesfield is an old town which experienced considerable growth in the first half of the nineteenth century with the construction of two- and three-story terrace cottages for the workers of the town's textile industries. Although many of these original houses have been demolished, the majority remain and most are in need of some form of repair and improvement. Some were in such a bad state of repair that the local au-

95

thority could see no alternative to full-scale clearance. Those in the Black Road area of the town, bordering the Macclesfield Canal, were considered to be some of the worst. They were all built about 1815.

In 1968, the Council prepared a case for the clearance of over 300 houses in the Black Road area in order to promote a comprehensive scheme of redevelopment incorporating new semi-detached houses and accommodations for old persons. Because of insufficient funds, no action was taken on this

Brian Ollier

2a

2b

2c

scheme, and both slum clearance and new house building were suspended generally throughout the town. In 1972, Macclesfield Council decided to resume its program, and the Black Road area was one of four areas to be cleared first. This fact was publicized at a Town Hall exhibition in June, 1972. The residents of the Black Road area had made representations to their Aldermen and Councillors in 1968 and inquired regularly about their fate during the four years that followed. This exhibition, however, spurred them to formalize their organization. They established an Action Group in order to present their own points of view to the Council and the townspeople.

## The Action Group

The Action Group first circulated a pe-

tition to find out where its support lay and to test local feeling about the Council's clearance plans. It quickly learned that most people in the affected area wanted to stay, and in one specific part of the area *all* the residents expressed the wish to improve their homes rather than have them demolished. The Action Group decided to concentrate its case in the area where it was guaranteed unanimous support.

The Group met with elected representatives and local government officials and explained their improvement ideas. Most summer evenings were spent visiting the homes of the 48 Aldermen and Councillors in Macclesfield. The Group enlisted the support of their local Member of Parliament, and extended an invitation to him to visit the area, thus securing front-page coverage in the two local newspapers. Car stickers and cam-

2a,b,c,d. Views of the project area streets and courts prior to rebuilding.

2d

paign posters were prepared by the Group and distributed throughout the town. Public meetings were held to gain support. A publicity team was set up to feed the local press with news items continually. In short, the Group made out a very convincing case to illustrate their preference for improvement of their homes. It adopted a slogan, "KEEP IT UP, BLACK ROAD!"

### The Residents' Technical Report

The Action Group asked me, the resident architect, and the resident builder to prepare a technical report on the condition of the 34 houses in the pilot area. The Group also appointed its own surveyors to inspect in detail all the houses and itemize lists of improvements required to bring the houses up to standards. The Action Group included in its report a proposal for declaring their area a General Improvement Area.* This report included a comprehensive list of environmental improvements for tidying up the area around the houses.

As "qualified persons," the Group is allowed to present a technical report to the Council for its consideration. The 54-page report, outlining the case for

---

*Designation as a General Improvement Area (GIA) brings with it an array of government grants and loans. Important among these are maturity loans—20- or 25-year balloon mortgages requiring annual payments only of interest—and option mortgages, under which the government subsidizes interest payments for low income families—EDITOR.

improvement and not clearance, was printed and copies were circulated to all elected representatives and local government officers; copies were also sent to the local and national press and others whom the Group considered would help it in its campaign. The report was well received. The Council's Planning and Development Committee and the Housing Committee met jointly to consider the report. They decided to recommend the setting up of a Housing Strategy Group consisting of officials from the former Slum Clearance and General Improvement Area groups to consider the case of the Black Road area residents and make recommendations for the full Council to consider.

The economic criteria affecting older housing had changed radically with the 1969 Housing Act. The expansion of the Improvement Grant system had shifted a much greater share of public investment into repair of older houses and their surroundings. In the same Act, cooperation between residents and the local authority was encouraged in order to decide upon the desirability of area improvement and to gauge the local residents' support for the implementation of general improvement schemes.

The Housing Strategy Group spent six months in its preparation of recommendations. They first asked the public health department to reinspect the Black Road properties. They searched out the Department of the Environment's opinions. They later checked the

credibility of the Action Group's guarantees of support.

The public health officers found that, while the bulk of the properties in the Black Road area were in such a bad state as to be only suitable for clearance, there was a concentration of improvable properties within the area outlined for improvement. The Department of the Environment's reaction to the Action Group's proposals was that the houses were borderline cases but that, "resident solidarity and an ambitious scheme of environmental improvements has been noted . . . to such an extent that while reservations about detail proposals, scope and cost still exist, social argument cannot be excluded in the balance of physical deficits and potential."

The Housing Strategy Group's report noted three major points that had to be considered when determining the future of the Black Road area:

1. The Residents of the Action Group still accept that their houses are viable homes, and consider these houses capable of improvement at reasonable cost to give a life of at least 30 years.
2. Residents' confidence is matched by their willingness to invest in the dwellings.
3. Legislative and economic conditions have been altered sufficiently since 1968 for the local authority to reconsider their earlier decision to clear.

97

The Housing Strategy Group also acknowledged the residents' desire to carry out the scheme on a self-help basis. The Action Group had indicated that the residents wished to manage both the house and site improvements, and the Action Group had its architect who would manage the entire operation.

## The Declaration of a General Improvement Area

After the Housing Strategy Group submitted its report in April, 1974, the Macclesfield Council declared the Black Road Area the first General Improvement Area in the town. Among the Council's resolutions were the following:

1. "That the Town Clerk be authorised to complete the necessary legal documents." The Action Group had earlier agreed to sign dedication documents agreeing to accept improvement grants. The Group had also proposed to give up its private lands for collective site improvement. This was then prepared by the Town Clerk and the Action Group's solicitors, signed by all the owners, the Mayor, and the Town Clerk. The Action Group also changed its name to the Black Road Area Residents' Association, created a trust organization, and voted in four trustees to administer the improvement scheme and subsequent maintenance of the environmental improvements.
2. "That the Local Authority authorise an expenditure of £250 per house for general environmental works." The residents later calculated that if they had contracted out their ambitious scheme it would have cost about £ 23,000. Using residents' labor and only contracting for specialist work, i.e., stone walling, brickwork, asphalt laying, reduced this to £8500.
3. "That the Housing and Estates Committee be asked to make housing available for rent to the occupants of the Black Road area properties as temporary accommodation while the improvements were being carried out."
4. "That the Council be prepared to give maximum improvement grants where appropriate . . . and that the chairman and vice-chairman of the Housing and Estates Committee be given delegated powers to approve grant applications." This facilitated approval of the residents' grant ap-

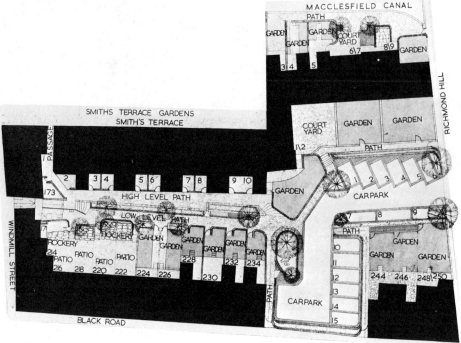

3. Plan of the Black Road General Improvement Area: 34 houses in all.

plications and ensured smooth continuity of the improvement works.

The Council agreed to make maturity loans available for the first time to the hardship cases in the Black Road area. For others, they promised loans to cover improvement costs over and above the grant amount. In short, the Council endorsed all the proposals of the Black Road residents plus additional proposals to safeguard the implementation of the scheme. It was now up to the residents to prove themselves and carry out their improvement scheme.

While the Councillors had been making up their minds about the area, the residents had been busy finalizing plans for the GIA. The most important early achievement was to persuade most of the tenants to purchase their homes from the absentee owners. House prices, while the area was threatened with clearance, were very low and the Action Group managed to get all the tenants to buy prior to the increase which was bound to come when the Council's clearance proposals were replaced with plans for improvement. In one particular terrace the tenants were able to raise £1600 for the five houses in which they lived. Although this was not a large amount, the Action Group's financial advisers working with the agents of the landlady were able to show that £1600 invested in an annuity policy

would bring the landlady twice as much in interest as the rent she would receive—plus the advantage of not having to maintain the houses and repair them when the improvement scheme began. Interestingly, the £1600 was not divided equally by five, but rather made up of amounts each tenant could afford. The two pension-age tenants contributed £200 each. The younger couples paid more for their houses. These Robin Hood financial arrangements worked a treat, and in addition the Council was pleased that the actual residents would get the grant and not some absentee landlord.

Both the Council and the residents needed convincing quickly that the works would start immediately after the declaration of the GIA. As the architect, I agreed to alter my house first with the help of the other residents and a local contracting firm. The improvements to my house also helped "educate" the other residents in chimney breast demolition, house replanning, carpentry, etc., so that they had a little experience when it came to doing their own houses and helping the elderly residents who would require substantial assistance.

After three months the Show House was complete. The Council was impressed with the first conversion; so were the residents. Builders were invited to see what had been done with a view to offering them negotiated contracts for work the residents themselves would not be carrying out. This way they were able to see the desired standard of workmanship and visit the other houses which were to be improved.

## The Residents' Program

While drawings and specifications were being prepared for all the houses, roof-works were begun, and the Council agreed to pay interim grants for this part of the works. This allowed complete project reroofing prior to the start of internal house improvements. I drew up itemized specifications for each house, and contractors were asked for itemized prices. This meant that residents could see where the costs lay and, from the nature of the price breakdown, where their labor could be best utilized to save the most money. Some contractors were a little skeptical of the approach, especially as there was an abundance of work at the time. Most refused to participate, but, nevertheless, the residents managed to secure all the assistance they required, and in addition got builders to agree to penalty clauses and completion dates for each house.

The builder who lived in the GIA agreed to carry out one complete terrace. Another small local contractor agreed to take a second terrace, and a larger firm from the town took the third terrace. The first two turned out to be great successes because they were able to adapt to the strange site management conditions and to residents' participation in the improvement works. The third, larger firm proved more difficult and unable to accommodate the wishes of the residents in the same way. This resulted in all kinds of difficulties, including delays in the completion of the works with subsequent mortgage offer lapses, lengthy stays in temporary houses by these residents, and, indirectly, a reduction in the standard of workmanship. Experience has shown us that in self-help schemes, larger contractors cannot participate as well as smaller firms because of their long chains of command and inflexibility.

Mention has been made of mortgages. No scheme of this nature can be attempted without the full financial backing of a local authority. Building societies refused to contemplate finan-

4. The architect's house done first to show what could be accomplished.

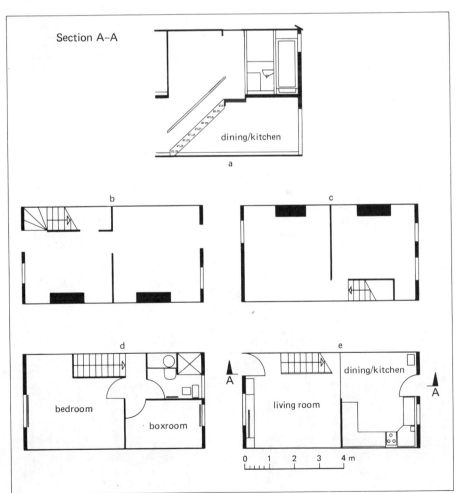

Section A–A

dining/kitchen

a

b

c

d

bedroom

boxroom

e

living room

dining/kitchen

0   1   2   3   4 m

5. Original plans of the architect's house: a ground floor, b first floor. c,d. Alteration plans. e. Section A-A.

cial assistance for the improvement of this 160-year-old terrace housing. The local authority, on the other hand, could not declare a GIA and then not back it to the hilt with financial aid. Everyone who needed assistance in the Black Road area got it. The elderly took up the maturity loans. The less well-off younger people received option mortgages and the remainder either took advantage of normal mortgages or, in a few cases, they paid cash. When the contractors' bids were submitted, they were, of course, higher than the figures submitted in the residents' original report. Apart from inflation, the residents had upgraded their requirements, with many deciding upon central heating at the last minute. Average mortgages, to cover the costs of the works, (over the £1500 grant level) were about £1300–£2000, and the average maturity loan was about £600. These figures suggest that the elderly paid less for their house improvements. This is true because, in general, less work was done to these homes, not because they were in better condition, but because the elderly did not want as comprehensive an improvement job as the younger residents. In addition, the local authority agreed to interpret the need for improvements in the elderly residents'

6

6. Self-help at Black Road.

7. Work just starting at Black Road.

houses rather liberally, thus again reducing cost. This manifested itself in upgrading, rather than complete replacement, of staircases, retention of low door head heights, and so forth.

Once a mortgage had been given by the local authority, it was up to the owner to keep to the agreed figure. If he wanted extras, then the amount would be calculated with the contractor, and the owner would have to put in more man-hours to compensate for the additional costs. Residents found that much of contractors' site time is spent in nonskilled work that really anybody can carry out if given direction. It was the responsibility of the architect to program all of this and ensure that the owners and the contractors were equally aware of what each was required to do. Most of the residents worked on the building site during the evenings and weekends. A few took time off from work to complete their house improvements. In the case of the elderly, the younger residents pooled their labor and demolished chimney breasts, outhouses, etc., and then later helped with house decorations.

7

## An Assessment of the Scheme

Now that all the house improvements are completed, the results can be assessed. No house is the same. The completed improvements reflect the individuality of each occupant. It would have been much easier to standardize the scheme, but in Black Road perhaps the greatest single success is the individual house types produced. The windows and doors are different, there are many types of staircases—some open riser, others solid riser—some kitchens have large areas of floor, others have breakfast bars. Some houses are open plan, some have all the improvements accommodated in the original house structure, others chose to extend either in the form of a one-story or two-story additions. Some residents decided upon a shower rather than a bath. Most chose gas wall-mounted boilers, while others preferred solid fuel central heating, and still others decided on more conventional forms of house heating.

Even with this apparently anarchistic design approach, the overall appearance of the improved houses still reflects the period in which the houses were built. Their common sense approach has helped the residents avoid the easy trap of ruining the house proportions by changing the original window sizes. Instead, the existing window and door proportions have been kept and no one has inserted bow windows or gone for porches over their doorways.

The local authority has acted responsibly in its interpretation of the building regulations. Rigid and inflexible standards have not been asked for. No Parker Morris room dimensions here, and no attempt to make the houses into something they were never designed for. Shared external manholes and soil vent pipes, relaxations on room heights, and the like have all helped to make the scheme possible.

The environmental works are now completed, and they are complementary to the individual house improvements. Off-street car parking has been provided, common seating and play spaces, tree and shrub planting, and new paths and private garden areas have been provided as well.

The scheme was completed on time, and it is a credit to all concerned—the residents, the local authority, and the contractors. It has shown what happens when residents and the local authority work together, with mutual respect and

8. Smith's Terrace after restoration.

9. Black Road's courts transformed into private gardens and public walkways.

trust, to see a scheme through. Both the Black Road residents and the Macclesfield Council feel justly proud of the success of the Black Road General Improvement Area No. 1.

## Lessons for Other Areas

1. The presence of a "qualified person" (a resident, qualified architect), as referred to by the Ministry of Housing and Local Government, within the area was of immeasurable value when it came to negotiations with the Council and later the contractors. There is, therefore, an argument here for calling for architects-in-residence in future areas of General Improvement or Housing Action.
2. Concentrating on a small compact area and making sure that all the houses were improved was clearly a correct strategy and enabled the project to move ahead quickly. The scheme would no doubt have failed if a large pilot area had been chosen and only random house improvements within each terrace had been carried out.
3. The Group decided at the outset to establish a precedent. Other tenant groups were expected to adopt a similar course as long as the financial incentives remained available for house and area improvement. Here, too, the Group has been successful.
4. The manner in which the Group tackled the Council and the emphasis they put on cooperation undoubtedly persuaded local government officials and elected representatives to listen more willingly to its ideas. The insistence on avoiding criticizing individuals within the local authority had a great bearing on the outcome of the residents' fight to save their homes, and subsequently their successful management of the General Improvement Area.
5. Lastly, the residents embarked on a campaign to save their homes knowing that they were right in what they wanted. They were willing to sacrifice personal gain to see the joint effort succeed.

Since the completion of Black Road General Improvement Area No. 1, another successful scheme has been completed up the road using similar management techniques. At Black

Road General Improvement Area No. 2, local leaders again organized themselves into a Residents Cooperative and Building Cooperative and carried out the scheme themselves, taking three years from start to finish. Again a community architect was involved, working on site 24 hours a day, and the scheme has benefited by learning from the first scheme down the road, and also by having a little more money to spend on site improvements.

Community architecture is now a recognized job description in the United Kingdom, encouraging architects to work within their communities, learning to understand the needs of the residents, and then implementing technical proposals to meet these needs. As the main thrust of the work is to break through the normal bureaucratic blockages which restrict the development of self-help work, it is very labor-intensive, and as such is uneconomic if the normal fee regulations are applied to the professional service.

The Royal Institute of British Architects has therefore written to the Secretary of State for the Environment asking for financial assistance in the form of a Community Aid Fund, which would allow Residents Groups up and down the country wishing to carry out schemes similar to Black Road General Improvement Area Nos. 1 and 2, to apply for funds to employ professional

Community Architects. The approval of such a fund and the general expansion of the use of Community Architects in the United Kingdom will make great inroads into the problem of our older housing communities.

# Commentary on Black Road

Tom Kay RIBA, London

## WHERE CAN BLACK ROAD TAKES US?

Rod Hackney is a persuasive publicist for self-help . . . which is not to devalue the work he actually did in Macclesfield. The question is, has it wider applications? Can it, for instance, be applied to public housing built over the last 50 years? If it can, does that imply the propriety and practicality of selling all local authority housing, an idea which would certainly be approved of by Mrs. Thatcher? In fact, if Hackney can solve that riddle, the present government will certainly ensure his future prosperity.

Hackney appears to believe, as do many others, that it is inevitable that public money spent by a public authority must produce an unsatisfactory, i.e., bureaucratic, solution. To answer this would require a book; however:

1. Most Council (public) housing does not make the news and is not infamous.
2. The really gruesome housing has been brought about by a number of decisions, none of which relate to the lack of occupant participation.
    a. High urban land values and thus local authority decisions to raise residential densities in the 1950s and 1960s.
    b. Government loan sanctions / subsidies which, through the Housing Cost Yardstick, involved larger subsidies per person for higher densities, and additional subsidies for taller buildings. When taken together with a "bandwagon" decision by central government to subsidize large-scale prefabrication during the 60s, the inevitable monster estates were built—and then found wanting.

The lack of participation of the occupants in the planning of each accommodation was "incidental" by comparison to these policy decisions. (Self-help in these "monster estates" would, I presume, involve the tenants demolishing the blocks with their own bare hands. A positive view of vandalism?)

Rod Hackney refers to two- and three-story (new) terrace housing as expensive substitutes for the dwellings which they replace. What does this mean? I'm afraid he is saying that they cost more to build than a rehabilitation scheme—in which we will accept lower standards and a shorter life. These new dwellings *are* expensive, but they are still too cheap because of the level of cost set by government; this forces reductions in technical standards—even where these reductions are known by the designer to lead to problems in use. The shift to rehabilitation over the last 10 years has done little to alleviate this problem. A different scale of costs is employed, but it is now recognized that, in many instances, the 30-year, relatively trouble-free life expected of these properties is hopelessly optimistic. In this context, the wisdom of dropping standards even further, as suggested by Hackney, in order to suit individual householders' pockets may be very shortsighted.

Hackney has addressed himself to the problem of a limited range of houses within the private sector—houses that can be bought very cheaply because of the laws governing sitting tenants and controlled rents (a very rapidly decreasing sector). Would his Macclesfield scheme have been viable if the selling prices had actually reflected the value of the existing houses (freehold vacant possession) at, say, £10,000? (Depending on location, i.e., in which city and where in that city, Black Road houses might have sold for anything from £5000 to £50,000).

Hackney is proposing a method of organizing and designing that is at least as labor intensive ("professional" time) as that traditionally paid for by middle and high income clients when providing themselves with accommodation. Such tailoring, not surprisingly, does produce more ultimately satisfying living conditions. Given current government cutbacks (and I do not foresee any great expansion, even with a change of government), it would seem very unlikely that funding would be forthcoming in sufficient quantities to have more than a marginal effect on the provision of advice and skills suggested by the term *Community Architect*. I have made the assumption that Hackney's clients would not be able to pay for such "expanded services." The proposition of Community Architect / Architecture has built into it an acceptance of architecture for the poor, which I find worrying. It is, of course, very much in line with Conservative thinking on state housing provision only for the "needy and destitute"—old people, the chronically ill, one-parent families, and so forth. The proposition seems to accept the fact that the majority of architects do not work for the community and are not concerned with the political implications of their work. In this context, Hackney's evangelical mission would be better directed against the RIBA and its membership in an attempt to encourage or *force* all architects to be community architects.

Self-help rehabilitation should clearly have its place in the armory of housing solutions. Black Road itself is an achievement of which Rod Hackney and the occupants should be proud. But to put this up as a prototype solution to Britain's housing problems is naive, or at least, shortsighted. Hackney assumes that State housing provision has failed and that nothing should or can be done about it except to sidestep it or abandon it. He gives up just at the point when we have learned enough lessons about bureaucracy and its failings to propose radical change to the system rather than scrapping it.

# UHAB in Harlem
# New York

We too often assume that self-help is the province of the United Nations housing office, something suitable for the Third World. And yet, in advanced industrial nations like our own, self-help continues to play an important role in the development of housing for almost all sectors of the population. In the following article, Charles Laven, former Urban Homesteading Assistance Board Director, describes the successful effort of a group of Harlem residents to acquire a pair of abandoned tenements and to convert them into individualized apartments, collective services, and a mosque (the residents are practicing Sunni Moslems).

Although the process was inordinately complex, slow, and required tremendous inputs of professional time, Laven argues that self-help is essential in the present urban housing situation and that it can be made to work. He concludes:

The elements at work in a self-help housing project are complex: job skill development, decentralization of housing control, cooperative ownership, and architectural design and construction process directly controlled by the users, and the creation of political awareness among neighborhood residents. It is this combination of objectives that makes self-help difficult. It

is, however, this potential that makes it worthwhile.

New York architect and housing activist Tony Schuman read Laven's report in draft and responded with the critique that follows it (see Commentary). Laven, in turn, has tried to provide answers to the critical questions Schuman raises. Their debate is an important one for the present moment in housing.

All photos Beverly Hall

# Self-Help in Neighborhood Development

**Charles Laven, Director**
**Urban Homesteading Assistance Board,**
**New York**

In the form of urban homesteading, self-help housing has received widespread attention as its scope has grown in the past 10 years. In deteriorating neighborhoods of New York City and in similar areas across the country, more and more people are directly contributing to the process by which housing is produced. This is not a new phenomenon, nor is it a previously unrecognized one. What, however, is unique is the wide range of self-help activity, its place in a growing neighborhood movement that emphasizes local control of planning and service delivery, its focus on seriously distressed urban neighborhoods and very low income people, and finally the measure of official recognition it is receiving.

Self-help is, of course, the oldest and most traditional manner by which people provide shelter for themselves. It takes place in highly industrialized as well as in developing countries, and across all social and economic classes. It cannot be blithely dismissed as a quaint anachronism, nor minimized as a desperate and only ameliorative response to overwhelming need. Even in the United States, self-help is surprising in its scope and constancy.

In 1969, a study commissioned by the Department of Housing and Urban Development reported that fully 20 percent of all single family new construction starts are by owner-builders. Owner-builders are found across the country, in rural, suburban, and urban areas. They provide houses at lower cost and of equivalent quality to those professionally developed and built. Importantly, owner-building provides a means to home ownership for lower income groups. In a 1979 study of census data by the National Association of Realtors, it was again confirmed that owner-builders account for 20 percent of all single family housing starts. What is remarkable is not only that activity has remained constant, but that it continues strongly without support structures and in the face of significant obstacles.

Self-help housing activity includes "back-to-the-city" brownstoners, suburban owner-builders, and the mutual self-help projects which have long been a key mechanism in providing housing for migrant farmworkers, native Americans, and other rural poor. The focus of this article is the application of similar self-help principles in a seriously deteriorated urban neighborhood.

Urban homesteading is a programmatic response to the problems of housing abandonment and neighborhood decline. It builds upon the organized efforts of residents of distressed neighborhoods. I will first discuss abandonment and neighborhood change as the background and origin of self-help homesteading. A case study of an urban homesteading rehabilitation project will be presented; the government support needed for homesteading, the role of the Urban Homesteading Assistance Board (UHAB), and some of the new directions that urban homesteading has started to take will be discussed. Finally, a series of conclusions as to the limitations and replicability of this sort of urban self-help will be drawn.

Self-help is not seen as a cure-all, substituting people's own energies for the failures of the private housing market and government assistance programs alike. It is not a panacea, capable of operating in isolation from other kinds of political and economic change, nor is it a solution for all types of people and neighborhoods. Rather, self-help is seen as a starting point, where housing programs precipitate and inform other types of development. Groups of people are brought together through self-help actions, beginning a process of neighborhood organization and response. The individuals who participate in self-help projects end up with job training, higher quality housing, and greater self-confidence in their own abilities. As a housing program, it is more a human story of people's own efforts at change than a record of dwelling units produced and technical innovations implemented. Compared with

the widespread failures in federal efforts to date, it can only be seen as an important step forward.

## Housing Abandonment and Neighborhood Decline

The sheer numbers are staggering. In New York City, it is conservatively estimated that over 30,000 dwelling units per year are abandoned. The municipal government has reluctantly become the largest slumlord in the city, perhaps in the world. Indeed, some entire neighborhoods are under municipal control. In *Loisaida* (a 56-block area on the Lower East Side of Manhattan), it is estimated that almost 70 percent of the housing stock is in City ownership.

Housing abandonment is by no means only a New York City problem. A report prepared by the federal General Accounting Office reported that abandonment is a major problem in over 20 cities across the country. Although some recent attention has been given to the problem of displacement of low income families through gentrification, a more serious problem is the continued displacement of low income families through abandonment.

There is no unified analysis as to why housing abandonment takes place. The New York experience, however, has led to a general conclusion: alternative modes of ownership and management must be developed. It can be simply stated that the private, profit-motivated ownership of low income, multifamily housing no longer works. The numbers do not add up, the costs of maintaining property continue to outstrip people's ability to pay. There is no way that this type of ownership can be profitable again. Conventional financing and ownership structures cannot make this housing work. New mechanisms must be developed to rehabilitate, manage, and operate residential property. New government subsidies and professional resources must be found. This is where New York City's self-help homesteading comes in.

## Urban Homesteading

Single family urban homesteading began in 1975 as a federally sponsored demonstration in a few cities. The concept is simple: vacant, publicly owned properties are made available to low and moderate income would-be homeowners. Support may range from mere advice on the rehabilitation process, to the actual contracting out of the process by the agency on the homeowner's behalf. Financial assistance in the form of below market interest rate mortgage loans is often made available. The effort quickly grew from a demonstration in 23 cities to an institutionalized program in 99, and became one of the more popular federal housing assistance programs. Its emphasis is on direct user control of the entire housing process, from project inception and design, through development and construction, to ownership and management.

Like the single family program, multifamily homesteading is the reclamation of previously abandoned property by the future residents. Obviously, multifamily homesteading operates in multiple dwellings: buildings that range in size from 3 to 80 or more units. More complex forms of organization are required, in human as well as legal and financial terms. Multifamily projects are often organized as cooperatives, usually on a nonprofit basis. Lower income groups are frequently served, as well as more distressed neighborhoods. Most significantly, the origins of multifamily homesteading are not in a government-initiated demonstration, but rather in a grassroots response to serious neighborhood conditions.

## The Urban Homesteading Assistance Board

Virtually all of the self-help homesteading activities in New York have been aided by the Urban Homesteading Assistance Board (UHAB). UHAB is a nonprofit housing service which assists low and moderate income New Yorkers in developing self-help solutions to their housing needs. Formed in 1973 as a professional response to grassroots initiatives, UHAB's beginnings were a recognition that the initial two or three projects in the City would remain only interesting quirks without organized assistance. UHAB's goal was not to provide handouts, but to give technical assistance to self-helpers willing to salvage buildings and create their own homes.

The scope of UHAB's activities is threefold: advocacy, resource development, and technical assistance. UHAB has acted as an advocate for self-help homesteading efforts, coordinating presentations, developing policies, and encouraging support from a variety of institutions. In order to make multifamily homesteading a functional program, UHAB has worked with federal and local agencies to organize the necessary resources. This has involved analyzing existing programs, proposing changes, and arguing for the set-aside of special funds to support multifamily homesteading.

UHAB's initial focus has been on the City's most deteriorated neighborhoods. As a counterpoint to the current theories of planned shrinkage, depopulation, and triage, UHAB has focused on the incremental strength of seriously distressed areas. The planning theory behind the initial homesteading efforts was to start from a small kernel of strength, building from one project to a neighborhood level of activity. Throughout the planning and processing period, and during the subsequent phase of housing rehabilitation, all major decisions are made by the homesteaders. UHAB helps in locating suitable city-owned properties for rehabilitation. We prepare projects feasibility studies, including estimates of the rehabilitation costs and identification of appropriate loan and subsidy programs. We assist homesteaders in securing reduced rate architectural and legal services. Loan applications are prepared in our office and processing is expedited. During construction, UHAB assists homesteaders in securing building permits and, eventually, certificates of occupancy, and in developing essential construction management and accounting systems. Training in cooperative self-management is offered to homesteaders as projects near completion.

UHAB has a professional staff of 16, including architects, planners, developers, community organizers, and researchers. The staff is supplemented by consultants in accounting, management, law, and architecture. UHAB has been sponsored from the beginning by the Cathedral Church of St. John the Divine. Support comes from foundation and corporate grants, as well as contract work for government agencies. UHAB's overall policy is set by a Board of Directors consisting of representatives from the Cathedral, foundation backers, and community housing organizations.

## Self-Help Rehabilitation Project in Harlem

The severely distressed neighborhoods in which multifamily homesteading operates are plagued by the dual problems of housing abandonment and underemployment. Housing is viewed as a starting point for an overall development process, the point through which a variety of resources are coordinated. The best way to portray the interplay of program elements is through a study of one project, for in reality the effort is more difficult than the concept, and the people involved are more important than the theory.

Just north of Central Park, in a deteriorated area of Central Harlem, there are two buildings recently renovated by a group of New York City self-helpers. The neighborhood consists of tall, formerly elegant buildings lining Central Park North and the broad avenues. Housing abandonment has hit this section of Harlem hard, and there is not a street that does not show signs of the ills associated with severe urban distress: population loss, high unemployment, extreme poverty, decline in social and commercial infrastructure, and high crime rates. Yet much of the housing stock is beautiful and basically sound, and the neighborhood has locational advantages.

2. 113th Street and St. Nicholas Avenue.

3. Mosque of the Islamic Brotherhood: self-help housing in Harlem.

2

3

On 113th Street and St. Nicholas Avenue, two buildings stand out. Freshly painted windows, a shingled canopy over a newly occupied store, and carved wooden front doors distinguished them from the rest of the deteriorating tenements. The buildings were previously abandoned and had been vacant for over five years. They now contain 14 apartments, shops, and a variety of communal spaces for the residents. How 14 units of high quality, rehabilitated housing managed to get built on a corner in Central Harlem is a complicated story. But it illustrates the kinds of programs needed to support self-help, the goals of self-helpers, and the problems raised by the urban homesteading.

The project is sponsored by the Mosque of the Islamic Brotherhood. Formed in the early 1960s, the Mosque is a religious community of orthodox Sunni Muslims. A rapid growth of Islam in American black communities has taken place in the past 20 years, paralleling a worldwide Islamic revival. The 60 families who form the Mosque had quite different personal histories prior to coming together to practice their faith. Most were low income, although many members had high levels of skill and there is a range of educational backgrounds. A few were involved in construction and participated in trade union-sponsored apprenticeship programs. One was employed as a drug rehabilitation counselor. Others worked as secretaries, clerks, and helpers in small businesses. Some were unemployed.

As a religious community, the Mosque emphasizes strict self-reliance, independence, discipline, and self-improvement. Islamic religious tenets and practices are rigorously studied and followed, including strict observance of the Muslim sabbath, of all religious holidays, and of periodic fasts. Iman K. Ahmad Tawfiq, religious leader of the Mosque and a well-known Islamic scholar, often speaks of the Islamic emphasis on self-reliance and self-improvement as a direct response to the cycle of dependency in which he sees many Harlem residents caught. The Mosque perceives that one of its goals is to present an alternative to the community.

In pursuit of this goal, the Mosque sponsors a number of services in the community. These include a restaurant and the first health food store in Harlem. Public events, street fairs, and educational programs are also part of the

4

4. The spiritual leader of the Mosque.

5

5. The Iman greets the children.

6. 6a.b.c.d. Sweat turning into equity for Mosque members.

Mosque's outreach activities. Self-help urban homesteading fit well into the structure and goals of the Mosque. It was a natural progression from the development activities that the Mosque began with, and was one of the few ways in which the Mosque could solve its unique housing problems. A central location for the Mosque, in the form of cooperative housing project, would help build its organization and community identity. And many of the members of the Mosque lived in substandard housing and were overcrowded, as they tend to have large families.

The Mosque was put in touch with UHAB through a network of neighborhood contacts. This started a long development process, which began with choosing a site. After examining a number of city-owned buildings, the two on the corner of 113th Street were selected. They had architectural merit in their exterior brickwork and detailing. They were extremely wide by New York standards, so that family apartments could be easily accommodated. These two buildings had been designated as an urban renewal site for rehabilitation. After some negotiations, the rights to develop this property were assigned to the Mosque, and a price of $1000 per building was set. The detailed procedures for purchasing abandoned property from the City of New York could begin.

UHAB's role in the entire development process was critical. The Mosque had never been involved in a housing project before, so the technical aspects of housing finance, development, and construction were unfamiliar. A number of the initial procedures and negotiations were handled entirely by UHAB. Everyone involved knew that the Mosque's members would be the builders and owners of the project and therefore were ultimately responsible for its success or failure. However, in order to get started, UHAB took the lead, allowing the Mosque to build up capacity and knowledge prior to taking full responsibility for project implementation.

## Putting The Project Together

To start, money was needed to hire an architect. UHAB arranged for the Mosque to borrow $10,000 from Community Funding, Inc.—a consortium of private institutions, including Columbia University and Barnard College, formed to make no-interest loans to community

organizations for development projects. The Mosque's was the first such project it supported. Later, the Mosque borrowed additional funds from the Consumer-Farmer Foundation, another private organization that supports community housing efforts. In total, over $25,000 in seed money was advanced to the project.

Some of this seed money was used to hire Kaminsky and Schiffer, a New York City architectural firm. The design of the building turned out to be a difficult task with a complex set of needs and ever-changing requirements. The two buildings selected were old law tenements, built prior to 1901. Because of their age, the buildings required major work, including some new structural elements, a new staircase, a new fire escape, and complete replacement of all interior finishes. New York City building code requirements, perhaps the most rigorous in the world, dictated room sizes, allowable materials, and construction methods. Finally, the financing agency for the project had its own set of design requirements, emphasizing large units.

The design process was an interactive one. Kaminsky and Schiffer would propose a series of layouts to the Mosque, work out with them a reasonable program, and make a submission to the government agencies. The agencies, in turn, would comment on the submission and require changes from the architect and the Mosque. Many schematic designs were presented to the Mosque so that they could become familiar with the process of reading plans and evaluating their needs.

Members of the Mosque spent long hours with UHAB's staff, the architects, and reviewers from the City's housing agency analyzing options and refining the design. The final plans include 14 apartments in two buildings, as well as day-care/community center, and a place for religious services. Over one-half of the apartments have four bedrooms and all are extremely spacious.

While the architectural design process was going on, rubbish removal and demolition of the buildings' interior started. This preceded final mortgage commitments. Starting the long, diffi-

6a

6b

6c

6d

cult job served as a way to consolidate interest in the project and as a negotiating tool—working in the buildings established site control and pressured government agencies to support the project. And demolition work is good training for future tasks. It is labor-intensive without requiring a high level of skill. It allowed the group time to develop work habits and to get organized. Importantly, it can be done on very little money. As one member of the Mosque put it, "At times it seemed as if the funding for our project would never come, so we just started, so we could show people what we could do."

The development of financing mechanisms to permit construction to begin was not simple. There was a recognition from UHAB, the Mosque, and government agencies that the demands of completely unassisted self-help construction would be too great. Earlier successful urban homesteading projects in New York had shown that some experienced labor to assist the homesteaders was necessary. In 1976, the City of New York began to receive significant amounts of job training funds. The federal Comprehensive Employment and Training Act (CETA) allowed cities to contract with nonprofit groups to provide work experience and job training for unemployed persons. CETA funds would also pay for the hiring of a construction manager, crew chiefs, and for general overhead and administration. To obtain CETA funds, the Mosque formed a coalition with United Harlem Growth, another neighborhood-based nonprofit organization with similar goals and objectives. By applying jointly, the Mosque and United Harlem Growth increased their political power, created a program of the scale preferred by government agencies, and reduced the administrative burden each would have to bear. The completion of negotiations for the CETA contract created an organized labor force to rehabilitate the buildings. This supplemented the sweat equity volunteer labor of Mosque Members. All that was needed now was a mortgage loan to purchase materials for construction.

Just then, New York City's fiscal crisis intensified. The Municipal Loan Program, a bond-financed rehabilitation loan program, had traditionally been the major source of housing loans in the City. In October, 1975, it was cancelled, leaving the Mosque project with no source of financing. The Community

Development Block Grant program (CDBG) had been created by the federal government in 1974. These funds had just begun to come into the City, and we therefore had the opportunity to design a rehabilitation financing mechanism to replace the Municipal Loan Program.

The new program was the Participation Loan Program which structured a combination of resources to finance rehabilitation projects. During the period of construction, interim financing was to be provided by private commercial banks. Long-term financing would be provided jointly by savings banks and the City. The City would participate with CDBG funds, offered at an interest rate of 1 percent. The private funds would be loaned at market rate, then 9.5 percent. The combined interest rate to the homesteaders would work out to 5.5 percent.

The implementation of the Participation Loan Program as a replacement for the Municipal Loan Program began extremely slowly. It took over a year for all the parties representing three different banks, a government agency, the homesteaders, and UHAB to reach agreement on the financing and subsidies necessary to allow the Mosque to begin construction.

Finally, a loan commitment for $338,970 was made. Of this amount, two-thirds came from the City of New York and the balance was provided jointly by the New York Bank for Savings and the Bowery Savings Bank. Chemical Bank, a major commercial lending institution, took care of the interim financing for a projected 18-month construction period at an interest rate of 10 percent.

The loan works out to $20,000 per unit, including the commercial space, the religious meeting room, and the day-care center, or approximately $18 per square foot. This compares favorably with similar gut rehabilitation work going on at the same time in New York City that was running about $42,000 per dwelling unit, or $36 per square foot. The 50 percent saving is due to the low acquisition cost, the value of the sweat equity volunteer labor, and to the job training funds provided to the project.

No labor costs, except for small subcontracts for licensed tradesmen, were included in the project mortgage. The value of the CETA training funds provided to the Mosque was $495,934.

These funds allowed for the enrollment of 85 project workers. More than 35 of those trained in this program got regular jobs upon completion. (This is about equal to the national average for such training programs.)

Before construction finally began, a major problem resulting from the long period of negotiation arose with the CETA funding. The CETA contract had been negotiated and signed over a year before construction loan closing. It first ran out in August, 1977, and had to be extended twice, with significant additional funding. Although the Mosque's project was a single development, the two different sources of money, one for labor and one for materials, were extremely difficult to coordinate on a single time schedule. CETA funds were expended unproductively while the Mosque waited for the mortgage loan that would allow materials to be purchased. The administrative problems of managing federally funded job training programs are at times nightmarish.

Finishing the Job

Individuals from the Mosque spent untold extra hours working on their buildings. From beginning to end, they provided 24-hour guard service. This meant having someone sleep in the buildings each night, even before it was enclosed or heated. Every weekend was spent working on the buildings. The Mosque had extremely rigorous and demanding standards. During the entire course of the construction, they were improving layouts, upgrading the materials used in the buildings, and adding amenities. Items added included special entry doors, quality tile work, special paint jobs, exposed brick walls, spaces for individual washing machines in each kitchen, carefully laid and finished oak flooring, and apartments redesigned to fit the needs, and at times even the furniture of the future owner. This is the kind of work that a conventional developer would call uneconomical and unnecessary. A traditional job training program might not see it as useful training experience. But, for homeowners building their own space, it is a natural activity. For the members of the Mosque, rehabilitation was a full-time occupation for over 18 months.

By summer, 1978, the buildings were 90 percent complete. The final portions took a significantly longer time, a result

111

of the group becoming tired after a long period of tough construction work and becoming satisfied with new apartments that, although unfinished according to conventional standards, were quite habitable. The homesteaders began to move in January, 1979. Everyone involved with the project, and indeed everyone who has visited the buildings, is overwhelmed by the size of the apartments and the quality of the construction. The buildings have been occupied now for over three years. They are extremely well managed and immaculately maintained. They are current on all financial obligations to the City and the banks. Final monthly carrying charges for the cooperatively owned units do not exceed $280 for a four-bedroom apartment.

## Drawing Conclusions

Most of the Mosque's members are now fully employed, some in construction, others in the expanding small enterprises of the Mosque itself. The project as a training ground for unemployed persons has been successful. As a way to provide low-cost, quality housing, it is unmatched in the neighborhood. And perhaps, most importantly, it was a way for individuals to develop skills and self-confidence.

The project worked despite an organizational and administrative structure of appalling complexity. It took over four years from project conception to final occupancy. The resources of two local government agencies were required, as well as those of three different banking institutions. An additional five support organizations were involved in one way or another. Yet only 14 units were created in this project.

The complexity of the program as designed should not be seen as inherent in self-help efforts, but rather the result of very tentative government commitments, reflecting bureaucratic fears of the risks involved. And, indeed, there are many risks associated with the development of any self-help project. Some of them are economic: Will the project be affordable given the level of subsidy available? Over the long term, will the residents be able to manage and maintain the housing? Will family incomes rise as costs rise? There are also risks related to production: can inexperienced self-helpers really do extensive rehabilitation? Can CETA workers trained in this setting find jobs? Others relate to neighborhood conditions: can

8a,b. Tiles and moorish arches. Surely self-help is the only way to create Islamic housing in New York City.

the rehabilitation of one building generate supportive activities around it? Can it survive alone in the meanwhile? Finally, there are risks associated with the people themselves: will they lose their commitment? How will new people be integrated into the project? The Mosque answered these questions sufficiently well so that their project could ultimately succeed. The replicability of self-help efforts like the Mosque's is dependent on our ability to reduce these risks.

The first and foremost question to be confronted is economic. In 1974, when the Mosque project was planned, the average cost of self-help rehabilitation was $12,000 per dwelling unit. With a modest subsidy (in the form of a below market interest rate loan), this led to average monthly carrying charges of $130 per apartment, covering all maintenance, operating expenses, and debt service. Using the standard rule of thumb, this is affordable for families earning $6240 per year, and thus made economic sense for large portions of the population in our inner-city neighborhoods. By 1980, the cost of running a rehabilitated apartment, *exclusive of debt service,* had risen to $165 per month. The materials necessary for gut rehabilitation now cost $20,000. With the identical below market interest rate loan, a monthly charge of $280 is now required to carry the same apartment. This is too much for a family earning less than $13,000 per year. Yet, the median income for families in the same neighborhoods has not doubled from the $6000 figure of 1974. In order to make apartments available to these families, the level of subsidy must be increased three to four times. Of course, the inflation that has made self-help projects less feasible has also raised the marginal cost of subsidies.

The increased cost of subsidies does not affect self-help housing projects alone. All low income housing developments are having economic difficulty. New projects are difficult to start because of the layer upon layer of subsidy required to achieve feasibility. Older projects are in difficulty because of the astronomical rise in maintenance and energy costs. The limited resources allocated to subsidize housing must now serve significantly fewer units at far greater unit cost.

Self-help, however, still retains a number of cost advantages that are unique to cooperatively owned, self-run projects, and are true savings not attributable to subsidy. Foremost among these is the value of voluntary labor. This can reduce total development costs by as much as 50 percent. In addition, self-help homesteading projects eliminate much of the overhead and profit charged by general contractors. Because of cooperative ownership, overhead and profit can also be eliminated from management. Cooperatives show lower vacancy rates and turnover than other projects, further reducing costs. Finally, repair costs can be reduced because the knowledge gained by the future residents during construction leads to reduced reliance on outside personnel.

These cost advantages were one of the initial selling points for multifamily urban homesteading. Not only would the residents control the process from inception to completion, but they would not forever be dependent on unpredictable handouts. It was this notion of independence that encouraged participation and enticed wary government agencies to invest. However, the concept of self-sufficiency and independence must be carefully treated. It does not mean that affordable, quality housing can be created solely by the sweat of low income families. At times, conservative government housing agencies, disenchanted with conventional delivery systems and unhappy with the high cost of subsidy, have supported self-help because of a mistaken belief that this was possible.

Who can be against self-reliance and independence, especially when it costs less? But, as long as operating costs rise faster than people's incomes, the independence will be transitory.

The subsidies required to ensure economic success must be large enough to allow for a margin of error in the production process. They must be flexible enough to be applied to the vastly different requirements of each self-help group. The allocation and grant process must be quick enough so that people's energies are not drained by inordinate delay. Finally, they must come in a form that creates an incentive for involvement and encourages control of the entire process by the residents. Perhaps the best guarantee of the long-term success of a self-help project is not in the subsidy mechanism alone, but in the availability of jobs after training for the new cooperative owners. The Mosque's project had parallel goals of quality housing and skill training so that the owners will be permanently employable.

9. With its neat shop and well-cared for building, the Mosque of the Islamic Brotherhood hopes to be an example to the community.

The government support we need must have a similar direction: sufficient subsidy to ensure initial feasibility, and a commitment to neighborhood economic development so that jobs will be available.

A focus on the neighborhood is of critical importance to the success of urban homesteading projects. Each project, like the Mosque's, has begun without any public commitment to an overall neighborhood rebuilding strategy. We view each project as a starting point, anchoring committed individuals to the neighborhood, who then become advocates for additional rebuilding. Although the process is slow, every urban homesteading project has spawned similar efforts in adjacent buildings. For example, the Mosque is rehabilitating a nearby property. Other buildings in the area are now self-managed by tenants. And the neighborhood's potential has been recognized by conventional developers. A number of projects are being planned.

## Lessons from Self-Help

A program to rebuild our neighborhoods, thus restoring the infrastructure and creating jobs, is critically needed. A useful analog might be the original homesteading program in the western territories. The Homesteading Act of 1862 gave every family willing to occupy and farm it 160 acres of land. After a period of five years, they were given clear title. Success was extremely varied. Farmers in the eastern areas were extremely successful. The land was rich and sufficient water was available to ensure large crops. Further west, however, the land was dry and subject to the vagaries of yearly rainfall. Successful homesteaders in the western plains were significantly fewer until the government invested in dam-building and irrigation systems during the latter part of the 1800s. The cost and difficulty of installing those systems was far beyond the capacity of any single homesteader. Without massive subsidy and government support, individual attempts at self-help were doomed to failure.

If we create subsidies sufficiently large and flexible, and if individual housing projects are related to a neighborhood planning process, is success assured? What about the people themselves involved in such self-help efforts? Some would argue that self-help is only

possible for the young and energetic among the poor, the ones able to take on difficult construction work. Others contend that only unusually committed groups like the Mosque can succeed. Still others say that small-scale cooperative efforts, even within the context of a neighborhood development strategy, are doomed to failure for a variety of financial reasons—a lack of economy of scale being the foremost. A careful reading of the experience to date, however, refutes many of these arguments.

Self-help and urban homesteading, in the final analysis, means control of the housing process. That may range from participation in site selection, design, and the packaging of the project, to voluntary construction, and finally to ownership and self-management. Participation and control need not mean that one has to be young and healthy. What is needed in order to make self-help applicable to a wide range of people is a variety of entry points into the process. Control and participation can be created without ever picking up a hammer.

For example, much homesteading work in New York City is now focused on self-management in abandoned but occupied buildings. The City of New York has transferred the management of over 250 publicly-held properties to low income tenant associations. Many of the tenant managers are elderly, many are women, and some are on welfare. They are responsible for all the financial affairs of the building—hiring and firing contractors, arranging for repairs, collecting rent payments. They have proven to be enormously creative and successful. The quality of the housing is improving, and the level of user satisfaction with it.

Another innovation in New York focuses on the use of private contractors to do the bulk of actual reconstruction work in vacant buildings. The homesteaders are responsible for initial demolition and finish work. The contractors, often minority and neighborhood-based, do all structural work, carpentry, and subsystems installations. This reduces the burden of construction work, and allows working families to participate without giving up their jobs.

Finally, we come to the issue of the size of these projects. the Mosque project was average. Others UHAB has helped have ranged from three dwelling units to 30. There are a variety of reasons for cooperative housing tradi-

tionally focusing on large-scale developments. First, the amount of work necessary to package the financing for a project is often the same for 10 dwelling units or 1000 dwelling units. In addition, in a coop, the financial success of the project as a whole is dependent on each individual member. In a cooperative of five members, one person late with the monthly rent represents a loss of 20 percent of building income. In a large coop, the financial leverage of each individual is far less. Finally, the economies of housing production and maintenance work better at a large scale. Increased purchasing power leads to lower cost and better ability to withstand inflation.

Small-scale cooperatives have the potential, however, for real participation by the members. Everyone knows everyone else, and direct democracy is possible. The alienation that members of large cooperatives can feel is eliminated. The economies of scale that mark large-scale cooperatives can be developed also for small-scale projects. The notion is to create a series of *secondary coops:* small cooperatives banding together in order to generate the purchasing power of a larger project. Such secondary coop projects may focus on fire and liability insurance, fuel costs, and other items common to all. They may become support groups for administrative problems, and conceivably could share maintenance personnel. The potential of secondary cooperatives is just now being tested.

Self-help efforts similar to the Mosque's could be expanded rapidly. They need only the creation of adequate subsidy programs, the relation of individual projects to neighborhood planning efforts (including economic planning), and the development of government procedures that support local commitment. The combination of elements at work in a self-help housing project is complex: job skill development, the decentralization of housing control, cooperative ownership, an architectural design and constructions process directly controlled by the users, and the creation of a political awareness among neighborhood residents. It is this combination of objectives that makes self-help programs difficult. It is, however, this potential that makes them worthwhile.

# Mosque of the Islamic Brotherhood
# Multifamily Homesteading Project

## Project Summary

| | |
|---|---|
| Project sponsor | Mosque of the Islamic Brotherhood |
| Location | 55 St. Nicholas Avenue/132 West 113th Street New York, New York |
| Number of dwelling units | 14 |
| Number of commercial spaces | 3 |
| Total construction cost | $338,970 |
| Value of job training contracts | $495,934 |
| Total number of trainees | 85 |

## Development Costs

| Item | Cost |
|---|---|
| Materials | $253,160 |
| Land acquisition | 2,000 |
| Construction interest and financing fees | 34,293 |
| Architectural and professional services | 19,000 |
| Miscellaneous development costs | 30,517 |
| TOTAL | $338,970 |
| Cost per unit | $19,939 |
| Cost per square foot | $18 |

## Project Financing

| | |
|---|---|
| City of New York mortgage | $201,038 |
| Private mortgage | 137,932 |
| TOTAL COST | $338,970 |
| Monthly carrying charge per two-bedroom apartment | $240.00/month |

## Sweat Equity Urban Homesteading
## Status Report
## May, 1980

### Total Number of Projects

|  | Projects | Dwelling Units |
|---|---|---|
| Occupied | 23 | 233 |
| In construction | 11 | 97 |
| In planning | 13 | 97 |
| TOTAL | 47 | 427 |

Only projects where construction is expected to begin within four months are included. The projects include an additional 18 commercial spaces and community rooms. Over 13 different neighborhood organizations have been sponsors.

### Location of Projects by Borough

| | |
|---|---|
| Manhattan | 29 |
| Brooklyn | 13 |
| Bronx | 5 |

Neighborhoods include the Lower East Side, Harlem, East Harlem, and Clinton in Manhattan, Williamsburg and Oceanhill-Brownsville in Brooklyn, and Morrisania in South Bronx.

### Public Financing of Projects

|  | Projects | Dwelling Units | Aggregate Amount |
|---|---|---|---|
| Municipal Loan | 11 | 160 | $2,171,177 |
| Section 312 loans | 18 | 130 | 3,260,800 |
| CDBG loan | 18 | 137 | 2,701,361 |
| TOTAL | 47 | 427 | $8,133,338 |

Municipal loans were provided by a New York City bond financing program with an interest rate of 8 percent for 30 years. Section 312 loans are direct Federal loans with terms of 3 percent for 20 years. CDBG loans are made available under the Community Development Block Grant at a rate of 1 percent for 30 years.

117

# Commentary on UHAB/Self-Help

Tony Schuman, architect, New Jersey
School of Architecture

## THE AGONY AND THE EQUITY

Criticism of self-help is a heretical undertaking in the context of Western moral and social thought. Who can offer anything but encouragement to those who, neglected by both the private market and inadequate public programs, provide shelter for themselves and their families by the sweat of their brows? But a problem arises when this individual solution to the housing question is elevated to programmatic dimensions, suggesting wide applicability and success on a mass scale.

The scope of self-help activity is broad, ranging from tenant management to development and sponsorship of rehabilitation and new construction. The two programmatic ideas common to most forms of self-help housing—a desire to reduce costs and to guarantee security of tenure—are clearly combined in the project described by Charles Laven of UHAB. As UHAB's sophisticated efforts serve as models for similar programs in many cities, it is worthwhile to look carefully at the pitfalls and shortfalls of its sweat equity approach.

## BENEFITS OF SELF-HELP

There are four potential benefits claimed for self-help housing:

1. Reduced construction and operating costs resulting from the donated labor of the participants in construction (and eventual maintenance) and the use of public subsidies to produce below-market mortgage interest rates.
2. Employment and skills training. Residents working under the supervision of experienced builders learn skills useful in building maintenance and are prepared for employment in the construction industry.
3. Control of urban land. With the housing shortage forcing rents upward and making working class neighborhoods ripe for redevelopment, cooperative ownership offers the hope of retaining a part of the housing stock for low and moderate income families.
4. Strengthening of community and individual identity. The effort required to carry out a rehabilitation project in the face of adverse economic conditions, bureaucratic delays, and inevitable construction snags are powerful molders of consciousness and self-esteem. The process serves to decommodify both labor power and housing, providing an opportunity for dignified work whose product is appropriated directly by the workers. Self-help housing also offers design flexibility and, hence, is capable of meeting the needs of unusual groups like the Sunni Moslems described by Laven, who cannot easily be served by conventional housing.

## PITFALLS

All of these potential benefits have been realized to some extent in every self-help project, and this is the great merit of the approach. At the same time, however, each has also revealed serious problems. The problematic aspects can be explored by reference to the benefits described above.

1. Reduced costs. Recent trends indicate that the gap between housing costs and income continues to grow. From 1973 to 1977, rents rose nationally 9.6 percent per year, while incomes rose only 5.6 percent. The picture is even bleaker for UHAB in New York City, where median rents rose 23 percent between 1975 and 1978, with only a 7 percent rise in median income. Inflation in construction materials, interest rates, and fuel oil prices suggest the situation will only worsen in the near future. The net result is that those who need it most are increasingly unable to afford even self-help housing, despite the reduction in initial costs and the economies involved in cooperative management.

   There is no reason to believe that the gap between income and housing costs will narrow. On the contrary, the historical inability to correlate costs and incomes indicates that the discrepancy is a structural aspect of capitalism, viewed as a long-term secular trend. Because housing costs are affected much more by mortgage rates than by construction costs, sweat labor itself is unable to solve the dilemma posed by the rent-income gap. As a result, self-help housing is heavily dependent on government loan subsidies. Neither the economic nor the political climate suggests that these subsidies will soon be available in sufficient quantity. At least one self-help advocate now acknowledges, "We are getting blown out of the water by costs."

2. Employment. The potential benefits are restricted at the outset to the younger and more energetic of the poor. Excluded are the elderly, the disabled, women with child care responsibilities, and employed people who could not support themselves and their families on the modest stipends provided to self-help labor through the CETA program.

   For the participants in self-help, training in the building trades offers little beyond its eventual application in building maintenance. With the construction industry in difficult straits, and the minority groups who are most active in self-help housing largely excluded by racism, there is little likelihood that self-help training will lead to permanent employment.

   It has been argued that there are more than enough potential construction jobs available in rehabilitating the housing stock of our beleaguered cities. The idea is appealing for both economic and social reasons. However, there are several substantial obstacles to realizing such a program on more than a token scale. First, there would be substantial competition from the construction unions wanting a piece of the action. Second, if the rehabilitated housing is to meet the social goal of sheltering low and moderate income people, it would require deep operating subsidies and a commitment to the right of people to remain in their communities regardless of their status in the economy. This last concern goes right to the heart of the question of control of urban land.

3. Control of Urban Land. The sum total of sweat housing in New York, currently some 583 apartments in 50 buildings, is negligible compared with the wave of coop conversions and gentrified brownstones that are transforming the class and racial character of New York's older neighborhoods. In more remote and derelict communities, like the South Bronx and Central Brooklyn, where gentry fear to tread, a policy of "planned shrinkage" has been proposed to spur outmigration of poor residents. From an accounting standpoint, this would rid the city of dependent, service-consuming tenants and open up vast tracts of land for redevelopment.

What is at issue here is the very definition of a city. While community residents see the city as a place to live, work, raise children, and pursue their educational, cultural, and recreational needs, the private sector sees the city as an opportunity for investment, a locus for the accumulation of capital. In this context, the ability of the urban poor to remain in the city at all depends on their willingness to subsidize their own existence. Self-help housing cannot compete with private interests. A few buildings may be salvaged, but urban land is controlled by capital.

4. Community and Individual Identity. Self-help housing is an intense, energizing, and creative undertaking. In the absence of public and private support, community residents have taken a stand in defense of their communities. People have been "reborn" in a socially–conscious and collective manner. Newly rehabilitated buildings stand as rays of hope amid piles of rubble.

The impact of the experience on its participants is difficult to measure, and varies widely from group to group. The most passionate advocate of self-help is the English architect John F. C. Turner, whose book *Freedom to Build* has been a bible for the movement. His view stresses the values of autonomy, self-sufficiency, and decentralization, and suggests that self-help housing is an expression of individual liberty. Adherents of this viewpoint present optimistic assessments of the process, and support the concept with a fervor approaching "sweat ecstasy." There is an implicit assumption that small communities can be sustained internally and *independently of larger economic and political forces.* The model calls for an expanding number of local efforts, leading to the eventual incorporation of similar communities in a new, self-governing network: society is transformed from the bottom up.

This view reflects both a populist orientation, distrustful of a government controlled by giant corporations, and a conservative anarchist perspective, distrustful of centralizing tendencies in large-scale organizations. Unfortunately, self-help frequently works at cross purposes to its goals. There is an inherent tendency in self-help to reduce the value of labor power and to have a depressant effect on wages, despite a general agreement that the maldistribution of income is a primary source of our housing problems to begin with. The willingness of self-help workers to labor for low wages, or even without compensation at all, competes with the demand for an adequate living wage.

By assuming the burden of providing shelter for themselves, self-help groups reduce pressure on government to maintain its legitimacy by correcting the failures of the private market with social programs. This implicit willingness to manage the contradictions of the capitalist housing market is sometimes acknowledged explicitly, for example, by Rod Hackney in his account of the Black Road project in England.

The precarious financial picture of self-help housing has led more than one community group to enter joint venture agreements with private investors through the sale of equity shares, a process discussed by John Sharratt in his report on the Mission Hill and Villa Victoria projects in Boston. The joint venture approach, while outside the pure sweat model, demonstrates the pressures to conform to the private market for housing. While no neighborhood group can be faulted for seeking crucial financial assistance, there is at least an element of irony in the attempt to solve housing problems by reinforcing the tax shelter and investment mechanisms that maintain a housing system based on profit rather than need.

If the pitfalls of self-help housing are predominantly economic in nature, the shortfalls stem from its failure to challenge the structure of the economy. The root of the dilemma is the privatization of the housing questions, the attempt to solve a collective problem on an individual basis.

## SHORTFALLS

Because the housing question arises from the disparity between housing costs and income, there are three logical means of addressing the problem: raise wages, lower costs, or subsidize the difference. As self-help groups complete the construction phase and take on the management and maintenance of their housing, the underlying economic problems come to the fore. It is especially instructive, therefore, to see how the groups approach the question of maintaining financial solvency.

Because self-help groups tend to view the housing problem as lying outside the labor market, the issue of wage levels and income distribution is generally not addressed. Most efforts focus on easing the size and terms of the mortgage itself. In this light, the most encouraging development in self-help housing circles is the recent call for permanent operating subsidies. This demand at least acknowledges the existence of the cost-income gap. The underlying premise is that rents should be based on income—an obvious point of unity with all low and moderate income tenants. The idea is hardly radical. Both public housing and HUD Section 8 subsidies were based on the principle that tenants should not have to pay more than 20 or 25 percent of income in rent.

The demand for permanent operating subsidies is attractive for several important reasons. The first of these is that it is national in scope and addresses the housing problems of millions of needy families in addition to the relatively small number engaged in self-help. The subsidy demand also calls into question two prevalent notions: that subsidies are only for the poor and that ownership equals control. The present beneficiaries of federal housing subsidies are overwhelmingly middle to upper income investors, landlords, and homeowners, not low income housing consumers. The principal vehicle for federal subsidy is the income tax system that offers deductions to owners for local taxes and interest payments and gives housing investors generous allowances for depreciation. These indirect subsidies are geared to reinforcing the unequal distribution of income under capitalism.

The link between ownership and control is more complicated. Self-help groups are hostile not only to private-for-profit ownership of housing but also to public ownership. But the obvious alternative to indifferent public agencies or rapacious land-lords—control through cooperative housing—will turn out to be an illusion if residents cannot meet rising carrying costs. The independence which makes self-help housing so attractive is seriously compromised by hard economic reality.

## A STRATEGIC ROLE

Despite its shortcomings, self-help is a useful training ground for housing activists. Participants are brought into direct confrontation with market forces and financing mechanisms. In this sense, it is precisely because self-help doesn't "work" as a solution that it has potential. The fighting spirit of self-help housers couples with their manifest commitment to their neighborhoods and leads them to defend their physical and emotional investments. The self-help groups must inevitably take the lead in pressing for the targeting of *existing* housing subsidies for buildings in not-for-profit cooperative, community, or public ownership. They will also be the forefront of the demand for vastly increased housing subsidies, having demonstrated that hard work alone cannot overcome the failure of the private market. And the demand for permanent operating subsidies socializes the housing question. It insists that housing is a necessity and not a luxury and therefore must be treated as a public good and not as a commodity.

It has been argued by some that advocacy of self-help is a dangerous diversion, shunting attention from the structural aspects of the housing problem into a bottomless pit of small-scale self-exploitation. To the extent that self-help is seen as a solution to the housing question, these fears are well grounded. But in the absence of a mass movement for decent housing as a public responsibility, self-help is a valuable starting point.

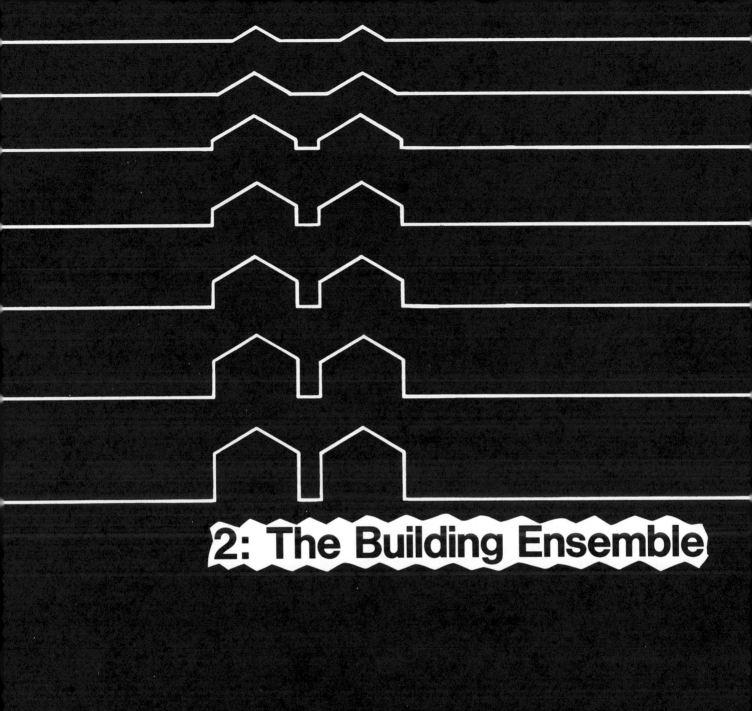

# 2: The Building Ensemble

# Cluster Housing
# Mexicali, Mexico

Christopher Alexander's Mexicali project—the construction of five houses in northern Mexico—represents the first practical application of his complete theory. In his earlier work, which culminated in the publication of *A Pattern Language*, Alexander and his co-workers concentrated on the development of a mode of analysis and communication which would permit fruitful collaboration between users and architects. The subtitle of that influential book is *Towns·Buildings·Construction*, and implies that users' involvement in the creation of environments should extend beyond design. Now in this report, Alexander tells how five families came together in a new institution, the builder's yard, to work side by side with architect-constructors to make their own houses, guided by a pattern language which was their joint creation.

The story of the project and the changes it wrought in the lives of the participants are deeply moving. Alexander himself has said that when he looks back upon the tiny community that was created, he is "filled with something which is as close to a religious feeling that any social act in our society can bring me to. Here are these five families . . . They have become powerful, and are powerful, in a way which almost takes the breath away." In the Commentary that follows, Karl Linn and Alex Tzonis define the kind of political society Alexander's process implies, and translate the experience in Mexico into terms useful in our own country.

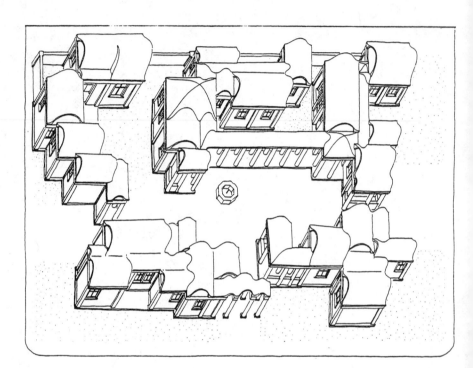

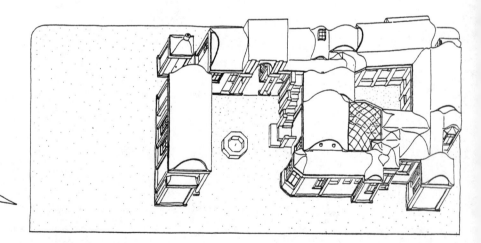

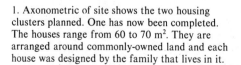

1. Axonometric of site shows the two housing clusters planned. One has now been completed. The houses range from 60 to 70 m². They are arranged around commonly-owned land and each house was designed by the family that lives in it.

# The Production of Houses*

Christopher Alexander, Howard Davis,
Julio Martinez, Don Corner
Center for Environmental Structure
Berkeley

In the modern world, the idea of beauty, the idea that houses can be loved and beautiful, has been eliminated almost altogether. For most of the world's housing, the task of building houses has been reduced to a grim business of facts and figures, an uphill struggle against the relentless surge of technology and bureaucracy in which human feeling has almost been forgotten. Even in those few houses which openly concern themselves with their appearance, beauty also has been forgotten. What happens there is something remote from feeling, an almost disgusting concern with opulence, with the taste of the marketplace, with fashion. There too, the simple values of the human heart do not exist.

The real meaning of beauty—the idea of houses as places which express one's life directly and simply, the connection between the vitality of people and the shape of their houses, the connection between the force of social movements and the beauty and vigor of the places where people live—this is all forgotten, vaguely remembered as the elements of some imaginary golden age.

Yet strangely, little of the literature on so-called "housing" and few of the efforts being made today are trying to bring these things into the world again. There is a great deal of concern about the price of houses. There is a vast concern with the millions of homeless people on the earth. There is a widespread concern with industry and technology and the ways in which these can help to solve the so-called housing problem. There is concern with the importance of "self–help." There is concern with political control of people over their neighborhoods. But all this is strangely

*This article is taken from the preface and introductory chapter of a book with the same title that describes in detail a project embodying a new form of housing production that was carried out in Mexicali, Mexico by the Center for Environmental Structure in 1975–76. The article is printed with permission of Oxford University Press. © 1982 Christopher Alexander

abstract, without feeling. It deals with the issues, but it glides over them. It does not concern itself with feeling; it creates a mental framework in which solutions are as mechanical and as unfeeling as the problems they set out to solve.

We recognize the value of many of the efforts people are making to solve "the housing problem," but we are concerned, here, with the feeling at the root of it. We have tried to construct a housing process in which human feeling and human dignity come first, in which the housing process is reestablished as the fundamental human process in which people integrate their values and themselves, in which they form social bonds, in which they become anchored in the earth, in which the houses that are made have, above all, human worth, in the simple, old-fashioned sense that people feel proud and happy to be living in them and would not give them up for anything because they are *their* houses, because they are the product of *their* lives, because the house is everything to them—the concrete expression of *their* place in the world, the concrete expression of themselves.

To be clear, we have chosen to illustrate this process with one particular project we have built recently in northern Mexico. In this particular Mexican example, the houses have an area of 60 to 70 square meters, they are arranged around common land owned jointly by the families. Each house is designed by the family that lives in it, and is therefore different from the others. The houses are built from interlocking soil cement blocks, produced by us in our own yard, and have ultralightweight concrete vaults built over a lightweight woven wood basket. They cost about 40,000 pesos each, which was equivalent to some $3,000 U.S. dollars at the time of construction.

However, the specific details of our Mexican project are quite unimportant. What matters is the system—our seven general principles. These principles con-

cern the overall organization of a production process, the relation between people and the design of the houses, the fact that the houses are planned by the families themselves, the fact that there is a new kind of architect guiding and managing the process, and the fact that construction is undertaken, and money controlled, in an entirely new way.

We believe that these principles apply to all kinds of housing, in all parts of the world. They are independent of the particular construction details that are used. They apply equally to houses that are expensive and to houses like ours which are very cheap. They apply equally to houses which the people help to build for themselves, as they have done in our Mexican project, or to houses which people design for themselves and then have built for them by professional builders. They apply equally to houses built at low densities of two to four houses per acre, or to houses built at medium densities of 15 per acre like those in our Mexican project, or even to houses built at much higher densities, of 60 per acre in complexes four stories high.

The single largest element of our environment is that created by our houses, or by "housing." Today, most of this "housing" is produced by mass means. That is, it consists of hundreds of houses produced by one form or another of semi-automatic process—either the repetitive construction of tract houses, or the repetitive construction of apartments in apartment buildings.

There is no doubt that the alienation and despair which many people feel is created in large part by the depressing burden of this "mass housing" in which people are forced to spend their lives. It is commonly assumed that mass housing is essential in our time since it is not possible to produce houses in sufficient numbers, or to produce houses cheaply enough, without resort to "mass housing." And, finally, it is assumed that it is indeed necessary for us to go further and further in this direction in order to solve the problems of housing shortage felt by most countries in the world.

## Today's Housing Systems

If we consider the systems of housing production which exist in the world today, we find that almost all of them lack two necessities fundamental to any human society.

> First, recognition of the fact that every family, and every person, is unique, and must be able to express that uniqueness.

> Second, recognition of the fact that every family, and every person, is part of society and requires bonds of association with other people.

These two complementary necessities are almost entirely missing from today's houses. On the one hand, the houses are identical, machine–like, stamped out of a mold, and almost entirely unable to express the individuality of different families. They suppress whatever is wonderful and special about any one family. On the other hand, the houses also fail, entirely, to give people a basis for small, local congregation. The houses, placed and built anonymously, express isolation and lack of relationship. They fail altogether to help create human bonds in which people feel themselves part of the fabric which connects them to their fellow men.

We must recognize, to start with, that the houses in any society are always given their character by the system of production which produces them. If the character of the houses is inadequate, as it certainly is today, then it can only be improved by modifying this system of production.

At any given moment, the system of housing production is a coherent system. It is not designed by any one person or group of people. But it is, nevertheless, a system—a system of rules, habits, laws, and accepted procedures, taken for granted throughout society, and responsible for the production of most of the houses in society.

Although there is no one institution responsible for the invention of this system, still, the process which the system embodies is in no way informal. It is highly organized; indeed, so highly organized, that any departure from the

system is likely to lead to almost interminable difficulties, delays, objections. . . . In fact, only a trickle of nonconforming houses can be built outside the system in any given year.

Like all systems, the system of production is always recognizable by its products, that is to say, by the *form* of housing which it produces. For example, the housing production system currently most widespread in the United States is the one which is called "tract development:" it can be recognized, exactly, by the tracts which it produces. Within this system, developers buy land, develop roads, and then build houses, more or less identical, in quantities of hundreds at a time. These houses are owned by individual families; they have private lots. The process is based on the existence of federally-insured bank programs which lend money on these kinds of houses and on the tax incentives which encourage families to make these kinds of purchases. The houses are designed, ahead of time, as "model homes," on the drawing board. The model houses are then built, many times over, by contractors, working with crews of specialized labor, themselves most often working as subcontractors. The construction techniques emphasize speed; many of the construction workers are novices, working essentially for money, not for the love of what they build. All this, ramified throughout society, in a million details—in what can be bought in a hardware store, in what a subcontractor can legally do, in the forms of management approved by the state licensing board for contractors and architects—all this together forms the system of production which produces some 400,000 houses per year in the United States alone.

Another common system of housing production, more widespread throughout the world, is the system which produces publicly–financed apartment houses in France, Sweden, the USSR, and many other countries. In this system, apartment houses are built for the government by developers (either private or government controlled); the individual dwellings are identical "cells" arranged in several stories of apartments, the cells typically smaller than houses. It is taken for granted that the apartments will later be rented by families who have nothing to do with the process of their production. Again there is a well-developed system of loans for this type of housing, again the contract-

ing procedures, the title transfers, the loan execution, the process of advertising, the legal form of rental, are all institutionalized, in more or less similar form, throughout the world. This process of production is even more widespread than the process we call "tract development." Families do not have the right to change their dwellings, they cannot undertake any form of improvement, they do not have security of tenure, they have to get permission for any change from management. Apartments are identical, because they come from a standard set of drawings.

*We assert, categorically, that neither tract houses nor these apartment houses can be made more human merely by "improving their design" so long as the underlying systems of production which create them remain unchanged. . . .*

Of course, it is true that in either one of these systems the designs of the buildings can be made *slightly* more intelligent, *slightly* more respectful of human needs, *slightly* more personal in feeling. *However, the alienated character of the buildings which are produced is, in the end, a direct consequence of the deep structure of their production systems—and this character cannot be substantially improved until the systems themselves are altered at the roots.*

## Developing the Biological View

The arguments which have led us to this conclusion have been presented, during the last few years, in a series of books. Volume 1, *The Timeless Way of Building,* provides a fundamental analysis of the adaptation between people and buildings, and shows that the human environment can only come to order under circumstances similar to those which existed in most traditional societies, where people are directly responsible for shaping their environment, and where they also have the necessary common "pattern languages" which make it possible for them to cooperate in producing a coherent structure.

Volume 2, *A Pattern Language,* gives one example of a detailed language of the type called for in *The Timeless Way of Building.* It specifies patterns at a wide range of scales, including the largest patterns of a city, the detailed patterns which govern the layout of land and buildings, the patterns which govern the shapes of rooms, and patterns which govern the construction details. The families who designed the

## Table of Housing Operations
## (Prices and Maximum Allowed Quantities)

| Operation | Units | Price/Unit | Maximum Allowed Per m² | Price/m² | Percentage of Total |
|---|---|---|---|---|---|
| 1. Layout and Tools | 1 | 2800 | | $ 42 (Mexican) | 7 |
| 2. Excavation | m² | 8.3/m² | 1.00 | 8 | 1 |
| 3. Cornerstones | # | 26.6@ | .53 | 14 | 2 |
| 4. Wall Foundation | m¹ | 19.2/m | 1.05 | 20 | 3 |
| 5. Slab Preparation | m² | 9/m² | .77 | 7 | 1 |
| 6. Underslab Plumbing | 1 | 600 | | 9 | 2 |
| 7. Slab | m² | 18/m² | .77 | 14 | 2 |
| 8. Columns | # | 41@ | .53 | 22 | 4 |
| 9. Walls | m¹ | 93/m | .97 | 90 | 15 |
| 10. Door Frames | # | 120@ | .08 | 10 | 2 |
| 11. Perimeter Beams | m¹ | 30/m | 1.10 | 33 | 6 |
| 12. Roof Basket | m² | 38/m² | 1.00 | 38 | 6 |
| 13. Gable Ends | # | 112@ | .08 | 9 | 2 |
| 14. Electrical Circuits | rooms | 110/room | .10 | 11 | 2 |
| 15. Roof First Coat | m² | 66/m² | 1.00 | 66 | 11 |
| 16. Roof Top Coat | m² | 44/m² | 1.00 | 44 | 8 |
| 17. Window Frames | m² | 121/m² (windows) | .18 | 22 | 4 |
| 18. Windows | m² | 148/m² | .18 | 27 | 5 |
| 19. Doors | # | 250@ | .08 | 20 | 3 |
| 20. Plumbing Fixtures | 1 | 3300 | | 50 | 9 |
| 21. Electrical Fixtures | rooms | 85/room | .10 | 8 | 1 |
| 22. Painting | m² | 10/m² | 1.94 | 19 | 3 |
| 23. Paving | m² | 20/m² | .30 | 6 | 1 |
| | | | | $ 589 (Mexican) | |

This Table of Housing Operations was prepared by Alexander and his associates and used by the families in the Mexicali project to make cost estimates at every stage in the design process. It is also a guide to the step-by-step operations that order the construction work.

houses and common land in our Mexicali project did so using this pattern language.

Volume 3, *The Oregon Experiment,* describes the way that a community of 15,000 people (The University of Oregon) is now using a pattern language to govern the planning of its communal land and buildings, and the administrative procedures which make this possible. This experiment has been going on for five or six years now, and is improving all the time as the process matures.

Another volume, *The Linz Cafe,* describes a public building recently built in Austria, which embodies many of the ideals of *The Timeless Way of Building,* and shows, in a simple case, what such a building really can be like in our time, and at a reasonable cost.

All of the books published so far, implicitly (though not explicitly) point out that the production process which produces an environment is given its fundamental character by its internal distribution of control. That is, each production process is a human system which distributes control over decisions in a certain manner.

Some kinds of distribution of control work well to produce very beautifully organized, orderly, and lovely environments in which people feel satisfied. Other kinds of distribution of control work badly; they produce environments in which there are abundant mistakes, failures of adaptation, impersonal expenditures, in which money is spent by the wrong people, in the wrong place, at the wrong time. But in every case, the key to the success or failure of the system lies in the *way* that control is distributed. Above all, it is this that determines the quality of the environment.

*The argument which leads to this conclusion is, in essence, biological.* To understand it, let us compare the housing projects that today make up a major part of our man-made world with any typical part of the biological world—a forest, a plant, an organism, an ocean. In the biological world, there is always an immense complexity, and this complexity comes about as a result of a process of minute adaptation, which, painstakingly, slowly, ensures that every part is properly adapted to its conditions.

In this sense, even though, of course, biological systems are all imperfect, there is nevertheless an extraordinary extent to which each part, each form, is "correct," in which each decision, each peculiarity of form required by local adaptation, is "just right." The system contains huge numbers of variables, huge numbers of components. And the process which produces it, the living process of adaptation which is typical in all biological systems, guarantees that each part is as nearly as possible "just right," appropriate to its local conditions, and appropriate in the large, so that it also functions well as part of some system larger than itself.

On the other hand, if we compare a modern "housing project" with a typical part of the biological world, the contrast is stark. Where the biological system shows minute and lovely adaptation at every point and at every level, the typical housing project shows a high level of disastrous failures of adaptation. The houses are "just wrong" in almost every way that matters, even though they are often thought out in broad general terms which should make sense.

A biological system is able to achieve its sensitive and complex adaptations, because control over the shape of components is widely distributed at a great many levels throughout the organism. For instance, in an animal, major arrangement of limbs is under one level of genetic control; location of organs is controlled at a lower level by a lower-level center; the detailed form of organs—for instance the exact shape of the lung wall—is controlled by the hormones at the level of the tissue itself; clusters of cells are controlled at an-

The Mexicali project proposes seven principles for the design and construction of proper houses (the descriptions are Alexander's):

1. *The Principle of the Architect-Builder.* The subtlety of the designs which come from different families . . . can only be made if there is a direct process where the elements are decided on the site. . . . The great complexity needed by a human settlement cannot be transmitted via paper, and the separation of functions between architect and builder is therefore out of the question.

2. *The Principle of the Builder's Yard.* The architect-builders of a small community have their base of operations in a builder's yard, a place that combines the functions of workshop and material storage, that is a demonstration of the local building system, and that can be used to make experiments and refine it. The builder's yard, once it is working, becomes the nucleus of growth and development and repair of the entire surrounding community. It is a permanent place in the community.

3. *The Principle of House Clusters.* The cluster is a well-defined social and physical entity . . . and the buildings open from this common land and not from the street outside so that the common land forms a transition between the public street and the individual house . . . it is more like a courtyard or enclosed garden with its own distinctive character . . . . The cluster is at the same time a product—a social reality that exists after the construction is finished—and the organ of production itself. It is the unit of production, the living cell through which the process of design and construction realizes itself. Families who form the cluster have active social relations with one another from the start.

4. *The Principle of Individual House Design.* The uniqueness of each family is clear from the house it designs. Here is an example:

Lilia [Duran] and her husband, Jesus, who is a barber, had only one child, about two years old, when they started construction. Their daughter is everything to them; they protect her, love her, and in the finished house, she is, metaphorically and literally, at the center. The house is the smallest of the five and shaped like a Greek cross, with a family room in the middle of the cross, and their daughter's bed, in an alcove, right off the family room, at the heart of everything, where "they can watch her." The house is small, because the Durans hope to build a barbershop one day for Jesus—and so decided to save their money. And between the place right next to the cluster's entrance—where they hope to put the barbershop one day—and the front door of the house, there is an immense porch, similar to the one Lilia had in her house while she was growing up.

5. *The Principle of Step-by-Step Construction.* The construction system is not defined by a system of "standard details" nor by a system of "components," but is instead defined by a system of operations to be performed one after the other in sequence. The individual steps or "operations" are so defined that they can be applied freely to any plan with certain minimal constraints and will, when properly executed, make a complete and structurally sound building from that plan.

The process is therefore capable of organizing the mass production of a large number of buildings which are all entirely different down to the smallest details of layout; yet the order of the process is capable of maintaining firm discipline, schedule control, and cost control within the project. Further, the individual steps of the process are chosen to be simple enough so that members of the family, friends, and paid, unskilled laborers can help to any desired degree, or even complete the process by themselves, under the supervision of the architect-builder in charge.

6. *The Principle of Cost Control.* [See the Table of Housing Operations on the preceding page—Editor] Our experience has shown that with our system of cost control it is possible to hold the prices of the buildings to a firm cost per square meter that is lower than the typical square meter cost for housing of comparable finish. The secret of this cost control system is that it is perfectly congruent with the system of operations. It is based on these operations, it follows these operations, it makes sense in terms of these operations. Thus the backbone of the entire cost control system lies in the close connection between the operations defined above and the cost accounts.

These figures are reliable enough so that we can make a detailed estimate of the price of each house simply as a function of its area. The estimate is reliable enough for us, as the contractors, to use it as a bid. As a result, even though the houses are all different, we were able to make a detailed cost estimate for the bank the moment the houses were laid out.

7. *The Principle of Human Rhythm.* Finally, of course, the architect-builders are responsible for guiding the actual process of construction. And the process itself is carried out as a human rhythm while design and construction are going on. And it is lived as a continuing, ongoing rhythm once the houses are finished. Even when the houses are finished, the same process which has created them then extends into the lives of their occupants. The process not only builds the houses, but repairs them. The houses are never finished; they exist, in an imperfect state, constantly changing and improving, just as we ourselves also exist in an imperfect state, constantly struggling to improve ourselves.

. . . The essence of the process with the families is a human thing. On the one hand we have to be sure that they understand how much work they have to do and that they will do it. On the other hand, we also have to convey to them that it is a circus, a party, a wonderful time.

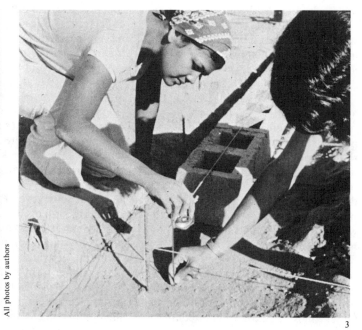

All photos by authors

2

3

4

5

6

7

*Step-by-step construction* in Mexicali:

2. The cluster was designed by the families using stakes to mark the location of the houses and the form of the common space. The pattern language was used as a guide.

3. Next the wall foundations were laid using blocks made on site in the builder's yard.

4. After the floor slab was poured, columns of interlocking soil cement blocks were erected. Note reinforcing rods.

5. Simple block walls span between columns. Each individually-designed house begins to take shape.

6. Porches and door frames go up next. The building technology selected permits family members to participate fully in the construction of their houses—and to enlarge or modify them later on.

7. After the perimeter beams have cured, the wood roof basket is put in place, ready to receive its two coats of dense concrete.

other level; and the fine tuning and arrangement of individual cells is controlled, at least in part, by a homeostatic process at the level of the cells themselves. *In short, there is fine grain control over the details of the organism at every level, just where it is needed to produce the right result.* It is this fact, above all, which is responsible for the beautiful and subtle adaptation of the parts which form the whole.

By contrast, the production systems which produce housing in the modern world are too centralized: there is insufficient control at the levels which should control detail. And if we ask ourselves why modern housing in the world is so often "just wrong," instead of just right, we shall quickly see that the failures of adaptation are caused, most often, by the fact that the decisions which control the form of the houses are almost all made at a level too remote from the immediate people and sites to allow reasonable and careful adaptation to specific details of everyday life. Most of the processes which govern the shape of the houses and their parts are controlled at levels of government, or levels of industry, or levels of business, which are remote from the minute particulars of the house and family itself . . . so that, inevitably, they create alien and abstract forms, bearing only the most general relationship to the real needs, real demands, real daily minute–to–minute reality, which the members of the household experience.

Of course, all this abstract, arm's length control of the housing process is typically justified by the argument that low cost and high volume production require it. It is argued that even if the machine of industry and the machine of development are incapable of paying attention to the local particulars which proper adaptation, and which proper biological wholeness, would require— nevertheless these machines are still essential, still useful and efficient, because they can produce houses in such enormous quantities.

Let us repeat this more clearly. Present systems of production are organized in such a way that most decisions are made very much "at arm's length." Decisions are made by people remote from the consequences of the decisions. Architects make decisions about people whose faces they have never seen. Developers make decisions about land where they have never smelled the grass. Engineers make decisions about columns which they will never touch, nor paint, nor lean against. Government authorities make decisions about roads and sewers without having any human connection at all to the place about which they are making these decisions. The construction workers who nail the boards and lay the bricks have no power of decision at all over the details which they build. Children, who are going to play between houses have no power of decision at all, over even the sandpits where they are going to play.

Families move into houses which have been laid out "for" them and have no control whatever over the most fundamental and most intimate aspects of the plan in which they are going to live their lives.

In short, the production systems which we have at present define a pattern of control which makes it almost impossible for things to be done carefully, or appropriately, because *almost without exception* decisions are in the wrong hands, decisions are being made at levels far removed from the immediate concrete places where they have impact . . . and, all in all, there is a colossal mismatch between the organization of decision and control and the needs for appropriateness and good adaptation which the biological reality of the housing system actually requires.

*If we are to put this situation right, to bring our production systems into order, we must therefore concentrate, essentially, on this human problem of the distribution of control. What we must find is a system of production which is capable of giving detailed, careful, at-*

8. With the application of the second coat of lightweight concrete the roof vaults are finished and the house completely enclosed. Windows and interior finishes are the next steps.

9. Paving is the final operation, creating the private patios and the cluster's common space. In accordance with the *Principle of Human Rhythm* which states that the construction of houses must be a joyous affair, the conclusion of each operation is marked by a group celebration.

8

9

*tention to all the particulars which are needed to make each house "just right" at its own level, at its own scale, and which is yet at the same time efficient enough, replicable enough, and simple enough so that it can be carried out on an enormous scale, and at a very low cost.*

## Seven Principles of Housing

Specifically, we believe that there are seven forms of control—seven principles—which play a crucial role in the production proess. To identify these seven types of control, we may ask the following seven questions:

1. What kind of person is in charge of the building operation itself?
2. How local to the community is the construction firm responsible for building?
3. Who lays out and controls the common land between the houses and the array of lots and houses?
4. Who lays out the plans of individual houses?
5. Is the construction system based on assembly of standard *components,* or is it based on acts of creation, which use standard *processes?*
6. How is cost controlled?
7. What is the day-to-day life like, on site, during the construction operation?

We believe, very simply, that there is an objectively sensible answer to each one of these questions.

1. *What kind of person is in charge of the building operation itself?*

In today's production system, there is no one person in charge. There are various officials, architects, engineers, contractors, each one carrying out his duties, but without any one of them having an overall view of the whole. What results, inevitably, is a bureaucratic and inhuman situation in which feeling cannot prevail, because each person's feelings are submerged by the bureaucratic process.

However, for adaptation and control to be correct, it is possible to imagine a new kind of master builder, who controls all aspects of planning, design, and construction, in a very immediate way—but who has direct charge of no more than a few dozen houses at a time, with direct responsibility to the

10

10. The first cluster completed at Mexicali, seen from the road.

11. Paths and patios: the *Principles of Individual House Design and of Clusters* aim for a balance between community and privacy.

12. The architect-builders in the builder's yard celebrate the successful completion of the work with the five families and the group of Mexican architecture students who assisted.

11

12

families who are going to live in those houses, and with the power to respond directly to their wishes.

## 2. *How local to the community is the construction firm responsible for building?*

In today's production system, the actual contracting is most often carried out by large corporate combines, with offices and directors far from the neighborhood. Of course these men, and these organizations, cannot be responsive to the wishes of the neighborhood, nor to the individual families.

However, for proper adaptation to occur it is possible to imagine a system of decentralized builders' yards, one or more for each small neighborhood, every few blocks, each one responsible for the physical development of its local neighborhood. This is a human solution, which places control within reach of the people who are affected.

## 3. *Who lays out and controls the common land between the houses and the array of lots and houses?*

In today's production system, this is a process carried out in an entirely abstract manner. The city controls the common land between the houses. The administration responsible for the building project lays out this common land by assigning it to a draftsman. The subdivision of the land into lots, or apartments, is done by an official in an office entirely remote from the real situation. Inevitably, what is created by this process is inhuman and abstract.

However, for proper social connection between people and their community, it is possible to imagine a building process in which groups of families, of a size small enough so people can talk to each other and reach agreements, can themselves work in clusters, have control over their own common land, and lay out their own lots according to their own wishes. This is a human solution, which places control over the essential issues in the hands of the people who are most affected by these issues and who understand them best.

## 4. *Who designs the individual houses?*

In today's production system, the individual houses are most often designed by architects, remote from the people, often not even able to know the families

because very often the families have not yet been chosen; and the houses are designed to be standard—as well-designed as possible, of course—but essentially standard cells. This is bound to be inhuman. Families who are vastly different in their needs end up living in boxes designed for average families all with the same walls, the same windows, the same–shaped bedroom, the same–shaped kitchen.

However, it is possible to imagine a much more flexible process, in which families design their own houses or apartments, within a fixed cost limit, and with certain necessary ground rules, but in such a way that each house is a celebration of the spirit, a mark on the earth, of that family and its special story. These houses would not only be treasured by the families who designed them so long as they live there, but because they have a human touch, because they emerge from some specific human situation and have the touch of life to them, they will also be more human, more full of life, for any other family who comes to live there in the future.

## 5. *How are the construction details themselves actually produced?*

In today's production system, it has become common to expect houses to be assembled from mass-produced components. Some of these components are small, others are very large. But the variety which can be produced by mixing components is always still variety "within the system," which tyrannizes the design so that we have twenty different cells instead of one kind of cell, but they are still all cells, still all essentially the same.

However, to avoid the tyranny of parts over the whole, it is possible to imagine a system of construction, technically far more advanced, in which what is standard are the *operations* (tile setting, bricklaying, painting, spraying, cutting . . .), but where the actual size and shape of what is done can vary according to the feeling and requirements of the individual building. This is more human, because it allows the builders to make a work of art, which captures feeling and spirit.

## 6. *How is cost controlled?*

In today's production system, the importance of cost control is used to cen-

tralize as many operations as possible—design, construction, purchase of materials—and to drastically limit local initiative and prevent local spirit from entering the buildings.

However, to prevent cost control from inhibiting reasonable and careful design of individual buildings, it is possible to imagine a more flexible cost control system, one which benefits from local initiative, which allows each house to be made, step–by–step, within a fixed budget, but without controlling the exact way in which this budget is spent, thus allowing each house to be different, in the ways it needs to be, in order to satisfy the family.

## 7. *What is day-to-day life like on the site?*

In today's production system, the site, during actual building operations, is merely a place where "the job is being done." There is no special cause for happiness because houses are being built. None of the workers have any immediate connection with these houses, and no special pleasure in them: for them it is "just a job."

However, to overcome the vast alienation of these "housing projects," it is possible to imagine a much more human situation in which the spiritual importance of these houses becomes a real and effective daily part of life on the site, in which the families themselves contribute, as much or as little as they want to, and in which the construction process is a "house raising," a time of special importance for the families, lived through by the families and the builders together in a way that celebrates its happiness.

We believe that these seven principles of control together must govern any reasonable housing production system. This does not mean that there are not other, still larger questions capable of having even greater impact on the production process. For example, it is clear that the distribution of money in society, the flow of money for housing in the economy, the design and manufacture of building materials, and the political structure of local regions all have massive effects on the production of housing. In this sense, we certainly do not claim to have dealt with the totality of "the housing production system."

However, we do believe that the seven principles we have identified to-

13. Christopher Alexander says of the five families who participated in this house-building project:

They have made themselves solid in the world. They have shaped the world as they have shaped themselves. And they live now in the world they have created for themselves—changed, transformed, opened, free in their glory, stamping their feet, watching the water trickle through the common land, looking after their neighbors' children, waiting now to help friends take part in the same kind of process—on this piece of land or in another corner of the town.

They have become powerful, and are powerful, in a way which almost takes the breath away. They, they themselves, have created their own lives, not in that half-conscious underground, interior way that we all do, but manifestly, out there on their own land. They are alive. They breathe the breath of their own houses.

gether form the necessary core of any production system and must be present whether these other larger variables are changed or not. Even if other major social changes were to occur—in which the flow of money, the distribution of political power, and the nature of manufacturing were all to change—even then, we believe that those changes in themselves, would still not bring about an adequate approach to the production of houses *unless accompanied by these seven kinds of changes in the system of housing production.*

# Commentary on Mexicali

Karl Linn ASLA, New Jersey School of Architecture

## ADVENTURE CITIES

Each time I read Christopher Alexander's story about his Mexicali Project, I'm filled with a sense of both joy and concern. Alexander describes compassionately the engagement of five families in the building of their own dwellings clustered around a common area. I empathize and rejoice with Alexander as he was deeply moved when one participant told him:

... in words of almost inexplicable warmth and fervor that this was the most wonderful process he had ever experienced, that he had always a desire to work more, that he wanted to help the other families complete their houses ....

Whenever I hear of people's meaningful involvement in building their own habitat and the resulting sense of accomplishment, mastery, and dignity they experience, my sense of faith in the potential of such processes is renewed. Often enough in my own work over the last 20 years, I've witnessed a sense of community develop when people join forces to build a common environment. The potential that participatory building processes have to generate human strength and community has haunted and inspired me all these years.

The building process that Alexander initiated must have been extraordinarily successful, touching all involved, including Alexander, the catalyst, at the very core of their beings. Alexander exclaims:

... when I look at these five houses and the cluster I am filled with something which is as close to religious feeling as any social act in society today can bring me to ... [The families] have become powerful, and are powerful, in a way which almost takes the breath away.

Having let myself feel, through Alexander's words, the exuberance that the Mexican families actually experienced, I'm also left with a sense of anxiety about the fate of the families. What will happen to them if officialdom reacts, provoked by the "rambling appearance" of the houses and by the growing sense of liberty that the families express? What will happen to the families' sense of powerfulness? What will Alexander's new friends do if political and economic pressures mount against them? Have they been able to inform themselves as to the uniqueness of their position in the midst of violent political and economic forces organized to keep poor people in their places? How long can such a system tolerate this life-affirming nucleus?

I have worked with grassroots communities in the United States and have witnessed people-removal through slum clearance, planned shrinkage, and gentrification (a process often triggered by the success of self-help rehabilitation efforts). I'm convinced that today, as the polarization of poor and rich and of underdeveloped and developing countries intensifies, any engagement of people in the development of their habitat has to be accompanied by political consciousness-raising, so that the consequence of property development and the dialectic of property improvement (as illustrated by the gentrification process) are made clear. Having registered these reservations, I would like to focus on the fundamental programmatic contributions Christopher Alexander has made in his Mexicali experiment.

## THE SYSTEM OF STEP-BY-STEP OPERATIONS

Alexander has succeeded in developing a self-help housing production system that "respects human feeling and human dignity first." The buildings are also cheaper than most, more in reach of the masses, costing only about $3000 each. And the system is capable of mass production, drawing optimally on local resources as it did.

Architects' only actual physical contact with their work is the sharp point of a pencil. In grassroots work, people become much more intimately involved with building materials and building processes; a building system that encourages sensuous hands-on contact with materials fosters greater creativity. An architect-builder—a person sensitive to the organization of space as well as one intimately connected with materials—can nurture such a process. Christopher Alexander has carried this people technology a step further with his development of "step-by-step operations," a process with which I am eager to experiment in my own work. By organizing not the components but *the operations*—bricklaying, plastering, painting, etc.—into a functional system, he shows the way to tap community creativity fully: "If we cannot make adequate houses of identical components, then what we mean by the same way must somehow be deeper, more basic, and capable of more fluidity. . . ."

Through his use of the concept of step-by-step operations, Alexander was able to engage people who had never built before, unleash latent capabilities, and teach new ones, thus transforming building into an ongoing celebration of the builders' full humanness.

## THE BUILDER'S YARD

Contrary to the static relationship between passive consumers and the preconceived housing products generated for them by architects designing for defense, prestige, profit, and regimentation, the Mexicali project aspires to reestablish the functional relationship between dwellers and their habitats common in indigenous architecture. Alexander has written:

The process not only builds the houses, but repairs them. . . . The houses are never finished; they exist, in an imperfect state, constantly changing and improving, just as we ourselves also exist in an imperfect state, constantly struggling to improve ourselves.

To facilitate labor-intensive grassroots construction processes, to encourage intimate contact with construction material and personal contact between the builders themselves, Alexander created a builder's yard. The yard contained building materials and design guides (the pattern language), and also functioned as a gathering place for the education of the larger community.

This is a timely invention, a process-oriented institution evolving out of the contemporary need of people to participate actively in the design, construction, and management of their own habitat. Environmental self-help is an idea being catapulted into prominence in all countries caught up in economic crises, including the United States. The expansion and overcentralization of cities and their top-heavy bureaucratic organizations have begun to generate counterforces that emphasize grassroots citizen participation in the revitalization of neighborhoods. But to conduct broad-based environmental self-help programs effectively, including urban homesteading and open space development, support systems have to be established. Alexander's builder's yard must be considered a central component of such a system.

In the United States, another significant sociocultural development is the positive emphasis on cultural pluralism. Now that the deracinating concept of an American melting pot has been outgrown, the consequences for environmental design are staggering. Communities are beginning to differentiate themselves: some Italian neighborhoods now feature urban arbor-vineyards, Hispanic neighborhoods, mosaic plazas. This ethnic renaissance will most dramatically express itself in the homes and streets of residential neighborhoods; again, a neighborhood-based builder's yard is the essential *catalyst* for the process of individual and collective environmental self-expression.

Some years ago, I visited the new residents of an urban renewal section of Washington, D.C. They pooled the tools from their suburban basements in order to equip a most elaborate cooperative workshop, and over the years this workshop has helped them to change completely their new and rather impersonal quarters into intimate, personal habitats. The emphasis on hands-on environmental production systems capable of personalizing human habitats is not limited to residential neighborhoods and is more than a measure for solving the problems of what to do with leisure time created by increasing unemployment—or wealth. The impetus for labor-intensive engagement in production processes is generated by a fundamental spiral development in technologies worldwide. So far, machines that save people from backbreaking work have also caused people's hands to be disengaged from the production process. We need new kinds of machines and processes to spare people backbreaking labor, but reengage human hands and minds.

I can foresee a time when builder's yards—offshoots of the Mexicali project—are integral parts of every neighborhood, contributing to a fundamental transformation that will enable neighborhood residents to control their habitat. In the same way that Adventure Playgrounds—initiated in Scandinavian countries and in England—enable children to discover their creativity in the making of their own environments (thanks to the availability of salvage materials, tools, and compassionate play leaders), architect-builders and builder's yards located on every block might one day transform our desperate urban agglomerations into Adventure Cities.

At the end of the First World War, architect Bruno Taut envisioned the Alps constructively engaging the millions of soldiers who were to be released from military duty. He proposed transforming their aggressive energies into cooperative action in the sculpting of mountains and glaciers. Adventure Cities, through a network of builder's yards, could become a new channel for the energies of millions in the unending process of environmental growth and change.

14. Drawing by Bruno Taut, from *Alpine Architektur,* Hagen, 1919.

This 'alpine architecture' proposed to use the energies of the demobilized armies of the First World War to transform the entire chain of mountains into crystalline monuments to peace. Universal participation in urban design and rebuilding could equally well transform the social and physical realities of our cities.

# Klostermuren
# Göteborg, Sweden

Klostermuren is a small residential community not far from the center of Göteborg, Sweden's second largest city. In a nation with an already notable history of progressive housing measures, Klostermuren represents an important step forward. It was entirely designed by the families that live there.

Brought together by architect Johannes Olivegren, future residents visited similar housing developments, studied *patterns* (based on the work of Christopher Alexander), and walked the 1.3-acre site to study its trees and hillocks before design began. This way, neighbors-to-be came to know one another very well. The creation of a community, not merely housing, is the goal at Klostermuren. This is not an unfamiliar objective for architects. But we know little about how to achieve it.

As Olivegren says:

As soon as we build for more than one person, we build a community. What methods and tools do we have for building such a social structure? Nearly none. We've attempted to build a social structure with houses, streets, and infrastructure, rather than with people. . . .

So Klostermuren is an experiment, and one carried out with university and government involvement. The Klostermuren experiment involves site selection, a specific means for bringing families into the program, a well-thought-out design methodology, an interesting way to en-

able participants to calculate costs as they design (a Swedish Crown, by the way, is worth about 20 cents), and an effective technique for dealing with the group dynamics. The design system, by concentrating on site organization and building volumes, has produced a remarkably pleasant and coherent scheme, but one in which individual differences can still be clearly read. Toward the end of the experiment, the families made the mutual decision to face all their entrances toward the common land at the center of the site. They also agreed to adopt the pattern, Uniting Footpath. It seems clear that a community has been created at Klostermuren—and architecture has given it form.

# How a Little Community Is Born

**Johannes Olivegren, architect**
**FFNS-gruppen, Göteborg**

## Problem, Goal, and Hypothesis

As soon as we build for more than one person, we build a community. What methods and tools do we have for building such a social structure? Nearly none. Without really recognizing what we were doing, we've attempted to build a social structure with houses, streets, and infrastructure, rather than with people. This hasn't produced a particularly good social community. What we are looking for instead is a social process which brings people together in new relationships and patterns of living. In other words, a continual community building process where individuals and groups develop by giving each other support and stimulation as they work to design their immediate environment and take responsibility for its maintenance and future development.

This is the background for a long-range design research project, and the present article is an account of one application of the theoretical program. This particular experiment was commissioned by the local authorities of the city of Göteborg and was carried out during 1973–1975 and took place on a site called Klostermuren on the island of Hisingen. Our intention is to continue with larger projects involving several different types of housing, as well as working places and community facilities of different kinds. The aim of our research is to be able to apply the same participatory procedures to the living and working environments of all segments of the population. Due to existing legal, political, and economic conditions, it was practical for us to begin with single family houses. However, given the proper framework, the methods and procedures of this project can be used for designing all types of housing. Other applications are already in progress.

The basic principle for the construction of a community should be that all the inhabitants in the area are given the opportunity to participate in continuing development. This can be accomplished both in renovations and improvements to existing neighborhoods and in the building of new areas. Inhabitants of the area are relatively well acquainted with its conditions, and they are very capable of contributing to improvements in their own interest and in the interest of the community. Newcomers to the area should be first referred to existing housing. After a time, they will have the opportunity to contribute to the planning and design of old and new areas. In this way, a community grows from the inside with the help of its own residents and in harmony with its particular characteristics. This type of community development must, of course, occur in balance with regional, national, and international conditions. But the development and growth of a society should not be primarily driven from above or from the outside, but from the inside by its own inhabitants and their commercial and industrial activities.

## The Elements of the Klostermuren Process

Users can be solicited to participate in the construction of such a community through newspaper advertisements and municipal institutions. Those who show interest are invited to a general meeting for further information and to have their questions answered. Those who continue to be interested are selected to join the new community in the order that they have registered, or according to the size of the household and other criteria that the local authorities wish to apply. At Klostermuren we used a list of families who had requested housing sites from the city agency to invite participation. First come, first served was the basic rule for membership in the group.

Our objective was the design of 12 houses and the creation of a working community and the process involves some specific techniques and concepts.

## Techniques for Working Together Cooperatively

These are essential tools for this social process. Seven simple techniques are outlined in a pocket-sized pamphlet that the participants carry with them from the beginning of the project. The techniques are as follows:

1. Introduce yourself. What's your name? Where do you come from? What's your occupation? What are your special interests? What kind of support would you like from your neighbors? What kind of support are you able to give?
2. Round the group. Here, avoid discussion and polemics. Give each person about the same amount of time. Give everyone attention and show appreciation for their ideas. Discussion is then often unnecessary.
3. Discussion. If discussion is necessary, give each subject a time limit and everyone about the same amount of time. No one should speak four times before all have spoken twice. Finish with "round the group."
4. Avoid majority decision. If 2. and 3. are used, in general a solution can be found which meets different needs. Majority decisions are often unfair to the minority. Seek consensus.
5. Taking someone aside. If you become unhappy or angry with someone, take someone else aside and express how you feel. (The listener should avoid making comments and should keep the session private.) Afterwards, it will be easier for you to speak with the first person in a relaxed way.
6. Take the opposing point of view. When two parties are locked in their attitudes, i.e., continually repeating the same arguments, have each try for a while to defend the other's point of view. Attitudes will soon become less one-sided.
7. Encouragement is the best form of criticism. Harsh comments and criticism, even in the name of honesty,

shut the door to flexible thinking. Give encouragement and appreciation and the door will be opened.

*Professional Assistance.* Architects play an essential role as advisors and group leaders.

*Step–by–Step* is our working schedule which divides the design work the users have to do into relatively short periods during which a substantial result is achieved each time. About 30 steps are needed for users to design their environment and their houses in single family housing areas.

*Patterns* are design tools taken from Christopher Alexander. Patterns are employed especially to make future residents aware of all the issues involved in site planning.

*Field Trips* to existing housing areas are essential so the participants are able to see good and bad solutions to common design problems. Through such field trips, the architects gain an understanding of the preferences of the users and are able to discuss them intelligently.

*Price Lists* of different kinds are introduced so that the users can get an idea of the costs of their own houses and common facilities at any point in the process.

*The House Design Procedure* is a system for determining the form of the house in general. Styrofoam blocks of different shapes are used in this process. These are tools for the design process only. They are not intended to represent prefabricated building units.

*The Procedure for Interior Planning* involves the use of Styrofoam pinboards and yarn (for trying partition locations) and paper cut-outs for utilities, staircases, furniture.

## Execution of the Project

By March, 1973, the development of the method had come far enough so that our group could investigate the interest among local authorities in Sweden's three largest city areas—Stockholm, Göteborg, and Malmo. The Klostermuren site in Göteborg was finally chosen as the location of the pilot project. On November 20, 1974, after presentations and political negotiations, local authorities approved the project and appointed a committee to follow its progress.

2. The architect (left) discussing house plans with future residents.

The work began with the preparation of a map that illustrated the building site boundaries. The neighbors were informed of the project and gave their written approval. The local authorities invited eight builders to bid on a simulated project so that costs could be determined and price lists could be made up.

Invitations were sent out to 800 households on the list for sites for single family houses. Fifty-five households responded and were called to an introductory meeting on April 3, 1974. About 20 of the most interested families then got together at another meeting in order to get better acquainted before making a final decision. After further considerations (size of the household, economic status, etc.), 12 families were selected with four in reserve. These 12 households paid 500 Swedish crowns each as a deposit before designing started.

At the end of the design period (which took two months), a second general meeting was held on June 27, 1974, where the households reviewed their work. By that time, the group leader (who was the architect) had executed professional drawings of the users' designs that were delivered to the local authorities for approval and to the selected builder for final estimates and contracts. During the summer, working drawings were made, and on September 24 the households signed individual contracts with the builder. Up to this point, the local authorities had been responsible for the contract with the builder. Now each family took over this responsibility. On October 1, 1974, ground was broken. Construction had begun about four working months after the households had started their designing. They moved in in two stages, May 15 and June 27, 1975.

The intention is that the households will, even in the future, use the cooperative working techniques to help solve problems they may have in common. And by using our design tools, they can also create additions and alterations to their homes and common areas. If new households move in, they will be welcomed and introduced to the other households and the manner in which the project was developed and functions will be explained to them.

### Description of the Area and the Houses

Klostermuren is about 5000 m² and is situated five kilometers or a 20-minute tram ride from downtown Göteborg. The site is surrounded by single family houses from the 1930s and 40s, apartment houses from the 50s and 60s, a grammar school, a green area, a ball park, and a playground with animals. At 450-m distance is a day-care center, post office, shops, and a bus stop.

The 12 new houses are organized in four groups of three each. In the center of the houses is a common area with a playground, sitting areas, and birch trees which were saved during construction. All entrances face the common area to promote spontaneous contact between neighbors. The entrances to the garages face outward to the surrounding streets. At the main entrance in the southwest corner is a house shared by all, the use of which is open-ended. (It is often used for visitors, or for communal celebrations.)

The houses are different in design and vary in size from 112 to 151 m² of living space. The houses are covered with board siding and are stained or painted in yellow, brown, red, and blue. Roof materials and colors are the same within each group. Almost every house has balconies and outdoor sitting areas in two different locations.

The floor plans closely follow the needs and wishes of each household. The heights of the houses vary from one to three stories and the space is used to full advantage. Several households have designed rooms with double height ceilings and contact between the first and second floors. Some have extended the house depth. Others have widened different parts 30 cm from the original Styrofoam block proportions. The plans speak for themselves.

### The People and Their Environment

The 12 families which took part varied in size from two per household to five people per household. The adults ranged from 24 to 55 years of age. There were 19 children, of whom three were above 16 years of age. One of the adults was from Japan, one was from Hungary, and the others were Swedes. Six of the women were housewives, two women had part-time jobs, and four had full-time jobs. All of the men had full-time jobs. The occupations included office worker, nurse, carpenter, taxi driver, engineer, teacher, and architect. The household incomes for 1973 varied from 40,000 to 100,000 Swedish crowns

### Summary of the Residents' Role

Each family introduces itself.

The families inspect the area.

Their observations are transferred onto a model of the area at the scale of 1:100.

The families study *patterns* for the area.

Each family designs three different proposals for the overall organization of the site and evaluates them with the aid of patterns.

Three or four site plans are chosen by the group as possible solutions.

The final plan for the site is chosen through careful review of the patterns and detailed discussion.

Each family chooses a site.

With the help of Styrofoam blocks, each family organizes roughly the volume and layout of the house it can afford. (Each design volume has a label showing its construction cost.)

The houses are placed on the model of the site.

Neighbors confer with each other about the interrelationship of their houses.

Adjustments are made with respect to neighbors, terrain, sunshine, vegetation, and so forth.

Each family designs its floor plan on Styrofoam pinboards at the scale of 1:50.

Discussion of floor plans with next-door neighbors.

The families make improvements.

Vertical sections are studied on the pinboard at the scale of 1:50.

The house forms are completed with windows, doors, balconies, colors, and so forth.

The project's external design as a whole is discussed; improvements are made.

The architect/group leader executes working drawings of each family's design. Each family then checks the drawings and may add further details.

A professional model builder completes the model.

The contractor calculates prices.

Each family chooses interior materials and colors.

The contractor's calculations are checked by the architect and presented to the residents.

Negotiations with the contractor.

Review of working drawings. Negotiations with banks and approvals from local authorities.

Each household signs its own contract with the builder contractor. . . .

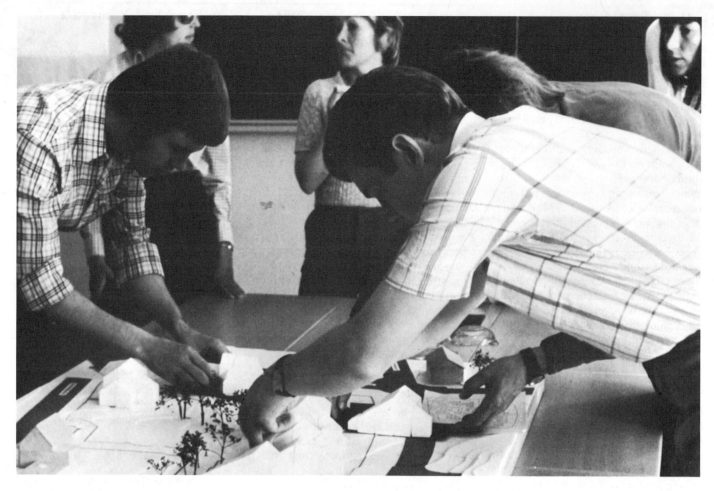

per year. Most were in the middle of this range. (This income generally represents the average for households looking for housing sites in Göteborg.)

Meeting attendance during the design phase was very high. No household dropped out during the process (nor to this date). The excellent participation was due to the stimulating and fruitful social interaction, the relatively short design time, and the expected quality of the homes at a comparatively low cost. The households were generally very positive about the project and its methods. They particularly appreciated that they had the opportunity to get to know each other before moving in.

The more unpopular aspects of the process were: the time limit which was experienced as a pressure by all, having to wait to know about the final costs of the house, and in some cases, expectations about techniques for working together toward consensus were not satisfied as we hadn't the time necessary to use all of them entirely successfully. Conflicts concerned mainly the communal house and the choice of house sites.

The nearby neighbors took part mainly in formal presentations and by approving the map of building limitations and the drawings that had to be delivered to the local authorities for building permission. In general, their attitude was positive toward the project. They were astonished that their opinions were asked and that their participation was invited. One family, which already lived on the site, took part more than the other neighbors by coming to some of the design meetings and some of our parties.

The common house has been located by the residents on the outer edge of the site, and has, among other things, the aim of facilitating contact with the surrounding areas.

## A Review of the Design Process

Design meetings were held twice a week, which seemed to be too often. (One evening a week should be enough. Extra design meetings and study evenings could then be added as the need arises.) The time, 6 to 10 P. M. with a half-hour break, was excellent. The two design weekends during the early stages

3. Participants used a simple model to test alternate site plans.

of the project were successful. They provided the project participants several opportunities to meet outside of work/ study periods under free and easy circumstances, during meals, walks, volleyball games, and evening parties. Three design weekends would perhaps be an improvement. Work to be done at home was assigned between nearly every design meeting. These two design months were quite intensive—enough so that the harmony of some households was put under stress.

The techniques for working together became the essential tool for the social interaction within the project, especially 'round the group which was used some 100 times with great success. Majority votes were used very rarely. As a rule, the group found flexible solutions for its problems which could satisfy individuals in different ways. Formal decision-making procedures were used less than originally expected, mainly as a result of using the techniques for working together. However, this sometimes cre-

ated confusion about what had been
decided. In the future, a clear distinction has to be made between informal
discussion and formal decisions.

The step-by-step procedure proved
invaluable, but should never become
rigid, a ready solution once and for all.
It's essential that every step contain neither too little nor too much to do. When
a step contains too little, the interest of
the participants slackens, and when
there is too much to do, they feel
stressed and dissatisfied. The participatory phase of planning and design at
Klostermuren took two months. (This
was too short. Three months would
have been about right.) The time spent
in group work amounted to 120 hours.
Already after 65 hours or less than one
month after the start of the designing,
the designs for the site, the houses, and
their interiors were nearly completed.
The rest of the time was used for choice
of materials and utilities, review of final
drawings, negotiations with the contractor, and the preparation of contracts.

The procedure for designing the site
worked well. In one session, 11 households made 33 variations for the layout
of the site. After evaluation and elaboration with the help of patterns, one of
these solutions was selected as the design for the area. Then the time came
for each household to choose a site. A
tentative choice of site went quite well;
no serious conflicts arose. When the
choice was to be final, the situation became different. Real conflicts came out
which previously had been covered up.
The conflict was resolved by choosing
sites in the order that the households
held in the original queue for obtaining
a site. An interesting thing was noted at
this time. Those who had the opportunity gave equal importance to who their
neighbors would be as to the physical
location in their selection of a site.
Even in this small-scale society, social
groupings in the physical environment
appeared to some extent.

The procedure for designing the
houses with Styrofoam blocks also functioned well. An essential quality of this
method was that the households didn't
get caught up in details at the outset.
Each family placed the main volumes of
the house on the site, concentrating on
orientation with reference to the neighbor's houses, the grounds, and the sun.
They could make rapid adjustments
with help of Styrofoam pieces that they
were able to group and regroup very
quickly.

4. Modular styrofoam blocks prepared by the
architect aided residents in designing their
homes.

5. The blocks combine to create diverse, but
related, house forms.

6. The finished houses are of varying sizes, but
the common vocabulary of materials, forms, and
colors speaks to the desire for community.

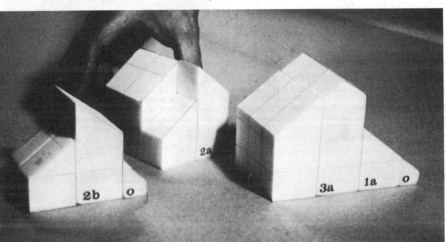

139

The procedure for laying out the interiors also worked quite well. The closer we came to the details of the dwelling, the more experienced and proficient the members of the households became. All of the dwellings ended up being very different inside. Choice of materials and utilities took a comparatively long time—about 41 hours of the total 120. Here the variety was, of course, the greatest.

The patterns were generally considered to be a valuable design tool, but due to the shortage of time they weren't used as much as they might have been. We found, by the way, that it was not necessary to describe every pattern in great detail. We did a list of patterns and discussed them as we went through the list. People were able to keep in mind what the different patterns contained, the problems, and the solutions. They also seem to have subconscious patterns that showed up when they worked closely with their site plans and houses.

The field trips (project visits) proved to be educational in the same way, but due to time limitations they were too few. On the other hand, the families

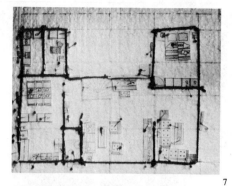

7. Knitting yarn was the preferred material for sketching plan ideas.

7

8. An interior at Klostermuren.

8

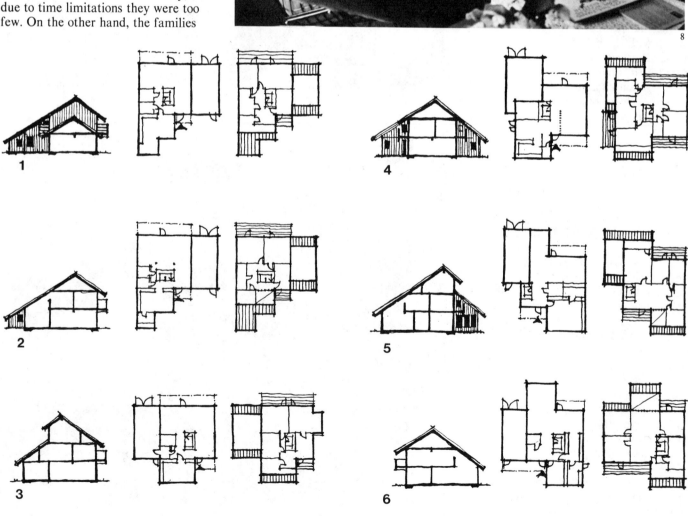

1

2

3

4

5

6

made several field studies on their own during the project.

The general contractor collaborated in the design work and made regular cost calculations. The personnel of the construction firm had the delicate and laborious task of helping the users at the same time as they looked after their own interests as builders. The prices written on the design volumes that were used in the beginning can only be used in the very first stage as they represent gross estimates. As soon as possible, estimates should be based on prices per square meter. We found that this gives more precise figures.

The development and research costs for this project were considerable—about 300,000 Swedish crowns. The cost of future applications will be more reasonable. With projects of 40 to 60 households, the cost per household will vary from 3500 to 5000 Swedish crowns ($900 to 1250). This is quite reasonable if one thinks of what the families get in exchange—a supportive and democratic community.

9. The individuality of Klostermuren's residents shows up in the plans and sections of their houses which vary from in size from 112 m² to 151 m².

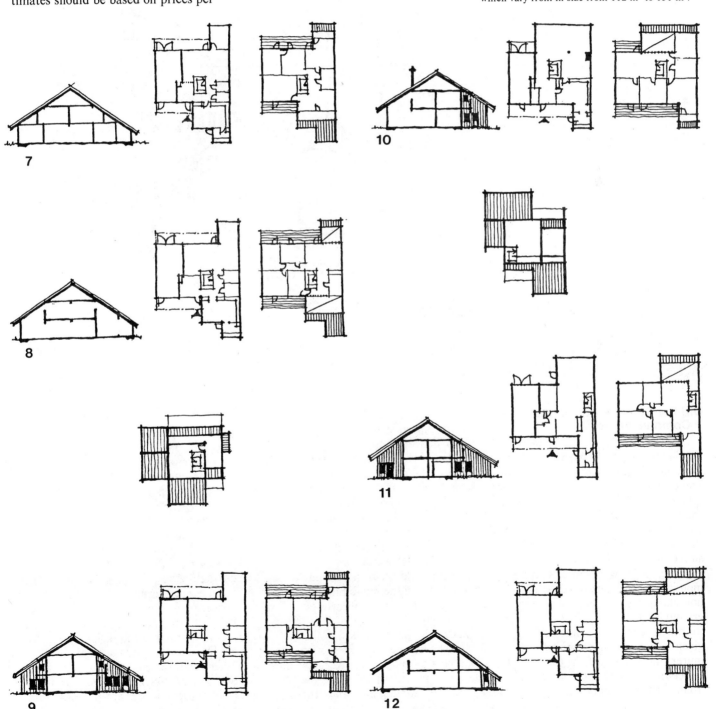

141

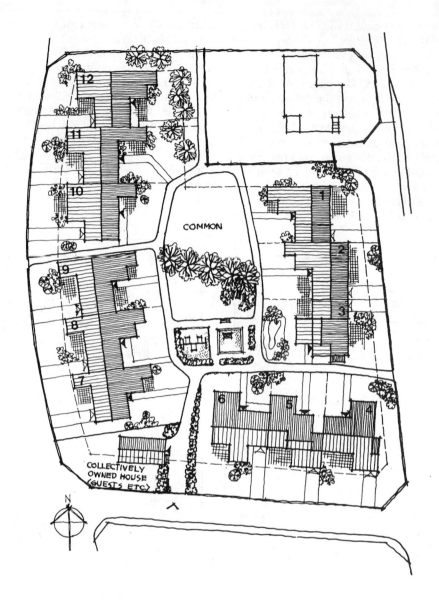

10. The final site plan is based on the concepts of a common garden and "uniting footpath." Note the community-owned guest house at the southwest corner of the site.

## Did the Social Process of Building a Community Work?

Application to this project was voluntary, and the choice of households was made somewhat at random as they were taken in the order of their position on the public list for sites, as well as according to the size of the household and the age of the adults. This procedure resulted in a relatively heterogenous social mixture. We have observed that common interests or lack of such among the households have influenced physical groupings. The attraction people have for others with similar interests was given a chance to develop at Klostermuren and influenced the creation of the community. The method of going 'round the group in order to give everyone a chance to speak at meetings was

an essential aspect of the social process. Most important perhaps is that design work done collectively involves a great deal of problem-solving toward a common goal (the construction of a small community). The end result was that we all got to know one another quite well as human beings. The contact within Klostermuren today is far greater than in a usual housing area where people have been neighbors for decades. And this will continue to be true because the inhabitants decided to turn their entrances inward toward the common area in the middle. The users made this choice in spite of the fact that the garages are entered from the street, and that visitors will have difficulty in finding their way to the front doors. By coming and going through the common space the chances for friendly

encounter will be considerably greater than if they had turned the entrances outward toward the streets. (The pattern after which these entrances have been designed is called by Alexander "uniting footpath." This is one example of how patterns have been used in the project.)

What one recognizes at once while approaching the area is that all of the houses are different and have individual characteristics, but that there are some architectural forms in common. The houses vary from one to three stories, have different colors and also different roof material and roof colors for each group. One house has one balcony, another has three, and the rest have two. Some houses form a row (similar to town houses), others are set back from each other in varying combinations.

11

Some have small sites; others have bigger sites. The specific quality of this area is that all the variation is genuine. That is, the variations arise from the different needs and wishes of the inhabitants and have therefore a real background—they are not the imposed imagination of a single architect who is trying to make an environment more interesting. This factor alone means that there is a very substantial difference between this area and other areas planned by people who don't use them.

A quick visit to all 12 houses reveals that no house is like any of the others, either outside, in plan, in section, in interior decoration, or in utilities. The construction of the houses (post and beam) is such that the users are free to change the arrangement of rooms on both floors to some extent. Evolution according to changing needs has, in this way, been allowed for. Walking through the houses, one is able to experience that people are different, unique, and have personal opinions and wishes that they want to keep as they, at the same time, form something in common with others. In conclusion, one could say that this small area expresses both individuality and community in the physical environment.

12

11,12. Klostermuren: architecture and community through a careful attention to process.

# MHGA/rue Duméril
# Paris

This is the story of a housing movement soon surely to spread to the US. It had its beginnings in Paris about eight years ago when the architect Guislain called together 10 families to discuss a new way of living. All were educated, serious, and active on the left in political and environmental movements. All agreed that Paris apartment life was lonely, isolating, and hard on children. They wanted to "décloisonner le système travail/famille/militantisme"—break down the barriers between job/family/political work. Perhaps a more communal lifestyle in a neighborhood where their abilities would be well used. . . .

Ground breaking was in April, 1974, but it was not until July, 1975, that they were able to move in at last. They say, "C'est long ... mais c'est tellement mieux!" Their collective home, called Jardies, seems always to be humming with activity. The workshop doors are open, and children from the neighborhood are learning to paint under the supervision of one of the artists who lives at Les Jardies. Other members of the group can be seen preparing one of the public rooms for an evening film showing or a meeting about some problem that has come up on the block, in Paris, or even in some remote part of the world.

From his office (at 4, sentier des Jardies, 92190 Meudon, France) Yves de la Gausie issues a constant stream of pamphlets and letters of encouragement to the many groups throughout Europe who want to share in the spirit of Les Jardies.

The article that follows tells the story of the most recent collective project, at rue Duméril in Paris, and of the development of the Movement which animated the group and supported it through the difficult process of creating a new way of life in the city. The author, Jean-Claude Prinz, is a graphic designer and a member of the group. He worked closely with well-known architect and group member Pierre Colboc on what will surely be a handsome and exciting place to live, at quite reasonable (at Paris rates) cost.

A short while ago, Marc Emery, Editor of *Architecture d'Aujourd'hui*, surveyed these designs for collective living and wrote:

They bring something new [to housing] in their architectural language, in their spatial organization, and in the mode of production which they propose (and sometimes realize). These architects have rediscovered a sense of propriety, the subtle balance between scale and density, between public and private space, between individual and communal facilities ... anticipating a foreseeable cultural evolution, they have set out to find the way to build the collective habitat, renewing in this way the utopian tradition which has so long been intimately connected with the history of architecture. Isn't this a sign that the profession of architecture, so generally condemned, can, when required, renew itself?

In her Commentary on Les Marelles and MHGA (see Part 1), Katharine Coit sees both as part of the *courant autogestionaire*, the desire for self-determination that is sweeping through France in opposition to the tradition of autocracy, hierarchy, and centralization. It is a necessary movement, says Coit, and it offers "an example of the role of architecture in the struggle for social transformation. . . ."

1. From storage yard to collective housing: a model of the Duméril project in Paris.

144

# The Movement for Collective, Self-Managed Housing

**Jean-Claude Prinz**
**La Duméril, Paris**

The Movement was launched in November, 1977, at a national meeting on self-managed housing organized by a group of architects and students at the school of architecture in Nantes. At the core of the movement were six groups that had already built housing for themselves. They came together again for a second time in February, 1978, in the new town of Cergy-Pontoise at the invitation of the "Jardies" group from Meudon and of a local group, "Atelier Communautaire." Shortly after this meeting, the *Mouvement de l'Habitat Groupé Autogéré* (MHGA) was formalized and adopted a written charter.

In October, 1978, a national meeting was held at Orsay. There were two full days of fascinating ideas, of experiences, and of projects. More than 250 people took part. In the meeting room were potential participants, journalists, and elected officials, but above all there were representatives of successful groups from all over France and from foreign countries with the same desire: to take control of the design and management of the collective habitat.

The following groups are active members of the MHGA in France:

- Village 6, Alençon
- La Calaria—la Croix Falgar (Toulouse)
- Les Jardies, Meudon
- Palaiseau (Essonne)
- Betton—Les Gilles Pesset
- Saux les Chartreux
- Nanterre Chevremont
- Lorry les Metz
- La Salucéenne, Saux les Chartreux
- La Fabrique, Paris 12$^e$
- La Duméril, Paris 13$^e$

These groups are at various stages in the development of their housing. Some are complete and occupied, others are in construction; the last names on the list have just purchased land and begun the process of design. The list grows longer and longer every day.

## Case Study: The Conversion of a Workshop into Housing and Common Spaces in Paris

The latest group to start the MHGA process—La Duméril—consists of seven families. In the beginning, the group, then only four families, visited numerous locations in Paris (factories, warehouses, garages, etc.), but because we were not well organized, nothing came of the search. Then, in June, 1978, ap-

2. The original project by architect Guislain: Les Jardies in Meudon outside of Paris.

145

propriate land and buildings were found in the thirteenth *arrondissement* just off the Boulevard Saint Marcel. The locale was big enough to house more than four families, so we decided to enlarge the group to seven. As two of the original families had by now dropped out, this meant finding five families to complete the group, and this created a number of problems.

The new group gained cohesion slowly through a series of meetings, some simply social, others political, others organizational, but all having the same spirit. There was a desire to make a new kind of habitat and new social relationships through the mutual planning, organization, and managment of a residential community—rejecting all ideas of real estate speculation and putting forward the alternative of communal property.

When we were ready, we incorporated and began the search for a bank that would provide the same conditions of credit and interest for each member family in the group, regardless of its actual income. Eventually such a bank was found. The site was purchased. Design work could begin.

At our regular, biweekly meetings, each family began by listing its needs and expressing its expectations. The two graphic artists wanted to work at home and wished to have their studios near the public entrance. All of the professional studios had to be located so as to receive the maximum amount of light. The architect wished to organize his dwelling around an open courtyard. Some families wanted to live on the ground and others on the first floor. The floor-to-floor heights of the old buildings and the fact that there were no windows to the rear made some of these choices difficult.

At the same time, cost considerations and technical constraints forced us to keep our design project largely within the limits set by the existing construction. Laying out new apartments in the old buildings brought to light numerous curious nooks and crannies that now function as shared spaces for storage, wine cellars, and so forth. Across the courtyard from the new housing is a former projection cabin from a movie theater long since demolished. It is being preserved and enlarged to serve as a common space and a place to welcome neighbors. We will hold our biweekly meetings there, and occasionally

3

4

3. After a long search, the Duméril group found this neglected builder's yard and its sheds.

4. Pierre Colboc, the architect in the Duméril group, sketches for comment.

146

we will use it as a gallery to display the works of the artists among us. The remainder of the site (approximately 600 m²) is to be preserved as open green space.

In October, 1978, we filed all the drawings and papers required for a building permit. However, it took us nine months to get it, and there were innumerable difficulties along the way due to the unusual nature of our project. During our long wait, our designs were further elaborated in group sessions. Many different proposals for the facade were studied, discussed, and finally agreed upon by the group as a whole. The design of the individual dwelling interiors evolved in a similar way, with ideas found, thrown away, restudied, and eventually pinned down. Each proposal was discussed by the group in great detail, and this helped the individual families to make their decisions. All those matters that affected the collective as a whole were agreed upon by consensus.

In July, 1979, we finally received our building permit and each member of the group searched for contractors willing to bid on the job. This didn't work very well because our project turned out to be too small for large firms and too large for small ones. In the end, we selected a brand new firm that had been organized to do a similar project nearby in the twelfth *arrondissement*. Work began in December, 1979. This means that it will have taken us two years and five or six months from the time that we

5a,b,c. Collective housing begins with collective design.

5b
5c

located our site to the time that we finally occupy our new community. Our apartments will be delivered to us semifinished by the contractor, that is, they will have plumbing, kitchens and bathrooms, heat, and electricity—the things that were needed in common. Any additional charges for finish materials or equipment will be borne by the individual families.

Most of the dwellings are on two floors and many have interior balconies, due to the form of the original buildings. The interior spaces in the apartments are substantially different from each other. We designed our housing so that all the principal windows look out onto the common space, the entry, and the main walkway. We hope it will be a sort of village square.

## Financing Issues

In this project we worked out what we believed is an equitable way of sharing the financial burden. Some costs are shared on the basis of the floor area occupied by each family, and others are divided equally among the seven families who form the collective. The average price for each apartment, including purchase, construction, legal fees, design fees (engineering and construction supervision only), and insurance came to 4600 francs m² (about 90 dollars per sf). For this each family receives a dwelling, storage areas, a laundry, and the common garden.

## MHGA: The Charter of the Movement

### I: In Key Principles

The Movement is made up of the groups of families or individuals who have built or who wish to build or transform their habitat in order to give it the following characteristics:

1. Each group is to be of limited size (between 5 and 10 dwellings) so that true mutual understanding and collective decision making are possible. The group will collectively design its habitat. It remains in charge of all the decisions concerning the planning and the management of its habitat.

   Several groups may come together in a federation to carry out operations at a larger scale.

2. A portion of the construction budget is set aside for common spaces and facilities (between 10 and 20 percent of the built area) which will permit a collective life to develop.
3. The group does not seek to isolate itself from the rest of society, and the common spaces that it builds should be shared by the different organizations and individuals who contribute to the social life of the neighborhood or the village.
4. From the time of its formation and throughout its life, the group will try to break down the system of social segregation in which we live. This means that in the beginning, each group should organize around common objectives, rather than around common tastes. This principle also requires that the group use all possible means to provide the same quality of habitation for all its members regardless of income. Further, for each member it means respect for, and willingness to listen to, different ideas, and the progressive transformation of the fear of social contact into a *plaisir de la différence.*
5. During the planning period and afterward, the group will manage its own affairs. The word *autogestion* is used specifically to mean the search for a true equality of power that respects the differences between people. It requires the following rules: All decisions which affect the entire group are taken according to majority rule. Each family and each individual retains full control of decisions which do not affect others. Responsibility for the project and its management is shared by all the members of the group and each has the right of initiative. All the tasks and responsibilities are redistributed frequently.

### II: The Role of the MGHA

The Movement is at the service of groups and individuals who wish to carry out projects of this sort or who already live in such habitats. Its role is:

1. To facilitate meetings between people who wish to carry out this type of project, and to help in the organization of groups for this purpose.
2. To give support to groups who ask for assistance on problems of finance, law, organization, and techni-

cal matters with respect to the creation of this form of habitat. To serve as liaison between various groups within the Movement and to make the experience of all available to each.
3. To provide information, counsel, and training to municipal governments, social agencies, and all groups which support this program.
4. To work with the public agencies, community groups, housing organizations, and all other groups, political parties, unions, or associations interested in our work to help them aid the development of self-administered, collective housing.

### III: The Organization of the Movement

In its own organization, the Movement respects the principles of self-management:

- Autonomy of each local group within the framework of the Charter of the Movement
- Regional coordinating committees that decide on development activities to undertake at the level of the region
- A national coordinating body that sets policy at the national level, following the direction determined by the General Assembly of the Movement that meets each year
- Each coordinating group applies the same rules of organization that were listed above for the groups of inhabitants: the distribution and rotation of tasks and of responsibilities and a balance between group decisions and individual initiatives

6a,b,c,d,e. The construction phase: a contractor did the heavy work; the collective was involved all along the way. Celebrations built community spirit.

6a

6b

6d

6c

6e

**1**

Ma chambre,
mon coin où je travaille,
où je lis, où je réfléchis,
où j'aime !

1. My room, the corner where I can work,
read, and think quietly.

**2**

La vie de la famille ou du ménage.
Le séjour, on mange ensemble.
On fait la cuisine, on discute.

2. Family life: the living room and dining
room—places to sit together, to cook, to eat, to
talk.

**3**

On se réunit : un groupe de six à dix familles
pour faire des choses ensemble..
Jouer aux cartes !
Faire nous-mêmes nos meubles
dans l'atelier de menuiserie !
Discuter, recevoir un groupe de l'extérieur
sans déranger la famille !
Pour ça aussi il faut de la place
c'est le groupe qui est responsable de ce qui s'y passe.

3. Families also want to get together in groups
of six to ten to play cards, to discuss politics,
to build furniture.... These activities need
their own special spaces.

**4**

4. The idea of a proper social life requires that
several such groups of families come together
to build collective housing with the support of
local government. Each group will have its
special way of life, its own culture. But
common facilities will bring them into contact.
This kind of housing program encourages "le
plaisir de la différence."

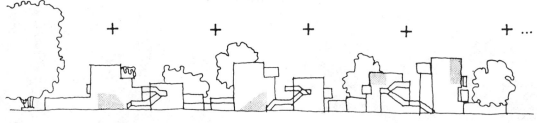

**5**

Une crèche, un club de jeunes...
Ce sont des équipements construits et gérés par la municipalité
mais qui peuvent être intégrés à l'habitat.
Les habitants peuvent participer à leur gestion.

5. The day care center, the young people's
club.... These usually belong to the city.
They should be a part of the housing and
under the control of the inhabitants.

7. A panoramic shot as the project approaches completion.

## The La Duméril Group

| Occupations | | Age | | Children |
|---|---|---|---|---|
| Men | Women | M | W | |
| Graphic Artist | Computer Programmer | 35 | 37 | 1 |
| Lawyer | — | 35 | — | |
| Salesman | Nurse | 32 | 30 | 2 |
| Theatrical Producer | Government Worker | 35 | 33 | |
| Architect | Choreographer | 40 | 38 | 2 |
| Economist | Press Attaché | 40 | 29 | |
| Designer | Graphic Artist | 35 | 31 | |

## La Duméril: Division of Project Costs

| | Purchase | | Construction | | "Carrières" | Taxes | Legal Fees | Design and Engineering/ Construction Supervision |
|---|---|---|---|---|---|---|---|---|
| | Dwelling | Common Areas | Dwelling | Common Areas | | | | |
| Pro rata on basis of area occupied | ● | | ● | | | ● | ● | |
| Shared equally by the seven families | | ● | | ● | ● | | | ● |

8. From *Habitants*, the Movement's publication.

# Lycée David
# Angers, France

A few years ago, Yona Friedman was asked by the *Vins du Postillon* group to convert a large industrial building in Paris into offices—with the participation of the office staff. Friedman decided in fact *to make the employees into designers* of their own workspace. To this end, he developed a set of manuals and graphic communication techniques which would permit them to conceive the workplace as they wished it to be and to communicate their ideas to their fellow workers and to the architect. Before the experiment could be carried out, the sponsoring wine company was swallowed up by a larger conglomerate. Fortu-

nately, the people involved in planning a new secondary school in Angers had heard of Friedman's proposals. He was invited to try out his concept of user design with the school's students, their parents, and the faculty.

The procedures evolved by Friedman not only generated a handsome school that pleases those who use it, they also generated a hot debate with another exponent of design methods, Geoffrey Broadbent. In his Commentary and in the architect's response, Broadbent and Friedman confront the knotty issues of user design: the possibility of manipulation, the illusory nature of design free-

dom within bureaucratic regulations. . . . Whatever the reader's conclusions, Friedman's experiment in Angers represents a unique example of a public building created by its users—and a step toward a public language of architectural design.

1. Planned by faculty, students, and parents, the Lycée David approaches completion.

# Communicating with Users

Yona Friedman, architect
Paris

The planning of the new Lycée David (a large secondary school) in Angers, about 300 km southwest of Paris, represents an important experiment in user planning. First the conception of the program, and then the design of the building, was done entirely by the future users: faculty, students, and parents. The project was carried out in the following steps:

1. As the architect appointed by the Ministry of Education, I prepared a detailed instruction manual.
2. The pupils, their parents, and their teachers, individually and in groups, used the lessons in the manual to program and design the Lycée.
3. The architect adapted their plan to the industrialized building system selected by the government agency.
4. Finally, there was a series of working meetings with the future users and the architect to work out the definitive plans.

This effort in user planning led to the organization of the Lycée in four "mini-lycées." The buildings are presently nearing completion and will be in use during the coming school year.

## The Problem of Communication between Architect and Users

The making of plans (in the largest sense of the term), is an act which has at its beginnings the desire on the part of one or more persons to improve the quality of life. Now, people—architects call them "users"—can't envisage such improvements without also conceiving an image of their future environment. This image (it is the goal of planning) is the result of thought processes in which the user brings together in his mind everything that seems important. To make satisfactory architecture, then, means that the resulting environment prefigured by the plan should approach as closely as possible the image conceived by the user (and which exists only in his imagination).

It is clear that the materialization in real terms and in three dimensions of this image is only possible if the user has been able to communicate his image to those who must elaborate the final plans. Good communication between user and designer is the key to successful architectural results. Note that we are talking largely about communication from the user to the designer. The all-too-common case, where it is the designer who persuades the user of the excellence of his plan (a plan created without taking into account the image in the mind of the user), ought to be considered the original form of bad communication. The architect who sets out to elaborate a plan which approaches a user's image runs up against numerous difficulties. Many images can't be turned directly into buildings. Internal contradictions and external constraints may involve alterations to the image conceived by the user. It is very important then that the user be able to communicate clearly how he evaluates the importance of the various trade-offs required for the realization of his image.

Unhappily for the entire design profession, these conditions of communication are practically never achieved. Users don't ordinarily know how to explain either their images or the acceptability of trade-offs. These communication conditions are rare also because the time available for contact between architect and user is too brief (not to mention the frequent case in which the designer must serve an unknown user). Due to the lack of satisfactory communication, the designer can't help but introduce errors into his plans. However, it is not he who will suffer the consequences of these errors, it is the users.

It is evident that the difficulties inherent in communication (and hence the risk of errors resulting from these difficulties) would disappear if the designer and the user were one and the same person. This is the process that we call *autoplanification* (user planning). It is a perfect solution if one is dealing with a single user or a small group of users who can by themselves make a plan: they know what they want and they know what is unacceptable to them. But any group of user-designers lives in the midst of other people who are frequently not involved in the development either of the image or of the plan until too late, when actual construction brings its inescapable consequences. It is very important that these others be involved from the outset. So another kind of communication should be added to the process: that which should take place between the initiating user-designers and those who will be affected by the project. Let me add that, clearly, the "language" that one can use with oneself and the "language" which is appropriate for use with others are not the same.

In a more academic fashion, we can say:

- Part of the process of user design requires an intrapersonal language. This is particularly important during the stages of the conception of the desired image and the evaluation of trade-offs.
- Another part of the user design process necessitates an interpersonal language. This is crucial during the negotiations over possible trade-offs.

Before user planning is possible, the following conditions must be satisfied:

- A system of notation (a vocabulary) must be found which works well to express both general and personal criteria.

2. From Friedman's user manual: Why user planning? (Because one is never so well served as when one serves oneself.)

People use buildings in widely different ways.

And the organization of the building's elements help them or prevent them from using the building as they wish.

- Rules of application (a syntax) must be established. They must be relatively simple and must permit users to recognize specific consequences (for themselves and for others) arising from the choice of particular criteria.

## The Language of User Planning

It is not possible to create this language without agreeing on certain fundamental architectural operations:

- The designation of a specific area for specific activities, whether enclosed or not. Such an area is in reality part of a total space (which existed before being subdivided into particular areas).
- The provision of access, direct or indirect, to the area designated, connecting it with all other parts of preexistent space.
- The assignment of appropriate functional descriptions to each area designated within the total space.

After that, it will be easy to establish a simple notation corresponding to each of these operations:

- A *designated area* within the space will be represented by · (a point).
- Any means of access connecting two designated areas within the space will be represented by a ——— (a line).
- The particular functional properties of each designated area within the space will be noted in special labels.

The use of these fundamental operations and their corresponding notation makes it possible to denote any plan

whatsoever for the organization of space. For each plan there will be a corresponding unique figure composed of points, lines, and labels. Each figure is, of course, a planar graph with its points labeled. Such a graph, which is a representation of the organization of the elements of a plan, will be the basis of the interpersonal language mentioned above.

The representation of a plan by such a graph tells us not only the character of the plan, but clarifies certain of its fundamental properties:

- The use of graph notation automatically separates interpersonal factors and intrapersonal factors in the plan. In fact, it is the graph that indicates the spatial implications of the plan that might have consequences for others. And the labels, apart from the graph, indicate the characteristics of the elements of the plan that are not ordinarily communicable except in an intrapersonal language. These characteristics, unlike those contained in the graph without labels, don't ordinarily create conflicts.
- Planar graphs (without labels) reveal the following potential problems: the necessity to introduce corridors (or stairways) to connect various elements of the plan in the manner desired, the possibility or lack of possibility of having a window or a door that opens to the exterior from any place located on the plan, and, given their relative positions, which rooms can have substantial dimensions and which cannot.
- The representation of a building plan by a planar graph facilitates the user's ability to comment objectively

This problem grows in seriousness as the number of future users increases. A school is a case which involves a great many users.

on how he would use the building.

When they have understood the functions of the building to be planned, it is relatively simple for the future users to make such graphs, and through these graphs to make plans. The reason for this simplicity lies in the abstract quality of the graphs, which draws on the visual training of the users (which has nothing to do with the architect's way of combining preconceived forms; if such training were necessary, this proposal would be impossible). The language of user planning that utilizes labeled planar graphs can, then, be taught with the aid of training manuals, just as the alphabet is taught to children (in the course of this training, the word *graph* is never mentioned).

Here, for example, is part of the manual which was used in designing the Lycée David d'Angers in Angers. And here are several drawings that the user designers made after reading it.

Buildings are built according to specific plans which show where all the elements of the building shall be.

Plans are conceived by architects with an eye to serving the future users . . .

. . . But it is impossible for the architect to know all the future users well.

In order to make design decisions, the architect may have to say that all the users are alike. This leads to the idea of the average teacher . . .

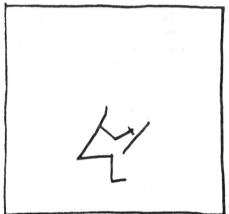

. . . The average student . . .

. . . And, even, the average maintenance crew.

But, in fact, teachers all have their own idiosyncratic ideas about teaching.

Just as students have their own ways of learning.

And the maintenance people know more about keeping a building clean than anyone else.

*The remainder of the manual illustrates the use of graphs to guide users in making their own plans.*

## More Reflections on the Language of User Design

The principal characteristic of the proposed language lies in the distinction made between interpersonal factors and intrapersonal factors. The first are represented by topological properties of the graphs, the second by the labels which the designer gives to the points and lines. The interpersonal elements of this language reveal the constraints that the designer can't avoid—the necessity of corridors, the ability to have openings to the outside from various rooms, and so forth. The situation is different if we examine the intrapersonal factors (those that are described largely by the labels). Each label defines the properties of a room or an area, and its importance depends above all on who has written the label for the space. This suggests that we should consider the labeling as the notation of user desires, which are not ordinarily so easily made apparent.

If we examine the different types of descriptors that are possible in labels, we find that their ability to communicate varies according to the case. For example, a user-planner, in order to define the image that he desires for a certain space, might employ the following label: this space should be large, round, pleasant. Now, round is reasonably comprehensible to everyone, but large is only comprehensible in relation to the dimensions of other spaces, and pleasant is a word which would be interpreted differently by every participant. Labeling a space pleasant, then, doesn't communciate very much.

If I go beyond the communicability of these descriptors to consider for a moment just how much the quality described by each depends on the position of the space within the graph, I will find that the requirement "large" is completely dependent upon the position of this room in the plan (that is, the position of the point which corresponds in the graph to the room in the plan). The term *large*, then, is related to the graph (we call this sort of descriptor *dependent*). The requirements that the space be "round" and "pleasant" are neither demanded by, nor prevented by, the position of the room, or, in our context, the point in the graph.

This explanation, surely too dense because of the need to summarize, is not necessary for the user-planner. I am describing it here only because of the interest that it might have for the architect—because the concepts described here have a great role to play in architectural aesthetics. To bring this discussion to a close, let us agree that a quality expressed in a label can be either communicative and dependent, noncommunicative and nondependent, or even communicative and nondependent. There are no examples of qualities that are noncommunicative and dependent.

A diagram may help us to summarize our reflections on the problems of communication between the architect and the user. This communication can be assured within certain limits, but no architecture is possible if one does not accept these inherent limits. However, the evident desire to overcome these limits is surely laudable—we must never forget that it finds its origins in the unhappiness of users and the architectural mediocrity that is swallowing up our cities.

3. To soften the industrialized building system called for by the local education authority, Friedman proposed painting the exterior walls in a lively fashion. The public elevations were

## The Manual

The final problem remains: How does one teach this language to the user-planner?

In a number of different experiments, I have made use of a manual. In the case of the Lycée David it was called, *User Planning and the School*, and it lays out, in the form of a comic strip, the essentials of the language that I have described here. The user-planners followed the manual and its language to develop an organizational scheme for the Lycée that served as the basis for the final plan. The questions of form, in this case, were largely preempted by the construction system that was selected by the public agency that financed the project.

### The Sequence of User Planning

The design of the Lycée David d'Angers is the first experiment in user planning following the method described here for a public building. And insofar as we are dealing with a government agency, there were certain special constraints to be respected:

- The price of construction was limited by a national cost yardstick
- We were required to use an industrial building system selected by the City
- The dimensions of classrooms and other spaces had to follow the norms established by the Ministry of Education

The user-planners (once again, stu-

designed by the architect, but the courtyard murals will be planned and executed by the students and teachers.

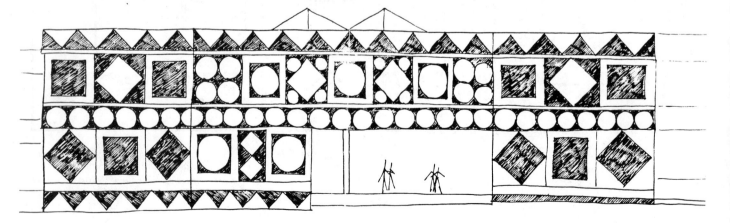

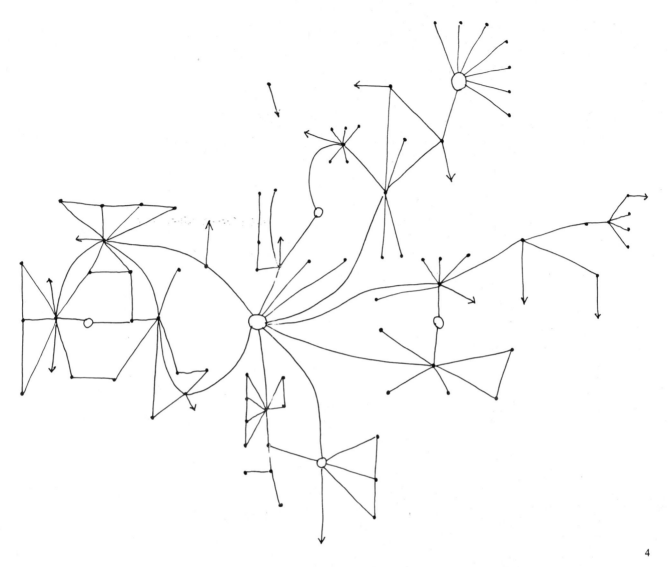

4

dents, parents, and teachers) were given the manual to use in planning the school, a task they carried out in groups that they themselves organized. A special group was designated to assure the coordination of the plans made by each smaller group. Following the manual, they first did organizational schemes and then moved on to do *patates* (bubble diagrams). I used their final bubble diagram as the basis for construction plans that met the requirements of the industrialized system and the norms of the Ministry of Education.

The work of the user-designers led to the organization of the Lycée in four "mini-lycées" each containing seven classrooms on the upper level. This same level contains an independent group of preparatory classrooms. All the specialized spaces such as laboratories are located on the ground floor. The five teaching units (mini-lycées and pre-

paratory classes) are independent, while the rooms on the ground floor serve all of the units equally. Each teaching unit has its own courtyard (two of them are roofed and three are open). The covered courtyards connect with a roofed central forum. The mini-lycées are grouped around this forum.

It was particularly important to be sure that the plan could be reorganized or remodeled. The next generation of teachers or students might well want to use the building in different ways. This is a principle that I have been defending since 1957, a time when it was particularly difficult for architects to accept this notion, and my theory of "mobile architecture" is the development of this idea.*

The nature of the plan and of the fa-

cades helps us to avoid the monotony that often characterizes industrialized school construction. The plan gave us contours in place of great long walls. The facades are painted with geometric compositions. The courtyards will also be ornamented, but the decoration has been left to the initiative of the students and their art teachers. These same students have already completed in their old school some excellent decorative panels.

The paved surfaces (parking areas, recreation spaces, etc.) will also be painted with ornamental motifs, the cost of which will be very small. This is a technique that I believe to have general application and that I call *urban carpet*.

*Friedman, Yona, *Toward a Scientific Architecture,* MIT Press, Cambridge, 1975.

4. The graph developed by the user-planners to illustrate their conception of the school's organization.

## Some Final Notes

It is important to know that planning decisions were made without anyone but the concerned users present. I was not there, either. No user represented a group, but only himself or herself—this is very important. No general meetings were held; users met together to negotiate decisions when the areas they were planning were in direct contact with those of others. When this happened, they negotiated a mutually acceptable plan.

The users themselves invented the mini-lycée concept because:

1. They considered the proposed school too large (it was to have 1100 pupils).
2. They realized that as a group they were interested in several different conceptions of pedagogy that were not necessarily compatible, so each mini-lycée will be able to experiment in its own way.
3. The vertical separation of normal classrooms and specially equipped spaces is a consequence of traditional security rules in French schools.

Nobody took the lead in planning. No power was present. The reason for the horizontal extension of the school is the desire to avoid creating constraints for the future expansion of any function. As for the painted decoration of the building, this was deliberately left to me, because if the inside of the building is seen and used by the users, its outside is seen mostly by the larger public.

It is worth mentioning that the cost of the building is within the established budget.

I would like to add a final comment: the use of an industrialized construction system and planning on the basis of a grid simplifies user design. It is advantageous for the construction system to separate Support elements and Infill elements—for which the largest possible choice is desirable. The secret of almost all the important architecture of the past lies in the juxtaposition of a strict three-dimensional structural order and a free system of enclosure. The industrialized building systems that are available at this time are still very far from this ideal. For example, the systems used for school construction are closed systems that are not compatible with the majority of facade elements

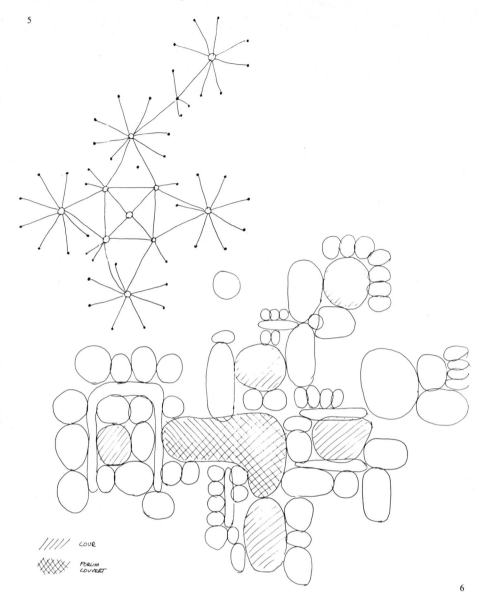

5

6

and interior finishing materials on the detached from the other parts, and the market.

User design becomes possible thanks to a method of communication, and thanks also to the introduction of discipline in building technology. The ideal of combining discipline with liberty remains on the drawing board, but the industrialization of building is only beginning.

## Postscript

The Lycée David d'Angers has been in use since September, 1981, and we have the first comments from the users about the building.

The *teachers* observed that, in the new building, pupils are "more relaxed than they were in the old one." The staff attributes this fact to the design

5. A graph of the ground floor as the user-planners wanted it.

6. The user-planners transformed their graphs into bubble-diagrams. Now the architect is ready to step back in.

where "all parts of the new school are relatively large distances between departments give occasion for walking." The "pupils and teachers meet only when they desire it." The school has thus "internal streets," where chance encounters are possible.

*Parents* consider that "their children feel at home in the new school." *Pupils* are already asking the school administration to permit them to "continue the self-planning process," and they want to propose small modifications to the buildings. They have also asked that a course in self-planning should be a regular part of the future curriculum.

My remarks, as the *architect*, are the

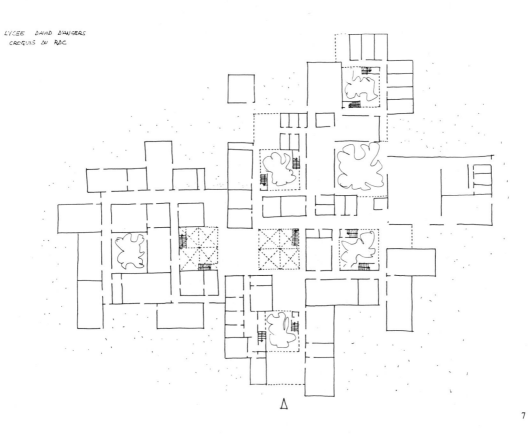

LYCEE DAVID D'ANGERS
CROQUIS DU RDC.

7

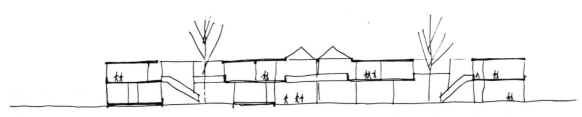

COUPE PAR L'ENTRÉE

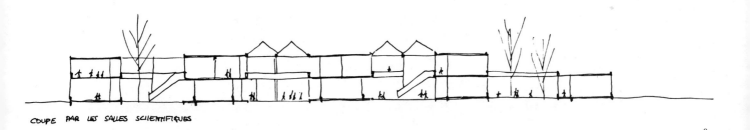

COUPE PAR LES SALLES SCIENTIFIQUES

8

7. Using the graphs as a guide, the architect
sketched this ground floor plan.

8. Two sections through the school: the upper is
through the entrance, the lower, through the
science laboratories.

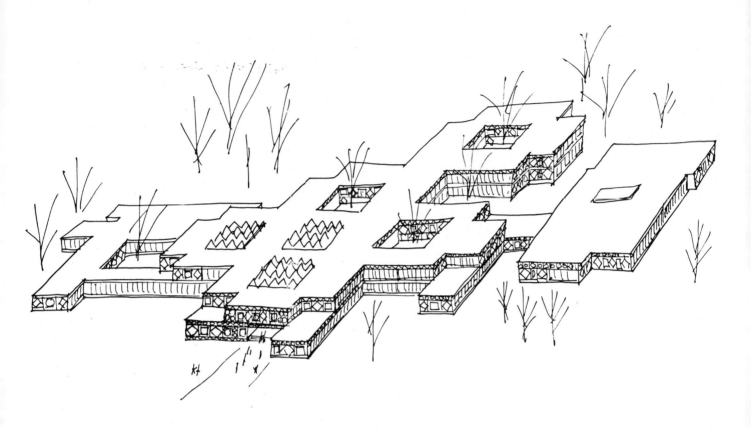

YONA FRIEDMAN, 1979

9. Axonometric view of the Lycée David. The school is organized around roofed and open courtyards.

following: the building was done in order to please the user and not me, the architect, or the architectural magazines. In spite of certain alterations by the local authorities, the users recognize the building as their own conception.

Architects should encourage future users of buildings to be built to dare to *conceive* the plans—to accept their own preferences instead of what the architect wants and finally to dare to feel confident about what they have created for themselves!

# Commentary on Lycée David

Geoffrey Broadbent, Head of School of Architecture,
Portsmouth Polytechnic (UK)

## GRAPH SPREE

One extreme attitude toward participation, of course, is raised in Henry Ford's famous statement concerning the Model T Ford: "You can have any color you like as long as it's black." In other words, he was laying down the parameters within which you could choose: in this case, no choice at all—take it or leave it. But anyone concerned with participation is stuck with Ford's basic problem, of how to lay down the parameters within which participation *may* take place. In the past, a number of theorists, including Yona Friedman, have "offered" people choices by designing an infrastructure into which people then were supposed to build; in one extreme form of this—such as Le Corbusier's Obus scheme for Algiers—they could build whatever they pleased. At the other extreme, such as Archigram's Plug-in City, *they* designed the pods which you, the user, would plug in. All these solutions, or so it seems to me, are variations on the theme of "expert knows best," and I am by no means the only one to ask Friedman a basic question: If *we* do not like *your* infrastructure, shall we be able to refuse to build into it?

Some say these problems have been transcended in the shantytowns of the Third World. There, people build what they want with no constraint at all from anyone else's infrastructure—or do they? Of course they don't, for they are constrained by another kind of infrastructure—not a crude, physical framework in this case, but an equally crude economic one. They don't have a slick Archigram plastic pod; instead they have the bits and pieces that advancing industrial societies think of as

waste—bits of wood, corrugated iron, oil drums, packing cases, cardboard, and so on. But they do, at the end of the day (or rather, in this case, the night, building as they must from dusk to dawn), have a house and a sense of possession: this is *my* house, and *I* made it.

All attempts at participation are compromises at some level or another between a *laissez faire* "let it be" and the other extreme: this is what *they,* the state, have "provided for *us.*" That certainly seems to be true of Friedman's Angers procedure. Self-planning, he says, is quite different from simple user participation, because in conventional participation the designer either asks people what they want and then plans what he thinks they should have, or he prepares a design in the first place, asks the users what they think of it and then, perhaps, modifies it accordingly. But Friedman claims that in his system, the users actually do the designing for themselves.

This was possible at Angers because Friedman had *taught* them to do it, much as Kroll in Brussels taught his medical students how to plan their *zone sociale.* The differences lie in what was actually taught. In Kroll's case, it was the manipulation of little plastic blocks—color-coded to represent different kinds of activity spaces—on a basic model of the contours. Friedman taught his "users" *graph theory,* with which he believed they would be able to decide the disposition of everything in the building: rooms, doors, windows, staircases, and so on. In order to do this, he had to make two rather massive assumptions. Firstly, that the users actually care about such relationships more than anything else, and secondly, that once you have related a set of rooms together on plan, then (in Le Corbusier's words) "the plan is the generator."

Plans, of course, *can* be represented in graph theoretic terms, as a host of writers from Jean Cousin to Lionel March to Phillip Steadman have shown with great clarity. So Friedman prepared a manual, explaining with even greater clarity, by carefully annotated, comic strip-like sketches, just how graph theory works in its applications to planning. He explained that a *bouton* (a point, a vortex or whatever) might represent, say, a space (indoors or outdoors), and that a *fleche* (a line or an arrow) might be used to represent a link or connection between two such spaces. He doesn't elaborate much on what kind of connection he means, but there's a strong implication in his diagrams that he means the "walk-through" connection of adjacency. He quite rightly explains that a point might mean virtually *any* kind of space from a mean little cell to the interior of what looks like a Romanesque church, so of course each point will require a label (an *etiquette*) describing just what it is.

He then shows how a single graph might generate many different forms, much as March and Steadman have demonstrated that three quite different Frank Lloyd Wright houses, the "Life" house with its rectangular rooms, the Jester house with its circular rooms, and the Sundt house with its triangular rooms, all conform to and could have been generated from the same graph. Indeed, Friedman takes a simple graph and makes from it a rectangular plan, a circular plan, and a triangular plan. But the problem is that his three plans are topologically different, for while his triangular and rectilinear plans each consist of a single large space divided into three, his circular plan consists of three concentric circles nesting inside each other. Graph theory *doesn't* allow such transformations!

He then goes on to explain how labels attached to his various points such as garden, kitchen, and so on describe what they are and give some indication of their function, and, in some cases, their necessary sizes and shapes. He then shows how the planning relationships of his graphs may take into account sunpath, orientation, aspect, and prospect, and he shows how each point may be expanded into a space to make a bubble diagram.

Obviously, you can teach people graph theory by this simple step-by-step approach, and I have no doubt that, as a charismatic teacher, Friedman would have had some most assiduous pupils. But the question with all graphs, bubbles, and other abstract representations of built form is: then what? How do you convert them into three-dimensional built form? In my book *Design in Architecture,* I have proposed the following approaches:

1. Pragmatic Design—design, that is, in dialogue with the materials.
2. Typologic Design—repeating what is an established type.
3. Analogic Design—drawing visual or other analogies with forms from nature, painting, or whatever.
4. Geometric Design—using two- or three-dimensional geometric systems.

Friedman seems to have chosen—or was obliged to use—that favored twentieth century form of design that combines numbers one and four above into a prefabricated building system—using in this case a frame with infilling panels.

And therein lies the nub of the rub. I may not like the built, physical form of his system any more than I would have liked the infrastructure I might have been asked to build into some of his earlier schemes. And in fact, years of experience have convinced me I do not like *any* prefabricated, light frame system. Not only do they present the starkest, bleakest, and most hostile environment that has ever been "provided" for real live human beings, but I have yet to find even a single one that was anything like adequate in the crudest of physical terms. All suffered from leaks, solar overheating, heat loss, noise transmission, horrific problems of maintenance, and so on. This gross imposition of a system seems to me so remote from any *idea* of user satisfaction that trying to convince people that they were doing the designing by teaching them graph theory is nothing but window dressing.

The physical planning of a building is by far the easiest part, quite trivial in comparison with the working-out of its three-dimensional reality. For the simple fact is that if you have enough rooms, in a reasonable range of sizes and shapes (bearing in mind Peter Cowan's quite crucial observation that something like 70 percent of *all* human activities can be housed in rooms of around 150 square feet), and, if within that distribution of sizes and shapes you have enough "specials" such as laboratories or gymnasia, *then the management of the school—the deciding of who shall use each part—after it has* been built—plays far more part in user-satisfaction than anything to do with the original plan. So, however well-intentioned this scheme of Friedman's may be, it gets us little further forward than Henry Ford's theoretical "How many seats do you want?" "Four." "How arranged?" "Two in front, two in the back." Ford could have taught his customers graph theory so *they* could have designed such relationships. Friedman's answer is similar to Ford's: You can have any building style you like as long as it's in my system!

He knows, of course, that he's got a problem. He tries to deal with it (tongue in cheek?) by suggesting that while the volumes of the building may be fixed, what people actually see is the "decoration." So the users *can* have any color they like—literally—and, what's more, they can have any pattern, for the "decor" is meant to be ephemeral, painted on and then changed at the users' whim! But what group of users could agree on such things? Do we have your decor for six months and then repaint it with mine? And suppose we can't design it. Well, having gone to the trouble of teaching us graph theory, I suppose Friedman could go on to teach us supergraphics! In fact, the aspect that really worries me is precisely that *of the* designer as teacher. Graph theory obviously has its uses, and for school buildings these days it's literally kids' stuff. But how can *they* visualize from their graphs room sizes and shapes, arrangements, the sizes and shapes of the windows and doors, the colors and textures of surfaces? They *can't,* and neither can I until I've gone to the next stage of drawings, models, and other simulations of what the building will be like. These steps are included in those participatory modes, which Friedman dismisses so lightly, in which the users tell the architect what they want, he interprets more or less accurately what they said, and offers back for their comment drawings, models, and so on that *they can understand.* It's the familiar Popperian model of Conjectures and Refutations which, given honest simulations and rigorous refutations, means that *nothing* can get built that the users have not approved.

Consider, for example, other cases where an architect has acted as a catalyst in the realization of designs by participatory processes, such as Erskine at Byker in Newcastle and, at the level of rehabilitation, Rod Hackney's Black Road in Macclesfield. These architects designed a range of samples (the Janet Square pilot project, the architect's own house) that people looked at to see what most nearly met their personal requirements and suggested such modifications as would bring them closer to their preferences and needs. So these two are examples of Conjectures and Refutations that transcend the serious problems that arise when even the most sensitive designers produce the most intelligible drawings and models they possibly can. But limited as drawings and models obviously are in showing the architect's three-dimensional concept of what he thinks *they* want, they seem to me a good deal better than the dots and lines of a graph. So, however distorted a perspective might be, however glamorous a model, when used in the Conjectures and Refutations mode they still seem to be a good deal more honest than teaching people graph theory to make them think they are designing and *then* imposing your system!

## REFERENCES

Geoffrey Broadbent, *Design in Architecture*
Lionel March and Peter Steadman, *The Geometry of the Environment*
Karl Popper, *Conjectures and Refutations*

# Response to Broadbent

Yona Friedman

Geoffrey Broadbent has written a lengthy Commentary on my article about the experimental *autoplanification* implemented for a school building in France. I was surprised to find how enormously he misinterpreted both the article and the experiment itself. I cannot easily explain his reaction except by assuming that he did not understand the paper, so I feel somewhat guilty not to have explained the operation clearly enough. It is possible, of course, that Broadbent understood my paper and that he deforms on purpose both my intention and the paper's content. In this latter case, his motive might be to defend the designer's monopoly on the design process by trying to demonstrate that people cannot do their own design without the expert making drawings and models to make them understood. Drawings and models were at all times the devices by which designers, willingly or not, deceived future users: how many lovely "drawings, models, etc.," resulted in awful buildings! Architects always talked with their clients, using a language (visual or verbal) mastered by the architect alone, one which serves his interests and not necessarily those of the future user. In other words, drawings and models are much too often a salesman's technique.

My conception about design is a simple one:

1. *There is a future user of an object to be made, and this future user knows perfectly the nature of the object he wants.* If it is he himself who materializes that object, he knows how to make the necessary compromise between his image about the object to be designed and the inevitable contextual difficulties.
2. *If the object will be materialized by people other than him, the future user generally has some difficulties in communicating his wishes and decisions to the persons charged with materializing the object* that will serve him, the future user. *Thus, design process is dependent upon a nearly unsolvable problem of communication.*
3. *Communication problems are not theoretical problems;* they manifest themselves in concrete cases and proposed solutions have to be tested in such cases (as cakes are tested by eating).
4. Face-to-face communication, verbal or nonverbal, often works well. Communication that uses visualization might be good, too. But these *techniques of communication are not adequate if only one of the partners of the dialogue masters the language used,* or if both partners each use a different language. In such cases, the *stronger partner will always manipulate the weaker partner.*
5. *If there are more than two partners involved in the communication process, manipulation will increase.* If there are many people (the future users of an object to be designed), the resulting noise in the communication process (future users expressing their respective and often contradictory wishes) becomes overwhelming. *The design process will be completely manipulated by the designer who will take on the role of the arbitrator.*
6. *This is the reason why designers in participatory design take always on themselves the role of the arbiter*—the one who decides (generally in an arbitrary way) what voices to listen to within the general noise, and who justifies (by drawings and models, etc.) the arbitrary choice he himself made.
7. *This manipulation can be practically avoided if all partners in the communication process master fairly equally the language to be used* (if all future users know how to design, at least on a very fundamental level). In order to achieve this goal, it becomes necessary:
   - to agree on a language (verbal or visual) to be used *which can be mastered by all partners without difficulty*
   - to exclude the "experts in design," who are liable to manipulate the *future users, from participation in that basic conception of the object to be designed*
8. *Thus, the future user, instead of being asked to approve or disapprove the design made and defended by a professional designer* (who agreed graciously to listen distractedly to the future user's wishes), *should instead conceive and sketch (if even in unskilled manner) the object to be designed.* By working on this "sketch" he will do all the analysis that matters to him. *The technician's role becomes one of materializing the object by following the sketch he gets from the future user.*

The language I proposed because of the ease with which unschooled people can use it, is a simple application of certain aspects of graph theory. This language is very similar to the sketching technique that architects have used for centuries. The test of this process is not the architect (even not Broadbent), but the future user's satisfaction. If the future user gets the design product he expected, this proves that he is a good designer. That is what happened with the Angers school.

*User planning does not mean a procedure through which the future user can participate in the architect's work, but one that makes the architect into a simple technician assisting in the future user's work.*

To further expand the comparisons with Henry Ford with which Broadbent honors me, the process of user planning would be similar to Mr. Ford's not constructing a series of cars, but instead his trying to initiate people in building their own cars—if they want a car—from materials and parts they find or they can improvise. I permitted myself the liberty to read Broadbent's comments to a group of user planners; they laughed that Broadbent evidently considers them idiots incapable of expressing themselves with a pencil.

There is no better way to understand something than to do it by yourself. It is more important to leave scope for imagination (but not for phantasms), than to explain and explain and explain. Imagination is not the designers' monopoly, and conceiving a building is a question of imagination. To be able to express what one imagines—this is the main problem—and this is wherein lies the rationale for the user planning procedure used.

I would like to cite here, in the defense of the method I employed in Angers, something one of the users said to me after the work was over: "We have learned now what self-direction (*autogestion*) means."

# A Last Word

Geoffrey Broadbent

I am delighted to see that although in principle Yona Friedman rejects the idea of Conjectures and Refutations, in practice he adopts it with great vigor. He put forward an initial series of conjectures, I attempted to refute them, putting forward further conjectures; he has then tried to refute me, and so on. That is how knowledge grows. I am sorry he thinks that I misunderstood him; his further comments suggest that I understood him only too well, but he seems unwilling to accept the implications of his argument if followed through to its logical conclusion.

My chief argument with Yona Friedman is this: he says he is committed to the view that designers should not manipulate other people, and he seems to think that even *offering* them possibilities is a form of manipulation. He suggests that the designer should withdraw from presenting his ideas and *educate* "the people" to design for themselves instead. In that way it seems to me he is deceiving both himself and the very people he is trying to serve. He writes books, which is a form of manipulation. So do I, and as a teacher I know that education is the biggest manipulator of all. Why, Friedman even uses that most manipulative of all educational devices: encouraging his pupils to laugh at ideas *he* doesn't like. Yet, one thing is very clear: he and I are both seeking the same ends—to provide the best possible living and working environment for people. It's just that we differ in the ways we think this can be achieved.

Of course, I agree with him that "drawings, models, etc." have been and continue to be used by designers for quite nefarious purposes, as part of their "salesman's technique," as devices for deceiving future users, and so on. But that does not mean that they always have been used in this way and will continue to be so used. Books, too, have been used for nefarious purposes, but they have also been used to spread knowledge and to express man's deepest emotions. They have been used to incite revolutions, and even Friedman has used them to disseminate his ideas on what he calls a "Scientific Architecture."

My comments on some of his key points are as follows:

What kind of future user *"knows perfectly the nature of the object he wants"*? I am a future user of all kinds of things: books, records, clothes, houses, places of work, means of transport, and so on. I certainly don't know what I want in most of these fields until I see what other people, more creative than I in those areas, are actually offering me as things to choose. How *can* a user know what he wants until he has seen what is possible? Each of us obviously knows very well a particular environment, and we may have a more or less passing acquain-

tance with a number of others. We form our ideas of what we want entirely on the basis of such experiences. Most of us are habituated to the environment we know, and it *may* be so perfect that we cannot envisage any possibilities of improvement. In that case, we shall want to stay exactly where we are. Others, with reason, will dislike what they have and will have positive ideas on how it can be improved: a roof that doesn't leak, a better kitchen, a better distribution of space between living, sleeping, and so on. But people's horizons of expectation are always limited by what they know. An expert will know what has been going on worldwide, and so he will be able to introduce all kinds of other possibilities. The key word is *introduce,* and only the most arrogant expert would want to do more than that. I think it insulting to the people one is trying to help to withhold from them conjectures as to what *might* be possible.

That is true if one is trying to help an individual; it is even more true if one is trying to help a community. A community, in deliberation, will agree on some things and disagree profoundly on others. The collective view by definition must be the lowest common denominator. Karl Marx pointed this out. He showed that popular taste, by definition, must be conservative, especially in times of social upheaval (see *The Eighteenth Brumaire of Louis Bonaparte*), but even few Marxists seem to believe him.

A sensitive mind can give a community "what it never dreamed it could have"—to which more of them *might* agree than they would to the tried, tested, familiar, and mistrusted. We accept this in the fields of literature, music, painting, clothing, automobiles, and so forth. People constantly are being offered new things, most of which sink without a trace. But occasionally, something new catches on because it *is* "what people never dreamed they could have." They didn't know it was available until it was presented to them—as a possibility—by a creative mind. Such creativity is the result of special experience. As Marx and Engels put it (in *The German Ideology*):

In the case of an individual, for example, whose life embraces a wide circle of varied activities and practical relations to the world, and who, therefore, lives a many-sided life, thought has the same character of universality as every other manifestation of his life . . . not at all because the individuals by their reflection imagine that they have got rid of, or intended to get rid of, this local narrow-mindedness, but because they, in their empirical reality, and owing to empirical needs, have been able to bring about world intercourse.

As for prefabrication, I am extremely pleased to hear that Yona Friedman does not like it in principle any more than I do, but what about the users of his school? Surely, they also had views. If they are anything like the users of prefabricated schools and houses in Britain, his users must dislike the system very much, yet feel quite impotent to do anything about it. The only ones who can fight governments over such things as this are experts of the kind which Friedman—despite his protestation to the contrary—so obviously is. Again it seems to me a dereliction of duty not to exercise that expertise. Friedman, with his knowledge of what is so bad about such systems, should be *teaching* the French Government that these systems are uneconomic and environmentally and architecturally disastrous ways to build schools. If the *experts* can't refute "received wisdom" in this way, then certainly nobody else can.

So, where does all this leave us? We ought to be concerned with three levels of urban development. I *like* cities, and like Aldo Rossi I believe each city is given its identity by the "monuments" it contains. We neglect our responsibilities to the future if we do not add our own monuments, such as the Sydney Opera House, John Portman's hotels, and the Beaubourg. These will always be the work of the creative designer. You don't even have to *like* them, individually, to appreciate the role they play as twentieth century monuments.

Then there is the general texture of the city in which, as Rossi suggests, we place "insertions" from time to time. These, too, demand a kind of expertise that *only* a professional designer can offer—in the spirit of Conjectures and Refutations that I have been advocating.

But beyond that, literally at the margins of the city and in the countryside, I should like to see freedom of an even more extreme kind than Friedman seems to be advocating, based on the Third World "sites and services" approach. Of course, it is precisely in areas which were started like this that people move fastest towards copying—by visual analogy—what *architects* had been doing in the richer parts of the city. See, for instance, my example from Santo Domingo. [See also Eduardo Leira on housing design in Orcasitas in Part 3 of this volume.—EDITOR]

The more I see of such things, the more I am convinced that on the urban margins and certainly in the rural community the *only* sensible approach is to let people build for themselves. If they seek our advice as experts, then by all means let us give it, but otherwise we should not interfere. If we are invited, however, let us recognize that this is *because* we are experts and share with them our full expertise.

# UCL *Zone Sociale*
# Woluwé-St. Lambert (Brussels)

*Diversity which does not merge into unity is negation. Unity which does not depend upon diversity is tyranny.*

*Blaise Pascal*

At the edge of Brussels, unfinished in a sea of winter mud, stands the *zone sociale* of the Catholic University of Louvain Medical School. The completed buildings are a dense accretion of living spaces, shops, offices, restaurants, theaters, workshops, infant schools, and cafes. The architecture is as rich and varied as the city itself, from which it takes its materials and forms. Like the city, it is a metaphor for collective effort in a plural society. And it is one of the canonical works of the participatory movement in architecture.

In 1969, as the medical school prepared to extend its conventional modern architecture to the construction of traditional dormitories and dining halls, the students rose up. Influenced by the *événements du mai* in France the year before, they were forming new ideas of medical practice and of collegiality. They demanded an architecture that would mitigate the impact of the massive hospital.

Willing to learn and teach, Kroll spent months meeting with students both casually and in committees to develop the program.

Encouraging creativity and celebrating diversity, Kroll has made his spaces with flexible partitions and kits of parts, reflecting the influence of SAR in nearby Eindhoven. Students can choose a range of accommodations—from the traditional single room to multilevel suites. Married and single students live side by side; children are part of everyday life. The facades are largely movable panels. Fortuitous terraces and setbacks provide space for aerial gardening and chance meetings.

Communication is the theme and connections are stressed: ladders, stairs, and bridges punctuate the elevations. The most discrepant uses are made to touch: a ground floor houses a nursery school, administrative offices, and a bar. A subway to downtown Brussels (the station, designed by Kroll, is now under construction) has a place of honor in the site plan. It is there that the student quarter and the neighboring village will meet.

Fearing loss of authority, the UCL administration chose a moment when the students were away to fire Kroll, accusing him of practicing "anarchist architecture." Work has stopped. The aloof modern architecture favored by admin-

istrators jealous of their status and power can be seen in the earlier research and hospital buildings that frame the *zone sociale*. The site is a battlefield of ideologies, with architecture as the weapon and students pitted against bureaucrats.

Kroll has written, "Relationships between people in a space that suits them—that is architecture." And he has gone on to apply his architectural principles to projects as diverse as a large brewery for Kronenbourg, a residential sector of the new town of Cergy-Pontoise outside of Paris, and, perhaps most interestingly for us here, the revitalization of barracks-like public housing in the French city of Alençon. Whatever the scale, his work continues actively to involve people and to achieve high aesthetic quality. Kroll says, "One needn't choose between art and participation—although should they come into conflict, one must always choose people as they are now—because each has a role and the roles are complementary. Users participate as themselves—so should architects (as artists)."

1. Mémé and "Fachiste"—diversity of forms, functions, and living arrangements in a single structure.

# Anarchitecture

Lucien Kroll, architect
Brussels

Two *politiques d'habitat*—social approaches to housing design—are possible. One is that of a maternal authority whose specialists determine needs, make objects to live in (rational, comfortable, hygienic), and reinforce the industrial division of labor and the apathy of students. The other is participatory, pluralist. It embraces each participant as a function. It is based upon mutual comprehension, willingness to teach and learn, an exchange of responsibilities, a sharing of roles. It generates enthusiasm. With a view to incorporating the decisions of residents, it is a process which must remain open, flexible. It must free creativity, not constrain it. Having blindly followed the path of functionalism and technology, architecture senses the impasse in which it has ended and now seeks to become the expression of a new kind of collegial and plural society. Architecture wishes to shed its previous harsh and authoritarian aspects.

This latter *politique* is written and can be read in the environment we have built. Architecture is an instrument that can encourage or block hu an behaviors—all the more powerful because its language is addressed to the unconscious. If it is designed entirely by specialists, if it is fixed and untouchable, it cannot possibly respond to the diversity and creativity of those who use it. Therefore, we have used every possible means to design and build this residential quarter with the people who will use it: chance meetings, both informal and highly organized, study groups, and so forth. (If there is to be a many-sided architecture, many must be involved in making it!)

Many independent decisions taken over time come together to form the texture of ancient towns. With deep conviction, we set out to express the diversity of individuals and not the authority of institutions—as much in the juxtaposition of spaces and uses as in the possibility of future change and growth. Putting ourselves in the place of the residents, we moved far from the traditional role of the architect as maker of isolated objects. Relationships between people in space that suits them, that is architecture. An empty box is not architecture. Construction finds its meaning only in the social relations it supports. Communication through architecture becomes politics.

## Design as Politics

About 1968, the Catholic University decided to leave the old city of Louvain and set up in Brussels a large hospital, a medical school, and the residential facilities necessary for around-the-clock use. The university planning office drew up a master plan very "nineteenth century" in style (rigid zoning and institutional glory were the leading ideas). Sincerely open (at the time) to the idea of participation, they proposed this plan to the medical students, who rejected it, not wishing to be involved in this kind of project—and anxious to avoid turning into comfortable, socially irresponsible, over-privileged, and over-specialized doctors. They found the institutional image too strong, and demanded that the project be broken up and mixed in with the functions and families of the adjacent neighborhoods. They asked that planning proposals coming from the local residents be received in a spirit of mutual cooperation. This proposal was rejected by the authorities (technical requirements are such . . . ), but they did agree to allow the students to propose the architect for the job. It was then that the students discovered and arranged for the University to hire us, and for a while the customary hierarchical relationship between the parties involved in a major design project became instead a kind of amicable cooperation. At first the University authorities accepted us without reservation, even though we had no connections to the Catholic university milieu. They saw in us a solution to their problems, an alibi for the inflexible architecture they had insensitively proposed. Through sketches, memoranda, meetings, and conversations, we made ourselves as clear as we could be about our objectives and our methods. The authorities cheerfully approved everything, and we began construction of the first buildings. These were rather miraculous circumstances. We worked closely both with highly motivated students, and, at the same time, with representatives of the institution who were intelligent, competent, and exceptionally open. (It was only later that they became bureaucratic.)

We were just coming to that moment when a choice has to be made. On the one side, tranquilizing, and with its artificial image, was the authoritarian, paternal order. We went in the other direction—toward diversity, everyday culture, decolonization, the subjective, toward an image compatible with the idea of self-management, an urban texture with all its contradictions, its chance events, and its integration of activities. Ours is primarily a political project and not an aesthetic one. It is more or less ungeometrical, anti-authoritarian, anarchical *(anarchitectural)*, that is to say, human—as organic as a family of plants, and as ecological. It seemed to us that a great number of diverse intentions (above all, the most contradictory ones) could come together to create an urban landscape which is more like a growing thing—spontaneous, colorful, involved—than any formal geometry. We are convinced that a complex kind of order (the simple repetition of identical elements represents to us a disorder, a sickness) encourages a more responsible, autonomous sort of behavior than the usual dormitory for nice young men and women.

## Plant Ecology and Social Ecology

There are two ways to create space for plants, just as there are two ways of organizing social space. The first aims at a single, predetermined objective. It is authoritarian, rational, and reductive. It corresponds to the desire to control

2. Kroll's architecture is a polemical challenge to the abstraction of the medical complex which preceded it.

3. Communication marks the architectural concept; there are rich connections within the *Zone Sociale* and between it and the medical center.

4. *Zone Sociale* site plan. The structures shown in outline are as yet unbuilt. Those in gray—from north to south, the restaurant connected to the Mémé-Fachiste, the "Ecole," and the "Ecumenical Center"—are occupied. Despite the names, each contains living accommodations, offices, shops, cultural facilities, etc.

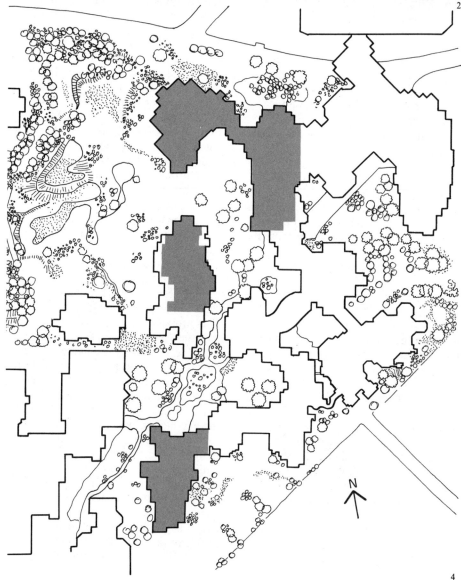

3

4

events and people on the part of those whose task it is to conceive, organize, and produce. It contains an unconscious will to enclose life within geometrical schemes, to leave nothing to chance. At best, this approach to design divides the richness of life and reorganizes it by subject, like the books in a library. At worst, it turns the world into a kind of storehouse of replacement parts. This is the approach which has built our formal city parks (where everything is strictly planned; there are, of course, no weeds) and the artificial spaces of our housing projects (every function pigeon-holed, all eventualities provided for). It reproduces the image of the military camp where the spatial order grows in a rigid grid from abscissa and ordinate. Some people like this. It responds to a wish to manipulate and be manipulated.

The other way of making social space (or, for that matter, a green space) is a living process which implants only key centers of activity in a clear spatial configuration and with an intensity of form and meaning that favors (and expresses) what we believe essential: living relationships and activities which spring from diversity, unexpected initiatives, and, above all, that something in social man that leads to the creation of community. This way of working is at once subjective, holistic, and spiritual. It uses rationality, but recognizes its limitations. The other is objective, normative, egocentric, and utilitarian. These two views coexist: their counterpoint evolves with the times.

They met, startlingly, at the Medical School in 1969. The students made clear the nature of the responsible society they wished to see take form on the new site. The University was able to understand their political project and to believe it compatible with the grand geometrical project they had already begun [for example, the hospital facilities—EDITOR]. They decided to build it. Harnessed together for a time were exceptional intelligence, energy, and trust.

5. The main courtyard with the Fachiste (so-called because it contains ordinary dormitory rooms for students not interested in group living) in the background.

6. A view of the Ecole from the roof garden of the Mémé.

## Organic Architecture

The forms of the buildings we proposed were conceived in an ecological fashion. There were few elements of simple geometry, no regular repetitions. They grew from the interior toward the exterior. The facades incorporate many different forms and colors. The massing of the scheme is not the result of artificial stereometry, but rather like a natural pile of mossy rocks, sliced through with circulation in all directions. Even the concrete structure is conceived in the form of mushroom columns placed irregularly.

A subway station opens onto the middle of the site. A concrete slab covers its 100 yards of platform. It, too, has the quality of plants—columns freely located, slab decoration modeled according to the load supported. The columns have branches that pick up eccentric loads, and they are cast in forms lined with the actual bark of trees. It is terribly important that the exterior spaces express the same intentions, be shaped to reproduce varied microclimates, to receive plants of all kinds—cultivated plants and those brought by the wind, the birds, or even the students from their country gardens. The density of construction is almost overwhelming. Only an explosion of plant life covering the ground, the walls, the balconies, the windows, and the roofs can soften it. It will blunt the sharp edges and hard surfaces, hide one building from another, multiply distances and spaces. Already by 1971, the students had planted more than 1000 trees on the site with us.

Continuity—the unification of spaces, forms, and materials—is for us one of the most fruitful design concepts: it calls on us to join the architecture with the gardens and the gardens with the facades (nothing is as fascinating as a climbing plant which follows its own laws of space and growth). The materials of the facades pour out onto the ground. The materials of the ground plane cling to the walls (paving stones from the walkways which crawl up the walls, brickwork and stones which climb down to form pavements). In the same fashion, the roof tiles descend down along the walls and the concrete walls turn corners and stretch out irregularly to tie together the different parts of the project and break down the brutal geometry of modern architecture.

Trees are planted against the facades. (The old myth that they ruin foundations has no validity with current technology, nor does the notion that vines destroy the walls they climb. When lime masonry was in use, ivy fed on the masonry joints. Today, the poor things can't cling to smooth cement or continuous oven-baked brick. One first needs a "scaffolding" of Virginia creeper to help them attach themselves!) The vines covering the wall give protection against cold, heat, and humidity. They shelter a great number of birds, and they do more for photosynthesis than the products of industrial culture. These plant analogies indicate the nature of the society that we were anxious to shelter and whose development the architecture should support and express.

Through meetings, letters, and drawings, we were as explicit as possible about the visual and social qualities of the architecture we believed in. We thought it had been understood and approved by the authorities. Only some years later we learned that certain officials had decided very early on to put an end to participation and use the nature of our architecture as an excuse should students react against being put back in their place. So instead of helping us to get on with the project, they bogged us down in the increasing bureaucracy of their offices. In fact, these same authorities had resolved to "begin again at the beginning, in order to better divide student residence into small groups and surround them with the effective and discreet presence of faculty." They seemed to have calculated that, in stopping work on our site and abandoning it in a sad, unfinished state (there are only 20,000 m² built of the 40,000 m² designed), in not completing this busy center, but directing their funds towards completion of other parts of the medical school in which there was no student participation, they were going to be able to reconstitute a passive and compliant student body: "The party is over, we must establish order again." The first thing they did was to destroy our ecological gardens with a bulldozer and a formidable group of surveyors. In a battle of ideologies, not even flowers are innocent. . . .

## The Honeymoon: Cooperation and Participation

However, during the first years some of the University officials encouraged us and joined in the discussions we were having with the students. It was only thanks to an extraordinary chain of events, to the reasonableness, imagination, and objectivity of this first group of officials, and the thoughtful behavior of the students who wished to have a say in their way of living and in their professional and political education, that our designs could be conceived and in part built.

A great number of visits, meetings, chats, and notes exchanged with the students of the "Mémé" (the *Maison Médicale*), headquarters of the medical students then still in Louvain, helped us to understand and to frame a way of life, before drawing precise plans. "No washbasins in the rooms, we don't want to live like the bourgeoisie." "To feel that I'm in the city, I'd like to wake up to the smell of bread fresh from the oven." "I'd like to grow parsley and chives outside my room." "Stores—not hard sell, but economical. . . ."

To reinforce the creative process, we

organized "thinking groups" made up of friends, assistants, students, and specialists that met several times for entire weekends. They came easily to imagine themselves as residents, living on the site, giving it its character. "A subway platform is a bit lonely, and an underground parking garage can be sinister—but if one opens onto the other, they'll be more human." "Organize scattered day-care centers. They'll be more familial and more accessible. They'll avoid becoming hygienic parking lots for babies." "Let's have a vegetable or a secondhand market." "Contact between the parts of the school, and above all with the city."

## The Program

They took apart and put back together again the simple program established by the University: 20 apartments, 60 studios, 200 rooms for single students, 200 single rooms grouped into apartments, six communal houses of 18 rooms, and headquarters space for the Mémé. In addition, there was to be a 750-seat restaurant, places for worship and culture (a cinema and a theater), a day-care center, a kindergarten, student services, and offices for the administration. Finally, serving the entire neighborhood and covering 3500 m², a post office, offices, shops, and a few small restaurants. This program called for 40,000 m² of construction, not including the city subway station. To expand participation to include students other than those who came forward eagerly, we organized a number of formal meetings which appealed to the less motivated students. The University, at our invitation, sent an official representative to each of these meetings.

As these meetings caught the imagination of the participants, they generated extraordinary creative thinking which we could fit directly into the design and then check very quickly with the future residents. Those who were truly motivated were few, but convinced that they must bring their best professional judgment to bear on each design decision. In working to create "ordinary" dwellings, they meant to attach themselves visibly to the local, popular culture and give their medical profession a human scale, an openness, an acceptance of those it served which medicine in a class society had forgotten.

Architecture would serve them as a language—standard windows, sometimes with flowered curtains, common materials, no high fashion design, domestic scale, gardens—these quickly make things welcoming. What sick person would leave his little house in Kapelleveld to confide in a doctor in the University's enormous hospital? He'd only be able to speak of his "mechanical problems," and not of his life. How would he act in a more familiar sort of space? This desire to make the *zone sociale* feel comfortable to those from the outside was felt to be very important. It guided our design work throughout the stormy history of the project.

## The Image of Autonomy

Encircled by tough, modern buildings, backed up against the little village of Kapelleveld, our group of buildings seems a bit like a sponge, without exact form, of a soft vegetable texture, and run through with different sorts of hollows. The building forms are not static. Walking through the site they change constantly, always in an unexpected fashion. The materials of the windows, their colors, curtains, balconies, and plants increase the sense of diversity. They reinforce the individuality and the autonomy of the occupants, and not the power of the central administration. This architectural "irregularity" enables everyone to find the spot that just fits his needs. It also permits residents to modify the facade to suit. (Who will notice a window repainted by an inhabitant to his taste?) Participation doesn't work against the architecture, but with it.

No architectural volume can be said to be dominant (the composition is not hierarchical). There are many important places, many centers, each connected to and integrated into the others by an elaborate network of circulation. One thing we had in mind was the possibility of a police raid against the politically active students. Here it is impossible to cover all the exits. Everything connects: roofs, floors, basements, terraces. The stairs aren't necessarily continuous, following some abstract rule. They follow more organic laws, like animal trails or the paths in an older neighborhood.

## Anarchitecture

Without meaning to diminish the tradi-

tional responsibilities of the architect, we were trying to develop a relationship of friendship and trust with all those concerned with the project—even those from the University who were dissembling, hiding their true feelings behind facades alternately strict and holy. We hoped to express this open relationship and prove that architecture can be a joyous experience for all those who get involved in it: first the students who will use it, then the official clients, but also the construction workers, and even the bankers. Architecture need not be the tragic or sordid affair that one might believe from seeing the buildings now in fashion.

## System of Construction

We could not accept a system of construction which was either too repetitious or too limiting like most systems of prefabrication (which are rarely economical anyway). On the other hand, the use of self-managed teams of artisans could jeopardize our objectives or lead the project to break down in disorder. Now, traditional construction expresses a more-or-less organized, more-or-less habitual sequence of building acts and the richness and skill associated with them. And heavy prefabrication presents a slightly Stalinist image and involves a loss of workers' skills and abilities as machines take over the building site. But open industrialization joined to craftsmanship shows us the way to participation and self-direction, and enables us to demonstrate in the act of construction the possibility of a decentralized society.

Our effort was related to the studies done by SAR (Stichting Architecten Research) and John Habraken at Eindhoven. We stripped away everything that was too Dutch, and we resolved to accept and use whatever unforeseen opportunities cropped up in the course of construction. We thus adopted the SAR distinction between structure (Support) and Infill (but which structures which?) in order to reserve a substantial domain for design participation: the Structure fixed and unchangeable, Infill independent of structure and totally flexible. The Infill elements could come from various sources: they may be selected from the large number of elements which are available on the market, or they can be made by an artisan or knocked together by the occupants themselves. The struc-

8. (left) The back of the Ecole: workmen changing facade panels to accommodate a new use. At the base, a nursery nestles beneath the Rector's office.

9. (above left) Planting beds—for flowers or vegetables—to "soften the overwhelming construction."

10. (above right) Students worked with the architects' team to create a contrasting natural landscape.

11. Site model shows planned construction.

12. The upper section of the Mémé is a three-story volume of space in which students create their own lodgings using a kit of parts designed by the architect.

12

13. An almost unlimited arrangement of spaces and levels is possible within the block-long loft.

13

14. A view upward through the loft. Random windows in the exterior wall permit floors to be located at any level.

15. Typical floors in the residential portions of the project employ a SAR grid and movable partitions to encourage user involvement.

14

15

ture was designed to accept these three possibilities simultaneously or successively.

Structure and Infill are related by dimensions and zones. Modular coordination ensured that building elements would fit easily either into one another and into the structure. The dimensions are based on a module of 10 cm, with a preference for 30 cm (one foot), and upon a tolerance proper to each technique and material. We banked on open prefabrication and organized everything around it: it is a cultural revolution as important as the one which brought interchangeable parts for machinery. The architectural image which results appears to have been made over the course of time by a great number of personal and yet compatible decisions.

The apparent disorder of the facades is also extremely organized. In fact, it is obtained through a severe discipline: we based our design on a coordinating module, creating a Scotch grid in the manner of SAR with 10 and 20 cm zones running in both directions in plan. Structural members and mechanical equipment find their place in the 20 cm and the partitions in the 10 cm zones. All the windows are multiples of 30 cm with their frames. They fit neatly with the partitions.

We have used, side-by-side, windows in wood and in aluminum and still others in plastic, and also solid panels with colored surfaces. There are never two windows of the same dimensions or two panels of the same color next to one another. The juxtapositions of the windows and the panels were determined by chance, sometimes by using playing cards (I didn't have a table of random numbers). But once in a while we had to improve on chance, which sometimes lined things up too neatly.

## Mixed Masonry

We asked the masons to mix concrete blocks and bricks. To give force to that idea, we laid down very precise constraints: "To reach the middle of the window there, begin here." (The two points weren't at 45° from each other, otherwise one gets a simple stair.) "All the blocks should touch each other." Making a wall became a conscious act. The masons couldn't do it while thinking of something else. Here they performed as artisans. The forms created belonged to them, they weren't drawn. It wasn't the work of the architect, or

16–19. Participation extended to the construction workers. Here are some examples of the masons' inventions. The two figures which guard the stair to the married students quarters are the result of a friendly competition between two foremen.

175

the contractor, or the foreman. This architecture encourages the inhabitants, too, to leave their mark.

## Schizophrenic Concrete

"Beautiful" masonry is traditionally regular, abstract, "schizophrenic." But today the quality of masonry is no longer measured in terms of geometry or mechanical precision. Concrete, poured in place, even under impossible conditions, used to be expected to come out smooth, without a joint, without a trace of its formwork, the instrument of its production. However, one must note with admiration that the same persons who have demanded this sort of construction, when they begin to perceive the value of the marks of the potter's fingers or the brushstrokes of the painter, suddenly recognize the incoherence into which the division of labor has led us. And they realize that buildings produced under this system unconsciously influence behavior, to the point where anything an inhabitant adds to his dwelling is seen as embarrassing and inappropriate.

## Fossil Concrete

We asked the men who made the shuttering to put unusual materials on the forms. They tried it out first at small scale, then on a bigger section of concrete, forming it with very rough pieces of wood (the first planks sawn from the log with the bark still on—very irregular in thickness, form and texture). They even used branches and leaves to make sure the formwork would not be smooth. One of the carpenters told me, "You see how nice the forms are? But I'm going to fix it up over here because there's a little spot that doesn't look so good. . . . " They made sculpture.

We wanted a great concrete wall, 7 m long on two levels. The carpenters went out into the neighboring fields very early in the morning to collect various things—leaves, pine branches, saplings—and fixed them delicately with nails and staples to the formwork while it was laid flat. When we removed the formwork, we found an extraordinary fossil wall. The carpenters showed us details of branches, the exact impression of the fragile leaves of the plantain. Some brought their families to the site on Sundays to show off their work. One can imagine teams of specialists trained in this work who would go from site to

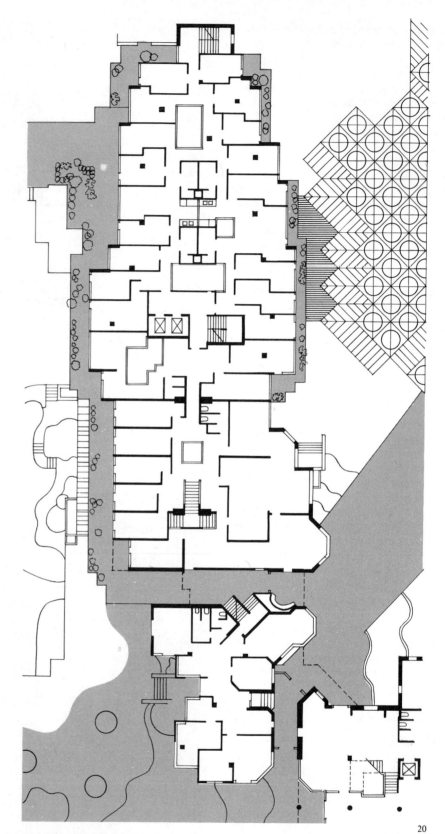

20

20. A typical floor in the Mémé. Note the random column location intended to encourage planning freedom. Partition locations shown are only suggestions.

21. Partial plan of typical residential floor shows use of SAR grid and degree of flexibility.

22. The facade recapitulates the city and responds to the diversity behind.

176

site as the guild craftsmen did, giving life to walls.

Only after having exorcised the technocratic illusion of the complete industrialization of building can we move to democratize the act of building once again. Instead of allowing the technical processes to control everything, we could set about decentralizing decisions and actions—generating, bringing together, and supporting all the individual initiatives and all the lively differences of both the workers and the future inhabitants. In this way, the centralized authority of a ruling class *and* of a ruling technology could be done away with. And one could move ahead with all the technical and human means we have now to create step by step a new, human environment, more participatory, more in keeping with socialist precepts.

## Economic Considerations

Below we give the costs of building the *zone sociale* of the Medical School at Woluwé-St. Lambert. These figures (in Belgian francs/m²) are as of January, 1978. They are limited by strict cost ceilings imposed by the state on university housing organizations, which are considered low-rent housing corporations (Société d'Habitations à Bon Marché).

The budget was 16,503 Bfrs/m². For three of the buildings we succeeded in staying below the budget (for example, the Ecumenical Center at −2.67 percent, the *Mémé* at −1.51 percent)—but the *Fachos* came in higher, at +1.95 percent. The building called *École et Administration* ran into bad luck. The firm which contracted to build it at below maximum allowable cost had barely begun when it went bankrupt. It was replaced by an expensive and disorganized operation. Here are the costs, by category, for the first three buildings:

|     |                             |         |
| --- | --------------------------- | ------- |
| 1.  | Site work and grading       | 4.07%   |
| 2.  | Masonry, concrete, floors   | 38.51%  |
|     | Partitions                  | 6.46%   |
| 3.  | Roofing                     | 9.63%   |
| 4.  | Finishing of surfaces       | 8.15%   |
| 5.  | Carpentry and glazing       | 11.85%  |
| 6.  | Water, gas, and sanitary facilities | 6.30% |
| 7.  | Electrical work             | 7.03%   |
| 8.  | Heating                     | 4.08%   |
| 9.  | Painting                    | 2.96%   |
| 10. | Walkways, parking, etc.     | 0.96%   |
|     |                             | 100.00% |

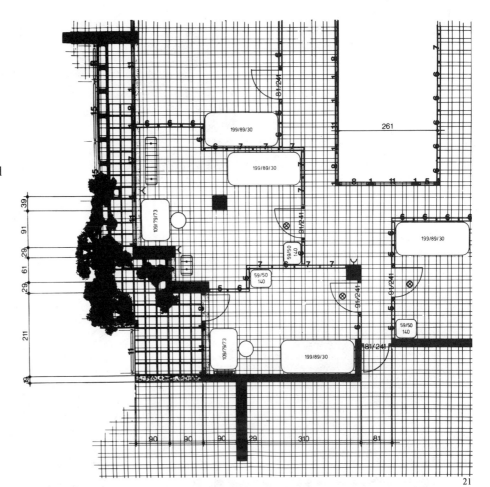

21

22

23. The Metro (subway) station is at the heart of the *Zone Sociale* and gives it importance to the surrounding community. Its undulating, organic roof involved the workers in design and color choices.

24–25. Construction underway on the station.

26. The column as tree: workers brought natural materials to line the forms.

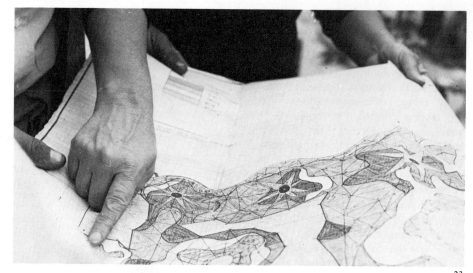

23

24

25

26

We wanted to give the expenses in some detail because many observers like to believe that our architecture must be very expensive. For obscure reasons, this relieves their anxiety.

## The Engineers

The structural engineers on this project were decent people whom the University imposed upon us. We quickly ran into trouble over our random structural system, conceived as a group of mushroom columns of different diameters joined by a thick floor slab with continuous reinforcing (a flat plate). Nervous surprise. What's logical about this? For us, a regular grid of equal bays risked producing unimaginative behavior. The engineer swore that our scheme would cost 43 percent more. Bitterness. A University official found a mediator in the person of a paternal engineer-arbitrator who had useful advice for his suffering colleague: "First imagine that the columns are in line, calculate them like that and then add reinforcing where you think necessary; I trust your instinct as an engineer. . . ." I got my "promenade" of columns. Little by little, the engineer came to understand our logic and collaborated. He works with us still in an extremely intelligent and reliable fashion.

## Popular Arts and Traditions

On the one hand, architecture should decondition inhabitants, at once from the present industrial-social-legal model *and* from nostalgia for the past, and on the other, it should place them in a contemporary, ordinary, generalizable environment. For this reason we sought to utilize materials which suggest popular culture: slates of common cement asbestos for walls subject to dampness, window frames out of the catalog, exposed concrete, ordinary bricks and block, standard glazing on the balconies, some plastic, and so forth. We wished to employ what future archeologists would recognize as the "popular arts and traditions" of our epoch.

Inside the Mémé, the rooms are all different. It didn't seem appropriate to make them the same. It is irrational to impose identical architecture on diverse inhabitants; it will tend to make them identical, faceless—or rebellious. The partitions that form the students' rooms are placed in a rather irregular floor plan, between the unaligned columns.

27. An architecture of accommodation: a cafe designed by its owners fits neatly into the Ecole.

They are easily demountable and permit the residents to take them down and to replan the floor as they would like to have it. That is, this system gives the residents the ability to adopt a natural and creative attitude in their dealings with the institution and to move beyond the traditional and oppressive landlord-tenant relationship.

In opposition to the ordinary tendency of individuals and institutions to be closed, shut in on themselves, here in the *zone sociale* everything communicates, everything connects, everything is open. It is possible to see, to hear, to encounter one another. The floor slabs are cut through, connecting the levels, the walls open up, the balconies are joined. There is access from every side: through the basement, through the attics, with ladders on the terraces, by little bridges.

To avoid the monotony of a student city, we mixed together, in a diversified urban texture, all the elements called for by the program. A large meeting room is shared by the *Maison Médicale* and by the restaurants. When he opens his window, the Director of the Medical

School will be able to hear the voices of children coming from the primary school which is on his ground floor. Above his offices are apartments for young married couples. Shops and places to eat are inserted in the residential sections. Even though it is somewhat difficult to tell where one building begins and another ends, the key points in the plan are reinforced by collective facilities which create landmarks, and by the variation of forms, spaces, materials, and colors which visually tell one where one is.

## Summing Up

Both we and the students had wanted to avoid creating a university ghetto. We believed in continuity between our *zone sociale* and the village of Kapelleveld. To create "good urban habits," we decided to build, as our first step, a diverse and animated center for our new neighborhood. The hazards of planning and of financing produced the opposite of what we intended: the central meeting place around the Mémé is now too

homogeneous and university-like. It doesn't have enough people to be lively and, a more tragic thing, it is completely isolated in a sea of rubble, parking, and mud. The University has not been able to accept its responsibilities and carry out its plans for a truly urban milieu: it lets men and things fall into despair and ruin.

We now have the feeling that this entire project rested on a misunderstanding. The authorities never really believed that we would carry out our announced intentions and that participation would create an environment which was so foreign to them. One doesn't see in what we have built enough of the kind of order which would lead the inhabitants to obey unconsciously, to hold back from mixing in anything which wasn't their immediate concern. Also, our architecture probably doesn't confer sufficiently the social status which is supposed to distinguish the Catholic student from all those good people who are neither one nor the other. The University decided, then, to change architects as one would

change shoes. They fired us with the same casualness with which they hired us, thus admitting the failure (or misunderstanding) of their policy of friendly participation and aborting the plan which expressed it. Of course, the students resisted firmly but politely the redoubtable group of more "civilized" architects brought in by the authorities. With these architects, the students saw their chances of realizing a convivial environment evaporating. But who will win?

Last March, during the only sunny week, the students put up a tent with 1500 seats, and for a week they put on shows: theater, song, a little sport, beer, sausages, and a protest exhibition. They created an extraordinary atmosphere (it should be normal, really). The authorities were upset. They protested their good faith: if there hadn't been revival of cooperation, it was because of lack of time or absentmindedness. They only wanted it to begin again, as soon as possible. They weren't withholding in the way they went about it: they sent in Prof. R. M. Lemaire himself—more an

archeologist than a planner (the Romulus of Louvain-la-Neuve*) —and charged him with renewing participation: "Tell me if you prefer gray or white paving blocks? As far as the overall plan goes, trust me. I know." Response: "We want the Kroll plan." "That, no—but what about the paving blocks?" And so forth . . . a dialogue of the deaf!

Lemaire proposed a plan and was turned down by the students. This plan gave up the idea of the center which had been seen as connecting the *zone sociale* with Kapelleveld. It moved most of the future construction back against the hospital (which is hardly welcoming)—to take advantage of the lively atmosphere provided by sick people and their visitors! A retreat: we'll be better off by ourselves. The plan also massacred what was left of the densely planted hills and gardens (lawn and paving, it's better . . . ). It introduced a *cordon sanitaire* (parking spaces and grass) to maintain a certain distance between the campus and the town (the students speak once again of a ghetto). It also plans to let our existing buildings rot under their temporary covering of tar paper.

*At the time the Medical School moved to Woluwé-Saint Lambert, the remainder of the University was transfered to the new town of Louvain-la-Neuve, designed under the direction of Lemaire, a professor in the School of Architecture and Planning.

The group leading the resistance to this plan is composed of representatives of the various residential buildings, employees, local businessmen, and families who live on the site. It functions like a neighborhood committee—it invited the mayor and not the University officials to its annual celebration. It also acts like a study group—it is researching its own recent history (the generations succeed themselves and pass on their accomplishments). "Revolutionaries, they don't hold back, but now they're demanding *possible* things: that's much more dangerous." Civilized in all respects, they calculate, they reflect, they don't do anything suddenly. The authorities are no doubt waiting for the final examination period to take action against the students who oppose them.

Fortunately, we never wished to see the spaces we created as a work of art, a merely intellectual achievement, but as a living process, a perpetually unfinished place (a battlefield?) to which each generation adds new meanings and further, rich contradictions.

29. A student leaflet calling for a mass meeting following the appointment of another architect to continue the project after Kroll's dismissal. It asks, A new master plan for the area?

30. The remarkable completed buildings stand in unkempt fields awaiting resolution of the conflict.

Un nouveau plan directeur pour le site ?

ASSEMBLEE GENERALE des utilisateurs.

29

30

# Commentary on UCL *Zone Sociale*

Alex Tzonis and Liane Lefaivre

## PARTICIPATORY ARCHITECTURE AT THE CROSSROADS

It has been almost two decades since the relation between designer and user of buildings emerged as a key issue in architecture and the populist movement* reversed contemporary values and attitudes, giving the user a new, central place in the creation of his environment.

Populists criticized contemporary architecture for its forbidding paternalism. To them, its designs—whether academic or modernist, functionalist, or decorative—falsely claimed to embody universal norms suited to the good of society as a whole. In fact, the populists argued, these norms merely reflected the official culture and the interests of a self-perpetuating profession. Populists also charged that behind the image traditionally associated with the profession of architecture—heroic devotion, calling, disinterestedness, discipline, service, and universality of man**—stood an elite attitude, alien and even hostile to most people. To support their attack, they pointed to the rapidly deteriorating modern structures which, although built according to the established rules and measures of the new architecture, were being neglected, defaced, or abandoned out of indifference or resentment by users seeking to shape their places in keeping with their own sense of dignity and their own canon of quality.

To populists, contemporary architecture was an anomaly and a scandal, its authoritarian benevolence seemed out of place in a democratic society, its arbitrary order unacceptable in a culture devoted to individualistic realism. Populists felt that contemporary architecture deprived man of a basic satisfaction by splitting designer and user into two different people. Many of them looked with nostalgia to an idyllic architecture that had existed before the division of labor, industrialization, and state intervention had spread monotony, oppression, and alienation, and of which one could still see traces in so-called anonymous, vernacular, indigenous, or popular settlements.

Populists concluded that, *in the name of the people,* of dignity, and of democracy, professionalism in architectural thinking and practice had to be limited, if not eliminated. In return, the intervention of the user had to become broader and more powerful. Moreover, the old set of professional ideals had to be replaced by new populist ones—disinterestedness by involvement, discipline by liberation, service by expression, and universality by community.

The arrival and rapid spread of the populist movement during the 1960s brought hope as well as panic. While to some it was a long-awaited event, infusing new vigor in architecture and, even more, instigating social change, setting up democratic institutions, and acting as a catalyst for a more humane everyday life, to others it was an *agent provocateur* that threatened the fragile existence of architecture, and even of a delicately balanced postwar society.

For all the clattering, the takeover never happened. Populism and its polemics underwent a quiet but rapid decline almost a decade after their first appearance. No apocalyptic visions appear on the horizon now. Only a few people in not very centrally located places seem to be discussing the problems of architecture and freedom, architecture and democracy, architecture and dignity, architecture and social change. The mood is considerably different.*

Yet, now we have at hand actual projects that have been designed according to principles that a decade ago were only ideas. In addition, although the major platforms of architectural debate seem to have been successfully disinfected from the spread of populism, most of the questions to which populism tried to respond (albeit clumsily) remain without an answer. We feel, therefore, that there is a double reason for a critical discussion of these projects.

Populists not only criticized, but they tried to reshape architectural theory and practice. One wing of the movement took a relatively conservative position, focusing on aspects of visual form and disregarding plan and construction. They tried to develop a "pop" style—the notion of style remaining defined in a traditional manner—emulating objects of popular appeal with whose design professionals had had nothing to do. Another group ignored style altogether. They thought of it as an elite notion, demanded the complete liquidation of the architect, and espoused the ideal of buildings made solely by users through a "self-help" process. Finally, other populists took the middle of the road in the debate. They viewed architecture as being reformed through the "participation" of the users in the generation of buildings on equal terms with the architects.

The projects we have in front of us fall largely into this last category. In them, the architect enters a polity with the user through a series of discussions of varying length and content: longer and more involved in the case of Alexander's Mexicali project, shorter in the case of Kroll's. In theory, this eventually leads to the fusion of ideas from the two sides and finally to a compromise plan that is said to represent a consensus.

Another approach to participation is through the introduction of "open," "half-determined" structures. This is the Supports system of Habraken and was the method followed in the SAR projects: while the architect defines a general shelter and a system of services, the user fills in the rest of the fabric. Thus, official standards, professional norms, and industrial requirements are interlocked into one "participatory" whole. The user may complete his part on his own, taking his time over the years, or he may arrive at a final plan during a series of meetings with the architect.

---

*Tzonis, A. and Lefaivre, L. "In de Naam van het Volk" (The Populist Movement in Architecture), (Dutch) *Forum,* no. 3, 1976; (German) *Bauwelt,* January 10, 1975. Also published in English in *Papers by the Faculty of the Department of Architecture, Harvard University,* Cambridge, 1978.

**Larson, M. S. *The Rise of Professionalism. A Sociological Analysis.* Berkeley, Los Angeles, and London, 1977.

---

*Tzonis, A. and Lefaivre, L. "The Narcissist Phase in Architecture" *Harvard Architectural Review,* no. I, 1980; *Wonen-TA/BK,* no. 23, December, 1979; *Arch +*, Aachen, January, 1979.

Certainly, the user may participate at a very early stage, influence site arrangements, and even the selection of technology. The SAAL, Mexicali, and the Brussels Medical School projects opted more for this approach. Local, pragmatic constraints—materials, technology, site, and zoning considerations—define the dividing line between the parties. In the case of the Mexicali project, there were also theoretical constraints. The architects arrived with a doctrine contained in the manual, *The Timeless Way of Building,* to which they had to adapt the participatory process. In all cases, however, it seems that agreement was finally reached in a way satisfactory to both sides and the final plans completely fitted the users' needs.

But a discussion of these projects ought to go beyond this immediate reaction. We must be sure that the diffused sense of satisfaction in the user does not really arise from nonarchitectural factors such as location of the project or the equipment installed. (Alas, after a long discussion with the inhabitant of a unit of Infill housing in Holland, I found that what proved to be the main attraction of the house was the new sanitary equipment it contained.) In fact, we must see to what extent the euphoria of the user is in reality the result of the architectonic product at all. We have to be careful not to become victims of the famous fallacy pointed out by the researchers in the Hawthorne Project back in the 1920s.*

As is well known, Elton Mayo and his team showed that what had been initially accepted as an effect of good environmental conditions on productivity in the factory was only the result of the "democratic" atmosphere, of the therapeutic effect of interviews and counseling, and of the personal contact—the meeting, talking and caring, the interest in the other, the sense of not being alone, of being worthy—which ran parallel to the modifications in the physical environment.

Before praising participation as a means of developing better architecture, we ought to know more about such sociopsychological phenomena. We might find out that attitudes toward modernist architecture could be different if moving to a new apartment regularly involved such an intense experience in group relations as that accompanying the Mexicali or the SAR projects. Of course, we might find the opposite to be true. Whatever the case, we will want to know more about the relative impacts of design and participation.

But there is a more basic issue in developing a framework for criticism. These projects ought to be seen not only in terms of their current performance—as isolated individual products—but also in terms of their ability to perform as parts of a larger system of human relations and social change. Was not such a framework, after all, the context within which populism made its demands for a new architecture? Within such a framework, we may question whether offering the choice to the user to determine his or her environment—at least in the ways it was conceived and carried out here—is a great contribution to improving the human condition.

The authors of these projects seem to be departing from a rather limited point of view about the nature of needs and aspirations in the user. They only go so far as to criticize the idea of universal norms of architecture. They focus on new ways of satisfying the needs of the individual and not the norms of an outside power, of opening up freedom of choice and trying to find means to keep individual choice from conflicting with the freedom of others. There are contradictions in this approach.

Ideally, in systems of double-scale intervention—such as the Supports/Infill system of SAR—the designer himself assumes the responsibility of guaranteeing that each individual choice can be fulfilled to the same extent without troubling any other. Conflicts may also be resolved through long meetings between users and designers. During these discussions, the users modify their initial demands either by bargaining between themselves or by simply becoming aware of the possible consequences of their choices. In both cases, they become more conscious of the context within which they operate. As the authors of the Mexicali project stated, there is a development of "human association," of "relationship to other families." But this interaction and awareness can be very limited, despite the assurances that its limits are "society" itself.

There are at least two cases where it might *not* be possible to satisfy human needs, where freedom of choice is curtailed, and which lie beyond the narrow conception of the world of user-architect relationship offered here. Populists, like the designers of the Welfare State they criticize, seem to apply all their efforts of analysis to the arbitrarily-isolated domain of consumption in relation to the habitat and to ignore the fact that this freedom could not be found outside the structure of dependencies in society which is determined by the organization of control over the means of production. Thus, while some early modern architects of the Welfare State saw users almost as a well-ordered regiment awaiting their rations, some populists and participatory designers see them as clients of a well-serviced supermarket. According to this model, people would be free to acquire from shelves what they need without control, supervision, or bureaucracy. If only that little cashier were taken away from the entrance—as Herbert Read once remarked.

The second most important limitation comes out of the fact that while individual needs, demands, and desires are identified as different, what makes them vary is never discussed. They are viewed as springing out of a private self, independent of the social self.* In fact, a person does not create his own needs, demands, and desires. These are not autonomous constructs maintained outside social ties and outside the structure of power in society. Its lines of persuasion and inducement are significant determinants of what an individual perceives and chooses. To rely completely on the perceived norms of the user may lead as far away from freedom and human dignity as does the list of the official norms and institutional standards that are so despised.

One may even argue that participatory architects not only looked at this larger social framework through the glass darkly (although a better view was not impossible), but that they even projected this narrow attitude onto their users. Housing, for example, tends to take a central position in all discussions at the expense of other issues. Why not urge people instead to adopt the approach of the citizens of ancient Athens? During the time of Pericles, they were accustomed to private poverty and substandard housing within which they spent minimum time in return for the luxury of a public place where most of everyday life was spent discussing common affairs, "national" and "international" questions, even humanistic issues and epistemological, aesthetic, and moral problems.

The following argument, however, could conceivably be made in favor of the projects: Welfare State architecture, with its em-

*Mayo, E. *The Human Problems of Industrial Civilisation,* 1933. Mayo, E. *The Social Problems of an Industrial Civilization,* 1945. Dixon, W. *Management and the Worker,* 1939.

*Brittan, A. *The Privatised World,* London, 1979. Holland, R. *Self and Social Context,* London, 1977.

phasis on universality of design norms and rigidity of standards, has been to a large part of the population both a way of distributing "shelter goods," and also a socialization process. It was a means of directing the loose proletarians from a wholesome agrarian past and a scoundrel urban present to a future of well-disciplined industrial production. Similarly, it can be argued that the value of the projects at hand does not lie in how many architectural services they supply, but in their educational role. The authors themselves have stressed that they see their projects as schools for liberation, places where the scared, the passive, and the deprived will gradually feel the sweet taste of freedom and sense the dignity of being independent. In other words, the space appropriation by the users, which takes place in terms of the arrangement of their own immediate environment in these projects, serves as a paradigm for appropriation on a much vaster scale and on a much higher level of the social life.

Unfortunately, there is much historical evidence to support the opposite. The acquisition of home, especially if one identifies with it, accelerates the privatization of self and intensifies conformism and a passive attitude toward efforts that affect general social issues. The ambiguity that surrounds such experimental efforts only reinforces the fear that these projects, like most participatory and populist architecture with their emphasis on variety, flexibility, and uniqueness of the product, only contribute to the transformation of a sober, regimented population into an enthusiastic crowd of unbridled purchasers. The projects may play therefore only a socialization role in preparing the user for a consumer society. This may be argued also in the case of another group in the population which has not yet been integrated into contemporary society, the so-called marginals. Participatory and populist approaches may succeed where even the Welfare State has failed and where traditional processes of the enforcement of order do not seem to have worked very well in overcoming the resistance to social integration for several historical reasons.

Deep in all participatory and populist architecture lies the narrow idea of society as an aggregate of private units struggling to maintain independence, while at the same time trying to form a unity. The idea of the social contract, an elegant logical construct of the eighteenth century, as a substitute for ties of affectivity and bonds of devotion still survives. It may have slightly modified the earlier concept of liberty of the individual into that of freedom of the group, but it is still a picture of a world of fragments with no framework. It is an abstract model inherited from the old bourgeois revolution, far from the historical reality of man which proceeds in the reverse, from a collective whole to the personal identities which branch out of a main trunk.* It makes no reference to the evolution of subjugations and dependencies, to roots, myths, memories, and conceptual and institutional frameworks that make up a substantial part of society, and which each individual carries within himself almost like a second constitution.

Whatever theory or practice of architecture may be developed, its accomplishments will be few as long as it misses the picture of the whole, the social and historical essence of design. Its campaigns of liberation may demolish some of the walls of the prison house of contemporary social life, bringing an air of release. But the freedom is only provisory; brand-new walls are quickly erected between social groups and between individuals,

the result of privatization, neotribalism, consumerism.

This limitation can be seen even more clearly in the visual effect of the projects we are discussing. It seems that all but Kroll's *zone sociale* let beauty take care of itself. There is no conscious effort to incorporate meaning into built form, with the exception of the implicit statement banning aesthetic indoctrination, the ostracism of the international style or any uniform visual vocabulary, and the invitation to the users to externalize their personal desires and aspirations.

Kroll's social center and housing is a work charged with meaning. It joins a whole variety of materials and assembles numerous plan types and components that user participation seems to have brought back to memory and to have sewn together in an intricate variegation, as if in a petrified, collective stream of consciousness. It is a haunting vision more than a plain statement about the world as it is. It is a fabulized neighborhood, melting together a student's bohemia and a fiddler's shantytown, where there is no moment of boredom or meanness, no law ordering public and private property, only lives which grow and interlock with each other, branches in a human grove, in an *espace végétale*.

Kroll's vision of an anarchic, organic society is strongly reminiscent of another Belgian's social, "vegetable," architectonic image of freedom and harmony: Victor Horta's art nouveau masterpieces. And as certain buildings of Horta's are the best monuments to the reformist efforts of the dawn of this century,* Kroll's housing complex may emerge as one of the most expressive memorials to the humanistic campaigns of the 1960s. His vision, however, also has its limitations. His world is a setting, an absorbing fable, tempting to walk into and linger in. It has the attraction of a kindly magic land of escape, as Horta's buildings have. But seen as works of art, there are few difficult dilemmas posed, very little conflict, and no catharsis. It is an architecture of poetic illusion, but not of tragedy; it fails, therefore, to capture the essence of art as a cultural phenomenon.

The projects under consideration here share certain aspects of image and visual organization. They are all unable to present a public face. It seems that none of them make up for the loss of the deep joy that this public face of architecture brought about in the past. True, there is some sense of relief achieved in them through the avoidance of styles that make painful or embarrassing references to a dominant class. The designs have no formal facades, no decorum, no overt insignia of a ruler. This absence may be considered positive from the social point of view, an expression of egalitarianism. On the other hand, they stand as street altars to the solipsism and to the conformism of the modern private self. Eventually there may be a soft drink bottle of a well-known multinational brand resting on the window-sill, but one may overlook it as an unnerving hint of a bondage not yet resolved. Although a sense of unity arises out of the interlocked units and the overlaid grid, as in the case of Kroll's and the SAR projects, respectively, this unity does not make up for the absence of what Durkheim called "*représentations collectives.*"** It fails to reproduce the social code of environmental organization that weaves the deeper ties of human community, affective ties. In the absence of a truly public face, these architectonic efforts at total composition remain episodic

---

*For a critique of the individualistic view of society, see: Ekeh, P. *Social Exchange Theory*, London, 1974. Lukes, S. *Individualism*, New York, Evanston, San Francisco, and London, 1973.

*On Horta's political ideas and architecture see: "Extraits des Memoires de Horta," in Hoppenbrouwers, A.,Vandenbreeden, J. and Bruggemans, J. *Victor Horta. Architectonographie*, Brussels, n.d.

**Durkheim, E. and Mauss, E. "De Quelques formes de Classification. . ." *Année Sociologique*, Volume VI, Paris, 1901–02, pp. 1–72.

and strangely mute. Such compositional patterns recall a calendar with pauses but without holidays, with intermissions but without collective celebrations.

Still, in a time of such pessimism, escapism, hedonism, fear of the modern, conformism, and avoidance of human commitment—what we have called the narcissist phase of architecture—*these finished projects are some of the most hopeful signs in architecture today. Despite all the objections and criticism aimed against their fallacies, omissions, and inconsistencies, these projects are the bridge over which any humanistic architecture of the future must pass, even if the path moves in completely different directions. They are the genuine inheritors of the movement of modern architecture in its original efforts and not the reductive version of modernism represented by the so-called international style, nor the narrow architecture of control and surveillance of the Welfare State workshops. They are children of deeper aspirations linked to the vision of architecture as a social art.

Any humanistic architecture to come will have to pursue the ideas materialized in these projects and originating in the populist and participatory movements. But it will have to join these ideas to the ideals of a renewed professionalism—knowledge, discipline, service, and universality of man. These ideals will have to be stripped of their associations with earlier stages of social development and previous private interests. The split between user and designer and the flight from old professional ideals have had their day. They came as a spontaneous break with past routines and doctrines and as an automatic resistance to the use of the institution of architecture to serve private interests. But they were also the outcome of lack of knowledge of the larger framework, of a reading of architecture outside of society and history.

*Tzonis, A. and Lefaivre, L. op cit.

A humanist architecture will have to be based on the reality of the concrete user as a source of knowledge and as the ultimate authority, but it will also have to develop a broader notion of social accountability. It will have to accept the concept of delegation on which professions are built. On the other hand, its notion of accountability will have to be broadened to cover not only the interests of a special group, but those of society at large. A renewed humanistic professionalism will reflect not the retreat to previous traditions of arbitrary authority, but the new social approaches of cooperation and reciprocity, of trust and devotion.

A humanistic architecture, in addition to creating and implementing design, will also have to generate knowledge about the instruments through which its intervention may be most effective. It will have to see projects—mechanical constructions, containers of activities, microenvironments, complexes of signs—as petrified human associations, as controls of relations which channel the flow of power and reinforce or weaken dependencies, dominations, and reciprocities. It will also, inversely, have to view them as results of such a network of power. To this will have to be joined the historical point of view. Historical studies demonstrate, better than any others in the social sciences, the relation between built form and social formations.**

From such investigations, a new typology of buildings will develop to replace the old formalist one that is currently being adopted as an expression of nostalgia for an authoritarian past. It will be a typology that will reflect instead the collective origins of social needs and the collective participation necessary to satisfy these needs.

**For further discussion on this topic, see Tzonis, A.: "Architecture as a Social Science" in *Department of Architecture, Harvard University Faculty Paper Series,* Cambridge, 1979.

# Byker
# Newcastle-upon-Tyne, UK

*Byker Hill and Walker-Shaw—Collier lads forevermore!*
*Traditional Tyneside Song*

Byker Hill overlooks the factories, shipyards, and quays of Newcastle-upon-Tyne. Since it was built in the nineteenth century, its narrow, cobbled streets and undersized, back-to-back row houses have been home for the men and women of the mines and of the port and its industries, and for the pubs, bingo halls, swop-shops, baths, and laundries where people meet. Byker is now being rebuilt around the people and the social life that give it an indelible character.

In 1968, after 50 years of plans to replace the decaying houses, Newcastle's officers were inspired to ask Anglo-Swedish architect Ralph Erskine to take on the challenge of Byker. Erskine agreed on the condition that he work for the city only long enough to review the situation and prepare a "plan of intent." If the Byker residents approved this plan and agreed to replace the city as his primary client he would proceed. The plan of intent set out the following objectives:

● To build a complete and integrated environment for living in collaboration with the residents
● To maintain valued traditions and relationships with surrounding areas
● To rehouse those in Byker without breaking family ties and other valued associations
● To exploit the physical character of the site and its views and to emphasize pedestrian connections
● To give the new Byker character, a clear physical form, and local individuality within groups of houses

It is hardly surprising that Byker accepted Erskine. Erskine then found Vernon Gracie, an architect who had worked with him on earlier schemes. Gracie agreed to live in Byker. He has been there now ten years, personally testing the results of their designs.

The architects' first action was to open an office in an unused funeral parlor. There, behind plate glass windows, they worked in full view of the community. The door was always open. Erskine has written:

People, kids, the chief planner—they all come in and out. We often took in kids who had been "chucked out" from home and it was raining. . . . And you could walk out on site and talk to people and contractors. We exhibited plans, drawings, and models in the window—but also local notices. "Anyone lost a tricycle? Ask the architect." "Guinea-pigs . . ." and so on. Much less important was the RIBA sign-plate.

To test the match between the architects' ideas and the people's needs and to minimize displacement, Byker is being renewed in stages. The pilot scheme, Janet Square, was severely criticized by its volunteer-occupants. Later phases incorporate the lessons learned.

The architects convinced the city to allocate houses before they were designed so families could follow the entire process from drawing board through construction, eliminating unpleasant surprises. The care lavished by tenants on private gardens and public landscaping, the total absence of vandalism, and the record of investments (parquet floors and elaborate kitchens—in rental housing) are proof that the architects have gotten it right.

The famous Byker Wall for which the development is widely known originated as a response to a proposed and possibly still-to-be-built motorway along one edge of the site. It provides housing for elderly persons, and neatly incorporates a number of Byker landmarks (the Shipley baths and a Catholic church). And, like the wall of a medieval town, it gives form and identity to the entire redevelopment area (approximately 2400 d.u. and all sorts of community services on 200 acres). This massive building—it is more than 3000 feet long—is now enlivened with flower boxes and grounded in the past by the traditional north country red paint with which the tenants have marked their doorways.

Byker is now largely completed. A new building for "sheltered housing" has recently been occupied; the last of the ancient brick houses is disappearing. But the vital social life remains.

Ralph Erskine was one of the founding members of Team 10 that reminded us some years ago that architecture was about people, that it was meant to create a sense of place, and that it could be recognized as "built homecoming." In her Commentary, British social scientist Alison Ravetz concludes that Vernon Gracie and Ralph Erskine's architecture "is in every sense humane: it creates a place to be homesick for, a place to come home to." Byker sets a new, high standard for mass housing.

1. The reconstruction of a working class
neighborhood: new low rise housing encircled by
the famous Byker wall.

# Designing between Client and Users

**Ralph Erskine, architect**
**Drottningholm**

It was with considerable doubts that I, in 1968, considered the offer to replan Byker, a central part of Newcastle with a resident population then of 12,000. What could we find out about their needs and how could we help them fulfill their dreams? Our backgrounds were so different!

As often before, I suggested to the town fathers that the traditional client is an administrator and sponsor, but that the true clients for an architect must be those who use the buildings, streets, and towns which he helps to form. I had not yet met the people of Byker, and, at my request, I was given a month so that in talking with them I could discover whether we might be able to make a valid contribution to their future community. My daughter, Jane, and Arne Nilsson came over from the office and lived there a month and I made several visits, and at the end of this period we had learned a little and felt we could learn more. I therefore proposed a number of objectives, and a method of work which included the establishment of an open office in Byker—proposals which were enthusiastically accepted by Newcastle city officials.

There was still much to learn about Byker—much that we expected and much that surprised us. We found that, as is usual in Newcastle, many who lived in Byker, regardless of the problems there, wished to remain, and that many who had left wished to return. We realized early on that we ourselves, middle–class professionals, would never be accepted as "Byker people," but hopefully might come to be called by the residents "our architects." Contrary to our expectations, they did not share our or other outsiders' interest in the existing houses and streets—they wanted their Byker, but a new Byker, and expressed this vocally. For them Byker was a special place in Newcastle,

2. The original Byker—back-to-back housing from the mid-19th century.

3. The new Byker—some of the feeling of the old, but with green space, light, and emphasis on the pedestrian.

a strong local culture, and the neighbors, friends, and associations they knew. They rejected the old houses and all they stood for, and were confident that we could give them far better new homes and surroundings.

As I had earlier in Sweden, I realized again that it is only when time or circumstance distances us from an evil history that we forget the evil and admire the forms it created, or, as so often today, uselessly seek to escape from a threatening reality in nostalgic and unrealistic dreams and imitations. It is, inevitably, only safe and comfortable intellectuals who speak of the strong aesthetic of slums, or foreigners who romanticize forms created by the injustice and poverty of other worlds. *Once they have seen alternatives,* the inhabitants of Byker, the Eskimo in an igloo, or the slum dweller of Venice can judge if, and at

what expense, their dwellings could be adapted to their needs. Aesthetic appreciation is linked to one's experience of life.

We found that Byker people wanted their corner shops, pubs, laundries, and the Shipley Street Baths, all of which were scheduled for demolition. They wanted functional spaces that were also places for meeting friends and neighbors, places "for a good laugh," as well as for practical use. But they also asked for privacy and quietness and "flowers outside my window," things they could not find in the old Byker. They felt that despite their inconveniences, limiting internal streets to pedestrians would be acceptable— quiet, safe, and pleasant, "and anyway not many of us have cars." They were skeptical about play areas with sandboxes for children, however, fearing there would be dirt, mess, and noise.

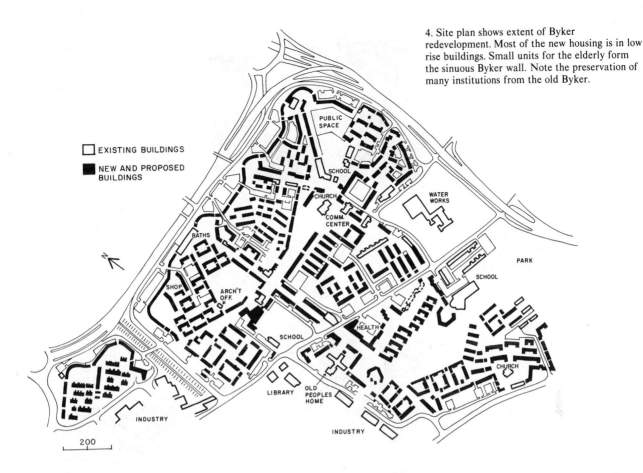

4. Site plan shows extent of Byker redevelopment. Most of the new housing is in low rise buildings. Small units for the elderly form the sinuous Byker wall. Note the preservation of many institutions from the old Byker.

□ EXISTING BUILDINGS
■ NEW AND PROPOSED BUILDINGS

PUBLIC SPACE
SCHOOL
CHURCH
COMM. CENTER
BATHS
WATER WORKS
PARK
SHOP
ARCH'T OFF.
SCHOOL
SCHOOL
HEALTH
CHURCH
LIBRARY
OLD PEOPLES HOME
INDUSTRY
INDUSTRY
200

Their requirements were many—and many (though not all) we have been able with time to meet. But first and foremost, they wanted rapid action, instead of the "endless talk" of many past decades. They wanted a new house to live in as soon as possible, and had preferences for its location, for its planning, and for having their old neighbors around them.

**Changing the Program**

Before accepting the commission, I wrote my own revised program which incorporated what we had learned and included our setting up our office on a corner in Byker, with the provision that meetings with authorities should be held there rather than in the Town Hall of Newcastle—a strange and foreign place for Byker folk! Clearly, those who are "strong" should meet those who are at a disadvantage in their own familiar surroundings. All this the city accepted. We set up shop and started work.

It was then, fortunately, that Vernon Gracie, who had earlier worked with me in Sweden, agreed to join me again. He was fascinated by the task and more than willing to reject a lucrative offer in the Middle East and move to Byker.

During the first seven years he lived above our office and, helped by others in the team, he carried the main load of maintaining contact with the Byker people. Vernon, Roger Tillotson, and a team of professionals from Britain and Sweden who shortly joined us and for whom Byker has become a way of life, have been responsible for running this complex project. My role, after the initial stages, has largely been limited to an intensive design involvement with Vernon and the team, first in the master plan and then in each of the following stages. Vernon's design involvement was especially strong in the Dunn Terrace area. Roger and the other job architects have had the lead in other parts of the project.

*I cannot overemphasize the extraordinary dedication and persistence of Vernon and Roger and the other members of the team over so many years, a degree of involvement in all aspects of the project which they maintained despite quite exceptional and, at times, most unnecessary difficulties. I feel that it is of great importance to realize that, without this tireless defense of our objectives and of the project's qualities and their lack of "self-interest," much of the success of Byker would have been*

*impossible. If, as I am convinced, such a level of professional dedication is bound to be an exception, it would indicate that environmental quality, with the extraordinary effort it requires, can only be common if it becomes an important objective for the community at large and for its politicians and administrators. Left to individual architects' good will, it will remain the occasional "one-off" phenomenon.*

Realizing that we were "outsiders" and that the architect-planner role did not give us the right to destroy ruthlessly the traditions of others, our first Byker plans maintained the familiar street pattern—the front roads, back alleys, and house groupings of old Byker. These initial plans were rejected by local inhabitants who explained the deficiencies of orientation (all the original streets ran up and down the steep hills; half the living rooms faced north), and the nature of use patterns and social exchange in old Byker. Their opinions were confirmed by certain intellectuals we met who were born and bred in such environments, and by our own observations in our pilot project that reproduced certain of the characteristics of the back lanes and the somber color of that grimy community.

189

Under the impact of these opinions and insights, we scrapped our plans and let the desired patterns of association, people's expression of their needs, our previous experience, and the physical characteristics of the site form the plans and buildings that are now the structure of new Byker. Our studies also showed that the old houses were extremely difficult to rehabilitate and there seemed to be no economic advantage in the exercise. We, therefore, only revitalize buildings of obvious economic or environmental value—our own office is (very symbolically?) established in the former shop of a gentleman who arranged funerals . . . or weddings!

## Collaborative Design

Clearly, the intent of our moving into old Byker was to make it possible for us to work in as full collaboration as possible with the users of the new Byker. While architects plan physical structures which communities use, it is the inhabitants who build communities. They can be helped or hindered by the structures, and it is my experience that their participation in the process of planning and building increases the value of a project for them immeasurably. The understanding of what the buildings and streets can do when built, and what is not possible and why, the realization for people that they can contribute and influence instead of merely accepting, and the easing of the architect's load in that he can inquire about preferences instead of guessing in the isolation of his office are obvious advantages of this process when it works well.

When at an early stage we discovered an empty site outside our project area, I suggested that we could build a pilot scheme (Janet Square), showing people some early action, and giving us the possibility of learning from the experience to the advantage of later development. We designed and built 46 houses in extensive contact with the future residents, maintained contact with them after occupancy, and learned and adjusted our plans as a result. The perimeter block, on the other hand, which was to be built first in order to get Byker under way on land cleared earlier for a motor road, was the subject of information rather than participation. This was regrettable, but everyone, and not least the Byker people, wanted quick action. There was therefore no time for, and little interest on their part

5. Well-tended gardens everywhere indicate the affection the residents feel for the new Byker.

Jeremy Preston

6a

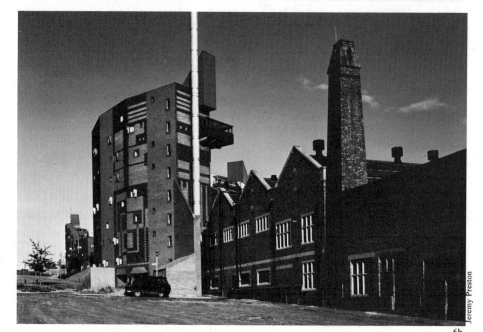

Jeremy Preston

6b

6a,b. Two views of the Byker wall. The wall was conceived as protection against a planned expressway (which might still be built on the open strip seen in the upper photograph). Note the inclusion of the Shipley Street Baths into Erskine's wall of housing in the lower photograph.

190

7. The inner face of the Byker wall is softened by timber access balconies and planting boxes.

in, an effective discussion on planning and other problems. Participation is not an easy process when the residents are already under stress of clearance from a proposed motorway and the City's earlier redevelopment planning.

Where we have fundamentally disagreed with the residents, we have—as we always do with clients—tried to convince them by fair methods. For example, we find that British children, like all others, enjoy swings, and sand, and water-play places, while grownups and parents will not have them for reasons good and bad—dogs fouling, noise, mess (and, in other projects, the negative effect on property values). We therefore planned rather inadequate facilities for children, leaving space for further provision. But we built a functioning and dog-free playground that included guinea pigs, sand, climbing frames, trees, etc., outside our office and trusted that the message would get home. This method did prove successful, and we are now asked to equip areas better for the children.

Ever since my first fairly successful attempts some 25 years ago at involving whole communities in participation in the planning process in Sweden, I have been convinced of its importance for the satisfaction of both individuals and communities. I find this confirmed in our later projects and especially in our most far-reaching collaboration with the Eskimos and settlers of arctic Resolute Bay.* But it was first in Byker that we

*For a general presentation of Erskine's work, see *Architectural Design,* **47,** 11–12, 1977.—
EDITOR

were fully to realize its political importance. Many political observers have noted that working–class culture in England is strong on personal contacts and group loyalties, but not so strong on abstract thinking. Since the modern world is to a large degree formed by the manipulation of abstract concepts, those to whom such concepts are foreign will tend to be governed, and those who can work with ideas will be the governors— be they politicians, trades union leaders, technicians, businessmen, or architects.

As time passed in our work in Byker, we realized that while our task of providing a physical structure for the community to use was important, the pedagogic side of participation was at least of equal importance. In doing our normal architect's job, we could also help people to understand the thought process involved and help them realize that they could insist on changes in plans if they could understand how and why decisions are made and analyze and justify their needs. This has begun to happen and we have—as we hoped— sometimes been given considerable trouble, changing our ideas and finding new solutions at their request. The community has certainly become more active, and this activity takes many forms—of which most, though not all, are positive.

Simultaneously, there is a parallel process that we half expected and we view with mixed feelings. Despite the fact that there is no ownership in Byker—it is all rental housing—there is a discernible tendency for Byker people to put down new roots and quickly be-

come contentedly "middle class" in their attitudes towards home, gardens, and neighbors. Surprisingly perhaps, not only do most of the people make beautiful gardens, but some also make considerable investments in their rental flats and houses—laying parquet flooring, putting in better kitchen cupboards, and so forth.

The pleasure we have in this comes from believing that they feel equally at home now as they did before, that they mean it when they tell me that the new Byker is so much better than the old, that they do enjoy the houses, the planting, the outdoor equipment, and the familiar neighbors around them. The worry we have is that this degree of satisfaction may lead to apathy—it has happened before. However, we cannot build poor environments so that activating dissatisfaction is maintained. . . .

We never expected our success to be immediate or sensational, and where possible have encouraged all involved to realize that there will be troubles, disappointments, and failures in the course of our mutual achievements. We are, however, after more than 10 years of continuous effort, inclined to feel that a reasonable level of success is the result. It seems to us that a large number of those who live in the new Byker do so with considerable satisfaction.

We assume that any general dissatisfaction on their part would make life for us "on the site" unbearable! Instead, we find we are welcomed to visit them, both in houses and flats; we are invited to tea and feel ourselves accepted by the community, at times, indeed, as "our architects."

In our original program and in our reappraisal of the City's earlier plans, we had, apart from our presence in Byker, stated certain other aims of importance: to rehouse the present inhabitants, to maintain as far as possible the present structure of a community with close-knit subgroups, to provide a varied environment, to give encouragement to corner shops, small enterprises, and variegated activities and meeting places, to protect against traffic noise and winds, to utilize the south slope and its views, to introduce generous vegetation and traffic-protected walking and play areas while maintaining reasonable car access, and to maintain contact with the surrounding areas and especially with Shields Road, the traditional shopping street to the north. Much of this we have achieved.

As a result of our discussions with people in Byker, the considerable number of flats which were envisaged in an earlier project by the city have, in our scheme, been limited to those in the perimeter block, and these are intended for elderly persons. The rest will be almost entirely single family housing—mostly row houses for economy, but with some that are semi-detached and even detached.

As earlier explained, our original suggestion that we could revitalize houses and follow the spirit of the existing street pattern was, under the impact of resistance from the residents, soon discarded. We feel that our experiences since then have confirmed that it was important to break with old and unpopular traditions. Sadly, the unnecessary delays in the construction of several stages of the scheme have had consequences within the community that are impossible to counter. Families have moved away from Byker and, despite the fact that many could move back later, our original objectives of rehousing about three-quarters of the community within Byker will not now be met.

Fortified more by previous experience of social-psychological studies and user-reactions than by a well-defined request from Byker, we have also planned for a considerably greater degree of traffic separation than was envisaged in early City plans. It seems clear that pedestrian areas give a positive environment for the easy social exchange that Byker people desire. They themselves confirm this strongly, and state that in these well-equipped areas and pedestrian streets they have much more social contact than in the old Byker. The walkways and parks are generously planted, all houses have gardens, and there are flower boxes (partially planted in a nursery a year before the completion of each building) on all access galleries of flats. Our office has even set up a service for landscape advice and for the sale of plants at wholesale prices.

The flourishing of flowers now in the new parts of Byker is a joy. Compared with the almost total lack of plants in old Byker, and considering the residents' lack of gardening experience, this can be considered something of an achievement! This is a complete disproof of my initial skepticism when people said, "We want gardens and flower boxes, and we *will* cultivate them." My reservations were seconded by "experts" who said, *they* will never plant a flower box. In Sweden or Austria yes, but it is NOT DONE in England, and never in Byker. These same "realists" told us, "Corner shops are irrational and out," or "They will want cars outside their doors," or "It will be ripped to bits by vandalism and all the trees broken off," or "Wood on balconies, friendly at first, yes, but fragile and soon carved to bits," etc., etc.—all the attitudes that lead to Good Tough Modern Medievalism for the Lower Classes, and perpetuate antiquated ideas and social structures. Here, as before, we have at times and with demonstrable successes listened to the wisdom of residents, rather than to the wisdom of experts. When we have foreseen that due to lack of experience or funds people would find difficulty in using and maintaining their new environment, we have managed to give them the necessary support. Our garden advice and plant purchase schemes are, we feel, examples of such necessary contemporary architectural practices.*

In this, as in other matters where it seems that a certain degree of success has been achieved with somewhat unconventional methods, it must be emphasized that the constant encouragement and support we have received from key officers and officials of Newcastle have been factors of vital importance to all of us in the Byker office. I wish I could with equal warmth and sincerity give them responsibility for all our failures!

---

*At Hammarby in Sweden, we have recently gone even further, giving users design assistance in planning dwelling interiors and selecting furnishings.

8. The base of the Byker wall is a row of maisonettes with private gardens for families with children.

9. (right) The wall steps down at intervals to provide a transition to the predominantly low rise development.

Jeremy Preston

8

# Pitfalls in Participation:
# A Cautionary Tale (of Success)

**Vernon Gracie, architect**
Byker

From the standpoint of 10 years' involvement with the Byker Redevelopment, with some years still to go, certain factors stand out and I have set them down the way I see them.

## The Price of Time

Old Byker had a mixed occupancy with only about 6 percent owner-occupiers; the remainder lived and live in rented property. By 1969, blight,—accelerated by the City's planning activities of the early sixties—had already cut deep in the form of two huge "compulsory purchase order areas" that had the effect of severing the residential areas from the main shopping street, Shields Road, to the north. The political objective that came into focus in 1969 was to allow as many as possible of the residents who wished to remain in the area to be rehoused in the area. But even at the time the objective was being formulated, it was only capable of partial realization, particularly as the land cleared was designated for an urban motorway.

Delays in the early years of the redevelopment helped deepen the depression being experienced by the community at that time, and contributed to a higher percentage of the people leaving the area than had been envisaged. We had thought at the outset that about 60 percent of the people would wish to stay in the early stages, rising to about 75 percent during the later stages if the new housing was suitable and well liked. In practice by 1976, 50 percent of the original population of about 17,000 had moved out of the area, most of it between 1971 and 1974 when the major delays in building occurred. Since early 1976, movement away from Byker has virtually ceased, however. In the light of the delays, it was very difficult to retain credibility with the residents when information they had been given proved

to be woefully optimistic on the dates on which they were likely to be rehoused.

## There are Many Bykers

The redevelopment has been phased to try to achieve the political objective of rehousing Byker people in Byker, but the staging pattern of clearance/redevelopment was drawn up without a clear understanding of the importance of status or of the differences between neighborhoods within the area. Like many cities in England with industries along the riverbank, the low-status areas in Newcastle are near the river. In general, the farther away from the river and the higher up the slope people lived, the higher their status.

This was marked in Byker because the shopping facilities on Shields Road are also at the high northern end of the area. Problems arose when people in clearance areas of high status were offered new houses in an area of low status. (If you are rehousing people, remember that they take their prejudices with them. The pattern of redevelopment should take this into account, and by recognizing that certain areas will be considered low status by residents, try to build in certain compensations.) At Byker this meant locating new shops and community services at the bottom of the hill.

## Alleviating Anxiety

Where clearance is taking place, then, in addition to the uncertainty people feel about their futures, the stress induced by vandalism and theft and demolition,* the disintegration of the

---

*Here are some of the main things we have learned about the clearance phase of a project like this. It is often much easier to burn rubbish

social fabric of the area, and not knowing where they stand on the priority list for rehousing, an element of competition for the new houses can be observed which increases the stress levels experienced by some to the point of desperation, even mental breakdown.

To counter this, first a Code of Practice for demolition was introduced, which was drawn up with local residents, the Community Redevelopment Officer, and the various departments of the City, so that a much more vigorous control of demolition could be exercised, not least by the people affected by it. Secondly, and with much more far-reaching importance, we managed to engineer a change in housing management policy to allow allocation of new houses at least six months before completion. It allows neighbors to be rehoused together and an element of social stability to be carried over into the new areas. It provides adequate time for people to plan the move and fi-

---

in or near gutted houses, but the blown debris and smoke cause a great deal of upset to people affected by it. If empty property isn't boarded up, it can give thieves access to the roof, and in the Byker terraces it is a simple matter to get from roof void to roof void. People who lock and bolt their doors and windows still develop real fears of entry through the roof. It also exposes residents to loss of electric supply when the wiring in the roof is removed by vandals for the copper. The residents were happier when they were involved in what should be demolished, and when. Onslaught with a bulldozer on the property next door can be pretty terrifying at 7 A.M., even if you are prepared for it. Proper cordoning-off of buildings being demolished is obviously important, and nonchalance by the demolition contractor can have serious consequences. We observed a near-miss outside the office when a large lump of brickwork fell from a building under demolition, narrowly missing a passing pedestrian. As it is virtually impossible to prevent children playing in the evenings in semi-demolished buildings, it is important to ensure that they are left in safe condition at the end of the day.

nance it, and it gives them an involvement with their home long before they move. It is a policy that has worked well and is now being used elsewhere in the City. It is also interesting to observe that where groups of houses in Byker were not allocated early, i.e., were allocated to tenants on completion, the social cohesion of groups is far more fragile.

We have discovered that there is nearly always a disparity between the housing mix planned for a stage of the redevelopment and the requirements of the people who come to the top of the priority list and expect to be rehoused there. Requirements can change quite drastically in as little as three months, and this has led us to a more pragmatic approach to housing mix. The mix is now worked out during discussions on the program for each stage between the City Housing and Planning Departments and ourselves. Some flexibility is gained by a policy of initial "underrenting" and some by the use of house types that can convert from small to large or vice versa. We have, for example, a house type that starts as two two-person flats, but can readily be made into one five-person house. Some have already been converted.

## Problems of Democracy

Our method of working closely with the community can call into question the role of the locally–elected politician who traditionally acts on behalf of the people of his ward. Officers of the Council have had a long-standing involvement, so that many are known personally in Byker and are often approached directly by people requiring help. But we also refer matters brought to our attention to the relevant officers, and the Community Development Project Office does likewise. If the Councillors, through a lack of sympathy for or misunderstanding of the process, feel that their traditional democratic role is being jeopardized and their position undermined, then political backlash can occur. This can manifest itself in a variety of ways, including withholding needed support. In Byker it remains a problem.

## Project Evaluation

The general principles we have adopted in layout seem to work well. The semi-private courts, with private gardens

1. Shops and offices are inserted into the small housing blocks. They provide places to meet and chat, and maintain the lively urban character of traditional Byker life.

with low fences, are well liked. A beech hedge is planted outside each garden fence, and tenants can let these grow up if they desire additional privacy. So far there is little evidence of this happening, and nearly all the beech is being clipped to fence height. The relationship of the house type to neighborhood layout is important as we have observed that the concept of territory is different in single-aspect house types and dual-aspect types.

In the pilot scheme there is a square onto which both single– and dual–aspect house types face. The square is, or rather was, a main pedestrian route through the scheme, and as part of the general landscaping provision there was a table and a couple of seats more or less in the middle of it. The sitting place was put to considerable use by youngsters in the evenings, to the point that they disturbed residents. It became apparent that the families in the single aspect houses felt the intrusion on their privacy much more than those in dual aspect types, where the possibility of retreat to the other side of the house ex-

isted. The inference is that a single aspect house type may produce a sensitivity to the use of space beyond the immediate property that residents in dual-aspect types don't exhibit to anything like the same extent. The alternative of increasing privacy by, say, shutting off the garden by a wall or high fence, has to be evaluated within the context of the social mechanisms of the community, the need to display, and the importance of visual contact (children playing, etc.). Possibly a fence with operable shutters so that the residents can control and vary the degree of contact they have is the answer.

We have also found that groups of elderly people prefer to live together as neighbors and friends with a short walking distance to their families. The extended family network is still an important part of Byker, but layouts planned this way allow the elderly to live in groups with a lower child density. We try to locate them near corner shops and services. Hobby rooms and space for "nonhousing" are used well, and we continue to provide them. So far, they have always been attached to houses so that if they were subjected to vandalism, abuse, or just did not work, they could be incorporated into the body of the house. This possibility of "retreat" does not now seem to be necessary, and we are now designing them free-standing and sited so that they can be put to a wider range of uses. We are also planning some special industrial units as parts of future stages to encourage light industry, the "back street workshop," the clothes dealer, etc., to continue in the new Byker. Some of these spaces are already being looked at as work space for the recently formed Residents (management) Cooperative.

In 1970, we wrote, "Our main concern in the redevelopment is for the people in Byker, and our task is to provide the right physical framework to enable them to maintain the relevance of their community in the future." Is this being achieved?

Surveys that have been done in Byker over the years have shown a better than 90 percent satisfaction rate with the housing and general design of the redevelopment, so from the viewpoint of the physical framework, the objectives do seem to be being met.

But our continued contact with the community makes us aware that the factors determining the success or failure of a housing scheme ultimately rest on the social forces generated by the community, and the relationship it has with the local authority. Apart from the broader social issues, housing management, maintenance, and cleaning are important ingredients that I feel will require considerable work in the next few years if areas like Byker are to remain viable communities for a long time. While the Housing Department has a commitment to Byker, within the constraints of present national policy, work needs to be done to explore alternatives forms of tenure,* so that tenants can

Jeremy Preston

2

Jeremy Preston

3

2. With the automobile nearby but out of the way, Byker's streets are places to stroll and play.

3. Architectural reminders of the old Byker mark important paths.

---

*We are looking at a different approach to the development of tenant control. In particular, we are at the early stages of discussing ideas for an optional scheme for individual tenants. Briefly, in exchange for taking on all responsibilities for their homes, externally and internally, tenants could look forward to a housing pension based on an annuity funded from both administrative and work costs "saved" by the Council throughout the years of tenancy. With the wealth of experience and expertise on superannuation insurances and welfare economics that exist in Britain, it should be possible to devise a scheme which all tenants, regardless of income, could take part in. We have prepared an initial discussion paper,

giving a somewhat oversimplified outline of how such a scheme might work and are optimistic that the Housing Department will initiate a broadly-based working group to examine this and other proposals.

The motivation for work on such ideas has roots in our approach to and understanding of the responsibility of the architect in a major housing redevelopment. An essential aspect of the responsibility is to ensure as far as possible that the social potential inherent in the physical design will be realized and in pursuit of this, our attention is frequently drawn to the problems of housing management.—CAROLINE GRACIE

have the opportunity to go beyond the present, limited management cooperative, take the degree of responsibility for their environment they want and the power to take their proper part in the decision-making process and the determination of policies affecting them.

## On-Site Architecture

It is undoubtedly important to have "the architects" present within the community to cope with the day-to-day problems and stresses experienced by the people. It provides a continuity of

contact that can produce feedback from the informal and chance contact that is often difficult to get in more structured meetings. This has most certainly been of value in our approach to design.

Possibly the most important role the on-site office plays is that of a meeting point between the users and the local authority which has contributed over the years to the resolution of conflict and a degree of consensus between the user/client and the sponsor/client. It has been said that consensus is the enemy of participation, that participation should be about uncovering conflicts of interest, discovering differences of opinion. In Byker, the local Council, by adopting participation as its own policy, gained the initiative in controlling its structure and course. Participation in this context is therefore an aspect of urban management, rather than of giving people a decisive voice in their areas.

We have had as great a commitment to the user/client as possible, while recognizing that our objectives are constrained by the necessity to work within the "establishment" power structure, and that our ultimate responsibility when all is said and done is to the sponsor/client. Our abilities to bring about change as we might wish it are bound to be limited. We have acted on occasions as "hidden advocate," pressing the case for policy changes on behalf of tenants. Our position in the middle of Byker, which has often given us insights into user requirements, has also on occasions created levels of expectation among tenants that it has not always been possible to fulfill—partly because we have been unable to make an impact on decision making because of the structural constraints of our position, partly because the local authority wishes to retain its traditional role, partly because of changes in national housing policy, and partly (let it be said), because we also make mistakes.

We are all-too-aware of the political passivity of Byker people, who are fairly typical of the British working class in this respect. The "progress through conflict" philosophy can, I think, only work on a power-sharing basis, and in the circumstances that prevail in Byker, could possibly have led to a polarization of opinion and difficulty in making any progress at all. The traditions and background of the community, and the stress under which much of it lives during clearance, militate against a cool and reasoned debate on planning and architectural matters; the time scale is too long from inception to handover of houses to expect a wholehearted commitment from each family. We, for our part, only claim a modest advance in humanizing the processes of redevelopment.

## Byker Now

We still have our office in Byker. Apart from the possibilities it offers for contact with the users, it also enables us to give a level of care and attention to the physical environment as it is built that people seem to respond to well, and it enables us to exert pressure on the authority to see that areas are maintained (though in the present economic climate this can be an uphill struggle). And people now have a good idea of what an architect is and does, so our presence has undoubtedly helped to demystify the professional's role—a very good thing.

One final warning: Byker residents'

involvement in the redevelopment process results from the goodwill of the professionals—who are involved by choice, not by requirement. While things go right, the degree of involvement and commitment of the professional team to consultation and the giving of information will be considerable. But if things should go horribly wrong, it is difficult to see a professional team taking a hammering for year upon year without the goodwill vanishing and the more traditional approach to redevelopment reemerging.

We are very fortunate that the redeveloped Byker is well liked by its residents. People understand that the "community" has now shifted from the old housing areas to the new and seems even to have gathered strength from the process.

4. Recently completed "sheltered housing" at the western edge of Byker. The huge redevelopment project is now complete.

# Commentary on Byker

Alison Ravetz, Hull School of Architecture (UK)

## BRITAIN'S "BEST KEPT VILLAGE"

A mile or so out of Newcastle, with its motorways, "precincts," and glassy towers, is Shields Road, a traditional traffic-torn high street left over from an earlier era. Just behind its busy stores, on the riverwards side, is a swath of cleared land waiting for a motorway. All along its far side on the brink of the hill is Ralph Erskine's Byker Wall, and behind the wall are old and new Byker, tumbling down the escarpment to level out in factories and warehouses that clutter up the banks of the Tyne. On one side is the new estate, still being built and occupied; on the other, the parallel ranks of Tyneside flats, looking almost vertical from Raby Street. Only the ghost remains of what was once the nerve center of a dense working–class neighborhood. Old Byker is being hacked to pieces while the new Byker first confronts, then encircles and engulfs it. This could be the familiar rape and pillage of a working–class neighborhood, with eventual replacement by today's standard version of housing for the masses. But Byker, as they will tell you in Newcastle, is something special.

## THE ARCHITECTS' APPROACH

The inspired choice of Ralph Erskine was due to the chairman of the new Conservative planning committee, and to the chief officers of planning and housing. Erskine's design philosophy was expressed in his plan of intent ( *Report on the Byker redevelopment area,* January 1970):

> The present neighbourhood of Byker, though economically depressed, has a self-respect which, though eroding fast, is still evident. There is a strong feeling of attachment to the community . . . Our main concern in the redevelopment is for the people in Byker, and our task is to provide the right physical framework to enable them to maintain the relevance of their community in the future.

The city architect had already carried out studies that showed the necessity of a perimeter block to baffle the motorway noise, and Erskine accepted this as "a basic design decision, like the motorway, or waterworks, or densities . . . outside the scope of participation." Other than this, participation was fundamental to his way of working: his aims would be made public, showing the range of choice and giving a time scale for representation. "The public would be informed as to what their representations had achieved, and where and why suggestions had not been accepted." This was endorsed by the corporation, and the con-

*Alison Ravetz is a social historian and research fellow at Hull School of Architecture. This is condensed from her review in The Architects' Journal (April 14, 1976) and adds a recent postscript*

sultants were given a small annual allowance for participation.

Meanwhile, immediate planning and design decisions were being made. Erskine rephased the demolition program to cut down clearance areas to about 250 dwellings, in order to minimize further loss of population and to enable people to move across to the new estate in manageable numbers. He established the guidelines of what was a predominantly low rise environment, with all its community facilities intact. The architects at once set to work on a pilot scheme of 46 dwellings on a cleared area, Janet Square, which they hoped to make a joint exercise with residents, from initial planning to occupation and use.

Today Janet Square has the ailing look of many council "schemes" up and down the country. The consultants are still regretful about this; they feel that they themselves learned a lot from the mistakes made, but that residents have to continue to live with these as there is no money to rectify them. The architects hope that when Janet Square is engulfed by the new estate, they can bring it up to the same standard as the rest. Meanwhile, after much doubt about taking over the council's responsibilities, the residents there have accepted grants for improving the common spaces, and this has created a precedent in the City.

The perimeter block, as we have seen, was decided on without any consultation with Byker people. Further attempts to involve the users in design on a large scale proved abortive, though the architects' presence on site has enabled a constant two-way dialogue to take place. The "link" blocks stepping down from the Wall to the terraced cottages below, and the cottages arranged in rows and squares, emerged with a confident and finished style after the pilot scheme. The low rise housing accounts for far the greater part of new Byker, and gives it a distinctive atmosphere: intimate, intricate, enticing, and highly colored. Often one does not reach one's destination, because on the way yet another interesting possibility presents itself. We are guided by changes in the shade of the flowers. Private and public gardens spill into one another. The cars are kept at bay, often in amazingly tight spaces. There are intriguing wicket gates and glimpses of washing hung from poles like ships' masts. Every few yards there is a corner where a table and benches invite conviviality.

In spite of being a small minority of the whole, the Wall has dominated discussion about Byker, as it dominates the upper slopes. Since it provides a vivid new image for the city, it is only fair that it should attract highly colored comments. It presents an austere yet soberly patterned face to the, as yet nonexistent, motorway, but turns a fair face to the south, where its white upper stories are hung with private balconies, plastic-roofed access terraces, and crazy little stairways. There are "conserva-

## Daybook Record

| Time | Name or Description | Reason for Visit | Action | Comment |
|------|---------------------|------------------|--------|---------|
| 8:50 | Mrs. Smith | Asked for sand from sandbox for grandchildren to play with | Got some | |
| 11:30 | Mrs. Spraggon | Reported gas leak at Mrs. Smith's Carville Road | Phoned Gas Board | |
| 12:45 | Billy Bucket | Came for matches | Got them | |
| 5:30 | Thomas Something | Playing "hide and seek" wanted to hide here | Hit under table | Difficult to throw out |
| 11:20 | Man from first handover | Wanted his fence altered as rubbish blows under it | Said we'd think about it | |
| 11:30 | Mr. Campbell | To murder Arne because of trowel | Arne was not in unfortunately | |
| 2:45 | Mrs. Smith | Lady had fallen in Gordon Road, broken wrist and shock | Called ambulance, came after five minutes | |
| 3:00 | Mrs. Rogerson and friend | She wanted some grass seed | Got some in a very nice paper bag | Will come back with bag later |
| 6:10 | Eddie | To wash | Washed | |
| 7:10 | Mrs. Wann | Upset—kids broke window—news of move too much, broke down | Sherry and a chat | |
| 9:15 | Two men (NEEB?) | Said they had a cooker to fix in Shipley Place | Told them Shipley Place not yet built | They left in a confused state |
| 10:00 | Ian Muckle, Action Centre | To call meeting about Shipley Rise play area | Roger, Caroline discussed | Arranged for another tenants' meeting |
| 10:10 | Tenant, Gordon Road | Collected the key from Action Centre | | Very happy man |

tories'' where terraces abut landings, and each threshold has its own bench, flower trough, and screen. In summer, the terrace is a tunnel of flowers and creepers.

The Wall is not very high—its maximum height is eight stories, and no children live above ground level, which contains family houses with gardens. In spite of all the insults and jokes, and in spite of some real faults such as the weathering of the asbestos cladding and the rain which falls between the cladding and the terrace roofs drenching the thresholds below, the inhabitants love it. They are mostly elderly and they bask in the view and the sun. ''It's like the Costa Brava. Whoever would have dreamt that Byker could look like this?''

### REHAB OR REDEVELOPMENT

The architects did consider renovation, and at first were inclined towards it. Technical obstacles, together with an independent piece of research showing that 80 percent of the people wanted clearance, dissuaded them. It was the same message that comes from many of our old working–class neighborhoods: that the people do want new houses, but on the same site. And here they would have settled for considerably less conspicuous houses than Erskine's gave them.

There was never any question but that new Byker was for Byker folk. In Newcastle, every clearance tenant is entitled to a new house, so there was no obstacle in principle to moving them

across from old to new. The cost of the new homes is often a strong argument against total redevelopment. Here, this is brushed aside by officials, perhaps a little too airily, when they say that rebates take care of those who cannot pay, while the rest are glad to pay.

The other main argument against total redevelopment is the callousness with which it is commonly done. This slow ritual murder of a working–class neighborhood and its culture was already under way here, and Newcastle deserved the usual outcome of planning blight and social demoralization. That it did not quite happen is due partly to the game spirit of the Byker people, and partly to the work of the many voluntary and statutory agencies in the area. But a major part was played by the consultants' unorthodox view of architecture and style of working. They set up office in an old shop which was open to all comers. Vernon Gracie lived for several years over the shop (he now lives in one of his own maisonettes), and there he experienced the terrors of demolition and vandalism, knowing how much worse these must be for the elderly, the alone, and the poor. This experience contributed towards the drawing up of a code of conduct for clearance, to mitigate some of the hardships to residents, and this is now used in other parts of the city.

### PARTICIPATION

Meanwhile the new estate was quietly absorbing the churches, schools, and other community buildings. The architects, social administrator, and other members of the staff concerned themselves with every aspect of its life, from shopkeeping to pigeon fancying. Perhaps as much thought and imagination has gone into easing the social transition to new Byker as into its physical design. When it is finished, it will, if the architects have their way, have a liberal supply of corner shops, craft workshops, and light industries. That is, it will be a complete neighborhood, not a dormitory suburb.

New Byker has been helped by many people: a special officers' group of the corporation, the Byker Action Centre, set up by the Council of Social Service, from which the community development officer works, the local clergy, and many other formal and informal groupings. These could and do exist in many redevelopment areas without the benefit of resident architects, but for many there is no doubt that their presence here has been a catalyst. While other architects still fumble towards the concept, or else refuse outright to admit it, the Erskine/Gracie practice works in the full acceptance that there is both sponsor/client and user/client. Not only that, but they are quite clear that it is the user/client they are designing for, and, with the same quiet insouciance that shows in their buildings, they get the sponsor/client to approve, at least so far, what they do for the user.

Perhaps it is this commitment, and their reservations over Janet Square, that gives the consultants their faint sense of failure when it comes to participation. For this is not a situation where a local community decides what it wants and gives the architects orders. It is very much a case of an architect leading a community—a community that, like all communities, is not a harmonious whole but a collection of differing and often bickering groups. Accounts of Third World self-build housing and blueprints for tenant takeover may indeed shape our practices tomorrow, but in England now most professionals, whether they like it or not, have to work with an acquiescent population which expects authority to take decisions and which is roused to militancy only when the decisions are appalling. In time, perhaps, the balance will change and the professional will more truly become the servant of the people.

Nevertheless, the fact of the architect living on site, of the office being open to full view of all passers-by, the accessibility to anyone of every single member of the staff, staff involvement in many local organizations, and especially the presence of a social administrator, create a style of participation, as extracts from some record sheets kept in May, 1974 help to show (see box).

At present, participation in Byker centers around a Liaison Committee, chaired by residents in rotation. Slightly to the concern of some of the professionals, who would have preferred a properly constituted association, it has no formal structure. Anyone professionally involved in Byker and any interested resident may go along. Normally there are 30 to 40 people at meetings. The residents do not wish for anything more structured than this, and the truth is that residents' associations, of which there are several in Byker, function only in the uncleared areas. Their active members relapse into private life once they get a new house—one of the penalties of successful rehousing.

The mechanisms for participation here have grown up so naturally under the unobtrusive and sympathetic presence of the architects that one sometimes wonders whether Newcastle appreciates the very real innovation it has going on here. The work connected with participation undoubtedly takes up many man-hours, amounting perhaps to a full working week for one person.

The special fee allowed cannot cover this, but Erskine's regard themselves as working on a nonprofit basis and they are helped by the extremely low overheads of their office.

At Byker, it took the importation of a foreign firm, the strong support of the Council, and the unique outlook of Ralph Erskine and Vernon Gracie to initiate what amounts to a new kind of architectural practice. In theory, there is no reason why their methods should not be repeated by any local authority using its own staff. Neighborhood offices could be set up where planning, housing, architectural, and community development personnel, as well as voluntary agencies, could "open up shop." This should not greatly raise the costs, and indeed, if the results were more effective than under the centralized system, it should bring savings. The strongest barriers would be the interdepartmental rivalries for which local authorities are notorious, the suspicion of local councillors jealous for their own relationship with their constituents, and the absence of the guiding intelligence that has been so outstanding at Byker.

The consultants' initiatives in participation are part of their own expanded view of architecture. In spite of its whimsical appearance, the resulting environment conveys a feeling of confidence that no design decision has been taken without meaning and sympathy. At the same time, one has more faith in it because it has room for doubt. Thus it has mechanisms for advance or retreat: the liberal number of hobby rooms, for instance, if they are unused or vandalized, can be reduced by incorporation into adjacent dwellings. The private spaces may be advanced or the public spaces put to different uses. Cars may be brought closer to the houses if people find the distances unacceptable; if the idea of light industries does not catch on, the shells can be used for garages. The architects are creating a living environment. It is up to the people, professionals, and politicians to let it change in sympathy with social needs.

## POSTSCRIPT, DECEMBER 1980

With over 1900 dwellings and over seven and a half thousand people, Byker is now an established part of the city, and this summer it won an award as the "best kept village" in the *Britain in Bloom* competition. All the overt signs are that it is a good place to be. There is little vandalism, and the residents are "personalizing" their houses and even taking over some of the smaller public open spaces with the tacit sanction of the authority. The main problems have nothing to do with design (apart from difficulties with the area heating plant), but concern poor maintenance of houses and the inability of the Parks Department to understand what is needed to maintain the landscaping. The crux is that the city persists in working in a centralized way that does not meet local needs very well.

In retrospect, the shortcomings of Byker lie not in the environment—which will obviously continue to be a place of pilgrimage for years to come—but in Newcastle's failure to extend this brilliant experiment and in the failure of other authorities to use it as a prototype.

It is not possible to judge Byker independently of its design, which is outstanding by any criterion. Even the pilot project has worn well, and the Wall, though still the butt of jokes, can be justified on its own merits. But the design could not have achieved the success it has without the architects' local involvement, the advance allocation of housing, and the active participation of people. Byker came about through a unique combination of political circumstances and a special architectural practice and commitment, and the present indications are, sadly, that this will never be repeated.

# Mission Park
# Boston, Massachusetts

In the 15 years since John Sharratt gave up "conventional practice" to work for Boston communities—first as an unpaid advocate and now as their professional architect—he has saved hundreds of homes and built still more new ones. His success as a community architect, which he would attribute to the determination of the neighborhood groups for whom he works, is outstanding. In his Commentary, Tunney Lee cites Sharratt's neighborhood redevelopment work as a key factor in the

profound changes in the political climate of Boston . . . . The city and developers must now deal with [active community groups] and sometimes include them in the development process. The design methods, institutional

arrangements, and financial tools for active community control were developed in large part in the Sharratt projects.

Sharratt's most recent major project, in the Mission Hill section of Boston, prevented the Harvard Medical School and its associated teaching hospitals from wiping out a stable residential neighborhood. Although Sharratt and the members of the Roxbury Tenants of Harvard Association (RTH) were successful in creating a compromise plan that permitted the expansion of the medical complex while providing better housing and community facilities for the threatened families, still he says, "The most significant fact that has been made clear to me during my experience with

RTH is that institutional expansion has replaced urban renewal as the key threat to working class neighborhoods."

The approaches to community participation, to programming, to design, and to the complex process of large-scale development that Sharratt has developed through his experiences at Madison Park, Villa Victoria, and Mission Hill—and which he describes in his article—indicate the multiple skills necessary for the successful community architect and provide fruitful lessons for those who wish to rebuild our cities with and for the people who live in them.

1. Mission Park--successful rebuilding by the Roxbury Tenants of Harvard Association.

# Preserving the RTH Neighborhood

**John Sharratt, architect**
**Boston**

Between 1960 and 1975, institutional expansion threatened to destroy the residential community that adjoins the Harvard Medical School complex in Boston. There are 13 major teaching hospitals of the Medical School within a four-block radius. This tremendous educational/medical center has brought the area economic and employment benefits, but also congestion, pollution, and pressure for expansion. The expansion plans of these independently governed but associated institutions produced an active, speculative real estate market in the area. The institutions knew that they needed to grow, that land was limited, and that they had competition. This led to "land banking" efforts which drove prices up—and residents into the streets.

Since it was built in 1899, the neighborhood has been inhabited by Irish Catholics and Germans. Recently a number of black and Spanish-speaking families have moved in. The people in the community are of moderate means, holding jobs in the manual trades or small businesses. Most of the homes are two- and three- family dwellings in which the owner generally lived on one floor. Many of the present residents grew up in the neighborhood and later set up households near their relatives and friends.

Beginning in 1964, Harvard's real estate agents began buying houses in the neighborhood. They gave priority in rentals to transients (students, hippies, and young staff members at the hospitals) instead of families. Rents increased; poor maintenance practices accelerated the physical deterioration of the properties. Families who had lived in the neighborhood for many years found it difficult to remain. In 1968, Harvard announced its plans to build a new hospital complex. Residents received eviction notices stating that 182 apartments would be vacated and torn down by 1971. But Harvard officials had not clearly explained why the new hospital needed to be built on land oc-

2. Harvard's Affiliated Hospitals Center looms over old and new Mission Park.

cupied by housing, rather than on nearby empty land. There were no plans for relocation housing.

The student strike at Harvard in 1969 publicized the threat to this neighborhood. The students demanded cancellation of the eviction notices and a promise not to destroy housing. During the strike, student organizers met with community residents to form a tenants' union, the Roxbury Tenants of Harvard Association (RTH). By the end of 1969, RTH sent Harvard a petition affirming the tenants' desire to remain in their homes and requesting a change of the new hospital's location.

The RTH neighborhood (25 acres) that was threatened with extinction was part of a larger natural community known as Mission Hill (150 acres), which had similar religious and ethnic characteristics. Between 1960 and 1970,

Mission Hill medical institutions acquired over 70 acres of both vacant land and residential properties. This is almost 98 percent of the entire RTH neighborhood. By 1969, the Mission Hill community was afraid, paranoid, and rapidly deteriorating. When the district planner for the Boston Redevelopment Authority (BRA) was asked in that same year about plans for Mission Hill, the response was, "Forget it. It's going institutional. It's too late to save it as a residential community."

Immediately following the 1969 student strike, the students working with the residents asked me to come to a community meeting and outline possible development options for the RTH neighborhood. Up to this time, the task had been defined simply by the residents: "Save our Neighborhood." What this meant or how it was to be accomplished was not known. There were no clear social or political objectives, just the human needs of families and friends struggling to maintain their identity, roots, shelter, and urban fabric of life. But this real crisis would lead to clear objectives as the residents began to understand their problems, weaknesses, strengths, and aspirations. This community meeting turned into more than 10 years of meetings and the relocation of my office and home to the RTH neighborhood.

## Earlier Experiences

My work in the RTH neighborhood from 1969 to the present has built upon and been a part of my involvement with similar problems in other Boston communities since 1966. A brief outline of these other community efforts is included here as background to my experiences and the political setting of the RTH effort. It should be noted that these neighborhoods are in close proximity, and especially in the period of 1969 to 1972 were in close contact and gave one another political support.

## Madison Park

The Campus High Urban Renewal Project in the Madison Park area of Lower Roxbury, which is contiguous to Mission Hill, was approved by HUD in 1965. This area is at the southern edge of the great nineteenth century Boston landfill project. It was originally a healthy, middle class, residential area of mixed racial and ethnic composition. The social mix was maintained until 1965 when Urban Renewal drove the majority of the nonblack residents away. The project called for the demolition of 400 homes to make room for a 5000-student high school. No relocation housing in the neighborhood was to be provided—in fact, there would be no neighborhood. The residents were not allowed to participate in this "urban renewal" and refused to accept it. This neighborhood was also to be bordered by two new, major expressways. After serious deterioration, community leaders began to understand the severe havoc that these paper plans were creating in their lives.

It was at exactly this time that I became disenchanted with conventional practice and opened my office, John Sharratt Associates, Inc. (JSA). I began doing small renovation work and

offering my skills to community efforts. In 1966, the Lower Roxbury community asked me to assist them in developing reasonable alternatives to the Campus High Urban Renewal Plan. The problem was clear: the residents were being denied their homes, neighbors, churches, and roots without representation, participation, consent, or fair compensation. The solution was less clear. In some form, in some manner, the neighborhood must be saved.

The residents had their unifying crisis and became organized. I interpreted the plans of the Renewal Authority and presented alternatives for the neighborhood, the proposed high school, and the expressways. Political action in the form of community meetings and demonstrations resulted eventually in a memorandum of understanding being signed by the then-Mayor of Boston, the Boston Redevelopment Authority, and the community; it provided that on-site relocation housing would be provided for all the existing residents. The 56-acre urban renewal project was replanned by the Lower Roxbury Community Corporation (LRCC) with my assistance to meet their needs.

The residents were made aware of the new housing currently being built elsewhere in the city, and began forming opinions and expressing concerns. It was agreed that they must have the authority to approve who was to build their new homes and how they were to be designed. The Boston Renewal Authority at first refused to allow LRCC approval of the developer for their new housing. After visiting many new developments, talking to the residents, and interviewing developers, LRCC decided that not only would they approve the developer for their new housing, but it would be they who would build and own their new homes. This was a critical decision, and one totally unacceptable to the city government and its urban renewal authority. A community build and own its own housing? It can't be done! But given the residents understanding of their real goals and needs, and the housing that was currently being produced, there was no alternative.

The decision that the community should develop and own its housing opened an entirely new arena of problems and opportunities. Convincing the BRA to accept LRCC's concept of ownership took two years, numerous public hearings and demonstrations,

and intervention by the Model City Agency. In 1969, LRCC was finally designated developer for the 15-acre parcel contingent upon BRA approval of the development team.

After 11 years, the residents of Madison Park own and manage $10 million worth of mixed-income housing; 383 units are occupied with another 200 units on what used to be "future expressway" land about to be completed. The renovation of an existing 212-unit public housing project and a large commercial center are in the planning stage. The new high school that was to replace the residents has not yet been completed. The two expressways have been made streets. There have been six directors of the BRA and two Mayors since this all began. LRCC has outlasted, outpositioned, and outperformed those who were out to destroy their neighborhood.

All phases of the housing development have been financed through the Massachusetts Housing Finance Agency with HUD Sections 221(d)3 and 236 interest subsidies, and HUD rent supplements for the elderly and very low income residents. The neighborhood was assisted by a "for-profit" developer (as a consultant on a fee-for-services basis) and a church-based, non-profit housing corporation that provided the necessary front money for architectural and engineering fees, surveys, soil tests, and legal costs.

The issue of form of ownership was important from the very beginning. The residents were initially afraid to enter into a limited partnership (for the sale of tax shelters to wealthy partners) for fear that they would lose control. They wanted nonprofit, cooperative ownership. The funding agency would not accept a cooperative, and the compromise was a straight nonprofit, rental structure. Since these early years, the residents have gained more confidence and sought opportunities for local development. Because of this new confidence, all the new housing has been syndicated through a limited partnership, with the residents maintaining control as general partner. The cash earned from the sale of tax shelters has permitted LRCC to pursue economic development within the neighborhood. This form of development enables the community to play the private developer's game with United States tax laws while maintaining neighborhood control.

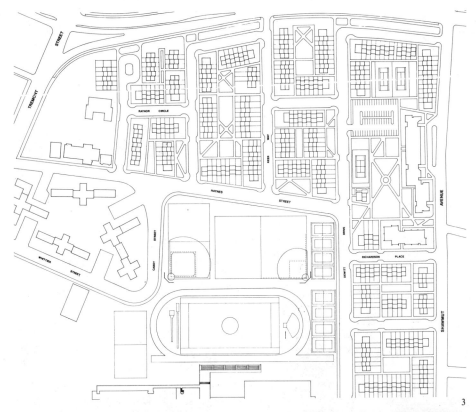

3. Madison Park site plan shows the Campus High School and new housing.

4. Development includes a new multi-purpose community center.

5. Family units are two-story rowhouses.

6. High- and low-rise housing seen from the high school playingfield.

205

## Villa Victoria

Boston's South End Urban Renewal
Area abuts the Campus High Urban
Renewal Area and was also approved
by HUD in 1965. The central section of
this renewal area was in the worst condition and had the greatest percentage
of absentee owners. The 1965 BRA
plan called for total demolition of this
area, to be replaced by upper income
housing and institutional uses. At just
about this time there began a large migration of families from rural Puerto
Rico to Boston and primarily to this
central section of the South End. These
new Bostonians found cheap rent, good
welfare benefits, low-skill jobs, a new
community speaking their language,
and often friends and families from
their home towns. The housing was
cheap, but services didn't exist. Adequate heat was rare, and eviction was a
constant threat. A local Episcopal minister helped organize the residents, and
in 1968 invited members of the LRCC
to tell them of their experiences. I was
consequently asked in 1968 to provide
technical services to save and rebuild
the community.

The problems and solutions for this
area were almost identical to those in
Lower Roxbury. The process has also
been similar, although somewhat easier
due to my experience, the success of
LRCC, and the City's more sensitive
community posture. But the residents'
continued existence in this section of
the South End faced a second major obstacle: being close to the downtown
business area and having good public
transportation, this area is considered
valuable property by private speculators
and developers and by a recent wave of
"gentrifying" home purchasers.

It was evident from a quick review of
the 1965 plan that there were many
buildings scheduled for demolition that
should be saved. There was a massive
relocation problem that had been ignored. Clearly, the plan was wrong for
the city, the South End, and the existing residents. While learning about new
life styles and needs, we set about to reconsider all the information that had
been gathered by the BRA to justify
their 1965 plan. My associates and I
surveyed and mapped building conditions, land use, ownership, traffic, employment, and residency, with size and
location of all families. We engaged in
an extensive process of design participation. Formal techniques such as slide

7. Villa Victoria occupies a key location in
Boston's fast-gentrifying South End.

206

presentations, models, architectural plans, and renderings were useful, yet the real information flowed while playing shortstop for the baseball team, attending weddings and birthday parties, sharing informal meals, and drinking many beers.

A new plan was carefully developed by and for the neighborhood with the presence, absence, participation, frustration, and mostly objection of the BRA. Everyone knew the issue being talked about was land use but that the real issue was control and ownership. The idea of community groups being able to attain control and ownership without finances or politicians, but through simple homesteading and moral or political arguments, was not spoken, but was ever-present.

We produced a plan with the local residents that received formal approval at their annual meeting in 1968. Mixed income housing, onsite relocation, and a true Puerto Rican plaza were the primary ingredients. The residents, organized as the Emergency Tenants Council (ETC), received supporting letters from every existing organization in the South End, from Puerto Rican groups in Chicago and New York, from state and federal senators and representatives, and from clergy and civic leaders to back up their inevitable request for designation as redevelopers of this 20-acre parcel. Their request was denied many times before finally being accepted.

These South End residents started their action a year later than their neighbors in Lower Roxbury, and yet received designation a month earlier. Lower Roxbury unfortunately paid the price for being first to ask for what was unheard of in 1960s urban renewal—community control. An informal coalition was, and is still, in effect between these two neighborhoods. Maintaining their primary objective of good, mixed-income housing with on-site relocation, the ETC residents have executed four phases of housing development, totaling 492 homes and 26,000 sf of commercial space, and a six-story office building. Two hundred additional new housing units, 20,000 sf of new commercial space, renovation of a large church, and total rehabilitation of an existing public housing project are in the works.

Phase One was financed through a local bank with a HUD Section 221(d)3 interest subsidy and the local housing authority leasing units for low

income residents. Phase Two was financed through the Massachusetts Housing Finance Administration (MHFA), and sold to the local housing authority using the HUD "Turnkey" program. Phase Three was financed through MHFA with HUD Section 236 interest subsidy and HUD rent supplements for low income families. Phase Four was financed through MHFA with the HUD Section 8 rent subsidy program. Three of the four projects were executed as limited partnerships, with the residents as the managing general partner, resulting in a significant return of tax shelter syndication proceeds to the community for use at its discretion. Joint ventures with the building contractors were formed to establish net worth for the limited partnership prior to sale of the tax shelters. One of the four projects was executed by the community residents as a precontracted, developer-owner sale to the local housing authority for a normal—but significant—developer's fee. The economic approach of this group has been very sophisticated and successful. This neighborhood has been assisted on all phases by a housing development consultant on a "fee-for-services" basis. The necessary front money was again provided by local church organizations.

The residents' group manages all of the developments, plus 300 units owned by the local housing authority, and has contracts for the provision of social services to the area, resulting in a full-time staff of over 70 residents. This does not include the construction jobs secured through their Neighborhood Priority Hiring Program.

## Back of the Hill

This community on the south side of Mission Hill has probably suffered the greatest damage from institutional acquisition and expansion. The neighborhood, which was only 35 acres in extent, has had 27 of these acres acquired by institutions that consequently demolished all but six of the existing homes. The institutions involved are: Lahey Clinic, the Ruggles Baptist Church, and the City of Boston. On the very top of Mission Hill sits the New England Baptist Hospital. This hospital has provided the beds and facilities for Lahey Clinic, and consequently the Clinic purchased 13 acres of land, evicted the residents, and demolished the homes in expectation of building a new clinic adjacent to

the hospital. The Ruggles Baptist Church saw as one of its missions religious support for this same hospital, and consequently purchased approximately 12 acres of land, deteriorated the homes, and cleared most of them in anticipation of building a new church adjacent to their hospital. The City of Boston acquired another 4 acres through tax foreclosure as a result of the blight caused by the other institutions.

John Sharratt Associates was asked by a neighborhood group, now the Back of the Hill Community Development Association (BOHCDA), to help save what was left and to replace what had been removed. The city, by this time (1970), had become reasonably supportive of community groups, including BOHCDA. But resistance from the Church and the Clinic was solid. They would not listen or talk. They did what they did because it was right. They were representatives of God. They were life-givers. Rational argument and political embarrassment gradually weakened the Church, which finally sold the few existing buildings to the residents and entered into an agreement with the BOHCDA for the remaining land. The Clinic was much more difficult. Eight years later, perserverance by the neighborhood finally resulted in the Clinic believing the BOHCDA was capable of developing the land and paying a fair price for it. An option agreement for the entire project was signed, and construction was started in October, 1979, on 125 units for the elderly and handicapped. An additional 400 units is awaiting funding, and a third phase is in the planning stage.

## RTH:Struggle/Planning/Participation

Our most recent project is the RTH struggle with Harvard to which I will now return. I believe the RTH Neighborhood Mission Park effort has been true participation in design and planning and has great significance for two reasons:

1. This is a most successful resolution of urban neighborhood/institutional conflict.
2. This conflict properly identifies institutional expansion as replacing urban renewal as the key threat to working class neighborhoods.

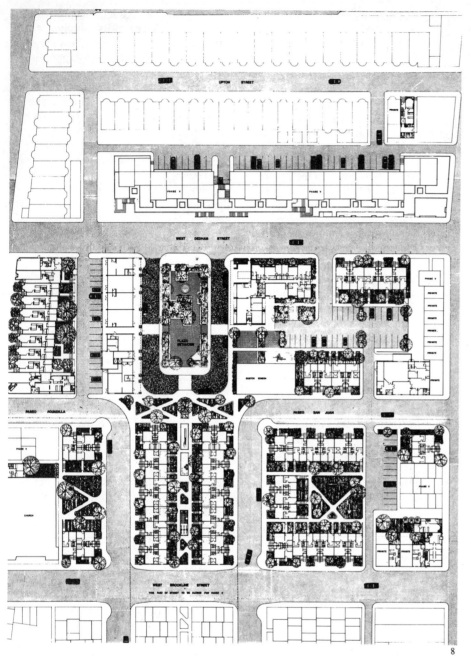

8

8. Villa Victoria site plan.

9. Site section shows incorporation of existing rowhouses with new medium- and high-rise housing around a central plaza.

10. Victorian townhouses on Shawmut Avenue were preserved and rehibilitated.

11. The plaza with elderly housing behind.

12. Small units and commercial space occupy the tower at the center of Villa Victoria.

13. Rowhouses are organized along a park-like spine.

14. Interior of a rehabilitated townhouse.

15. Getting ready for a community meeting in the central plaza.

9

10

11

12

13

14

15

16. Apartments for the elderly and the handicapped in the Back of the Hill district.

Steve Rosenthal

In response to the 1969 student strike, Harvard announced its decision to build 1100 units of new housing, part of which would accommodate residents displaced by the proposed Harvard Medical Center. The financing of the project remained vague. Critics questioned whether apartments could be constructed for the large families who lived in the neighborhood. Before the announcement about new housing, University officials did not talk with tenants to learn of their housing needs or obtain their participation in planning.

On the other hand, after the decision was announced, the University set up several committees involving tenants, students, and health workers. The residents and I worked in good faith on the Housing Committee, formulating goals and objectives. For at least one year, the Committee remained powerless to affect either hospital expansion or housing policies. Actual decision-making power remained in the hands of the Harvard Corporation and high-level administrators. Frustrated by a lack of progress, tenants and their supporters then turned to more aggressive tactics. Community residents worked with student organizers in door-to-door canvassing and with our staff to develop their own neighborhood housing plan. Frequent meetings took place in people's homes and at the local church. A strong leadership group emerged. The leaders, who numbered about 10, were of mixed

ages, had families, and were long-term residents of the neighborhood. They came from different ethnic and racial backgrounds, but generally similar economic positons. None of the leaders had been politically active prior to the expansion conflict. All had deep attachments to the community.

Gradually, RTH gained more members and emerged as a durable tenants' association. Membership eventually included most families in the neighborhood. Monthly meetings regularly have attracted 40 to 80 members. Each year, the membership has elected officers and board members who have worked together on specific strategies, negotiations, and organizing efforts.

During late 1969, RTH demanded direct negotiations with the Harvard Corporation. RTH sent delegations to the Corporation and to the Dean of the Medical School. Together with student and faculty supporters in Cambridge and at the Medical School, tenants organized three nonviolent demonstrations and a "mill-in" at the Dean's office involving more than 100 participants. The demonstrators asked that the Dean visit the neighborhood to inspect the deteriorating housing. After a delay of several weeks, the Dean toured the community with a group of tenants. RTH, with our assistance, prepared a lengthy document recording the history of the conflict, the relevant problems, and the identity of key interests. Existing code

violations were photographed and recorded. A development proposal, management plan, and comprehensive physical plan for the entire area was presented. The community also sponsored a City Council public hearing (at the local church) that documented institutional acquisition and neglect, and presented its own neighborhood development plan. Newspapers, radio, and television stations publicized the demonstrations, the tour, the plan, and the hearing.

This combination of events was the turning point. The University did not change its actual policies until RTH, with supporters among the faculty and student body, showed an ability to disrupt University business, challenge its experts, and attract embarrassing attention in the public media. The Harvard administration, headed by a new president, became convinced that its agents had served it poorly and that the tenants' positive commitment and power base were strong enough to be taken seriously.

Since 1970, the tenants have obtained written agreements that respond to their needs. The Harvard Corporation assigned one of its members and a staff person to take responsibility for negotiations with the tenants. In general, the Corporation has honored agreements between RTH and these negotiators.

The Corporation agreed to roll back

and freeze rents at their 1969 level. In addition, the Corporation guaranteed that all future rent increases would be subject to RTH approval. By 1972, Harvard's real estate agent had made repairs that met most of the safety standards of the Boston Housing Code. At the tenants' instigation, Harvard also began a program of housing rehabilitation funded by the University. By 1972, with JSA as the architect and RTH in control of the design, one-half of all homes had a complete exterior renovation. Their varied and bright colors were symbols of the community's achievement.

RTH obtained an agreement that established screening procedures, favoring rentals to families who wanted to remain in the neighborhood. Vacant apartments were to be rented again as soon as possible. A real estate office was opened in the neighborhood so that problems could be settled promptly. Because RTH members have participated actively in rental practices, the community has overcome pressures that discouraged families from staying in the area. As a result, the composition of the neighborhood has again stabilized. In 1971, after a long series of negotiations, the Harvard Corporation promised in writing that no tenants could be evicted until suitable relocation housing was available and approved by RTH.

Early in 1975, after five years of negotiations, RTH and the Harvard Corporation finalized agreements concerning new, tenant-controlled, mixed-income housing. RTH, as a codeveloper, gained control over architectural plans, rental policies, and maintenance. Residents were aware of the potential problems of community-controlled housing, but were committed to this goal as an important means to stabilize the neighborhood.

Ground breaking took place in October, 1975. Construction of the new housing was completed in 1978. The wood homes that did not receive exterior renovation (85 units) will be transferred to RTH as the general partner for a HUD Section 8 total renovation. The homes that did receive the 1972 exterior work will be transferred to a privately financed RTH cooperative to serve the residents not eligible for Section 8 assistance.

Over the past ten years, people have not only changed their community, but subjective changes and politicization have also occurred. When the struggle

against medical school expansion began in 1969, most residents wanted to remain in their homes. But they doubted their ability to win in a struggle against powerful and wealthy institutions. They had seen similar neighborhoods destroyed by the Government Center in Boston's West End, by highway construction in various parts of the City, and by urban renewal projects. But residents no longer feel powerless; they have witnessed a series of concrete achievements. People have developed pride in the community and the sense of personal efficacy that results from continued success and mutual support. The political awareness and strengths of the RTH neighborhood have skyrocketed. This group is now a significant and coherent voting block well able to make its wishes known.

The threat to housing was a clear-cut issue around which residents could unite. But there were many other areas of concern. For example, hospital expansion focused attention on the fact that many residents had no regular source of health care. Other issues included drug abuse and alcoholism, irregular police services, limited shopping facilities and the need for cooperative food buying, recreational facilities, and local economic problems and unemployment. The leaders of the tenants' association resisted pressures toward diffuseness. They directed their primary efforts toward the housing issue and encouraged their neighbors to do the same. More recently, after obtaining definite housing commitments, people have begun to work on other problem areas. During the construction phase of Mission Park, the neighborhood has focused on developing sound service programs.

Programs now in effect, provided, and managed by RTH are:

- Senior Citizens Food Program
- Senior Citizens Health Program
- Library and Tutoring Program
- Youth Program for all ages—focusing on teenagers
- Child Care
- Crime Prevention Awareness Program

Throughout the RTH events, organizers and community leaders have been careful to cultivate a reliable power base among both residents and outside supporters. New people have participated each year on the RTH

Board of Directors. Whenever major policy matters are to be decided, members canvass the neighborhood to assure that people have a chance to express their opinions. While the residents' power has rested on unity within the community, help has also come from other sources. Politicians representing the community in the state legislature and City Council have organized public meetings where people could state their feelings and form ties of solidarity. Although people in the neighborhood have taken the primary initiative, student and staff support within the medical center and University has also strengthened the community's power.

Another reason for the community's success has been the residents' flexibility in using a variety of tactics as warranted by different situations. For almost a year after the formation of the tenants' association, University officials did not respond seriously to residents' demands. Under these circumstances, confrontation and obstruction were necessary. Residents switched to negotiations and bargaining once their position and strength were recognized.

## RTH Accomplishments

The 1972 complete exterior renovation to 75 apartments by Harvard was the first real physical evidence of positive change in the RTH neighborhood. The completion of Mission Park in June of 1978 has secured the permanent existence of the RTH neighborhood, and proven to be a successful resolution of the classic urban conflict between a large institution and an old, but valuable neighborhood. The project design grew out of this conflict, the major interest groups' real needs, and the tools available for execution. The value of the available land required the construction of approximately 800 units. The neighborhood wanted the existing neighborhood saved and a minimum of 150 new townhouse units built. The medical center and the new housing together required approximately 1500 parking spaces. The University also required a minimum of 300 units for hospital staff. The final program resulted in 775 new units of housing, a 1274-car underground garage, 40,000 sf of rental office space, 5000 sf of community services and office space, two tennis courts, two basketball courts, six tot lots, a swimming pool, and a plaza. The buildings include a 27-story high-rise, three

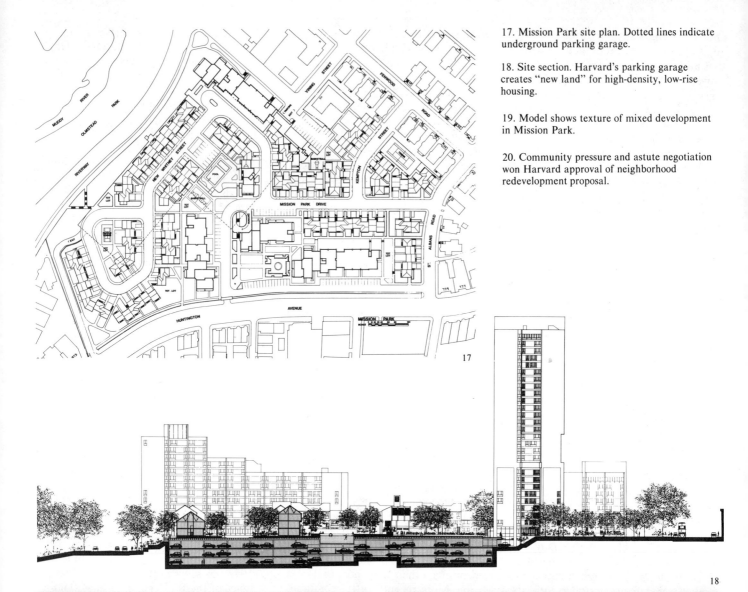

17. Mission Park site plan. Dotted lines indicate underground parking garage.

18. Site section. Harvard's parking garage creates "new land" for high-density, low-rise housing.

19. Model shows texture of mixed development in Mission Park.

20. Community pressure and astute negotiation won Harvard approval of neighborhood redevelopment proposal.

17

18

19

20

21

21. Harvard-owned garage shares the site with moderate income housing.

22

22. Community involvement produced a plan with unexpected amenities.

23. A quiet residential street right in the city.

23

stepped mid-rises, family townhouses, a three-floor underground garage, and a community building. The residential buildings contain 391 1-BR units, 228 2-BR units, 128 3-BR units, and 38 4-BR units.

The integration of this large program into a complex physical and political urban setting resulted in:

1. Building the parking garage beneath the site, with access from the large buildings and the hospitals that are to lease the major portion of parking spaces.
2. Placing the townhouse units throughout the site as the unifying fabric between the existing neighborhoods, the mid-rise buildings, and the neighboring park system.
3. Stepping the mid-rise buildings from 4 to 13 floors in an attempt to relate the two- and three-story townhouses to the high-rise building.
4. Shooting the high rise building up 27 floors to relieve surface density and allow ground space for the townhouses and recreation.
5. Placing the community building with the swimming pool and playground at the center and focus of the neighborhood.
6. Developing a formal plaza at the entrance as a community meeting place, as opposed to a more selective "neighborhood" meeting place.
7. Setting an additional six playgrounds, two basketball courts, a paddle tennis court, a tennis court, numerous benches, site lights, and landscape trees and plants throughout the site.
8. Tapping the new, hospital Total Energy Plant and taking advantage of off-peak loads and "by-product" energy.

The development has been financed through HUD Section 8 rent subsidy guarantees. The codevelopers have been RTH, the general contractor, and a private development group. The limited partnership that owns and manages the development is Mission Park Associates (MPA). RTH is one of the three managing general partners and is also a limited partner with substantial equity interest. RTH responsibilities include the right to determine or approve the following:

- Number and type of housing units
- Unit mix
- Subsidy financing
- Site plan, elevations, specifications, exterior materials, and building systems
- Tenant relocation plan and affirmative marketing plan
- Management plan and contract
- Selection of management company
- Tenant leases

The codeveloper fee from syndication proceeds for RTH came to $320,000, plus an additional $1.25 million if the development runs smoothly. Harvard advanced the price of the land, nearly $800,000 in front money, and was instrumental in securing the Section 8 subsidy. After a difficult start, Harvard clearly got behind the development and was deeply involved in making it happen once an identity of interest was established. The 1969 objective of "Save our Neighborhood" has been fulfilled and surpassed. The number of new and rebuilt homes has tripled. Social services and security are close to optimal. Political awareness, sense of neighborhood, and individual dignity have been greatly increased. RTH is, and should be, proud of its accomplishments.

The entire RTH struggle has been framed and formed by institutional pressures and the means available to deal with these pressures. As the architect/planner for this project, I believe that the manipulation of the available programs has produced a project of lasting quality. And the effort has produced a community and a leadership that can adapt and enrich this physical environment continually.

The most significant fact that has been made clear to me during my experience with RTH is that institutional expansion is replacing urban renewal as the key threat to working class neighborhoods. The problems are real:

- The institutions have the resources to buy up urban neighborhoods.
- Educational and medical institutions are extremely influential politically.
- Local planning agencies cannot be relied upon because of the political nature of these agencies and the powerful influence the institutions can produce.
- Few experienced, independent professionals will donate their time and risk the wrath incurred by challenging the institutions.

Specific legislation beyond the influence of the institutions is needed to prevent them from arbitrarily and unnecessarily expanding into our precious urban neighborhoods.

## Conclusion

Working with community clients, I have refined the following straightforward process to guide planning and decision making:

- Carefully identify and fully understand all sides of the problem.
- Seek out the most honorable/moral/political/correct/defensible solution.
- Frame the solution with sound technical arguments, documentation, and presentations.
- Seek public forums for presentations, discussions and negotiations.

My concept of neighborhood participation in design and planning focuses on economic control and the degree a neighborhood is able to affect real issues. The position I take as an architect/planner/friend/political strategist with a neighborhood is constantly changing. My introduction is usually as an expert, a professional with a useful skill for the situation. My participation in the early to middle phases, as the group is gaining new confidence, is as a part of the group contributing differently, but equally. In the later phase of development, as the residents' leadership has gained recognition, skills, and confidence, my position shifts back to more of a standard professional role which can easily be replaced or terminated. The trajectory of the development of my position is not a conscious plan on my part, but is the natural result of my filling the needs of the moment and of community groups growing into a new sense of their own power and importance.

# Commentary on Mission Park

Tunney Lee, Professor of Architecture,
Massachusetts Institute of Technology

## CITY SPACE AND CLASS STRUGGLE

The struggles of ordinary people to control urban space have gone largely unrecorded—partly because they are seldom successful and partly because architectural history is of and for the dominant classes. Even when there have been successes, as there were in the late 1960s and early 1970s they have been effective mostly in stopping some catastrophic action such as highway construction or clearance for urban renewal. These anti-actions are difficult to visualize. For instance, it takes a deliberate effort of historical reconstruction to stand in Central Square in Cambridge and see in the mind's eye the swath the elevated Inner Belt would have cut. There are no plaques on the thousands of houses still standing that say: "Here, but for the valiant and persistent efforts of neighborhood people, their organizations, and their friends, would be a six-lane elevated expressway."

However, there are exceptions. The three projects designed by John Sharratt for the Lower Roxbury Community Corporation (LRCC), IBA's Villa Victoria, and Mission Park for the Roxbury Tenants of Harvard (RTH) are concrete realizations of the struggles by poor and working class residents to control their neighborhoods. The successes of LRCC, Villa Victoria, and RTH are reminders of the profound changes in the political climate of Boston that reflect changes in the physical environment. Although the class struggle for space in the city continues, the battleground has changed in size and scope. Large-scale clearance and public displacement of entire neighborhoods are no longer attempted. Where there are active community groups, the city and developers must now deal with them and sometimes include them in the development process. The design methods, institutional arrangements, and financial tools for active community participation and control were developed in large part in the Sharratt projects. By now, those tools have become part of the standard kit of the numerous community development corporations that have sprung up all over the city.

What was the historical context within which the Sharratt projects were conceived and built? The three neighborhoods have in common only the threat of displacement and access to friendly professionals. Otherwise, they represent three different racial/ethnic groups with different problems of creating or maintaining a community in the face of overwhelming odds and strong pressures for total demolition. By the mid-1960s, Boston's neighborhoods were in the final stages of a process that had begun in the nineteenth century. In order to accommodate the immigrants (first Irish, then Italians and Jews) pouring into the rapidly expanding manufacturing economy, Boston exploded exponentially in size and population. Neighborhoods passed through successive stages of growth and decline as waves of newer immigrants replaced immigrants who moved to growing suburban areas. By World War I, textile and shoe manufacturing had stopped expanding in New England. There started a slow, but nevertheless painful, decline into a prolonged economic depression. This economic decline, coupled with the enactment of national quotas discriminating against all but Northern European immigrants, effectively froze change in the inner city and brought about the era of the "urban village." Romanticized by writers and studied by sociologists, the urban village was the epitome of the natural community, with its close-knit family, ethnic, and cultural life. It served as a safe haven from the harsh depersonalization and discrimination of mainstream American life. Living in parts of the city abandoned by more prosperous groups, the urban villages of Boston (e.g., the West and North Ends, East and South Boston, Chinatown, South End, Lower Roxbury, and Mission Hill) existed precariously, but were ignored and unmolested.

This period ended with World War II and the major upheavals in the American economy and the subsequent effects on urban space that followed the war. With postwar recovery, the Boston economy finished its transition from textile, shoe, and machinery manufacturing to a predominantly high technology manufacturing and service mix. Most of the expansion was in the suburbs, and where the jobs went, the housing followed. The educated and mobile, especially families with school-age children, went first. The great exodus from the inner city began, leaving behind those who did not want to or could not leave. At the same time, the southern agrarian economy was being transformed, and black tenant farmers were being displaced by the millions. Puerto Rico was wrenched from an agricultural into an industrial economy which needed fewer workers. These two groups—blacks and Puerto Ricans—flooded into the northern cities looking for work, and occupied the urban villages that were vacated by the new suburbanites.

In Boston, as elsewhere, the recovering economy also looked to downtown and its surrounding neighborhoods. Ignored during the Depression, they were now seen as desirable middle class housing areas and essential commercial and industrial space needed to compete with the suburbs. New highways were also required to carry the suburbanites and their automobiles downtown. The urban villages were now slums, and the space was much too valuable for working class people. Thus, the twin programs of Urban Renewal and the Interstate Highway Program began to wreak their havoc on the city. The first projects (West End and New York Street Urban Renewal Projects, the Central Artery and the Massachusetts Turnpike Extension) met with strong but ineffectual opposition. Residents attended raucous public hearings that were duly recorded, but ignored. However, these experiences were not without importance. The plans were abstractions, but the displacement of families and the demolition of neighborhoods in the late 1950s were realities that Bostonians could see for themselves and had to learn slowly to resist. The proper strategy and tactics had to wait to be developed in the coming together of the civil rights movement and the anti-war movement with the struggles over urban space.

216

By the time the second round of urban renewal and highway planning was started in the 1960s, neighborhood residents were apprehensive about their fate and became increasingly skeptical of the promises made by public agencies. Despite the more sophisticated "participatory" attitude adopted by the Boston Redevelopment Authority (BRA) with its slogan of "planning with people," residents were putting up more resistance and becoming more adamant. Sensing this, a handful of professionals and academics in the design and planning professions began to organize as advocate planners to provide technical assistance to neighborhood groups. The first battles were over highway construction (in Boston and Cambridge—the Inner Belt), but soon expanded into struggles with the BRA over urban renewal.

John Sharratt was one of these professionals and, as he has described, he volunteered his design services to LRCC and its advocate planning group, Urban Planning Aid (UPA). Later, he was to work with the Emergency Tenants Committee (ETC, later changed to *Inquilinos Boricuas en Acción*—IBA) on Villa Victoria, and then RTH. The three neighborhoods were quite different in their situations. Lower Roxbury was a black residential area in the process of becoming a neighborhood, but confronted by total clearance for a citywide high school and two highways. Villa Victoria was built in an area of poor tenements in the South End occupied by recent immigrants from Puerto Rico who organized to stay together in better housing. RTH was part of Mission Hill, a true urban village that had survived into the 1960s but was threatened by the expansion of the Harvard medical complex.

The three neighborhoods had a common characteristic: their continued occupation of their space was threatened. What further distinguished them was the desperate need to rebuild existing housing or build new housing—and this was the lever with which the activist architect could affect the process. The combination of increasing neighborhood confidence and dedicated and sensitive professionals produced a set of related strategies that have now become the modus operandi for Boston's new wave of community development corporations. In outline, these are:

1. Broad and democratic involvement of all affected residents through active organizing—in all aspects of the planning, including architectural design.
2. The development of ways of communicating that break down the professional barriers and demystify the design process. Underlying this is the recognition that if people do not understand the work of the professional, it is the professional's responsibility to bridge the gap.
3. With the residents' input, to create housing that is more than dwelling units, but that contains a full range of social services.

4. Institutional and financial arrangements that enable the residents to share development profits and to control ownership and management.
5. A strong organizational base with indigenous leadership that is prepared for the long run and that is flexible, changing tactics as necessary from protest to management.

These lessons continue to be useful, although the conditions of the struggle for space have changed and are still changing. The new struggles are more subtle; the targets are smaller and more diffused. Government has withdrawn from large-scale projects. Institutions have lowered their profiles. The most serious issues are now the destruction of the poorest neighborhoods through neglect, and market-induced displacement (gentrification) in well-located neighborhoods. These problems are more difficult to combat because there are no prominent targets against which to organize. But there is a continued proliferation of community development organizations willing to fight for their turf. For these groups, the Sharratt projects have become important in several ways:

1. LRCC, Villa Victoria, and RTH illustrate how to involve people and how to gain control of land and management.
2. The Sharratt projects stand as inspirations to new groups and are continually referred to as reasons for continuing when the struggle becomes protracted. For Boston's new Hispanic, Cape Verdean, and Asian immigrants, the projects represent what people can accomplish for themselves in the face of adversity and governmental opposition or indifference.
3. The projects are catalysts for further work. Villa Victoria and RTH are bastions of low and moderate income housing in gentrifying areas. They assert the right of working class and poor people to live in good housing convenient to downtown or services. LRCC and Villa Victoria are close to public housing projects and will be able to contribute to the salvaging of those low income units through their example and technical expertise.

The Sharratt projects thus represent a substantial part of the legacy of the participatory/advocacy period of the 1960s and 1970s. However, it is clear that they have succeeded well beyond "participation in design" or "user needs analysis." The projects have had substantial input from their residents and represent models of how to do "participation." But their significance lies in the crucial precedent of ownership and control established by the tenants—with the help of their architect.

24. Mission Park today.

# Cabrillo Village
# Saticoy, California

Here, in reports from the community organizer, the architect, and the landscape architect, is the continuing story of Cabrillo Village and its people. Ninety farmworker families of Mexican origin had lived for years in a dilapidated labor camp outside of Saticoy, California, earning meager livings picking lemons in the surrounding groves. Now, with the help of Cesar Chavez, the United Farmworkers Union, and the Catholic Migrant Ministry, they have formed a cooperative and purchased the 18.5-acre site from the Lemon Grower's Association. With support from the California Department of Housing and Community Development, the Farmers Home Ad-

ministration, the Department of Labor, and Rural America, they have begun to rebuild the old homes and build new ones, to create shops and day-care services around a central plaza, and to manufacture decorative tiles both for "export" and to express their heritage in the redesign of Cabrillo Village.

There are nearly 250,000 landless farmworkers in California and hundreds of thousands more in other agricultural areas of the US. Cabrillo Village and its sister projects—the San Jerardo Cooperative in Salinas, Blue Goose Camp in Brentwood, and others—point the way to a better future for these forgotten people.

Jaime Bordenave was the project director at Cabrillo Village. He is on the staff of the Rural Community Assistance Corporation, a Sacramento-based private, nonprofit corporation that provides technical assistance for housing and community facilities throughout the western states.

John V. Mutlow is a British-trained architect working in Los Angeles. He and his firm have long been involved in the housing and renewal problems of the Chicano community.

Frank Villa Lobos is a Los Angeles landscape architect and a principal in Barrio Planners, Inc., a nonprofit Community Design Center active since 1970.

# A Village for Farmworkers

Jaime Bordenave
Rural Community Assistance Corporation,
Sacramento

Cabrillo Village was built in 1937 as a private farm labor camp. Originally consisting of 100 cabins for single men, it was quickly converted to a family camp. Each of the cabins housed one family, predominantly legal permanent residents with Mexican citizenship. A number of other buildings were added over the years, including three dormitories which permitted migrant single men to live at the village. Many of these single men later married and returned with their families to live in one of the 480 sf cabins. Some of the tenured residents, and especially the foremen, were able to acquire the larger 660 sf units, which were three-bedroom units.

Located on 18 acres of reclaimed bottom land adjacent to the Santa Clara River, the Village had its own (inadequate) water and sewer systems, indicating its isolation from the neighboring towns of Saticoy and Ventura. The river and the railroad tracks have the village sandwiched in-between, accentuating the physical isolation. There have been other forms of isolation as well. The Mexican-American community of Saticoy generally considers itself "superior" to the village community, since the latter are not yet US citizens. The Saticoy and Fillmore Growers and the Saticoy Lemon Association maintained the camp well, but the drab colors and the cyclone fence, topped with barbed wire, around the perimeter did not help develop pride in the community.

The people of Cabrillo Village participated by-and-large in the joint Mexico-US Bracero Program, and when it was terminated, they decided to try to make a life here in the United States. A typical family is that of Jesus Guzman, who immigrated in 1960, after the termination of the program. In 1965, he brought his family to Ventura County and began working with S & F Growers, which provided housing in the Village for a minimal cost that was deducted from his paycheck. Many of

the men living in Cabrillo Village have lived there much longer than the Guzman family. Don Cruz Muro, age 74, was one of its first residents. The average is close to 20 years' residency at the Village, working with the same employer and picking lemons in the citrus fields of Ventura County.

On October 15, 1975, the Saticoy Lemon Association sent a letter to all 90 families living in the Village (10 houses had been destroyed over the years), advising them that they were to vacate the premises within 30 days. An offer of $500 was made to help with relocation expenses. The reason given for the eviction was that the State of California, which licenses labor camps, had reviewed the camp and found it substantially in need of correction of health and safety violations. The Saticoy Lemon Association had decided that, rather than repair the camp, it should be torn down, as it was estimated that compliance with the State order was not cost efficient. This action unified the residents of the Village and catalyzed the development of the cooperative at Cabrillo Village.

The eviction notices did not come as a surprise to the families, as their relationship with their employer had been deteriorating over the last several years. In September, 1974, the workers went on strike for a better wage and better working conditions. Having heard of the work of Cesar Chavez, who had lived in neighboring Oxnard, a union organizing committee was formed, which included Jesus Guzman, Luis Magdaleno, and José de la Rosa, among others. Don Luis Magdaleno was elected Chairman of the workers' committee. Under this leadership the strike was successful, with the workers receiving all their demands, including recognition of the committee as their representative.

Almost all of the workers signed authorization cards for United Farmworkers Union (UFW) representation and were waiting for the

effective date of new California labor legislation for an election to be held. On August 28, 1975, the day the election was to have taken place, there were only 90 workers, as 190 had been laid off—which meant that the election could not take place. Thus, when the eviction letter came on October 15, it was not difficult for the families to conclude that the growers were using the evictions as a means of retaliation and as a means of preventing the workers from organizing themselves for the union election. If the workers had to move to Oxnard, Santa Paula, Fillmore, and elsewhere to find housing, it would be much more difficult to organize themselves.

Most of the families in the Village had nowhere to go, as housing is scarce in Ventura County, particularly for farmworkers and more particularly for large farmworker families. The families decided to fight the eviction. Many people were consulted—the local county supervisor's office, the UFW, the Catholic Church, the Migrant Ministry, the California Department of Housing and Community Development, the local Community Action Agency and Human Rights Commissioner, the Housing Assistance Council—the list can go on. A flurry of activity began: protest marches were held, and there were all-night vigils at the home of one of the grower's representatives, newspaper articles, radio spots, and food collections.

On November 11, 1975, Father Pena, a Catholic priest from Texas who was working with the Migrant Ministry, suggested that the solution to the problem was for the growers to give the camp to the families, for they had paid for it many times over with their labor. As Cruz Muro says:

I have lived in this camp for 31 years, and I believe I have paid for it more than once already with the sweat I have left out in the field, working for these growers and mak-

ing them rich. I have made them rich and now that I no longer am willing to put up with them, they ask me to leave my house. Their excuse is because it is too expensive to repair it. I'll pay for the repairs if the company allows me, but where will I go if I am forced out?

It was Cesar Chavez who took the idea a little further. The UFW was working with the State to have the State purchase the camp. At a meeting on November 17 at the Village, Chavez reported that an extension had been given until the end of December (1975) to resolve the problem. He suggested that if the State did not purchase the camp, the families themselves should buy it!

In between these two meetings in November, the growers began bulldozing some houses at the Village that had been vacated by residents who broke ranks with the majority, took the $500, and left. On November 24, the bulldozer appeared again and tore down the building used as a preschool. In light of the stay of eviction, the families decided not to let any more buildings be torn down, and formed a human circle around the next building scheduled for destruction. The struggle solidified the group, and its convictions and strength grew rapidly.

## The Camp is Purchased

Families met on a daily basis, and Mass was celebrated afterwards by Father Ralph Woodward, who had come to live at the Village during these difficult months (in a poor community, there is always room for one more). "Although we had faith, we could not help the anxiety that we felt looking ahead in the future and not seeing what lay there," said Rosa Guzman.

By this time, the families had realized that buying the camp was the best way out of their predicament, and for that purpose they formed a corporation and chose a Board of Directors. On January 1, 1976, the Saticoy Lemon Association agreed to meet with the Village representatives to discuss the sale of the Village, and on January 9, a telegram was sent to the lemon growers offering $80,000 to buy the property. Each family was to loan $1000 to the corporation for the purchase, and the families began seeking their own loans for the first $500 contribution.

As the negotiations for the purchase were going well, the families turned their attention to the question of what form of ownership they would have. In late January, at a meeting in the Village church (a converted lemon warehouse), with 60 families represented, a vote was taken to form a nonprofit corporation. Twenty heads of household refused to vote and did not join in the newly formed Village association. This subgroup formed a loose association under the leadership of José de la Rosa and decided to attempt to buy the Village themselves, as a profit-oriented group. An offer was made by them to the Saticoy Lemon Association, but on March 5, when escrow was opened, it was the offer of The Cabrillo Improvement Association, under the direction of Luis Magdaleno, that was accepted. Incorporation papers were received on March 16 for The Cabrillo Improvement Association, Inc. (a California, nonprofit corporation). During these discussions regarding profit or nonprofit ownership, the decision was made to also form a Housing Cooperative Corporation, so that both options were open to the residents.

*Cinco de Mayo* (the Fifth of May—Mexican Independence Day), 1976, was a particularly joyous day for Cabrillo Village and its 450 residents. Escrow closed, and Cabrillo Village became the first farm labor camp purchased by the families that lived in it. The 20 dissident families did not contribute their $1000 toward the purchase, and the Association had to borrow $23,000 to close escrow. The United Farmworkers Union loaned $8000, and other families loaned the remainder. Ultimately the local Housing Assistance Council gave a two-year, low-interest loan so that

220

these families, as well as the United Farmworkers, could be repaid. The corporation assessed member families $16.13 per month to repay the loan.

The Association now had ownership, and along with that ownership came the responsibility for solutions to the problems that existed: water, sewage treatment, housing rehabilitation, and the "20," to name the obvious ones. The Campaign for Human Development agreed to fund the Cabrillo Improvement Association for $100,000 to cover the costs of hookup to the City of San Buenaventura water and sewer systems, as well as to pay for a full-time coordinator for a one-year period.

## A Visit to Cabrillo

A visit to Cabrillo Village today tells of the advances in the two and one half years since its residents made history. The Village speaks for itself. The main entrance strikes the visitor's eye with a several-hundred-foot long tryptic mural that tells the history of Cabrillo Village in bright colors. It was started in the summer of 1978 by the youth workers of the Village and was completed with weekend volunteer work. Rounding the corner, one enters the business center of the Village. La Cooperativa de Consumo, a cooperative food store, stands as a sentry. The building has been given a facelift, with fresh paint and a suspended ceiling. The small space is crammed with all the same items as a Ma-and-Pa corner grocery store, except that Ma and Pa in this case are villagers, and prices are lower than in the large chain stores.

Facing the coop store is the ceramic tile factory, which provides tiles for the housing rehabilitation project as well as the new "quadruplexes" that are being built. Through a complicated combination of financing, including a nonsecured loan from the neighborhood Bank of A. Levy, eight village workers produce wall and floor tiles with Mexican designs. After the village need has been met, the factory will operate on a commercial basis and intends to offer attractive prices to other housing cooperatives. The factory will also provide part-time work to village residents during the time when lemons are not being picked.

Next to the large shuttle-kiln is the office and meeting hall of the Association. Social services, employment train-

Tim Street-Porter

5. Village residents work on housing rehabilitation.

6. . . . While others record progress in the community mural.

ing, English classes, health clinics and nutrition classes, as well as the administration for the various programs of the Association, are provided here. Six young people from the village currently receive work experience training. The business office of the Cooperative is here, and all Board and membership meetings take place here, on a monthly basis. The families' monthly payments of $40 are sufficient to cover the costs of these operations.

The single men's barracks have been converted to community uses. One serves as the preschool, which until recently has been run by the women of the Village. The local Head Start Program has assisted the preschool, and now this 1100 sf building houses two full classes. The rehabilitation was done by the men of the village, except for the bright colors, which were done by the youth. Bilingual graphics describe what

is going on inside: ESCUELA/ SCHOOL.

On the south and west of the preschool are two other barracks that have been converted to temporary housing for a maximum of four families, to be used until the housing program is completed. A crew of workers, mostly from the Village itself, does the rehabilitation. Training funds from RURAL AMERICA help provide an experienced work force, and the California Department of Housing and Community Development continues to help with money for materials. The workday begins with a formal class that outlines the work to be done and the principles involved in the current phase of construction work. The membership recently approved the purchase of a large flatbed truck that helps assure that materials will always be available—and somewhat less expensively, since they

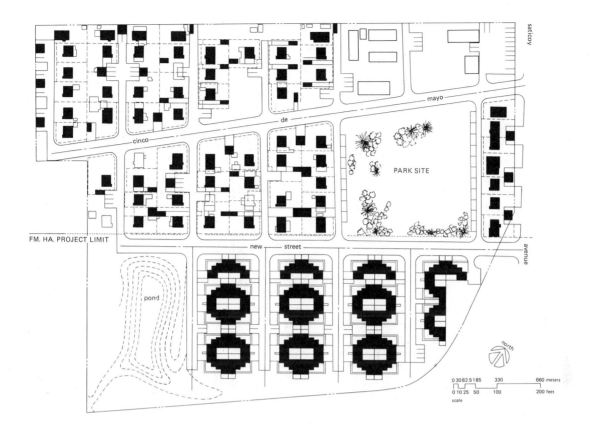

7. (left) The tile shop was set up to supply Cabrillo Village's needs. It now exports its products all over the state.

8. Site plan shows new quadruplex houses to the south. Rehabilitated houses are north of New Street. Families moved from the park site get the first of the new houses.

can now shop around for lower prices.

The men have divided themselves into four maintenance crews, rotating Saturdays to sweep, rake, and water in the common areas of the Village. Volunteers take care of the soccer field, the church, and the sewer system, in addition to their other duties. A new park has been designed that will include a plaza, as well as places for the youth and the elderly. It will be built after the 35 new units are completed. Since this was the first time that the Farmers Home Administration made a grant and loan to a farmworker cooperative under Sections 514 and 516, it has been a long and tedious process. But there is activity everywhere in the Village—activity that benefits its people. Plans are being made for future cooperative business ventures, including the opening of a cabinet shop and the conversion of the rehab crew into a cooperative contracting business.

## Conclusions

In April, 1979, a resolution of the con-flict was finally reached, with the 20 dissidents becoming members of the Cooperative. Undoubtedly a long time will pass before the division is healed. Yet in a certain sense it has been productive, for it has forced all of the residents to study the issue of a housing cooperative: what it is, how it functions, what it means in terms of ownership. There has been a clarification of values, and both groups have learned from it. The majority of the families saw the limitations of their own income and realized that only with the benefits of being a nonprofit corporation could they afford to rebuild the Village. Their poverty level incomes could barely support a deeply subsidized building program, let alone one with market rate interests and no subsidies. Again, the Cooperative was the closest thing to individual ownership available to the group (some of the Association members and most of the "20" still feel that individual ownership is a realistic possibility). It is understandable that not all of the families living within the confines of Cabrillo Village at the time of that decision would agree, and they did not. The Association has taken a conciliatory position and hopes that all of the families will someday share equally in the benefits of the Cooperative, as well as bear its responsibilities.

Having addressed their own internal needs and difficulties, the Association is now able to focus some attention on the needs of other farmworkers in the area. With Village staff providing backup, the Association has begun the search for land to develop other farmworker housing projects. And with this, the drama has gone full circle. From its feeble beginnings in 1975, the Cabrillo Cooperative has grown strong. Not forgetting its own struggle, it now begins to help others.

# Designing Cabrillo Village 1

Frank Villalobos, landscape architect
Barrio Planners, Inc., Los Angeles

In spring, 1977, I met Mike Cardenas of the State of California Department of Housing and Community Development (HCD) in Coachella, California. We had come to meet here with farmworkers from this desert region. I had recently completed a report for the Department of Migrant Housing, a branch of HCD. This report was part of the Development Master Plan for making new communities out of 25 migrant camps owned by the State of California. Its work in rural communities had gained Barrio Planners Incorporated a good reputation with farmworkers' groups throughout the State.

At the time of our meeting in Coachella, Cardenas mentioned to us that a little farm town called Saticoy had recently applied for funding for the construction of 82 new houses. His department had done a feasibility study which supported the farmworkers. In fact, a development budget of $1.4 million had been recommended, and he had instructed the Cabrillo Improvement Association to start looking for architects and landscape architects.

I contacted the Cabrillo Village Improvement Association in summer, 1977, and Barrio Planners was placed on a list of consultants to be interviewed for the project. Jaime Bordenave, the director of Cabrillo Village, mentioned to me that five consultants had been put on the short list for interviews by the Board, and this list included John Mutlow. This was not a surprise to me because John Mutlow had worked with Better Communities Corporation in the preparation of the migrant housing study for HCD, and his reputation in housing ranked high at HUD and with local groups in Los Angeles.

I called John and suggested an association with his firm in the Cabrillo presentation. The team was received well. John's experience in housing and our approach to planning and design was well regarded by the Board. Naturally, three-quarters of our presentation was made in Spanish. We were given a contract in the fall, and we began our work a few weeks later.

Our process started with a series of weekly meetings, since naturally we had proposed a major citizen participation component. We began with an educational role. This included the development of an architectural vocabulary which could be understood by the people and through which we could communicate. Our process also included "two-way instruction," which allowed them to learn about us and us to learn about the people of Cabrillo Village at the same time. Cabrillo Village people are proud, they are hardworking, and they know what they want. At meetings, their statements were short and to the point. Opposition was echoed by those who shared the same feelings. The expressions of agreement were equally loud. During the breaks and after the meetings, one at a time the men would approach us with ideas. They did not always wish to present their ideas before the group, but we carefully included them in what later became the Architectural Standards Manual. Another instrument we used in obtaining input was the architectural program survey. Each of the 83 families received a questionnaire. In a graphic format, it depicted typical house space use alternatives, and asked each family to indi-

1. Part of the housing questionnaire used to determine residents' preferences.

cate its preferences in the design of the new housing.

As you know, nothing is easy in the world, and such was the case with the Cabrillo Village plan. Ventura County enforced the zoning and parking code, thus establishing that Cabrillo Village cannot grow in number of residents and keeping the total number of units at 82. In addition, the planning department required the development of a park for the residents. The most expensive requirement was the expansion and resurfacing of all the private streets in the existing Village and the improvement of Saticoy Avenue, the main road leading to town.

The Farmers Home Administration required that its project be clearly designated a development site with identifiable boundaries and with its own infrastructure, essentially separate from the rest of the site. Other Farmers Home Administration requirements conflicted with the needs identified by the residents, making it very difficult to please both sides. For example, the residents wanted to have tile in the bathrooms (not a great demand, yet a costly one), but Farmers Home said no tile—with the exception of bathtub areas. Residents asked for tile on countertops in kitchens, and Farmers Home said they couldn't have it, they need more modest countertops, and so on. Such debates led to a one-year delay in the completion of working drawings. Cost hikes caused by inflation brought us to a great dilemma by 1978. $1.4 million could only provide funding for 35 new units. All 82 families were now forced to confront the problem of who gets the new housing. Anticipating the budget problem, Jaime Bordenave asked and obtained a self-help grant through HUD. This started the rehabilitation of the existing houses.

The question of relocation became an important topic of discussion at almost every meeting toward the end of the participation effort. The central questions asked were: who gets the new houses? Who has to move to make room for the park? Whose house gets rehabilitated first? The choice of new housing was voluntary. Fifty percent of the families wanted new houses (approximately 38 families), but only 35 could be built. The rehab program was begun with a lottery for those people who opted for rehab housing. Names were drawn, and the lucky 10 were in

the first phase of rehabilitation.

It was our job to prepare the rehab plans for the reconstruction and expansion of the existing units. In addition, our services included the development of an Architectural Standards Manual. This manual will be useful for the residents in the construction of amenities such as fencing, signage, street furniture, light fixtures, and so forth. We are also in charge of the landscape design of the new park. The creation of the park means that 18 families will eventually have to move to make room for it. This problem was caused by using the undeveloped portion of the site for the new housing to minimize initial relocation.

The residents' criteria for park site selection required:

1. That it be centrally located (like parks in Mexico).
2. That the park be close to the church and child care center.
3. That the park be an extension of the existing playground and be able to physically link the two areas during

special celebrations.

The 18 families on the site will be given the option to go into new housing and so they will be moved only a short distance. The material from the houses to be demolished will be cleaned, sandblasted, and stored for use by the people in rebuilding their community.

The use of tile and brick in the new Cabrillo Village is a strongly felt need, connected with the culture of the residents of the Village. The need is so strong that it goes beyond the economic barrier. And as they say, where there is a will, there is a way. So, the Village hired us to design a tile factory, and we converted an existing steel storage building. The initial goal was to manufacture enough tile for all 82 houses, old and new. The factory is so successful that it is now selling tile to construction companies throughout the area. It also provides employment for farmworkers during the off-season.

The Cabrillo Village story is unique, and great credit must be given to the residents of this extraordinary community.

# Designing Cabrillo Village 2

**John V. Mutlow AIA**
**Los Angeles**

Cabrillo Village is laid out as a series of single family dwellings along private streets, each with a well-maintained private garden. The church, child care school, office, and single workers' housing are located at the main entrance. When we arrived, the dwelling units were in a state of deterioration. Construction quality had been poor from the beginning (30 years ago), with exterior walls of redwood siding barely covering 2″ × 3″ studs. The units had no interior finish or insulation and, due to poor design, many wooden bathroom floors had begun to rot.

The first step we took as architects was a survey to ascertain the real desires and needs of the farmworkers.

The survey was based on a previous highly–successful survey that we had done in the Spanish community of Pico Union, located in downtown Los Angeles. The survey clearly revealed several important demands that were incorporated into the final design solution:

1. The typology of the single family dwelling should be preserved if possible.
2. Automobile parking should be adjacent to each unit, not grouped in parking courts.
3. Each unit should have a front and rear garden.
4. All living and bedrooms should face the street.

5. The existing lot lines, areas, and dimensions should be clearly identified and preserved.

A mixture of 2-, 3-, and 4-bedroom units was also established as a direct result of the responses to the questionnaire.

The initial decision to replace all of the 92 original dwelling units was reversed by the community as a result of the survey and the uncertainty that certain families were expressing. Ten dwellings had already been demolished, and only 38 families wished to move to the proposed new units. This hesitation reflected three fears: that the new units would not be single family structures, that the rents would be higher, and

1

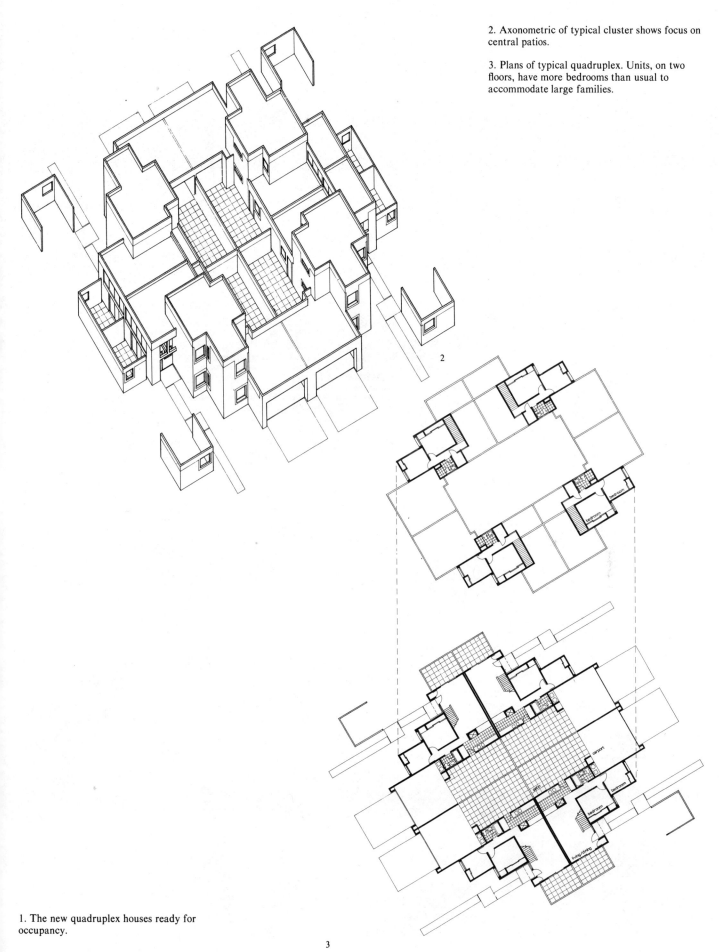

2. Axonometric of typical cluster shows focus on central patios.

3. Plans of typical quadruplex. Units, on two floors, have more bedrooms than usual to accommodate large families.

2

1. The new quadruplex houses ready for occupancy.

3

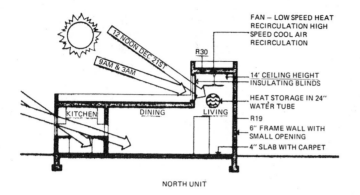

FAN — LOW SPEED HEAT RECIRCULATION HIGH SPEED COOL AIR RECIRCULATION

12 NOON DEC 21ST

9AM & 3AM

R30

14' CEILING HEIGHT INSULATING BLINDS

HEAT STORAGE IN 24" WATER TUBE

R19

6" FRAME WALL WITH SMALL OPENING

4" SLAB WITH CARPET

KITCHEN

DINING

LIVING

NORTH UNIT

4

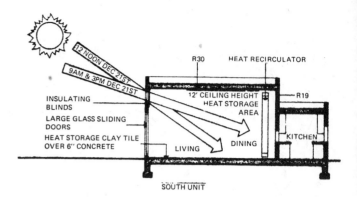

12 NOON DEC 21ST

9AM & 3PM DEC 21ST

R30

HEAT RECIRCULATOR

12' CEILING HEIGHT HEAT STORAGE AREA

R19

INSULATING BLINDS

LARGE GLASS SLIDING DOORS

HEAT STORAGE CLAY TILE OVER 6" CONCRETE

LIVING

DINING

KITCHEN

SOUTH UNIT

5

6

that a change in their social ties would occur.

Because the allocation from the Farmers Home Administration, the financing agency, was for multifamily housing, single family housing was, in fact, ruled out. Row housing would not provide the independence desired by the farmworkers, so a series of "quadruplexes" was developed to satisfy the users' requirements. The decision was made to follow the lot line dimensions and sizes of the old lots in the new housing so that continuity would be provided through similarity to the existing Village.

Three alternative quad plans were developed and presented to the group. The first was a cost-effective solution consisting of rotating rectangles. The second contained a series of L-shaped units arranged in different configurations around a common space. The final solution was a series of stepped L-units that provides greater individuality to the dwelling unit. The repetitive nature of the units minimizes cost. Each unit has all its bedrooms facing the street. Two bedrooms are on the first floor, with the third and fourth bedrooms stacked over them, if needed. A two-textured and integrally–colored stucco facade of simple forms and shapes with whitewashed trim provides a visual relationship to familiar Mexican architecture.

As the design was being finalized, the Association inquired about the possible reduction of utility bills, since this cost represents a large percentage of the families' income. We then investigated a number of possible solutions, using active and passive solar systems. Our studies indicated that with the use of active hot water heating and passive space heating, 60 to 70 percent of the utility costs could be saved. An application was made to the HUD solar office for all 35 dwelling units and was successful: 50 percent of the new units will have individual active systems, and 50 percent a group (quadruplex) system. This way we will be able to test the efficiency of each system.

The passive system proposed directs the sun's rays through a large glass area onto a storage mass, a 6-inch concrete floor, which absorbs the heat during the day and releases it during the night. Increased wall and ceiling insulation, plus insulating blinds for the windows, retains the heat in the winter and controls sun penetration in the summer. Natural ventilation was carefully planned to alleviate excessive heat buildup in the summer.

The efficiency of the north-facing units was 10 percent less than their south-facing counterparts. For these units, alternate systems of storage, either solid or liquid, were examined. Due to the capacity of water to store five times more heat by volume than does concrete, it was found that a wheel water tube, placed behind a south-facing clerestory window, was the only alternative that could match the projected savings of the concrete mass storage system of the south-facing units.

The rehabilitation of the older houses is coming along nicely. A responsible management employee trains CETA workers under a Village program to carry out the work. New foundations are installed. Wood floors are replaced where they had rotted away. Structural walls are reinforced and insulation and interior surfaces (drywall) are put in. Old ceilings are removed and new ceilings installed. Bathroom and kitchen plumbing are replaced, and all new fixtures and cabinets are put in. A new service porch is added with a hot water heater and a hookup for a washer and dryer. And in most cases, one or two new bedrooms are added. A major rehabilitation job is being completed every three months. More than 25 houses have been finished to date.

# Experimental Housing
# Havana, Cuba

Paul Jacob, an American architect working in Cuba, describes the design and construction of a SAR-influenced experimental housing project in Havana. When we apply the term "experimental" to residential projects, we mean usually to call attention to a new use of materials, an innovative structural system, or the flexibility of dwelling layouts.

Jacob's project involves these, but much more as well. It is, in addition, an experiment at the level of urban design, in the allocation of dwelling units, and in the direct participation of people in the building of new homes. These experiments are aimed, in part, at overcoming the legacy of underdevelopment that is the heritage of Cuba's colonial past, and

at expanding the supply of housing for a growing population. But they have cultural and political purposes also. Jacob writes, "User participation in a country undergoing profound social change is a basic factor in the development of a new consciousness."

This housing experiment, with its concerns for efficient use of scarce materials, speed of construction, adaptability, integration of urban functions, and participation, is part of a larger, ongoing effort to define a physical framework for a socialist society. In such a setting, architecture is as much concerned with content and process as with form. But the end result, the form of the environment, is hardly unimportant. After all, it is ex-

pected to speak about equality, solidarity, and hope for the future.

Paul Jacob's article should be read in parallel with that of Roberto Segre on revolutionary architecture in Cuba which appears in Part 3. Speaking against a background of rural poverty and urban squalor shortly after the triumph of the Cuban Revolution, Ché Guevara said, "I am not interested in dry economic socialism. We are fighting against poverty, but we are also fighting against alienation." Jacob and Segre show us that architecture can play an important role in that fight.

1. Calle 3ª, Vedado (Havana): experimental, prefabricated housing.

# Participation and Experimentation in Housing

**Paul Jacob, architect**
*Comité Estatal de la Construcción,*
**Havana**

The development of the experimental LH prefabricated housing system was undertaken in the 1970s in the Cuban Building Research Center in an effort to confront limited national production capacities and the ever-increasing housing demand in Cuba. The LH system, *conceived to respond to the participatory nature of construction* and to satisfy the varied requirements of urban development plans, was based on the industrialized production of prestressed, hollow core concrete slabs applied in bearing walls, floor and roof slabs, and spandrel walls.

The basic low rise building unit is formed by two apartments with an interior width of 7.20 m and an intermediate staircase. The free span between the bearing walls is 6.00, 7.80, and 9.00 m, defining apartments with one, two, or three bedrooms, respectively. The superstructure is formed by transverse bearing walls employing six slabs placed vertically in a continuous double contention wall-type foundation. The floor and roof slabs are simply supported on prefabricated rectangular beams anchored to the walls by steel bolts. The sanitary, hydraulic, and electrical installations are of preassembled plastic components, connected at each level to a stack which contains the corresponding service lines for each vertical unit of apartments. Lightweight interior partitions are used to divide the apartments, and standardized window units are employed as exterior enclosures.

The design collective was composed basically of four architects, two structural engineers, four technical assistants, and various draftsmen. The developmental process, from the initial engineering analysis to the construction of the first prototype (a 16-unit, four-story building), took approximately four years. Construction of the small urban

2. A precast concrete spandrel.

3. Wall slabs slip in place.

4. Interior space (7.2m × 9m) between bearing walls prior to installing light partitions.

231

project described here began a year and a half after the first prototype was completed.

## Theoretical Considerations

As a result of initial discussions, the design collective formulated a series of technical premises and architectural concepts as the basis for design development. The technical premises included:

- Elaboration of a building system with a minimum number of generically different and interchangeable components
- Use of large spans—from 6 to 9 m
- Maintenance of structural components and the structure as a whole free from the limitations normally imposed by mechanical installations, interior divisions, and so forth
- Subdivision of interior spaces with lightweight, interchangeable partitions to adapt to changing family needs and space standards
- Use of preassembled and containerized concepts in the erection of structural as well as nonstructural components
- Maximum use of factory finished components

The architectural concepts included:

- Maximum volumetric and spatial flexibility in the application of the building system
- Acceptance of unlimited facade and interior finishes
- Combination of different living unit sizes (including duplex apartments) to satisfy varied demographic requirements

- Grouping of two, three, and four living units around vertical circulation in low rise buildings and an unlimited number of units around vertical and horizontal circulation in medium and high rise buildings
- Maximum flexibility in building forms and types (linear blocks, units permitting horizontal growth in one and two directions, variation in heights, adaptability to grades, and so forth
- Applicability of the systems' basic principles to other architectural programs (institutional, industrial, and cultural buildings)*

---

*This is not only an economic, but a political precept in Cuba. The use of a similar architectural vocabulary for housing, schools, workplaces, and cultural institutions underlines the unity of these aspects of urban life and the contributions of the people working together to build socialism.—EDITOR

5. Model of factory-built service core.

6. Flexible 3-bedroom apartment in experimental building.

7. A basic 1-bedroom unit.

## The Participatory Project

An area of approximately one and one-half square blocks in a residential zone of Havana was chosen for the urban project. The site contained some existing buildings that had to be retained, thereby limiting the volumetric possibilities in the application of the system. Because of the site's proximity to the Havana sea wall, excellent natural ventilation was assured. The direction of the sea breezes and the sun's trajectory were considered in the urban design, as well as the need for:

- Maximum density without sacrificing green spaces and recreational areas
- Use of a portion of the ground floor space for commercial and community facilities
- Providing vehicular passages through two of the buildings

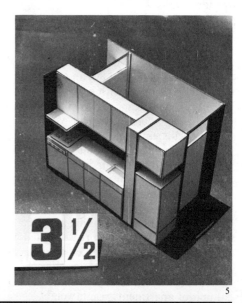

5

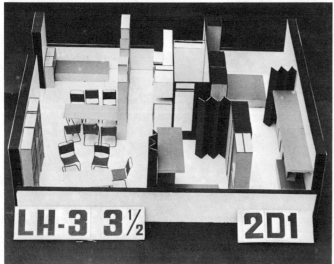

6

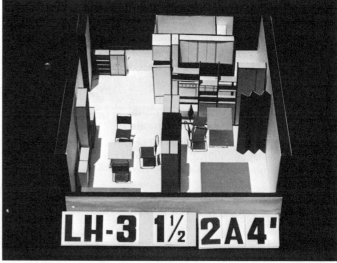

7

- Maximum use of the site's natural conditions (views, breezes, urban location, etc.)

The urban project was designed in collaboration with architects from the National Institute of Urban Planning, thereby guaranteeing compliance with existing urban codes as well as permission for the experimental aspects related to the limitations of the urban site.

The main objective of the project was the application of the experimental building system on an urban scale, taking into account the sociopolitical and economic principles of a developing country undergoing social change.

### The Microbrigades

Once the main objectives of the urban project were defined and the working drawings begun, a *Microbrigade\** was formed to construct the project. Due to the size (170 dwelling units) and experimental character of the project, the Microbrigade was organized with a series of special conditions. However, the basic regulations and sociopolitical aspects were maintained.

A Microbrigade normally consists of approximately 35 men and women from one or more work centers who voluntarily participate in the construction of housing units for their factory or office collective. To participate in a Microbrigade, construction experience or skills are not required, and, in most cases, the workers learn during the actual building process.

The official formation of a Microbrigade takes place in an assembly in the participating office or factory. The building team is elected by the group. The workers who remain behind in their normal jobs guarantee to make up the production of those who form the brigade. With the organization of the Microbrigade, a building site, working drawings, materials, tools and equipment, and technical assistance are guaranteed. The building site and size of the residential project are determined by the location and needs of the work center.

A foreman is elected from the brigade's members, and responsibilities are distributed according to abilities and preferences. Three or four workers are

*For more on this mode of housing production, see the report by Roberto Segré in Part 3.— EDITOR

8. Microbrigade workers and volunteers mount a stair beam.

incorporated into special joint brigade units that construct shared social and community facilities (schools, clinics, shops, etc.).

Because of the size of the experimental urban project, a brigade containing twice the normal number of workers was formed through the participation of a number of work centers. A small administrative force that controlled production schedules, training, participation, and the supply and use of materials was organized, as were a labor union and political and social organizations for the participants in the project.

The building site, type, and distribution of living units for the experimental brigade were defined by the design collective in conjunction with the workers in the participating work centers, based on an analysis of the workers' needs and the structural and architectural characteristics of the LH system.

The relationship between design collective, Microbrigades, and work centers became extremely close during the construction process since the design collective was involved not only in the conception of the project and the organization of the Microbrigade, but also manually participated in the construction work. The project's concepts, premises, and design solutions were explained and analyzed with the brigade

members prior to ground breaking, and monthly progress meetings permitted the direct participation of users in the evaluation and solution of the problems encountered during the construction. This interaction taught the designers a good deal about needs—and about the organization and simplification of various technical and functional aspects of the experimental system.

The brigade workers were divided into specialized work teams and trained in the construction activities. Although this is normal procedure in the Microbrigades, in this experimental project the subdivision of the work forces was of special importance to the organization of the construction process. The units formed were:

- Assembly of prefabricated structural components
- Finishing of structural joints
- Mounting of lightweight interior partitions
- Carpentry (windows, doors, kitchen equipment, etc.)
- Interior finishes (tile, paint, etc.)
- Plumbing
- Electrical work

Once the site was prepared and the foundations poured, construction began with the mounting of the prefabricated units, reaching a rhythm of approximately one apartment per day including the staircase elements. Interior finishes and the positioning of the lightweight partitions followed immediately after the completion of the second-story floor slabs and reached a level of approximately one apartment every three days. Theoretically, the first apartment was ready for occupancy 10 days after the assembly of the structural components was begun and a 30-unit apartment building was completed in 40 days.

The workers from the associated offices and factories participated in massive voluntary work sessions with their corresponding Microbrigades. These sessions, usually scheduled for Saturday afternoons or Sunday mornings, proved both an educational and practical experience. They not only accelerated the building process, but also allowed these workers to participate actively in the making of their homes and to become familiar with the problems inherent in construction. Voluntary participation is taken into account in the assignment of living units.

## Distribution of the Living Units and Community Integration

The distribution between work centers (when more than one work center forms a Microbrigade) is based on the proportional participation of each center. For example: if three work centers construct 30 living units and each has had equal participation, each receives 10 apartments. If, on the other hand, one contributes 50 percent of the work force, the second 30 percent, and the third 20 percent, each would receive 15, 9, and 6 living units, respectively.

The distribution of the dwelling units among the workers is an internal matter for each work center to decide. A commission is elected in a workers' assembly to which administrative, labor union, and party representatives are added. Workers with a housing problem make their formal requests to this commission. Each request is exhaustively analyzed on a basis of the worker's participation in daily tasks, his or her housing need, and the family's general involvement in the revolutionary process. Being a member of the Microbrigade does not automatically entitle the worker to an apartment. A preliminary selection is presented to a workers' assembly and each case is accepted or rejected by a majority vote of the work-

9

10

9. A Type A building takes form.

10. The 30-unit experimental building nears completion.

ers' collective. An individual worker can appeal to the commission and his or her case will be reanalyzed and presented a second time for the workers' consideration.

Once this process is completed, those who are entitled to apartments receive their contracts from the local government* housing agency and take occupancy of their new homes. With the occupancy of the new building, another organizational process is begun: community groups are formed. Basically there are three:

• CDR—Committee for the Defense of

---

*Microbrigade housing rents are set at six percent of family income.

the Revolution
• Residents' Committee
• FMC—Federation of Cuban Women

Each organization elects officers from within its voluntary membership.

Each committee plays a different role within the revolutionary social structure. The CDR is basically a political organization through which various functions are performed on the neighborhood or community level. These include:

• Development of political awareness through study circles

11. Ready for unit assignment to families.

- Neighborhood guard duty to prevent antisocial activities
- Health control by assisting in mass vaccination programs, and other measures
- Organization of political activities and festivities (for example, the traditional block parties celebrating the 26 of July, etc.)
- Voluntary work to guarantee the development and maintenance of common areas (streets, gardens, parks, etc.)

Residents' committees are formed in each multifamily building for the usual reasons: to oversee maintenance, to settle disagreements between neighbors, and to organize common services.

The FMC, on the neighborhood level, is designed basically to incorporate women into the revolutionary process through education or involvement in community activities.

Once the experimental urban unit was constructed and the apartments distributed, these social-political organizations were formed. Due to differences in the cultural levels of the occupants and problems arising from adjustment to a new way of life, various social problems arose. To cite an example: the teenage son of one of the families

exhibited antisocial behavior in his family and community relationships. The case was brought to the attention of the neighborhood organizations. The situation was discussed privately with the boy's parents, as well as in an open community meeting. It became clear that the boy had a psychological problem, and steps were taken to assure him the treatment he needed for proper adjustment to community life.

Periodic voluntary work units are formed through the residents' committee and the CDR to keep up the apartment buildings and their common areas. Community feeling, as well as individual and collective pride in the new living units, assure the participation of the entire family—each member being assigned a job according to age and physical abilities.

## Project Evaluation

The experimental building system proved extremely satisfactory and fulfilled the majority of the premises initially set out. It was agreed that some technical details had to be simplified and that the workers' experiences in the building process should be incorporated into design revisions. The urban design project opened new possibilities for the

use of tight urban sites and the inclusion of social and service facilities within residential buildings.

After a period of use, functional aspects of the apartments were discussed with the occupants. An evaluation of space per person, functional relationships, incorporation of new concepts of flexibility in traditional living areas, and the value of user participation in the project was made. Generally speaking, the results were positive. However, it became clear that more early education should be included in the future so that user participation can be more firmly based on technical understanding rather than on emotional response, thereby facilitating the acceptance of new materials and concepts. This aspect is of extreme importance because traditional concepts will dominate in user participation if those involved do not thoroughly understand the possibilities that new technologies and materials offer.

User participation in a country undergoing profound social-political change is a basic factor in the development of a new consciousness. Democratic participation, although focused in this article on the construction of housing, must be considered an integral part of *all* productive and social relationships.

# 3: The Neighborhood and the City

# Historic Preservation
# Bologna, Italy

Bologna's historic core is among the largest collections of medieval and renaissance buildings in Europe. It is the scene of the largest preservation effort anywhere. What is noteworthy is that Bologna is seeking to preserve far more than its architectural heritage. It plans to preserve an entire way of life.

Aware of the fate of most European and US cities, Bologna's progressive city government has managed to avert both demolition for speculative development and social destruction caused by gentrification. Acting just in time, a master plan for Bologna was drawn up in 1969 under the direction of architect Pier Luigi Cervellati. It stressed:

1. Redevelopment in the core rather than growth at the periphery, to minimize transportation and infrastructural costs, and to preserve the special quality of Bolognese life (Bologna contains the finest restaurants in Italy).
2. The need for careful historical analysis to classify culturally valuable buildings for future uses and to establish rules for restoration.
3. The strategic use of public housing funds for conservation and rehabilitation.
4. Adaptive reuse of nonresidential, historic buildings to provide comprehensive educational and social services in every neighborhood.
5. The importance of democratic participation in planning at every level.

The plan defines the city as a *bene pubblico*—a public good, something like our old-fashioned notion of a commonwealth, created by all, and intended for the benefit of all.

Throughout the extensive urban transformation that has taken place, the attention to architectural detail and traditional construction methods has been extraordinary. In fact, the policy of "conservative restoration" may raise hackles even in advanced postmodernist circles. But the status of a building as art is not more important in the decision to restore than its function, its role in the cityscape, its meaning in its context. In Cervellati's words, the historic city represents "the collective memory of the population." A better future requires an understanding of the past.

It also requires an active, involved citizenry. To encourage participation, power must be shared. In 1974, the City Council adopted a new *Ordinamento del Quartiere*. It gave each neighborhood the right:

- To elect its local officials
- To formulate its portion of the City budget
- To make plans for physical and economic development
- To control traffic
- To grant or withhold building permits
- To administer its education, health, and cultural institutions

Direct democracy, self-governance, elimination of slums and speculation, popular demand for environmental quality—these are the hallmarks of the new Bologna. In its historic core, young couples, workers, and elderly pensioners—not architects and art directors—occupy carefully renovated houses. A colleague of Cervellati's sums up: "This is admittedly not the revolution, but it is revolutionary." And a lesson for American cities.

To place this experience in the broader context of European politics and to connect it to the US situation, two planners who have long-standing connections with the Bologna plan have been asked to respond to Cervellati's report. In his Commentary, which appears following Eduardo Leira's presentation of Orcasitas in Madrid, Manuel Castells discusses participation in Bologna and some of the political problems that accompany it. Bruce Dale's Commentary focuses on the articulation of Bologna's program with the concerns of progressive planners and architects in this country and suggests some fresh strategies for us.

1

# Preservation with Participation

**Pier-Luigi Cervellati, architect**
**Chief Planner, City of Bologna**

The focus of these reflections is the relationship that has grown up between the people of Bologna and the decisions made in the planning and execution of a program to restore the historic core of the city. The contribution of ordinary people to the development of an architectural project or an urban design proposal is not easy to predetermine, in the sense that it is difficult to define a set of rules to regulate the relationship between the designer and the users. In fact, almost any piece of architectural or urban design is ordinarily held to come out of the creative mind of a single artist, while the purpose of participation is the expression of a collectivity. How can we bring together opposites such as individuality and collectivity? How is it possible that the collective presence can influence a program of conservative architectural restoration, a program that must be guided by a rigorous methodology, by a fixed set of rigid practices that tend to be scientific in nature? How can one introduce participation into a form of urban intervention that is objective and not subjective, and of limited flexibility? I can try to answer these questions by relating the recent history of urban revitalization in Bologna, a city in which preservation and participation are practiced together.

Our program of historical preservation affects, above all, a specific part of the city, the *Centro Storico* (the historic core). The historic core, of course, is the preindustrial city of Bologna. Socially and functionally stratified, but still a spatial unit, the historic core is considered to have achieved its definitive form by the middle of the nineteenth century, in that later changes, both quantitative and qualitative, reflect different economic laws and cultural values than had informed the earlier development.

The appearance of industry and motorized transportation profoundly changes the space and the time of human settlements, leading to the breakdown of continuity. For this rea-

2

1,2. Piazza Maggiore and the famous towers: the historic core of Bologna contains the largest collection of medieval and Renaissance buildings in Europe.

son we define the historic core as that which was realized before this moment, before the great population explosion that profoundly affected almost all older cities. For Bologna, the period that marks the passage from the historic city to the contemporary one coincides with the steady unification of Italy, that is, the second half of the nineteenth century. This was the first era of rapid population growth and the first residential and industrial developments were built outside the old wall that once encircled Bologna.

It is essential to come to an agreement about just what is the historic core and to fix a moment after which changes in urban form and in the buildings themselves can no longer be considered part of the history. This is important because many people in Italy believe that everything is historic, or is destined to become so in the future. Following this line of thinking, ultimately one could find the entire historic core replaced by new construction. In any case, it is not easy to explain these individual parameters with criteria derived from urban history and economics. The concept of an historic core is anything but widely understood. Imagine trying to explain it to the people of the city when there is no agreement among specialists!

## The City as Memory

Let us talk for a moment in philosophic terms. Toward the end of the 1960s when we undertook the master plan for Bologna, we wrote that the center represented the historic "memory" of the city, the collective memory of the population. The historic core, we said, is that symbolic place that gives character to the entire city—both the new and the old sections. And we gave some examples: "Try to imagine Bologna without its two towers, without the piazza Maggiore, without . . . ," and so on, citing places and streets, well-known buildings that everyone has seen, even on illustrated postcards ready to be sent around the world. The response was obvious. It was No, it would no longer be Bologna.

But it was more difficult to explain that these monuments without the surrounding minor buildings, without the so-called "connecting urban tissue" would lose their meaning and no longer have any reason to exist. It was difficult to make the case above all because the

minor buildings that we referred to, the houses of workers and artisans, the narrow streets and the alleys, were (and are) the locus of all wretchedness. Here are the homes of the poor, of the urban underclass. "These houses, these streets, what is artistic about them?" we were asked. "Even if they are historical, these are dog holes, the rain comes through, they are full of cracks, they lack sanitary services, they are terrible places to live." Yes, it's true, we responded. However, once restored, put back in order with all that one expects in a modern house, one could live in them beautifully. Naturally, no one believed us. For most of the people, the historic core remained only piazza Maggiore, the two towers, the monuments—and not even all of these.

In 1970, we put on an exhibition with large photographs showing well-known monuments and minor buildings, famous places and others so little known that one had to turn to the exhibition notes to find out what and where they were. Together with these photographs we displayed the entire master plan that had been adopted the year before. However, the photographs were the dominant part of the show. To put on a show of the historic center in the middle of the historic center is a bit like an exhibition of mirrors in which the audience ends up looking at itself, but perhaps begins to notice details which until that time had escaped attention. The impact was immediate. Leaving the show, people began to look at the historic center as if for the first time. In those same houses and in those same streets that they had considered a disgrace a short time before, they began to discover positive elements: the colors, the scale, details that brought back memories of when they had lived in a certain house, or of a friend who had lived in another. These recollections of the past helped everyone to understand the abstract definition we had given of the historic center as the collective memory.

These houses and these streets were ugly, uninhabitable . . . but how many memories they raised, how much emotion—and the feeling one has for one's own city is always very deep. Even those who live in a city in which they were not born have these feelings and are pleased to find that they live in a place others find valuable and worthy of being photographed and publicly exhibited. The show was tremendously suc-

cessful with the people of Bologna. Through the exhibition, Bologna became pleasing to them. The people had finally seen the city and begun to understand it.

We did not do these things in 1970 merely to avoid the accusation that we wished to transform the historic core into a museum, however popular (and in Italy the museums are anything but popular; they are generally considered cemeteries for art). Our ideas were accepted because a new consensus was created in Bologna. The people had begun to understand the city, to see the historic core as a whole, requiring precise methods and rigorous criteria for its restoration. Even those who knew nothing about historic architecture now said yes, the historic core must be seen as *a single monument,* without distinctions between famous buildings and less important ones. And so in this way, the little houses and the background buildings became just as important as Bologna's famous towers.

At this point the reader will be saying to himself: this is not participation, this is manipulation! Actually, it is education. We believe that the restoration of the city can only spring from a profound understanding of the structure to be preserved both on the part of the designers and the people who live in the historic area, the users themselves. For many years in Italy, the care of the cultural heritage, and in particular the historic city centers, has been seen as the protection of the historic, artistic, and natural patrimony menaced by barbarous society that has lost its feelings for beauty. The failure of this aristocratic concept of historical conservation was inevitable, because it is the demand of a narrow elite, only those who have the privilege of understanding and appreciating the value and the meaning of high culture. Important monuments, entire historic buildings, parks, and gardens were destroyed with almost no protest because the great majority of the Italian people believed that destruction was necessary, was the consequence of progress and economic development.

It was only in 1956 that an association was formed to care for, defend, and explain the importance of the patrimony. Since its beginning, Italia Nostra has been involved in very important battles, even if the results have frequently been modest. Despite the outcries, demolition and wholesale environmental destruction continued. The opponents of this organization—largely developers and real estate speculators—called it an association of countesses, and they were almost right. There *were* many countesses on the board of Italia Nostra, but not one worker. How could one expect Italia Nostra's cries of pain to interest the urban poor? Why should the working class be expected to defend the cultural heritage if, not understanding it, it cannot benefit from it?

A policy of urban conservation, then, begins with knowledge and understanding. To be effective, it must be based on widely accepted cultural values concerning the "why" and the "for whom" of conservation. Only when the values of the historic core have entered the popular consciousness can one plan its restoration and expect that the results will be well cared for.

The quality of a conservation program is therefore an index of common perceptions and popular knowledge, and the first step in any historic preservation program is to make sure that the people who live within the historic area understand it thoroughly. Why? Because everyone is able to think about the issues and contribute to their solution.

## Participation in Preservation

Let me take a step backward and explain that the modern city of Bologna is divided into 18 districts, 14 outside the old walls and four in the historic core.* In each city district there is a neighborhood council, made up of 20 people of different political backgrounds with an elected council president, which discusses all of the administrative affairs that affect the area. The members were originally chosen by the City Council, but as of 1980, they are directly elected by the local citizens. These neighborhood councils are involved in the schools, in retail services, in the organization of sports, in social welfare, in the making of the city budget, and also in all matters affecting urban development within their areas. All local people are encouraged to participate in the discussions of the council and to express their views.

The councils spend hour after hour discussing neighborhood redevelopment in order to come to agreement about

3. The historic core of Bologna, characterized by its well-known arcades, is still made up of vital working class communities.

Bruce Dale

4. The arcades shelter a rich social life. They are retained as a prominent feature in the new infill housing.

*The total population approaches 480,000, of whom about 70,000 live in the historic core.

5,6,7,8. The historic core of Bologna is not merely a collection of landmark buildings. It is also the ordinary structures that provide their context—and the pattern of daily life that they support and contain.

how the environment should be, what changes ought to take place within the community. Through these discussions, a majority opinion is formed and becomes the position of the neighborhood on projects and proposals. The decisions of the neighborhood councils are usually, but not always, respected by the city administration which, in any case, has always sought the neighborhoods' opinions on measures that come before the City Council.*

It is difficult for the City Council not to take into account the views of the neighborhoods for the simple reason that if these views are not respected, the city government would lose its credibility, participation would become an academic exercise, and the people would stop participating and withdraw their support.

Some have said that even this participation can be manipulated, in particular by the organized political parties—an order from the party and the neighborhood councillors who are members of the party are expected to rush to the meeting to carry out their orders. In Bologna we really believe in participation, however defective and imperfect it may be, and the problems of neighborhoods take priority over the needs of the party. Mistakes, and mistakes there have been, can always be traced to efforts to interfere, precisely to manipulate participation. Nothing could have worse consequences than fictitious participation, and the administration and party leaders in Bologna are quite aware of this.

Issues of urban planning have become little by little of general interest in Bologna, or better, of interest also to those who don't ordinarily think about such things. The mechanism of participation functions very well when we are dealing with the development of a new neighborhood, or when the issue is a road or a garden, a school or a sports field, but it even functions well when it comes to preservation—in the sense that the people have understood the meaning and the why of conservation. Today they would be the first to oppose the violation not only of a well-known monument, but even of a small piece of less important construction. Nevertheless, the plan for the historic core is still inadequate. It works well as far as pres-

*Such a procedure, called the Uniform Land Use Review Procedure, is now required in New York City. See Commentary by Bruce Dale.—EDITOR

ervation goes, keeping up the face of the historic city. But it is unable to respond satisfactorily to the other disquieting question: for whom is this preservation being done? We continue to say: for all the people of Bologna, for all the people of the world, because cultural wealth belongs to everyone. This is clear. But an historic core is not the Santa Cecilia of Raphael carefully hung in the national museum for everyone to share. It is not enough to be able to view an historic core the way one views a painting. It is essential to be able to make use of it. The historic core must not be a place for Sunday visits. It must be a place to live all the time.

## The Struggle against Speculators

There have been problems from the very beginning. In Italy at that time,

7

they were accustomed to buying a building site, constructing a building, and selling it quickly at a price four or five times the cost of production. So they opposed the plan for the historic core. Too many regulations, they said. They wanted to tear down and rebuild and now they were being asked to maintain, in addition to the facades, the same building volume, the same floor area. They were being required to use traditional building techniques and materials, and they could not change the typological characteristics of the dwellings. They argued that our conservation plan was "fetishistic" and impractical.

Then the Superintendent of Monuments got involved. (The Superintendent is a functionary of the State, and has the job of taking care of all of the designated monuments in Italy, and in Italy only those buildings which the

Superintendent has designated are monuments.) The Superintendent said we were trying to preserve too many buildings in our plan. An entire historic core! Unheard of. To preserve everything is to preserve nothing. "There are hierarchies which must be respected," said the Superintendent. There are monuments (Architecture), and there are buildings of no value. Ours was a plan, he said, that should be redone from the beginning.

Certain of our popular support, we did not back down, and gave authorization to build only to those projects that rigorously followed the standards called for by the plan.* Standards in the plan have the force of law, and reluctantly the Superintendent and those who wished to build in Bologna had to adapt to the will of the City.

The first preservation projects were an enormous success. The public was very pleased. Builders quickly realized that historic preservation could become a gold mine. The upper middle class, which after the Second World War had left the historic core to live in the surrounding hills or in new suburban areas, were ready to return to live in the City, and they didn't care about cost. To live on the periphery was to live in an environment that was being made uglier every day. These were the years in Italy in which the fad for antiques and old houses reached its height. The rich, both the new rich and the old rich, wished to be surrounded by things that indicated their distant family origin . . . and they wanted to live in an historic area. All of a sudden the historic core was under attack.

The speculative builders, who up until this time had been interested only in large open sites outside the core, suddenly saw a new El Dorado. They recalled what had happened in other European cities, starting with Haussmann's transformation of Paris and quickly were hot on the trail of every building that might be for sale. They had in mind a big killing: buy the houses, throw out the tenants, restore

---

*One of these standards was singled out by the opposition to demonstrate the supposed madness of our plan: We required the use of the Italian trowel (a steel tool that traditionally had been used for smoothing plaster walls in the place of the trowel *all'americana,* the same tool made in wood). Steel trowels were no longer available on the market and the plasterers were accustomed to using the wooden ones. But the correct finish is important to a valuable structure.

8

the buildings, and then sell them for extremely high prices. And those regulations and standards in the plan that were supposed to get in the way of development? Water over the dam. In fact, the more careful the restoration required by the plan, the more valuable a building became when it was completed. They went so far in some cases, supposedly pursuing restoration, that they introduced elements from other periods in the buildings they were redoing. To fifteenth century houses they added baroque iron gates taken from the demolition of Venetian villas, they installed precious marble in the place of the traditional tile floors, they added statues where statues had never been.

All of a sudden, and for the first time in Italy, the speculators were in favor of public housing construction. The miserably small quantity constructed up to that time would no longer be enough. The motive behind this sudden interest in housing the poor was anything but humanitarian. A greater number of public housing units meant that a larger number of families could be pushed out of the historic core. As there was a law in effect at that time that prohibited all private evictions, people were offered substantial sums to give up their apartments. But now it was the state that was to pay for emptying the historic core. The work of careful restoration could not be done with tenants in residence.

Real estate deals were soon being described as cultural intervention, as a defense of the historic and artistic heritage. In short, the speculators became the true defenders of the historic core. Official circles of high culture were silent. They were satisfied with the protection—an end in itself—of the architectural heritage of the City. But could it be a real defense? Can an organism as complex and interwoven as the center of the city be reserved for a single social class? And once it becomes the home of the well-to-do, how can it be considered the *bene culturale* (the common cultural heritage) of all the people?

The protest of the people who lived in this part of the city was immediate and vocal. In fact, the housing situation was so acute that a nationwide movement was able to force the government to develop new housing programs. The new housing law was revolutionary in that it gave city governments the right to expropriate land for development as public housing *at the price of agricultural land*. The new law accorded cities other useful powers as well, for example, the right to acquire completed buildings at the price of their construction, as long as they were to be reused for public purposes.

9

## Preservation as Public Purpose

Toward the end of 1971, we began to think about how to use the new law to avoid the expulsion of the working class from the historic core. Our reasoning was very simple. In addition to planning public housing developments on vacant land in the periphery, we would do the same thing in the historic core taking not land, but buildings. We were prepared to argue that housing is the most important public purpose.

In fact, the choice of buildings to expropriate had already been made back in 1969 when we drew up the master plan for the historic core. At that time we had identified the blocks of buildings that had homogeneous characteristics and that exhibited a high degree of refinement. In these blocks, the master plan called for piecemeal interventions, each to be carried out following the approval of a specific small-scale plan. The data from the national census of 1971 were used as the basis for a careful study of each family that lived in each apartment. It turned out that the buildings we had identified housed the poorest people in the city, and in the worst conditions. The expropriation of these houses seemed to us humanitarian, as well as urbanistically correct—finally a portion of the public budget would be used to eliminate social and physical degradation in the city. Furthermore, the neediest social groups would be permitted to continue to live in the historic core in renewed housing.

Having explained the "why" of preservation, now at last we were able to be precise about the "for whom." We made careful studies of the designs, checked out their practicality, estimated the costs—these turned out to be substantially less than the cost of new housing—and then we presented our proposal to the councillors and the people of the neighborhood. Their reaction was positive, but not enthusiastic. They were in agreement with any action which would block speculation, but in their hearts they doubted that these houses, as unsanitary and run-down as they were, could ever be restored and transformed into proper dwellings. Yes, they thought the houses should be preserved, but they themselves would prefer to live in a house more or less like the ones that were being built in the periphery.

The design drawings we showed didn't seem to offer sufficient guarantee

of final quality (and then who understood the drawings anyway?). Even the three-dimensional model we had made seemed little understood. In any case, they accepted our proposal, even though they didn't quite believe that the landlords would be expropriated. In sum, their response to us was a kind of "wait and see."

In the meantime, the reaction set in. It was anything but wait and see, and it brought together not only the owners that we had in mind, but landlords in general. With every passing day their response became angrier. Centering around a group called *Proprietá Edilizia* (this is the association in Italy that represents those who own rental housing), backed by Christian Democratic politicians, and supported by the local press, the opposition to our plan soon took on the aspect of a crusade.

It was rumored that the city government was beginning to invoke Marxism: after the houses everything would be expropriated—jewelry, paintings, even clothing and furniture. The city government, under the control of a Socialist-Communist coalition since the end of the War, was, they said, at last showing its true face, its Bolshevik heart. During the Fascist period, of course, many buildings were taken in order to carry out street widenings and other urban planning programs. Then the expropriations were done to favor the big urban developers. This time we proposed to answer the need for low-cost housing. And above all, it was this that they were contesting. It was always assumed—and not only in Italy—that working class housing belonged on the periphery of the city, not at its center.

The opposition was clearly also a form of public participation. A rigged sort of participation, obviously, but one that developed a wide consensus. Even members of the Socialist and Communist parties who were owners of the buildings in which they lived became extremely nervous. We had to repeat over and over again that no, we did not wish to expropriate the entire city, but only the specific areas shown in the plan—the very poorest blocks.

However, suspicion is an insidious worm. In fact, in not listening carefully to the protest, we had broken faith with our own ideal of participation: to be a city in which the involvement of the citizens, all the citizens, is determinant. Bologna was the first city in Italy to organize a new type of participation

10

through which local communities could select and implement their own programs. Now we were being accused of not wanting to hear the protest, of invoking participation only when it was convenient, of being indifferent to negative reactions to our plan.

We moved away from the notion of expropriation and made a new proposal: contractual agreements. The contracts we proposed would be between the city and the property owners. Each property owner who agreed to restore a building would also have to agree to re-rent it to its original tenants. In exchange, the city would provide technical assistance and, if needed, financial aid.

With the idea of the contract, we found a balance between opposed interests, we avoided a perhaps irreparable political rupture, and at the same time we did not compromise our objectives. The concept of historical preservation without the removal of any social classes had been preserved, and we had laid the groundwork for beginning the "integrated conservation" that two years later, in 1974 and in Bologna, the Council of Europe was to adopt as the only valid criterion for renewal in historic urban areas.

9,10,11. Deteriorated conditions in the historic core prior to the beginning of the preservation program.

11

## Participation in Design

There was public participation in design from the outset, and in a major way after the completion of the first projects. But let's proceed in order. It has been said that the preservation of an historic area involves analysis and careful cataloging of all its elements. An old city is an organism developed according to definite political logic, reflecting various stages of urban praxis and ways of building, each generating specific residential forms. All of these components must be identified and understood in order to organize the technical and design means that will lead to the proper treatment of the architectural heritage. But not only knowledge is needed: a political program for implementation is also necessary.

A plan for Bologna's historic core, because of its social and economic implications, must not be abstract, subjective, or backward looking. Instead it must facilitate the present and future use of the historic area, in the conviction that there is no proper preservation without respect for human needs. Hence, the conservation of an historic core requires the planning of the entire city of which the historic core is an integral part. If the historic core becomes isolated from its environmental and spatial context, there is a serious risk that the plan will become merely architectural.

The face of the traditional city is in large part an index to its social structure. The city is a complex mixture of human existences tied to places and specific activities that can be carried on only in this space and only with that person. The character of an historic center cannot be saved without seeing to it that the popular use of the center will continue into the present. If this cannot be ensured, the preservation program will be sharply limited and risks total failure. For these reasons, in Bologna we have fought for integrated conservation in which the human element has a value greater than that of the buildings. We never stopped saying that unless the original social order remains intact, there is no historical preservation.

We have already introduced an equation that explains our goals in relation to the cultural meaning of the historic core:

To understand = to preserve
To preserve = to determine future use
To determine future use = to take control
In sum: to understand is to take control

Understanding, then, is the necessary and indispensable condition for returning the historic city to the control of the people.

Professionals must play their own special role, a role that cannot be turned over to anyone else. It is their job to determine the exact methodology of preservation. To do this, they must develop a deep knowledge of the existing environment. They must examine every structure and every space, draw it up, classify it in precise typological cat-egories, and catalog it in order to establish the design process that precedes implementation. It is a process that runs backwards: it starts from existing buildings and groups of buildings in order to arrive at a knowledge of the models, the proportional canons, and the rules of composition that controlled their design in the distant past. This knowledge of historical design and the construction methods is sought in documents—old maps, tax records, and deeds—from the study and careful drawing of the buildings themselves, and from a direct analysis of the characteristics of traditional materials and building systems. When this is done, one can proceed to define the specific design program for each restoration. (The architects are always able to find ways to insert new components to satisfy contemporary needs: for example, sanitary services and mechanical systems and ways to lay out new dwellings while respecting the characteristics of the old buildings.) In the end one has the architectural documents required for preservation—and a preservation which is rigorous and scientific.

At the same time, architects must not behave as those who know everything, who transmit special knowledge, special culture. This is especially true in historical preservation projects where many of the groups involved in implementation—masons are an example—have an historical competence greater than that of the architect, or where the users know with great clarity what is required in a satisfactory dwelling. Preservation ought to give rise to a reciprocal com-

12. Old records were searched to determine the original form and use of each building in the core.

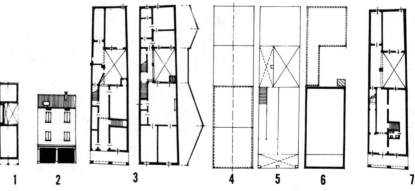

13. Prior to restoration, buildings were subjected to typological analysis. The drawings show a typical example: 1: Diagrammatic plan 2: Elevation 3: Plan at grade, typical floor, and roof form 4: Diagrammatic site plan 5: Site-organizing elements (arcade, stair hall, courtyard) 6: Initial structure and later additions 7: Rehabilitation drawings

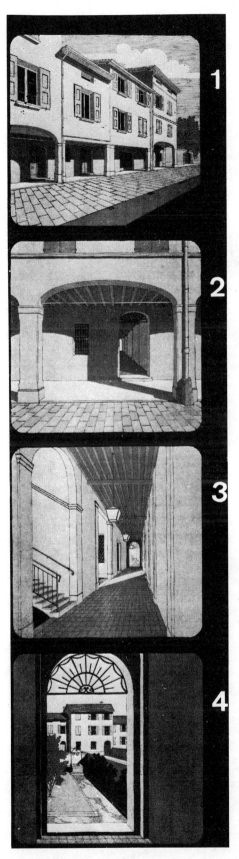

14. Drawings show spatial sequence from street to garden court. The traditional Bologna house emphasizes collective space.

munication of knowledge—an indispensable condition if we are to avoid manipulation and oppression, trickery and mystification.

Operations of integrated preservation such as Bologna's provide opportunities for authentic participation, both in the determination of the program, as we have been noting, and in the implementation itself, because it impacts directly the residents of the places to be restored. It is true that in Bologna neither our drawings nor our three-dimensional models were well understood, nor should we have expected them to be. Their presentation didn't generate much discussion. No one came forward to say that the size of this or that dwelling was inadequate; no one asked for specific explanations. Everyone was waiting to see the real things, the finished construction. In the first place, restoration projects, no matter how broad the overall program, are usually limited to a few buildings at the outset—and these are the buildings in which no one lives—the buildings on the verge of collapse, in which the architectural effort assumes the characteristics of an experiment both for the designers and the local citizens.

## A Debate over Style

Construction was started on sites where there were only shells, or in fact where nothing remained because the ruins had been cleared away. For areas such as this, the plan called for a form of conservation redevelopment, that is, the reconstruction of buildings with typological characteristics much like those which had occupied the site. The new buildings were not to be identical in the sense that they were designed in an historical style, but they were to reflect the architectural and structural order of the surrounding buildings.

Why did we call for conservation redevelopment? There are technical, cultural, and social motives involved. Now, if in a building there is a wall, a column, or other element which is no longer structurally sound and cannot be restored, it must be replaced. It is the same when one deals with a registered monument: if in a cloister a wall should collapse, it is rebuilt. In our case, dealing with urban restoration, we consider the single building to be much like the architectural element. Therefore we can replace the element (in this case a new building) where one has been lost or

found to be physically unsound.

There were only 13 such cases within the blocks we had chosen to start with, while there were hundreds of buildings ready to be restored. Our policy of conservative redevelopment irritated those architects in Italy who live and design in order to polemicize with the past, and those critics who believe that all new construction in historic areas should contrast with that which exists, creating a certain "dissonance." Diatribes of architects and incompetents, arguments without any cultural significance made only to exhibit the antipathy that many still feel toward integrated conservation! These objections might have carried greater weight if our choice had not been made for social as well as cultural reasons. In fact, this form of reconstruction was a response to a specific request from the community.

The mechanics of our preservation program called for the first houses to be rebuilt, and then for the tenants who lived in the second phase of the work to be moved into them. More houses would then be vacant and ready for reconstruction. In turn, when completed, they would house tenants from yet other buildings in need of work, and so forth. This was our way of ensuring that the tenants would not be pushed out of their own neighborhoods. Had these first buildings been "dissonant" modern structures in the historical context, they would have constituted a form of discrimination between the tenants of the modern dwellings and those who would continue to live in the old houses, however much restored. We would have created two sets of weights and measures, as they say, and would have generated potential conflict by rehousing families in very different conditions. Our policy of typological conformity put everyone on the same plane, and the neighborhood demand finds a precise reply in the concept of the historic core as a unitary monument.

These new-old buildings became the neighborhood's point of reference, a full-scale model everyone could understand better than the formulas in the plan, and therefore that everyone could criticize and use to make suggestions for improvements. If the architectural drawings had left the local people indifferent, the completed houses encouraged them to express their opinions and permitted them to evaluate with facts

15

16

17

15,16,17,18. Views of typical buildings undergoing restoration . . . and a satisfied resident.

248

the historic preservation program proposed by the City administration. It is of little importance that these first buildings don't please modernist or "postmodernist" architects, that they caused the noses of insensitive and arrogant critics to wrinkle up.

For those who moved first, the contrast between the house they got and the house they moved out of was extremely positive. It could not have been otherwise. These families were finally able to live in houses with bathrooms, with heat and hot water. An old lady remembered sleeping only once before in her life with a bathroom near her bedroom—and that was during her honeymoon voyage, in a hotel. After that she had lived in a three-story building with one toilet on the ground floor for the tenants in 12 apartments.* For the first time, she was able to live

in a proper house, without having to move out of her neighborhood where over the years she had built up a series of relationships and personal contacts.

The urban scene in the old core is familiar and understood; it speaks a comprehensible architectural language with a comprehensible message. When people are forced to move to the new quarters in the periphery, for them it is as if they had gone to another world, one where it is difficult to reconstitute a social network. For the great majority of the people, the new city on the periphery presents an image that is not easily accepted. At the same time, because of deterioration and speculation, many people feel they have only the most precarious hold on the historic city. Things were not always this way.

The traditional city was not only the expression of the collectivity, it was also the common property of its residents, and as such it was held to be a *bene pubblico.* The presence of different social classes integrated into the same urban fabric and at times into the same building was testimony, perhaps proof, of the undifferentiated and collective character of the city. The historic core was then the entire city. It was not divided between its center and a periphery as is the contemporary city. The location of churches and other buildings

representing power (which was anyway collective and public in the deepest meaning of the term) avoided hierarchical subdivisions.

The extension of the modern city and the complexity of its communications and its differentiated land uses has greatly increased the significance and desirability of the central core. Subdividing the urban land and merchandising the building sites result in the privatization of this *bene,* this city previously collective and undivided. Exactly in this moment of accelerated urban growth, of convulsive expansion, the city becomes center and periphery—to be bought and sold by speculators.* The original inhabitants and their traditional activities are pushed out and replaced. Building public housing in the historic core was our way of restoring certainty to the poorest residents that they would be able to live in the center. Perhaps this explains why the social goals of integrated preservation took precedence over architectural concerns.

## The Issue of Architectural Typologies

But design problems were not eliminated. The type of housing to be built remained an open question, and only with the first completed projects was it possible to evaluate in the real just what we had meant when we had talked of holding onto the historical typologies. Let us consider architectural typologies as the result of a number of functions required by human activities, that is, as an expression of a very particular way of life that becomes concretized in buildings, where, for example, the dwelling and the act of dwelling become analogs of one another, ultimately defining a typology. Each architectural typology, as a result of the close reciprocal relationship between physical organization and social meaning, generates in each period a specific structural

*It may seem strange that in a city as well off as Bologna, where per capita incomes are reasonably high, that there are still areas so deteriorated as to remind one of the poor cities in the south, but one should not forget that the dwelling conditions in the centers of cities like Milan and Turin are often worse. It has been calculated that in Italy there are eight million rooms in run-down condition. This is certainly the result of the particular form of capitalist development in this country, of a perverse housing policy, of the excessive power of the speculators, who created an enormous production of new houses, but only for the middle and upper middle classes. The clusters of poverty inside the historic centers have been, and continue to be, functional for this kind of uneven development. These are the areas held in reserve, which on the one hand demonstrate the importance of constant expansion of production of new housing, and on the other provide an active field for investment as speculators buy these run-down houses at low prices, later to reap great profits from the central location. Responsibility lies in any case not only with speculators or local municipalities. Even intellectuals and professionals have—in bad faith—encouraged this process with their design projects aimed at demonstrating the appropriateness of building solutions that can be "neatly inserted" in the historic urban fabric. Many Italian architects consider themselves veritable *virtuosi* in the art of cutting the heart out of a city. They see these run-down areas as providing the great test for new designs in glass and concrete (but mostly glass), such that the monuments which remain can be reflected in their new architectonic inventions. And it is, of course, just these professionals who most sharply question our conservative restoration. They called our first houses scandalous and false, saying that they were an embarrassment to modern art and architecture. Social issues seem not to have importance. Anyway, they say, all new houses, and even low income housing on the periphery, have baths, heat, and hot water. But the people who live in the center were not influenced by these banal arguments. They understood that something completely new was taking place.

*A preservation program such as ours will only succeed if the expansion of the city can be controlled. In Italy, particularly, urban growth must be reduced to zero. If the city is permitted to grow, the cycle of redevelopment and relocation will continue. Offices will continue to take over the city center, taking away yet more of this common cultural heritage from its traditional users. It is not by chance that one of the basic decisions made by the neighborhood councils during the debate on the master plan for the city was to limit further expansion. If the program of conservative preservation has been able to move ahead, it is due to this wise choice.

19a

19b

19c

19. In Bologna, conservation was felt to require adherence to traditional materials and techniques as well as building form. Medieval and Renaissance builders' manuals provided guidance.

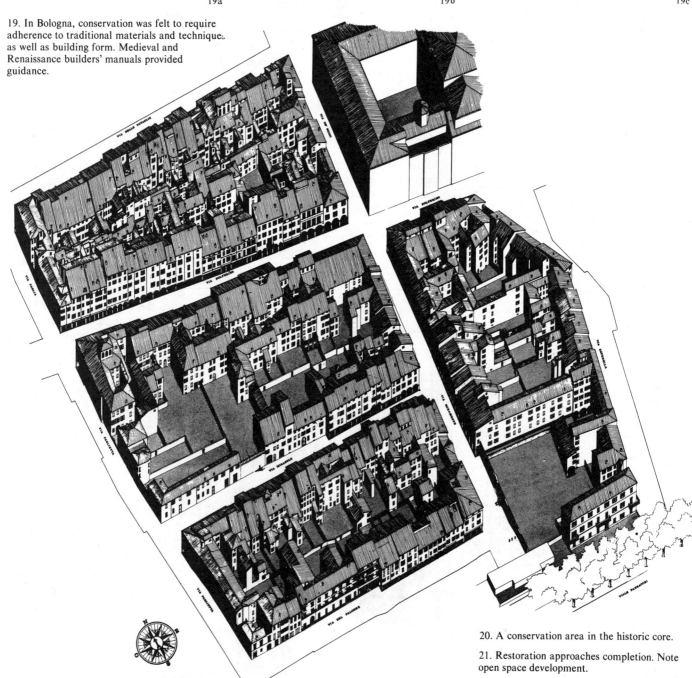

assonometria 1:200

20. A conservation area in the historic core.

21. Restoration approaches completion. Note open space development.

20

system and spatial form which we then identify as a building type: a church, a convent, a dwelling, a hospital. Now, the use of an historical dwelling typology for contemporary ends, with, of course, the introduction of modern services, is the methodological approach to conservative restoration. It has a certain scientific logic, but it is also a way of providing new housing that is not the conventional and standardized modern product. Above all, it is a way of affirming the right of every social class to live in a setting of cultural value, to live in the historic city. And it reaffirms once and for all the people's power to reconquer the city that a powerful few wanted to take away from them. In the existing buildings, the perpetuation of the historic typology enables us to join modern functions and the old building. These functions are essentially unchanged, they are the functions of dwelling. To rebuild the structures that grow out of a "natural consciousness," that is, out of a collective system of meanings and functional separations (the historical typologies), is clearly a technical-scientific task, but it also, and

to a high degree, involves an understanding of society. An expression of a material culture of a people, a residential typology is a demonstration of their will to live their lives outside the control of the dominant power. An historical building typology belongs to the people: it is their history.

This is not mere rhetoric. Think for a moment of the not-so-conservative restorations carried out in many European cities in the recent past. The architects' attention has been focused largely on the exterior, on the building facades. On the interior, the replacement of the families that traditionally lived in these buildings with others from higher income groups corresponds precisely with the replacement of the historical structure and spatial forms with an architecture identical to that found in brand-new buildings. This way a double expropriation is achieved, both social and cultural. The working class is driven out, and its culture is destroyed. The result is disastrous. This is not the beautification of the city, but its sterilization.

The concept of typology was nothing

more than an abstract architects' and engineers' notion to local residents until it was translated into clear, dimensioned drawings. Then we were asked, "Why this bedroom? Why these dimensions? Why this stair?" The answers no longer needed to be technical and abstract. At the outset, we measured and drew up the furniture that each household possessed. We cut the little paper shapes, and together with the future residents we placed them on the plans we had drawn to make sure they had sufficient flexibility. This, too, is a form of participation. But there is more. The relationship between the dwelling and the exterior spaces, the replanting of the gardens behind each house, connecting these gardens with the main entry by a large corridor—all these things became the subject of much discussion and common reflection on their use.

We had decided to make use of the traditional Bolognese arcade in our project. The immediate understanding that these could be more than covered walkways, that they could be a collective extension of the private dwellings, a once-common way of using space now

21

251

fallen into disuse in Bologna, was the ultimate demonstration that the return to the historical typology would have profound social and human consequences.

The proof that our program of integrated preservation in Bologna was successful came when we were called upon by the neighborhood councils to speed up the pace of reconstruction. Everyone who lived in an old house wanted now to live in a restored house, and they wanted it restored as we had been doing it. Beyond any intellectual propositions, they found these dwellings pleasing. And they found them pleasing just as they had been restored, even with the stairs that critics said were too steep, and even though the fact that we had made the attics habitable perplexed them. They may have continued to be ignorant of the significance of the historical typology, but they were happy to live in a dwelling that responded to their traditional way of life.

There was criticism of the colors chosen for the facades—many were not accustomed to the strong colors found in original stucco work. Many suggestions were put forward with the intention of improving some aspects of the apartments, above all the quality of finishes, and these comments improved the entire program. It is important to emphasize the interest shown in the work of restoration. In some cases, people went to the job sites to beg the masons to finish quickly. In others, groups of future residents made regular visits to check on the quality of the work. This is not

something that is known to happen in the popular zones of the periphery!

## Toward a New Urban Community

In the final analysis, a program of integrated preservation is always carried out in a terribly complex context where social needs, economic demands, and profound cultural questions are interwoven. Our experience convinces us that the economic, cultural, and social mix that created the historic city core must continue, in the future as in the past, as the only guarantee of the continued viability of the environment. This point of view gives rise to a corollary: the built results of a restoration project must not create inequalities. As in the past, every family must come to live in equally dignified and comfortable dwellings, and the historic core must not be permitted to develop hierarchical subdivisions. If the people of the city are not constantly aware of the threat, there's a risk that the kind of mechanical separation between inhabitants that is characteristic of the so-called modern city will come to mark the old centers as well.

No, it is not with architecture or urban planning that social problems are resolved (as Marx and Engels have explained so well), but it is with an understanding of social issues that one should approach the process of designing the modern city, both as a cultural and as an economic entity. Here, then, is the great and revolutionary discovery: a historic city core becomes, with the in-

volvement and impact of its residents who will be sure that it retains its traditional nature, the only modern part of the metropolitan area.

With respect to the destruction of much of the urban environment, to the social segregation of the new and unplanned residential districts, to the squalor of the outlying areas, the historic core, even with its internal contradictions, is becoming the truly modern, authentically livable part of the city. We are not interested, then, in studying and preserving the historic core merely because it is beautiful or because it is old, but because it represents the design model that we can use ultimately to transform the remainder of the city. The historic core has become the point of reference in changing the way we do urban planning and the way we understand the role of architecture.

Through the involvement of the citizenry, through public participation, it is possible to set in motion the revolutionary project—not revolutionary in the technical or methodological sense, but in the sense of a challenge to all those forces that would destroy urban civilization. Above all, a challenge to speculation, that most powerful enemy of the city and of urban culture. And urban culture, through participation, becomes comprehension and consciousness for an ever-larger number of people interested,

22,23. Nature in the city: careful attention is lavished on collective space.

24. An interior view of integrated conservation.

22

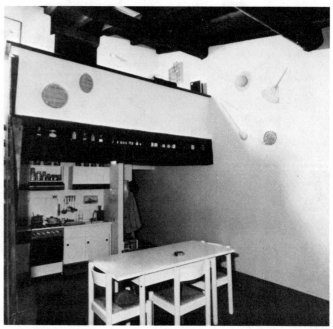

23

strongly interested, in the future of their city. They wish to become once again the controlling force in the environment in which they live and work, and they will fight against indiscriminate and chaotic development and the power of technocrats, administrators, and traditional bosses.

The people understand that only through the reconquest of the space of the city can they transform quantity into quality, the quantity of urban activity into the quality of life. People are not interested in abstract, utopian plans. They are looking for a reality that will help them to change their condition from those who are acted upon to those who act—from being the objects of history to being its subjects. This requires active participation. This does not eliminate the need for plans or for designers, but at the same time (and the story of our work in Bologna dramatically demonstrates this) no architect or planner can consider himself to be the interpreter of the popular will. To the architect who says, "I understand what the people want and now I will draw it up," we say no, participation is not merely the choice between forms or apartment layouts.

Real participation involves research on everyone's part, including architects and planners about the nature of the city in which we wish to live. It is the search for the form of city that will lead to a rebirth of community. The presence and the participation of the people in this search goes way beyond architectural considerations. It is a political struggle and it comes face to face with urban reality: a reality that consists of the city which is already built, the city that is growing around us, and the city that is still to be created.

The experience in the historic core of Bologna demonstrates the feasibility and the success of this struggle. A tiring effort, frequently difficult, even more frequently ill-understood, that somehow moves ahead, that day-by-day, house-by-house, marks the steps of this reappropriation of the city by its people. It happens because the people of Bologna play a leading role in the battle for the city. Participation, then, is to be understood as the daily struggle to defend the city, to retake and reuse together the places in which the community can aspire to greater dignity and self-awareness.

25. "Large containers"—major buildings such as *Il Baracano*—are converted to public use.

26. The courtyard of a "large container." These structures commonly house branch libraries, clinics, nurseries, and the meetingplace of the local Neighborhood Council.

254

# Commentary on Bologna

Bruce Dale, architect, Department of Housing
Preservation and Development, City of New York

For some time in the early 1970s, I worked as an architect in the Bologna regional planning office. From this vantage point I observed with admiration the workings of the Bologna Neighborhood Councils and municipal agencies. Later, when I returned home and began to present the now-famous plan for Bologna's historic Center to American architects and planners, I quickly became aware that something in the material was overwhelming my audiences. It had been my intention, in presenting this example of both ideologically clear and successful planning by the Communist municipal government of Bologna, to demonstrate that it was possible to combine economically feasible urban redevelopment with the highest level of social concern. Yet somehow the lectures, even when addressed to sympathetic audiences, did not generate the enthusiasm I hoped for. Listeners were overwhelmed. Being confronted with the reality of a city where apparently anything was possible depressed American planners and students: "It can only happen there because they have a Communist government . . . it can't happen here . . . it's inconsistent with capitalist society . . . it's unrealistic to expect so much. . . ." Only after reading Pier Luigi Cervellati's article did I realize that I had been leaving out an important part of the Bologna story—one which would have helped in translating that experience into the American context.

I have often pointed out that Bologna is only one of Italy's many cities. The country as a whole remains predominantly capitalist. But I had neglected to underline the long struggle Bologna's planners had carried on and the strategic victories they had won before they earned the right to implement their program. In leaving out that part of the story I had made it difficult for my audiences to grasp the process used in Bologna and prevented them from understanding that we could adopt similar strategies. For architects and planners who are committed to social values and who believe it is correct for government to lead the way, there is a good deal to learn from the Bologna experience.

There are three essential themes that emerge from Cervellati's discussion and that parallel planning concerns in the United States: decentralization, participation, and advocacy. All three of these concepts have represented a significant part of planning ideology in the United States since the 1960s, yet none has fulfilled its promise. Although positive in their influence, they still remain insufficiently developed.

Decentralized government (and subsequent community control) was a major battle cry in the 1960s' struggle to reduce the impact of racism on both public education and neighborhood development. One measure of the success of these movements in New York City was the development of councils not dissimilar to those set up in Bologna in 1964. These councils, called Community Planning Boards, are comprised of residents who advise municipal government on local issues. The recently revised New York City Charter has strengthened the Boards by giving them a statutory role in a new Uniform Land Use Review Procedure. This new participant role assures each community that no land use change will be approved by the City Planning Commission without first consulting with the local community board. Here we have a good beginning, but when we remember that recent reform laws in Italy require regular public elections for neighborhood councils in *all* cities we recognize how far we still have to go.

Participation has also become an important concern of planners and architects in the United States, as evidenced by the array of techniques concerned with information-gathering and user participation in design employed, for example, in Boston's Southwest Corridor Project. Such experiments make it possible for people to play a useful role in determining how their environments should look and function. They must be made the rule, not the exception.

In the United States, the advocacy movement attempted to offer technical expertise to low income communities. This form of practice failed, however, due to the withdrawal of financial support by local power structures and the lack of stability in poor communities required to sustain a form of participation which did not have the power to confront the basic issues of survival. [On this subject, see Chester Hartman's Commentary below on the Pratt Center.—EDITOR]

The Bologna experience suggests some ways to make these strategies more effective. Cervellati has attributed the success of the Bologna plan to the assertive advocate role played by the City's own planners. By taking the initiative and working with the Neighborhood Councils, they were able to develop public awareness and consciousness of the planning process and its goals. By organizing public exhibitions and participating in long hours of public debate, the planners were able to overcome local lethargy. Once the plan was developed, understood, and accepted on a neighborhood level, it was relatively easy to organize a political constituency capable of withstanding subsequent counterattacks from conservative political forces.

One of the most politically impressive aspects of the strategy of participation was the City officials' commitment to be responsive to the Neighborhood Councils. But Bologna's belief in decentralized government is reflected not only in the inclusion of the Councils in the planning process, but also in giving them substantial administrative roles. For example, the negotiation of individual contracts between the City and the property owners are handled by the Councils as are the administration of rents, the determination of priorities for renovated apartments, and management of many social and cultural services.

If it is true that local participation is necessary to give force to progressive programs, and if it is also true that decentralization of control is a desirable goal, then it is clear that community-based organizations wherever they are need capable advocates *within government.* To survive the ups and downs of public policy making, community-based planning organizations must receive a continuous flow of information and technical assistance. Without it, it is difficult to maintain an organized political constituency capable of influencing the decision-making process. With it, the superior effectiveness of neighborhood-based programs will lead to growing credibility in the community, which in turn leads to greater political influence. When the community-based organizations perform well, the agency-based advocate will be able to point to their success in his or her defense, and perhaps mobilize them when under attack. But, even with such defenses the progressive planner runs the constant risk of being removed from government.

I am tempted to say that the Bologna plan is both successful and overwhelming to American professionals and students of urban planning and restoration planning for the same reason. That reason stems from the fact that the City's employees had become political organizers working to achieve an ideological goal: the returning of a *bene pubblico,* the built environment of the city itself, to the low income residents of the historic district, rather than to real estate interests for speculation or gentrification. Bologna's planners faced sharp attacks and questions on many aspects of their plan, importantly its high cost. Their response was consistently assertive; they actively defined and defended their own decision to include *social costs* in the benefit analysis of their proposals. In an age of growing shortages, local government cannot remain neutral.

Bologna has set an example of good government for much of the Western world. It has done this largely because of its socialist ideology. The realization of its social goals, interestingly, depended less on the role of the Communist Party, which withdrew its support at several crucial points in the program, than on the personal commitment of professionals who were willing to get their hands dirty to implement their ideas. Their choice was to become first-person participants in their own society, rather than hired technicians attempting to maintain a facade of objectivity.

Cervellati concludes his article by stating that participation must be understood as "the daily struggle to defend the city, to retake and reuse together the places in which the community can aspire to greater dignity and self-awareness." The process of reclamation that aims at preserving social as well as cultural values in the built environment he defines as *integrated conservation.* The historic preservation movement in the United States shares Cervellati's interest in the meaning of the built environment, but exhibits little concern for people, and as a result has not achieved the same levels of success and of community support in low income neighborhoods.

In our country, cultural value is generally attributed only to the architecture of educated elites. In Bologna, all of the historic district's buildings, not just the masterpieces, are seen as the historic fabric of the city; it is in the buildings where people lived and worked that history was made. If it is the whole that is worth saving as the container of history, then this important task is best accomplished by facilitating its continued use as a living environment.

In many other cities, the sacrifice of the historic urban fabric in order to spotlight a few "important" buildings has only led to the creation of sterile "museum districts" that serve a small fraction of society. The process of clearance, of course, drives out working class families who cannot afford to remain in these glossy, new areas. The result is what Cervellati has called double expropriation, first of place and then of culture. In a similar manner, many emigrant cultures in the United States were lost after being uprooted by urban renewal or major preservation projects in such places as Society Hill, Philadelphia, Old Town in Alexandria, Virginia, or the Vieux Carré in New Orleans.

Large-scale historic preservation has all too often created situations in which isolated buildings lose their contexts, their functions, and a large part of their historic value as well. Unfortunately, much of the preservation movement in the United States has lead to results of this sort. This is due in part to the limited financial resources available for restoration, but also to the limited concerns of elitist preservationists. With the recent increase in the number of entire districts given historic designation, the scale of the problem has increased geometrically. Designation, despite HUD's recently published denial, has been followed by displacement of low income residents who are unable to afford the higher rents demanded for the renovated dwellings. The result of preservation is almost always gentrification.

The profitability of restored buildings in American cities has been further reinforced by the passage of the 1976 Historic Preservation Tax Reform Act and the 1981 Tax Act. These tax incentive programs ensures a financial return for the preservation of single landmark buildings and hence adds impetus to speculation. However, instead of attacking government support for restoration in the United States, we would do better to learn from the Bologna experience and develop mechanisms which will also ensure the preservation of social values.

257

# SAAL/Curraleira Lisbon, Portugal

We remember the Portuguese Revolution of April, 1974: roses in rifle barrels, dancing in the public squares, the end of a long period of fascist rule first under Antonio Salazar and then Marcelo Caetano. In the vanguard, architects in large numbers came forward to play an active role in the reconstruction of Portugal's cities and society. Organized into "ambulatory support groups" under the direction of Nuno Portas, they set to work immediately in the squatter camps and central slums of Opporto and Lisbon. Their results frequently were of high architectural quality (see, for example, the reports of Alvaro Siza in *Lotus 13* and Alves Costa in *Lotus 18*). They always created active communities, better housing, educational facilities, and social services. It should be noted that the SAAL teams were made up of many disciplines—all those necessary to help a neighborhood help itself.

As Portas tells us, the basic SAAL principle was "the prior organization of demand": the SAAL groups' first task was to enable the residents to articulate their needs, to take the leadership in finding solutions, and to apply the political pressure necessary to implement their programs. This organization of political demand eventually came into conflict with the needs of the ruling coalition. Under pressure from the ever-present right, the dominant Socialist Party dismantled SAAL step–by–step. But not before it had had a chance to prove the validity of its approach to planning and design and to build significant projects.

In the following articles, Nuno Portas describes the objectives and organization of SAAL and one *Brigada* (work team) tells the story of the redevelopment of the Lisbon district known as Curraleira. Stressing the collective nature of their work, the report on Curraleira is signed by the team as a whole, and not by its individual members. In his Commentary, Manuel Castells, who was in Portugal at the height of SAAL and who now teaches planning at Berkeley, argues persuasively that the SAAL experience has significance for us. We are in an historical period of structural scarcity, he writes, and "in this sense we will all be Portuguese for many years. The example of Portugal should stimulate our thinking."

1. New housing—by and for the residents—rises out of the rubble of the Curraleira squatter settlement in Lisbon.

1

# SAAL and the Urban Revolution in Portugal

**Nuno Portas, architect,**
**formerly Secretary of State for**
**Housing and Urban Planning, Lisbon**

The Ambulatory Support to Local Residents Program, known in Portugal as SAAL, was launched a few months after the beginning of the Revolution of April, 1974, and aimed at introducing a new process in housing policy—new relationships between the different agents acting in the production, distribution, and use of dwellings—and, through the change of process itself, at altering the final product in both form and management systems.

The traditional concept of housing separates the builder entirely from the user, therefore separating the latter—residents—from both the design team and the work of construction, ordered by the government and completed before the tenants enter the premises. Very seldom have the dwellers had a voice in the choice of site, organization of the community, or building types, and dwellers have had even less say in the allocation of investment, in the choice of construction company, and in the assignment of dwellings. In traditional housing, everything is done by the time the tenant arrives. Under the SAAL program, he arrives *before* any decision has been taken. In other words, the new program starts with the *prior organization of demand,* that is, with a group of dwellers, and nearly always on a basis of an existing "social ecology," since the program was directed mainly towards already structured communities "living" in slums or shantytowns. The same principles are being followed for the cooperative associations of future residents who are not necessarily already living in zones of planned clearance and reconstruction.

The direct participation of future dwellers in the elaboration of the dwelling designs is only one of the expected consequences, and is not the main purpose of the program. The original objectives of the SAAL program were:

1. To transfer the leadership of administrative and technical processes to the users (organized demand),

thereby creating new relations of force within the project administration. This requires that a sufficient legal margin for local decisions be given to the users. Only within this area of autonomy can one talk of participation. Elsewhere, participation is no more than a demand for political change.
2. To link each housing program to the problems of specific urban situations, so that the technical solutions of the planners must take into account the rehabilitation of the building stock, full use of the existing infrastructures, environmental conditions, and, last but not least, the stability of a specific, structured community of users.
3. To create conditions for the mobilization of local community resources—not only initiative and management resources, but also materials and labor (unemployed and subemployed, volunteer work, etc.)—in a long-range process, enabling us to create more adequate forms of housing construction.

As an offshoot of the principle of resident participation, we posit a change in the conventional one-way process of town design, from top to bottom, from general to particular, and tending towards "grand design," excluding all local involvement. In the SAAL program, a flow of information in the opposite direction was established, supported at the grass roots level, and starting from an analysis of local resources and forms. A more-or-less dialectic synthesis of the two courses of action depends on the political views and quality of the municipal leaders and planners—their capacity to adapt to more interactive dynamics between large-scale plans and the local proposals arising out of dialogue with inhabitants of the areas. One must not forget that a new view of urban economy underlies this interactive methodology: a principle of austerity emphasizing small-scale,

incremental benefits as opposed to the capital-intensive, new infrastructures characteristic of urban plans of the 1960s.

## Financing the SAAL Program

These principles take form in a public finance scheme that should be more beneficial to the residents because less capital is needed per dwelling built or improved. The SAAL program stimulates not only the incorporation of the residents' own resources, but also the savings arising from the direct management of the works or from contracts with local companies given out by the residents' associations. The reduction of costs that comes from choosing nonprofit construction companies such as local cooperatives has been remarkable and much greater than the benefits normally associated with standardization and prefabrication. The SAAL approach also aimed at changing rigid codes and national project criteria, leading to the incorporation of existing structures (road networks, old buildings, etc.) and to the design of "evolutionary" structures to defer part of the necessary investment.

The goals of the new housing policy were not focused on global, quantitative targets, nor did they anticipate either dependence on the conventional, private entrepreneur system (in Portugal, limited to a few powerful enterprises, more in the habit of controlling than being controlled by the state), or the creation of a massive state agency for planning and construction—the typical solutions used, respectively, in the European Common Market and Eastern European countries. Instead, they would form a new system of diversified and complementary policies, in which the implementing agents would include:

1. The organized residents (cooperative channel).
2. State services and, later on, municipal services (direct public channel).
3. Private enterprise, through construc-

259

2. Process, content, *and* form: the high quality of SAAL housing production.

At left, from top to bottom, S. Victor (Opporto), architect, A. Siza Vieira; Antas (Opporto), architect, P. Ramalho; Leal (Opporto), architect, S. Fernandez.

At right, housing by SAAL *brigadas* in Lara and Maceda. SAAL flourished only briefly, but generated dozens of projects of high quality.

tion contracts, with preestablished sale prices (concession channel).

One concern was to make the results of the three channels compatible by establishing common design standards and defining a single rent system based on family income. The production targets to be attained through each of these channels were not fixed, since the main problem was not the lack of financial means, but the shortage of available land, adequate projects, and the threat of high unemployment (in both major construction firms deep in debt from speculative practices and smaller ones unable to compete). When we started, no national and regional development plan was available to establish priorities between the productive and social sectors. Similarly, no urban plans

reflecting the new social policies giving priority to low income strata had yet been devised.

In organizing a system of parallel and complementary policies rather than one favoring only a single formula from the start, an effort had to be made not only to avoid an unfortunate time loss in restructuring the entire construction sector, but also to make sure that the residents (and their representatives) would be able to assess the different quantitative and qualitative results of each channel. It turned out that *all* the alternatives had, at the start, handicaps or at least unforeseen areas of resistance.

The "concession channel," already tried in Italy, had the advantage of not requiring prior public acquisition of land and project design approvals, since

the enterprises already had both in hand. It did, however, depend on the willingness of the enterprises to comply with price limits and standards set by the government—that is, with their willingness to exchange high profits for the guarantees of credit and demand offered by the state and banks. At the same time, the new administration would have to agree to accept many urban sites and projects approved by the former regime, but not meeting the new criteria that stress minimizing transportation costs and preserving ecological balance.

The "direct public channel" depended on the efficiency of government technical and administrative agencies, exclusively central, which under the former regime had given no proof of leadership, of ability to control costs, or of interest in urban coordination. These agencies did not own significant amounts of land and had generally employed the familiar architectural typologies of great collective buildings—the sort that were profitable for the big enterprises, but are inappropriate to most urban environments. Their typical product was the *grand ensemble* on the 1960s French model, without connection to the urban grid and with housing blocks scattered in vague exterior spaces, thus entailing high maintenance costs. This logic would only be altered later by transferring the design functions to the municipalities and to the regions.

The "cooperative channel" had no tradition in Portugal, and at the outset suffered from the same lack of buildable land as the second channel of direct public development. It depended not on the good will of the government, but on the capacity for mobilization of the residents in question. It was expected that, once the period of initial organization was passed, the cooperatives themselves would become collective pressure groups working on public agencies to get the necessary land and financing. This did, in fact, happen. The dynamics of this third channel led to the first state expropriations of land— frequently in inner-city areas—and eventually to the passing of laws that created a faster land acquisition process.

It was assumed that the results of the cooperative channel would be seen in smaller-scale building operations, integrated in the urban grid and appropriate to smaller construction enterprises, and in projects specifically designed for each site, and therefore better adapted to their physical contexts and to the communities to which they were directed. It was also probable that the production cost would be lower. This, in fact, was the case. As expected, the program "SAAL–Cooperatives" allowed Portuguese architects to carry out innovative experiments in participation and design methods, as well as in the formal relations of the projects to specific human and urban contexts. We will now discuss some of the cooperative projects and briefly assess their results.

## The SAAL Teams

In calling on the residents to associate themselves in cooperatives to manage and control projects involving dwelling rehabilitation or new construction, the government created a technical assistance organization that supplied a specialist team for each association, i.e., for each area intervention. About 100 technical teams were formed, each including architects, engineers, social workers, and students of different backgrounds. The associations had the right to choose a compatible team on the basis of knowledge of its methods and experience.

The technical teams, generally headed by architects, were to provide:

1. Initial support in setting up the residents' cooperative associations and in delimiting the social and urban areas of the project, community organizing activities, generation of the building program through surveys and interviews and in general assemblies, and public discussion of the alternative courses of action for its implementation.
2. Assistance in preparing the proposal for acquiring the necessary land, assessing buildings suitable for rehabilitation, and in obtaining other resources.
3. Aid in the elaboration of the program from its development stages to architectural work on both the dwellings and community facilities.
4. Elaboration of the site plan for approval by local authorities, following the guidelines of the cooperative association.
5. Assistance in the bidding process and advice to the associations on either the selection of the general

3. SAAL favored the "cooperative channel" for housing production. In many cases, as at Curraleira, unemployed workers were helped to organize and run producer cooperatives.

contractor or the direct management of the project.
6. Supervision of construction and any eventual modifications.
7. Help to the association in calculating costs and in contacts with local agencies regarding public services.

The technical teams were compensated on the basis of time and not percentage fees, and were prepared to attend residents' meetings and official interviews, as well as to carry out normal professional work and construction supervision.

The entire system of local teams was subordinated to a simple structure of regional coordination (Oporto, Lisbon, and Algarve) specifically created for this purpose. The regional SAAL offices were in charge of choosing the technical staff, monitoring costs, giving suggestions respecting on-site experiences, proposing technical solutions, and supplying standard components using the best local designs.

This unusual extension of professional services to the community even in areas which exceed conventional project responsibilities—e.g., administrative and management support to social and cultural actions of the community—was

an important innovation, involving the designer in the political and institutional context. This involvement probably had at least indirect consequences for design solutions and for keeping the team in touch with the sequence of production operations and the use of the built structures. This provided important feedback, which under conventional contracts can never be obtained. But it also involved the risk of extra-professional "custody" of the communities along political and sometimes partisan lines. Such attempts at ideological control by teams did in fact occur and were used by critics of SAAL to denigrate the entire program.

Changes in the national government and in the municipalities during mid-1975* increased the confrontation between state institutions and the "teams and residents," including the regional

*The author ceased to have responsibility for the implementation of the program in March, 1975. At the end of that year, the coordination structure that had been created was formally dissolved and several teams stopped receiving pay. Most SAAL projects, however, continue.

The Constitution of 1976 decentralized planning and housing to the municipal level. In some places, this has meant a return to the imposition of familiar bureaucratic building types and the end of participatory design.—EDITOR

coordination structure. The conflict that occurred was not between the government and the residents, but within the state apparatus, between its conservative, legalist part and a progressive faction, somewhat less institutional, which "took the side" of the residents. This was no more than one reflex among others of the divisions that occur in a state during a period of transition.

In our opinion, the scheme proposed to the residents a form of cooperation with the state in which success was not guaranteed from the start. On the contrary, it necessitated continuous pressure from organized residents to defend their interests through democratic institutions—a sort of "cooperation-under-conflict" whose results necessarily depended on the evolution of the state as well as on the maturity of the social movements involved.

## Scope of Participation

The innovation of the SAAL program in the area of project methodology was to put face-to-face from the very start users and designers. This situation is not original in the liberal professions, but is not commonly used in public housing programs. In most projects, the designers have, at the best, a statistical knowledge of the socioeconomic characteristics of the future users, codified through a typology of households (in which only the nuclear household is taken into account), and a set of standards that "analyzes" the needs and aspirations of the users. Thus, until the end of the project, the design team does not have direct access to the users, who therefore have no possibility of expressing what makes them differ from the standard or of making known their wishes and views on the design proposals made by the team. Nor, finally, are the future residents encouraged to make any alterations during the construction stages, or even later during the years of use of the houses. Feedback on what concerns inhabitants is practically nonexistent. At present, projects that should express the ways of life of their inhabitants are in fact monotonously and invariably repeated, as if there were nothing to change or improve. We do see, however, changes in style or fashion from architect to architect and from year to year.

In conventional housing programs, criticism of the solutions is a matter for peers, through administrative hierarchies, or the response of the builders, or by selected professional magazines influential in spreading trends. In the last few years, this practice has created a sort of closed shop and has been justified as reaffirming the "autonomy of architecture." This attitude increasingly leads to an historicism that avoids all attempts to articulate architecture with its context. This tendency can be altered only if the following changes take place:

1. *Organization of the social demand* which a project is directed to satisfy *before* design is started, and the involvement of these project users not only in discussion, but also in the elaboration of the program and the essential production decisions (form of financing, type of construction, use control).
2. *An increase in citizens organizations' power* in decision making within the local political and administrative structure, including the control of the planning and development apparatus in matters of common sense by elected neighborhood representatives.

If this participation is not to become just another illusion, or a more sophisticated form of cooptation, it is necessary that there be real political influence or power of decision on the part of those who wish to participate. In the SAAL program, this capacity comes from delegating management to the residents' associations. This is perhaps its most original characteristic.

Desperate housing conditions have a negative effect on the possibilities of participation: "What we want is houses, the architect knows what is best. . . ." The architect explains his solutions as usual, trying to convince the client that his solutions are in fact the best: "If it is not done this way it will become more expensive; this way it will fit better in the environment." A mysterious verbal code and numerous half-arguments are frequently used. But drawings or, better, models, or better yet prototypes of the dwellings that prospective residents can visit have proved to be a useful stimulus to the architect–resident dialogue.

The new role that the residents take in the SAAL process, although it includes an active dialogue about design, is not always sufficient to give architectural results notably different from those of the conventional process. To go beyond the familiar but outmoded solutions, the designers must be predisposed to learn with unskilled "partners," and these new partners must have a true interest in participating in qualitative aspects of the environment and in establishing a patient discussion on what they want and how to express it.

The experience of dozens of projects that have reached the building stage has not yet been fully assessed, so it is dangerous to jump to definitive conclusions. The dialogue established was, in some cases, primarily of a political and ideological nature, opening little of the black box of environmental design concepts. However, many of the completed projects reveal positive results of dialogue with the residents in decisions about the functional organization of buildings—high or low rise, with or without private yards, with the kitchen opening up to the street or to the back, with or without an entrance-hall, and so forth. These are important aspects of housing typology, and ones that have direct connections with desired patterns of life or with the mental images that the residents have of houses they like.

In some cases—such as the one chosen for a more detailed presentation—in the initial stage, the decision was made *to build a set of possible solutions,* from which the residents could select a model instead of having to accept a unique type without the possibility of choice based on experience. How can one better understand the advantages and disadvantages of each design alternative than through visits to the construction works, and through the experience of the first inhabitants?

Curiously, it was in the external architectural expression—volumes, openings, finishes, and even color—that the residents allowed the opinions of "their" architects to prevail and which caused to appear in these SAAL projects the inevitable references to central-European housing of the 20s and 30s, which was neither known to them nor among their preferences.

## The Solutions and the Contexts

The diversity of urban situations in which the dozens of SAAL operations were begun or completed does not allow us to make a synthetic, typologic classification. However, we can say that the majority of the projects differ from the solutions adopted in earlier public housing programs in which post-CIAM layouts predominated (multistory slabs or towers with interstitial open spaces). Although no common guidelines were given to the teams, the majority of the solutions are of low rise, high or medium density type with well-defined exterior spaces—reducible to the archetypes of street, square, or patio—and continuous or connected buildings instead of the usual isolated slabs and towers. Part of the exterior space was frequently used for private gardens.

Some research was carried out by several teams on duplex and terrace houses with narrow frontage to obtain the best economies of land and infrastructure. The predominance of two-story row houses or patio houses is intended to allow a margin of adaptability and provide for future expansion. Further, whenever areas for rehabilitation were inserted into the historic urban grid, the preexisting urban morphology was respected. At times, the projects included rehabilitation of old houses which were expropriated. This was the case of the *ilhas* (blocks) of Oporto—back-to-back working class housing of the nineteenth century—where, in some areas like Antas and San Victor, recovery of the rows through infill with new dwellings was attempted.

In cases where the new housing developments were located in suburban areas characterized by high-density, arbitrary sets of buildings separated by vast semirural spaces, the forms chosen were many, ranging from patio grids to streets with row houses, such as in Seixal.

The slum of Curraleira is one of the most characteristic and extensive shantytowns in the inner city of Lisbon—physically marginalized from the bourgeois city, but near public services and facilities. It was one of the first to be organized into a cooperative association in 1974, and its leaders showed a remarkable capacity to manage the operation, even during the long period in which the municipality was hostile toward the SAAL program. Instead of radicalizing their demands in a partisan manner—which would probably have led to the rupture and demorilization of the residents of an area to which before April, 1974, many promises had been made but not kept—the leaders of the association managed to keep housing construction going, open a consumer cooperative, and organize a women's craft workshop—all measures aimed at maintaining the self-reliance of the local population.

From the urban point of view, the Curraleira design project tried to solve the difficult problems caused by irregularities of land crowded with slum houses and difficult access by working in a pragmatic way and using two or three types of buildings. One, a duplex with galleries, was used to fill in the existing borders of the bourgeois city and to increase the density on the most buildable strips of land. The others, maisonettes, row houses, and extendable patio houses were adopted where indicated by the slope of the land. The buildings are correct, though less photogenic or stylish than some other projects in Lisbon or Oporto and obviously less brilliant than, for instance, those of Alvaro Siza Vieira, the present Portuguese architect of greatest international prominence. But this example results from a process of careful participation in the discussion of the solutions and in the art of reconciling the objectives of the residents with the concrete local political conditions. A national program should be assessed by the average quality of its operations, and not only by its occasional formal architectural successes.

4. Young residents of Curraleira watch their new community rise.

# Designing Curraleira

**SAAL Curraleira Team**

Architects in charge: José Antonio Paradela
Luis Gravata Filipe

Sociology: Cecilia Vaz
Matilde Henriques

Civil engineers: Antonio Almada Guerra
Eduardo Fonseca Almeida

Assistants: Alvaro Costa
Francisco Quintanhilha
João Dionisio
Maria De Deus Damião
Paulo Braula Reis

The object of this SAAL project was the redevelopment of a large slum area of the shantytown type, homogeneous at first sight, but containing several different urban settlements, each with its own identity: Curraleira, Covas, Pinheiro, Carrascal. . . . This squatter settlement is fairly old (about 70 years) and contains 760 families, 70 percent of whom have lived there for more than 10 years. It sprawled across urban land that had escaped development due to its steep topography and vast areas of loose fill that make construction difficult.

Owing to its central position in Lisbon, many social and religious organizations had made efforts to improve conditions and promote development. When in November, 1974, the SAAL *Brigada* (work team) took up the job, we found an already organized community with a certain degree of institutional complexity. A "Householders' Committee" had been elected by the residents in May, 1974, and with members of a local community development association and others, it met twice a week. The Committee had already decided to form a social housing coopera-

1. Curraleira: the squatter settlement occupies the steep valley sides ignored by conventional builders.

2. Project by the SAAL Team for the redevelopment of the area.

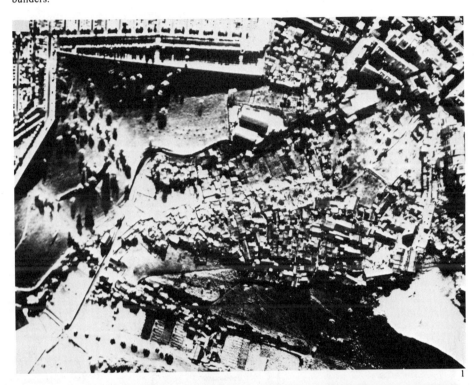

3

3. Site section shows building types in relation to ridge and valley.

tive, had defined some needed programs, and agreed on the main objective: new housing development should take place within the community.

The *Brigada's* planning intervention was limited by this prior decision, and hence focused on proposing areas in which building should take place, given the existing soil conditions, topography, condition and value of existing struc-

tures, relocation issues, and so forth.

## Building a Working Relationship

When important planning decisions were to be made, the people of Curraleira were always asked to assemble. The community was informed of these meetings (which attracted 200 to 300 people) through posters made with the help of the *Brigada*. Since the great part of the population is illiterate, a group of residents would also go through the streets with megaphones to announce each assembly.

In the early phases of the project, the residents' lack of experience in dealing with technicians and also the experimental nature of the SAAL program gave rise to lengthy discussions about the right way to work together. After all, besides creating an efficient physical plan, the idea was to achieve the specific social goals of the revolutionary process launched on April 25. People did not expect only designs from the *Brigada,* but also advice and technical assistance on a wide range of problems, even getting rid of mice, improving lit-

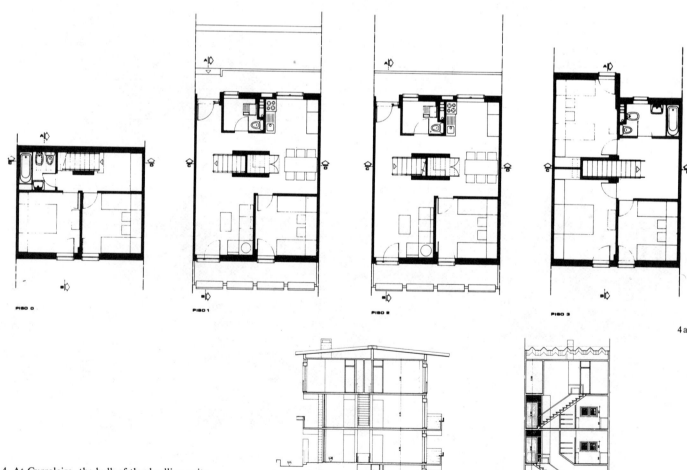

PISO 0    PISO 1    PISO 2    PISO 3

4a

4. At Curraleira, the bulk of the dwelling units are in four-story, maisonette-over-maisonette buildings with gallery access (Piso = Floor).

4 b          4 c

eracy, and salvaging shacks in near ruin. This, of course, required alterations in the composition of the work team in order to be able to respond properly.

The final composition of the Curraleira *Brigada* was two social workers, on architect, one cival engineer, and four architectural students from the local university. Their first task was to form neighborhood subcommittees, each with a delegate to work closely with teh SAAL team. The creation of neighborhood delegates was very important for the acceptance of the *Brigada* by the population, eapecially in gathering needed imformation and getting feedback to our design proposals.

- Teaching people to read and write
- Creating an informative newspaper for the area
- Helping the victims of a fire that took place in the area to take over empty houses in the vicinity
- Leading discussions about the architectural projects proposed for different areas of Curraleira

The SAAL group did a good job in the many newly–defined phases of the project:

As the SAAL team got going, several tasks were initiated almost at the same time:

1. The design and construction of utility services, such as house and street drainage, water, and electricity.
2. A sociological survey on housing preferences and data for the relocation and social service programs.
3. The plan for redevelopment.

The first resulted in immediate benefits (water fountains, sewers, street pavement, and getting rid of litter). These actions gave prestige to the residents' committees and encouraged people to get involved.

The social survey was intended to have a didactic character, making both the community and the City aware of the numerous problems of the areas, such as crowding, unemployment, ill health, low education levels, and the lack of community facilities. It was divided into two parts. The first con-

cerned the family, its socioeconomic status, and its needs, including housing needs, while the other was aimed at revealing the feelings of the population about the improvement of daily life and towards discovering its image of the new homes.

It was expected that interviewers would not only gather information, but would teach the people about the redevelopment process that was now underway.

The redevelopment plan, which by its nature involved technical concepts outside the normal experience of the population, involved intensive discussion, both with small groups and with the neighborhood assembly. We made several models and many perspective drawings of the site and the new houses at different scales with the objective of making clear our proposals. If in certain cases the team's technical arguments were accepted because of the confidence established by the *Brigada* and the knowledge people had of site restrictions and difficulties, in others very fierce opposition and argument were put

forward. For example, people rejected prefabrication systems and apartment blocks more than four stories high. There was also a lot of debate over locations and programs for the new community facilities.

**Building Design**

The data from the social survey gave us useful information for the design of buildings. It turned out that preference about type and form of buildings varied largely from one family to another. A few preferred high buildings, perhaps reproducing the image of the city around them. Most others, still retaining their original rural outlook, or because they had pets, or used parts of their homes for artisan production, preferred row houses or maisonettes. The Lisbon planning agency initially opposed this scale of development because of its low density, alleging lack of space in the city for housing. Fortunately, a satisfactory compromise was reached that resolved some difficult community situations before violent confrontations might have arisen. It is curious to note

5. A typical main living floor as designed by the Curraleira Team and the residents. The openness of the connection between cooking-dining-living departs from the traditional formal isolation of family space and signals a shift in familial roles.

6

7

8

9

that, although the vast majority wanted to live in maisonettes or on the ground floor of a block, the survey didn't show much interest in private gardens. On the other hand, there was a strong demand for children's playgrounds.

The sociological survey also helped resolve certain issues connected with interior design, such as the need for a large kitchen space for sewing and washing. It was specifically suggested that living and eating spaces be separated by walls. Although required by Portuguese standards in houses with more than two sleeping rooms, more than one bathroom was considered unnecessary by the residents of Curraleira. Almost everyone agreed about the importance of verandas or terraces to put flowers, sit outdoors, or for children's play.

For the development of designs, meetings were held with participation of householders in a first pilot phase of relocation (34 families). This was to be a test of the overall redevelopment plan, giving the community and the *Brigada* an opportunity for a comprehensive trial of all the steps involved. Meetings were held with housewives in small groups of four where more detailed problems were solved, such as relations between kitchen, living room, and work space by changing partitions, doors, or equipment. Alternative finishes were also discussed and defined at these meetings.

Field trips to other SAAL schemes in progress (Setubal and Sines) were organized in this phase and to some housing component prefabrication plants as well. The same process of meetings and interviews was extended to the next phases, organized in all cases through the neighborhood delegates.

Of the various alternative building types presented by the *Brigada,* two were ultimately selected that corresponded to different residents' needs and ways of life:

● Four-story apartment blocks formed by two maisonettes (duplexes) with open gallery access and oriented along the street. These dwellings are for families with four to eight members. They will be allocated to the more "urban" families, able to adapt easily to the typical city block of apartments.

● Expandable dwellings forming clusters of 30 to 40 houses grouped into neighborhoods, these are quadruplex dwellings with one or two floors and connected private space (patio). Each has independent access from the street or footpaths. These houses are designed for young families still growing, or for families of great size (up to 12 persons). Quality and comfort levels were defined by each family involved according to its requirements, aims, and financial possibilities. In every case, however, we made sure the houses would have *at least* the standards of those built by the state. It is out of the question therefore, as was at a time argued by political opponents of SAAL, that the Curraleira houses are substandard

buildings. They are, however, not the usual standardized product, and this is surely part of the reason they are so successful.

About the time these design decisions were being made, the original Householder's Committee was transformed into a social housing cooperative (*Cooperativa de Habitaçao Economica*—CHE), having elected to become the collective owner of the new dwellings. After many public discussions, both privately owned housing and self-help construction* were rejected by the

*It was also argued that self-help would perpetuate the high unemployment in the construction sector.—EDITOR

residents' assembly. It was thought that these conservative proposals might very well initiate a return to the prerevolutionary situation, acting against the motivation of the people for collective development and their newly discovered ability to make demands on the state.

## Technical Conception

The Curraleira redevelopment project was initially to be carried out in three phases, each with 250 dwellings. This solution was intended to permit the use of a prefabricated concrete box-frame system, potentially more economical and quicker to build. On the other hand, it would require a more highly organized work site and the quick completion of roads and foundations. As the local authority was responsible for these items and as we could not guarantee the timetable required due to financial and land expropriation problems, designs were prepared for two alternatives: prefabricated frame and traditional building system.

We ended by adopting the traditional solution in this first phase as it proved better adapted to circumstances. It gave us flexibility in bidding, and it permitted us to work with local, small-scale building cooperatives offering even lower construction costs than the industrial prefabricators. The second contract for 134 dwellings was won by a local cooperative made up of unemployed workers from the area. This underscores once again the necessity of integrating the physical and technical aspects of architectural projects with social goals.

Signing the contract for the construction of the 34 dwellings of the pilot project gave new impetus to the Curraleira process. As we moved into this more practical phase, people began to realize their aims would be achieved and the collective spirit was strengthened. This led to a more conscious and dynamic control of the process on the part of the residents' cooperative—in a moment when financial and legal support started to fail and SAAL was buffeted by political pressures. After this time of apprenticeship, project direction has been assumed by the CHE, which today has responsibility for the entire redevelopment program. As of early 1981, over 100 houses are complete and occupied. And more are underway.

10

11

6–11. Views of the new Curraleira.

269

# Orcasitas
# Madrid, Spain

The success of Orcasitas in Madrid is a legend in European community development circles. A haphazard squatter settlement only a few years ago, today it has 1500 new dwellings with terrazzo floors and sunny terraces in elevator buildings. These new homes are owned by the former squatter families, who also manage the project, supervise the children's playgrounds, and operate the new shops and services that fill the ground floors.

One would have expected a different result, especially as the residents of Orcasitas started their struggle for new housing under the fascist regime of Francisco Franco. They were fortunate to receive the support of dedicated left-wing lawyers, and through them with CETA, the *Centro de Estudios Territoriales y Ambientales*, and its leader Eduardo Leira, a US-trained architect. CETA is a cooperative architectural and planning office that was created out of the Spanish student movement of the late 1960s to provide technical assistance to then-emerging movement toward neighborhood associations. These *Associaciones de Vecinos* sprang up with the Franco government's emphasis on economic development and the timid liberalization that accompanied it. They eventually played a major role in the restoration of constitutional democracy in Spain.

The important point, of course, lies in what Leira calls the "parity of needs." Architects and planners have a concept of the good life and the physical setting appropriate to it; people, organized into neighborhood associations or similar pressure groups, have environmental needs and, given strong leadership, the political influence to implement plans, to get buildings built. The story of Orcasitas is the story of pressure and negotiation, of architects as strategists as well as designers, of participation as mobilization. It addresses the issue of the roles of professionals and of the community. And, although the project is a triumph in the eyes of the residents and CETA can

be justly proud of its role, it also raises some important questions about populism and architecture. Should architects subordinate their vision to the desires expressed by their community clients? How might designers educate clients without manipulating them?

Eduardo Leira has recently left CETA to take the job of Director of the municipal office responsible for the new master plan of Madrid. We can be quite sure that it will be more responsive to the needs of the City's population than are the earlier plans he describes in his article. The people of Orcasitas and the project presented here did much to make this new plan and the policies it embodies possible.

Manuel Castells, who is from Madrid and has followed the progress of Orcasitas closely, discusses in his Commentary

some of the political and architectural problems raised by Leira's article. He finds that the experience

clearly shows that there is a way out of the dilemma between free market urban barbarism and the . . . bureaucratic takeover of the city. Cultural innovation, grassroots mobilization, and political change could produce a major leap forward to a new urban frontier—on the assumption that only if people control the city will cities actually be built for people.

The report on the Orcasitas project was prepared by Eduardo Leira in collaboration with CETA colleagues Jesus Gago, Luis Mapelli, Ignacio Solana, and Daniel Zarza.

# People, Building, Democracy

**Eduardo Leira, architect and planner,**
*Centro de Estudios Territoriales y*
*Ambientales* **(CETA);**
**Chief Planner, City of Madrid**

Orcasitas today is a legendary name in Madrid, the vanguard of the neighborhood movement. A "myth" with 1500 new dwellings created through the collective struggle of its residents, who previously lived on the same site in a *barrio de chabolas* (squatter settlement). These residents, with a good deal of technical assistance, fought for 10 years to get their new community. They held a general assembly each week—surely a participatory record.

Is the completed project any different from one carried out by a public agency without the participation, without the initiative—both of which have been marked here—of the residents themselves? On a formal level it may not appear so. One finds no *avant-garde* architectonic solutions. There are few substantial innovations in spatial organization, either of the site or the individual dwelling units. But will there not be substantial differences in the resulting community? Is it possible that the life lived in this neighborhood will be the same as that in speculative developments or ordinary public projects?

The process that led to the creation of the new Orcasitas would appear to guarantee that there will be major differences. The first and most essential is that *the neighborhood itself remains*—when everything would have led one to believe that today, in the best of cases, these residents would be living each one isolated from the others in new dwellings even further out on the metropolitan periphery. And this outcome would have cost even more years of economic denial and the hard work of self-help construction and shantytown life.

The process that created Orcasitas, however, must not be permitted to remain shrouded in its mythic qualities. Orcasitas emerged in the context of *franquismo,* as part of the powerful movement of opposition that developed on all fronts for democracy and against the Franco dictatorship. Its political importance arises from the fact that it was a major landmark in the urban strug-

gles that created the well-organized network of Neighborhood Associations. In this case, it should be made clear that we are not dealing with a movement that was specifically political, nor in its beginnings was it connected with any political organization. It arose directly out of the people and grew steadily with its outstanding leaders and broad participation as key elements in its success. Perhaps because of the spontaneous nature of the process, the role of technicians—architects, lawyers, planners—was also crucial. This role was minimized by the residents, partly because for them militancy was the ultimate value, and partly because of underlying class suspicion. We were only fully accepted after we had worked side by side with the residents, after we had "drunk wine" with them. Nevertheless, we technicians prepared the legal and planning framework on which the residents mounted their demands. In addition, we contributed the design projects and financed their development out of our own pockets. (We were only paid after great delays by a municipal Administration mistrustful of professionals working for the people of Orcasitas and which threw in our path numerous obstacles that their usual architects and planners never had to face.) The Orcasitas residents were accustomed to thinking of the Administration as an inaccessible Olympus and to receiving only rebuffs or repression from public agencies. We served an additional essential function by bringing the residents and the Administration together.

Yet the question arises again: does the final built result constitute an advance over ordinary public housing development? CETA has succeeded in providing housing for the residents. But is it architecture? We hope that the following analysis of the experience at Orcasitas will help to answer this question. We, the architects and planners, who participated in the project have written it with all our capacity for rationalization, but also with our propensity for

self-criticism.

There are similar projects under way today under the democratic regime. The change of political context makes certain things easier, but it also makes some forms of action and some government responses that were deemed appropriate under Franco unacceptable today. Will residents and their professional advocates know how to act effectively within the new constitutional framework? Have the lessons of the citizens' movement in the major Spanish cities been incorporated in the policies of the new public agencies? These are the questions that are raised for us today.

It is necessary to tell the whole story. In the first place, one must understand the nature of the urban movements that arose under Franco. Only then can we answer the questions that have been posed. And even so, the answers cannot as yet be definitive.

## The Beginnings of Orcasitas

Some six kilometers from the center of Madrid, in between the roads that lead to Toledo and Andalusia, lies the little plateau of Orcasitas. It is on the far side of the long-awaited greenbelt called for by the master plan of 1946. In 1950, it was just outside the built-up metropolitan area.

At that time, the owners of the land decided to divide it into parcels and sell it for urban uses, although it was zoned for agriculture. Each parcel was 40 to 50 m², and only a very few of the poor immigrants coming from the south of Spain were able to buy as much as 200 m² of land. Although it is not clear that dividing the land into parcels for sale was against the law, surely construction of housing was. Only by getting a roof built in one night and moving in quickly could these new landowners keep from being thrown out. Makeshift construction, lack of elementary services, overcrowding, muddy roads—here were found all the usual characteristics of

marginal urbanization for the flood of rural workers surging into the big cities.

In the case of Orcasitas, the original owners of the land held onto some key parcels: those which connected with the highway, and building sites lying between the parcels that were sold and the major streets. In this way, they created the basis for the revalorization of the land and the future removal of this precariously settled population should urbanization be legalized at some later time.

Settlements like Orcasitas are quite different from their counterparts in the Third World. During this period of substantial migration into Madrid from the rural areas, settlements like Orcasitas became the most important form of residential community for the new arrivals. There was a great demand for manpower in construction and also in the new industries that were growing up around Madrid.*

The residents of settlements like Orcasitas were not socially or economically marginal, even though they were not part of the conventional housing market. The extraordinary growth of Madrid brought Orcasitas, like so many of these new areas of urbanization, relatively close to the center of the city within a few years.

The inhabitants of Orcasitas soon found themselves, in the words of others, in a location "too expensive" for them. Like other working class communities caught in the expansion of Madrid after 1965, Orcasitas began to attract the attention of developers looking for new sites for middle class housing. The expulsion of the original population and the reconstruction of the area became the objective of both the original owners of Orcasitas and private promoters.

## The History of an Urban Struggle

The master plan for Madrid prepared in 1971 by the municipality accorded precisely with the objectives of the orig-

*Madrid, a bureaucratic and service city, was converted in the postwar period, with conscious political intent, into the second most important industrial city in Spain.

The Franco government hoped to create an economic base for its fierce political centralization and also to create a counterweight to the two developed industrial areas, Catalonia and the Basque country, both then as now centers of movements for autonomy.

272

2. A street in the original squatter settlement of Orcasitas.

3. A courtyard in the old Orcasitas.

4. Opposition headquarters—the Proprietors Association in Orcasitas.

5

6

5,6,7,8. Evidence of the apartment boom of the last years of the Franco regime. The demand for space caused land prices to soar. Thousands of working class families were displaced. The constant threat of eviction spurred the rapid growth of the Neighborhood Association movement.

7

8

inal landowners. The goal: to construct new housing, to remove the squatter populations and clear their communities. The method: give control of the redevelopment process to the largest land-holders in each zone, including the power to expropriate small holdings that stood in the way of realizing their plans.

Just at that time, the residents of Orcasitas were beginning to fight for services. Because each ordinary service was the responsibility of a different organization, there was in Madrid no uniform program of area development. The *Canal de Isabel II,* a private corporation, finally put in water mains, and eventually the municipality supplied sanitation services. Road paving came much later, and only after numerous vocal demands from the community.

In carrying out these operations, the agencies and private companies involved looked for a community spokesman to simplify dealing with each of more than 1000 families that by now lived in Orcasitas. This functional demand reinforced the need for an *Asociación de Vecinos* (Neighborhood Association). In fact, its leadership arose spontaneously in the process of dealing with the water company.

Ultimately, two things substantially altered the pattern of development anticipated by the master plan. The first and most important was the existence of this Neighborhood Association— which became progressively stronger in the face of every threat of expulsion. The second was solid legal, architectural, and urban planning support which, together with direct neighbor-

hood struggle, permitted the residents to carry on their fight effectively before the courts.

The 1971 master plan made the mistake of saying—in passing and without giving it much importance—that the new dwellings ought to be for the people who lived presently in the areas to be redeveloped. This would have been merely anecdotal and without importance if it had not been for existence of the two things we have mentioned and the community's readiness to fight for its rights. This support from the plan itself for the demands the residents were making reinforced the struggle which had already begun. The struggle itself and the political consciousness that the inhabitants developed through it continuously raised the level of demands. From an initial fight against removal,

273

10

9. One of many demonstrations organized by the Orcasitas' Neighborhood Association.

10. The Neighborhood Association movement spread quickly through the major cities in Spain. One of its missions was a broad program of public education on urban issues.

11. A poster put out by the Neighborhood Association in Hortaleza—a district in Madrid—calling for a demonstration against speculative luxury development.

11

that we did for them calls for a staged development in which new dwellings are completed for whole sectors of the original settlement before residents are asked to move.*

The design of the new housing itself was later assigned by the Ministry of Housing to a team made up half by professionals selected by the Neighborhood Association and half by the Ministry from among its friends and political supporters. Even after this point, the process was neither simple nor direct.

The right to have new housing had been won step-by-step by the residents. They then found themselves up against official housing policy which was disposed to leave the construction of social housing to private developers (who, logically, would not have bothered to produce it). At the same time, there were neither precedents nor mechanisms for involving the users as participants in the design, an essential part of the entire

---

*Without doubt, INUR's willingness to accept in the end the professional team proposed by the residents was influenced by its previous positive experience working with CETA.

12. Architects and graphic artists working with the Neighborhood Associations produced powerful mulitmedia presentations on development problems and alternatives.

13. A presentation and debate in the streets of Madrid.

14. Orcasitas' leader Lopez Rey demands results from the then Minister of Housing at a street meeting.

process. Only the constancy, the ability, and the unity of the residents have led to a positive outcome. They were forced to negotiate with a variety of successive administrations that were more or less—usually less—receptive to their demands. With each political change at the top, there was a crisis with the Ministry of Housing and, starting almost from the beginning each time, the old agreements had to be reaffirmed. In one period in 1973, there were five changes in the top administration of the Madrid provincial housing agency in a period of a few months. Through all this, the Neighborhood Association was able to hang on and in fact to get its agreements with the agencies set down

in writing.

To get the project approved by the Ministry, to make sure that the budget was not reduced, to see that the prices of the new dwellings were fixed beforehand, and to see that the work was finally begun and that it was completed with satisfactory quality—all these steps, one after the other, have required the residents' vigilance and pressure. The total process has already taken 10 years, from the first demands in 1970 to the completion of the first dwellings at the end of 1979. And it is not yet over. Although 1500 dwellings are complete, a second phase of 760 apartments is yet to begin.

## A Strategy for Action

The renewal program demanded by the residents, involving new dwellings at prices they could afford in the same place where they had previously lived, is now essentially accepted by the Administration, if not as a general housing policy, at least in this case. But things were very different at the outset of the struggle in Orcasitas. First, it was necessary to persuade government agencies to take action to control the speculative real estate market, and then to convince them that the project was feasible.

The neighborhood strategy throughout the process followed two complementary lines: pressure and proposals, action and negotiation. Pressure took all the usual forms: lists of signatures, press conferences, frequent visits to agencies, and mobilization in the streets. The absolutely indispensable other side of the coin for the Neighborhood Association was to be prepared always to take the initiative in planning and design, stating clearly what was needed and showing how to do it, offering a way out to the public officials each time they reached their wits' end. This meant hours in the offices and corridors of ministries and municipal agencies. It meant proposals and more proposals. The politicians and functionaries, with their lack of imagination, frequently required the residents to invent brand-new ways to carry out their plan, ways before which the administrative machinery nearly shuddered to a stop. In addition to being responsible for the action proposals, the Neighborhood Association had to arrange the necessary coordination between agencies, something the agency directors themselves could not do.

Another essential feature characterized the development process at Orcasitas: the insistence on partial and short-term victories. New housing was the final objective, but not the only one. The neighborhood was lacking in many things and it made no sense to wait for its total transformation at some time in the future. In the meantime, there were water, sewage, paving, and garbage collection to be won—and all in a way that wouldn't put off the longed-for day of complete reconstruction. Success in obtaining these things constituted perhaps small, but absolutely essential, victories. Through them, the Association gained in negotiating ability and recognition of its central role as organizer

and channel of the residents' demands.

## The Creation of the Neighborhood Association

The renewal process the residents had in mind required solid organization. In its early stages, the Neighborhood Association did not understand the role it would have to play. It had been formed by immigrant workers with very limited education, and perhaps more importantly, it was born under a regime in which all collective associations were proscribed. The fight to hold onto both their dwellings and their central location in the growing metropolitan area called for organization. It was in the responding to this attack that the Association was formed and the demand for a new Orcasitas formulated. The idea of a new Orcasitas was the result of a new consciousness, collective in a certain measure, but developed above all among the leaders of the Association, especially the long-time President of the Neighborhood Association, Felix Lopez Rey, the true author of the process at Orcasitas. He is a living demonstration of the vital importance of leadership.

A jewelry maker who worked in his home, Lopez Rey was in the community all day every day, and had a flexible schedule. Without doubt, it was these things that permitted him to dedicate himself regularly to the struggle. Learning on the way, Lopez Rey rose to become a key figure in the citizens' movement in Madrid. He knew how to bring together the ideas of his technical advisers, improve and orchestrate them with his criticism, make them known to his comrades at Orcasitas, and then transform them into programs that would mobilize the community. At the same time, he learned how to manage the press and to negotiate ably with the government agencies. Such a leader served to galvanize an authentic mass movement. Utilizing the community assembly as a constant instrument of democracy, he forged a unified movement at Orcasitas with a great capacity to make its demands felt.

In this fundamentally democratic process, a crucial milestone was the construction of the Neighborhood Association's headquarters. It was a time when civil rights were unknown and public meetings were strictly illegal. In the beginning, assemblies were held in the small houses, or, on occasion, in a local school. That is, until it was

decided that the residents themselves should build a headquarters. A great many of the members worked in the construction sector and had building skills. All that was lacking was land and materials. The materials came from nearby construction projects (even employees of the Public Works Department took part in collecting the necessary materials). Then, on a piece of vacant land owned by the municipality, they built their headquarters without permission (the city officials looked the other way).

This community building was conceived as more than a meeting hall. It was also to furnish necessary services to the community, such as showers and toilets. The building quickly became a landmark in the neighborhood. It became a place for chance encounters and the creation of a collective life. Its construction was a great victory for Orcasitas, the more important because it was the fruit of a common effort.

## The Neighborhood Movement

In the absence of elementary freedoms, how can such a powerful collective movement spring up? The development not only of the Neighborhood Association in Orcasitas but of the entire citizens' movement in Madrid and throughout urban Spain is only understandable as a reflection of the political and social situation during the last years of Franco's reign. If the harshness of an authoritarian regime is a great obstacle to the development of such a movement, it also explains the need—and the reasons for its rapid growth.

Among the timid measures of political liberalization that had to accompany rapid economic development, the Franco government approved a so-called Law of Association (1964). It was seen as a substitute for a real measure of organizational freedom, in so far as all types of political associations continued to be outlawed. In fact, the government envisioned the creation of associations of sporting groups, artists, and the like. It was under the letter of this law that the Neighborhood Associations claimed legality.

In an effort to appear modern, even city governments, which at the time had no autonomy and whose officials were appointed by the central government, began to show a greater tolerance for criticism and discussion of urban problems. By the beginning of the 1970s, a

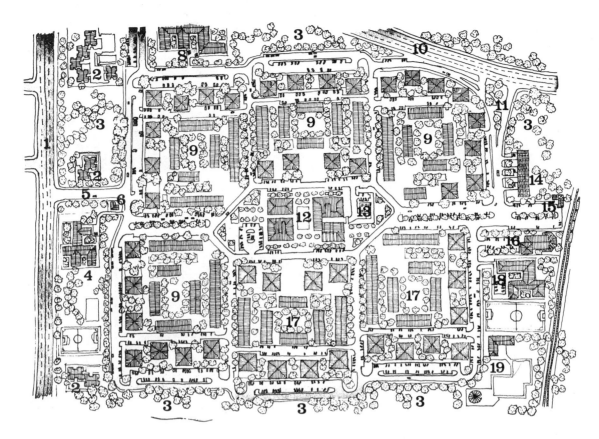

large number of Neighborhood Associations had been formed, but without any particular focus or demands. In the case of Orcasitas, the legalization of the Neighborhood Association was not easy. It was necessary to get the support of persons with influence in the regime: a curate, a member of the Falange. . . . Fortunately, the Neighborhood Association was still seen as something innocuous, and not as a political association, so a legal charter

It is important never to overlook the fact that in the final years of Franco, the regime's internal contradictions were notable. The harsh repression of earlier periods was no longer possible. It had to be balanced by a certain permissiveness demanded by ever-larger numbers of people and by the need for legitimacy. Only direct political activity was repressed and, consequently, collective initiatives (which were ultimately, of course, political in intent) tended to arise by indirect routes: student groups, Neighborhood Associations, professional organizations. The first Neighborhood Associations were organized around living conditions in squatter neighborhoods. Some time later, the left parties in the underground opposition, which until then had been focused on the workers' movement, began to diversify their areas of political work. It be-

15. The new Orcasitas: 1. Calle Ibarra 2. tower apartments 3. open space 4. school 5. entrance road 6. medical clinic 7. entrance from the Madrid highway 8. EGB center 9. mid-rise housing, first phase 10. Carabanchel Expressway 11. entrance road 12. commercial and civic

center, including the headquarters of the Neighborhood Association 13. district heating plant 14. workshops 15. train to Madrid center 16. church 17. mid-rise housing, second phase 18. EGB center 19. public pool.

came steadily clear that the citizens' movement was taking on notable importance in the fight for democracy.*

The development of the movement has been and continues to be highly important in the development of consciousness. The struggle for housing is the key to mobilization. In it residents discover a means of social participation at many levels. Political demand soon moves from the individual dwelling to community facilities and public services. While at the forefront of the struggle a Neighborhood Association generates an enormous number of activities. It becomes a center of collective life. This creates the possibility that the new community that is arising out of the process of struggle may be a significant place apart from its architectural character—a place inhabited by transformed people who have not only be-

come part of the municipality and wrested from it the right to new housing, but have won full citizenship for themselves and their children. Recognizing this, many politically oriented professionals like us rushed to offer skills to support the growing movement.

## The Role of Professionals

Throughout the entire process of alternating demands and proposals, professional advisers have played an essential role in the success of the Neighborhood Associations. In a situation such as this, where there is an initial lack of communal consciousness and a low level of education, things cannot really be different. But what of these professional advisers? Playing their role well requires a very particular understanding of professional involvement, and even then all too frequently it laps over into paternalism.

Recent years in Spain have seen the rise of new professionals who use their knowledge as an instrument of social transformation. Under Franco, working

---

*The decline of the neighborhood movement during the democratization of Spain makes clear its character and calls into question the political insight of those parties of the left which, after they became legal, largely abandoned such popular movements to concentrate on electoral politics.

in underground political parties, they sought new forms of professional activity, hoping to break down the traditional dichotomy of professional and political work. The liberal professions offer the greatest possibilities for combining these forms of work, and in the last years of the 1960s many collectives of lawyers, doctors, and architects appeared.* It is not by chance that these new professionals come out of the student movement which reached such heights in Spain 10 or 15 years ago. It was there that university students learned to combine underground political struggle with forms of mass action.

Among architects and planners, professions that until then had been highly elitist, a number of collectives were formed in the late 1960s to pursue this new concept of professional work. They frequently tended to take on an interdisciplinary character, which is particularly necessary for city planning. This is the case with CETA, which from the very early stages has been the technical assistance group behind the Neighborhood Association in Orcasitas, and in later years for many other similar groups.

## CETA

A word about the nature of the collective seems necessary. Like other groups formed at the same time, CETA from its very beginnings has been a cooperative in which all the workers, whether professional or not, are equal partners. The group was formed almost without any initial capital. In its place, members contribute unreimbursed hours of work. Salaries are quite low, and the income spread between various members of the team is small. We have no outside sources of financial support. Our clients have almost always been public agencies, even when their members were almost entirely of the right wing. Only the professional competence of the team and the contradictory internal needs of the Administration enabled us to obtain commissions in the early years.

In Orcasitas, at the beginning we were even asked to help frame the issues for the residents' struggle. As this sort of process was brand-new to us

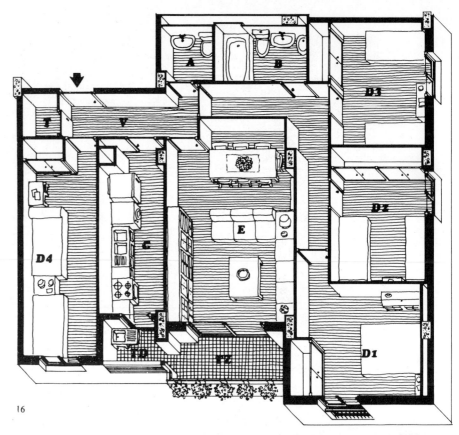

16

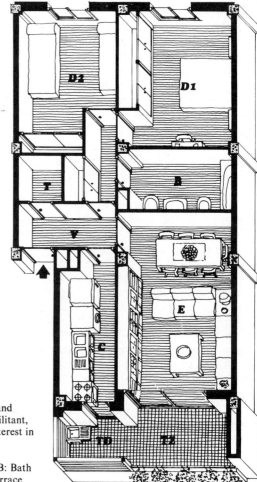

16,17. Apartment layouts for the towers and mid-rise blocks respectively. Politically militant, the residents of Orcasitas showed little interest in architectural experimentation.

E: Living Room C: Kitchen D: Bedroom B: Bath A: Half-bath V: Foyer T: Storage TZ: Terrace TD: Drying balcony

17

*For example, the first labor law offices, which played such a crucial role in the union movement during the last years of the Franco regime, were formed in this manner.

both, residents and technicians worked closely to determine what to do. In addition, we were able to make a contribution which turned out to be fundamental throughout the process: our professional relationship with people in the government, and the fact that we were personally acquainted with certain officials, enabled us to get negotiations started. The residents' first small victories led them to understand the importance of technical support and steadily to gain confidence in themselves. In no instance did the architects and planners attempt to act in the place of neighborhood leaders, insisting instead that the struggle be directed by the residents themselves at all times. Even so, in a project of this sort, when there is constant collaboration, roles will tend to overlap on many occasions. For example, we professionals attended all neighborhood assemblies to report on developments. There is no doubt we acted as proponents of particular programs or directions, playing an important role not only in the direction of the struggle, but also in the progressive development of political consciousness among the residents. At Orcasitas, the professionals were expected to participate in militant political actions and to share closely the life of the residents. In the beginning, this helped us win the confidence of the neighborhood and made working together easier. But in the end, it complicated our relationship. In the later stages, when the planning was done and it was time to start building, the moment arrived when the technicians quite properly began to focus on strictly professional activities. The Neighborhood Association expected the continuation of militant involvement. This caused problems that we are working out to this day.*

Even when the relationship between the residents and the technical team was functioning smoothly, conventional architectural and planning tools proved inadequate means of communication. We even found it difficult to formulate the questions that would get us information we needed to come to agreement about the project we were to

Bedroom 2,40 x 4,30m.
Kitchen 2,40 x 2,70m.
Closet
Bath
Half-bath
Closet
Bedroom 2,40 x 4,30m.

Drying area Terrace 2,10 x 1,80m.
Bedroom 2,40 x 4,30m.
Closet
Multiple-use space 4,30 x 3,70m.
Entrance
Living-Dining 22m².
Terrace 2,10 x 1,80m.

18. The revised apartment layout proposed by the architects for the second phase of construction. The major change involves the substitution of a central multiple-use space for the traditional formal entrance foyer.

design. The participatory process at Orcasitas has shown us just how undeveloped are the means for involving residents in design, especially when their educational level is low. The role of the professionals as proponents of new architectural solutions runs first up against this difficulty in communication, and then against the influence of the mass media, which is more powerful in establishing cultural models and desirable lifestyles than is the experience of the residents themselves in their struggle. For the most part, the conventionality of the architectural results achieved reflects the decision of the technicians to stick closely to the opinions and aspirations *expressed* by the people of Orcasitas. We will return to this issue.

Architects have come to regard participation as essential, and without doubt it introduces a new form of professional work quite different from the traditional Enlightenment attitudes which have characterized architectural practice in this century. Even so, what kind of technical support is needed? How can the participants avoid manipulation at the hands of their professional servants? In other words, how

*Here is an example that all architects should consider: as the residents were in no position to offer us financial support, we had to count on the fact that the Administration would pay for our work once the housing project actually went forward. Of course, the long preceding phase of consultation and planning was not compensated, and the collective was required to finance it internally. In the case of Orcasitas, this phase lasted for a number of years during which the level of effort was constantly high. Later, when the architectural projects were actually commissioned and we began to receive fees, there were numerous misunderstandings with the residents who had worked so long without any hope of pay. Clearly, collaboration between residents and professionals is not easy. The social position of the professional, even if it is a mythification of the role, leads to half-hidden class antagonism, particularly when what in the eyes of the residents seem to be very large fees are involved.

279

19

20

21

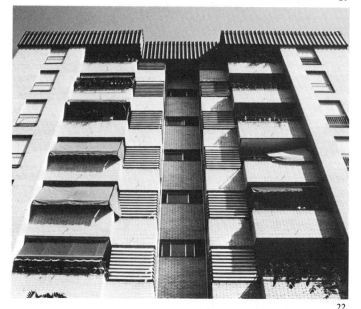

22

23

24

25

26

27

28

29

19. Step-by-step, new housing replaces the squatter settlement.

20. A courtyard in the new Orcasitas.

21,22. Views of the housing blocks.

23,24. The new primary school.

25–29. Shops, streets, and courts in the rebuilt community: a triumph for the people of Orcasitas.

many final decisions are accepted by residents because they believe in the "goodwill" of the technical group? In order to look at these questions, let us briefly analyze the experience of participation at Orcasitas.

## Neighborhood Demands and Participation

The goal of the struggle was to get new housing built on the site of the original dwellings. It was the residents' purpose to force the government to pay as much for the expropriation of their old dwellings as they in turn would pay for the new ones. Although it was not said straight out, the objective was an even exchange of an old house for a new one. In Orcasitas this concept was the subject of much careful thought (involving residents and professionals), and in the end the people did receive payments sufficient to purchase new dwellings outright.* Furthermore, it was soon understood that the fight was for a well-

*This has been the approach in a number of Madrid neighborhoods. The inhabitants argue that they don't live in substandard housing or neighborhoods without services because of their fault, but because of the government's. Hence, if the government wishes to bring the neighborhood up to standards required by law, it must exchange house for house. Given that the new dwellings in Orcasitas are in apartment houses, this form of tenure itself constitutes an exceptional demand. The housing policies of the Franco government, which were directed almost entirely at promoting private ownership, ultimately made this a general expectation.

serviced and complete neighborhood, and not merely for housing, the one thing the residents already had. Each objective—new housing, high expropriation prices, outright ownership, a planned neighborhood—represents a distinct stage in the struggle, and a different process of participation.

At CETA, it was our hypothesis that *the quality of the plan,* presented at frequent neighborhood assemblies, could play an important part in broadening demands beyond housing as an issue. Our experience here, particularly when we compare it with other cases in which the role of the plan itself has been minimized, confirms this hypothesis.

Following this, establishing the value of the existing dwellings came to be the central focus of the struggle. This was a two-sided issue. On the one hand, there was the desire to obtain the maximum possible indemnification for the old houses at the time of expropriation (but not for the land itself as high land prices would result in enormous increases in the cost of the new dwellings without significant offsetting income for the residents). On the other hand, the residents were looking for the lowest possible price and the best possible terms for purchasing the new dwellings. Both objectives were achieved. In many cases, the residents will pay, in constant pesetas, less than they have received for their substandard dwellings. Clearly, the resulting project involves a very high level of government subsidy.

These unusual financial conditions were won from the government just before the first democratic elections in 1977, following the death of Franco. They were written down as fixed prices that could not be changed at a later time. They must be considered exceptional, and are largely the result of the populist position taken by the then Minister of Public Works and Urbanism, M. Garrigues, who had his eye on the mayor's office in Madrid. In accepting the residents' demands, Garrigues created a precedent that has created more than a few later conflicts because the Socialist-Communist municipal government that was elected (and still is in office) could not make such prices a general rule.

During the struggle over house values and financial conditions, participation was limited to pressure on the agencies and the objective was simply to obtain the maximum possible. The residents

themselves carried out a careful study of each family's financial circumstances, and they calculated the monthly payment that each family could properly make for new housing. Duly analyzed by the Administration, these data were the basis for the establishment of differentiated formulas for purchase. The total subventions obtained in this way probably amount to not less than 80 percent of the real cost of the new dwellings.

## Participation in Design

Until the moment arrived to give form to the new housing, no one realized just how limited the residents' participation in matters of design might be. The people of Orcasitas had demonstrated over and over again that their direct involvement in the management of the entire project was indispensable. The neighborhood renewal project would not have gotten off the ground without them, of course, and they played the central role in determining exactly how the program would be carried out. The government had neither the will nor the mechanisms necessary to undertake this large project. The residents forced the Administration to find the will and the way through constant pressure.

When the day came, however, to decide what the new dwellings would be like, neither the residents nor their leaders appeared to have anything to say. Their most immediate reference was some apartments which the government had recently built nearby. The architects found much to criticize in them, but the residents of Orcasitas found them to be wanting only in two minor aspects. These apartment houses had no balconies, and, as the original houses at Orcasitas were one-story high and on the ground, the residents felt the need for a place where they could get a breath of fresh air and grow a few flowers. Also, a low-quality vinyl flooring had been used and it had quickly begun to deteriorate. This led Orcasitas to demand nothing less than terrazzo! In fact, the slogan *terraza y terrazo* quickly became the rallying cry in the neighborhood. However, that was all.

Even after many discussions and elaborate investigations, not much more became clear. For families living with mud and garbage and leaky roofs, what counted was to get an apartment right away and at an affordable price. Ques-

tions like, "If in your apartment you can have sun only in the living room or the kitchen, which would you prefer?" were completely without meaning for them.* They were all too willing to leave the answers to such questions to the technicians in whom they now had confidence, having worked together through many years of struggle.

Even so, because the ideology of participation was so strongly rooted in both the neighborhood leaders and the professional team, we put on exhibitions of what we felt was good quality housing, handed out information sheets of all sorts, and built *full-scale models* for the people to "try on." But the result was always the same: as soon as the architects showed a preference for a particular option, it became the choice of the leaders, and the residents would vote for it in almost unanimous fashion.

As construction went forward, however, it became easier to present the residents with alternatives and to get them to voice their opinions about specific problems, such as finish materials, colors, and type of windows. Although numerous decisions were made in this way, they are not of great importance. The crucial design decisions were made by the architects, although they were aware at every moment that they were acting on behalf of the residents.

A deep sense that we were making decisions for the residents because a more direct form of participation had proved to be impossible deeply colored our feelings toward the work. Perhaps it is here that one will find the real significance of the neighborhood's participation. We knew the people well, but still we had to make a constant effort to put ourselves in their place, to interpret their future needs, their desires, their most profound preferences—while trying always to see clearly through the veil of distortions that came from advertising, from deeply rooted cultural symbols, from the common desire for emulation. . . .

The discussion of the brick facades provides a simple example. We had two brick samples laid up, one with raked joints and the other with flush joints. We, although we expressed no preference, were inclined without doubt toward the second. (We preferred flush joints because they tended to hide de-

---

*This is in fact question number 14 from the interview form used in our thorough Housing Needs Investigation.

fects in construction.) But to our grief, the residents overwhelmingly chose raked joints because they are regularly used in luxury residential construction. When in doubt, the residents always adopted the solution which was the most familiar, the most orthodox. The first sketches we produced contained a clear architectural idea. Most of this remained on paper, and little by little we moved toward more neutral solutions with minimum risk and gave up the hope of producing anything of great architectural interest, at least from a formal point of view.

## An Evaluation

The economic and technical problems in a project of this scope are so limiting that a conclusion is forced: it is one thing to make architecture in the traditional sense of the word, it is another to build hundreds of dwellings. What quality of architecture can be achieved in the construction of mass housing? What kind of architecture can one get when participation is the watchword? In both cases, the answer from Orcasitas will always be less positive from architects than from sociologists and planners—*and much less positive than from the residents themselves.*

The authentic design innovations are to be found not inside where residents' conservative views prevailed, but outside the new dwellings. The open spaces on the site are no longer treated as something left over, as in speculative developments. These spaces are not simply the "negative" given by the form of the buildings, but have collective meaning and purpose in themselves. Here the participants gave the architects absolute control, much more so than in the buildings, and we were able to design with freedom.

The next and final phase of construction at Orcasitas will consist of 760 units. This has been designed by CETA in collaboration with a team of young architects designated by the Society of Architects. Here, without doubt, the question of architectural quality has a high priority. In any case, the same technical and economic constraints remain, as does the desire for the same quality of life exhibited by the first phase.

Let us close with a few words about the most recent form of participation. With the new Orcasitas substantially

complete, the residents today find themselves faced with the necessity to create new kinds of organizations to handle the numerous problems of management and maintenance of their dwellings, open spaces, and community facilities. In the occupied buildings, the residents have already organized themselves by entries, handling the problems that affect each group of apartments in this way. The next step will be to group the entries together in block associations that will take care of garbage collection, gardening, playground equipment, and so forth. At the top, bringing them all together will be the Neighborhood Association, which will continue to represent the neighborhood in its dealings with the government, and will handle responsibility for such community-wide functions as the central heating plant that services the entire neighborhood.

Two other initiatives should be noted. The residents themselves have organized a large furniture store in one of the new buildings where they sell at

very low prices. Having gotten their wish for terrazzo in all of the apartments, they have also created a company to handle the regular cleaning this material requires. In making the community work, just as in bringing it into existence, the participation of the residents is the central fact. The support of professionals—architects, planners, and lawyers—has given their participation *power*.

# Commentary on Bologna/Orcasitas/SAAL

Manuel Castells, Professor of Urban and Regional
Planning, University of California at Berkeley

## PARTICIPATION, POLITICS, AND SPATIAL INNOVATION

Community participation has generally been considered a kind of moral gadget to animate the popular soul of urban programs. The experiences of Bologna, Orcasitas, and the SAAL program, some of the most innovative cases of urban participation in Europe, present a very different picture. There, participation is the basic ingredient that makes urban innovation possible. But we are not dealing only with political resistance to urban change. Cities deteriorate socially, functionally, and physically because of the ultimately negative effects of urban development patterns dominated by private real estate interests and by the logic of self-affirming power of public bureaucracies. Unless there is a social force counterbalancing the power of capital and of the state, no sensitive planning, no large-scale architectural creativity can be implemented.

People's interests—expressed through participation—introduce three major new elements in the process of urban production:

1. They are going to be the users of new buildings, and therefore, their response is the ultimate *criterion* about the adequacy or inadequacy of any architectural project.
2. They are likely to judge the city in terms of use-value—rejecting the logic of exchange value. They question the right to decide what value is through the exercise of private economic power.
3. They are potentially able to mobilize and hence put pressure on decision-making bodies, thus creating alternative sources of legitimacy—constituencies for an alternative politics.

The combination of these elements makes it possible to counteract the prevailing structural trends in urban form. The three experiences related here are very different, but they all dramatically reverse the usual trends of market-dominated and bureaucratically managed development. These elements preserve and construct the city as a use-value oriented form that articulates design, culture, functions, and people. And they all are able to proceed in such a manner because they can rely on organized and mobilized popular support. To be sure, there are crucial differences between the three experiences, not only in terms of scope, but also because of the source of initiative in each program: the national government in Portugal, the local government in Bologna, a voluntary Neighborhood Association in Orcasitas. But whatever major distinctions could be made according to the levels of autonomy of popular participation, the common fact is that because of grassroots mobilization, some major urban changes could be carried out.

In Bologna, it was demonstrated that preservation need not necessarily imply gentrification, that public housing does not automatically mean new peripheral development, and that monuments include local culture, and, therefore, people. But to overcome the bitter resistance from real estate interests and Christian Democrats, the city not only had to back away from its original expropriation scheme, but to mobilize grassroots

support by using the neighborhood councils. These councils, originally thought of as mechanisms of administrative decentralization, became the sources of active social participation.

In Orcasitas, the long urban struggle that united neighbors *and* architects made it possible to break down the fatal cycle of shantytowns and speculative developments. The program, as described by Eduardo Leira in his remarkable article, really meant that urban value was granted to those who build the city with their effort, and not to those who own it with their property deeds. If we remember that this movement actually succeeded under a fascist dictatorship, we can measure the capacity of neighborhood struggles to modify the usual patterns of urban development.

In Portugal, the initiative of the revolutionary government provided the opportunity to combine limited resources with people's enthusiasm and technical assistance to produce more and better housing than had been built by public programs in 20 years of the former fascist government.* Furthermore, by articulating public policy to neighborhood control, Nuno Portas avoided the apparent contradiction between efficiency and democracy. Urban mobilization was used as a productive resource. Public policy was intended to stimulate neighborhood political organization. It is precisely this combination that presents the most promising perspective for new urban policies in an historical period of structural scarcity. In this sense, we will all be Portuguese for many years. And the example of Portugal should stimulate our thinking. Should we request massive public urban programs at a moment when fiscal austerity seems to be a necessity and when large sectors of *popular* public opinion are deeply frustrated by the bureaucratic waste of most public agencies? Dare we pull back and dig defensive trenches in our neighborhoods only to see people fighting each other for an increasingly shrunken piece of an increasingly disgusting cake? Or should we develop a new, offensive *public* policy, based on intelligence more than on public spending, relying on participation and self-management more than on social welfare? If this is the right direction, the SAAL experience, instead of being seen only as a deliberate attempt to cope with an urban emergency, could be a source of inspiration and an experimental demonstration of the "soft-model" of urban planning that may be the only feasible alternative to the planned shrinkage of the neoconservatives.

Community participation obviously gives rise to problems, for instance, the classical problem about the quality of the urban environment. Given the cultural conservatism of popular sectors, as is natural because of their limited exposure to new information, their control over design, may turn out to be a source of aesthetic setbacks, as Orcasitas shows. But, at the same time, this observation raises the old debate about who decides what is beauty. As Orcasitas' residents put it when I interviewed

---

*Charles Downs, *Community Organization and Urban Policy in Revolutionary Portugal,* unpublished Doctoral Dissertation, Department of City Planning, University of California, Berkeley, 1980.

them, "We have our own right to ugliness." That is, they wanted above all to be like other new housing developments in the city, not to feel like experimental objects. They wanted to be "normal," not to exchange the marginality of the shantytown for the marginality of the architectural vanguard. Although one can understand this position, one is also happy that Bologna's architects did not accept the residents' taste for grand modern buildings. To deepen the dilemma, we should recall that, while in Orcasitas the Neighborhood Association was the real power, in Bologna, City Hall always had control of crucial decisions. Should we conclude that there is a negative correlation between grassroots power and architectural innovation? Things are much more complex, particularly if we again consider the question of how aesthetic standards are produced and measured. But the tension is there and should be carefully considered in all participatory design efforts.

Another major issue is the difficult relationship between professional work and social involvement with the residents. Most architects and planners willing to get involved in participation do so for ideological and political reasons. Residents know it; that is why they trust their architects and planners so much. But, at the same time, residents develop such demands and such an idealistic vision of the "good professional" that architects cannot fulfill their expectations for long. And then the crisis comes, sometimes with the passion of betrayed love. I think it is essential to clearly differentiate the three roles—political, professional, advocate—to avoid dramatic misunderstandings. People do not blame architects for being paid. But they do reject the idea that high fees should be a major consideration in undertaking a needed project. In that sense, there is a kind of primitive moral of "good and evil" that marks all relationships between people and planners.

The crucial thing is for architects and planners to really understand people's specific *cultural* needs and to accept them and fight for them. When the Orcasitas people complain that architects do not spend enough time "drinking with the residents," it is not a purely psychological demand. It is because they know it is the only way for architects to understand the basic needs that they cannot verbalize, but that they feel strongly about. For instance, Orcasitas' residents built collectively, using their free time, a large, simple building to be used as the Neighborhood Association's headquarters. For years it was a place for people to have a warm shower, to obtain cheaper beer, to chat, to meet, to play. When the new housing development was being built, residents asked and the architects agreed, that their handmade headquarters building be preserved and used as a public center, so "future generations" would know what the shacks were like and the residents might remember their own history. (So history is not only the Bologna core, it is also Oscasitas' shacks.) And yet, in July, 1980, when I talked to Felix Lopez Rey—the popular leader of Orcasitas—he expressed his disappointment because, after all, the architects' plans called for demolition and the construction of a new civic center, where the Neighborhood Association would be given two rooms. It was a whole new conception of what a public place is about. Sometimes it is difficult for designers to stand by a commitment to a multidimensional city.

The main underlying question in citizen participation is, obviously, the characteristics of the political process. Significantly enough, the Orcasitas, Bologna, and SAAL articles do not address that issue. In fact, participation cannot be a "transmission belt." When it is, it does not produce the desired effects of fostering innovation or increasing satisfaction. And truly active par-

ticipation is not a simple process. It requires previously organized, autonomous mobilization. One cannot imagine a participation scheme from the top. The Scandinavian experience here is quite revealing: when people are invited to join a participatory structure set up by a housing authority, they only participate actively after a problem arises that mobilizes them.* They do not see any reason to get involved in a participatory process without having first experienced their capacity to change things when necessary.

To say that participation depends upon the relationship between autonomous social movements and the process of political representation is actually to pose the most complex and crucial problem of current public policy. My position is that only when there has been prior, autonomous mobilization is the ground ready for successful participation. Social movements come first. People are better organized and frequently readier to be mobilized than is generally thought by the political establishment, largely ignorant of the world beyond the walls of power. The problem is to accommodate such an organized popular presence within state institutions, to be willing to risk disruption and conflict. There is no ideological choice possible. If one wants to manage effectively within established parameters, never accept participation: it will be a source of unpredictable trouble. However, if one wants *to change the rules of the game,* autonomous grassroots mobilization and its expression within the institutional system are essential. Without such a new source of social power, the limits of spatial innovation will be rapidly reached. And this is the major contradiction faced by social change-oriented parties in advanced industrial societies. To foster the social change on which their legitimacy is based, they ought to accept the participation of emerging social movements such as neighborhood associations in the decision-making process. But by so doing, they undermine their monopoly of political power. I would like to have seen these contradictions discussed in the fascinating documents prepared for COLUMNS by Cervellati, Leira, and Portas. Portas should have talked about the impossible situation of being a left-socialist professional within a government torn between revolutionary officers, social democrats, and communists. Leira should have referred to why Felix Lopez Rey refused to become PCE (the Communist Party of Spain) alderman in the Madrid City Council so as not to be distanced from his neighborhood: such was his level of trust in the new left-wing local government. Cervellati should have talked a little bit about the speculation indulged in by working class landlords in the historic core of Bologna to the detriment of the very large student population of the city—this was one of the factors behind the student riot of 1977. And although Cervellati's presentation is an honest and thorough analysis of the experience, I think that the tensions between the Italian Communist Party's national strategy [to bring the property-owning middle class into the Party—EDITOR] and the urban innovations in Bologna should have been directly expressed.

It remains that the three experiences, published here for the first time, clearly show that there is a way out of the dilemma between free market urban barbarism and the public-sector bureaucratic takeover of the city. Cultural innovation, grassroots mobilization, and political change could produce a major leap forward to a new urban frontier—with the understanding that only if people control the city, will cities actually be built for people.

---

*Tom Miller, "Citizen Participation in Sweden," *International Journal of Urban and Regional Research,* **2**, 1981.

# Roanoke Design '79
# Roanoke, Virginia

In the 1960s, Marshall McLuhan predicted that TV would make us a "global village." Today, Charles Moore and urban designer Chad Floyd are demonstrating, with a slightly more modest reach, that interactive TV can recreate the town meeting in the modern city and add a missing dimension to urban planning and design.

Moore is accepted by the aestheticians in the profession for his historical allusions (Kingsmill, Virginia housing), pop inclusions (UC Santa Barbara Faculty Club), and spatial effusions (Burns House, Los Angeles). He has now turned his hand to designing at the larger scale of the city. The familiar wit and imagination remain, but are joined to a concern for common goals in the environment. As partner Chad Floyd

says, "If we work under intense public scrutiny and with massive popular participation (an idea that is usually anathema to architects), we might be able to set free the inertia of public opinion and produce designs that the broad spectrum of citizens would rise up and support . . . "

In the *Roanoke Design '79* process, public scrutiny and participation involved a storefront architects' office, close contact with a Citizens' Workshop (50 people representing Roanoke's community life), and a series of "Design-a-Thon" television shows. Carried live over WDBJ-TV, The Design-a-Thons encouraged viewers to phone in ideas for their city. Over 3000 people called, suggesting everything from improved street lighting, to elderly housing, to a major

department store. As the ideas came in, Moore made design sketches while Floyd discussed their cost and impact. Idea by idea, sketch by sketch, TV show by TV show, the people and their architects built up an image of their city as it should be.

To write his Commentary, Michael Appleby interviewed people in Roanoke. In his interviews, he found that citizen participation had occurred as never before in that city due to the use of television—and that the result was strong commitment to the revitalization of the downtown area. However, in the conclusion to his report, Chad Floyd refers to TV design as "Pandora's box" and acknowledges the potential for manipulation. However it goes, he says, its impact on the profession will be far-reaching.

# Giving Form in Prime Time

Chadwick Floyd AIA, Partner,
Moore Grover Harper, Essex, Connecticut

Television has been blamed for the disintegration of community in America because it isolates us from the public realm in a cocoon of privacy. It is ironic, therefore, that this demon television is increasingly drawing us together in ways that bear the marks of community—albeit an electronic one. The annual Super Bowl ritual is shared by no less than 100 million Americans, and for good old-fashioned foot stomping community interaction, we have the daily "Phil Donahue Show," in which collective participation is the device that nails a national audience to its seats.

As an architect engaged in designing the public realm, I have been exploring ways to harness the interactive potential of television to the task of shaping real communities. Enfranchising citizens by means of TV has seemed to me a proper way to design in a democracy, and one that results in solutions that "fit" better. Now, after completing a total of 16 hours of live "Design-a-Thon" programs in four American cities, I am convinced that this medium is even more productive than I had once hoped. Not only has it helped us reach richer solutions to urban design problems, it has demonstrated a power to strike the collective imagination of a community and focus disparate energies towards a common goal.

For me, television has become the midwife of a new kind of urban design, one that permits the architect to shed his unfortunate mantle of "detached professional" and assume a place in the center ring of urban affairs where, under the klieg light of public scrutiny, he can demystify the arcane rituals of design. Where we have been able to work in this way, the result has been a tremendous increase in popular concern for urban design, an enrichment of our work, and a strong commitment among citizens to realize the fruits of our common labors.

To date we have undertaken four projects using TV—in Dayton, Ohio, (with Lorenz and Williams), Roanoke, Virginia, Springfield, Massachusetts,

2. Chad Floyd explains downtown design before a live audience on WDBJ-TV.

and Watkins Glen, New York. Roanoke is recent enough to represent the state of the art, yet it provides us with the perspective necessary for evaluation. I will begin by reviewing the urban design challenge we faced in Roanoke and will go on to describe how we employed TV as one part of a broad participatory design program. Then we will look at how and why it worked, what questions it raised, and what its implications may be for the future.

## Roanoke Design '79

Roanoke is a city of about 100,000 people in the Shenandoah Valley of southwestern Virginia. It is the largest metropolitan area in the western half of the state and is noted mostly as a transportation center. Beginning as a depot for western migration in the early nineteenth century, Roanoke became in that century's last decade a burgeoning center for railroading, largely because of its proximity to rich West Virginia mining country. Much of the downtown was built in the prosperous 1890s, with the result that the city's old buildings are dressed in Victorian finery. Like many American cities, Roanoke began losing its vigor in the 1950s when its affluent

population departed for the suburbs and the suburban shopping malls made their inevitable appearance. The downward spiral has been widening ever since.

We were asked to help the city reverse this trend and to do so with maximum public involvement. Our first step was to form a multidisciplinary design team by bringing aboard Mel Levine of The American City Corporation who took charge of market research and development feasibility analysis. When we got to Roanoke, we found a city whose downtown was made up of two depressingly familiar components—and an unexpected opportunity. First was the *retail core,* down from three to two department stores and barely holding its own. Threatened by the imminent opening of a one million sf suburban mall and suffering from 50 percent vacancies on the traditional downtown shopping street, the retail core was in trouble.

Second was *urban renewal,* 12 acres of it, all prime downtown land, cleared 11 years earlier of aging buildings. Except for one parcel that had been developed in 1977, the urban renewal area was still a surface parking lot (is anyone surprised?).

The unexpected opportunity was the *Market District,* inexplicably saved from urban renewal, a bit dilapidated, but charming nevertheless—except for a collection of vintage mid-1960s, plexiglass-topped farmers' stalls that looked very out of place. A neo-Georgian market building sat at the middle of it all fronted by a formal Plaza and surrounded by sympathetic commercial structures that housed a variety of small shops selling everything from Appalachian handicrafts to "marital aids." The market district was unique, a gem in the rough, and we could see immediately that it would figure heavily in the revitalization of the downtown.

## Participatory Design: the Conventional Wisdom

In his instructions to us, City Manager Bern Ewert stressed that community consensus was needed. Consensus is a tall order. While we knew that television could extend our process into the community, we had no idea if it would result in consensus. And we knew that, to be effective, the TV work would need to be supported by a full range of conventional participatory techniques.

Probably the most important was our full-time presence in the city, which helped us become familiar with the physical context and social and development climate. During the fall of 1978, I, as project architect, and Trip Wyeth, my assistant, lived in Roanoke. Trip and I worked out of a downtown storefront office in order to make ourselves available to the public and vice versa. The store was on a well-trafficked street and a big window gave passers-by the chance to observe us at work at the drawing board or around the conference table. Local citizens felt free to stop in and talk about the city. Their ideas were written down, along with their names and phone numbers, and were put in the window where they attracted more citizens. We collected over 3000 ideas this way.

All of our design work and most of our meetings took place in the storefront office. An expansive table just inside the front door provided a neighborly place to exchange ideas. We made it high enough so that a person could come in and chat for a few minutes without feeling obliged to sit. We found that by opening this shop and

3. A view of downtown Roanoke as the designers found it.

sharing downtown retailers' chores such as sweeping the pavement, worrying about trash pickup, deciding whether to stay open Thursday nights, or debating how much to spend on Christmas window decorations, we got to know downtown businessmen pretty well and earned their respect. We also picked up a feel for the downtown shopping environment that was deeper and more visceral than we'd have derived from formal urban analysis alone.

The storefront linked us with the man on the street, but without consistent interchange. What gave us a firmer feel for the place was our Design Workshop, a group of 50 people selected by the City Council and the City Manager as representatives of the community. The workshop had three roles: first, it was our resource for community attitudes, second, it was our design review committee, and third—at the project's end—it was our lobbying agent. We held six workshops that ran the gamut of involvement techniques: a downtown walking tour, role-playing sessions, a collective plan drawing of the downtown, brainstorming sessions, and regular design review.

Another important group was the Steering Committee, convened by the City Manager to act as our official client. This was not representative, but numbered among its members the movers and shakers: bank presidents, major retailers, top businessmen, and civic leaders, whose support for projects of consequence is essential. The Steering Committee met regularly every other week to guide us and to reach decisions on key issues.

## Television: That Extra Something

The use of these conventional techniques comes as no surprise to veterans of participatory design projects. They offer a workable means for understanding community dynamics, but they are inadequate in themselves, however, because their scope is limited to a fraction of the community. At the urban design scale, they can operate only on a symbolic level. Their inability to create broad public involvement can translate into lack of public support when money must be raised and, worse, suspicion that deals are being made behind the scenes. The case for opening up the process to the entire public was irresistible. We argued that by doing this no one would be able to say that he had been kept uninformed about the project, or that decisions had been made behind his back—both complaints that had been heard widely before.

Our very first act in Roanoke was a press conference, and our last act in Roanoke was a press conference. We went on the radio at the drop of a hat, ingratiated ourselves with local talk show hosts, and took care always to be newsworthy. If anyone needed a dinner speaker at the last minute, we were the one. We took ads in papers, gave interviews to magazines, and set up "idea tables" on the street. What it all meant, I think, is that *Roanoke Design '79* became a real issue for the average citizen.

## Producing the "Design-a-Thons"

No other public forum offers so useful a variety of communication techniques as television. The modern lens can widen in one second to encompass a city district and in the next second can fill the screen with the picture of an architect's hand . . . designing. Still images, moving images, graphic representations, statistics, interviews, models, sound tracks, computer simulations—any conceivable combination can be chosen by the director from a console of display screens. The age of TV is upon us and waiting to be employed.

The biggest discussion group that can gather in one room is limited to about 300 by the size of a projected slide on a screen. Such a group is an implausible surrogate for a city of 100,000 and very questionable in its makeup, because any participant in a meeting has to be already interested enough to be willing to leave his home and sit among strangers in some auditorium or Council chamber, an unattractive prospect. For the average busy person, this is too demanding, unless he has strong personal

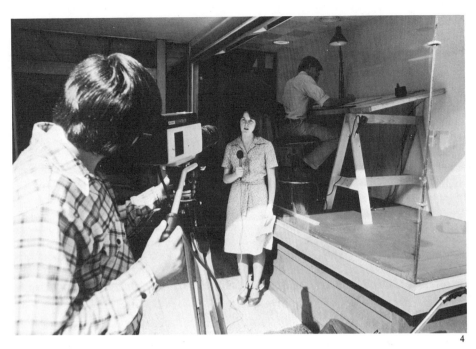

4

4. Trip Wyeth is local news as he works on downtown design in a shop window.

5. Members of the Design Workshop participate in an on-site discussion of future land use.

5

motives. But asking any of us to turn on our TV is not demanding. In the privacy and comfort of our own living room, where we can relax in the old lounge chair after a hard day's work, we are more willing to listen to unfamiliar material; it is in these familiar surroundings that new information is most likely to take hold. Virtually every household in Roanoke has a TV, so our design efforts could be elevated beyond the level of parochial interests to the higher plane of the public realm. Television offered symbolic creation of community through communication.

To design on TV, you first have to get time from a local station. Time is the absolute ruler of television. Paying for commercial time is out of the question, because the rates outstrip most urban design fees. But getting time is not as hard as one might think so long as the design project qualifies as "public affairs." The decision to produce a public affairs series in *commercial* prime time (the only way to attract a good audience) can be made by a local station without network involvement. All commercial stations are required by the FCC to provide public affairs programming, and most are hungry for lively ideas.

Our Roanoke station was WDBJ-TV, a CBS affiliate. Once WDBJ was committed to the series, we received from them the time, facilities, and production staff necessary to get the job done properly. Assigned to us was Ted Powers as executive producer and Ken Ferguson as producer/director. Ted and Ken led us through a crash course in television production and opened many creative doors that otherwise would have remained shut.

Producing television shows takes effort beyond normal professional services. Fortunately, the extra effort can be reduced significantly by modifying the design process at the outset to meet the special requirements of television production. For instance, design presentations for television must be painted, not drawn, and in brilliant hues that pack a wallop (also with flat paint that does not shine under the lights). Just as important, the image must be made up of sufficiently different values that separate clearly on black and white sets. Precious time and money can be wasted by first making conventional drawings and later translating them into artwork appropriate for television.

Our first step was to tour WDBJ's facilities and hear about the production goodies available to us there. Then we made a scale drawing of the studio with cutouts for the floor cameras, which we arranged in various locations. We found that the control room (and its director who selects images for broadcast out of all those available from the cameras) has a grab bag of technical aids. Primary among them is videotape, which is prerecorded and filed away for use on the show. Ken had driven around the downtown area with a video truck from which he taped every street and landmark that we might want to talk about.

After working with videotape, we learned that it can be used for any number of short sequences, such as lists of ideas, which can be inserted for breathing space on a live show. The director also has a computerized character generator that allows him to display titles on the screen. A slide chain (nothing more than a complicated-looking carousel projector) enables the director to show 35mm slides. A film projector allows him to show film. These are some of the basic building blocks; out of them we fashioned together some effective communication techniques. My own favorite is a lap dissolve from slide into sketch (previously registered to the slide) so that the viewer sees the future appear before his very eyes!

An essential element in our Roanoke presentation was the telephone installation. We wanted a bank of six phones, and we wanted to be able to talk with callers "live" on the air. The system Ken decided on was a very expensive rig with space-age microphones that at-tached to eyeglasses (which we all wore anyway). The system required a switchboard in the studio. An assistant director screened calls, taking the caller's name and address, and checking to see that the caller could articulate his idea well and that the subject fit the moment in the show. We made no attempt to select subject matter to support our views. We also decided against the conventional wisdom that dictates protection from profanity by a seven-second delay. In other words, we hung right out there. Our equipment was very expensive; its cost, $2000 per show, was assumed by local sponsors. In more recent projects, we have found that a simple speaker phone system works as well and runs only about $800 per show.

## Four TV Shows

We produced four prime-time, hour-long, live television shows, all of them different, each reflecting one phase of the design process, and about 30 days apart. The first was a forum for receiving ideas. The key here was to get viewers to call in. We wanted to get a dialogue going with citizens about the future of downtown. We and our consultants were on hand to answer technical questions, and we were encouraging, non-judgmental, and open to anything. There is no way to predict what suggestions you will receive in this kind of a format. One fellow called to say that the reason downtown Roanoke fails to

6. The City Manager's Steering Committee reviews preliminary plans and financial projections.

7. To solicit citizens' ideas, Floyd mans an urban design booth at a local street fair.

compete successfully with surburban retail centers is that suburban facilities provide climate control. He was followed by a lady who lamented that downtown has little to offer in the way of attractive green space. These concerns were combined on a later show in a proposal for a botanical garden as the centerpiece of development in the new downtown. It was received with enthusiasm by the community.

Calls were answered by a panel of six Design Workshop members. We had time to take about 12 calls on the air; the rest were written down on questionnaires by volunteers from our Workshop. These questionnaires were rushed by runners to a copy machine. Copies were distributed to the key players, who were thus kept informed of viewers' thoughts. Copies also went to the director, who punched them into the character generator for airing during the show. The *idea* thus became a hot potato, rushed from hand to hand, displayed on the character generator, scribbled onto stage flats, and thrust into the hands of the architects. The problem became: what to do with this

mounting flurry of ideas? How do you even hold the growing pile of sheets in your hand, much less look through them? We have found since that an anchor desk for the lead architect provides a central clearinghouse where questionnaires can be reviewed in the confusion of the hour.

The first show began with an airing of goals and a description of the project area followed by phone calls and on-camera interviews with key public figures. City Manager Bern Ewert lent his aegis of civic authority. Video tapes of downtown played over phone calls from viewers. Mel Levine (our economic consultant) discussed the feasibility of viewers' ideas. Charles Moore, our partner-in-charge, worked at a drafting table, sketching ideas as they were called in. The atmosphere of the studio for this prime-time hour (it followed Walter Cronkite on Thursday nights) was controlled chaos, somewhere between "Wide World of Sports" and a Jerry Lewis telethon. The director played his cameras over the studio from telephone operator to architect, to interview, to videotape of downtown, to

7. To solicit citizens' ideas, Floyd mans an urban design booth at a local street fair.

close-up of the architect's fingers making a sketch, to runners bringing in sheet after sheet of new ideas. The result was pure excitement, a sense of something going on, of communications lines being opened.

The second show was very different. Where the first had been a call for ideas in an open-ended format, the second was a presentation of planning concepts and was tightly orchestrated. We provided the director with a closed format matched to a running time and calibrated in segments of 15 seconds. Our presentations of development alternatives on a 40″ × 60″ map ran to no more than 4½ minutes each (the audience's maximum attention span, I am told). Planning alternatives were grouped into VW and Cadillac schemes, but pieces from each could be interchanged on the flat map to create alternate schemes on the spot. We also included numerous interviews with citizens and politicians.

A questionnaire was published in the

8. Urban design live! The photo sequence gives the flavor of a Roanoke Design-a-Thon.

9. Anchor man Chad Floyd introduces the issues and calls for participation.

12. Viewers are taken to the problem areas downtown. Here is the Market Building.

13. A lap dissolve transforms the scene into the architects' proposal.

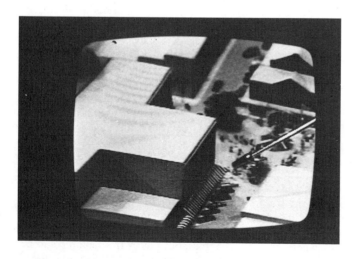

16. Close-ups of models helped viewers understand and comment on the design concepts.

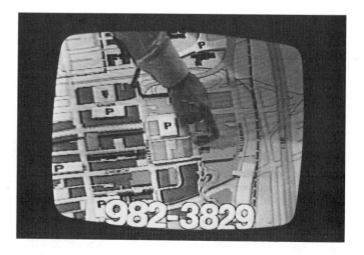

17. Models with movable parts enabled the architects to set up viewers' proposals.

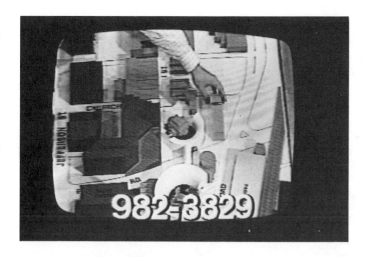

10. Models are used to describe alternative proposals. The call-in phone number appears on the viewer's screen regularly.

11. Design Workshop volunteers take calls from the public and rush ideas to the design desk.

14. The conversion of a large warehouse into a cultural center and the construction of a botanical garden on the vacant lot next door are suggested.

15. This interior sketch of the botanical garden was made for the TV show.

18. . . . And to present the cost implications of various options.

19. Charles Moore, who has been sketching viewers' ideas in front of the camera, joins Chad Floyd behind the downtown model to close the show.

Roanoke papers the same day as the show so that viewers could mark their preferences for proposals presented and mail them to our office. The 300 questionnaires that were returned gave us another sample of public opinion (it was not advertised as public balloting). After the shows, the Steering Committee made the final decisions, acting with the advice of the Citizens' Workshop, TV viewers, and comments from storefront visitors, as well as with market and other information prepared by us. The second show marked the end of planning and the start of architectural design.

The third round on TV a month later gave us our first chance to propose three-dimensional forms. Design concepts were presented by means of a nine-foot-long model of the downtown at a scale of $1'' = 50'$, fairly crudely made, but brightly painted. (The camera hides a multitude of sins, and crude craftsmanship is acceptable for a massing model.) Like the maps used on the second show, pieces of this model could be interchanged, and viewers were again invited to call in and comment. Afterwards, our Citizens' Workshop and Steering Committee gave their reactions, and we went on to refine the scheme for presentation on the final show.

The fourth and last show was a straightforward presentation of our completed scheme, along with a strategy for implementation, and a development cost schedule. Presentation was made with model and drawings. Cost information was superimposed by the character generator over a shot of each building as it was discussed. Telephone calls were not part of this show, but we welcomed a studio audience of persons who had participated in the development of the project.

**The Resulting Urban Design**

The final design reflects, I think, the uniqueness of its process. It is a pluralistic scheme. It accommodates a diversity of ideas and to some extent the messiness of the real world. It makes no attempt to neaten up reality by imposing an artificially unified formal structure. Rather, specific development sites have been identified, and proposals for them have been prepared that stand alone and are complete in themselves. We have dubbed this approach "Situa-

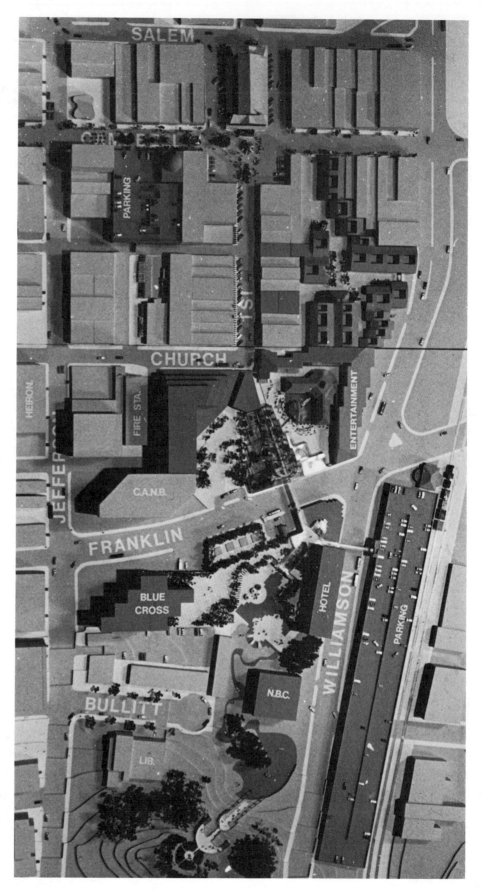

20. The final downtown revitalization plan. New office space and a new hotel are supported by cultural and entertainment complexes and a spectacular botanical garden, all tied together by landscaped malls and plazas.

tion Design," and we believe it provides a more feasible strategy than that offered by modernists of a decade or two ago who preferred the grand, and usually infeasible, concept. The trouble with the modernist approach was that it had to be implemented in its entirety to become functional. Since this never in memory happened, most of our cities now have a half-baked look. "Situation Design" more closely approaches the accretionary method by which cities grow and prosper.

Our development strategy (based in part on our market study) holds that downtown Roanoke will survive in the era of suburban malls only by becoming a complementary cultural and entertainment attraction. Downtown will not survive by competing with the malls. Specialty retail (in small amounts) designed to evoke Roanoke's Victorian railroad era was recommended (by a local resident), but new major retail was ruled out.

The Market District (downtown's true repository of history and atmosphere) is earmarked as the first-start project. It will be developed as a small specialty retail center under the direction of a central management entity. A plaza in front of the market building will become downtown's new "celebration zone." It will host a festival stage and new stalls where area farmers can sell their produce. The market building will be renovated as a sawdust-on-the-floor restaurant, and just across the plaza a spacious warehouse and adjacent lot will be developed as a cultural center. This center will include a science museum and planetarium, the historical society, a fine arts center, a repertory theater, and a parking garage.

Two other parking garages will be built under our development plan, the first on Campbell Avenue, the traditional retail street that has suffered vacancies recently. It will be tucked behind a row of historic buildings slated for revitalization as a retail mall. This mall will connect with Roanoke's most successful furniture store and bridge across the street to a department store. The third and largest garage proposed for the downtown area will be located within the urban renewal area. It will house cars displaced by future development of surface parking lots and will be linked to new office buildings and entertainment/tourist facilities. The latter are the essence of our urban design

scheme: they include a tourist hotel, a botanical garden, and an entertainment center. In the shaping of these all-important entertainment facilities, special attention was given to Roanoke's Centennial Celebration in 1982, our goal for project completion.

Each of these development components was suggested in some fashion by a viewer during one of the TV shows or by some other citizen in the course of our design process. We were in control of the forms the ideas took on. The community concurred strongly that downtown should be made into *the place to go.* This basic idea stimulated many others, so that by the time we got cooking, our problem became more one of sifting through mounting citizen suggestions than one of dreaming up ideas ourselves. Some suggestions were linked directly to potential developers, who were actively involved on the shows and were asked to give reasons for preferring one site over another. Involvement of developers throughout the planning process was important to us and sheds light, I think, on the logic behind the discreteness of our development proposals. We put ourselves in a situation in which, as urban designers, we had to answer to economic and political reality.

Prior to our involvement, public feeling on a couple of big planning issues had been badly misread by civic leaders, with serious conflicts as a result. We found ourselves resolving potential conflicts on TV with surprising ease. This was accomplished by getting the public directly involved in the debate, something that moved estimates of public opinion from conjecture to relative certainty. For example, our opinion sample, unscientific though it may have been, was helpful in resolving a raging dispute over a library building that was being threatened with transformation into a cultural center. Citizen questionnaires and calls revealed strong attachment to the library. So we found a central, less expensive, and more exciting home for the cultural center on the third show. It was among the first of the proposals to be implemented.

### From Design to Implementation

The final report for *Roanoke Design '79* was submitted to the City Council in April, 1979, and accepted two months later. Its presentation was not made by

the consultants, nor by the City Manager, nor by city staff, but rather by the citizens who worked on it: a group composed of housewives, a fireman, a schoolteacher, senior citizens, businessmen, a banker, and schoolchildren. After this group's presentation at an open City Council session, not a single word was raised in opposition—despite the plan's hefty price tag of $17 million in public investment.

Since then, many months have passed in a succession of large and small triumphs that happily show little sign of letting up. First, the Roanoke Garden Club implemented some small planting proposals. Then the Economic Development Administration awarded the City a $500,000 grant for the transportation center in one of our parking garages. The next good news came from HUD, which awarded a $4.5 million grant for the construction of two parking garages. Then Blue Cross—Blue Shield of Southwestern Virginia—having announced enthusiasm for one of the downtown sites on the third TV show— went forward with plans to build. Their new headquarters building is now under construction. The best and most impressive news came on Election Day, November 6, 1979, when Roanoke citizens overwhelmingly approved a bond issue that will pay for $15 million in public improvements—the majority of which originated in the development plan. Finally, $4 million has been raised from private citizens to pay for the new cultural center.

For a city with a population under 100,000 in a year of galloping inflation and imminent recession, that was not bad. To what degree it can be attributed to the use of TV is difficult to estimate, but what is certain is that together with the Citizens' Workshop, the storefront office, and the Steering Committee, our use of call-in television extended the range of our work from the intimate inclusion of a few to the involvement of many. This combination has quite obviously paid off.

In an interesting way, TV enlarged and dramatized what we were doing so that our work and even *we* were popularized. People paid attention to us. As architects, it was a bit hard at first to get used to this (harder still later to get over it). Working under intense public scrutiny made us evenhanded and objective. As a result, the public perceived us, rightfully I hope, as the public's professionals rather than as advocates of some interest group's viewpoint. This worked in our favor, because we gained in credibility and were not looked upon with the kind of cold suspicion with which we had been confronted in some other places. Television freed us from the chore of having constantly to present our credentials before the community, of having to argue our neutrality. It was a pleasure to be able to get on with the work at hand in a constructive atmosphere.

Our development plan's functional and social fit is as good at the macro-scale as our market, economic, and functional assessment of existing conditions. While I am confident enough of the accuracy of these estimates, what is more interesting, I think, is the micro-scale: how well does our design solution fit the person on the street, his hopes and dreams, his concerns? It is at this level that urban design so often breaks down, and it is here that an important benefit from participation lies. The population of a city is diverse. Desires within even a single social group are labyrinthine. Left to his own devices, a designer acting alone will be limited to his personal world view, his own way of making shapes, his own palette, his own childhood or other memories. For a city, the personal resource pool is enough. A city is a pluralistic tangle with more combinations and permutations than a single brain can sort out. The designer working alone needs help. Not in making form, that only he can do. He needs help knowing what he should be making forms about. In Roanoke, our citizen involvement helped us piece together a development program of sufficient richness to reflect the diversity of the city itself.

The use of television carried with it liabilities as well as benefits. One was the inescapable superficiality it imposed on treatment of all subjects, however complex. Even in an hour-long show, we found it impossible to delve deeply into the problems with which we were faced. We also worried that the television shows would give viewers the inaccurate impression that by calling in they could directly and instantly intervene in government decision-making processes, when in fact this was not true. The shows were our attempt at communication. We were in no position to make promises about what the City Council would decide to do. Were we unfairly raising hopes by creating the appear-

21. Architect as TV "personality." Where does it lead?

ance of action where it was not ours to offer? Was the tool too powerful?

The danger of this TV-aura credibility is that it can be misused, and it can be argued that our "Design-a-Thon" is a Pandora's box that never should have been opened. Within may reside a more serious evil than that familiar demon, lack of public interest: namely, the threat of manipulation. What part of our activities, one might ask, was selling and what part was participation? We certainly tried hard to make our proposals look good. In the hands of a dedicated charlatan the dazzling devices of modern television *could* be employed to perpetrate fraudulant schemes. Now that we have opened the box, we cannot escape these dilemmas, buy they are the same as those perennially debated by journalists: when does television report the news and when does it create the news? Innocence will not save us. The danger of manipulation by some should not prevent us from exploring this promising new technique.

Decisions may eventually be made on the spot by citizens in their own living rooms, as is already happening in Columbus, Ohio, where cable-TV viewers are connected to their station by means of a black box that registers binary votes for computer tabulation. The black box has yet to be employed for purposes other than station programming or public opinion polls, but its promise is clear: participatory TV may be the direction of democracy itself.

It remains for us to chart the way towards televised architecture, if we wish to. It may not be an easy passage. As

architects harness television to communicate directly with their community clients, they will have to add considerably to their inventory of professional skills. Like those unfortunate silent movie stars whose squeaky voices got them left by the wayside at the onset of talking pictures, some will not adapt well to the new medium. As John Sheahan, a CBS news correspondent, asked me in Roanoke, "Will architecture graduate schools have to offer courses in how to be an anchorman?"

But the big winner will be the public, those millions sitting even now at their TV sets flipping the dial searching for something worthwhile to watch. They may soon tune in to something really valuable: a chance to help shape their cities. As Bern Ewert, Roanoke's City Manager, pointed out to us in the afterglow of our work there: "Cities, like people, have spirits. That's gone unrecognized for too long by planners and architects. They usually try to solve urban problems with technical solutions. *Roanoke Design '79* tapped the inner spirit and ignited the imagination of our city. What was transmitted over the airwaves was not just a lot of technical information, but hope and optimism for the future. It moved our people in a powerful way."

# Commentary on Roanoke Design '79

Michael Appleby, Department of Urban and Regional
Planning, Virginia Polytechnic Institute & State
University

*"It's springtime in the mountains again.
Birds are flying, trees are flowerin', bees are a buzzin',
It's springtime in the mountains again."*

Jackie Wright, 1975

The feeling of optimism of this mountain song is especially applicable to the city of Roanoke these days. Another spectacular Appalachian spring has indeed arrived, but the difference this spring is a growing confidence in the downtown and an increasing commitment from local government to broad citizen involvement in neighborhood revitalization efforts. Among southern cities, these developments are unique, and *Roanoke Design '79* is related to both of them.

I initially brought a good deal of skepticism to the enterprise. I am trained as an urban and regional planner and have a considerable experience with citizen participation. I wondered whether *Design '79* would turn out to be a lot of show with little substantive effect. I also questioned whether the project had provided genuine participation opportunities to ordinary citizens.

I began my consideration of this experience with the question: Did *Roanoke Design '79* accomplish more than what would have occurred anyway? After all, the study area is charming, centrally located, and is highly accessible in an era of increasing transportation costs. Therefore, I decided to conduct a small survey of Roanoke residents. The intent was to gather a variety of perspectives on *Roanoke Design '79.*

It is now six months since the conclusion of *Design '79,* and it may be possible to identify its enduring effects. Care was taken that those interviewed had varied relationships to the effort. Those interviewed included:

1. The Director of Downtown Roanoke, Inc., an association of businessmen which was a sponsor of *Design '79.*
2. Bank finance officer—Acted as liaison between the planning consultants and the business community.
3. Television producer at WDBJ-TV who produced the "Design-A-Thon" programs.
4. Citizen activist and member of the Design Workshop committee.
5. Local minister, not involved with *Design '79.*
6. Physical planner, City of Roanoke—responsible for the first phase of the study and acted as coordinator and liaison with the consultants.

7–8. Two owners of stores in the study area.

Obviously, such a small sample is in no way representative of the Roanoke population as a whole. Nevertheless, it provides us with an impression of the continuing presence of *Design '79* in Roanoke.

The interviews were open-ended and included the following questions:

- What was your role with respect to *Roanoke Design '79?*

- In your opinion, what was most noteworthy about the project?
- What activities were the most successful in promoting citizen involvement? Least successful?
- Was your involvement worthwhile? Did it make a difference?
- In your opinion, what were the short-term effects of *Design '79?*
- Do you expect *Roanoke Design '79* to have a long-term influence on the future development of downtown Roanoke?

## SOME PROPOSITIONS ON PARTICIPATORY DESIGN

"Giving Form in Prime Time" offers us several propositions on the experience in Roanoke. The propositions are:

First:    As a result of *Roanoke Design '79,* a strong citizens' commitment to the revitalization of the downtown market area has emerged.

Second: Television has overcome the impossibility of involving vast numbers in the design process.

Third:    Citizen participation occurred in Roanoke as never before in that city.

The survey respondents can help evaluate these assertions.

*Is There Citizen Commitment to the Downtown Market Area?*

There is, indeed, considerable support for this proposition. Roanoke residents voted *for* a $15 million bond to refurbish the market area. Another $22 million in business investment is slated for the area. The merchants interviewed reported a significant increase in shoppers in the area. In addition, shop openings in recent months have exceeded shop closings in the downtown area by a two-to-one ratio. Moreover, nearly all who were interviewed spoke with optimism about the future of the market area and its ability to compete with a new giant mall on the suburban fringe. Several respondents (Businessman, Finance Officer, Planner) spoke convincingly of how previous attempts to obtain funding for redevelopment had failed, whereas the response to *Design '79* was altogether different. This time, there was a ground swell of public and private support for the area. There was no doubt for six of the eight interviewed that *Design '79* had turned things around for the market area. If the current indications of this commitment continue (as they appear to be doing), *Roanoke Design '79* will truly be an exemplary urban design effort.

*Is Television the Answer to Involving Vast Numbers of Apathetic Citizens?*

The television series played a major role in determining what was accomplished by *Roanoke Design '79.* Five of the six interviewed, who were both familiar with and active in the process, identified the television programs as the most effective mechanism for involving citizens in the design. Three of the six commented on the unique character of the Design-A-Thons. The programs created a public atmosphere.* They made concerns and issues highly visible and provided a vehicle for widely distributed "public ownership" of the planning process and its product. An economically viable downtown area was made into a believable dream. It's more important to understand how this was done than it is to speculate on whether television by itself is the answer to dilemmas of apathy among huge numbers of possible participants.

## Did the Participation Make a Difference?

Opinions vary as to whether citizen contributions made a difference. Thus, while one person questioned the control by the designers of the end product, several others indicated that with the storefront design office, the TV shows, the Design Workshop, and advisory committee, there was no question that there had been considerable direct citizen influence on what was proposed. In general, however, those interviewed perceived citizen participation to have been central in the *selection among possibilities* but not in the creation of unique new ideas never conceived of by the designers. It's hard to determine the extent to which the first television show was an important source of new ideas that influenced the final product. This is particularly true in *Design '79* where there were so many sources of citizen ideas and the number of citizen ideas contributed was so large. When asked which features of *Design '79* were the most successful in involving citizens and generating ideas, six of the eight suggested that it was hard to say because the methods were so complementary. When pressed on the question, the respondents rated the methods in the following way:

| Method | Most Effective for Involving Citizens and Generating New Ideas | Second Most Effective for Involving Citizens and Generating New Ideas |
|---|---|---|
| Television series | 7 | 0 |
| Storefront | 1 | 2 |
| Advisory Committee | 0 | 3 |
| No answer | 0 | 3 |
| **TOTAL** | 8 | 8 |

It is very clear that television was an essential ingredient of project success. Whether or not television is the answer to mass participation is difficult to evaluate definitively. It is certainly true that many more homes are reached by television than by conventional means of participation. And, the *potential* for interaction is impressive. Still, the normal viewer relationship with television is passive, and the notion of active response to a program in progress is foreign to most viewers. I suspect if a careful accounting of discrete ideas used in the proposed plan and a determination of the origin of those ideas was made, television respondents would not be the major source.

---

*The second TV show happened to be aired during one of the industry's rating periods. The official estimate of audience size was 54,000 adult viewers.—EDITOR

## Was the Citizen Influence Documented?

There is a paradox in the question of documentation of citizen influence. It was, after all, citizen support that passed the $15 million bond for the area. And some 3000 ideas were obtained from workshops, the storefront; and so forth. So while it is hard to point to the citizen origin of specific ideas in the plan or identify the extent to which important concepts were developed by citizens, it was, after all, citizen support that guaranteed public and private action.

## How Did *Roanoke Design '79* Make a Difference for the City?

I began with the question: Will *Roanoke Design '79* have an enduring impact on the development of the downtown? After interviewing eight Roanokers on the experience, I believe that the answer is a resounding *Yes!* There is ample evidence that *Roanoke Design '79* mobilized public interest in the downtown area, generated plausible solutions to its development problems, and put together a constituency that could *act* upon proposed development strategies. The results are impressive:

- A wide-ranging and substantial public and financial commitment to the area
- Significant private investment scheduled for the market district
- Federal grants for supporting parking structures
- Construction of a regional Blue Cross center in the area
- Immediate supportive responses from local civic clubs (beautification projects, etc.)
- Increased numbers of shoppers and visitors in the area and new shop openings
- A pervasive belief among Roanoke residents that redevelopment is workable and the area can become viable despite a proposed $100 million mall not far away

All of these accomplishments were noted repeatedly in the small survey (see Table 1).

Another result that is a little more difficult to substantiate in a definitive way is the growth of dialogue between the business community, citizens, and local government. Several of those interviewed mentioned an increasing collaboration between these groups. And the current interest of the city manager in developing systematic, in-depth citizen participation in a new *city-wide* neighborhood revitalization program is clearly a direct consequence of a highly successful experience with *Roanoke Design '79*. In fact, among local government staff, Chad Floyd and the project are viewed as ideal models of citizen participation, leadership, and method.

## OTHER ASPECTS OF *ROANOKE DESIGN '79*

This project was a success because of the variety of methods used, the development strategy, and the many roles played by the designers. First, there was a comprehensive set of participatory methods. A visible presence was established in the downtown area. An advisory group composed of influential business and civic leaders was established; workshops, guided tours, newspaper polls, and meeting upon meeting provided many avenues of involvement and considerable publicity. All of this contributed to a broad sense of participation and the emergence of a new, more confident public attitude toward the future of the city.

There was an additional aspect which, in my opinion, was of particular importance to the favorable outcome. Projects that require major resources, significant change, and public policy support must have strong advocates with ample economic and political resources. This was accomplished by *Roanoke Design '79* through the inclusion of developers, civic leaders, and representatives of financial institutions throughout the process.

The development strategy for the project was called *Situational Design*. This approach consists of many small, independent, but coordinated projects that make up a much larger whole. Aside from its inherent capability for responding to changing conditions, this approach also encourages the formation of strongly differentiated support groups, and is, therefore, an essential strategy for all hard-pressed local governments.

Another important ingredient in the project's success lies in the many roles the designers performed. While the designers alone were responsible for "shaping the shapes," there also were group facilitators, community organizers, public relations experts, small group-process designers, office managers, and media personalities. This made them accessible to great numbers of Roanokers, helped put a human face on the process, and contributed to the public "ownership" of both the process and its final proposals.

This was an exciting project. It has clearly affected the City of Roanoke. *Design '79* was well managed, innovative, highly visible, and ultimately very effective. For me, the most important contribution is the proof that the seemingly impossible task of turning around years of defeat and stagnation in the downtown of a southern mountain city *can* be accomplished.

**Table 1. Summary of responses to *Roanoke Design '79*.**

| | | | Questions | | | |
|---|---|---|---|---|---|---|
| Respondent | 1<br>Role in *Design '79* | 2<br>Most Noteworthy Aspect | 3<br>Most Successful Involvement Method | 4<br>Involvement Worthwhile | 5<br>Short-Term Effects | 6<br>Long-Term Effects |
| 1. Director, Business Association | Sponsor | TV | TV Advisory Committee | Yes | Public-Private cooperation | Revive downtown |
| 2. Bank Finance Officer | Liaison w/ *Design '79* | TV | TV Advisory Committee | Yes | Bond referendum | Confidence in downtown |
| 3. Television Producer | TV Producer for *Design '79* | — | — | — | Revived interest | — |
| 4. Citizen Activist | Member Advisory Committee | TV | TV Storefront | Yes | Bond | Revived downtown |
| 5. Local Minister | No role | — | TV | Yes/No | Revived interest | ? |
| 6. Physical Planner | Liaison Coordinator w/*Design '79* | TV | TV Storefront | Yes | Changes begun | New citizen participation efforts |
| 7. Businessperson | Observer | TV | Storefront | — | Increased sales | Viable downtown |
| 8. Businessperson | Observer | Storefront | Advisory Committee | — | Increased sales | Viable center |

# Atwells Avenue/Federal Hill Providence, Rhode Island

The Atwells Avenue project is a step in the revitalization of Federal Hill, an important Italian community in Providence, Rhode Island. After concentrating on citywide programs and participatory efforts involving national political agendas and mass mobilization, it is appropriate to come back to the ethnic neighborhood. This is the level where citizen involvement in environmental design usually begins. It is the place where every sympathetic architect or planner can be immediately useful. It carries, in this moment of the "new right"—with its budget slashing and its desire to return to the market's invisible hand—the hope of social democracy.

It is not without some irony, then, that the story of Atwells Avenue starts with a Republican Mayor looking for a stable constituency in a basically Democratic city and with a group of conservative homeowners and storeowners. Into the mix came an able economic development specialist—our first author, James Williams—and a batch of inventive architecture students from the Rhode Island School of Design. One initiative led to another (and this is really the moral of the story), and Federal Hill now boasts of new housing, better services, lively shops, and an active citizenry. Their latest achievement—designed with our second author, landscape architect Albert Veri—is the reconstruction of Atwells Avenue with new plazas, markets, fountains, and a grand entrance arch. In this example of urban design, the form expresses the residents' heritage, the content reflects the people's priorities, and the built reality proves their recently-gained political savvy and determination.

In his Commentary on Christopher Alexander's Mexicali project (see Part 2), landscape architect Karl Linn describes the positive aspects of cultural pluralism. He notes that "the deracinating concept of an American melting pot" no longer dominates US urban policy; communities are beginning to differentiate themselves. Linn calls for an ethnic renaissance. Atwells Avenue in Providence is evidence that communities, like individuals, now do assert the right to self-expression.

Albert Veri's project addresses itself to the problem of ethnic design in an Italian neighborhood. The line between ethnic expression and kitsch can be a thin one. Atwells Avenue narrowly avoids this danger—and is, in fact, both charming and enormously popular. It will be interesting to see where it leads.

# Federal Hill Revitalized

**James Williams, economic consultant**
**Barrington, Rhode Island**

Federal Hill is a strong, ethnic neighborhood in the city of Providence. It is geographically contiguous to downtown yet separated from it by Interstate 95. Federal Hill has been a haven for immigrants throughout the history of Providence, beginning with the Irish in the mid-nineteenth century. In the late 1800s the Irish were replaced by the ever-increasing numbers of Italians moving to Rhode Island. By 1930, 20 percent of the city's population was of Italian origin—more than 50,000 people, many of whom settled in the Federal Hill neighborhood.

By 1970, Federal Hill had been reduced to somewhere between 14,000 and 18,000 people, most of whom were still Italian. The outward migration was the result of the upward mobility of the Italian Americans who moved to the suburbs, as well as the highway construction project which gutted a large percentage of Federal Hill.

What remained of the Federal Hill neighborhood was marked generally by two- and three-story frame buildings housing from six to eight families. The main commercial street, Atwells Avenue, was a conglomeration of architectural styles, none particularly distinguished. Many stores were a bit frayed around the edges, and the streets that run off Atwells Avenue were crowded with triple-decker tenements, separated only by narrow alleyways. There were no front lawns to speak of and very few back-yards. In general there was a serious lack of green space throughout the neighborhood.

But an observer would miss the real essence of Federal Hill if he were to view only the physical characteristics. The Hill's heart and soul is not to be seen; it can only be felt. The sense of pride, the dedication to a way of life, and the joy of festivity and celebration make Federal Hill a very special place for its inhabitants. These almost spiritual attributes provide a quality of life that in many ways compensates for the lack of amenities. Even those people who have moved away from Federal Hill think of the Hill as their place of roots, their family home.

Approximately 70 percent of the people who patronize the stores along Atwells Avenue come from outside the neighborhood. Many people who moved from the Hill years ago come back on a daily or weekly basis to visit old friends or just to walk the streets and relive old memories. This strong level of identification with the Hill has been cited by many residents and businessmen as one of the primary reasons why Federal Hill should be able to attract people back to the homes and shops and narrow streets.

Urban renewal in the 1960s and early 1970s, following on the heels of the highway construction, destroyed Federal Hill's previously strong boundaries. These projects had a devastating impact, bulldozing dozens and dozens of homes. In addition, a number of "revitalization projects" proposed for the commercial corridor would have resulted in tearing down existing businesses and building a new shopping district, which one merchant characterized as an attempt to make Federal Hill "look like downtown Oakland." The community finally rallied against this invasion and began to organize a strong effort to "save the Hill." It was in this spirit of reaction that the Neighborhood Organization of Italian Americans (NOI) was formed.

## Community Organization Begins

In mid-1973, a trained community organizer was hired by NOI, and concurrently an urban renewal issue arose which aroused the interest of strong community leaders. Some homes along the western boundary of Federal Hill located at the top of a very steep hill were in danger of collapse due to the vibration caused by highway construction. The State Department of Transportation, working with the Providence Redevelopment Agency, moved to condemn all the buildings on the west side of Ridge Street. The Ridge Street neighbors, under the leadership of Lou Viti, banded together and met with the officials. They demanded that the Transportation Department build a retaining wall to keep the hill from breaking up. The issue was resolved in favor of the Federal Hill residents, and community organization now had a firm footing in Federal Hill.

In 1975, leaders from Federal Hill became aware of a home improvement program that had worked successfully in Hoboken, New Jersey. The Hoboken project was unique in that it used public grants to reduce interest rates on conventional home improvement loans from banks. This scheme had the advantage of making available about five times the amount of home improvement money that a revolving loan fund could produce. Community leaders and staff approached City officials with their idea for a home improvement program using Providence's CDBG funds. In addition, the neighborhood demanded the right to control the program and the funds. All of their demands were eventually met by the City, and an organization—New Homes for Federal Hill—was created with Lou Viti as President. He has done a tremendous job of restoring old houses and building new ones and of holding the ethnic community together.

The concept of a commercial revitalization program was first introduced on Federal Hill in late 1972 by the National Center for Urban Ethnic Affairs. A meeting of Federal Hill businessmen was organized, and an outside consultant discussed the need for merchant involvement in a revitalization program and suggested that $50,000 to $100,000 of private money would be necessary to begin. The reception was less than enthusiastic. Store owners replied that anyone who would expect to raise that kind of money among the Federal Hill merchants was naive at best.

During fall, 1974, NOI made a new attempt to revive the concept of neighborhood economic development on Federal Hill. A preliminary meeting was held to discuss submitting a proposal

2,3. Atwells Avenue is the heart of Providence's largest Italian community.

for federal funding. As a result, local store owners Tom DiPippo and Lom Gasbarro began walking Atwells Avenue, talking to merchants to interest them in revitalizing the long-dormant Merchants Association. A reorganization meeting was held in the basement of DiPippo's store, and a new slate of officers was elected. The election introduced a completely new and young element to the businessmen's Association. President Tom DiPippo, then in his mid-thirties, runs a music and jewelry store that has been on Atwells Avenue for three generations. Vice-president Lombard Gasbarro is a member of the third generation of Gasbarro's in the wine and liquor business in Providence. Secretary Norma Walsh is the daughter of Vincent Pantalone, the owner of Vincent's Specialty Shop, a long-established children's clothing shop. In January, 1977, almost 50 years to the day on which her father opened his store, she opened a separate clothing store of her own. Ben Renzi opened a new restaurant on the avenue just a few weeks prior to becoming Treasurer.

The newly elected officers of the Federal Hill Businessmen's Association realized the importance of neighborhood support and the need to do something that would rally Federal Hill. March 19 is the feast of St. Joseph, the patron saint of Italian-Americans. Gasbarro and DiPippo quickly set about creating a community-wide Saint Joseph's Day festival. Six neighborhood butchers agreed to act as statue bearers and a statue carriage was quickly put together. They had a red, white, and green line (the colors of the Italian flag) painted down the middle of Atwells Avenue for the day. Rhode Island School of Design students came to Federal Hill and painted the fire hydrants to look like *carabinieri,* Italian policemen. On the day of the festival (a Wednesday), nearly 12,000 people showed up to watch the procession down Atwells Avenue. The merchants provided sandwiches, wine, and cheese, and almost everyone was giving away *zeppole,* the traditional Italian festival pastry. This festival has since grown to the point where it attracts nearly 250,000 people during the three or four days of celebration each year.

## Neighborhood Revitalization

In April, 1975, the federal Office of Minority Business Enterprise, in conjunction with the Economic Development Administration, contracted with the Diocese of Providence to organize a neighborhood economic revitalization program in the neighborhood of Federal Hill. The National Center recommended a local staff consisting of an executive director, a planning assistant, and a clerical person. In addition, the Center called for a Neighborhood Economic Revitalization Commission. The underlying concept behind the Neighborhood Revitalization Commission was that community representatives—those

people who live in the neighborhood— have the same right to participate in the revitalization as do the local merchants. Not surprisingly, there was considerable antagonism between those two groups. Businesspeople felt that community people did not support them, did not like them, complained too much about prices, and did little to encourage the development of business within the neighborhood. Conversely, community residents tended to feel that merchants simply took from the neighborhood rather than giving to it—they came, made their money, moved to the suburbs, and cared little about the neighborhood. The Neighborhood Economic Revitalization Commission was one way to get these two groups to recognize that they each have a vested interest in the neighborhood, that they share common concerns, and that only by working together could they encourage redevelopment.

Around this same time, another event took place that was to affect greatly the future of Federal Hill: the election of Mayor Vincent A. Cianci, Jr., the first Italian-American Mayor of the City of Providence. Cianci was 33 years old at the time of his election, and he was determined to see highly visible, physical changes in the City. Within a week or two of taking office, Mayor Cianci met with representatives from the National Center for Urban Ethnic Affairs and prospective board members from the Providence Business Development Organization (PBDO). That meeting resulted in the Mayor's support for the principle of neighborhood economic revitalization and his agreement to allow PBDO to function as an autonomous neighborhood development corporation.

## PBDO: Economic and Physical Design

In June, 1975, I was hired by PBDO as its first executive director. My first job, after finding an office and hiring a staff, was to secure the confidence of Federal Hill's Merchants Association and to make that Association a strong organization within the overall Federal Hill community. In fall, 1976, arrangements were made with a design studio at the Rhode Island School of Design for students to survey the physical characteristics of the Atwells Avenue commercial corridor and prepare design studies for needed improvements. These students surveyed the Hill, took many photographs, and prepared a slide presentation pointing out the less-than-elegant appearance of the Hill—and opportunities for physical changes, including storefront redesign. This eventually became a City grant program with a 33 percent reimbursement for improvements merchants made to the facades and public areas of their businesses. The program has grown in scope, and now serves all of the City of Providence.

Another part of the RISD students' work centered around a new lighting system proposed by the City for Atwells Avenue. They found that the new lighting system would simply overlap the existing system and would not greatly improve the quality of the avenue. The students prepared their own plan, proposing a pedestrian lighting system that dramatically changed the feeling of the street. It was this proposal which initiated the overall physical improvement plan for Atwells Avenue.

Upon review of these student proposals, the Merchants Association agreed to establish a Neighborhood Economic Revitalization Commission (NERC) to work on this and other area improvements. The Commission was formed in January, 1976, and consisted of 12 members from the Merchants Association, six representatives from the Congress for Ethnic Neighborhood Organizations (the successor to NOI),

and two representatives, one lay and one clerical, from each of the three churches along Atwells Avenue.

Mayor Cianci played an extremely important role in helping to make the Commission work. If any group from Federal Hill made a request to the City for aid, he would ask community people what the businessmen thought of it, or if the businessmen made a request, he would say, "Have you taken this around to the Churches and to the community people? What do they feel about it?" His reasoning was sound. Whichever group he neglected would be envious, and would exploit and play up conflicts. It was, in fact, the realization that individually neither the community groups nor the Merchants Association was going to get the kind of commitment needed from City Hall that forced them to sit through the early meetings of the NERC and to build a single organization on Federal Hill.

## Financing the Design Proposals

At last serious discussions got underway between members of the business community and Mayor Cianci on how best to implement the design proposals made by the RISD students. During one of those meetings, Mayor Cianci committed himself to support any proposal for which the businessmen could find an appropriate funding source. When it became apparent that there was going to be a public works jobs bill passed by Congress during 1976, the businessmen returned to Mayor Cianci's office and asked if the City would submit a street revitalization plan to EDA. The Mayor agreed and instructed his planning of-

4. A parade drew crowds to the opening of the newly refurbished Atwells Avenue.

5. Atwells Avenue is only one of many citizen initiatives which are improving the Federal Hill area.

fice to work closely with Federal Hill.

It was in this atmosphere that NERC began planning the physical redevelopment of Atwells Avenue. PBDO hired two of the RISD students who had worked through the local Community Design Center on proposals for Federal Hill. These staff members began designing alternatives for Atwells Avenue revitalization, and at a June meeting of NERC their initial schemes were presented. Two planners from the City's Department of Planning and Urban Development also submitted design proposals to the Commission. The Revitalization Commission studied the designs as presented, suggested modifications, or in some cases total redesign, with the process continuing until a final design concept emerged. The process took eight weeks of regular meetings.

The final concept plan for Atwells Avenue proposed a pedestrian lighting system, a small park at the corner of Bond and Atwells Avenue with either a swimming pool or a boccie court, and the corner of Dean and Atwells Avenue was to be made into a Memorial Square. DePasquale Avenue was to be closed from Atwells Avenue to Spruce Street, and a fountain was proposed as the focus of an open air market. It was also decided that something should be done in front of each of the three churches to create piazzas along Atwells Avenue.

In September, outline plans were submitted to Mayor Cianci and enthusiastically approved. He instructed the Department of Planning and Urban Development to prepare an application for EDA funding and to contract with a landscape architect to complete the design. Representatives of the Commission asked the Mayor to allow them to hire their own professional so that they could continue to have maximum control of the process. As method of payment was an issue, the Neighborhood Commission proposed to interview only those who were willing to accept the job on a contingency basis. Under those conditions, the Mayor agreed to allow the Commission to select its own designer.

Four New England firms were recommended to the Commission. A meeting was held in October, 1976, in the basement of Holy Ghost Church to interview them. The local firm of Albert Veri Associates Landscape Architects was unanimously selected. The major reasons were Veri's obvious "simpatico"

Douglas Dalton

to participatory design process and his sensitivity to the ambiance of Federal Hill.

In December, EDA announced its list of approved projects. Providence received approval for its downtown development program, but not for the Atwells Avenue revitalization plan. At the next meeting of the Revitalization Commission, it was determined to aggressively seek local funding for the plan.

At the January, 1977 meeting of the Providence Redevelopment Agency, the Federal Hill Revitalization Commission again presented its street revitalization plan. The Agency approved the designs and instructed staff to prepare a redevelopment plan for the "Federal Hill East Project." On April 4, the Public Works Committee of Providence City Council held a public hearing on the Atwells Avenue Street Revitalization Plan. Nearly 150 residents and businessmen from Federal Hill attended the hearing, and the City Council Committee unanimously agreed to recommend financing of the project to the full Council. The first reading of that plan took place on April 17, with the second reading following on April 21. At both meetings the plan was unanimously ap-

6. New landscaping and street furniture on Atwells Avenue.

proved and adopted by City Council. At each of these meetings there were at least 50 to 75 Federal Hill residents.

The results on Federal Hill speak for themselves. There are currently over 140 businesses along Atwells Avenue. Of the 106 that were there in 1975, 95 remain. Of them, 88 have already been helped in some way by the project: storefront renovations, new signage, expansion, new product lines, and so forth. And the street revitalization scheme is now complete.

The most important factors in this success story were the following:

- The involvement of the merchants and neighborhood people throughout the process. The neighborhood people feel that it is their project, and, in point of fact, the control was always theirs.
- The commitment of a strong, aggressive Mayor.
- The availability of early funding to provide Federal Hill with a capable professional staff, RISD students' technical assistance, and finally a talented landscape architect.

# Tradition and Innovation

Albert Veri ASLA
Providence

Three factors can be identified which have led to the success of the Atwells Avenue revitalization plan:

1. An active mayor convinced that the strength of the city lay in the economic viability and environmental quality of its neighborhoods.
2. The neighborhood was organized. A team made up of 12 merchants and 12 residents (the Neighborhood Revitalization Commission), working with sensitive designers and experienced economic consultants from PBDO, did a thorough analysis and came up with a sound conceptual plan.
3. Funds for neighborhood revitalization became available when needed from new federal and state funding sources.

The following is a brief description of how, once the planning process was established, a conceptual plan approved, and priorities identified, we worked to prepare an urban design scheme that reflects the spirit of Atwells Avenue—the heart of the Italian neighborhood called Federal Hill.

7. Holy Ghost Plaza marks the end of the Atwells Avenue project.

Douglas Dalton

305

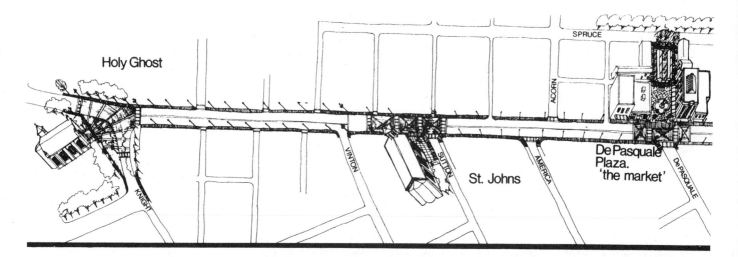

Holy Ghost

SPRUCE

ACORN

VINTON

SUTTON

St. Johns

AMERICA

DePasquale Plaza. 'the market'

DePASQUALE

KNIGHT

James Williams, then Executive Director of PBDO, and his staff of recent Rhode Island School of Design graduates began the task of preparing a conceptual design in 1976. These young and enthusiastic landscape architects, architects, and graphic designers devoted enormous time and energy to Federal Hill. They were invaluable in gathering base data, and in helping to organize the community. Their original plan emphasized lighting design, identified important intersections (that we later planned as major nodes along the avenue), and established the design concept of DePasquale Plaza as a pushcart marketplace with a central fountain.

At the time we were selected to carry forward this design effort, the decision was made to seek funding through the Economic Development Administration (EDA). Given only a month to complete the application, we began with a review of the concept plan and held many meetings with the Neighborhood Revitalization Commission, for it was understood that once the application to the EDA was approved by that federal agency, major changes to the design plan and scope of work would not be allowed.

Many late evening meetings were held and design alternatives discussed, including bus shelters, paving materials, maintenance, and the new image of the neighborhood. Inventory and analysis of the neighborhood was fast-paced, and the fantastic input from the neighborhood participants permitted us to file the application on time. The final plans emphasized five major areas:

1. The entrance from downtown Provi-

Douglas Dalton

9

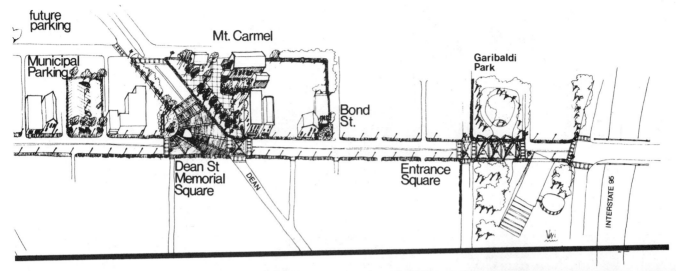

8

dence. Should there be a sign that says: "You are now entering Federal Hill," or should the image of the neighborhood be that sign? A triumphal arch was recalled to be a feature of many Italian cities. This suggestion from a neighborhood resident resulted in the design and construction of a magnificent archway over the road.

2. The intersection of Dean Street and Atwells Avenue, flanked by the Mount Carmel Church. This intersection brought a good deal of traffic into the Atwells Avenue neighborhood. These potential shoppers would be entering by "the side door." Recently this intersection was renamed in honor of the pastor of Mt. Carmel Church who did so much to improve the quality of life on Federal Hill.

3. DePasquale Plaza. A street approximately 300 feet long was to be closed and turned into a marketplace. Atwells Avenue's past was brought to light when some of the Commission members spoke of the pushcart merchants and sidewalk vendors who once gave character to the area. Some first and second generation Italian Americans apparently still were ready either on a full-time or part-time basis to sell their wares in a traditional street marketplace. The Capelli building on the corner of DePasquale Plaza and Atwells Avenue had been vacant for almost 20 years. Its importance on the avenue was significant since it was the only four-story building (most are two and three stories). A group of the merchants banded together,

10

forming a corporation to purchase the building and rehabilitate it to make the plaza work. In spring, 1980, the building was officially dedicated and now houses shops, law offices, and luxury apartments.

4. St. John's Plaza. Although less prominent than the other two churches (since it was off to one side of the avenue and was not a focal point), through the use of lighting, street paving, sidewalk paving, and landscaping, the character of this area became strengthened—and reflected the architectural style of the church. The church is now proceed-

8. The revitalization plan was a collaborative effort between designer and residents.

9,10. Two views of DePasquale Plaza with its new shops and offices. On market days, the frames become colorful stalls for pushcarts.

307

ON THIS LOCATION STOOD
THE FRUIT STAND OF
FRANCESCO GAROFALO
AND
HIS SONS LEO AND JOSEPH
CIRCA 1930 to 1960
"THIS WAS THEIR LIFE"
LEONARD A GAROFALO
1979

11

12

11. Goods for sale and people begin to appear on Atwells Avenue in greater numbers.

12. A reminder of neighborhood history.

13. Old traditions revived.

14. Dean Street Memorial Square with Mount Carmel Church in the background. A program of public events complements the physical revitalization.

13

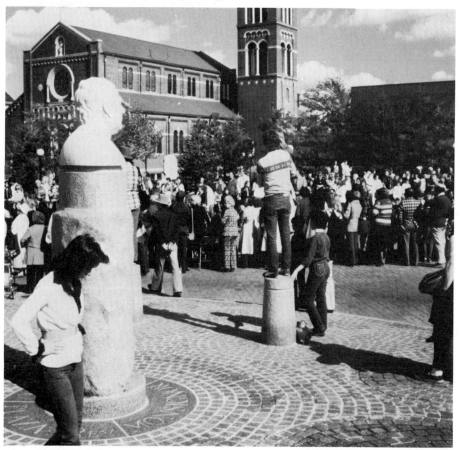

14

ing to deed to the city the area between the church and the street which will be made into a public plaza.

5. Holy Ghost Plaza. The project area terminates in Holy Ghost Plaza at the intersection of Knight Street and Atwells Avenue. Just before arriving at Holy Ghost Plaza, Atwells Avenue takes a slight turn to the left, enough to focus attention on the axis of this Florentine-style church and its new plaza.

## Participatory Urban Design

The design theme was established early in the meetings with the merchants. They wanted the neighborhood to speak for itself, to express the Italian-American heritage in art, culture, and economic contributions to America. Everyone has his own idea of what is art, and the Commission and the other neighborhood participants were not exceptions. Selection of materials and design elements such as lights, benches, bus shelters, trash cans, flower planters, and the like had to be selected by consensus and integrated into an overall design that was aesthetically appealing and in keeping with the neighborhood and its priorities.

Highly charged meetings were held to establish the design theme. Our assumptions and preferences and those of the participating merchants and residents were laid out clearly at the first meeting. We put together a slide presentation showing examples of revitalization projects in other areas, photographs from books and magazines, streetscapes from Italy, and materials and design details successfully used elsewhere in Rhode Island and New England. The presentation was quite long, but when it was over the butcher could talk to the clothing salesman, the architect to the resident. We had a common vocabulary.

At the next meetings, what had already been discussed was translated into thematic concepts and approved. Now all of the materials, design elements, and details could be selected on the basis of an accepted design theme. There was a common understanding, and ideas were encouraged. In fact, many of the best parts of the new Atwells Avenue began as comments from NERC members. The excitement of designing one's own environment within a realistic planning process was felt by all those involved.

We were constantly awash with input—mostly because we sought it. We encouraged participation and always mentioned in our presentations how a particular comment influenced our design or selection of materials. We also discussed why certain ideas would not work because of cost or incompatibility with the overall design. The difficulty the architect faces with this approach is being able to keep the overall design coherent—and equitable. Everyone wants his portion of the street to be well lighted, have a bench with no vagrants, and a trash can someone else empties. Some want trees, others absolutely no trees. Still others want bus shelters to encourage patrons (but not located in front of their stores). When the five nodes received the greatest embellishment and the most expensive lights, the areas between felt slighted. . . .

Numerous sketches and copies of the overall design plan had been distributed throughout the neighborhood. The Merchants Association and the NERC made sure each storefront displayed a copy of the proposed plan.

### Maintenance Problems

As final plans and specifications were being drawn up, questions came up about who would maintain the project area once it was completed. The architects had previously met with the various city agencies, including Parks and Recreation and Public Works, whose responsibility it was to take care of the City's public areas. As in all cities, these agencies are underfunded and understaffed, so to take on even a greater responsibility was questionable.

Who would replace the lights that were burned out? Who would empty the trash cans? Who would sweep the streets? Who would turn on the fountain? After spending nearly $3 million, would we allow this street to deteriorate due to lack of maintenance? (In Providence, as in other cities, the local utility company will supply electricity and maintain streetlights only if it is their standard light. When a different fixture and pole is used, the City must agree to assume all maintenance and repair costs and responsibilities.)

The three churches were the first to respond. Holy Ghost, Mount Carmel, and St. John's Church submitted written agreements to the Redevelopment

15

16

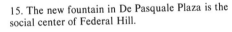

17

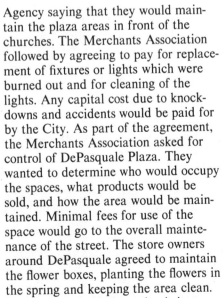

18

15. The new fountain in De Pasquale Plaza is the social center of Federal Hill.

16–18. Views along the avenue.

Agency saying that they would maintain the plaza areas in front of the churches. The Merchants Association followed by agreeing to pay for replacement of fixtures or lights which were burned out and for cleaning of the lights. Any capital cost due to knockdowns and accidents would be paid for by the City. As part of the agreement, the Merchants Association asked for control of DePasquale Plaza. They wanted to determine who would occupy the spaces, what products would be sold, and how the area would be maintained. Minimal fees for use of the space would go to the overall maintenance of the street. The store owners around DePasquale agreed to maintain the flower boxes, planting the flowers in the spring and keeping the area clean.

Although the construction is just completed, the private side of the equation is already beginning to explode.

Many storefront improvements have already been completed under the Mayor's Office of Community Development/Storefront Improvement Program. Marginal businesses have been renovated or taken over by more enthusiastic and enterprising businessmen. Atwells Avenue on Federal Hill is flourishing. The planning process used here does not minimize the importance of the designer, but I believe it puts him in his proper position. The revitalization of our nation's neighborhoods, indeed our cities as a whole, is a complicated matter. And it requires initiative from the neighborhood, professional assistance from landscape architects, architects, and planners, and most important, support from city hall.

# Southwest Corridor Project Boston, Massachusetts

The Southwest Corridor project started as a plan to build another link in the Interstate Highway system—a link which would have wiped out a number of Boston's proud neighborhoods. After years of protest followed by participation, the Southwest Corridor Project has entered the implementation stage. But today there is no highway mentioned in the plan. Instead, it stresses mass transit, job development, community revitalization, and an extension of Boston's famous "emerald necklace" of parks.

This is a massive undertaking, the subject of the biggest US Urban Transportation Grant ever. In the words of original project director Anthony Pangaro, it is:

Far bigger than the filling of the Back Bay in the last century . . . eight miles long and as much as half a mile wide, six years in the planning, the redevelopment of the Southwest Corridor is the largest single construction project in the history of Boston. . . . With a strong, productive role played by the neighborhoods involved, the project is a one billion dollar investment in Boston's future.

While the debate over the distribution of power between the public agency and the people who live in the Corridor is not likely ever to come to an end, participation there surely is. There are public committees and private committees, Section planning councils and Station Area Task Forces, and ad-hoc groups of all kinds pressing for educational facilities, better playgrounds, and low-cost housing. They work with over 30 consulting firms—geologists, engineers, architects, urban designers, and traffic planners.

Our group author, WFEM—Wallace, Floyd, Ellenzweig, Moore, Inc. (with especial thanks to Tom Nally)—is the consultant responsible for citizen participation in this sprawling and complex project. In addition to coordinating existing committees and organizing new ones, WFEM has developed a barrage of

techniques for informing and involving the people in the Corridor. Theirs is probably the largest effort of its kind in the US. And it works.

Tunney Lee, in his Commentary on John Sharratt's work (see Part 2), points to the key role of the highway protests of the 1960s in improving Boston's urban redevelopment climate and to the role played by advocacy groups like Urban Planning Aid in making those protests effective. Chuck Turner, a former organizer for the neighborhoods seeking to

control the Southwest Corridor plan, develops this theme in his Commentary and points out that the right to participate was not freely given; it had to be won. Turner's history of citizen involvement in the Southwest Corridor is also a demonstration of Manuel Castells' argument (see Commentary on Orcasitas in Part 3) that mobilization must precede participation. Architecture can play a role in mobilization, too, be giving people a vision of the urban environment as it ought to be.

*A joint venture of two engineering firms, Kaiser Engineers, Inc./Fay, Spofford and Thorndike, Inc. (KE/FST), is the MBTA's prime contractor for coordination of the project. KE/FST is responsible for overall project coordination, the preparation of engineering directives, and the design of Corridor-wide systems. They are also responsible for the review of subcontractor work and the work of the three section engineering firms.

Four consultants form the Urban Design Group and work as subcontractors to KE/FST. Each of these consultant firms is responsible for a portion of the overall work: Stull Associates, Inc. is responsible for urban design and coordinating the station architecture, Roy Mann Associates Inc. is coordinating landscape architecture, Charles C.

Hilgenhurst and Associates is responsible for coordinating land development, and Wallace, Floyd, Ellenzweig, Moore, Inc. is coordinating planning and community liaison activities.

Each geographic section of the Corridor is under the design responsibility of an engineering firm reporting directly to the MBTA: KE/FST for Section I; PRC Harris for Section II; and Howard, Needles, Tammen, and Bergendoff for Section III. The transit stations in each section are designed by individual architectural firms that are subcontractors to these engineering firms. Landscape architects have been contracted to prepare landscape designs for each section. Most station architects are associated with or are in joint venture with minority-owned firms, a reflection of the Corridor's equal opportunity policy.

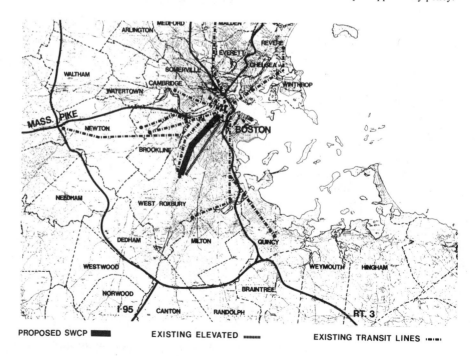

PROPOSED SWCP ▬▬▬    EXISTING ELEVATED ▪▪▪▪▪    EXISTING TRANSIT LINES ▪—▪—▪

# Managing Citizen Participation

Wallace, Floyd, Ellenzweig, Moore, Inc.
Cambridge, Massachusetts

Boston's Southwest Corridor Project (SWCP) involves the design, engineering, and construction of a major transportation system and the redevelopment of 120 acres of urban land. This vast swath cut through the city was originally to be a link in the Interstate Highway System. As a result of 15 years of active public participation, the project has taken a very different direction. It now calls for a new Massachusetts Bay Transportation Authority (MBTA) rapid transit line and nine new stations, reconstruction of Amtrak and commuter rail track and stations, 23 bridges, and an arterial street.

An integral part of the new SWCP is the neighborhood redevelopment that will occur along the Corridor. The projects that are already completed or are in the late planning stages include: two high schools, an occupational resource center, over 500 units of housing, a major mixed-use commercial complex, a new 5000-student community college, and a number of neighborhood-oriented retail facilities. Industrial development in the project's Crosstown Industrial Park will bring over 300 new jobs to the community, with more expected over the next few years. A new park will run the length of the Corridor and will include both active and passive recreation areas, a bicycle path, and a link to Boston's "Emerald Necklace" designed by Frederick Law Olmsted. The new Or-

This paper was prepared with the assistance of the MBTA staff, members of the several consulting firms at work on the project, and community residents, including the Station Area Task Force moderators. We gratefully acknowledge the help and insights of all the participants in the SWCP.

WALLACE, FLOYD, ELLENZWEIG, MOORE, INC.

Harry Ellenzweig, Principal in charge
Jacquelyn Hall, Associate, Project Manager
Thomas Nally, Planner, Assistant Project
    Manager
Lydia Mercado, Planner
Cheryl Myers, Planner
Wendy Landman, Planner
L. Duane Jackson, Planner
Dana Nottingham, Planner
Mauricio Gaston, Editor/Graphic Designer
Elizabeth DeMille, Research

ange Line and rail services, now in construction, are expected to be in operation by 1986, and will carry approximately 120,000 passengers each day. The public and private investment expected in the Corridor is on the order of $1 billion—making it easily Boston's largest public works project.

The 1948 Master Highway Plan for eastern Massachusetts called for the construction of I-95, an eight-lane, elevated highway connecting Route 128 to the proposed Inner Belt around downtown. Hundreds of thousands of vehicles were to have traveled on these highways each day through the densely populated communities of Somerville, Cambridge, and southwestern Boston. During the late 1960s, the Massachusetts Department of Public Works began the relocation of families and the demolition of the homes and businesses that stood in the path of the highway.

The destruction of neighborhoods and the spectre of the highway catalyzed community action. Urban and suburban residents organized through existing groups and formed new ones such as "Save Our Cities" and "Operation Stop." Recognizing their common interest, many joined the "Coalition to Stop I-95," later the Southwest Corridor Coalition. Community participation at this stage focused primarily on the negative effects of the planned highway. The battle cry was "Stop I-95—People Before Highways." Residents and businesspeople met in neighborhood caucuses and citywide meetings to develop strategies. Community groups used rallies, teach-ins, and wall posters to spread information, generate community involvement, and influence state and local officials.

In 1970, Governor Francis W. Sargent responded by declaring a moratorium on highway construction within the ring made by Route 128. He commissioned a regional study to evaluate transportation needs and propose alternative strategies. In 1972, as a result of the study's recommendations and strong community feeling, Governor Sargent

cancelled plans to build I-95 into Boston. The Governor recommended that the land already cleared through southwest Boston be used for the relocation of the elevated Orange Line and relocation of the railroad. The building of a new rapid transit line and the redevelopment of the highway right-of-way was made a top priority of State government and the office of the Southwest Corridor Coordinator was established by the Governor to guide planning and implementation. Community support for the new proposal was nearly unanimous.

The next step in the process was the securing of federal funding for the project. It took two years of intense negotiation between the federal Department of Transportation and Governor Sargent

and his successor, Michael Dukakis, to get the money earmarked for construction of I-95 transferred to the Urban Mass Transportation Administration (UMTA) for the building of the new Orange Line. This return of funds to the Highway Trust Fund and the withdrawal of general funds by UMTA was the first of its kind and marks an important change in federal policies governing urban transportation. No longer would highway building be the sole answer to urban transportation problems. The Boston case played a leading role in changing the course of American transportation planning.

Because the SWCP is federally funded, an Environmental Impact Statement (EIS) was required to determine the environmental, social, and economic effects of the proposed project.

The community played a major role in the environmental review process. The Southwest Corridor Coordinator's office held many formal, Corridor-wide public meetings and legally required public hearings to discuss major issues surrounding the project. More importantly, the Coordinator's office created neighborhood committees, smaller groups to discuss criteria for proposed transit stations, the profile of the transit line (whether above, below, or partially below ground level), and the precise alignment of the new track bed. Temporary and permanent reuse of community land and the design of the transit system were thoroughly discussed in these Community Task Forces.

The most significant commitment made to the community by local, state, and federal officials is embodied in a 1973 "Memorandum of Agreement." This agreement requires that all plans be reviewed publicly before adoption and that "10 percent of the planning and 5 percent (in dollar terms) of the basic design contracts let for the Southwest Corridor be designated for community participation and technical assistance . . ." (Final Southwest Corridor Environmental Impact Statement, Appendix). This document was signed by public officials and by numerous representatives of community organizations, many of which had been active in the Stop I-95 movement. These groups were to play key roles in the SWCP initial design phase, in the choice of development options, and in the formulation of a final Southwest Corridor Development Plan.

## The Neighborhoods

The Southwest Corridor cuts through a diverse cross section of Boston neighborhoods. For planning and design purposes, the Corridor's length has been divided into three subareas or *sections*. As far as possible, the geographical boundaries of the sections follow those of the major communities in the Corridor: the South End, Roxbury, and Jamaica Plain. In the past, railroad tracks and parks have functioned as neighborhood boundaries and the three communities have remained distinct, reflecting differences in population density, income, race, and overall living conditions. Each section contains a different set of community problems and attitudes towards the project, and different hopes for SWCP commun-

## COMMUNITY PARTICIPATION IN BOSTON'S SOUTHWEST CORRIDOR PROJECT

Southwest Corridor Chronology

### 1948
Massachusetts Department of Public Works issues a Master Highway Plan that includes an Inner Belt expressway and a link to Interstate 95 (I-95) South, called the Southwest Expressway.

### 1956
The Bureau of Public Roads and Interstate Highway Trust Fund is created by Congress. This provides the necessary funding to implement the Massachusetts Master Highway Plan.

### 1966–1970
Land is condemned and cleared in the South End, Roxbury, and Jamaica Plain for the Southwest Expressway. Organized citizen protest increases.

### 1970
Governor Francis Sargent declares a moratorium on the design and construction of all Boston area highways inside Route 128.

### 1971–1972
The Boston Transportation Planning Review (BTPR), a comprehensive transportation study for the metropolitan area, is conducted.

### 1972
Plans for the Southwest Expressway are cancelled by Governor Sargent.

### 1973
Governor Sargent appoints Anthony Pangaro as Southwest Corridor Development Coordinator and establishes a Southwest Corridor Project Office. Public meeting for discussion of the reuse of the Corridor begin. The Southwest Corridor Memorandum of Agreement is signed, formalizing a commitment to make community participation an integral part of Southwest Corridor Development.

### 1974
At Governor Michael Dukakis' re-

quest, the Southwest Corridor Project becomes the first US transit project funded with federal highway funds.

### 1976
Environmental impact analysis completed for the Southwest Corridor transit project. Public hearings held. Community members and public agencies help the MBTA interview and select consultants for design and engineering.

### 1977–1978
Draft and Final Environmental Impact Statement completed.

### 1977
Phase I SWCP design and engineering begins. Architectural and urban design criteria are decided on a neighborhood-by-neighborhood basis in public meetings.

### 1978
City of Boston begins industrial park construction in SWCP area.

### 1978–1979
UMTA formally announces $680 million total in federal grants and local funds for the SWCP. Phase II station and landscape design begins. Community is organized in Station Area Task Forces (SATFs) to participate in station and landscape design and adjacent development. SWCP Educational Training Program begins. Contracts for excavation, demolition, site preparation, and utility relocation are completed.

### 1980
SWCP station and landscape final design is completed. Construction begins.

### 1982
Construction of transit stations to begin.

### 1985
Orange Line scheduled to open. Amtrak operations and commuter service on the newly reconstructed railroad to begin.

### 1986
Scheduled date for completion of SWCP construction.

ity development.

Section I of the Corridor includes the inner-city neighborhoods of Back Bay, South End, St. Botolph, and the Fenway, and contains major institutions such as the John Hancock Building and the Prudential Center, the Christian Science complex, and Symphony Hall. A new hotel and shopping complex called Copley Place is currently being planned for a site adjacent to the Corridor at Back Bay Station.

Section I has the greatest ethnic, social, and economic diversity of all the Corridor communities. During the past 10 years, the central location and attractive row houses of the South End have attracted many young middle and upper class families to an area that was traditionally populated by poor and working class families. The South End has historically housed blacks as well as many new immigrants to the United States. Large groups of Chinese, Syrian, Lebanese, and Hispanic people still live there today. The disparity in life styles between the new upper income residents of the South End and their old neighbors has led to neighborhood tensions which have surfaced in discussions about SWCP design and programming decisions.

Section II includes the Lower Roxbury, Highland Park, and Mission Hill communities of Roxbury. The majority of residents are black and Hispanic and have lower incomes and higher rates of unemployment than do residents in other SWCP communities. This section has four large public housing projects along the SWCP right-of-way. These projects have special recreation space needs because of the large numbers of children and young adults. Section II suffered the most when the I-95 route was cleared. In Lower Roxbury and Mission Hill, more than 62 acres of land were taken for the proposed highway, and although 537 new units of housing have been constructed, most of this land remains vacant.

Section III is the Jamaica Plain area of Boston, home to a large working class Irish community. In recent years, significant numbers of black and Hispanic families have moved into the northern portion. It has the highest median income of the three SWCP sections. Jamaica Plain is bounded by several regional parks. It was a wealthy area of summer estates until the streetcar transformed the area into a middle class suburb. Section III has relatively

little vacant land in the Corridor. The community is concerned with maintaining its residential character, as well as with creating new places for work and commerce.

## Community Participation During Engineering and Design

The scale and extent of community participation in the SWCP is unprecedented in American urban redevelopment history. In order to address the varied interests of Southwest Corridor residents, new approaches to the community participation process had to be designed. Since 1977, we at WFEM have been responsible for the coordination of planning and community participation throughout the Corridor.* In this role, we review the activities of over 30 consulting firms working on the project and we work closely with the community committees. We establish procedures and schedules for public presentations and community review of consultant work. And we are heavily involved in getting information on all aspects of the SWCP out to the neighborhoods.

Community participation continues to be directed by the office of the Southwest Corridor Development Coordinator, initiated and directed from 1973 to 1980 by Anthony Pangaro. The organizational structure established in 1977 relies on a central planning staff at WFEM to coordinate the activities of three Section Planners. One Section Planner is employed by each of the engineering design firms and serves as the primary liaison between the Project and the community. The Section Planners co-moderate meetings, keep the community informed through regular mailings, and meet informally with businesspeople and community groups to discuss the Project. The responsibilities of WFEM's central planning staff include preparing Corridor-wide information, providing backup support of graphic and written material for the Section Planners, conducting special studies of issues such as zoning, and attending the numerous consultant and community meetings to coordinate liaison activities. Within our central planning staff, one planner is designated to assist each of the Section Planners.

### The Structure of the Process

The community participation process has been structured to include several

levels of community meetings. There are three section-wide Neighborhood Committees that meet periodically to review design issues and to be informed of Corridor activities. Topics such as construction scheduling or system-wide budgets are discussed at Neighborhood Committee meetings. Design review at these meetings involves system or section-wide elements such as park design, standards for stations, graphics, and engineering issues such as transit alignment and profile. Early in the design phase, Neighborhood Committee meetings and Corridor-wide Open Houses were the primary vehicles for providing information and community review opportunities to the public. Some of the more unusual early community participation "meetings" were the Corridor Walks. The Walks included project staff, consultants, and residents who together explored the path of the new transit line and its development parcels. We learned a great deal from one another about opportunities and constraints. Today, in the late design phase, the primary organizations for participation have become the Station Area Task Forces (SATF)—one for each of the nine stops on the new Orange Line. The SATFs advise the MBTA on station character, landscape design, and community development opportunities. Membership in each SATF is open to all residents, businesspeople, and agency personnel who live or work up to one quarter mile from the new Orange Line and within the area served by the new station. For each SATF, a resident has been elected Moderator and co-chairs meetings with the Section Planner. Since the fall of 1977, the Station Area Task Forces meet regularly every few weeks.

Other task forces have been formed as subcommittees of the Neighborhood Committees or SATFs to address specific or local concerns. For instance, a joint committee of the Green and Boylston SATFs was created to program the uses for a new deck over the tracks between the two stations. In Section II, a Parcel 18 Task Force was created to bring together community organizations and institutions to deal with development issues on the largest and most prominent piece of vacant land to the Corridor. A subcommittee of the Back Bay SATF was formed to study the design of structural canopies recommended to reduce noise in a residential area adjacent to the right-of-

313

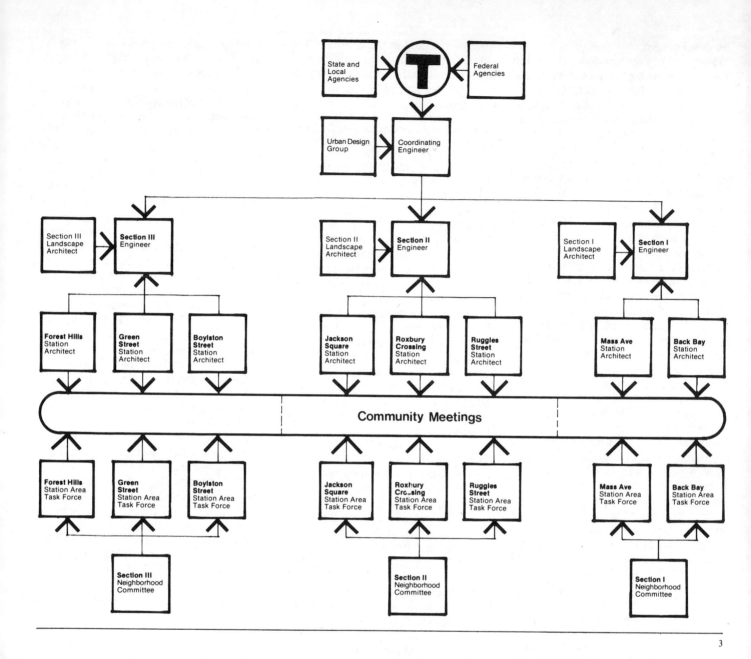

3

Map of new Orange Line showing station
locations and sectional divisions.

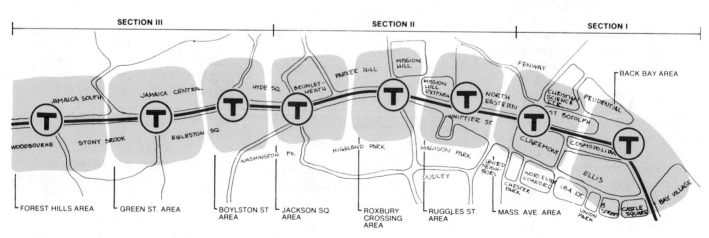

4

way. That subcommittee is also responsible for the programming and design review of a small street-end park next to the canopies. SWCP task forces have also been established to discuss Corridor-wide issues such as parkland management, art, and problems generated by construction.

Among the important items brought before the communities are major engineering questions about grades, tunnel versus open cuts, the reports of architects on their current work, and land use choices. The consultants and the MBTA formulate alternatives before the meetings (at work sessions and meeting dry runs), and often a preferred option arises that is most compatible with the rest of the design. Several options are frequently considered at the public meetings with the advantages and disadvantages of each presented and discussed. We look for consensus, and this often leads to protracted discussions, the restudy of a proposal, or creation of new ones as SATF moderators attempt to let every point of view receive a fair hearing. If necessary, votes are taken on specific questions. An MBTA official who is able to make commitments for the agency attends all community meetings and is often able to indicate which suggestions are possible and which are not and why, thus eliminating fruitless speculation and infeasible proposals.

## Participants in the Process

Participants in the community meetings have primarily been local homeowners. They may feel that they have a greater stake in their neighborhoods than renters, and they tend to be more active. Business people have been actively involved, though not as much as residents. In the Back Bay station area, representatives of the nearby insurance companies have been concerned about the effect of the project on their property, and with how well new Orange Line and commuter rail lines will serve their employees. Land developers who already own parcels or are interested in acquiring land near stations have also attended SATF meetings to promote their interests. Personnel from city agencies frequently attend SATFs as participants. In this way, all decision makers are brought to a central forum, both to hear and present information that might affect their agencies and the project.

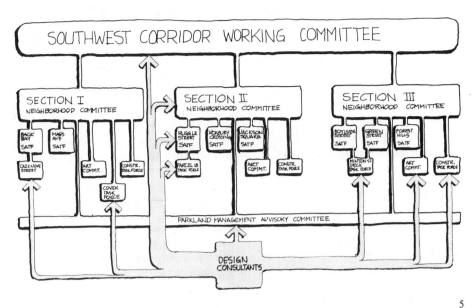

5

Redevelopment was an active issue in some parts of the Corridor and drew many people to community meetings. In Roxbury (Section II) where most of the land cleared for I-95 is located, land development is seen as positive force for the community, both as a source of jobs and income, and as a way of improving the area's physical condition. In Jamaica Plain (Section III), however, there has been a strong feeling expressed to maintain the *status quo*. The only development acceptable to most Section III participants is small-scale residential and commercial development.

Parkland programming and design held residents' interest longer than station design, perhaps because people perceived the parkland as a more significant part of their residential neighborhoods than the transit stations. In general, attendance at meetings to review and participate in landscape design was greater than attendance at station design review meetings.

The construction period will not be pleasant for many residential areas near the right-of-way. In response to community concerns, the MBTA has made some additional concessions that may raise the project cost, but will make construction more bearable. (Even before residents expressed their concerns, the MBTA incorporated noise controls into contract specifications.) Work will be scheduled to minimize night-time operations. And the MBTA will require contractors to provide sufficient parking for workers within the construction boundaries. During the construction period, the approach to community liaison

will shift in emphasis and technique. Section Planners will spend more time in the field monitoring construction, answering residents' questions, and responding to construction-related complaints. Community meetings will continue during construction, and we will remain responsible for keeping the communities informed.

## Community Participation Techniques

The community participation techniques described below have been used throughout the design phase of the project. The scale of the project demanded numerous ways of getting information to and from the public.

### Newsletter

The *Corridor News* is a free, 12-page tabloid newsletter written by project staff members, edited and produced by WFEM, and published by the MBTA every six to eight weeks. It currently reaches over 10,000 readers. The newsletter includes general information on design and technical issues, background stories, development plans, and coverage of milestones in the Project's history. Every issue includes reports on community meetings and the topics they covered. As construction approaches, the newsletter has informed Corridor residents of recommended construction techniques and schedules. The newsletter is distributed throughout the Corridor by the Section Planners. The distribution points include convenience stores, libraries, nursing homes, and barber shops. One Section Planner is a familiar figure to her neighbors as she bicycles from site to site delivering papers. A copy of the newsletter is sent to everyone who has ever attended a SWCP community meeting.

## SATF Notebooks

When the SATFs began to meet in 1977, there was a gap between the professionals' and the community's knowledge of design process and techniques. The Project staff wanted members of the community to get involved with the architects and engineers and not be limited to reacting to finished presentations.

The SATF Notebooks were written by WFEM to make genuine dialogue possible. Each notebook begins with an illustrated explanation of the station area design process and the kinds of design drawings prepared at each step. Material on landscape and urban design follows to provide site specific information on the stations. Reference material about who's who on the Project, a list of common abbreviations, and an illustrated glossary of terms complete the Notebooks. Although they were useful as reference books, the Notebooks could have served more effectively if they had been used on a consistent basis during SATF meetings.

## Handouts

Communication with the community often required the distribution of short, informational handouts. These were given out at meetings, through the mails, and at open houses or field offices. One-page flyers covering specific points of immediate interest have sometimes been distributed door to door along the Corridor, most often to announce meetings. Flyers were particularly useful during the programming process for the Section I Cover, in which residents became actively involved in determining the uses to be provided on a deck covering the right-of-way.

The handouts have often been used to supplement information presented at meetings. Some of them, such as "The Construction Story," describe the different construction techniques to be used along the Corridor. Other handouts dealt with reports of previous meetings, descriptions of new designs, and development proposals.

## Wall Graphics, Slides, Models

The many community meetings of the SWCP were enlivened through the extensive use of wall graphics, models, and slides. These three techniques were used to add depth and clarity to oral presentations. The models and wall graphics, prepared by us or by the station architects and landscape architects, also provided the community with the opportunity to have direct involvement with design by drawing on plans and sketches and moving elements of models around. This provided very good feedback and some interesting design ideas. Several of the graphics have been run off as posters for distribution in the community.

## Educational Training Program

Another innovative approach to public participation has been the design and implementation of an educational program for young people 16–21 years old. The requirement for some kind of training program was mandated by former US Secretary of Transportation Coleman for several projects throughout this country. The extent, depth, and duration of the SWCP program are unique. It was the first to be implemented and it has become the model for others throughout the United States.

The training program was planned and administered by the MBTA and

6. An example of the project newsletter which reaches 10,000 readers.

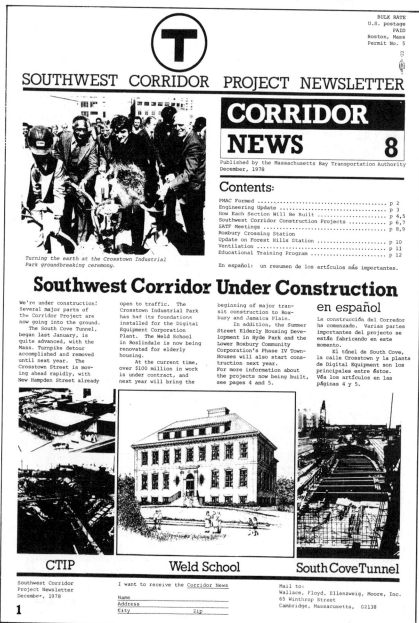

# ⒯ SOUTHWEST CORRIDOR PROJECT
### RELOCATED ORANGE LINE / RAILROAD IMPROVEMENTS

## The Station Area Task Force is your chance to influence design!

### WHAT is the Station Area Task Force (S.A.T.F.)?

■ **LOCATION**
THERE WILL BE ONE S.A.T.F. FOR EACH PROPOSED STATION; THE STATION AREA FOR EACH S.A.T.F. IS CONSIDERED TO BE THE AREA 1/8 TO 1/4 MILE ACROSS THE CORRIDOR AND HALF THE DISTANCE TO THE NEXT STATION.

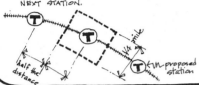

■ **PURPOSE**
A COMMUNITY FORUM FOR DISCUSSING AND EVALUATING ISSUES, DATA AND DESIGN RELATED TO NEW STATIONS. THE S.A.T.F. WILL ADVISE THE M.B.T.A. AND THE D.P.W. ON STATION CHARACTER (entrances, access, parking etc.), LANDSCAPING & OPEN SPACE, AND NEW DEVELOPMENT.

### WHO will participate?

■ RESIDENTS, BUSINESSES AND PUBLIC AGENCIES IN THE STATION AREA WILL DISCUSS THEIR CONCERNS AND REVIEW CONSULTANTS' WORK THROUGHOUT THE DESIGN PROCESS.

■ A NEIGHBORHOOD PERSON AND YOUR SECTION PLANNER WILL BE CO-CHAIRPERSONS AT THE S.A.T.F.

■ SOUTHWEST CORRIDOR CONSULTANTS WILL PROVIDE TECHNICAL BACKUP TO THE S.A.T.F.

- COMMUNITY RESIDENTS
- LOCAL BUSINESS PEOPLE
- PUBLIC AGENCIES
- M.B.T.A.
- CONSULTANTS

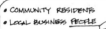

BARRIER FREE DESIGN

FUNCTIONAL REQUIREMENTS

SPACE REQUIREMENTS

**CONSULTANTS' INPUT**
- PROBLEM DEFINITION
- STRATEGIES
- DESIGN ALTERNATIVES
- DEVELOPMENT ANALYSIS

### HOW will the process work? REFER TO S.A.T.F. MEMO

(JULY 22, 1977 by W.F.E.M.) FOR A DETAILED EXPLANATION OF ORGANIZATION AND PROCESS.

■ CONCLUSIONS BY S.A.T.F. WILL BE REACHED BY CONSENSUS; IN CASE OF NO CONSENSUS, VOTING WILL BE USED TO DOCUMENT ALL POSITIONS.

■ RECOMMENDATIONS ON NEIGHBORHOOD-WIDE CONCERNS WILL BE SUBMITTED TO THE NEIGHBORHOOD COMMITTEE.

■ RECOMMENDATIONS TO THE M.B.T.A. AND OTHER AGENCIES WILL BE MADE TO THE SOUTHWEST CORRIDOR COORDINATOR.

■ CONFLICTS WITH S.A.T.F. RECOMMENDATIONS WILL BE BROUGHT BACK TO THE S.A.T.F. FOR FURTHER DISCUSSION.

PEOPLE WORKING TOGETHER

### WHEN will the S.A.T.F.s begin to work?

■ INITIAL MEETINGS WILL BEGIN IN OCTOBER '77.

■ IN PHASE II (Nov. '77 to April '78) MEETINGS WILL BE HELD ABOUT ONCE EVERY TWO TO THREE WEEKS.

■ MEETINGS WILL CONTINUE AS NECESSARY THROUGH CONSTRUCTION (1983).

FOR FURTHER INFORMATION CALL JACI HALL (864-3500) OR YOUR SECTION PLANNER

7. Above, one of the many flyers widely distributed describing aspects of the project.

WFEM together. The program has two main goals:

- To expose community youth to planning, design, and construction of public transportation and community development projects and to career opportunities in the design professions
- To assist community youth in acquiring the academic background and marketable skills necessary to pursue their interest in the design professions

The trainees, some of whom are part- and some full-time, work for one of the 30-odd SWCP consulting firms or for the MBTA. In addition to on-the-job training, the students participate in special weekly workshops with professionals in aerial photography, photogrammetry, engineering, city planning, and design.

## The Impact of Community Participation on Design

The design products of the engineers, architects, and landscape architects working on the SWCP all incorporate community criteria. The MBTA project staff and designers have presented their ideas to the community at each stage of development, and compromises have been made to reconcile conflicting needs.

One of the design consultants said, "Although it can be hard to design a house by committee, a large group can define building program elements, and at that point participation is useful." This represents an opinion prevalent among many SWCP designers—that the community should help to define criteria and program, but at some point the community must allow professionals to execute a design incorporating the needs of the user, the client, the budget, and the technical constraints. The community reviews the emerging design in all its stages. Some designers on the project have been more receptive than others, of course, to design review comments from the community. Members of the less receptive group would rather work from set criteria, complete designs, and present a near-final product to the community. Designers who prefer to work this way undoubtedly had more difficulty operating under the SWCP design rules than those who believe in a more open, interactive process.

The community's influence on design ranges from the large scale (location, use) to the details of station design. The consensus among the community, de-

## An Example of the SWCP Participation Process: The Section I Cover

The Section I Cover is a deck over the tracks of the Southwest Corridor transit system between the South End and St. Botoloph neighborhoods, both dense residential areas. The two neighborhoods are architecturally similar with streets lined by brick row houses, but they have always been dissimilar socially and economically, and physically separated by a railroad line. The right-of-way where trains have run in the past is open, noisy, dirty, and has had a negative impact on the area. The new Cover will reduce train noise to below 67 decibels (Leq)—equivalent to daytime city street noise—in the residential areas. Within the track enclosure, a ventilation system will eliminate the blue haze of smoke that used to come with each passing diesel train. In addition to controlling noise and air pollution, the deck will provide a lot of much needed open space. During the EIS phase, the decision to enclose the tracks was made in response to organized neighborhood demand.

The Section I Cover will be about one-half mile long, extending from Dartmouth Street at the new Back Bay Station to the new station at Massachusetts Avenue. The right-of-way between the ends of adjacent rowhouses is narrow—about 100 feet wide.

Since the design phase of the project began, community participation in the design of the deck has involved three different stages. Preliminary programming for Cover uses took place in summer, 1977. Examples of similar open spaces and recreational standards were pre-sented by consultants to community residents. Several intensive work sessions culminated in the gaming of three models by residents and consultants. Models were based on concepts of: "no use," "moderate use," and "high-intensity use," and were intended to illustrate the different ways residents felt the cover should be used.

Precise uses for the new public space on the Cover were programmed during the second stage of community participation, from March to July, 1978. Five community meetings were held to determine deck use and to address social and technical issues of importance to local residents. "Social issues" were those related to the historical separation of the two communities, which some people wanted to maintain by reducing or eliminating cross-Corridor pedestrian access. Security and surveillance were also on residents' minds. "Technical issues" included such matters as air pollution and the appearance of ventilation stacks. The MBTA and the consultants developed an approach to move toward a consensus on Cover uses. Common elements from the three models that had been developed earlier were emphasized, and convincing guidelines on privacy, security, and maintenance were prepared.

Activities for the Cover were to be decided by people on the street ends, as local orientation of the Cover was desired by the residents. Roy Mann Associates, the coordinating landscape architects, prepared large-scale design models of various street end uses, as well as sketches of options for landscaping. Stull Associates, coordinating urban designers, presented numerous alternate visual treatments for the venti-lation stacks. KE/FST, the engineers, reworked the ventilation systems and the street alignments. WFEM prepared information sheets on issues like security, surveillance, the MBTA policy on pedestrian access, and the planning process.

The basic planning strategy adopted by the consultants was to let the street alignment on top of the deck and the overall program uses emerge from the aggregation of locally determined street end uses. To avoid conflicts that could impede consensus, the MBTA policy on cross-Corridor pedestrian access essentially was to maintain the *status quo,* but provide in the design for the possibility of future connections.

After preliminary meetings, the local residents' Cover Task Force worked in small groups with models and drawings to agree on an acceptable program of uses. The consultants prepared large drawings to encourage people to record their design ideas and reactions to the suggestions of others. Eventually, a consensus emerged. This led to the preparation of the Coordinative Landscape Plan by Roy Mann Associates at the end of the summer (1978). This plan details the tot lots, community gardens, and paved sitting areas that reflect the largely passive nature of the Cover activities desired by the local participants.

The Third stage of participation was the review of detailed designs prepared by the Section landscape architects Moriece and Gary. After budget constraints and local input required some revisions, the plans were presented to the entire community at Section I Open House in February, 1979. Work is now underway.

**Partial Site Plan — Section I Cover**

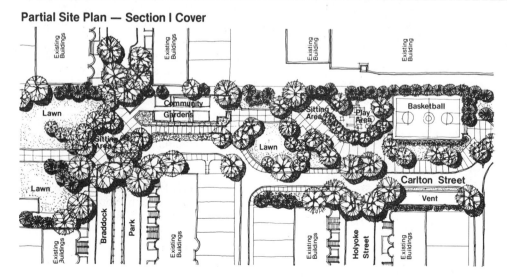

signers, and client is that the entire project is better because of community input. Some of the important design decisions strongly influenced by community input include:

- The introduction of decks to cover the tracks in Sections I and III
- The change of alignment of the arterial street in Section II
- The location and design of ventilation stacks in Section I
- The increased use of glazing (for vision and security) in many stations
- Increased attention to passive solar

heating in stations
- Changes in programming of Corridor parkland, with a general reduction in active uses and increase in quiet, green areas
- Reduction in the quantity of brick used in station landscaping in favor of plantings

The community has also had an indirect influence on design. The presence of an active, vocal community that cares about design has caused designers to be more thoughtful than they might otherwise have been.

9. The landscape architects present their work to the Neighborhood Committee.

10. Bringing design into the streets: the SWCP table at the St. Botolph Street Fair.

11. Trainees and staff of the SWCP summer program: a cross section of young people from the project area.

12. Trainees worked in all aspects of the project including architectural and engineering design.

9

10

11

12

## Green Street Station Design

The Green Street Station is one of the smaller stations on the new Orange Line. It is located in a quiet neighborhood composed largely of one- and two-family homes built in the early part of this century. The station is at the bottom of a hill and many residents will view the station mostly from above. The station location and design has evolved with substantial community input, and according to the planners, the architect, and the MBTA, the station is different and better because of it.

Sy Mintz of Mintz Associates and the Leon Bridges Company, the station architects, feel that community participation strengthened their understanding of the equal importance in the design of scale, character, approach to the station, and neighborhood security and surveillance. Community participation affected the form of the station, which evolved from a flat-roofed structure to a stepped profile of pitched roof sections. The area of glazing and of skylights increased after community discussions of daylighting and safety.

The size of the station was reduced for budgetary reasons, but also because of community desires. Other specific design elements that were influenced by community input include:

- Inclusion of commercial space in the station
- Orientation of the station entry to include persons approaching from the east as well as from the north and west
- Special attention to the fare attendant's location to ensure surveillance of bike parking and bus waiting areas in addition to the rapid transit platform

Sy Mintz feels that the SWCP participation process required the architects to be more responsive to people's concerns. And, says Mintz, "We certainly feel quite good about the final product."

13. The first scheme for the Green Street Station. The community had a number of objections.

14,15. Exterior and interior drawings of the final design. Greater visibility provides more security. Note the elevator for handicapped persons.

13

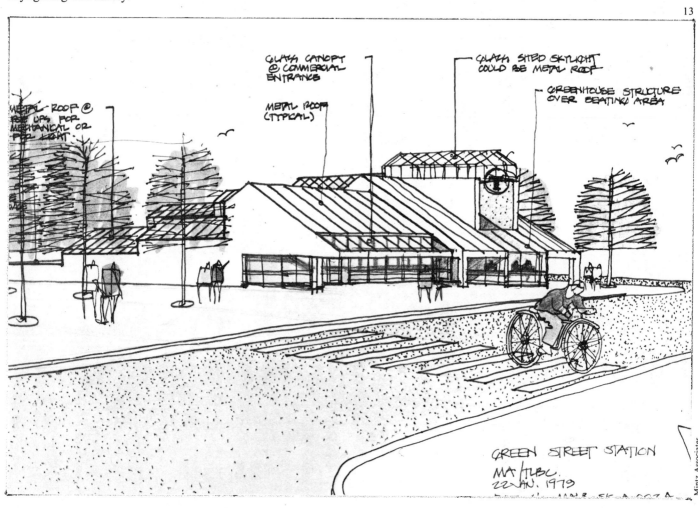

14

15

321

## The Community and the Future

One clear result of the SWCP community participation effort is a public educated in transit issues and public decision-making processes. Whether community people were frustrated or pleased by the process, they learned much about how transit systems are designed and how bureaucracies operate. Many participants believe that the SWCP process has taught Boston communities how to exert influence on public policy and convinced them they have a legitimate voice in planning decisions. Another positive effect of the participation process mentioned by Corridor residents was the growth in the sense of community. One SATF moderator feels participation in the process "brought some of the neighborliness back into the area." Several SATF moderators mentioned that local people had learned the importance of working together and that the potential influence of a group was now perceived to be much greater than that of individuals working alone.

The participation process also provided benefits beyond those directly related to the Project. Several people we interviewed mentioned that the process had taught the community to see the larger potential of rebuilding their neighborhoods, or, as one Section Planner put it, "The community received an outline for the possibility of total urban revitalization." The community participation process for the SWCP has been long and complex. Many people involved with the Project feel that the designers had changed and grown during the process. The MBTA mentions one other positive effect: the community has learned that some public servants are doing their jobs.

The community process has its critics, but an overwhelming number of people involved with the project seem to believe that participation was productive and successful.

## Conclusions

The project probably would not be being built at all, much less as presently designed, without an active participatory component. This conclusion can be drawn from examination of the Corridor's history, the nature of the Corridor communities, and the general current of the times. A major public works project located in a dense urban area in the

16

United States requires community participation to bring it to life. The SWCP demonstrates that a large-scale transit and development project involving thousands of participants and stretched over several miles of the city can have successful community participation if the process is flexible in dealing with varied communities and issues. One key planner on the Project put it simply: "This project demonstrated that large-scale design projects need large-scale participation processes to be effective."

Participation can succeed if it has support from top-level project management. In this case, the direct involvement of the MBTA's Project Manager was essential to the success of the process. As one Section Planner put it: "Tony (Pangaro) was always there . . . if a problem arose you knew he would be there to take the heat." Pangaro has stressed the importance of the community access to the Project Office: "Most projects have a layer of front line community liaison people. We refused to

hire people as public relations fronts and insulate ourselves from the community."

In any participatory process, it is important to state clearly at the start the overall limitations on participation and delineate those decision areas that are open to community recommendations. Past decisions must stand firm, unless significant new data become available, if there is to be progress. Constraints such as overall project budget or construction time schedule must be clearly indicated. By stating the rules first, and then following them, the process retains credibility. Of course, flexibility is required within these clear ground rules to allow for adaptation to changing conditions in a long-term project and to meet the unique needs of local communities. The participatory process for the Southwest Corridor evolved during the early planning stages, the EIS, post-EIS design phase, and will continue to change during the construction period. New techniques and meeting formats are constantly required. But the Project consultants have learned that project size and complexity do not significantly alter the basic principles of effective community participation. The overall success of the Southwest Corridor Project attests to the effectiveness of the effort here.

16. Welders at work on the entrance of the South Cove Tunnel.

17. Local roads in the area cleared for the highway are being reconstructed. In the background is the Occupational Resource Center, a City-wide vocational training school built on project land.

17

# Commentary on SWCP

Chuck Turner, former organizer for the Southwest Corridor Coalition

## WHAT PRICE PARTICIPATION?

The problem I have with the SWCP presentation by Wallace, Floyd, Ellenzweig, Moore (WFEM) is not so much what it says, but what it doesn't say. For example, the majority of their presentation deals primarily with the last three years. Yet to understand community participation in this recent phase, one must understand the nature of community participation in the earlier phases. However, it is perhaps unfair to ask planners who come in at the end to write the history of the beginning.

The plan in the early 1960s was to build a major highway and rail transit system through Boston and its suburbs. There was to be a major north-south highway that would complete the federal I-95 system and an east-west "Innerbelt" that would cut through Cambridge and Boston. While the effects would have been devastating throughout the region, Cambridge became the center of the early struggles against the plan. The reason for this was that Harvard and MIT had used their power to force the planners to run the system through the residential areas of Cambridge. This led to a very creative alliance between community activists, architects and planners, and Cambridge politicians. While this unusual alliance was effective at stalling construction during the early 1960s, by 1968 it seemed that there was no way to win the battle.

The reason for the gloom was that the then-Governor of Massachusetts, John Volpe, was selected by Nixon to be Secretary of Transportation. Since Volpe had been a major road contractor before being Governor, it seemed almost impossible to stop approval of the system. To make matters worse, Francis Sargent, the Lieutenant Governor, was to take over the Governor's chair until 1970. Sargent had been Commissioner of Public Works during an earlier Volpe administration (1958–1962). In this position, Sargent had successfully lobbied a bill through the State legislature that took away the rights of cities and towns to veto highway projects.

In the late 1960s an alliance, the Greater Boston Committee on the Transportation Crisis (GBC), was formed. This group pulled together a variety of interests and geographic areas to fight the system. Appropriately for Boston, it was headed by an activist Catholic priest, Father Corrigan. All these forces coalesced at the time of the inauguration of Frank Sargent and they tried to use the inauguration as a last-ditch effort to stop the highway system. Word was sent to Sargent through one of his liberal aides that the City of Cambridge would send fire trucks and thousands of demonstrators to his inauguration, with the support of the City of Boston, if Sargent did not give his support to the anti-highway decision. Word was sent back saying that if there were any attempt to embarrass the Governor he would never consider any alteration of the plan. The inauguration went smoothly, and shortly thereafter the Governor announced that he was appointing Alan Altshuler, MIT political scientist and writer on the subject of community participation, to head a special task force to examine the issues involved.

Anti-highway forces were very pleased until they realized that the task force was examining a narrow range of issues, not whether to build the system or not. Under the leadership of GBC, a meeting was set up with Altshuler. The meeting was hot and stormy as the community let the task force view the issues from the neighborhood perspective. The result was that Altshuler informed the Governor that the issues were much more complicated than he had initially assumed. He suggested that the Governor ask the Department of Transportation (DOT) to fund a study to reevaluate the plans for I-95 and the Innerbelt. The Governor accepted the suggestion, and petitioned DOT to make the money available, which it did. The Governor then established the Boston Transportation Planning Review (BTPR) with Alan Altshuler as head.

The BTPR ushered in a whole new phase in citizen participation along the corridor. Before BTPR, the activists were outside the system demanding that policy makers change their plans. BTPR's concept was to bring the community people into the process. They did this by setting up a study in which all affected groups would have access to information on the highways and an opportunity to make their viewpoint clear to the Governor— who would make the final decision. This transition from the streets to the planning room was aided by the early history of the highway protest in which there was an alliance between progressive architects and planners and activists from the community. This alliance had already developed great skill in making both moral and planning arguments against the highway. I question whether the community activists would have been strong enough without the alliance to endure the rigors of the 18- to 24-month planning process of the BTPR.

At the end of the study, Alan Altshuler presented an alternative to the Governor that represented *his own* compromise plan. The problem with it, beyond the technical issues, was that the planning group had never seen it! When it came to light through a series of articles in the *Boston Globe,* the new alternative was hastily dropped. And soon after, because of the BTPR conclusions and the political work of GBC (by 1972 there was not one town government in the region supporting the highways), the Governor cancelled the plans and called on the Federal government to let Massachusetts use Highway Trust Fund monies for rapid transit.

The decision by the Governor was applauded by the communities along the corridor and throughout the region. However, everyone realized that the most difficult phase of the struggle was in fact beginning. While in Cambridge and Lynn there was no longer an issue, along the Southwest Corridor numerous questions remained as to the design of the rapid transit as well as the road system. In addition, there would have to be plans developed for the vacant land that would remain after the transportation system was developed. (Keep in mind that by the time the Governor made his 1972 decision, *60 acres* of land had been cleared in the Southwest Corridor.) Obviously, to deal with such issues the community needed to have planning as well as organizing and political skills. The leadership of the anti-highway forces in Roxbury, a predominantly black community, reached out to the leadership of Jamaica Plain, a predominantly white but changing neighborhood with a relatively heavy Hispanic population, and the South End, a very mixed neighborhood in terms of race and income.

## THE PEOPLE TAKE THE INITIATIVE

Calling itself the Southwest Corridor Land Development Coalition (SWCC), the new group decided to focus on the potential development of the cleared land. In order to deal effectively with the land-use issues, they persuaded Boston's Model Cities Agency to finance a $30,000 study conducted by Dan Dimancescu, a young planner who had helped the Coalition with its early planning efforts. The team of planners hired by the Coalition involved people of all races, ages, and skills. One common feature was that almost all worked for wages far below what they normally would have received.

The planners met often and at length with the community in order to get a clear picture of the needs and the concerns of the residents along the Corridor. The Coalition was very fortunate in its early days in that people who had led the anti-highway fight like Gloria Fox from Roxbury, Ron Hafer, and Winky Cloherty from Jamaica Plain, and Ken Kruckemeyer (now on the SWCP staff) and Ellen Gordon from the South End played key roles in organizing participation in the planning process. Through these efforts, the Coalition was able to produce a sophisticated plan for the cleared land. The final land-use plan produced by the government at a cost of hundreds of thousands of dollars duplicates the 1971 recommendations of the $30,000 SWCC study. It is also significant that the first development to take place on the cleared land was a factory built by the Digital Equipment Corporation in 1978. The site used was shown in the SWCC study as being excellent for an industrial park. In 1974, the Community Development Corporation of Boston, a Model Cities spin-off and member of the coalition under the leadership of Marvin Gilmore, moved ahead with the development of the industrial park. Today, in addition to Digital, a second factory is being built by Health Company, a major hospital supplies manufacturer. Without taking anything away from the miraculous job done by Mr. Gilmore and the CDC of Boston, the hundreds of jobs that this industrial park provides must be seen as an outgrowth of the anti-highway work and planning activity of the Coalition.

After the dust of the BTPR cleared, SWCC attempted to organize itself for the long, arduous process of monitoring the development of the project. It formalized its bylaws and built the multicommunity leadership structure into its present form. In addition, it persuaded a privately funded legal advocacy group, Massachusetts Law Reform, to assign lawyer Elbert Bishop to the Coalition. Bishop was well known to the Coalition through the work he did on the SWCC study as a graduate student in planning at MIT. Once aboard, he helped the Coalition focus on getting local foundations to consider long-term funding for planners as well as organizers. Without such resources, the leadership of the Coalition felt they would be unable to effectively represent the community during the long design and construction phase. After much discussion, a number of local foundations under the leadership of Fred Glimp of Permanent Charities formed a consortium to fund the Coalition. They tentatively agreed to four-year funding with yearly performance reviews. However, they indicated that they would not be willing to fund the Coalition after this period and that it would be essential to get the government involved financially if the Coalition was to

be able to stay alive through the 10 to 15 years that it would take to develop the Corridor. While the Coalition worked on the issue of funding, it also focused on several other tasks. Perhaps the key task was the hiring of the project manager for the SWCP. The Coalition was also very involved in advocating for the community on unresolved issues. Uppermost in the minds of people along the Corridor during this period in 1973–1974 was stopping the development of yet another major roadway through Jamaica Plain. A second key concern was the securing of a government commitment that the replacement service for the rapid transit line to be removed would be completed as soon as possible. Another priority issue for the Coalition involved the railroad embankments along the Corridor. Governor Sargent had made the decision to depress the rapid transit and commuter rail lines. However, federal officials kept questioning the cost. The agreement to cover the depression in Section I came only after serious struggle. The vigilance and activity of the Coalition was well rewarded on all of these issues.

A crucial task was the development of the ground rules for participation and interaction of the numerous governmental and nongovernmental groups in the SWCP process. Since the Coalition was representing the arm of the alliance that had the least formal power and the scarcest resources for staff, it was essential that there be a clear initial agreement about rights and responsibilities. The proposal developed by the Coalition was eventually embodied in a Memorandum of Agreement signed by the various parties. While it hasn't worked perfectly, the framework established by the Memorandum was very helpful to the Coalition.

In the 1975 gubernatorial election, the Coalition took the position that since both candidates' records were good on the SWCP, the Coalition would not support either one but would instead keep the issues of the Corridor before the electorate. The election resulted in a victory for Michael Dukakis. For a while it seemed as if the Coalition and the Corridor were blessed since Fred Salvucci, transportation planner for the City of Boston, was named as the new Secretary of Transportation, replacing Alan Altshuler (who had become Secretary of Transportation under Sargent after the conclusion of the BTPR). During the BTPR, Salvucci had been a major ally of the community forces actively fighting against the highway system. In addition, he was

personally friendly with SWCP Manager Tony Pangaro and had worked with him when they were both starting as planners in the 1960s. It looked as if we had the perfect team to take the project to completion. Yet a few months into the Dukakis administration, the attitude seemed to develop that it was time to cut down the dialogue with the community and move on to build the system. This statement was shocking to many of us since while we wanted to "build the system," we felt that the community concerns had to be a continual part of the equation if the project was to be developed correctly. However, difficulties with the Washington transportation bureaucracy brought State officials to the Coalition to again plan close collaboration.

The strategy was to have a joint state/city/community delegation visit then Secretary of Transportation William Coleman, a Nixon appointee. The SWCP was to be promoted as a great opportunity for a quadrilateral partnership (federal, state, city, community) to develop a center city area in which live blacks, whites, and Hispanics of almost every age and income level. A key actor in this meeting was Senator Brooke, who since the early days of SWCC had been a loyal and hardworking ally. The strategy worked. Coleman directed the Urban Mass Transportation Administration (UMTA) to go forward with the project, and again it seemed as if we were about to enter the golden age of community participation.

After the years of fighting, everything seemed to be in place for the government and community to develop the Southwest Corridor as the model planning and development process for the new era. Tony Pangaro, grinning from ear to ear, told me how he and Fred Salvucci knew that without the work of Elbert Bishop and the Coalition, federal approval of the project would not have happened. Yet, a few months later when the Coalition initiated discussions about its role in the design process and monies to finance that role, the partnership had again cooled. After five years of representing the community on every level—including Secretary Coleman's—we were now told by our "friends" that we could not get paid for handling community participation in the final, critical phases. Ironically, Elbert Bishop and others from SWCC sat as community representatives on the review teams that hired the planners, including WFEM.

The WFEM article talks at length about SATFs and the process, yet never do they mention that the SATF was designed by the community through the Corridor Working Committee set up by the SWCC-initiated Memo of Agreement. Early on they allude to the formation of SWCC, but they neither describe what it is nor its historical role. In addition, it is mentioned in a manner that could have one believe that it was only formed in the late 1970s. Yet it was the ability of the community in the 1960s and 1970s to work with the bureaucracy that made the SWCP possible, and it is SWCC's ability to work with planners around design issues that make it of continuing value to the community.

WFEM gives the impression that it was the planners and their process that led to the growth in the community knowledge. The truth is that from the early days in the 1960s, both sides were constantly learning. The only difference is that people on the governmental side are getting paid. At times I might seem bitter, and I am. Because after 12 years of participating and helping to guide the SWCP process, I find that SWCC—praised so highly when its help was needed—for the second time in three years has had to release its staff because of the lack of funding. This at the time when the construction issues are paramount in the eyes of the community.

Gloria Fox, one of the original organizers, called last night from her office in Roxbury to say that the SWCC board has drawn up an agenda for the next meeting. The agenda reads:

1. How will design of new streets affect old traffic patterns?
2. How will dirt and noise control be handled?
3. Will pedestrian walkways be set up to provide safety?
4. How can workers and companies from the Corridor get jobs?
5. How will the old el be removed?
6. When will bikeways be completed?
7. What support can we get for the Community College which is supposed to go in the Corridor?
8. How can the community get access to usable materials from the Corridor?
9. What is the truck route for removing the refuse from demolition and construction?
10. Will there be sponsorship of another walking tour?

Obviously that's a tough agenda for an organization with no staff. However, as the freedom fighters on the African continent say, *A Luta Continua*—The Struggle Continues.

# Advocacy in the 80s
# Pratt Center (Brooklyn, New York)
# Tucson Community Development/Design Center

Covering the community housing work of Boston architect John Sharratt (see Part 2) *Architectural Record* recently wrote: "Advocacy planning, a phenomenon of the sixties, has all but disappeared in U.S. cities." Fortunately, this is not true. For without advocacy groups—more commonly known today as Community Design Centers—poor tenants, struggling neighborhoods, and decaying Main Streets in need of revitalization would have no access to the architectural assistance they need so badly. Underfunded and overworked, Community Design Centers can still be found in most large and many smaller cities providing design services, guidance through bureaucratic labyrinths, economic development information, and inspiration to countless urban neighborhoods. They are the conscience of the profession.

The Pratt Institute Center for Community and Environmental Development has been serving its Brooklyn neighborhood and the City of New York since the early 1960s. Today, students from Pratt's School of Architecture still flock to the Center for the experience of working with real clients on real buildings. From a once-elegant house on Washington Avenue, director Ron Shiffman and a staff of students and professionals carry on an exemplary comprehensive practice. A look at the Center's log for just a couple of months indicates the scope and importance of its work:

Los Sures, Williamsburg, Brooklyn

Gut rehab—45 d.u. in nine buildings. Revise working drawings.

Magnolia Tree Earth Center, Brooklyn

Conversion of three buildings for use as community environmental center. Design development complete. Started working drawings.

Dumont Avenue Homeowners, Brooklyn

Assistance in processing 312 loan application for six buildings.

Banana Kelly Improvement Association, Bronx

Sweat-equity gut rehab of three buildings (21 d.u.). Supervise construction.

Adopt-A-Building, Manhattan (Lower East Side)

Direct loan program: gut rehab of seven buildings; joint venture with Wai Chin, Architect.

Broadway Merchants' Chamber of Commerce, Brooklyn

Development of commercial revitalization strategy. Prepared Title VI grant proposal; funding approved.

Ridgewood Historic Society, Queens

Survey of historic structures in 25-block area.

Children's House of Park Slope, Brooklyn

Conversion of church rectory to day-care center. Drawings submitted to the Department of Buildings.

Park Hill Civic Association, Staten Island

Comprehensive planning study including housing improvement program. Market analysis begun.

In addition, the Pratt Center plays a vital role in citywide and national coalitions, lobbying for Community Development funds, fighting bank redlining, and encouraging the growth of groups like the National Association of Neighborhoods (NAN). Far from being a relic of another time, community design is on the rise. The conservative mood in Washington as well as the capitals of Western Europe will make it more necessary in the 1980s than ever before.

Jennings Hall Senior Citizens Housing, just now completed, is a good example of the valuable work of the Pratt Center.

In her companion article, Virginia Yang tells how Pratt Center and a Brooklyn community group fought for and won the largest Section 202 mortgage ever written, built 154 badly needed apartments, and created a convincing symbol of the power of neighbors working together.

In a second related article, architect Jody Gibbs describes advocacy in a very different setting. As director of the Tucson Community Development/Design Center, his clients are mostly American Indians and Mexican Americans fighting to hold onto their space and improve their housing conditions in a rapidly growing, free-wheeling sunbelt city. Gibbs and his staff have a very clear political perspective. It leads them to define the practice of community architecture broadly to include the preparation of illustrated urban histories, neighborhood newspapers, and area plans—but also striking buildings which embody their political beliefs.

The Commentary which follows is by Chester Hartman, former Director of the Urban Field Service in the Harvard Graduate School of Design and now the central node in the national Planners Network.

# The Pratt Center Now

**Ronald Shiffman, Director,**
**Pratt Center for Community and**
**Environmental Development,**
**Brooklyn**

The Pratt Center for Community and
Environmental Development was once a
community education program focused
on urban planning. It has evolved into a
public-interest, advocacy architecture
and planning office that provides a
broad range of technical assistance to
working class neighborhoods. The impact of the 1970s and 1980s on the evolution of advocacy architecture and
planning must be recognized if we are
to understand how and why the Center
functions as it does today.

The Center was established at Pratt
Institute in Brooklyn in 1963. It was a
product of, and a reaction to, the urban
renewal philosophies of the 1950s, and
it was fostered by the promise of the social revolution of the 1960s. The civil
rights movement, the "war against poverty," and the violent reminders of the
social and economic degradation of people residing in the Wattses, Newarks,
Harlems, and Bedford-Stuyvesants
affected the conscience of America—
began to raise questions concerning the
role of government, universities, and
individual citizens. That questioning
led to demonstrations in the streets, on
college campuses, and in professional
societies. We were jolted by reality—by
the severity of the social, political,
and economic problems.

Fueled by the belief that we could affect the course of domestic policy and
eliminate racism and economic deprivation, many of us joined the movements
for social change. We joined as citizens
and we joined in our professional capacities. We saw that our professions were
partly responsible for the problems, and
we asked how our skills could be used
to solve them. Out of this grew such
organizations as the Lawyers for Civil
Rights, the Medical Committee for
Human Rights, Planners for Equal
Opportunity, the Architects' Renewal
Committee in Harlem (ARCH), and
many others.

At the same time, campuses came
alive: first Berkeley's Free Speech
Movement, then Columbia and Howard

1. The dedicated staff—and baby—outside the
Pratt Center.

All photos by Kenji Takagami

327

Universities, and Pratt Institute. Interestingly enough, at Columbia, Howard, and Pratt, campus activism was centered in the schools of architecture. Progressives in the housing movement who were reacting against government urban renewal policies were attracted to the civil rights struggle, to anti-poverty efforts, and to the search for a more meaningful professional ethic. Together they set the base for advocacy architecture and planning. Their activities and philosophy helped to redirect the Pratt Center, which had initially been established to acquaint neighborhoods with urban development theory and programs. The events of the 1960s, coupled with the Center's direct involvement with low income, predominantly black neighborhoods, changed the focus dramatically. Together with our neighborhood clients and other advocacy groups the Pratt Center began to:

- Directly confront government, opposing policies and actions that adversely affected low income persons
- Participate in coalitions to bring about basic changes in urban renewal policies and housing programs
- Expand our educational activities to include direct technical assistance to neighborhood organizations seeking to alter or defeat urban renewal projects, as well as to initiate community-controlled neighborhood revitalization plans
- Plan the development of a socially relevant architecture and planning education program
- Utilize fourth- and fifth-year and also graduate students, supervised by a professional staff, to provide free planning and architectural service to local communities

National and international events continued to have an impact upon the growth of the Pratt Center. The Vietnam war, with its inflationary costs plus government substitution of "benign neglect" for social change, led to alienation, suspicion of government, and a massive retrenchment, with the virtual abandonment of the national agenda for economic and racial justice.

The vision, promise, and goals of the 1960s may have been tarnished for some, but for us they remain intact. Some immature optimism has been replaced by greater pragmatism, reflecting a realization that the issues that concerned us were complex, and the in-

2. The directors meet to review demands on the Center's time.

formation and technical capabilities we needed were more difficult to acquire than we originally anticipated. The goals of the Pratt Center at its inception and today differ only in degree. We have always been committed to a redistribution of power to those who have been denied, because of income, sex, race, or religion, effective control of their environments. We recognize that those traditionally denied access to technical expertise—that we as architects and planners possess—have a right to that expertise, and we have a responsibility to provide it.

Maximizing opportunities and the range of choices, particularly for low and moderate income people, is the common thread that weaves through the complex of activities that the Center is involved in. The philosophical base for the Center's work is a belief in participatory democracy—in grass roots decision making as the most effective means for improving the quality of urban life. We believe that improvement in the quality of our urban environment will be the result—but we see the processes of participation and transfer of control as the creative, visionary force in architecture and planning. As we develop a common language and a high level of community trust, we can develop a design aesthetic that is reflective of the rich mix of ideas, aspirations, and backgrounds that characterizes our cultural life. It is our experience that a common language and shared goals can only develop out of a long-term working relationship. This is an essential that most architects and planners cannot afford since they must work on a project-by-project basis.

## Pratt Center Programs

The Center functions on two levels: technical assistance to neighborhood-based groups, and policy analysis/program monitoring/coalition building. The neighborhood, as the focal point for individual and family identity within a city, is the place at which participatory democracy can be most effective. Therefore, the first and fundamental aspect of the Center is provision of direct architectural and planning services to neighborhood groups. We aid neighborhood groups in project design and invite, to the greatest extent possible, the direct participation of neighborhood residents in that design process. To do this effectively, we attempt to demystify design by: (1) bridging the language barriers—visual and verbal—between designer and client, so each can communicate clearly with the other, (2) broadening the experience of both neighborhood residents and designers, and (3) transferring to the neighborhood residents as much information and technical skill as they are willing to absorb. When the design process is really understood by the clients, they can have a meaningful role in decision making.

However, neighborhood-based organizations, unlike the planner's more traditional, affluent, and powerful clients, usually lack access to the funds necessary to implement their decisions. Therefore, the second level of Pratt Center activity concentrates on maximizing the resources available to city neighborhoods. This involves organizing local and national coalitions to monitor city, state, and federal programs. We regularly evaluate program alternatives and, when appropriate, mobilize support for administrative and legislative changes beneficial to neighborhood groups.

## Policy Watch

A major objective of the Center has been to have a broad impact on City policy, operating procedures, and attitudes. We use many methods to bring about these changes—research, community education, advocacy, development of alternative approaches, negotiation, conferences, seminars, research, and testimony—depending upon the issues involved. In addition to the continual evaluation of programs and the tracking of public expenditures traditionally associated with "monitoring" and policy analysis, the Center takes a much more activist role, including:

- Outreach to neighborhood groups and community-wide organizations actually or potentially affected by Community Development (CD) Block Grants, and related programs

- Liaison with city officials responsible for planning and implementation of the housing, CD, and employment programs to exchange information, resolve problems, and explore new approaches

- Consultation with federal officials involved in the oversight of the national CD program and the revision of legislation and regulations

- Direct challenges (legal and quasi-legal) to any city and/or federal actions that threaten to weaken the commitment of CD and other programs to low and moderate income groups

Complementing our policy work is coalition building, which is an ongoing, difficult process aimed at bringing local groups of differing capacities and orientation together to articulate common goals. The major objective of our coalition building has been:

- To share, collect, and disseminate information about neighborhood development ideas and projects, available technical resources, and developments within City, State, and federal government

- To advocate a redefinition of the city's development goals, and the design of programs to promote neighborhood-focused development

- To develop new sources of technical assistance to support neighborhood development

The Center, working through the New York City Housing and Community Development Coalition (which we helped organize and staff), has convened dozens of public meetings during the last few years. Participation in these sessions is open to the public, no fees are charged, and literally thousands of pages of information and hundreds of hours of presentation and debate are made available to thousands of inter-

3. The neighborhood economic development office.

ested individuals representing neighborhood development organizations, community groups, government agencies, banks, and foundations. We have also organized and participated in the:

- Unsafe Building Task Force

- Task Force on City-Owned Property

- Economic Development Task Force

- Coalition of NSA Neighborhoods

- Community Service Society CD Task Force

- Community Service Society *In Rem* Task Force

In addition to these efforts on the local level, the Center has played a leader-

ship role in a number of national coalitions that mirror our neighborhood orientation. These include the National Commission on Neighborhoods, National Association of Neighborhoods, Center for Community Change, Working Group for CD Reform, Citizens' Advisory Panel to HUD, Advisory Panel on the President's Urban Policy, and the President's Domestic Council (under President Carter). These national connections strengthen the Center's hand in encouraging the targeting of CD dollars to low and moderate income groups and maintaining a neighborhood focus for UDAG grants.

Involvement on the national level has in turn made us keenly aware of programs, issues, legislation, contacts, and sources of funds which enable us to be more effective in technical assistance. The work we do nationally has had direct benefits for our clients.

Over the years, the Pratt Center has put out a variety of citywide publications on community issues. For example, the Center prepares a *Community Information Bulletin* that provides a compendium of facts and references, as well as an analysis of CD issues. The Center publishes regularly revised editions of its *Housing Resource Manual* that provides a comprehensive guide to government and private programs that can be used by landlords and tenants. It defines terms, identifies organizations and resource people, and explains how various programs can be applied to local needs.

## Building Neighborhoods

With all this information available, the Center is able to function as a kind of switchboard—a contact system connecting people with resources and acting as an advocate for the neighborhoods. Neighborhood organizations come to the Pratt Center with a variety of needs, ranging in scope from the design of a single building to the development of complex plans integrating an area's housing, economic, and social goals. In many neighborhoods where we have started with a concentration on architectural activity, the Center has soon become involved in comprehensive planning. In areas where community planning is the starting point, the Center will often get involved in the programming and design of particular buildings. There are multiple points of entry from which the Center assists neighborhood-based organizations, and we try to help neighborhood groups achieve both short-term and long-term objectives within a planning context. The integration of architectural, planning, and economic development assistance that we are able to provide has been a major factor in helping our community clients achieve a modicum of success in their efforts.

The pattern for this kind of coordinated technical assistance was set with the Center's first major project in 1964. It was a referral from the Rockefeller Brothers Fund. A group of ministers from the Bedford-Stuyvesant community asked for help in evaluating a newly announced urban renewal project. The impact of the resulting collaboration on both the community and the Pratt Center was significant. A series of open community meetings was held to discuss the plan and the residents asked the Center to investigate alternatives to the City's renewal proposal. In cooperation with several community organizations, we conducted a series of field trips to other cities with active urban renewal programs. Using neighborhood facilities, we ran a 10-week course on community redevelopment. We attended numerous meetings to discuss alternative proposals for the revitalization of the area. As a result of this process, a community task force was formed. The efforts of this group, coupled with the energetic support of Senator Robert F. Kennedy, led to the establishment of the Bedford-Stuyvesant Restoration Corporation—one of the nation's first

and foremost community-based development corporations. The approach developed in Bedford-Stuyvesant, which integrated housing, economic, and social planning considerations, has been replicated by the Center in many of our subsequent planning activities.

Unfortunately, the publicity that surrounded the Bedford-Stuyvesant Restoration project raised unrealistic hopes in black communities about the speed and significance of social change that would follow and provoked envy within white communities. Black communities believed that white neighborhoods were

4. The chief planner discusses development in the Northside area.

given preference for city services, while white communities believed black neighborhoods were receiving disproportionate attention through anti-poverty and other federal assistance programs. Though there was some basis for each claim, the significant fact was that *none* of the communities had the resources to cope with the enormous backlog of needs.

In about 1969, the staff of the Center began to realize that limiting its efforts to black communities would lead to continued frustrations. Parallel support for social change in white working class areas was needed. By acknowledging the interdependence of neighborhoods, the Pratt Center took an important step. The staff began to look for issues that could bring people together and achieve the goals of social change.

## An Example of Advocacy

Our work in the Northside neighborhood in the Williamsburg section of Brooklyn enabled the Center to bring into focus several urban renewal issues and is a good example of Pratt's conception of advocacy planning. This old but vital Polish community opposed the planned expansion of a local manufacturing plant because it would require the destruction of homes and the relocation of residents outside the social neighborhood.

In 1971, the Center was asked to help save the homes and the neighborhood. We undertook an evaluation of the proposed facility and concluded that it would, in fact, be impossible for the plant to expand without demolishing adjoining residential structures. The community's alternate plan, developed with the help of the Center through numerous meetings with local organizations and the individuals directly affected, allowed for the plant to expand—but only after the construction of new housing in the immediate vicinity at rents each family could afford.

A series of violent confrontations between the City and Northside residents eventually secured the plan's reluctant approval. The residents were aided in their efforts by members of the press who worked diligently to publicize the plight of the families on the front pages of New York City's newspapers. The compromises reached in Northside led to important changes in City policies dealing with relocation, replacement housing, tax abatement, and mixed-use residential zoning. The new, low rise, medium density housing was built at a cost far below the average for new construction and stands as one of the few examples of stable, low rent, cooperative housing in the City of New York.

During the struggle between the City and the Northside neighborhood, the City frequently portrayed Northside residents as racists opposing jobs for black and Hispanic people. The Center, working closely with local organizers, made sure that this divisive tactic did not work. Through the combined efforts of the Pratt Center and the Education Action Center, the local anti-poverty group, black and Hispanic organizations from other parts of the City were enlisted to train the Northsiders to confront and negotiate with the City. The process of working with people from other racial and ethnic groups helped break down the stereotyped images that some Northsiders had and that others had of them. Furthermore, when the City undertook a series of violent, forcible evictions, telegrams were sent to the Mayor from all parts of the City—from black, Hispanic, Chinese, and Jewish communities—opposing the actions and joining in solidarity with the residents of Northside.

As a result of the victory in Northside, the Center was asked to assist other neighborhoods in the Williamsburg-Greenpoint area. One such request came through the Education Action Center and its Director, Jan Petersen, after a row of buildings adjoining the St. Nicholas Church was partially destroyed by fire. We were initially asked for assistance in evaluating how difficult it would be to rehabilitate the structures. Our investigation indicated that the buildings were beyond repair. Instead, we began working with residents in the area to see how the families could best be relocated and what options were available to create new housing. What ensued between the Pratt Center and the residents of the St. Nicholas neighborhood exemplifies the range of services that an advocacy architectural and planning office must provide.

As soon as the Center began working with residents to take a comprehensive look at conditions within the community, a number of major problems began to surface. The first was the impact of disinvestment or redlining—the process by which area savings banks and other lending institutions systematically discriminated against the neighborhood. There was also a need to provide more modern housing and related facilities for senior citizens who were residing in one- to four-family houses—large units that were desperately needed by young people starting families. This housing was not barrier-free and did not provide the level of comfort needed by the elderly population. A former nurses' residence was being used as a City detention center (a sore point in the area), and there were issues with the schools and other services as well. The Center considered these problems, and in collaboration with neighborhood residents, developed a number of planning options.

At the same time, the newly formed St. Nicholas Neighborhood Preservation and Housing Rehabilitation Corporation (affectionately known as St.

5. The Center is a training ground for social architecture.

Nick's) became a subcontractor of the local CETA sponsoring coalition and was able to employ about 20 staff people. The major drawback was that CETA did not provide funds for either supervision or for the operating expenses of the office. To make sure the new organization would be productive and successful, Pratt Center loaned St. Nick's one of its principal staff persons, Cathy Herman. She directed the activities of the corporation and supervised the new employees, and Pratt Center provided training for them. In turn, St. Nick's used some of its CETA funds to hire four young people from the Pratt Center to assist the director in a supervisory capacity. One of the first things the new St. Nick Corporation began was an overall assessment of neighborhood needs.

In late 1975, the State of New York announced that the Jennings Hall Shelter for Boys—the detention center—was to be closed. The St. Nicholas Corporation immediately began to consider alternative uses for this centrally located and dominant structure. Survey results overwhelmingly reinforced earlier perceptions of the need for senior citizen housing. The Pratt Center was asked to do a feasibility study and to help in the negotiation processes that would make this project a reality.

Of particular interest is the process by which the building designs were developed. Preliminary designs were done

by a group of architecture students working at the Pratt Center. About seven or eight alternatives were proposed, and each was discussed at length with neighborhood residents. Two approaches were selected and the Pratt Center architect—Virginia Yang [See her article following—EDITOR]—who had been hired through the CETA program to work in the St. Nick office began to develop the schemes. Because she was a recent graduate, she was assisted in this work by the staff of the Pratt Center and faculty members from Pratt Institute.

St. Nick's staff played a key role with the Center in encouraging community participation in every aspect of the design process. They organized a dialogue between the designers and potential tenants. When the plans and the HUD application were completed, St. Nick decided to hire the New York firm of Edelman and Salzman as project architects. Because of a widely shared desire in the community to recognize the central role played by women in the design process, Judith Edelman was named to head the team, and her firm made a commitment to hire Virginia Yang to carry on the project she had started. While federal requirements forced some compromises, the design today substantially reflects the community's input. Equally important, other CETA staff at St. Nick have developed what will be one of the first community housing management companies. This management program will provide employment for neighborhood residents, some of whom have already started their training. In addition to the senior citizen housing project, St. Nick's has now entered into contracts with the City of New York to manage a commercial revitalization project, including facade improvement, business development, and open space development. They are also successfully operating a community management program for City-owned residential property and have completed a study on the conversion of vacant industrial lofts into low rent artists' housing.

Today the dependence of the St. Nicholas Neighborhood Preservation and Housing Rehabilitation Corporation on the Pratt Center is diminishing rapidly. But we still continue to provide specific architectural and planning assistance to supplement staff efforts. Specifically, we have in the past year:

**Continued on page 337.**

# Jennings Hall: From Advocacy to Actuality

Virginia Yang, architect

The story of the new Jennings Hall is an illustration of the crucial role played by the Pratt Center in community revitalization—but it is also the story of people in a neighborhood discovering their collective strength by working toward a common goal. This goal, Jennings Hall Senior Citizens' Housing, is a tangible reminder of the individual experiences and group effort which are as much a part of the building as its bricks and mortar.

Jennings Hall, a hulking masonry structure of 1930 vintage, sits on the corner of Bushwick Avenue and Powers Street in the St. Nicholas area of Williamsburg. It is a solid, six-story building, out of scale with the neighboring two- and three-story wood frame row houses. Just as its scale is unusual in the area, so is its history important to the people who live in the surrounding houses.

Jennings Hall began as a home for the nursing nuns who served at St. Catherine's, once a nearby hospital. On the closing of the hospital in the late 1960s, the Archdiocese of Brooklyn leased the building to the City of New York as a home for delinquent boys. The people who lived in the neighborhood were uncertain about this use for the building. However, their fears were assuaged by assurances that the building would house only young children. In actuality, many of the new tenants were in their late teens. As a group, these troubled young men were rowdy, created tension, and caused problems in the quiet residential neighborhood.

At the time the Jennings Hall lease to the City of New York was about to expire in 1975, the people in the neighborhood had just formed the St. Nicholas Neighborhood Preservation and Housing Rehabilitation Corporation. This group, energetically led by Marion Wallin, Sal Abramo, and Father Vetro, saw the need to take an active role in determining the future of their neighborhood. Jennings Hall, about to fall vacant, offered an opportunity to the

6. St. Nick takes to the streets in defense of community.

Carl J. Wallin

fledgling organization to embark on a project of substantial importance to the community.

St. Nick asked the Pratt Institute Center for Community and Environmental Development for assistance, and together we reviewed the options. The owner of Jennings Hall, Catholic Medical Center of Catholic Charities, had no firm plans for the building. Rumors of demolition or acquisition of the property by a local bank circulated in the neighborhood. The uncertainty of the fate of Jennings Hall and the memory of its previous occupants stirred feelings of uneasiness in the community. These factors increased St. Nick's determination to see that those who lived in the neighborhood would have a strong voice in the next use of Jennings Hall.

Members of St. Nick and the staff of the Pratt Center brainstormed, entertaining numerous possibilities for the reutilization of the building: a multi-use center that would include continuing education and recreational facilities and possibly temporary shelter for homeless people, a professional building providing space for physicians, local service

groups, union organizations, health clinics, and a day-care center, or new housing. The structure itself could adequately accommodate a good number of these activities simultaneously. Jennings Hall occupied half a block and contained a total of 51,000 sf of usable area on seven habitable floors. It was quickly evident that it could be converted into housing and still have space enough left over to provide community facilities and offices for the St. Nick community organization, which at that time was crowded into the basement of the church hall.

Older people in the community, it turned out, were the group most in need of quality housing. In its proposal to the people of the neighborhood, the joint planning group recommended:

that Jennings Hall be converted into Senior Citizen Housing because . . . a great need for such housing exists and Jennings Hall lends itself to such a function . . . there is an unusually high number of senior citizens residing here; they generally occupy the

7. The new wing extends the old Jennings Hall to provide a total of 150 units for the elderly.

George Cserna

large rent-controlled apartments they rented many years ago because they want to remain in the community; these are the only apartments they can afford. The implication of this phenomenon is that there is a limited, perhaps non-existent, amount of housing available to young people who would like to remain in the neighborhood and raise their families here. In the St. Nick study area, this is a major problem because there definitely are a number of young people who want to stay in the neighborhood. Instead, due to the housing shortage, they are forced to move away; thus the average age of the population increases. A certain amount of potential and kinetic community vitality is lost as a result . . ..
In addition, lack of available housing, as well as the image of the area as "old," discourages any newcomers from moving in. The area begins to stagnate; the next step is decline.

Fortunately, HUD was just then reviving its program to provide low-interest

mortgages and rent subsidies for housing for the elderly and handicapped. After approval of the idea by the community in an open forum, Pratt Center played an important part in the preparation of St. Nick's formal application for HUD Section 202/8 funds,* supplying preliminary architectural plans that combined renovation of 54 units in the existing building and construction of 122 new units on the site. We worked on the formulation of the corporate structure and provided the lawyers to prepare the incorporation papers. In order to get the project approved by HUD, the Center convinced Pratt Institute to sponsor the senior citizen housing jointly with the St. Nicholas Neighborhood Preservation Corporation, the St. Nicholas Roman Catholic Church, and the National Council of Senior Citizens. The Center also assisted in the negotiations with archi-

*The Pratt Center's monitoring of national housing programs had alerted us to pending changes in the Section 202/8 program that enabled non-profit groups such as St. Nick to participate. As a result, we and St. Nick began working on the program prior to its official announcement.

tects, lawyers, and builders, and did the research for the Environmental Impact Statement. Our negotiations with the City led to official zoning changes that allowed the Jennings Hall project to proceed, yet protected existing houses and small businesses on the block.

## Programming with the Elderly

During the period between the request to HUD and the official notice of funds reservation, we worked together to formulate a comprehensive concept of housing for elderly people. It was based on the particular needs of those in the community who might someday live in Jennings Hall. Visits were made to all the Senior Citizens' Centers in the Williamsburg/Greenpoint area—about a dozen in all. At each session, staff gathered information from older people about what they would like to have in new housing. It quickly became clear to St. Nick that housing meant more than physical shelter. It must provide a broad spectrum of services to satisfy the social and psychological needs of aging persons. Ideally, all agreed, Jennings Hall should be a place which an older person could consider home for many years, even as his or her needs changed. The building itself should encourage residents to live independently, but services such as meals, housekeeping, social counseling, therapy, transportation, and recreational activities would also be offered to tenants. St. Nick hoped to include some congregate units so that those needing minimal nursing care could also live there in small groups of four or five with a caretaker. As it turned out, the idea was not feasible under this HUD program.

Upon official notification of a funds reservation from HUD for the development of 176 units in mid-1976, the firm of Edelman and Salzman of New York City was brought in to provide architectural services. This office was chosen because it had experience in housing for community sponsors and had assisted with the application to HUD by doing an assessment of the existing structure and a preliminary estimate of construction costs. I had worked on the project since its inception, first as a Pratt Institute architecture student, then as a Pratt Center staff member, later as a CETA worker at St. Nick. Now I joined the firm as project architect;

Judith Edelman was the partner-in-charge.

In order to ensure continuing input to the architects, a programming committee was organized. This group comprised people from St. Nick, the parish, Pratt Center, and the neighborhood. Under the leadership of Sister Thérèse Cordé, the committee was charged with turning the information gathered in the earlier phase into a final building program. It also had responsibility for tenant se-

lection criteria and the organization of management for the building after occupancy. The spirit, persistence, and thoroughness of the following people are at the core of the eventual success of Jennings Hall:

Theckla Burns
Marion Wallin
Salvatore Abramo
Sister Helen Brennan
Rose Crimi
Richard Macellaro
Pat Martone
Marie Leanza
Susan Burns
Gary Hattem
Gloria Olmo
Cathy Herman
Carl Wallin
Kenny Wallin
Marie Bueno
Pete Antonelli
Suzanne Wasik
Sister Thérèse Cordé

In addition to performing the traditional services of design and construction documents, we felt that an important component of the architects' responsibility was to educate the programming committee in the process of designing and building. The committee learned that design decisions were not only affected by users' functional needs, but were also shaped by other factors:

structural, mechanical, legal (building code and zoning resolutions), HUD guidelines, and economic considerations.

The programming committee directly determined many aspects of Jennings, from the nature and sizes of community spaces to the hardware and finishes in the building. Most significantly, the group's efforts ensured that the concerns of the neighborhood, such as security features, were not overlooked. The architects, on the other hand, were benefited by being able to work in a situation where immediate and regular feedback on a multiclient, publicly funded project, was an integral part of the design process.

## Symbiosis in Design

During the schematic design phase, the programming committee met weekly at the St. Nick offices. This group formed a symbiotic relationship with the architects. The programming committee provided the architects with information on the older people living in the area, as well as the feelings of the community in

8. Jennings Hall rehabilitated.

9. Jennings Hall extension in context.

George Cserna

general. The architects translated these concerns into spatial relationships and physical form. This description, however, does not fully convey the actual uneven course of events involving questions, definition, argument, misunderstanding, redefinition, probable solutions, continued discussion, and eventual resolutions. The process of determining the physical massing of the new portion of the housing provides an example of the complex working relationship between the architects and the programming committee.

Neighborhood people voiced strong feelings about the size of the new building, and also stipulated that the new and rehabilitated parts of the development be functionally one. The existing building would house 54 units; the remaining units would be in a new structure. We presented a series of massing studies illustrating alternatives ranging from 124 to 176 total units. These studies were presented graphically in plan diagrams and axonometric drawings, as well as through a study model which allowed the removal and addition of floors to represent each of the options. The manipulable model provided the committee with an extremely useful tool in visualizing the alternative forms of the new building. We were encouraged to minimize the apparent bulk of the structure by employing jogs and set-

10. The entrance to the new wing is a good place to sit in the sun.

11. Satisfied residents.

12. Federal budget cuts forced the sponsors to furnish Jennings Hall with donations.

backs. The committee wanted the street line preserved, and we found a way to hold it with a one-story portion containing community-related facilities. Above this, the residential floors, with double loaded corridors, rose six stories and then set back again for three more stories of units along a single loaded corridor. Through the articulation of the ends of the bearing walls between units, we found a way to echo the rhythm and scale of the neighboring rowhouses.

The result was a new building which, while not exceeding the height of the existing structure, would still contain enough units to make the project economically feasible in terms of construction and operating costs. Jennings Hall was designed to have a total of 143 apartments. Later, when the project faced financial uncertainty, seven additional units were added. This was accomplished not by building one story higher, but by filling in a setback corner and substituting more apartments for some ground floor community space.

The committee, as liaison between the architect and the community, spread the news of Jennings Hall's progress through St. Nick's newspaper, *Greenline*, by illustrated bulletins posted at gathering places, by periodic, open forum meetings to review the plans, and in casual, daily conversation.

Stanley Wisniewolski and others on the St. Nick staff constructed a model of the neighborhood so that the entire project could be visualized in context. They also built large-scale, furnished models of each typical unit. These were particularly useful in showing prospective tenants the features of the new apartments. This constant communication led the neighborhood people to feel direct involvement with this first major step in community revitalization.

Jennings Hall is now occupied and the architects' work is ended. But the work of the St. Nick community is continuing: they are busy reviewing the many applications from prospective tenants, resolving the details of managing the building, and thinking about their next construction project—knowing they can count on the continuing assistance of the Pratt Center.

13. St. Nick staff and volunteers—successful community redevelopment begins with people.

Continued from page 331.

- Conducted preliminary urban design studies for the Grand Street Commercial Revitalization Project. In return, Gary Hattem, St. Nick' director, has assisted other Center clients in their efforts to obtain commercial revitalization contracts from the City.
- Provided architectural and packaging assistance in the renovation of 137 Guernsey Street, a sweat equity coop conversion. The renovation of this six-family building was carried out by Westinghouse High School students supported by a Youth Employment Training Grant.

We are now attempting to develop a comprehensive approach to industrial building rehabilitation and job development. Our approach, modeled after successful efforts in England, will focus on the provision of space and services that will encourage new enterprises.

After our initial encounter with the problem in the St. Nicholas area some years ago, the Pratt Center has worked hard to create a coalition against redlining. In the broader Williamsburg neighborhood around St. Nick, we helped residents conduct a street-by-street *Real Estate Register* canvass to get information on bank lending patterns. Redlining evidence in hand, and armed with specific requests for financial assistance, a committee then approached a local savings institution, the Anchor Savings Bank. But initial discussions brought no progress. Pratt Center helped the neighborhood to challenge Anchor's request to merge with a Westchester bank. With the support of the local congressional leadership, an agreement was reached between the bank and the community in August, 1977. The bank agreed to provide $25 million over five years for mortgages in the area—and to advertise their availability. *Pratt Center now relies on the St. Nicholas staff to help us* to train other groups and to provide leadership in citywide groups fighting redlining and displacement.

As a result of a growing understanding of the importance of the issue, the Center began to work with other groups across the country on redlining. We helped to draft and obtain passage of the Community Reinvestment Act, which requires that banks keep records on their mortgage practices. Recently we have focused our attention on insur-

14. Pratt architecture faculty and students extend the Center's reach.

ance redlining and other forms of institutional and government disinvestment. Because redlining has a major effect on the potential for neighborhood-based planning, it has become an important issue for Pratt Center.

## The Future of Advocacy

The story goes on because the process continues. One event leads to the next, issues fade away, only to resurface in a different form. (For example, the relocation issue of the 1960s is similar to the gentrification issue of the 1980s.) The focus of our activity is the relationship of people to their physical environment. We provide professional assistance to help them understand their environment and make plans to improve it. We help them develop a grasp of the private and public resources available to aid them in implementing their ideas. We encourage them to forge the coalitions that can bring about progressive change in our society, so that their plans can indeed become a reality. Progress is slow, but real. Commitment is important, as are the quality and talent of the staff. The Center has been fortunate in being able to attract and retain a group of dedicated and skilled people, many of whom have been at the Center a significant portion of their professional lives. Supporting the work of the core staff are many hardworking students* and faculty members.

The Pratt Center, needless to say,

cannot do the job by itself. What must be created is a large number of practitioners and offices—public interest and private sector—focusing on social architecture and advocacy planning. Professional organizations staffed and directed by people committed to progressive social change and the enfranchisement of working class people and neighborhoods are desperately needed. We have found that effectiveness is dependent on the following factors:

- The ability to provide continuity of assistance over time to neighborhood clients
- Integration of technical assistance and monitoring functions so the client can be aided not only in the planning and design phases, but also in the implementation phase
- The development of *a broad range of interrelated architectural and planning services*, some of which have not traditionally been defined as in the architectural domain

One major question remains: How can this kind of practice be financed? The answer is not an easy one, and the un-

---

*Student involvement in the Center has continued unabated since the 1960s. Today we have about 70 students, 22 of whom are full-time at the Center, meeting all their academic requirements through their work. Others are enrolled in studio courses and take on well-defined projects that have a clear beginning and end. Still others combine course work and work-study programs, or are volunteers in our University Year for Action program funded by VISTA-ACTION.

certainty of funding has plagued the Center over the past 17 years, as it has other Community Design Centers. Fortunately, we have been able to develop a broad base of support, including private foundation grants, corporate gifts, and federal, state, and local contracts.*

While the need to develop a consistent source of funding for neighborhood architecture, planning, and other technical assistance activities is crucial, there are enough sources available to encourage new groups to begin. These include local foundations and contracts with local governments through their

Community Development Block Grant programs. In addition, many state offices of community affairs are finding ways to finance community design and development projects. If there is a commitment, there will be a way. We stand ready to help.

Ron Shiffman
Rudy Bryant
Rex Curry
Pratt Institute Center for Community and Environmental Development
275 Washington Avenue
Brooklyn, New York 11205

15. The Center's working environment reflects its values.

---

*In 1963, the budget of the Center was slightly over $35,000; today it exceeds $620,000, and has directly generated for its clients $14 for every dollar it received over the years.

Sources of funds shift from year to year and administration to administration. The Rockefeller Brothers Fund has, without any strings attached, funded the Center for at least 14 of the 16 years we have been in operation. Today, we have over 14 different sources of support, including HUD, the National Endowment for the Arts, the New York State Council on the Arts, the New York State Division of Housing and Community Renewal, and New York City's Housing Preservation and Development Department.

# Architecture and Politics in the Sunbelt

**Jody Gibbs, architect**
**Director, Tucson CD/DC**

About eight years ago, the Tucson Community Design Center was formed to address the architectural needs of the working class and poorer people in the desert border region of Southern Arizona. Our clients include Chicanos, Native Americans, blacks, and whites. And our projects cover a wide range of needs, including health clinics, food co-operatives, day-care centers, educational buildings, housing, neighborhood centers, libraries, and special facilities for the disabled, mentally handicapped, elderly, and other disadvantaged people.

Basically, we organize our clients to fight for equal services. The most apparent problem of our clients is that they don't have any money. Therefore, the majority of projects involves a political process of uniting the client group into a body large enough and strong enough to apply pressure for funds. When a client group comes to us, the program is generally to collect information with the client, analyze it together, determine with the client who or what is responsible for the problem, and then develop a strategy and implement it together. If this process is successful, then there follows a time when we do what is conventionally known as architecture. Approximately 75 percent of our time goes into the organizational work, information-gathering and analysis, and po-

2–4. An example of the Tucson Community Design Center's low income housing work. Environmentally-conscious design mixes units for families with elderly and handicapped households in single project.

5. Site plan. See following page for typical units.

Preceding page: an entrance into one of the courtyards.

2

3

4

litical action. About 25 percent of our time goes into conventional architecture.

The longer we work, the clearer it becomes to us that the form and function of the man-made environment is closely controlled by about 10 percent of the population. This small group seems to have power over the educational system, the economic system, the news, the law, and the ownership of the land. Thus, this same small group determines which industries, housing, transportation systems, and institutions do and don't get built. Our client group is in constant struggle with that 10 percent. It would not be an exaggeration to say that be-

tween these two groups a struggle exists and continues daily in all aspects of life—customs, culture, education, employment, health, food, information, material goods.

The 10 percent has many tools at its disposal to confuse our clients, but the three that we see them use most often are the government, the media, and racism. The government deploys a never-ending charade of programs that are supposed to correct the inequities of society. These have included the anti-poverty program, Model Cities, Community Development Block Grants, and many others. While the names change, the basic game is the same: that is, to

take one percent of the city budget and to toss it from the table like a bone for the poor to fight over, while the remaining 99 percent of the budget is used to address business as usual—rezonings, providing the infrastructure for commercial exploitation in the region, and maintaining a considerable police force to keep the lid on things.

I say these things without hostility. They are true, and in the quest for equality we try to get even without getting mad. As for the local media, the television stations and the newspapers add to the confusion of our clients with seemingly endless advertising, pseudo-politics, and "lifestyle" presentations,

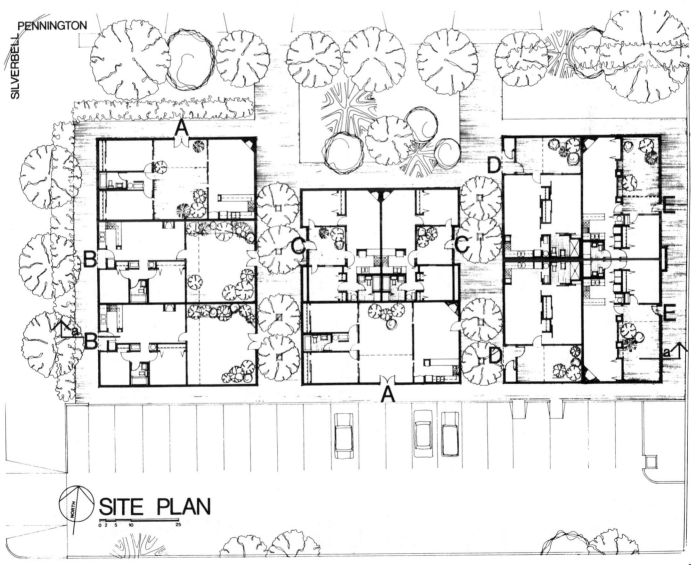

SITE PLAN

tripping people up on how they should or should not live. Both the media and the local government effectively use racism to divide our clients, brown from black from red from white, and our clients often fall for this in spite of the fact that they all occupy a similar economic position in society.

To counter the local government and media, we work with our clients to provide a counterstream of information. And much of our time goes into leaflets, posters, community newspapers, community meetings, and confrontation. It is impossible to be effective without some form of communications. It is equally impossible to be involved in ad-vocacy work without being involved in confrontation. Many architects and other professional people stay away from confrontation and pretend that they are neutral and impartial. We don't believe there is any such thing as an impartial professional. Those who believe they are impartial don't really know what is happening.

Each and every day we ask, "Which side are you on?" Of course, liberals wish to believe that they are on everybody's side—but that is impossible. Relative to the question at hand (Which side are you on regarding participatory design?), in our work our clients participate to a very large extent in in-formation-gathering and analysis, in development of aims and strategy, and in leadership in confrontation to see that funds are provided for projects. If they don't participate in numbers and to a significant degree, the projects will never happen.

In the design stage, the clients again have major control of the programmatic aims and requirements of a building. Generally speaking, we present alternative means of satisfying their program. We work a lot with models and renderings, in addition to plans and elevations and sections. Where possible, we like to show our clients an existing building we have done if it has similar elements be-

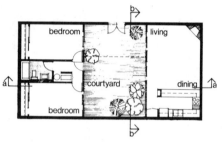

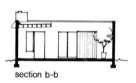

section a-a    section b-b

front elevation

UNIT A    FAMILY

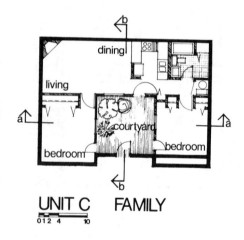
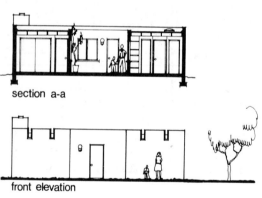
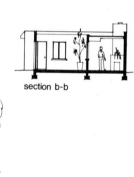

section a-a    section b-b

front elevation

UNIT C    FAMILY

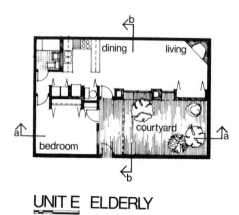
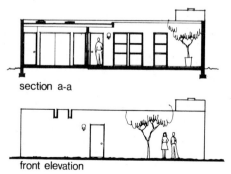
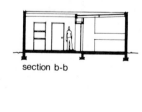

section a-a    section b-b

front elevation

UNIT E  ELDERLY

6,7. Part of the counterstream of information: cover and pages from the English/Spanish *People's Urban History of Tucson*.

Drawings by Daniel Zarza

7

43

cause even models are difficult to understand.

Most of our projects have very limited funds, and that possibly makes the decision-making process easier. Our clients wish to see that their project's aims are met. We use the building program we have developed with the client to evaluate design alternatives, asking them to consider how the building will be used at each hour of the day in the spring, the summer, the fall, and the winter. Our clients are very practical and they wish to see that they get the very most for every dollar. They generally want durable buildings that are well constructed, warm in the winter,

and cool in the summer. While aesthetics are important to them, they are usually secondary to practical considerations, such as more space for additional functions within a building. So far we have never tried having clients draw spaces or move furniture around in a model or that sort of thing. We would not oppose such practices if they produced good architecture, but so far we haven't used such methods. Some architects believe that such design methods confer freedom on the client. I suppose our concept of freedom has more to do with political economy, and we would like to see a participatory process where our clients—and the vast

majority of working people in the world—were able to participate with power and authority in the larger decisions concerning control of land, the economic system, the law, the media, and the educational system. Once the power relationships relative to these things change, we are fairly confident that the questions of participatory design will take care of themselves.

8–10. Three views of the South Tucson Adult Learning Center. Years of community pressure and advocacy architecture were required to get city, county, and state governments to cooperate in building this needed facility in the barrio. The murals are by Roberto Borboa.

8

9

10

# Commentary on Advocacy/Pratt Center

Chester Hartman, Planners Network

## ONE, TWO . . . MANY PRATT CENTERS

Commenting on Ron Shiffman's report on the Pratt Center puts me in an unaccustomed role. Usually I'm invited to be a commentator or panelist as the "dissenting voice," to attack some program, agency, or official representing the establishment. In this case, the Pratt Center has for nearly two decades been an extraordinarily valuable institution, both in terms of the concrete services it has provided to community groups in New York City and as a model for how to relate service to the broader issues raised by its advocacy work.

To summarize what I think are the key strengths and most important lessons of the Pratt experience:

- One is longevity and consistency. There's simply no substitute for being around for nearly 20 years and for the trust, respectability, and connections that are developed only over time. It brings about intimate knowledge of how the system functions and where the openings and opportunities are to be found, who the actors are, and how the game is played. The benefits of being a durable institution are to be seen in many phases of the Center's work—particularly in its ability to function within and help form coalitions, its effectiveness in the public arena with respect to expert testimony, and its overall ability to communicate with public bodies.

  While not a fan of great person theories, one important aspect of the durability factor is that Pratt has had the same director just about since day one. Ron Shiffman is an extraordinary person, and maintaining a single extraordinary person in the leadership role helps no end. It is fitting that *Village Voice* columnist Jack Newfield included Shiffman in his 1976 listing of "46 good people trying to save New York."

- The Center's continued adherence to clear and simple goals. A product of 1960s' consciousness and work style, the Pratt Center has steadfastly adhered to basic values of redistributive politics and participatory democracy—not just in form, but with the aim of maximizing people's control over their own lives and community resources. The way the issues of participation and control work themselves out in the Pratt Center's practice are transfer of skills through workshops, demystification of professional work, and community education. The aim over the long run is to work themselves out of a job. An example is given by the remarkable fact that one of their clients has become so able regarding the redlining/disinvestment issue that the Pratt Center now relies on it to provide training and leadership to other community groups dealing with these problems.

- Understanding the relationship of neighborhood problems to the political system as a whole, and constantly melding both ends of the spectrum in their analysis and their praxis.

- Institutional independence. Although its origins are with a university and the Center still is part of Pratt Institute, it is financially and functionally autonomous. How the Pratt Center

functions institutionally is perhaps a key issue to explore, particularly if one is to ask how we can help create and sustain many such institutions all over the country.

My own experience in the late 1960s as Director of the Urban Field Service (UFS) in the Harvard Graduate School of Design is perhaps relevant here.*

UFS was created in order to substitute collective, community-based work for the traditional studio-simulation planning and design form of education. Our clients were Boston-area lower income community groups that needed assistance with immediate problems, such as fighting a renewal project, creating a community development corporation, building a tenant organization, designing a center for teenage "street people," or forming a plan for resident control of a public housing project. Interdisciplinary teams of 4 to 10 graduate students from planning, architecture, landscape architecture, urban design, law, sociology, business, social work, and other fields worked for one or more semesters with and for the community clients. Instructors or team leaders were generally hired from outside the regular faculty (who, by and large, hadn't the interest, skills, sensitivity, or politics for this kind of work.) And the educational-socialization purpose of the experience—beyond the actual help rendered to the community (which usually was quite substantial)—was clear: to provide students with alternative models for professional work beyond the traditional private office and public agency slots. We wanted people to understand how community groups functioned and what their needs were. We wanted to de-professionalize our work, to get past the language, forms, and work styles that created barriers between planners/designers and those they were supposed to serve. We wanted to make the political forces underlying communities' planning and design problems explicit. We aimed to show how narrowly conceived professional roles, as normally taught in planning and design schools, had to be expanded to encompass at the least an understanding of, if not a commitment to, community organizing and working to resolve the local and national issues that created the specific community problem that brought about a request for UFS services.

All in all, UFS was very similar to the Pratt Center, in its work, political thrust, and educational purposes. Yet UFS was terminated (shortly after I was) in the early 1970s. Why did UFS expire and why does the Pratt Center flourish? One reason has to do with the role of education in our work. The Pratt Center initially was established as a *community* education project, while UFS tried simultaneously to achieve goals for and within the community and for and within the existing curriculum. Given the power that traditional faculty and administrators have over

---

*For a more complete description, see my article "The Harvard Urban Field Service: A Retrospective View" in *Eleven Views: Collaborative Design in Community Development,* Peter Batchelor, Ed. (Raleigh: North Carolina State University School of Design, 1971, pp. 120–130). The article is reprinted in the September, 1971 *Architectural Forum.*

curriculum and degree requirements, it is perhaps impossible to try to ride both horses at once. Competition for time from other course work, and resistance and hostility from other faculty members all tended to undermine the community-based activities. The Pratt Center, by contrast, has 22 *full-time* students (comprising half of full-time staff), who meet all their academic requirements through their work. *

Also, the differences in relations with "parent institutions" are substantial, as dramatically revealed by two contrasting incidents: UFS was deeply damaged by the reaction of the University administration to one of our projects that provided technical assistance to the Cambridge Housing Convention, an OEO-sponsored group seeking to halt Harvard and MIT takeover of the city's low rent housing areas. The Pratt Center, on the other hand, was able to convince Pratt Institute to become cosponsor of a senior citizen housing project with one of its client groups.

A second key factor is financial independence (the Center has a $620,000 annual budget). While UFS never had the money to mount a large-scale and long-term operation—although we did manage to squeeze some 20 largely successful projects out of a $25,000 budget over three terms—the Center has been able to draw on a wide range of governmental programs and private support. The diversity of its backing is a great strength, in turn a function of the contacts and success it has built up over so many years. We need to learn more about why Pratt has succeeded financially when so many other community design centers have been forced to close or cut back.

One important issue Ron Shiffman's article does not address is governance: how and by whom decisions are made at the Pratt Center with respect to what projects are sought out, accepted, and rejected, how resources are allocated, internal work relations determined, and so forth. Are the communities the Pratt Center serves represented in the process, and if so, how is the difficult question handled of playing off narrow interests of particular communities versus citywide strategy and policy-oriented work? Advocacy groups I am familiar with and have worked with have had some hard times around such questions—around centralized versus participatory practice within the organization and around the concrete issue of who gets paid how much and why.

The big issue, of course, is how to multiply the number of operations like the Pratt Center. For all its good track record, the service impact of a single center in New York City is minimal (although its policy-oriented work has of course had citywide and even nationwide impact.) Aside from a handful of cities

---

*In the UFS retrospective cited above, I suggested creation of "an autonomous institution to train students in community-based planning and design. Such a training institute ideally should be independent of the university...." See also my guest editor's introduction to the July, 1970 special issue of the *Journal of The American Institute of Planners* on planning education. I wrote:

To the extent that serious training in what has been called advocacy planning is desired—and more especially to the extent to which persons from powerless communities seek to equip themselves with the tools necessary to do their own planning and implementation—the university may be an inappropriate place for this kind of training.... In training these persons, universities are hampered by traditional admissions requirements and faculty criteria, inflexibility in course length and teaching methods, the highly political nature of community-based advocacy planning, and the inappropriateness of a student mentality—orientation to the university community and student life—for this kind of training. These considerations may make it more desirable to establish autonomous training institutes for students from the community . . . as well as for students from more conventional backgrounds who wish to receive training in planning skills but do not feel a need to travel the traditional academic and degree routes.

such as Tucson (as Jody Gibbs ably describes the work of the Community Development/Design Center there), too little of the kind of service and political work the Pratt Center does is to be found in other US cities, to say nothing of small towns and rural areas. I have no good or simple answers to offer to this problem. Funding is short, and will be more so, although successful work can produce big bucks (as Pratt has shown).There must be more conscious proselytizing work and technical assistance by successful advocacy practitioners toward the end of multiplying such centers in other cities and states. *

We will not easily solve the problem of how to provide paid work (even at relatively low salaries) for practitioners and students trained in community-oriented skills. But the organized demand by communities and practitioners for funds to support advocacy staff positions is a key ingredient in generating money from the public and nonprofit sectors. There also must be more efforts to relate this kind of work to the rest of our profession(s), and especially to the educational institutions where professional values and skills are formed. While relations with established educational and professional institutions entail risks and dangers, the resources, access, and legitimacy such institutions provide make them important potential assets.

People currently involved in advocacy planning and design need to focus their attention on the growth and expansion of these efforts. One or two such stories, important as they are, should not leave us feeling self-satisfied, but should inspire us to provide the means for expanding our work.

---

*Even in these times a fair number of Community Design Centers are keeping the idea alive, as indicated by the following list —**EDITOR**.

# NATIONAL DIRECTORY OF COMMUNITY DESIGN CENTERS

*Alabama*
**AUBURN COMMUNITY DESIGN CENTER**
Department of Architecture
Auburn University
104 Dudley Hall
Auburn, AL 36849
202/826-4516
R. Wayne Drummond/Dir.

*Arizona*
**TUCSON COMMUNITY DEVELOPMENT DESIGN CENTER**
316 South Convent, P.O. Box 1870
Tucson, AZ 85702
602/791-9361
Jody Gibbs/Dir.

*California*
**COMMUNITY DESIGN CENTER OF OAKLAND AND BERKELEY**
Department of Architecture
232 Wurster Hall
Berkeley, CA 94720
415/642-2676
James Vann/Dir.

**BARRIO PLANNERS, INC.**
5261 E. Beverly Boulevard
Los Angeles, CA 90022
213/685-6280
Frank Villalobos/Dir.

**LOS ANGELES COMMUNITY DESIGN CENTER**
849 S. Broadway
Los Angeles, CA 90014
213/626-1453
Gary Squires/Dir.

**NEIGHBORHOOD DESIGN CENTER OF OAKLAND**
1419 Broadway, Room 722
Oakland, CA 94612
415/834-7990
Maxine Griffith/Dir.

**COMMUNITY DESIGN CENTER**
2101 Bryant Street, 3rd Floor
San Francisco, CA 94110
415/647-1366
Chuck Turner/Dir.

**NORTH COAST COMMUNITY DESIGN CENTER**
301 Tesconi Circle
Santa Rosa, CA 95401
Bob Briscoe/Dir.

*Colorado*
**CENTER FOR ENVIRONMENT DESIGN, EDUCATION AND RESEARCH (CEDER)**
University of Colorado, Boulder
College of Environmental Design
Boulder, CO 80309
303/492-7627
Allan Wallace/Acting Dir.

**COMMUNITY INSTITUTE FOR DEVELOPMENT & DESIGN (CIDD)**
University of Colorado, Colorado Springs
Colorado Springs, CO 80907
303/593-3136
Paul Grogger/Acting Dir.

**CENTER FOR COMMUNITY
DEVELOPMENT AND DESIGN**
1100 14th Street
Denver, CO 80202
303/629-2816
T. Michael Smith/Dir.

**NORTH DENVER
NEIGHBORHOOD DEVELOPMENT
CENTER**
3401 Pecos Street
Denver, CO 80211
303/477-4774
Eric Glunt/Dir.

**NORTHEAST DENVER
NEIGHBORHOOD DEVELOPMENT
CENTER**
3313 Gilpin Street
Denver, CO 80205
303/825-1504
Bob Horn/Dir.

**WESTSIDE NEIGHBORHOOD
DESIGN CENTER**
825 W 11th Street
Denver, CO 80204
303/534-8342
Tom Edmiston/Dir.

**COLORADO RURAL DESIGN
CENTER**
2800 D Road
Grand Junction, CO 81501
303/243-8215
John Schler/Dir.

*Deleware*
**COMMUNITY DESIGN CENTER**
408 E 8th Street
Wilmington, DE 19801
302/658-4133
William Pelham, AIA/Dir.

*Florida*
**COMMUNITY DEVELOPMENT
DIVISION**
University of Miami
160 Mahoney Hall
1101 Stanford Drive
Coral Cables, FL 33146
305/284-2490
Joseph Middlebrooks, AIA/Dir.

**COMMUNITY DESIGN CENTER
OF JACKSONVILLE, INC.**
516 Adams Street
Jacksonville, FL 32202
904/354-8675
Bill Mauzy/Dir.

**TAMPA COMMUNITY DESIGN
CENTER, INC.**
315 Plant Avenue
Tampa, FL 33606
813/251-6167
Johnny Horton/Dir.

*Georgia*
**COMMUNITY DESIGN CENTER
OF ATLANTA**
836 W. Peachtree
Atlanta, GA 30308
404/885-1950
Kevin Johns/Dir.

*Hawaii*
**HAWAII CDC—KAUAI CENTER**
P.O. Box 542
Kapaa, HI 96746

*Illinois*
**COMMUNITY ADVOCACY DEPOT**
c/o Department of Architecture
University of Illinois
608 E. Larado Taft Drive
Champagne, IL 61820
217/333-7120
Professor Kaha/Dir.

**CHICAGO ARCHITECTURAL
ASSISTANCE CENTER**
502 N Wells Street
Chicago, IL 60610
312/661-1920
John Tomassi/Exec. Dir.

*Kentucky*
**LOUISVILLE COMMUNITY
DESIGN CENTER**
309 Speed Building
333 Guthrie Green
Louisville, KY 40202
502/599-0343
John I. Trawick/Dir.

*Maryland*
**NEIGHBORHOOD DESIGN
CENTER, INC.**
720 East Pratt
Baltimore, MD 21202
301/625-0123
Phyliss Sachs/Dir.

*Massachusetts*
**ARCHITECTURAL ASSISTANCE
PROGRAM**
MIT, Room 7-402
77 Massachusetts Avenue
Cambridge, MA 02139
617/253-7830
Debra Epstein/Student Dir.

*Michigan*
**KERCHEVAL—McCELLAN CDC**
10107 Kercheval
Detroit, MI 48214
Michelle H. Norris/Dir.

**NCPOA COMMUNITY DESIGN
TEAM**
305 Beakes Avenue
Ann Arbor, MI 48104

**COMMUNITY DESIGN CENTER**
Michigan Arcade
Suite 16
215 S. Washington Square
Lansing, MI 48933
517/482-0809
Arlena Hines/Dir.

*Minnesota*
**COMMUNITY DESIGN CENTER**
616 E. 22nd Street
Minneapolis, MN 55404
612/872-0727
Ruth Murphy/Dir.

*Missouri*
**COMMUNITY DESIGN CENTER**
School of Architecture
Washington University
St. Louis, MO 63130
324/889-6200
Hanns Webber/Dir.

*Nebraska*
**NEBRASKA COMMUNITY DESIGN
CENTER**
College of Architecture
University of Nebraska
Lincoln, NE 68588
402/472-3592
Jim Griffin/Dir.

*New Jersey*
**ARCHITECT'S COMMUNITY
DESIGN CENTER OF NEW JERSEY**
487 Orange Street
Newark, NJ 07107
201/483-2213
Toni Harris/Pres.

**URBAN PRACTICE STUDIO**
NJ School of Architecture
NJ Institute of Technology
323 High Street
Newark, NJ 07702
201/645-5321
Karl Linn/Dir.

*New Mexico*
**DESIGN & PLANNING
ASSISTANCE CENTER**
120 Yale SE
Albuquerque, NM 87106
505/277-3806
Edward B. Norris, AIA/Dir.

*New York*
**PEOPLES' DEVELOPMENT
CORPORATION**
Planning & Design Unit
1162 Washington Avenue
Bronx, NY 10456
212/993-0445
Ben Jennings/Dir. of Operations

**PRATT INSTITUTE CENTER FOR
COMMUNITY &
ENVIRONMENTAL
DEVELOPMENT**
275 Washington Avenue
Brooklyn, NY 11205
212/636-3489
Ron Schiffman/Dir.

**COMMUNITY PLANNING
ASSISTANCE CENTER OF
WESTERN NY, INC.**
1312 Jefferson Avenue
Buffalo, NY 14208
716/886-1400
Dick Prosser/Dir.

**COMMUNITY DESIGN CENTER**
106 Sibley Hall
Ithaca, NY 14853
607/256-7439
Stuart Stein

**PLAN/BUILD, INC.**
321 Highland Avenue
Syracuse, NY 13203
315/476-5636
Robert Charron/Dir.

**TAP (TROY PROFESSIONAL
ASSISTANCE), INC.**
2245 6th Avenue
Troy, NY 12180
518/274-3050
Joe Fama/Dir.

*North Carolina*
**COMMUNITY DEVELOPMENT
GROUP**
School of Design
North Carolina State University
Raleigh, NC 27650
919/737-2206
Henry Sanoff, AIA/Dir.

*Ohio*
**CONNECTION**
Department of Architecture
University of Cincinnati
Cincinnati, OH 45221
513/475-6426
David Smith/Dir.

**YOUNGSTOWN COMMUNITY
DESIGN CENTER**
107 W. LaClede Avenue
Youngstown, OH 44507
216/782-2646
H. Walter Damon, AIA/Chairman

*Oklahoma*
**NEIGHBORHOOD DEVELOPMENT
& CONSERVATION CENTER**
525 N.W. 13th Street
Oklahoma City, OK 73103
405/232-4626
Linda Ivins/Dir.

*Oregon*
**WILLIAMETTE COMMUNITY
DESIGN CENTER**
P.O. Box 10273
Eugene, Oregon 97440
503/345-2427
Richard Schields/Dir.

*Pennsylvania*
**ARCHITECTS' WORKSHOP**
401 North Broad Street, Suite 920
Philadelphia, PA 19108
215/574-9591
Augustus Baxter, Hon. AIA/Dir.

**MANTUA COMMUNITY
PLANNERS, INC.**
539 N. 36th Street
Philadelphia, PA 19104
215/387-4488
Tim Spencer/Dir.

**ARCHITECTS' WORKSHOP**
237 Oakland Avenue
Pittsburg, PA 15213
412/682-6360
Stan Kabala/Dir.

*Rhode Island*
**RHODE ISLAND SCHOOL OF
DESIGN COMMUNITY DESIGN
CENTER**
2 College Hill
Providence, RI 02903
401/331-3511 Ext. 350
Lester J. Millman, AIA/Dir.

*Tennessee*
**EAST TENNESSEE COMMUNITY
DESIGN CENTER**
1522 Highland Avenue
Knoxville, TN 37916
615/525-9945
Annette Anderson/Dir.

**MEMPHIS PLANNING & DESIGN
CENTER**
c/o Graduate Department of Planning
Johnson Hall, Room 226
Memphis St. University
Memphis, TN 38152
901/454-2056
Lindsey Albert/Dir.

*Utah*
**ASSIST, INC.**
218 E. Fifth South
Salt Lake City, UT 84111
801/355-7085
Chris Clark/Dir.

*Virginia*
**URBAN DESIGN PROGRAM**
Virginia Polytech Institute & State
University
College of Architecture & Urban
Studies
202 Cowgill Hall
Blacksburg, VA 24061
703/961-6415
Dean Charles Steger/Dir.

*Washington*
**ENVIRONMENTAL WORKS**
402 15th Avenue, East
Seattle, WA 98112
206/329-8300
Stevan Johnson/Dir.

*Wisconsin*
**DESIGN COALITION**
1201 Williamson Street
Madison, WI 53703
608/258-8866
Tom Starkweather/Lou H. Jablonski—
contact persons

# Microbrigades and Participation
## Cuba

In the following article, Roberto Segre, the well-known architectural historian and critic in Havana, looks at successive stages in architectural theory and practice since the Revolution as steps in the development of a socialist approach to the built environment. The effort is to define a framework for a socialist society, to transform utopia into reality, creating functional and culturally significant spaces for *el hombre integrado*—the new, integrated human being. Segre will speak of revolutionary architecture, but the revolution will not be primarily in form, as with our postmodernists. Here the revolution lies in the concept of architecture as a strategy to overcome the divisions in society, as a method of creating an egalitarian environment, as an instrument for economic and social progress, and as the key to involving people in making a world which is truly theirs.

Segre's concluding article should be read with Paul Jacob's report in Part 2 on an experimental housing project in Havana. Both Jacob and Segre make an effort to see architecture whole—as form, content, and process creating and reflecting the emergence of a new society.

1. A *campesino* and his son look out from the balcony of their new home. Tens of thousands of rural and urban workers in Cuba participate in the creation of new housing and new communities.

# Architecture in the Revolution

Roberto Segre, Professor of Architecture
Technical University of Havana

## Reality and Aspirations

Historically, the evolution of architecture has produced two levels of results: one practical and immediate, the objective response to the needs of society, and the other theoretical, based on hypothetical propositions that constitute aspirations and are an expression of desires. In its fullest development, the theoretical proposal becomes utopia, a concept characterized by two contradictory tendencies: idealistic utopia, never to be realized, and real utopia, a progressive conception of the environment.

Bourgeois ideologists have repeatedly elaborated idealistic utopias in the social, economic, and cultural spheres as an escape from the profound contradictions of the capitalist system. The history of the bourgeois utopia is this area of architecture and urban planning (setting aside for a moment certain progressive propositions realized in the nineteenth century) is characterized by a succession of ideal cities—technocratic images that are home to an imaginary society that has overcome the antagonisms of social class and of work as a human necessity. The images that come out of this tradition have very limited connection to objective reality. They can be said to represent an ahistorical confidence in the eternal persistence of the capitalist system.

From the moment of the October Revolution, Soviet architects and planners began to formulate new architectural and urban models reflecting the orientations of a socialist society. In these proposals, we find ourselves before the real and progressive utopia whose propositions do not arise out of abstract spatial and formal fantasies, but out of scientific predictions for the future of a society whose possibilities and nature can be interpreted through the methods of Marxist thought, that is, through historical and dialectical materialism. The early Soviet studies of new urban forms assumed the disappearance of the contradiction between the city and the countryside. They foresaw the need for "social containers" that would give form to the multiple and complex human functions which develop in a socialist society. The importance of providing for group social life in residential development, the close connection between production and education, and the possibility of planning the rational allocation of material and technical resources toward the satisfaction of social needs—these are among the socialist postulates which gave rise to the technical, formal, and spatial hypotheses of Soviet architects at that time.

In realistic utopias, the divergence between what is real and what is imaginary is not the result of insuperable difficulties, but only of limitations set by the objective laws of social, economic, and cultural development. In this case, it is not correct to speak of utopia as the image of the unrealizable—it becomes the embodiment of concrete aspirations. In the case of architecture and urbanism, these concrete aspirations are directed toward the creation of an environment that expresses the fullness of human life and the realization of a level of existence in which the basic necessities of all the members of the community are satisfied. This is not true of the utopias formulated within capitalism. These are almost always unrealizable because the desired social content, like the search for environmental coherence, runs head-on into a physical reality forged by class antagonisms, the exploitation of man by man, the iron law of profit, the cost of land, and the speculation which arises from private ownership—fetters that effectively block any urban development based on different principles.

In Cuba since 1959, gaps between reality and aspiration have always been small—not because of timidity in setting goals, but because of boldness and determination in carrying out the Revolution's program: for example, the rapid nationalization of the nation's productive capacity (which had been dominated by foreign monopolies), the announcement of the Socialist character of the Revolution only two years after the overthrow of the Batista tyranny (and under the watchful eye of the most powerful imperialist nation in the world), the campaign which brought literacy to 700,000 adults in a single year, the establishment of close ties between formal education and manual labor, and the development of international ties of solidarity and support with the countries of Asia, Africa, and Latin America. On the economic plane, reality has shown itself to be more complex and contradictory, and the transformations have not caught up with aspirations with the desired rapidity. The inherited past, centuries of exploitation and poverty, and the distortions of the former capitalist economic structure have left indelible marks whose disappearance will require profound and prolonged sacrifices from the entire society.

## Architecture and Dialectics

In the field of architecture, the difficulty in narrowing the gap between the present reality and realistic utopia has turned out to be equally difficult. Historically conditioned by the previous economic organization of Cuban society, one still sees today superstructural reflections which, individually, cause problems for architecture: the persistence of a system of cultural values established by the former bourgeoisie, outdated habits of thought that continue to create a frame of reference for building, and the quantity and permanence of our architectural inheritance that inhibits experimentation toward the transformation of the environment.

Cuban designers have accepted the objective parameters that define our architectural possibilities, and with the exception of a few visionary projects carried out at the inception of the Revolution (for example, the competition for Liberty Tower, 50 stories high and located in Alamar, and Residential Community 2 in Habana del Este, an enormous ensemble of residential, administrative, and cultural buildings—

349

thin slabs tied together by continuous horizontal platforms), theoretical development has closely followed improvements in the actual technical and economic base and the conditions created by the changes in social relations.

In the first decade of the Revolution, we find four principal tendencies in architectural development:

1. The introduction of careful economic planning to tie architectural solutions to the availability of human and material resources.
2. The acceptance of a dialectical relationship between local capabilities and high technology—a step-by-step development, starting with the environmental transformation required for social and economic growth.
3. A search for innovative approaches to the typology and construction of dwelling units.
4. The movement from closed industrialized construction toward the development of open systems in terms of production of components, construction methods, and design.

In the early years of the Revolution, the focus was on the production of housing. The parameters that limited the architect were, among others, the availability of manpower, the need to encourage the participation of users in construction, and the scarcity of building materials created by the imperialist blockade. At that time, the Technical Research Bureau in the Ministry of Public Works focused architectural investigation on simple construction systems easily assembled with manual labor and of lightweight elements using local materials and a minimum of imported components. This approach was dominant until 1965, when studies were undertaken to introduce more advanced prefabrication systems.

From within the team of technicians working in this initial period of research, the proposals of the Venezuelan architect, Fruto Vivas, stand out. The author of a book widely known in his country, Vivas had carried out successful housing construction experiments using light, prefabricated elements and artisanal construction methods, without the involvement of any skilled labor. Working in Cuba, his architectural experimentation had the following objectives: reduction of the weight of building components, the use of low cost materials, and the massive involve-

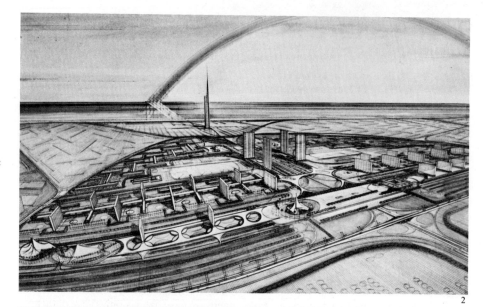

ment of popular participation in the construction of housing. This last is a *leit motiv* that runs through all his writings, an idea which anticipates the forms of participation which will be achieved later by the Microbrigades:

We can and we must create a construction technology which matches the actual state of development in Cuba, one which the Cuban people can use widely in bold programs of construction which involve the active participation of the masses; this is no utopia, it is an imperative necessity. . . . it is the people themselves who have in their hands the power to attack the problem of construction, and because of their needs we must not postpone the creation and appli-

2. In the first years of the Revolution, visionary projects were common. This is a view of the *Ciudad del Pueblo* by architects Fernando Salinas and Gonzales Romero.

3. A realized project from the early years of the Revolution: *Habana del Este.*

350

cation of simple methods of building which reflect the ability of the masses and the real economic possibilities, and which will permit the development of a building culture in the Cuban people. . . .*

The dialectical relationship between local capabilities and the demands of high technology as an element in the social and economic development of the people constitutes the basic postulate that has shaped 15 years of theoretical investigations and practical experiments by the architect Fernando Salinas. For Salinas, the solution to the housing problem cannot be sought in restricted technical or functional terms. Above all, one is dealing with a social, human problem that affects millions of inhabitants of the so-called Third World, whose subhuman conditions of existence are the result of the cruel exploitation imposed on underdeveloped countries by developed capitalist nations. The creation of a culturally significant human habitat requires first a social revolution:

> The first and most urgent duty of the architectural revolutionary in these times is to be involved actively in the struggle to transform profoundly both the economy and society, in order then to be able to dedicate all of his effort, his talent, and his heart to opening, together with the people, the road to a true and appropriate architecture . . . Transform man, and with him architecture will be transformed. . . .*

Salinas's understanding of the limitations that condition the practice of architecture in dependent, capitalist countries [such as prerevolutionary Cuba—EDITOR] led him to define 12 principles that focus light on the sharply restricted area of practice imposed on professionals by the dominant classes. According to Salinas, architecture and urbanism in dependent, capitalist countries is characterized by:

1. The contrast between the luxury of architecture intended for the minority and the poverty of that for the great majority, the working class.

*Fruto Vivas, *"Hacia una arquitectura de masas,"* Boletin de la Escuela de Arquitectura 516, Havana, September, 1966.

*Fernando Salinas, *"La arquitectura en los paises en viás de desarrollo,"* Speech given at the VII Congress of the *Union Internationale des Architectes*, Havana, September, 1963 (mimeo).

2. The inexorable growth of the housing deficit, with the consequent sharpening of the housing problem.
3. The marked differences between level of life and housing quality in the cities and in the countryside.
4. Speculation in land and construction for high profits that forces the majority of the people to find a solution to their housing problem in squatting and similar measures.
5. The minimum contribution of the state to the solution of the housing problem.
6. The parallel existence of an advanced technology used to solve isolated problems and a primitive artisanal technology used for the bulk of construction.
7. The concentration of building investments within the largest cities.
8. The generalized use of imported materials with industrial underdevelopment as a consequence.
9. Chaotic conditions in the construction sector, from the multiplicity of dimensioning systems and types of construction materials, to the diversity of architectural solutions to identical problems.
10. The dedication of the effort and talent of architects and technicians to the solution of the narrow problems of the wealthy elite.
11. A paucity of architects and technicians, reflecting the limited volume of architectural work.
12. The search for new aesthetic solutions concentrates on the city, the wealthy, and advanced technology.*

Counterposed to these principles, and as a consequence of the elimination of the antagonistic contradictions existing at the heart of capitalist society, new parameters arise that inform a new, popular architecture. Salinas has written:
The fundamental issues are these:

1. The necessity to produce an extraordinary volume of new construction in the shortest possible time.
2. The revolutionary transformation of society and the economy with the creation of new forms of social organization.
3. The creation through this revolutionary social process of a new type of human being.

*Fernando Salinas, *"La arquitectura revolucionária del Tercer Mundo,"* Tricontinental 1, Havana, July/August, 1967.

4. The particular conditions imposed by our climate and our building methods.
5. The cultural inheritance of our people and of the entire world.
6. A dialectical vision of the world and a practice guided by revolutionary ideology.*

From the general theory, specific characteristics of architecture can be derived; these are the ruling principles for the design of the habitat of the new, socialist society:

1. The principle of economy.
2. The principle of change and growth.
3. The principle of social transformation.
4. The principle of low-cost maintenance and operation.
5. The principle of adaptability.
6. The principle of variety within unity.
7. The dialectic vision of nature, thought, and economic society on the part of the creators of the new architecture.

These principles are complemented by the design methodology used in training our young architects and in orienting them toward the realities of practice, starting with the idea that:

1. Architecture is a part of the process of social development.
2. Architectural theory and practice must always be situated in a specific historic stage in the construction of socialism.
3. The architect must participate actively in the ideological struggle in the field of art and architecture.
4. The architect must play a leading role in the technical revolution that will permit the satisfaction of society's needs.

We are not dealing here only with technical changes, but with an entirely different conception of architecture, one based in a dialectic connection between designer and user who both participate in the different levels of environmental design. While the designer works at the scale of the ensemble, the grouping of rooms and spaces, the user determines the interior and exterior aspects of the rooms themselves: the form of the wall panels, color to be used, the level of equipment required, and so forth. One

*Fernando Salinas, op. cit.

object of research is a system of assembly of and fixing of exterior and interior panels that permits the substitution of new components for old ones as growth in the economy permits. What is aimed at in this way is a dialectical organization of the environment, one in constant transformation, a faithful reflection of the dynamic process that a revolutionary society exhibits. This new stage in the connection between designer and the user integrates the community in the creation of its own life space. In so far as the aspirations of the social collective are internalized by architects and given back to the community in terms of structures that are functional and culturally significant, utopia is transformed into reality; and, paraphrasing Fernando Salinas, spaces for the new, "whole man" *(el hombre integrado)* will be achieved—a framework of life for a socialist society.

## Building Socialism

The discussion of socialist principles and architectural theories in the 1960s and 1970s shows that an acceleration of the process of industrialization is essential if we are going to make up the deficits accumulated in the past. However, industrialization of the production of the habitat has proven to be slower and more complicated than architects had hoped in the early years. This initial optimism led the profession to undervalue the developments taking place within the field of artisanal construction.

After an early concentration on housing production in the first years of the Revolution, in the five years between 1965 and 1970 all available construction materials and manpower were directed toward the expansion of the production sector in order to meet the goals of the 1970 *Gran Zafra*. [The aim was to harvest 10 million tons of sugar.—EDITOR] During these five years, however, substantial investments were made in prefabrication plants, new cement factories were built, and the production of construction materials was increased; the effects of these investments began to be felt after 1970.

As a consequence of the priority given to the economic base, the number of dwellings constructed by the State was reduced in this five-year period. This, it should be clear, created pressure to find new methods to reestablish the index of construction. Set at three

4,5. Light concrete prefabrication systems such as the Sandino System shown here speed construction and permit the use of unskilled, voluntary labor.

6

dwellings per thousand inhabitants in the early years of the Revolution, the effort, in fact, was to raise the index to five per thousand, a level which would begin to cope with the demand for 35,000 new dwellings annually created by population growth, and at the same time to absorb part of the old deficit of 750,000 dwellings which were in deteriorated condition.

The national Census of Population and Dwellings of 1970 showed that for the nation as a whole the total number of dwellings in 1953, 1,256,594 had grown to 1,904,810 by 1970. This is an increase of approximately 600,000 units. If the State constructed just over 200,000 dwellings between 1959 and 1975, this indicates that the remainder were built by their residents. Even if this level is not comparable with the *increase* in State production, it nevertheless is a clear demonstration of the potential contained in popular initiative

and participation, especially if one considers that this production was carried out at a time when materials were scarce and that it was done without technical or professional support.

Traditionally, in the rest of Latin America, the system of self-help has been used to create rural dwellings and to upgrade the precarious dwellings in the squatters' settlements around the major cities. The typology is that of the individual dwelling, grouped in small clusters. They are constructed by the residents themselves, who in some cases carry out minimal infrastructural development work as well. Sociologically, these efforts are heavily permeated with the individualistic ideology of the petit bourgeoisie—the need for property and a private house—which has its roots in the unequal distribution of economic resources, and which in terms of design produces repetitive and anonymous solutions lacking in cultural signification.

7

6. A typical apartment house built by INAV, the state construction agency, in the early years of the Revolution.

7. Collective self-help: voluntary workers building new housing for themselves and their families.

8. Architect Fernando Salinas used on-site prefabrication to create these experimental dwellings in 1962. The interiors are completely open, permitting the users to plan their individual units.

What then is the alternative model that the Cuban Revolution proposes for the development of the habitat with artisanal methods and through the medium of popular participation? The answer was found by fitting housing needs to the economic, social, technical, and ideological objectives of a particular moment in the revolutionary process. The model is the Microbrigade.*

## Foundations of the Microbrigade

The availability of resources in the traditional self-help model depends entirely on individual income or on cooperative loans made to small communities. Self-help posits an economic system tied more to private initiative than to state aid, and one which severely distorts the distribution of national resources. It is not responsive to the need for coherent planning of the material base and the work force. The Cuban solution derives from a close relationship between social necessity and social possibility, and it is organized at the scale of the entire nation. In our case, the State allocates available materials and teams of technicians. They locate themselves in the different cities and towns which constitute the urban structure, and they do this in response to priorities that are established by the production enterprises which supply the manpower to construct collective housing.

The individual focus that characterizes self-help efforts requires that the labor in construction come from the

*For an example of Microbrigade housing production, see the report by Paul Jacob in Part 2—EDITOR.

worker's free time, perhaps with the collaboration of the nuclear family. In all too many cases, the availability of free time is a reflection of the unemployment or underemployment that is common in Latin America. In Cuba, by contrast, a direct relationship between the production center and the worker's need for housing is created. The solution lies in a rationalization of production—and an agreement by the workers to keep up the full production of the plant (or administrative center, educational institution, etc.) with a reduced number of *compañeros*. Then the extra workers are assigned to the task of housing in teams called Microbrigades. In this way, a dialectical link is created between the special effort made in the workplace and the availability of manpower that this frees up for construction. In the production center it is called *plus-work*, and it reflects the workers' understanding of the problems inherent in the economic development of the country and the importance of their direct participation in the solution of these problems. This has absolutely nothing to do with the exploitation of workers typical of an underdeveloped capitalist country. There, the worker, after selling eight hours of his labor power, must still take on the construction of his own home. This is a hidden form of appropriation by capitalist entrepreneurs, in that the building loans and materials purchases necessary to carry out the dwelling work are themselves sources of substantial profits.

In Latin America, because of the low level of construction technology and the millions of unemployed workers ready to engage in it, self-help is considered a

public health and education. The new stability of the productive infrastructure, the application of new technologies, and the rationalization of many tasks freed a considerable number of workers to be absorbed by the construction sector just as the expansion that characterized this past decade was beginning.

In Latin America, it is the unusual self-help initiative that has a collective or communitarian character. There are, of course, a few examples in Chile, Peru, and Mexico. However, in general the individualistic tendency dominates and the objective is to construct the private home, instrument of protection against a difficult and dangerous world, and at the same time a symbol of the value accorded to private property—ownership of land and buildings.

The socialist spirit of the Revolution, the disappearance of private ownership of the means of production, and the search for community define the ideological underpinnings of the new habitat. Its essential components express the collective character of the built environment. For example, apartment houses replace the individual dwelling, dwellings are given to families for their permanent use at a rent of only six percent of their monthly income, and the assignment of housing to workers is strictly on the basis of merit and need, independently of whether they have worked directly in a Microbrigade. The principle of housing as a social service is established. Construction is tied to a center of production, and it is the center of production that makes the assignments of apartments to workers in a democratic assembly.

# DISTRITO JOSE MARTI

MICRODISTRITO A
NEIGHBORHOOD UNIT A

**3**

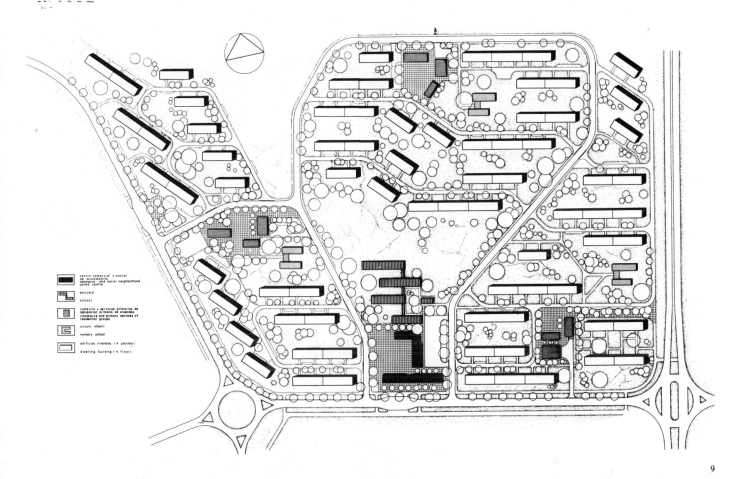

centro comercial y social
de microdistrito
comercial and social neighborhood
united centre

escuela
school

comercio y servicios primarios de
agrupación primaria de viviendas
commerce and primary services of
residential groups

circulo infantil
nursery school

edificios viviendas ( 4 plantas )
dwelling building ( 4 floor )

9

9. Following a devastating hurricane, heavy
prefabrication was employed to build needed
housing in the Jose Martí District of Santiago.

10. Jose Martí: "Gran Panel" apartments
grouped around shopping and services.

panacea. In Cuba, social mobilization
toward construction of this sort is considered an intermediate stage that will
tend to disappear with advances in industrialization and the utilization of
prefabrication systems. At the same
time, it is important to recruit workers
into the construction sector, and, after
1970, to reintegrate the mass of workers
who during the 1960s had been absorbed by the expansion of agriculture,
industry, and services—in particular,

10

355

## Microbrigades and Participation

Each Microbrigade is made up of 33 workers. (This is the group required to complete a building of five floors and 30 apartments in a period of nine months.) Each work team is of heterogeneous composition and only a few of the workers have a background in construction. Those who do, with the support of the technical assistance group, take on the skilled tasks and help in training the rest of the team. The building type generally employed—Model E14—is of simple construction, with block bearing walls and slabs of concrete prefabricated on the site. Even though this building type is standard for the entire country, the presence of architects on all the Microbrigade construction sites has permitted the introduction of variations on the original model, some improvements coming from the professionals and others from the inventiveness of the workers themselves.

An important aspect of the Microbrigade is its versatility in the creation not only of dwellings, but also of the social services required by the new communities. They also help in the erection of larger projects using industrial technology, as assistants to specialized Brigades. This has permitted Microbrigade communities to integrate buildings that reflect diverse technologies and that establish a dialectical relation with the usual simple construction. This is important both from the point of view of design and of the technical training of the workers, who through this direct ex-

perience learn a good deal about the technology and assembly of prefabricated elements. While the traditional forms of self-help, because of their social, economic, and theoretical roots, maintain the separation between artisanal construction and technological advances, the Microbrigade process is able to bring the two together to the benefit of both the construction and the construction workers.

In 1966, a search was initiated for solutions that could involve local communities in carrying out major construction through popular participation. But it was only in 1970 that the Microbrigades were created, following a speech of Prime Minister Fidel Castro on the 26th of July, 1970, in which he pro-

posed the integration of users in the construction of housing. In Santiago de Cuba, the workers in the cement factory "Jose Merceron" quickly organized the first construction brigade. In December, 1970, Fidel Castro, speaking to the National Conference of Basic Industry, laid out the structure and function of the Microbrigade, creating at that time the first Microbrigades in Havana. Soon after, all of the connections for support and technical assistance between the Microbrigades and government agencies were put in place.

By the beginning of 1971, more than 1000 Havana workers were involved in the construction of 1154 dwellings in the new areas of the city such as Plaza de la Revolucion, Altahabana, Boyeros, and Alamar. In two years, this work force had grown to comprise more than 1000 Microbrigades, and by 1975 there were more than 30,000 workers organized in 1150 Microbrigades throughout Cuba. In these early years alone, the Microbrigades built 25,600 housing units and a large number of social service facilities.

The past ten years has been dominated by the enormous construction effort of the Microbrigades. The enthusiastic participation of workers in the creation of new buildings and urban communities demonstrates the creativity contained in the concept of mass participation in the design and management of the built environment. This period coincides with the political organization of the socialist state and the creation of the organs of Popular Power

*(Poder Popolar)*, whose assemblies on the national, provincial, and local level successfully create direct connections between the communities and the different levels of decision making.

The immediate participation in the difficult task of constructing the houses and services they will use daily leads the Microbrigades to give particular care to the quality of the buildings they make, to the design and planting of the green areas, and to the search for solutions that will improve the functioning and significance of the immediate environment. In terms of urban design, the flexibility of the Microbrigade process has encouraged the design of new residential communities that are superior to the major undertakings of the earlier years (such as Habana del Este and the José Martí project). Today, buildings are grouped at different scales. There are small projects connected directly with a single center of production, medium-size ensembles which make use of free land at the center of the city and there are large, new communities in the growth zones proposed by the master plan. In Havana, these are Alamar, with 130,000 residents, and Altahabana, with 110,000. In general terms, the urban fabric of these new communities remains traditional in that it is made up of repeated blocks and because it must follow the preexisting infrastructure of roads and services.

Alamar is surely the most important example of the work of the Microbrigades. In addition to housing, it integrates production and educational functions of citywide importance, such as food and textile factories and a branch of the University focusing on architecture and engineering. This mix of functions permits the development of complex and diversified relationships, and as the possibility of employment now exists within the residential area, it encourages the full integration of women in production.

In architectonic terms, the repetitive use of the typical block model E14 leads to an excessive homogeneity, broken only by the community facilities structures and the occasional residential tower. The architects on the job, beyond experimenting with new exterior forms, have learned to differentiate the various buildings and groups of buildings through the use of color and super-graphics. The projects proposed for the sections of Alamar to be built in the

13

14

15

11,12,13. *Microbrigadistas* at work.

14,15. Two quite different residential types built by Microbrigades. The lower photograph of Alamar (Havana) shows the most common form of construction.

16

next few years show improved urban design solutions that create a hierarchy of interior green spaces, establish a greater continuity between the various residential buildings, and dialectically alternate different types of apartment blocks. The regularity of the grid that has been the basis for planning until now will soon be contrasted by the development of a new urban center. This linear structure in the form of a spine that runs through the different residential sectors is accentuated by the diversity of service structures that it contains, and also by the new 14-story blocks built with the IMS prefabrication system that visually signal the location of the core of social life.

The concept of environmental participation has not yet reached the level in which the designer and the user are linked as closely as they should be. This will become feasible as the number of design and construction specialists increases and they begin to work directly at the scale of the local community in concert with the levels of environmental planning established by the organs of Popular Power. While there can be no

17

16. A typical Model E14 apartment block at Alamar on the edge of Havana. Construction of this huge project was largely done by volunteer Microbridgades.

17. Alamar is a complete urban sector, incorporating schools, services, and workplaces. One of the goals of this integrated planning is to encourage women to enter the workforce.

358

doubt that the artisanal construction methods used by the Microbrigades are both less efficient economically and produce an architecture of less interest than that which results from advanced technologies (which must remain in abeyance until a higher stage in the development of the economy is reached), still, the positive experience of participation and the collective labor of the masses must be permanent parts of all future efforts in the production and management of the built environment.

## Conclusions and Perspectives

Since the Revolution, the concept of habitat in Cuba has been developed in a series of steps taken at the political, ideological, economic, social, and technical levels. Starting in 1960 with the Law of Urban Reform, the prohibition on speculation in land and housing, the shift from the private dwelling to housing as a social service, the integration of housing and social services, the participation of the masses in the process of construction, and the steady evolution from artisanal methods to advanced technology clearly demonstrate that the solution to architectural and urban problems lies in a complex interaction between the structural and superstructural elements which characterize an historically situated society.

Twenty-one years after the triumph of the Revolution, there exists a solid material base and a multiplicity of technologies with which to attack progressively the building needs of society. At the same time, the decentralization of political decision making and the increase in the number of architects and construction specialists throughout the country open new possibilities for architectural and urban design projects to provide the necessary identity and respond to the specific needs of each neighborhood and community that together make up Cuban society. That is to say, as both the material base and the cultural level increase, the new economic possibilities and the value systems of different social groups will require an architectural and urban design that expresses the mastery of advanced technology and its integration with our national cultural roots in the creation of new spatial structures that define daily life.

We are saying that the habitat will take on new significance and new de-

sign values will replace those historically established by the dominant class and imposed upon the dominated classes. Traditionally, the bourgeoisie gave form to its way of life, exploiting the material possibilities and adapting the ruling cultural codes of each period to establish its cultural hegemony.

18

19

18. Color and pattern are used to differentiate buildings and neighborhoods at Alamar.

19. Alamar.

Workers and peasants remained outside this orbit, without culture or with the poorest sort of cultural symbolism associated with handicraft production and folklore. The Cuban Revolution establishes as a point of departure functional standards for the habitat which are the same for all members of the community; this is a conception similar to that used in the design of education or public health programs. These functional and technical standards will eventually become part of the significant values that give specific meaning to the relationship *necessity-possibility-expression* within the community that generates them. We are moving, then, toward a superior stage in socialist culture, one in which the ancient contradiction between culture and popular art—a contradiction generated by class antagonisms—achieves synthesis in new forms that bring together the technical and artistic avant-garde with the popular arts to create an expression of habitat in conformity with the material and spiritual quality of life.

The building of socialism demands as a fundamental principle the creation of an egalitarian society that permits to each member the maximum personal development and maximum choice between alternatives in accordance with social necessities. The designers of the physical environment have the responsibility of interpreting these essential directives and transcribing them into forms and spaces appropriate for a social development which integrates all aspects of life, from the material to the cultural superstructure. We conceive of the built environment in terms of structures that are polyvalent and polyfunctional, whose practical value, symbolic references, and aesthetic values can be understood and appropriated by all the different cultural levels presently existing in society. Only with these principles firmly in mind is it possible to speak of a revolutionary architecture.

*Condensed and adapted from Roberto Segre, *La Vivienda En Cuba—Republica y Revolución*, Chapter 2.4, *"Teoria y experimentation...,"* Mexico: Editorial Conceptosa, 1979

20. "Long Live the Committees for the Defense of the Revolution"—a sign at Alamar. Each neighborhood has its own CDR, a combination civic organization, clean block club, adult education organization, and political discussion group.

# Commentary on Cuba

C. Richard Hatch

This commentary on Cuba concludes our presentation of the scope of social architecture. It is more than fitting that we end with an examination of architectural practice at the scale of an entire country. Louis Kahn said architecture was "the thoughtful making of spaces." In Cuba, architecture has become the thoughtful making of a people's national space—with the participation of all sectors of society. Whatever the shortcomings of the Cuban achievement in purely aesthetic terms, Cuban architects have played an extraordinary role in altering the relationship between the Cuban people and built space. This profound change in the content and process of architecture has given a former impoverished, colonial people a sense of proprietorship, the experience of collective responsibility, and an opportunity to make their own history and give it form.

Roberto Segre's discussion of Cuba takes us to the present limits of social theory and practice. He shows us architecture playing a central role in the transformation of an entire society. He demonstrates clearly how effective an instrument architecture can be in treating social ills. He reminds us that social architecture, in any place, must take its agenda from the historical circumstances that have shaped a people and their living space.

In Cuba, it is said that the Revolution began with the triumph of the revolution.* Political victory provided the opportunity to confront the legacy of underdevelopment. Segre has told us what is being done. Let me take a moment here to sketch in the historical background in order to clarify the relationship between Cuban practice and Cuban reality.

In the "Critique of the Gotha Programme" (1875), Karl Marx wrote with foresight about the situation which would be faced in Cuba:

> What we have here to deal with is communist society, not as it has developed on its own foundation, but on the contrary, as it emerges from capitalist society; which is thus in every respect, economically, morally, and intellectually, still stamped with the birthmarks of the old society, from whose womb it emerges.

The womb from which Cuba's socialist society is emerging is that of Spanish colonialism and U.S. neocolonialism. This long heritage of dependency and of exploitation to serve metropolitan markets left Cuba with a single-sector, agricultural economy. Essentially a monoculture prior to the triumph of the Revolution in December 1959, the Cuban economy was dominated by a small number of huge sugar plantations, many U.S.-owned. Most of the population lived in the countryside in squalid palm-thatch huts, working in the sugar fields and mills. The harvest season was known as "the time of the lights" since only then were wages sufficient to permit the peasants to buy candles. Sanitation and medical care were all but unknown.

And then there was Havana: frozen daiquiris, conga drums, the cha-cha-cha . . . prostitution, gambling, and the Mafia. Education, science, culture, politics, and medicine—these two were to be found only in Havana. The end result was two Cubas, the city and the countryside; two classes, the rich and the poor; and two governments, the one seen at the national capital and the other headquartered in Washington, answerable to the sugar companies, and using the annual sugar import quota as its instrument of control.

If the womb was dependency and exploitation, the birthmarks were those to be expected: Most people were illiterate, unemployment ranged around 50 percent, and the bulk of the peasantry was without land to farm. There were hardly any roads, railroads, or harbors except those that served the large sugar mills. There was almost no industry.

The social situation was equally problematic. With little experience of self-government, no tradition of democracy or political participation had developed. The separation of classes, and of manual and intellectual workers, was net. A sharp spatial segregation of classes and functions underscored the deep divisions within the city—and between city and coutryside. Almost from the start, the Revolution saw architecture as an instrument in the process of social transformation. At all scales, from the private to the national, architecture was called upon to do more than make up the deficits common to underdevelopment. It was expected to change the relationships between men. As Roberto Segre has written here:

> The building of socialism demands as a fundamental principle the creation of an egalitarian society that permits to each member the maximum personal development and maximum choice between alternatives. . . . The designers of the physical environment have the responsibility of interpreting these essential directives. . . .

In this early period, the need to build was overwhelming. The wretched slums of Havana and Santiago had to be eradicated, as did the disease-infested bohios of the Cuban countryside. Factories, schools, hospitals, roads . . . everything was needed. Traditional solutions from industrialized nations were tried, but found lacking. Construction was not enough. In 1963, Che Guevara would write:

> I am not interested in dry economic socialism. We are fighting against poverty, but we are also fighting against alienation.

After the first phase of reconstruction, architects would no longer focus entirely on quantitative deficits. The issues for a revolutionary architecture became the overcoming of the spatial segregation, challenging the narrow division of labor (and the low skill levels which it implies), and struggling against the lack of a democratic political ethos. Participation became the hallmark of the new era. Building programs were altered to maximize opportunities for popular involvement. Structural systems were invented which permitted intellectuals, farmers, and factory workers to join together in the rebuilding of the socialist

---

* Fidel Castro, in a radio address shortly after his entry into Havana in December, 1959, following the collapse of the Battista dictatorship, told the Cuban people, "Now the Revolution can begin."

Cuba. (Paul Jacob's description in Part 2 of a single experimental apartment development in Havana provides a concrete example.) Professor Segre tells us how popular participation was organized in new social institutions, culminating in the creation of the Microbrigades. Participation was not to be a substitute for development, but its complement. And if its overarching goal was the creation of an egalitarian society, the objectives of participation were many:

1. Nation-building: Participation in the creation of a modern Cuba was expected to build identification with the Revolution.
2. Growth of political culture: Involvement in decision-making and in negotiations between citizens and organs of the state was intended to lower the barriers between the governed and the government for the first time in Cuban history.
3. Women's liberation: Public participation provided significant roles for women outside the home and brought them into the mainstream of national life.
4. Eliminating class divisions: Carrying out common projects for the common good would open lines of communication between groups in Cuban society and overcome the traditional deprecation of manual labor.
5. Proprietorship: People who have built a school or hospital are unlikely to think of it as belonging to some mysterious entity such as "the state." They may come to see the state as themselves organized to carry out the work of society.
6. Transparency: Direct involvement opens windows into the structure of society, its institutions, and its technology. The formerly incomprehensible and alienating environment— conceived, built, and managed for and by others—is transformed into a place where people feel at home.
7. Competence: Emerging nations need the buoyant optimism and productive skills that arise out of successful participation in making needed things.
8. Overcoming material deficits: It can never be forgotten that along with alienation, Cuba was (and is) fighting to overcome its legacy of underdevelopment. Mobilizing the energy of the people is crucial.
9. Personal growth: Environmental participation is seen as an important element in the formation of the new Socialist individual, *el hombre integrado,* characterized by egalitarian values and collective concerns.

While the Microbrigade Program is the outstanding example of participation in the creation of the physical environment, the same spirit is manifested at many levels and reaches all Cubans at one time or another. The universal participation in the sugar harvest which characterized the heroic, early years of the Revolution has been replaced (the dangerous work of cane cutting has been taken over by machines) by wholesale involvement in social construction. A few examples from my experience may give the flavor of the Cuban approach.

Not far from the main square of Santiago there is a new, two-story apartment block containing a dozen dwellings. Painted sky blue with lighter trim, it was constructed using simple concrete elements prefabricated on site (the ubiquitous Sandino system) by the people who live there. The land, tools, technical assistance, and materials were provided by the local office of the national housing agency, without cost. When the new homes were complete, the residents participated in the demolition of the irredeemable slum in which they had lived. The initiative came from below, the support from above.

Only health care has a higher priority than education in Cuba. With the steady extension of schooling, it is said, in all seriousness, that by the year 2000 all Cubans will have a full college education. Secondary schools tend to be large and located in the countryside. This program is intended to mix urban students with the children of farmers and to make it possible for the teenagers to participate in agricultural work, the mainstay of the national economy. Parents in Camagüey, finding that their new secondary school had been pushed off to a future year because of budget constraints, organized themselves to do the job. The completed residential school contains facilities for 1200 students. With the aid of a sophisticated prefabrication system and a dedicated team of architects and engineers seconded by a government construction group, the volunteers did the job in eight months.

To overcome the traditional urban-rural division and the historic isolation of farmers, new towns tied to major cities by the new highway network are being built. No one is sent to live in these new towns. To encourage settlement, however, farm families are offered a town center with a clinic, a primary school, a cafe, and a cinema—and a *free* apartment, completely furnished (down to a 19-in. TV). The initial housing is built by the government to get the project moving. The first residents then join in the construction work. By the time the third wave has settled in, the professionals begin to pull back, leaving future planning and building to the residents. This achieves two primary purposes: It welds the new arrivals to town life into a community, and it introduces a peasant population to modern technology.

At Alamar, which Segre tells us is the largest Microbrigade project, work teams from all of Havana's varied enterprises and agencies meet on the site. Working side-by-side to build badly needed homes, one finds professionals and mechanics, teachers and truck drivers. As the finished apartments are allocated through their different workplaces, this same rich social mix will end up as neighbors under the same roofs.

Two more notes about architecture at Alamar: From their first years, student architects work on the site, first as laborers, then as liaison between the designers and the future residents, and finally as project architects—an exceptional professional preparation. Small factories, office, cultural institutions, and service agencies are woven into Alamar (and similar projects elsewhere). Sited close to schools and day care centers, they are there to encourage the participation of women, traditionally confined to the home, in the labor force and in public life. They have other important purposes as well. With the shops and cultural institutions, they are there to reduce the discrepancies between the historic core and the new periphery of the city. Their presence increases the *transparency* of the Cuban society and its economy, especially for the children who will grow up in Alamar.

In the first chapter, Herman Hertzberger showed what one architect working alone could do to encourage the human appropriation of dwellings in an alienated society. Roberto Segre, in the last, shows what a revolutionary architecture can do to support an entire people's appropriation of their habitat. His report on the Cuban experience helps to resolve the age-old debate about the role of architecture in society. Does architecture merely reflect the underlying structural organization of society? Or can architecture as process, content, and form be a driving force in the reformation of society? The acceptance of the power of architecture in social change contains a moral imperative.